terra australis 58

terra australis 58

West New Guinea

Social, Biological, and Material Histories

**Edited by Dylan Gaffney
and Marlin Tolla**

Australian
National
University

ANU PRESS

Australian
National
University

ANU PRESS

Published by ANU Press
The Australian National University
Canberra ACT 2600, Australia
Email: anupress@anu.edu.au

Available to download for free at press.anu.edu.au

ISBN (print): 9781760466718
ISBN (online): 9781760466725

WorldCat (print): 1460826244
WorldCat (online): 1460841771

DOI: 10.22459/TA58.2024

Cover design and layout by ANU Press. Cover photograph: Pottery designed by Beatriks Felle and Barbalina Ebalkoi
from Abar village, looking over Lake Sentani in background (Source: Dylan Gaffney and Marlin Tolla).

This book is published under the aegis of the Terra Australis Editorial Committee of the ANU Press.

Publication of this book has been supported by the ANU vice-chancellor's strategic funds for flagship titles
at ANU Press.

Contents

List of figures

List of tables

Preface

Marlin Tolla and Dylan Gaffney

West New Guinea—or Indonesian Papua—is a territory covering over 400,000 km^2, host to around 300 distinct languages and cultures. Despite this rich diversity, the human history of this area is almost totally unrecorded in the anthropological and archaeological literature, especially prior to the late nineteenth century. However, the area remains crucial for understanding how humans moved from Southeast Asia into the Pacific region, how descendent groups adapted to new environments, developed food production, exchanged languages, and traded objects, how people produced material culture, and how this material culture was collected and exhibited in museums. This volume seeks to bring these themes in West New Guinea's human past to light for the first time.

This book project was initiated in mid-2020, when both editors were studying for their PhDs. This was also a time when much of the world, including towns across Papua, was in lockdown owing to the growing COVID-19 pandemic. As such, the fieldwork programs of the editors and many authors were temporarily discontinued. With this paradoxical period of global stasis and profound change, we initiated this collaboration to take stock of Papuan and Indonesian research on West New Guinea, and to bring that work published primarily in Bahasa Indonesia into conversation with international researchers. As such, part of the purpose of drawing together this volume was to translate Bahasa Indonesia contributions to make this research available to wider audiences. Furthermore, an array of international research in archaeology, social and biological anthropology, linguistics, and museum studies had been accumulating in the years leading up to publication, which provided an opportunity to bring together a range of disciplinary perspectives on West New Guinea's human past. We thank all the authors for their perseverance in bringing their chapters to light, and to internal specialist peer reviewers for lending their expertise to the project.

Publication of this book has been supported by the Vice Chancellor's strategic funds for flagship titles at ANU Press. We also acknowledge Badan Riset dan Inovasi Nasional, Freie Universität in Berlin, St John's College and Hertford College, Oxford, the School of Archaeology, University of Oxford, and the Department of Archaeology, University of Cambridge, for their support. Finally, we gratefully thank the editorial team, especially Sally Brockwell and Sue O'Connor, two anonymous peer reviewers of the book, and copyeditor Beth Battrick for their efforts in bringing the manuscript to publication.

1

Introduction: The human histories of West New Guinea

Dylan Gaffney and Marlin Tolla

Abstract

This chapter is an introduction to *West New Guinea: Social, Biological, and Material Histories*. It first describes the sparse information available about the environmental and cultural history of the area before describing the boundary-making that has formed West New Guinea in the recent past. The chapter then identifies seven key research themes with implications for both global and regional anthropology: the early peopling of Oceania, human adaptation within varied and challenging ecologies, the emergence of food production, the dispersal of languages, the connections between the Pacific and global trade networks, the transformative lives of material culture, and the history of museums and collecting. Finally, the chapter provides an outline of the book structure and the chapters that follow, all of which contribute in important ways to the seven identified research themes.

Abstrak

Bab ini merupakan bagian pengantar judul buku "Papua bagian barat: Sejarah sosial, biologi dan budaya materi". Bab ini dibuka dengan uraian mengenai sejarah lingkungan dan budaya Papua bagian barat yang dilanjutkan dengan uraian latar belakang sejarah wilayah ini secara utuh hingga masa kini. Terdapat tujuh pokok tema yang dideskripsikan pada bab ini, dimana tema-tema tersebut berimplikasi pada studi antropologi baik itu dalam lingkup skala regional maupun secara global. Topik ini antara lain: penduduk awal Oseania, adaptasi manusia dalam keanekaragaman ekologi serta tantangannya, awal-mula produksi pangan, penyebaran bahasa, transformasi budaya materi, dan sejarah museum dan koleksi. Garis besar topik yang terdapat dalam 21 bab ini kemudian diuraikan pada bagian akhir.

Introduction

This is a book about the human histories of the western part of New Guinea and its offshore islands. When we speak of human histories, we mean the ongoing processes of social, material, linguistic, and biological transformation that have characterised the distant and more recent past, as well as those histories which continue to be made by living communities, and those which are yet to be carved out in the future. As it stands, West New Guinea (Figure 1.1) is superbly situated to address numerous unresolved anthropological questions about the early settlement of Australasia and the Pacific Islands via Island Southeast Asia, along with the subsequent processes of cultural diversification that have occurred within a range of distinct ecological zones, not to mention the emergence of dynamic interaction networks that connected these areas with other parts of the Pacific, Southeast Asia, and Eurasia. However, despite this latent potential, with respect to its archaeology, material culture traditions, languages, and human biology, this vast landmass remains poorly described and under-researched. In large part owing to West New Guinea's geographic and political context, the area is often left to the Southeast Asian specialists by Pacific researchers, and vice versa. As a result, it has been relegated to a conceptual fringe rather than featuring as an important link between the two regions. The wider discipline is therefore in serious need of published information from the western half of New Guinea to not only connect the scholarship of Asia and the Pacific, but also to tell more detailed and accurate stories about New Guinea's vibrant cultures.

This book focuses expressly on the western part of New Guinea (today administered by Indonesia), excluding, for the most part, the eastern side of this contiguous landmass (today the independent state of Papua New Guinea). It is the first volume of its kind, bringing together research from scholars, both within West New Guinea and internationally, who present novel regional syntheses, describe never-before-published archaeological sites, and provide fresh ethnographic insight into the material culture traditions of the region. To date, there have been no volumes dealing exclusively with the deep histories of West New Guinea as a whole. In the Dutch literature, *Papoea: Een Geschiedens* (Vlasblom 2004) summarised the area's social and political history from the time of European voyages through to the twenty-first century. Similarly, the French monograph *L'Indonésie et la Nouvelle-Guinée Occidentale* (Defert 1996) provides a detailed history of West New Guinea, especially covering the late twentieth century. In the Anglophone literature, an issue of *The Journal of Pacific History* (Volume 34, 1999) collected papers on the recent history of the region. *New Guinea: Crossing Boundaries and History* (Moore 2003) compiled archaeological literature from Papua New Guinea and historical sources from West New Guinea to provide a broad diachronic overview of the island's past. Several chapters included in *The Ecology of Papua* (Marshall and Beehler 2007) dealt with human culture and long-term interactions with the environment (Hope 2007; Hope and Aplin 2007; Mansoben 2007; Pasveer 2007). Previous multidisciplinary volumes have had a regional focus on the Bird's Head of New Guinea (Bartstra 1998; Miedema and Reesink 2004; Miedema et al. 1998), but contributions from archaeology, material culture studies, and human biology were generally peripheral. Greub's (1992) edited volume explored the art of Lake Sentani, Yos Sudarso Bay and Cenderawasih Bay, and is, to date, one of the most extensive explorations of the region's material culture. Finally, and most recently, Martin Slama and Jenny Munro's edited volume *From 'Stone-Age' to 'Real-Time': Exploring Papuan Temporalities, Mobilities and Religiosities* (2015) presented a range of anthropological papers which explored the changing face of West New Guinea (including the trope proliferated in both European and Indonesian societies that casts Papuans as living in the Stone Age).

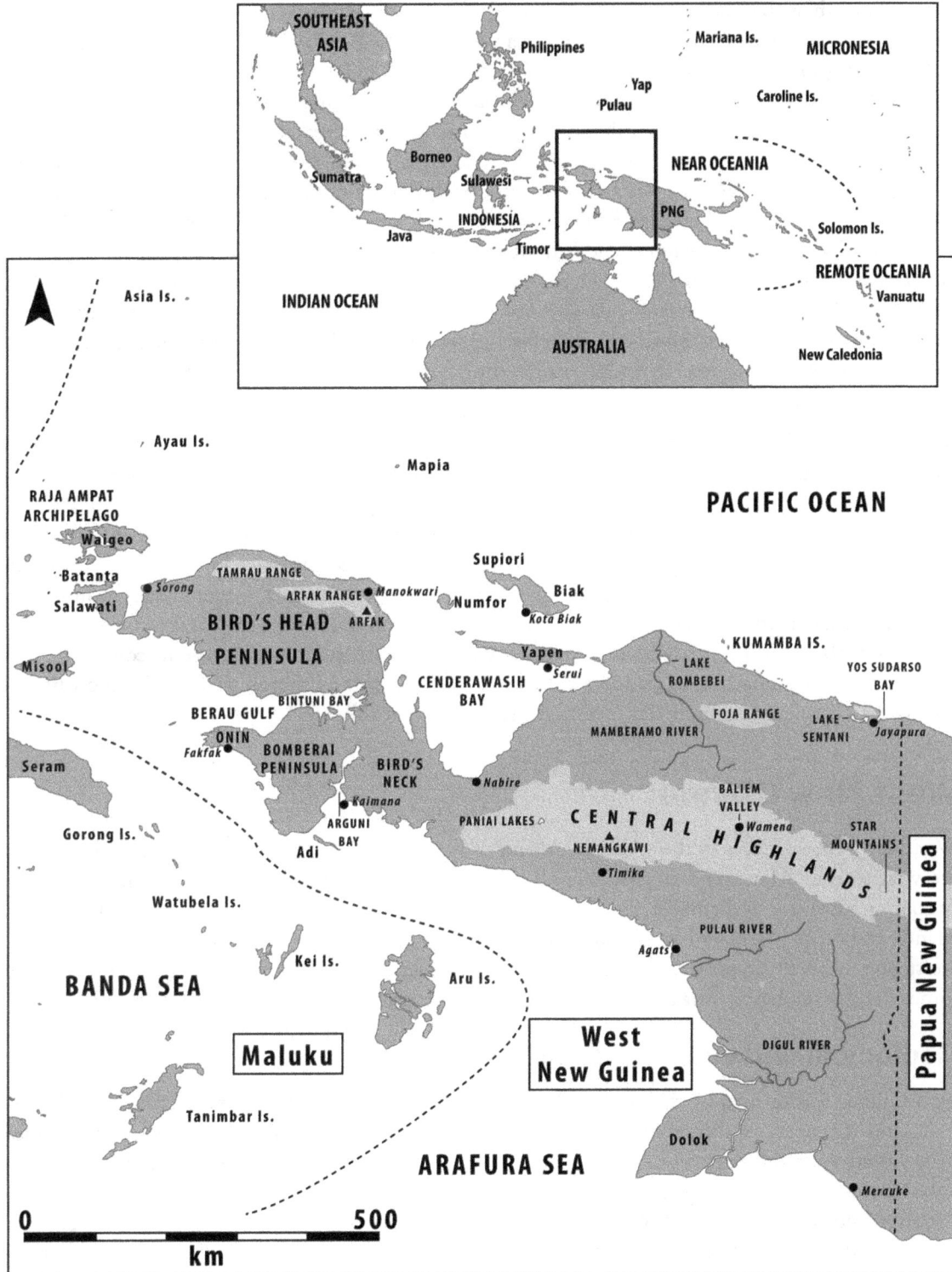

Figure 1.1: West New Guinea with key geographic features in the wider Asia-Pacific region.
Source: Dylan Gaffney.

Increasingly there has been a rich and diverse array of publications produced by Papuan and Indonesian researchers. In the Bahasa Indonesia literature, the <u>Balai Arkeologi Papua</u>[1] (Papua Centre of Archaeology, later subsumed within <u>Badan Riset dan Inovasi Nasional</u>, or BRIN) has, since 2009, produced a regular journal called *Papua*, which publishes archaeological and ethnographic research undertaken in West New Guinea. Numerous reports on this research are also available from the archaeological centre in Jayapura but many of these remain 'grey literature'. Additionally, a recent monograph deals with Melanesian migration around eastern Indonesia and West New Guinea, but this draws from existing literature rather than presenting new data (Abdullah and Paeni 2015). In social anthropology, several Papuan and Indonesian authors have published key papers in *Masyarakat Indonesia* and local journals published by Universitas Cenderawasih and Universitas Papua (see Chapter 2). Most of this archaeological and social anthropological material is written in Indonesian and one aim of the present volume is, therefore, to make available to an international audience the mounting evidence produced by Indonesian authors including Papuan researchers.

In this introduction to the book, we describe the West New Guinea area and tie together what little is known about the environmental and cultural histories of the region. We then describe colonial boundary marking and administration throughout the nineteenth and twentieth centuries, which has been responsible for how research in West New Guinea has diverged from the east of the island. The chapter then highlights several important research themes that have emerged in the wider Southeast Asian and Pacific literature, and which critically need to be addressed by research in West New Guinea. These themes include the early peopling of Oceania, human adaptation within varied and challenging ecologies, the emergence of food production, the dispersal of languages, the connections between the Pacific and global networks, the history of museums and collecting, and the active and ongoing lives of material culture. At the end of the chapter, we provide an outline of the book structure and a summary of the contributions that follow.

West New Guinea

West New Guinea refers to the whole mainland of New Guinea from the Bird's Head Peninsula in the west to the 141st meridian east, as well as its outlying islands in Cenderawasih Bay, the Raja Ampat archipelago, and smaller satellite islands and atolls. For our purposes, we exclude the Aru Islands and other Malukan islands like Gebe, Halmahera, and the Banda group, even though there are strong cultural, linguistic, and biological affinities between these areas and New Guinea, with some islands even being host to 'Papuan' languages ultimately deriving from New Guinea.

Geological and environmental history

New Guinea was formed by the rapid collision of two tectonic plates: the westward-moving Pacific Plate and the northward-moving Australian Plate (Baldwin et al. 2012). This gives New Guinea its distinctive central highland range, which runs like a spine through the centre of the island, flanked on its sides by lowland hills and alluvial plains (Figure 1.2). The mountains rise to above the snowline in some parts of West New Guinea, with the highest peak being Nemangkawi[2] at 4884 m above sea level (asl). These peaks are often interspersed with flat intermontane valley systems between 1200–2000 m asl (Löffler 1977), home to the vast majority of highlanders (Brookfield and Allen 1989). Although the northern and southern lowlands are characterised by swamp and

---

1   Throughout this and other chapters in the book, local language words are italicised and Papuan Malay or Indonesian words are underlined at first mention. Words from other languages (such as Dutch) are provided in single quote marks.

2   Puncak Jaya or Mt Carstensz.

mangrove forests, produced by large river systems, the north coast is generally emergent and looks over the Pacific Ocean, while the southern coast is subsiding and accreting into the Arafura Sea (Ellison 2005). As Terrell (2004) notes, the northern coastline of New Guinea, being precipitous and tectonically unstable, may have acted as a barrier to movements between the Pacific and Island Southeast Asia in the past. Prevailing winds, strong tidal currents, and expanses of mangrove forest may have similarly inhibited movements along the southern coast.

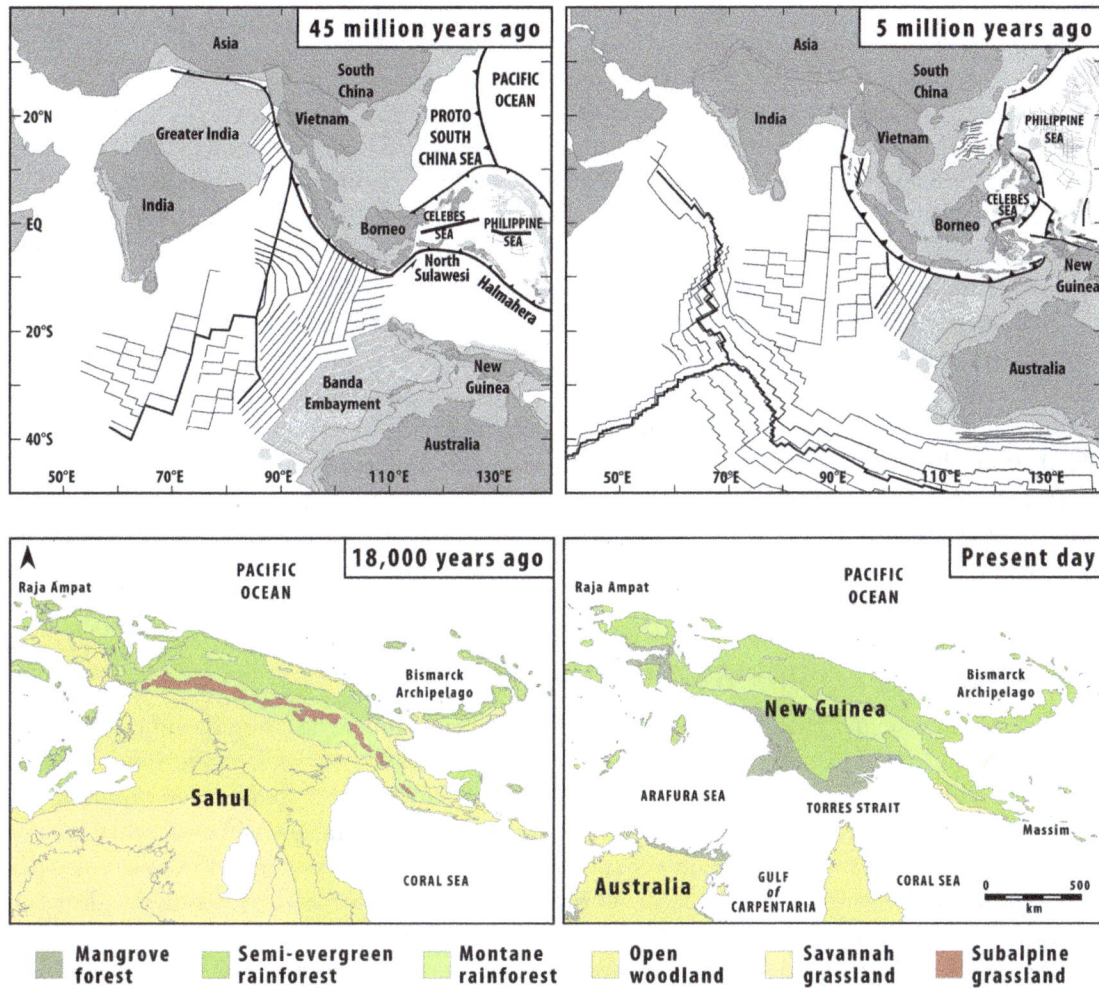

Figure 1.2: The formation of New Guinea.

Notes: Above shows the tectonic movement of New Guinea on the Australian Plate northwards towards the Pacific and Philippine plates alongside the westward movement of satellite islands of northern Raja Ampat and Cenderawasih Bay. Below shows the 'separation' of New Guinea from Australia owing to raised sea levels after the Pleistocene.

Source: Dylan Gaffney, redrawn from Hall (2017) (above) and van der Kaars (1991) (below).

Active tectonics have created the distinctive Bird's Head, or Doberai, Peninsula, connected to New Guinea by the relatively flat Bomberai Peninsula and the steep valleys of the Bird's Neck, shaped by the Lengguru fold and thrust belt (Dam and Wong 1998; Ratman 1998). This area offers a complex coastline with numerous sheltered bays and canoe harbours. Offshore, the northern Raja Ampat Islands—Waigeo and Batanta—have moved westwards along the Sorong Fault to their current position (Charlton 1996). This contrasts with the southern Raja Ampat Islands—Salawati and Misool—which sit on the Bird's Head microplate (Sapin et al. 2009). In Cenderawasih Bay, the islands of Biak, Supiori, and Numfor lie to the north of the Yapen Fault, while Yapen Island itself straddles the fault, along which these islands have been moving westward (Bertoni and Álvarez 2012). Uplift, subsidence, and lateral displacements have characterised these areas in the past, evident at several sites of raised coral terraces around the Bird's Head and on Biak, similar to the better-known Huon terraces of Papua New Guinea (Chappell et al. 1996). Smaller atolls—Ayau, the Asia Islands, and Mapia—have formed during the Quaternary and lie to the north of New Guinea, acting as stepping stones between West New Guinea and Micronesia (Milsom et al. 1992).

Today New Guinea is separated from Australia by the Arafura Sea, but owing to depressed temperatures and lower eustatic sea level during the Pleistocene period (2.58 million to 11,700 years ago) the two landmasses were formerly connected along with Tasmania, the Aru Islands, and the southern Raja Ampat Islands (see Boesl et al., this volume). In the archaeological literature this landmass has come to be known as Sahul (Ballard 1993). In areas with low relief such as the southern reaches of New Guinea, sea level changes at the start of the Holocene (11,700 to 8000 years ago) were dramatic and led to the flooding of the Arafura Plain, whereas the high-relief north coast broadly retained its shape. During the Last Glacial Maximum—the coldest phase of the Pleistocene about 18,000 years ago—temperatures in the central highlands and other mountainous areas, like the Cyclops range near Jayapura and the Tamrau Mountains of the Bird's Head, were on average 4–6 °C cooler than today, depending on altitude (Haberle et al. 1991, 2001; Hope 2007). This cooling compressed montane forest boundaries by about 500 m and subalpine grasslands commonly occurred in places 1000–1500 m lower than today (Figure 1.2). The lowlands, by contrast, experienced less extreme temperature depression (van der Kaars 1995). However, lower precipitation during the Pleistocene meant that the southern lowlands (now mangroves and evergreen rainforests) were likely woodlands and grasslands at that time (van der Kaars 1991) and some equatorial forests were less dense than they are today (Gaffney 2021).

Sociolinguistic groupings and cultural histories

Within these variable and changing environments, West New Guinea has long been host to highly diverse cultures (see Ronsumbre 2020 for a recent encyclopedia of indigenous groups in the region). Among most local communities, ethnic affiliation is usually signified by clan grouping and language use (Mansoben 2007). West New Guinea boasts over 270 languages (Arnold, this volume) and, although there have been dynamic population movements and intermarriages in the past (e.g. Donohue and Crowther 2005; Haenen 1998), the semi-isolated nature of genetic admixture between linguistic groups (Kusuma et al., this volume) supports the idea that language grouping provides one possible avenue to explore cultural variability at a very coarse resolution. This is not to say that cultural attributes are always delimited by language borders, because physical and social proximity, exchange networks, and shared communal practices are also crucial factors (see discussion in Moore and Romney 1994; Roberts et al. 1995; Welsch et al. 1992). Moreover, although the high ecological diversity of New Guinea is mirrored by a similarly high diversity of languages, the environment alone cannot explain the distribution of this diversity (Antunes et al. 2020). This is likely because, although some ecological features like rivers, mountain ranges, and malarial-prone lowland areas have contributed to shaping people's mobility (Summerhayes et al. 2017), in many places these features have not totally constrained people's settlement; linguistically related groups are often present on both sides of major rivers, mountain peaks and sea straits (Schiefenhövel and Vanhaeren 2017). Therefore, if we are to understand the complex distribution of West New Guinea's cultures, we must look to the contingent historical processes that gave rise to them.

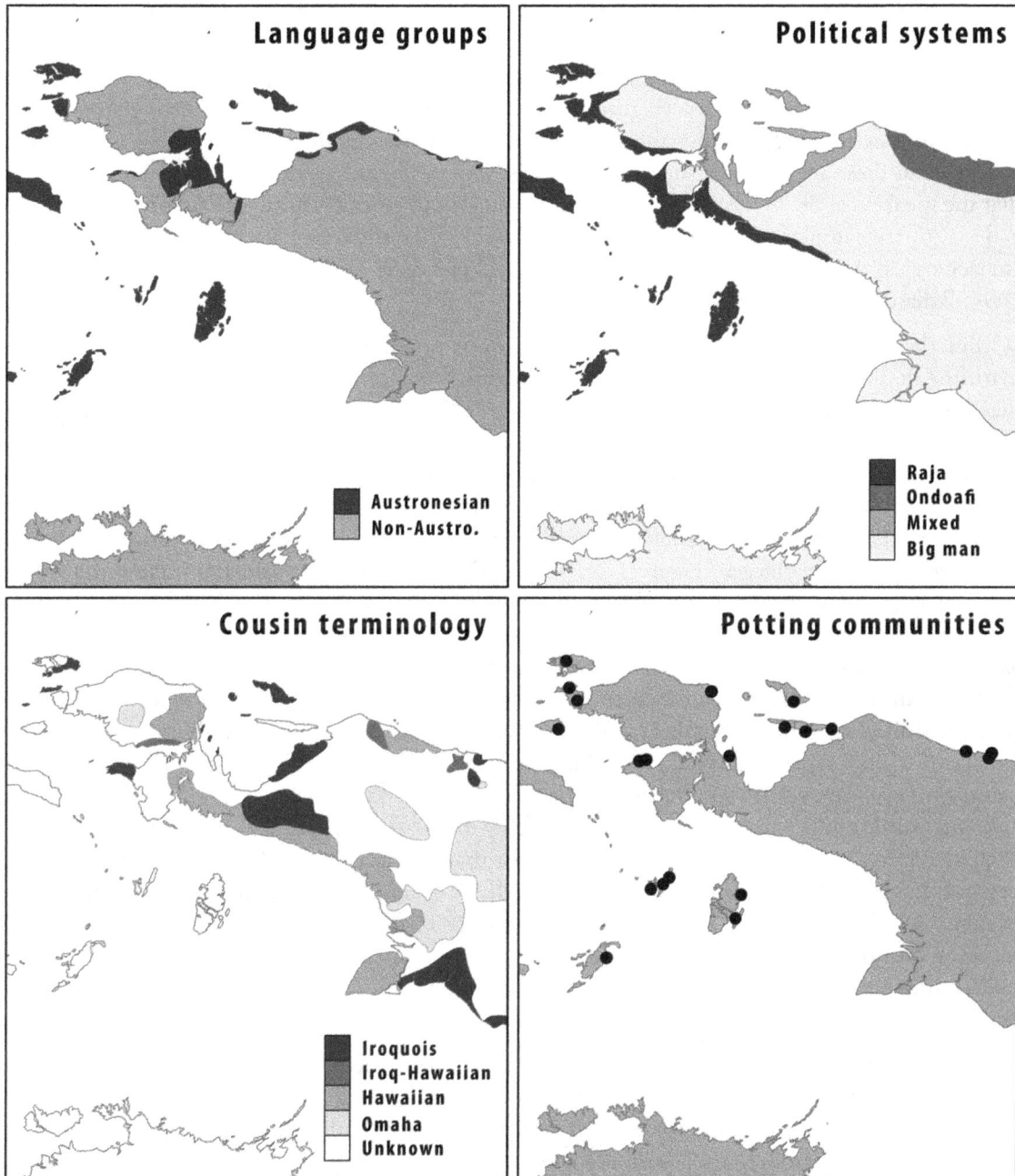

Figure 1.3: Distribution of four cultural attributes around West New Guinea.

Notes: Language grouping, whether Austronesian family or non-Austronesian (see Arnold, this volume); customary political system (Mansoben 1995); kinship as reflected by cousin terminology (Pouwer 1966); and historically recorded potting communities (Pétrequin and Pétrequin 2006).

Source: Dylan Gaffney, compiled from Mansoben (1995), Pouwer (1966), and Pétrequin and Pétrequin (2006).

In the north-western part of New Guinea, there are numerous groups that speak languages belonging to the Austronesian family. These include those in the Raja Ampat Islands, Bomberai Peninsula, Bird's Neck, on the offshore islands and coast of Cenderawasih Bay, around the Mamberamo River delta, and along the north coast (Figure 1.3). These speech communities are strongly associated with a complex coastal geography and, prior to the recent introduction of rice, fishing and shellfish collecting in these areas heavily supplemented sago processing and gardening. These factors suggest that the speakers of the first Austronesian proto-languages to enter the area were mobile seafarers and had a distinctive insular and coastal settlement pattern. This settlement pattern may be echoed in the archaeological record by extensive rock art on coastal cliff faces in this region (Arifin and Delanghe 2004; Ballard 1992).

Within the past few centuries, some of these groups produced pottery (Figure 1.3), developed maritime raiding and trading networks, and increasingly took part in globalising exchange systems that connected New Guinea with Eurasia (Swadling 1996). The presence of bronze axes and drums, ultimately of Vietnamese origin, around Lake Sentani and the Bird's Head provide material evidence for these exchange relationships (see Suroto, this volume). Until recently, many of the populations around Raja Ampat and the Bomberai Peninsula followed a raja political system, whereby power was bestowed by sultans from Maluku upon influential local leaders who held authority over several linguistically distinct villages (Figure 1.3). Those groups in Cenderawasih Bay followed a mixed political system whereby leaders could interchangeably arise owing to their lineage or their merit (Healey 1998). Meanwhile, around north New Guinea, there was a chiefly system, whereby an *ondoafi* (clan leader) held authority over a settlement or multiple settlements of the same linguistic group (Mansoben 1995). Around these areas, kinship tends to be expressed following Iroquois cousin terminology, wherein parallel cousins are classified in the same group as siblings, cross cousins are classified in a separate group, and fathers are classified in the same group as all maternal and paternal uncles (Pouwer 1966). The distribution of pottery making, more stratified political systems, and Iroquois kinship terminology, again, overlaps with coastal complexity, as well as the presence of dynamic maritime exchange systems in the past that connected New Guinea with Maluku and beyond (Ellen and Latinis 2012; Swadling 1996). These overlapping cultural attributes may provide evidence for the presence of a wider maritime network of interaction that brought Austronesian-speaking groups into contact with non-Austronesian (or 'Papuan') language speakers in the fourth millennium before present, and which facilitated increasing connections between eastern Indonesia and New Guinea.

On the mainland of western New Guinea and the Bird's Head, non-Austronesian languages are present. Many of these languages have likely descended—over tens of thousands of years—from the initial speech communities that entered Sahul. These people shared common genetic ancestry, which had diverged from that of Australians prior to the continent splitting into New Guinea and Australia (see Jacobs et al., this volume). Along the central highland range, southern lowlands, Bomberai Peninsula, and Bird's Head are numerous languages that may belong to a single family: the purported Trans–New Guinea grouping (Pawley and Hammarström 2018; Voorhoeve 1975). Although still hypothetical, it is possible that Trans–New Guinea expansions within the highlands were associated with demographic growth, leading to movements of people into the lowlands, which were more sparsely populated owing to less arable land, differing subsistence systems, and disease risk (see Attenborough et al., this volume). In the recent past, intensive field agriculture, horticulture, and pig rearing, sometimes supplemented by hunting and collecting, made the highlands distinctive from lowland areas (see originally Bulmer and Bulmer 1964). Large populations of highlanders were interconnected through trade and exchange, marriage, and warfare, and had indirect access to coastal products like shells (see Voirol, this volume; Tekege, this volume). These groups participated in decentralised and meritocratic political systems, commonly glossed as 'big men' and 'great men' societies (Ploeg 1966). Although systems of achieved status may have emerged millennia ago (Golson and Gardner 1990), big men groups as we know them may be an innovation reflecting recent material and political transformations—changes related to the adoption of sweet potato and the intensification of pig rearing in the central highlands (Bayliss-Smith et al. 2017), and the kain timur textile trade linking mountain people with coastal groups around the Bird's Head (Elmberg 1966; Healey 1998). Except for evidence of marsupial hunting in the Holocene (Hope and Hope 1976), there is currently no published archaeological evidence from the central highlands of West New Guinea. Therefore, the history of social and political change before the twentieth century remains an enigma.

In the northern lowlands and foothills, and the interior of the Bird's Head, are smaller populations speaking languages from distinct families and isolates. In swampy lowland areas, sago processing is common, supplemented by fishing and hunting, and in the foothills, horticulture may be supplemented by sago processing, hunting, and collecting. We currently know very little about the deeper past in the lowlands of western New Guinea (see Wright et al. 2013 for a review). Humans have lived around the hills of the Bird's Head since at least 30,000 years ago (Pasveer et al. 2002), and on the Aru Islands, at that time connected to Sahul, since 27,000 years ago (O'Connor et al. 2002). These people hunted in rainforests and grasslands, particularly specialising in wallabies, but also capturing cuscus, bandicoots, fruit bats and snakes, and collecting shellfish, seeds, and cassowary eggs (Aplin and Pasveer 2005; Aplin et al. 1999). Bone points were produced from the skeletons of these animals, whether for fibrecraft or projectile hunting, and stone tools were made in an expedient manner (Pasveer 2004, 2005). However, despite the clear diversity that characterises lowland material culture traditions today (see Jacobs, this volume; Kanem, this volume; Powell Davies, this volume), we know nothing about how this variability arose in the deeper past.

Colonial boundary-making and administration

West New Guinea has been witness to colonial partitioning for hundreds of years, with most of its inhabitants likely unaware of such pretensions until recently. There are tentative hints that settlements on the Onin Peninsula were tributaries to Java's Majapahit Empire by the mid-fourteenth century (Kern 1903), and parts of the coast and offshore islands paid tribute to sultanates around Maluku between the fifteenth and nineteenth centuries (Swadling 1996), but no attempts were made to claim land on New Guinea itself. Indeed, those Papuans providing tribute often conceptualised these relationships not as marking subservience but as facilitating new exchange possibilities (Andaya 1993, 108; Kamma 1982, 80).

In 1545, Yñigo Ortiz de Retez, who had travelled along the north coast of New Guinea to the mouth of the Mamberamo River, asserted ownership of the island for Spain (van der Veur 1966, 6). So too did Luis Váez de Torres in 1606 when he voyaged along the south coast of New Guinea (Hilder 1980); however, these claims remained symbolic with no capital invested by Spain to settle the island, convert its people, or monopolise its resources. Since the early seventeenth century, the 'Vereenigde Oostindische Compagnie' (Dutch East India Company, VOC) occasionally visited New Guinea, expanding from strongholds in Ambon and Batavia (now Jakarta), from which they controlled the maritime spice trade and occasionally organised raiding, trading, and slaving operations around coastal New Guinea (Wichmann 1909, 104). The Netherlands initially asserted ownership over West New Guinea only in so far as it appeased the Sultanate of Tidore, which laid claim to tributaries around the island's coast, and because it acted as a buffer to competing colonial interests in the region (Bone 1964). In the late eighteenth century, as Dutch naval superiority declined, the British began to make claims to the coast of New Guinea too, establishing Fort Coronation on Mansinam Island (Dore Bay) in 1793 proclaiming the northern part of the mainland 'New Albion' and under the possession of the Crown (Lee 1912). With rumours that the British had also established forts in the south-west of New Guinea, the Dutch established their first administrative post, Fort Du Bus, in Triton Bay on the Bird's Neck in 1828 and annexed all land west of the 141st meridian east. This fort was officially abandoned after less than a decade owing to high disease rates and mortality (Haneveld 1961). A later 1848 decree asserted that Dutch-controlled Tidore had a claim to this land with a line drawn from the 141st meridian in the south to Cape Bonpland in the north (van der Veur 1966, 1). Only in 1884 did the British and German empires formally acknowledge this boundary, thereby separating Dutch New Guinea from German New Guinea and British Papua. The Dutch administration initially remained small-scale in the late nineteenth and early twentieth centuries, with administrators, missionaries, traders, and some military personnel being the only real European presence, although Dutch, American and Japanese corporations increasingly sought natural resources for extraction from 1935 to 1960 (Poulgrain 1999).

During the Pacific War, brief occupation by Japan in 1942–1945 was primarily confined to the coasts. The interior was relatively unaffected except for harbouring Dutch intelligence and resistance groups and a small group of Japanese troops at the Paniai Lakes (Cheesman 1943). However, on the coast and offshore islands, the takeover and subsequent indentured labour used for infrastructure projects led to many local deaths (Rottman 2005). Following the Allied defeat of the Japanese in 1945, and the Indonesian struggle for independence from 1945 to 1949, many 'Indische Nederlanders' (i.e. Dutch and Dutch–Indonesian descent communities living in the East Indies) began to relocate to West New Guinea, and Dutch legislation encouraged this process of transmigration for several decades (Lugten 1985, 75). By 1961, the Papuan population was estimated at below half a million people (487,800), with Indonesian and Chinese migrants numbering 16,600 and Europeans numbering 15,500 (Pouwer 1999).

West New Guinea, as the territory was generally called after the war, became a focus of development and administration. It was placed under the authority of the governor and divided into 'Residentie' (provinces) led by a 'Resident' (district commissioner) (Jaarsma 1994). These provinces were divided into 'Districten' (districts) headed by a 'Controleur' (assistant district commissioner) (Figure 1.4). In 1945, only 5 per cent of West New Guinea was within reach of Dutch administrative centres; however, by 1962 this situation had changed, and the Dutch had made their mark on industry and urbanisation as well as language, culture, and education (Pouwer 1999). This process of nation-building increasingly fed a Dutch preoccupation with being perceived as compassionate colonisers (Rutherford 2009), despite events that reinforced ongoing suppression (e.g. the Obano uprising, the raid on Omadesep–Otsjanep, and so on). At that time, a requirement of the Netherlands being a member state of the United Nations was that they adhere to Article 73, which stipulated that colonial governments needed to work towards self-determination for non-self-governing territories as soon as possible (Jaarsma 1994).

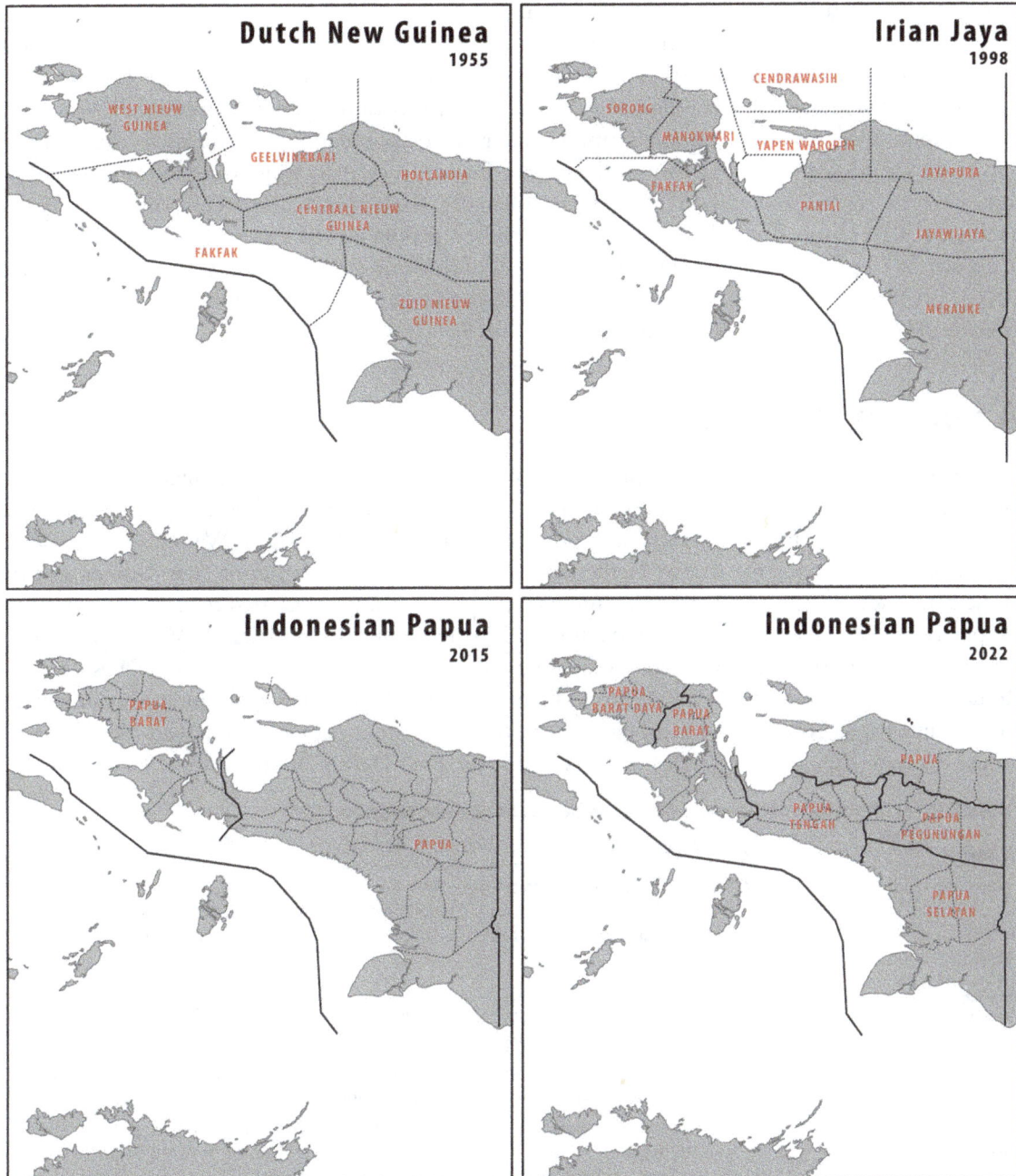

Figure 1.4: Administrative 'residentie' of Dutch New Guinea (as of 1955), regencies of Irian Jaya (as of 1998), and provinces and regencies of Indonesian Papua (as of 2015 and 2022).

Source: Dylan Gaffney.

Although the Indonesian independence movement laid claim to all of the Dutch East Indies from Sumatra to the 141st meridian, the transfer of control over West New Guinea to Indonesia did not occur until 1963. This process was facilitated by the United Nations Temporary Executive Authority (UNTEA) backed by the United States, despite being fiercely contested by the Netherlands (see Kuitenbrouwer 2016; Penders 2002; Webster 2013 for details). Then renamed Irian Barat and later Irian Jaya,[3] it was administered as a single province of Indonesia until 2001 when it was renamed Papua and given 'special autonomy' status. In 2003 the area was subdivided into Papua and Papua Barat provinces, and, in 2022, it was further divided into six smaller provinces (Figure 1.4), part of a gradual process of devolution and decentralisation (Kusumaryati 2019). In recent years, the demography of West New Guinea has rapidly changed: the population has increased tenfold since 1963 and has doubled since the turn of the twenty-first century, primarily owing to transmigration from western, central, and eastern Indonesia to urban centres in New Guinea (compare 1999 census data with 2020 census data). As of 2020, over 5 million people now live in an area of 415,000 km² (a density of 13 people per square km) with over half of those now being recent settlers (Ananta et al. 2016). For histories of Indonesian administration beyond what can be written here see, for instance, Gietzelt (1989), Timmer (2007), and Viartasiwi (2018).

A note on terminology

Owing to the turbulent and often violent history of colonial administrative changes in West New Guinea, the names used to refer to the western part of the island and its satellites can be confusing and contentious, carrying important social and political implications (Table 1.1). We refer here to West New Guinea to describe the former Netherlands New Guinea, the portion of New Guinea and its outliers now administered by Indonesia. Internationally, this is usually referred to as West Papua and has previously been referred to as Irian Barat (until 1973) and Irian Jaya (until 2002). Within Indonesia, the area tends to be referred to as Papua, comprising the provinces of Papua, Papua Barat (West Papua), Papua Barat Daya (Southwest Papua), Papua Tengah (Central Papua), Papua Pegunungan (Highland Papua), and Papua Selatan (South Papua). To describe indigenous people within West New Guinea, we use the term Papuan, to align with the commonly used self-identification.

Table 1.1: Terminology often used to describe parts of New Guinea.

Name	Description
West New Guinea West Papua Papua Irian Jaya (obsolete) Irian Barat (obsolete)	The former territory of Netherlands New Guinea (Nederlands-Nieuw-Guinea). Today Indonesian-administered Papua, Papua Barat, Papua Barat Daya, Papua Tengah, Papua Pegunungan, and Papua Selatan provinces including the mainland and outlying islands.
Western New Guinea (WNG)	The island of New Guinea west of the 141st meridian east, including the mainland of Indonesia-administered New Guinea but excluding outlying islands.
Eastern New Guinea (ENG)	The island of New Guinea east of the 141st meridian east, forming modern mainland Papua New Guinea but excluding outlying islands.
Papua New Guinea (PNG)	The modern nation-state of Papua New Guinea incorporating the eastern half of New Guinea and circum-New Guinea Islands in the Bismarck Archipelago, Southeast Papuan Islands, and northern Solomon Chain.
Circum-New Guinea Islands	Small islands peripheral to New Guinea, including the Raja Ampat Islands, Cenderawasih Bay, the Aru Islands, the Bismarck Archipelago, the Southeast Papuan Islands, the Solomon Islands, and the Torres Strait Islands, often extended to also include the Malukan Islands, Lesser Sunda Islands, and Sulawesi.

Source: Dylan Gaffney.

---

3   For clarification, the term Papua likely derives from a Spanish transliteration of the Biak term *sup i papwa* which denotes the 'land below the sunset', initially referring to the islands of Raja Ampat and Halmahera, and later mistakenly applied to the island of New Guinea and its people (Gelpke 1993). New Guinea, or 'Nueva Guinea', was first used by Ortiz de Retez, referring to the similarities he perceived between the islanders and those on the west African coast. Irian is an acronym for Ikut Republik Indonesia Anti-Nederland (Join the Republic of Indonesia Anti-Netherlands) that was, in 1945, associated with the Biak term *iryan* meaning 'the rays of the sun that drive the sea-fog away' by the brothers Marcus Wonggor Kaisiëpo and Frans Kaisiëpo on the suggestion of the Indonesian nationalist Soegoro Atmoprasodjo (Mote and Rutherford 2001).

Key research themes

As noted by Ballard (1999), the process of colonial boundary-making and naming has meant that historical narratives have been primarily produced at the macro scale from outside of New Guinea. As we will see in Chapter 2, these lines drawn up by competing colonial powers have come to shape the nature of academic research in the region, and in particular account for the long neglect of West New Guinea in the scholarship of the Pacific and Island Southeast Asia. Key debates in Asia-Pacific anthropology have been driven from research outside of West New Guinea; however, with systematic research being undertaken in the area, West New Guinea is now well placed to contribute in important ways to several research themes about the history of the region. Here, we identify seven key themes that have emerged from the wider literature, and which are the focus of chapters in the present volume.

Early peopling

The timing and nature of maritime dispersals by our species—*Homo sapiens*—out of Eurasia and into Oceania during the Pleistocene (Ice Ages) remains unresolved. During the hypothesised window of colonisation (>65,000–50,000 years ago), Australia and New Guinea were connected by lowered sea levels as one continent called Sahul. Recent computer modelling suggests north-western New Guinea would have been the most easily reached navigational target along a seafaring corridor of intervisible islands on the equator, in what is today Indonesia (Kealy et al. 2018). Moreover, genetic research suggests that these northern movements may have led to interaction and admixture between distinct hominin groups, especially between *Homo sapiens* and the Denisovans. The latter are known from fossil remains in Eurasia (Demeter et al. 2022; Slon et al. 2017) but Papuan people are host to some of the highest contributions of Denisovan DNA on the planet (Teixeira et al. 2021). Finds at Madjedbebe in north-western Australia may date human occupation to around 65,000 years ago (Clarkson et al. 2017), and certainly humans were present around other parts of Australia and Papua New Guinea by about 50,000–45,000 years ago (Norman et al. 2022; Summerhayes et al. 2010). We might, then, expect similar ages for West New Guinean sites, especially because genetic studies suggest there was a dual entrance into Sahul from the north and the south (Pedro et al. 2020). Toé Cave on the Bird's Head provides some of the only published radiocarbon dates from West New Guinea, which indicates occupation began just before the Last Glacial Maximum (c. 30,000 years ago; Pasveer 2004). This is consistent with the earliest archaeological sites from Maluku: at Golo cave on Gebe Island (c. 35,000 years ago; Bellwood 2019) and Liang Lemdubu in the Aru Islands (c. 27,000 years ago; O'Connor et al. 2005). However, it means that there is now a considerable temporal lag between West New Guinea archaeology and that of Australia and Papua New Guinea, which can only be resolved with ongoing fieldwork and publication, particularly from the Raja Ampat Islands and the Bird's Head Peninsula.

Human adaptation and transformation

The settlers of Sahul were the descendants of the world's very first maritime peoples, who crossed several biogeographic divides to populate their newfound continent. Important questions therefore abound about processes of human behavioural diversification as these colonists then moved into a range of novel ecologies around northern Sahul, including lowland tropical rainforests, high altitudes, mangrove swamps and small offshore islands (Summerhayes et al. 2017). A key marker of our species is our ecological plasticity, hyper-adaptable to a huge variety of challenging environments. We can ask similar questions about people's adaptive responses to fluctuating climates, sea level rise, the disappearance of megafauna and changes to tropical forest cover which occurred at the end of the Pleistocene period

(Hope and Haberle 2005). Another common feature of *Homo sapiens* is that we creatively transform our worlds around us. We can, therefore, ask how humans shaped these variable and changing ecologies which they came to live within, and how these long histories of ecological management contributed to the present distribution of flora and fauna around New Guinea. Similarly, we can explore how humans illustrated their experiences in these ecologies in the archaeological record; with that in mind, the connection between rock paintings and portable art dating to between 50,000 and 30,000 years old in Sulawesi, Borneo, and Timor (Aubert et al. 2007, 2014, 2018; Brumm et al. 2021; Langley et al. 2020), and similar, but as yet undated, paintings preserved around parts of coastal and highland New Guinea (Arifin and Delanghe 2004) remains totally unexplored.

Food production

Following climatic warming at the beginning of the Holocene period (11,700 years ago), New Guinea became separated from Australia and there is strong evidence from Kuk Swamp, in highland Papua New Guinea, that communities began to experiment with diverse forms of food production like cultivation, horticulture, and agroforestry, eventually leading the island to become an important setting for early agriculture at a comparable time when changes occurred in Eurasia and Meso-America (Denham 2018). The multidirectional exchange of vegetatively propagated plants like aroids, tubers, and bananas between the highlands and lowlands, and from New Guinea to its outlying islands, generated a wide array of cultivars (Barton and Denham 2011; Denham and Donohue 2009). Hypothetically, some of these crop movements may have been interlinked with the dispersal of the Trans–New Guinea languages across western New Guinea and even into Island Southeast Asia (Pawley and Hammarström 2018), alongside more intensive landscape modification and forest clearance (Haberle et al. 2001), and the emergence of technologically 'Neolithic' societies with polished stone, fixed structures, and exchange systems, in the highland zone (Shaw et al. 2020). There are no published archaeological sequences from West New Guinea that provide evidence for the emergence of agriculture, although ethnographic observations and palaeoecological research indicate that complex innovations in cultivation, like those at Kuk, may also have occurred in the Baliem Valley (Haberle et al. 1991). Further research is required to clarify when and how humans in West New Guinea began to experiment with cultivation and diversify their modes of plant food production.

Language dispersals

The coasts of western New Guinea are strategically located to address the migration of Austronesian-speaking cultures from Taiwan into the Pacific during the fourth millennium before the present. Based on linguistic evidence, Cenderawasih Bay in north-western New Guinea has long been posited as the immediate source of Austronesian speech communities before they skirted the north coast and migrated to the Bismarck Archipelago and the remote Pacific (Pawley 2003). Currently, the nature of these dispersals in Oceania is debated, with one group of scholars supporting a fast-track model, whereby highly mobile Austronesian speakers moved through Island Southeast Asia and the Pacific, bringing with them pottery and domesticated animals (Kirch 2017; Spriggs 2012), while another group supports gradual technological and language shifts that resulted from established social networks operating around New Guinea and Island Southeast Asia during the Holocene (Donohue and Denham 2010). The only way to resolve these issues is by investigating pottery-bearing sequences in north-western New Guinea and its offshore islands. Currently, there are only tentative hints at these connections, for instance in the presence of jade tools geochemically sourced to a western New Guinea origin but discovered at Lapita pottery-bearing sites in the Bismarck Archipelago (Harlow et al. 2012).

Exchange networks and the recent past

A rich record detailing the emergence of the Indonesian Metal Age and the expansion of Indian Ocean Rim trade networks also awaits publication from West New Guinea, which increasingly became interconnected with the globalising world economy in the last 2000 years (Bellwood 2019). These new connectivities especially involved the introduction of bronze axes, glass beads and later iron into West New Guinea (Elmberg 1968; Kamma and Kooijman 1973), interlinked with the expansion of the Maluku spice trade (Ono et al. 2018). In return, New Guinea communities sent highly desired goods such as bird-of-paradise feathers westwards where they became signs of prestige in south-west Asia and Europe (Swadling 1996). The involvement of New Guinea in these exchange networks further increased in the colonial period as traders from New Guinea, Maluku, Southeast Asia, China, and Europe situated themselves in strategic positions to facilitate the movement of goods back to their home communities. Fortifications and churches relating to the initial expansion of Dutch colonial control have been recorded in Maluku and Timor (Lape 2006; O'Connor et al. 2012; Veth et al. 2005) but remain sparsely reported from West New Guinea (Galis and Kamma 1958). There remains much to uncover about these globalising processes through archaeological, historical, and oral history records in the area. As Ballard (2010) notes, the heritage of the recent past can resonate with Papuan communities and become a meeting ground for local and academic interests that generate an array of novel questions to ask about the past. The necessary synthesis of archaeological and oral historical information about the recent past, in particular, could create important methodological innovations like those increasingly developed in Papua New Guinea (Tsang et al. 2022; Urwin et al. 2023).

Materialising culture

The careful examination of the technological sequences employed to produce ethnographically collected objects such as axes, pottery, and string bags can provide important information about group relatedness, mobility, and social boundaries across West New Guinea (Pétrequin and Pétrequin 2006). These observations can shed light on how their technological antecedents—those objects uncovered archaeologically—might have been made, and what their implications are for understanding society in the past. These art and craft traditions, some of which have long histories spanning hundreds or thousands of years, remain significant for many people in West New Guinea today. The manufacture, use, and display of such objects not only reinvigorates customary technologies but also creates new forms of tradition. Increasingly, organic materials are now substituted by synthetic ones and the growth of urban centres and large plantations are reconfiguring people's social and physical environments and access to resources (Chao 2018). As such, there is a real need to explore how people are navigating these changes and transforming their material worlds.

Museums and collecting

The Dutch colonial expansion into West New Guinea was initially stimulated by its strategic position to protect sovereign trade interests within the East Indies, but later became the focus of control, development, missionisation, and natural resource extraction from within New Guinea itself. Alongside this came early attempts at ethnographic documentation and a period of collecting, during which time thousands of art pieces and everyday objects were transported to museums in Batavia (now Jakarta) and Europe (Corbey 2017, 2019; Corbey and Weener 2015). The exploration of these museum collections alongside their historical documentation provides important insight into the day-to-day activities of the users and the cosmology and material expression of the makers, not to mention the peculiarly European practices of collecting in New Guinea (Haslwanter 2018; Jacobs

2011; Veys 2018). More importantly, things now housed in museums can resonate emotionally with visitors and connect Papuans—sometimes quite literally—with their ancestors. The records, photographs and collections produced by early ethnographers may similarly be powerful catalysts that connect people with their past (see examples from Papua New Guinea in Bell 2003; Gillespie 2017). The potency of these materials raises important questions about the ethics of display and storage; conversations which Papuans are increasingly part of (Hermkens and Timmer 2022).

Book structure

In the following chapters, the contributors bring to bear new archaeological, linguistic, biological, and ethnographic observations on the abovementioned research themes. First, we begin with macro-regional syntheses of West New Guinea's human histories from the perspective of historiography, linguistics, and biological anthropology. In Chapter 2, Gaffney and Tolla examine West New Guinea's ecological, cultural and colonial history before proceeding to outline how these have shaped social science research in the region from the sixteenth to twenty-first centuries. Arnold, in Chapter 3, provides the most comprehensive and up-to-date analysis of West New Guinea's languages and their historical relationships. Jacobs, Kusama, and Attenborough then present three linked chapters that examine the human genetic data from West New Guinea: in Chapter 4, they focus on broad-scale processes of demographic fluctuation and archaic hominin introgression during the Pleistocene; in Chapter 5, they examine local demographic shifts, and the geneflow between social and linguistic groupings; in Chapter 6, they present an overview of selective pressures acting on the human genome in New Guinea.

The volume then moves to area- and site-focused archaeological chapters primarily stemming from the work of Indonesian and Papuan archaeologists at BRIN who have been excavating in the region (Figure 1.5). Most of these chapters are provided in translation from the original Bahasa Indonesia. Other contributions come from international research teams who have excavated collaboratively at a series of key locations. In Chapter 7, Boesl, Adhityatama, and Wall describe the major landscape transformations that occurred around the southern Raja Ampat Islands and Bird's Head, formerly Sahul, at the end of the Pleistocene. They also speculate how future archaeological research in the area may help us to re-evaluate how Sahul was first colonised. In Chapter 8, Gaffney, Tanudirjo, Mas'ud, Novita Idje Djami, Razak Matcap, and Russell describe their results of a reconnaissance survey in the northern Raja Ampat Islands and examine how archaeological site distributions may document different settlement patterns in the past. Mene, Setiawan, and Gaffney then, in Chapter 9, provide provisional radiocarbon, lithic, and bone artefact results from Andarewa site on the Bomberai Peninsula, frequented from the Last Glacial Maximum to the Late Holocene. In Chapter 10, Tolla, Roberts, Lucas, Bonatz, and Posth present isotopic data from several lowland sites to explore changes to diet during the Holocene. In Chapter 11, Fairyo describes rock art from the lowland interior of Keerom, north New Guinea. Chapter 12, contributed by Suroto, describes recent survey and test excavations in the western part of Lake Sentani on the north coast of New Guinea; an area which may prove important in documenting expansions of Austronesian language groups into West New Guinea, alongside the emergence of globalising trade networks. With a focus on the area's recent material past, Fairyo then presents a brief report of decorated pottery recovered from burial cave sites in the nearby Kayu Batu area, in Chapter 13. Kawer and Gaffney next describe survey and surface artefact collections relating to the Pacific War on Biak and its satellite islands in Cenderawasih Bay. They note how Biak's extensive wartime archaeology not only reflects its importance for the Japanese and Allied military, but also the resonance of this event for local people.

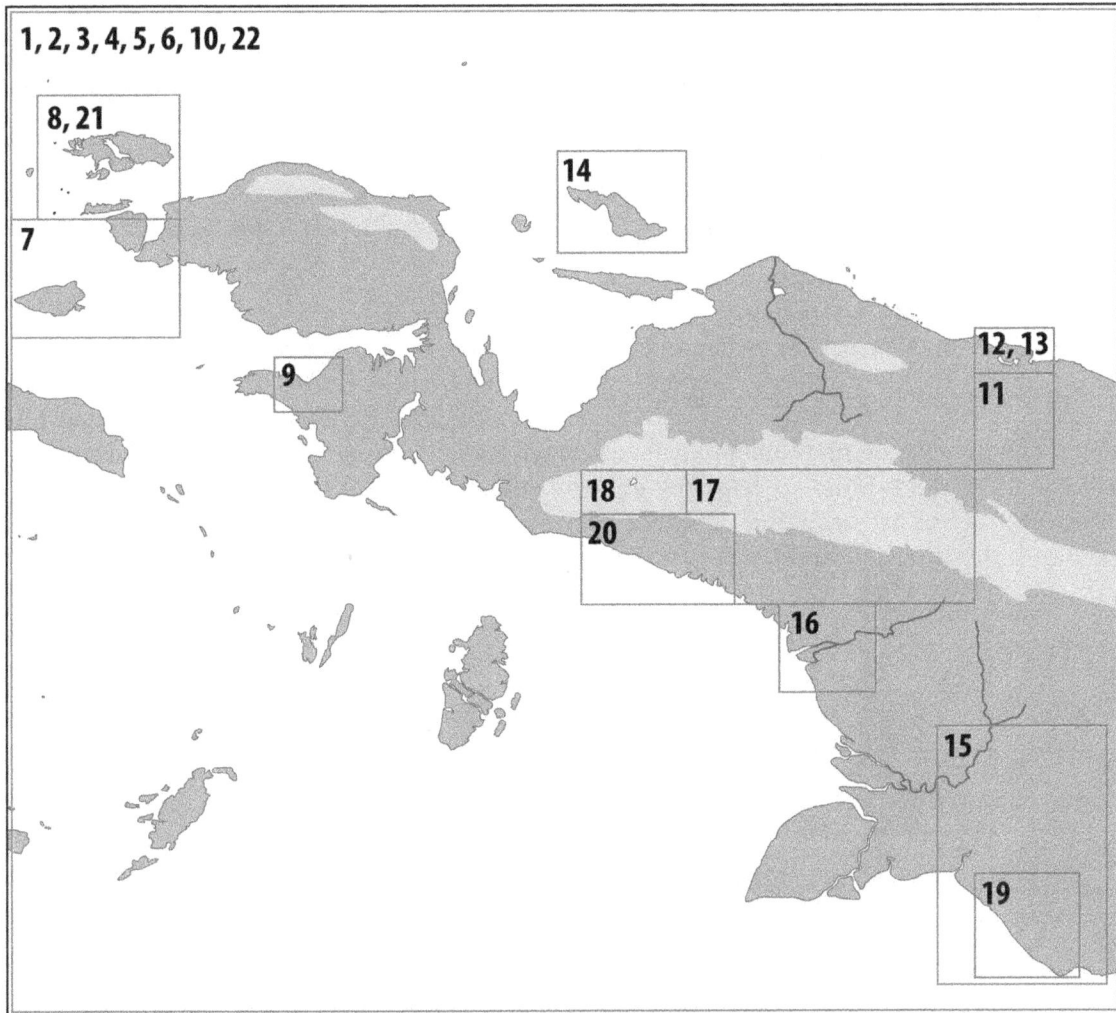

Figure 1.5: West New Guinea, highlighting study areas described in each chapter of the volume.
Source: Dylan Gaffney.

The book then moves to explorations of ethnographic material culture from the recent past, including its connections with deep time and the present, which brings Papuan, Indonesian, and international dialogues to the fore. These chapters provide vivid descriptions of how material culture can activate new understandings of West New Guinea societies, both historically and in the present. In Chapter 15, McNiven charts the social lives of Marind-anim canoes as they traded and raided along the south-central coast of New Guinea and in the Torres Strait. The author also speculates how these processes could be explored in the archaeological past through the sourcing of stone artefacts like axes and clubs. Powell Davies then presents an ethnographic account of the transformative ways in which Asmat carvers think about stone and steel tools in Chapter 16. Far from just revisiting the Stone Age trope, this chapter examines how Papuans conceptualise their materials, and themselves, in the wider context of state-level economic changes.

In Chapter 17, Voirol describes the marine shell trade in the West New Guinea Highlands, drawing from ethnographic, oral historical, and museum-based research among the Mee, Dani, Lani, Yali, and Eipo. This is followed, in Chapter 18, by Tekege's personal reflection on how shells are used as bride wealth among the Mee and how the perception of these practices has changed in the twenty-first century. In Chapter 19, Kanem describes women who make <u>noken</u> string bags in Merauke and how these processes have begun to change dramatically in recent years following, but not wholly related to, these objects being recognised by the United Nations Educational, Scientific and Cultural Organization (UNESCO) as intangible heritage. In Chapter 20, the social relationships that remain bound up in Kamoro material culture housed in ethnographic museums are described by Jacobs. Following on from this, in Chapter 21, Veys elucidates the politics of displaying West New Guinea ritual art in European museum settings, especially in view of both Papuan and pan-Pacific audiences.

Finally, Tsang and Summerhayes provide an afterword in Chapter 22 that reflects upon the significance of West New Guinea anthropology, archaeology, linguistics and material culture, in the context of the Pacific's deep human history. They also provide comments on future avenues for developing these disciplines within New Guinea more broadly. Given the current political and economic landscape, this process is likely to be a gradual one and attention should initially be directed towards meaningful community involvement, equitable knowledge exchange, and capacity-building. With this in mind, we hope that this volume will be of value to Papuans interested in their island's history and become a time capsule of information that will be available to future generations of Papuan archaeologists, anthropologists, linguists, geneticists, and curators.

References

Abdullah, T. and M. Paeni (eds.) 2015. *Diaspora Melanesia Di Nusantara*. Direktorat Sejarah dan Nilai Budaya, Direktorat Jenderal Kebudayaan, Kementerian Pendidikan dan Kebudayaan, Jakarta.

Ananta, A., D.R.W.W. Utami, and N.B. Handayani 2016. Statistics on ethnic diversity in the land of Papua, Indonesia. *Asia & the Pacific Policy Studies* 3(3):458–474. doi.org/10.1002/app5.143.

Andaya, L.Y. 1993. *The world of Maluku*. University of Hawai'i Press, Honolulu. doi.org/10.1515/9780824890599.

Antunes, N., W. Schiefenhövel, F. d'Errico, W.E. Banks, and M. Vanhaeren 2020. Quantitative methods demonstrate that environment alone is an insufficient predictor of present-day language distributions in New Guinea. *PLoS ONE* 15(10):e0239359. doi.org/10.1371/journal.pone.0239359.

Aplin, K. and J. Pasveer 2005. Mammals and other vertebrates from late Quaternary archaeological sites on Pulau Kobroor, Aru Islands, eastern Indonesia. In S. O'Connor, M. Spriggs, and P. Veth (eds), *The archaeology of the Aru Islands, Eastern Indonesia*, pp. 41–62. ANU ePress, Canberra.

Aplin, K.P., J.M. Pasveer, and W.E. Boles 1999. Late Quaternary vertebrates from the Bird's Head Peninsula, Irian Jaya, Indonesia, including descriptions of two previously unknown marsupial species. *Records of the Western Australian Museum Supplement* 57(57):351–387.

Arifin, K. and P. Delanghe 2004. *Rock art in West Papua*. UNESCO, Paris.

Aubert, M., S. O'Connor, M. McCulloch, G. Mortimer, A. Watchman, and M. Richer-LaFlèche 2007. Uranium-series dating rock art in East Timor. *Journal of Archaeological Science* 34(6):991–996. doi.org/10.1016/j.jas.2006.09.017.

Aubert, M., A. Brumm, M. Ramli, T. Sutikna, E.W. Saptomo, B. Hakim, M.J. Morwood, G.D. van den Bergh, L. Kinsley, and A. Dosseto 2014. Pleistocene cave art from Sulawesi, Indonesia. *Nature* 514 (7521):223–227. doi.org/10.1038/nature13422.

Aubert, M., P. Setiawan, A.A. Oktaviana, A. Brumm, P.H. Sulistyarto, E.W. Saptomo, B. Istiawan, T.A. Ma'rifat, V.N. Wahyuono, F.T. Atmoko, J.-X. Zhao, J. Huntley, P.S.C. Taçon, D.L. Howard, and H.E.A. Brand 2018. Palaeolithic cave art in Borneo. *Nature* 564(7735):254–257. doi.org/10.1038/s41586-018-0679-9.

Baldwin, S.L., P.G. Fitzgerald, and L.E. Webb 2012. Tectonics of the New Guinea region. *Annual Review of Earth and Planetary Sciences* 40(1):495–520. doi.org/10.1146/annurev-earth-040809-152540.

Ballard, C. 1992. Painted rock art sites in western Melanesia: Locational evidence for an 'Austronesian' tradition. In J. McDonald and I.P. Haskovec (eds), *State of the art: Regional art studies in Australia and Melanesia*, pp. 94–105. Occasional AURA Publication Number 6. Australian Rock Art Research Association, Melbourne.

Ballard, C. 1993. Stimulating minds to fantasy? A critical etymology for Sahul. In M. Smith, M. Spriggs, and B. Fankhauser (eds), *Sahul in review: Pleistocene archaeology in Australia, New Guinea and Island Melanesia*, pp. 17–23. Department of Prehistory, The Australian National University, Canberra.

Ballard, C. 1999. Blanks in the writing: Possible histories for West New Guinea. *Journal of Pacific History* 34(2):149–55. doi.org/10.1080/00223349908572899.

Ballard, C. 2010. Synthetic histories: Possible futures for Papuan Pasts. *Reviews in Anthropology* 39(4):232–257. doi.org/10.1080/00938157.2010.524865.

Barton, H. and T.P. Denham 2011. Prehistoric vegeculture and social life in Island Southeast Asia and Melanesia. In G. Barker and M. Janowaski (eds), *Why cultivate? Anthropological and archaeological approaches to foraging–farming transitions in Southeast Asia*, pp. 17–25. McDonald Institute of Archaeology Research, Cambridge.

Bartstra, G.-J. (ed.) 1998. *Bird's Head approaches: Irian Jaya studies—A programme for interdisciplinary research*. A.A. Balkema, Rotterdam.

Bayliss-Smith, T., J. Golson, and P. Hughes 2017. Phase 6: Impact of the sweet potato on swamp landuse, pig rearing and exchange relations. In J. Golson, T. Denham, P. Hughes, P. Swadling, and J. Muke (eds), *Ten thousand years of cultivation at Kuk Swamp in the Highlands of Papua New Guinea*, pp. 297–323. Terra Australis 46. ANU Press, Canberra. doi.org/10.22459/TA46.07.2017.16.

Bell, J.A. 2003. Looking to see: Reflections on visual repatriation in the Purari Delta, Gulf Province, Papua New Guinea. In L. Peers and A. Brown (eds), *Museums and source communities*, pp. 111–122. Routledge, London.

Bellwood, P. 2019. The northern Spice Islands in prehistory, from 40,000 years ago to the recent past. In P. Bellwood (ed.), *The Spice Islands in prehistory: Archaeology in the Northern Moluccas, Indonesia*, pp. 211–221. ANU Press, Canberra. doi.org/10.22459/TA50.2019.13.

Bertoni, C. and J. Álvarez 2012. Interplay between submarine depositional processes and recent tectonics in the Biak Basin, Western Papua, Eastern Indonesia. *Berita Sedimentologi* 23(1):42–46.

Bone, R.C. 1964. The international status of West New Guinea until 1884. *Journal of Southeast Asian History* 5(2):150–180. doi.org/10.1017/S0217781100000983.

Brookfield, H. and B. Allen 1989. High-altitude occupation and environment. *Mountain Research and Development* 9(3):201–209. doi.org/10.2307/3673510.

Brumm, A., A.A. Oktaviana, B. Burhan, B. Hakim, R. Lebe, J.-X. Zhao, P.H. Sulistyarto, M. Ririmasse, S. Adhityatama, I. Sumantri, and M. Aubert 2021. Oldest cave art found in Sulawesi. *Science Advances* 7(3):eabd4648. doi.org/10.1126/sciadv.abd4648.

Bulmer, S. and R. Bulmer 1964. The prehistory of the Australian New Guinea Highlands. *American Anthropologist* 66(4):39–76.

Chao, S. 2018. In the shadow of the palm: Dispersed ontologies among Marind, West Papua. *Cultural Anthropology* 33(4):621–649. doi.org/10.14506/ca33.4.08.

Chappell, J., Y. Ota, and K. Berryman 1996. Late Quaternary coseismic uplift history of Huon Peninsula, Papua New Guinea. *Quaternary Science Reviews* 15(1):7–22. doi.org/10.1016/0277-3791(95)00062-3.

Charlton, T.R. 1996. Correlation of the Salawati and Tomori Basins, eastern Indonesia: A constraint on left-lateral displacements of the Sorong fault zone. In R. Hall and D. Blundell (eds), *Tectonic evolution of Southeast Asia*, pp. 465–481. The Geological Society, London. doi.org/10.1144/GSL.SP.1996.106.01.29.

Cheesman, L.E. 1943. Japanese operations in New Guinea. *The Geographical Journal* 101(3): 97–110. doi.org/10.2307/1788873.

Clarkson, C., Z. Jacobs, B. Marwick, R. Fullagar, L. Wallis, M. Smith, R.G. Roberts, E. Hayes, K. Lowe, X. Carah, S.A. Florin, J. McNeil, D. Cox, L.J. Arnold, Q. Hua, J. Huntley, H.E.A. Brand, T. Manne, A. Fairbairn, J. Shulmeister, L. Lyle, M. Salinas, M. Page, K. Connell, G. Park, K. Norman, T. Murphy, and C. Pardoe 2017. Human occupation of northern Australia by 65,000 years ago. *Nature* 547:306–310. doi.org/10.1038/nature22968.

Corbey, R. 2017. *Raja Ampat ritual art: Spirit priests and ancestor cults in New Guinea's far west.* C. Zwartenkot Art Books, Leiden.

Corbey, R. 2019. *Korwar: Northwest New Guinea ritual art according to missionary sources.* C. Zwartenkot Art Books, Leiden.

Corbey, R. and F.K. Weener 2015. Collecting while converting: Missionaries and ethnographics. *Journal of Art Historiography* 12(12):1–14.

Dam, M.A.C. and T.E. Wong 1998. The environmental and geologic setting of the Bird's Head, Irian Jaya. In G.-J. Bartstra (ed.), *Bird's Head approaches: Irian Jaya studies—A programme for interdisciplinary research*, pp. 1–28. A.A. Balkema, Rotterdam.

Defert, G. 1996. *L'Indonésie et la Nouvelle-Guinée Occidentale: Maintien des Frontières Coloniales ou Respect des Identités.* L'Harmattan, Paris.

Demeter, F., C. Zanolli, K.E. Westaway, R. Joannes-Boyau, P. Duringer, M.W. Morley, F. Welker, P.L. Rüther, M.M. Skinner, H. McColl, C. Gaunitz, L. Vinner, T.E. Dunn, J. v. Olsen, M. Sikora, J.L. Ponche, E. Suzzoni, S. Frangeul, Q. Boesch, P.O. Antoine, L. Pan, S. Xing, J.X. Zhao, R.M. Bailey, S. Boualaphane, P. Sichanthongtip, D. Sihanam, E. Patole-Edoumba, F. Aubaile, F. Crozier, N. Bourgon, A. Zachwieja, T. Luangkhoth, V. Souksavatdy, T. Sayavongkhamdy, E. Cappellini, A.M. Bacon, J.J. Hublin, E. Willerslev, and L. Shackelford 2022. A Middle Pleistocene Denisovan molar from the Annamite Chain of northern Laos. *Nature Communications* 13(1):2557. doi.org/10.1038/s41467-022-29923-z.

Denham, T. 2018. *Tracing early agriculture in the Highlands of New Guinea: Plot, mound and ditch.* Routledge, London. doi.org/10.4324/9781351115308.

Denham, T. and M. Donohue 2009. Pre-Austronesian dispersal of banana cultivars west from New Guinea: Linguistic relics from eastern Indonesia. *Archaeology in Oceania* 44(1):18–28. doi.org/10.1002/j.1834-4453.2009.tb00041.x.

Donohue, M. and M. Crowther 2005. Meeting in the middle: Interaction in North-Central New Guinea. In A. Pawley, R. Attenborough, J. Golson, and R. Hide (eds), *Papuan pasts: Cultural, linguistic and biological histories of the Papuan-speaking peoples*, pp. 167–184. Pacific Linguistics 572. Research School of Pacific and Asian Studies, The Australian National University, Canberra.

Donohue, M. and T. Denham 2010. Farming and language in Island Southeast Asia: Reframing Austronesian history. *Current Anthropology* 51(2):223–256. doi.org/10.1086/650991.

Ellen, R. and D.K. Latinis 2012. Ceramic sago ovens and the history of regional trading patterns in Eastern Indonesia and the Papuan coast. *Indonesia and the Malay World* 40(116):20–38. doi.org/10.1080/13639 811.2011.648994.

Ellison, J. 2005. Holocene palynology and sea-level change in two estuaries in southern Irian Jaya. *Palaeogeography, Palaeoclimatology, Palaeoecology* 220(3–4):291–309. doi.org/10.1016/j.palaeo.2005.01.008.

Elmberg, J-E. 1966. *The Popot feast cycle: Acculturated exchange among the Mejprat Papuans*. The Ethnographical Museum, Stockholm.

Elmberg, J.-E. 1968. *Balance and circulation: Aspects of tradition and change among the Mejprat of Irian Barat*. The Ethnographical Museum, Stockholm.

Gaffney, D. 2021. Human behavioural dynamics in island rainforests: Evidence from the Raja Ampat Islands, West Papua. Unpublished PhD thesis. Department of Archaeology, University of Cambridge, Cambridge.

Galis, K.W. and F.C. Kamma 1958. Het fort te Jémbakaki. *Nieuw-Guinea Studien* 2:206–222.

Gelpke, J.S. 1993. On the origin of the name Papua. *Bijdragen tot de Taal-, Land-en Volkenkunde* 2:318–332. doi.org/10.1163/22134379-90003129.

Gietzelt, D. 1989. The Indonesianization of West Papua. *Oceania* 59(3), 201–221. doi.org/10.1002/j.1834-4461.1989.tb02322.x.

Gillespie, K. 2017. Protecting our shadow: Repatriating ancestral recordings to the Lahir Islands, Papua New Guinea. In K. Gillespie, S. Treloyn, and D. Niles (eds), *A distinctive voice in the Antipodes: Essays in honour of Stephen A. Wild*, pp. 355–374. ANU Press, Canberra. doi.org/10.22459/DVA.07.2017.13.

Golson, J. and D.S. Gardner 1990. Agriculture and sociopolitical organization in New Guinea Highlands prehistory. *Annual Review of Anthropology* 19:395–417. doi.org/10.1146/annurev.an.19.100190.002143.

Greub, S. (ed.) 1992. *Art of Northwest New Guinea: From Geelvink Bay, Humboldt Bay, and Lake Sentani*. Rizzoli, New York.

Haberle, S.G., G.S. Hope, and Y. DeFretes 1991. Environmental change in the Baliem Valley, Montane Irian Jaya, Republic of Indonesia. *Journal of Biogeography* 18(1):25–40. doi.org/10.2307/2845242.

Haberle, S.G., G.S. Hope, and S. van der Kaars 2001. Biomass burning in Indonesia and Papua New Guinea: Natural and human induced fire events in the fossil record. *Palaeogeography, Palaeoclimatology, Palaeoecology* 171(3–4):259–268. doi.org/10.1016/S0031-0182(01)00248-6.

Haenen, P. 1998. History, exchange, and myth in the southeast Bird's Head of Irian Jaya. In J. Miedema, C. Odé, and R.A.C. Dam (eds), *Perspectives on the Bird's Head of Irian Jaya, Indonesia: Proceedings of the Conference, Leiden, 13–17 October 1997*, pp. 235–256. Rodopi, Amsterdam; Atlanta. doi.org/10.1163/9789004652644_013.

Hall, R. 2017. Southeast Asia: New views of the geology of the Malay Archipelago. *Annual Review of Earth and Planetary Sciences* 45:331–351. doi.org/10.1146/annurev-earth-063016-020633.

Haneveld, G.T. 1961. De medische aspecten van het verlies van Nederlands eerste nederzetting op Nieuw-Guinea, Fort Du Bus 1828–1835. *Nieuw Guinea Studien* 5(1):104–110.

Harlow, G.E., G.R. Summerhayes, H.L. Davies, and L. Matisoo-Smith 2012. A jade gouge from Emirau Island, Papua New Guinea (Early Lapita context, 3300 BP): A unique jadeitite. *European Journal of Mineralogy* 24(2):391–399. doi.org/10.1127/0935-1221/2012/0024-2175.

Haslwanter, K.W. 2018. He who travels … Heinrich Harrer as an explorer through western New Guinea 1962. In M. Flitsch, M. Powroznik, and M. Wernsdörfer (eds), *Encountering—Retracing—Mapping: The ethnographic legacy of Heinrich Harrer and Peter Aufschnaiter*, pp. 40–49. Arnoldsche Art Publishers, Stuttgart.

Healey, C.J. 1998. Political economy in the Kepala Burung region of Old Western New Guinea. In J. Miedema, C. Odé, and R.A.C. Dam (eds.), *Perspectives on the Bird's Head of Irian Jaya, Indonesia: Proceedings of the Conference, Leiden, 13–17 October 1997*, pp. 337–363. Rodopi, Amsterdam. doi.org/10.1163/9789004652644_019.

Hermkens, A.-K. and J. Timmer 2022. 'We are not an emblem': Impermanence and materiality in Asmat lifeworlds. In H. Geismar, T. Otto, and C. David Warner (eds), *Impermanence: Exploring continuous change across cultures*, pp. 110–130. UCL Press, London.

Hilder, B. 1980. *The voyage of Torres: The discovery of the southern coastline of New Guinea and Torres Strait by Captain Luis Baez de Torres in 1606.* University of Queensland Press, St Lucia.

Hope, G. 2007. Palaeoecology and palaeoenvironments of Papua. In A.J. Marshall and B.M. Beehler (eds), *The ecology of Papua*, pp. 255–266. Periplus, Singapore.

Hope, G.S. and K.P. Aplin 2007. Palaeontology of Papua. In A. Marshall and B. Beehler (eds), *The ecology of Papua*, 246–254. Periplus, Singapore.

Hope, G.S. and S.G. Haberle 2005. The history of the human landscapes of New Guinea. In A. Pawley, R. Attenborough, J. Golson, and R. Hide (eds), *Papuan pasts: Cultural, linguistic and biological histories of the Papuan-speaking peoples*, pp. 541–554. Pacific Linguistics 572. Research School of Pacific and Asian Studies, The Australian National University, Canberra.

Hope, G.S. and J.H. Hope 1976. Man on Mt. Jaya. In G.S. Hope, J.A. Peterson, U. Radok, and I. Allison (eds), *The equatorial glaciers of New Guinea. Results of the 1971–1973 Australian Universities' Expeditions to Irian Jaya: Survey, glaciology, meteorology, biology and paleoenvironments*, pp. 225–238. A.A. Balkema, Rotterdam. doi.org/10.1201/9780203736777-11.

Jaarsma, S.R. 1994. 'Your work is of no use to us …': Administrative interests in ethnographic research (West New Guinea, 1950–1962). *The Journal of Pacific History* 29(2):153–171. doi.org/10.1080/00223349408572769.

Jacobs, K. 2011. Transacting creations: The Kamoro Arts Festival (1998–2006) in Papua. *Asia Pacific Journal of Anthropology* 12(4):363–382. doi.org/10.1080/14442213.2011.586358.

Kamma, F.C. 1982. The incorporation of foreign culture elements and complexes by ritual enclosure among the Biak-Numforese. In P.E. de Josselin de Jong and E. Schwimmer (eds), *Symbolic anthropology in the Netherlands*, pp. 43–48. Nijhoff, The Hague. doi.org/10.1163/9789004287266_005.

Kamma, F.C. and S. Kooijman 1973. *Romawa Forja, child of the fire: Iron working and the role of iron in West New Guinea (West Irian).* E.J. Brill, Leiden. doi.org/10.1163/9789004545243.

Kealy, S., J. Louys, and S. O'Connor 2018. Least-cost pathway models indicate northern human dispersal from Sunda to Sahul. *Journal of Human Evolution* 125:59–70. doi.org/10.1016/j.jhevol.2018.10.003.

Kern, H. 1903. Een oud Javaansch geschiedkundig gedicht uit het bloeitijdperk van Madjapahit. *De Indische Gids* 25(1):341–360.

Kirch, P.V. 2017. *On the road of the winds: An archaeological history of the Pacific Islands before European contact*, 2nd edition. University of California Press, Oakland. doi.org/10.1525/9780520968899.

Kuitenbrouwer, V. 2016. Beyond the 'trauma of decolonisation': Dutch cultural diplomacy during the West New Guinea question (1950–62). *The Journal of Imperial and Commonwealth History* 44(2):306–327. doi.org/10.1080/03086534.2016.1175736.

Kusumaryati, V. 2019. Adat institutionalisation, the state and the quest for self-determination in West Papua. *The Asia Pacific Journal of Anthropology* 21(1):1–16. doi.org/10.1080/14442213.2019.1670238.

Langley, M.C., B. Hakim, A. Agus Oktaviana, B. Burhan, I. Sumantri, P. Hadi Sulistyarto, R. Lebe, D. McGahan, and A. Brumm, 2020. Portable art from Pleistocene Sulawesi. *Nature Human Behaviour* 4(6):597–602. doi.org/10.1038/s41562-020-0837-6.

Lape, P.V. 2006. Chronology of fortified settlements in East Timor. *Journal of Island and Coastal Archaeology* 1(2):285–297. doi.org/10.1080/15564890600939409.

Lee, I. 1912. *Commodore Sir John Hayes: His voyage and life*. Longmans, Green, and Co, London.

Löffler, E. 1977. *Geomorphology of Papua New Guinea*. Australian National University Press, Canberra.

Lugten, M.M.C. 1985. 'Between two worlds'. Dutch Eurasians in transition from the "Indies" to the Netherlands: 1930–1965. Unpublished BA Hons thesis. School of Social Inquiry, Murdoch University, Perth.

Mansoben, J.R. 1995. *Sistem Politik Tradisional Di Irian Jaya*. LIPI-RUL, Leiden.

Mansoben, J.R. 2007. The socio-cultural plurality of Papuan society. In A.J. Marshall and B.M. Beehler (eds), *The ecology of Papua*, pp. 108–120. Periplus, Singapore.

Marshall, A. and B. Beehler (eds) 2007. *The ecology of Papua*. Periplus, Singapore.

Miedema, J. and G. Reesink 2004. *One head, many faces: New perspectives on the Bird's Head Peninsula of New Guinea*. KITLV Press, Leiden. doi.org/10.1163/9789004454385_017.

Miedema, J., C. Odé, and R.A.C. Dam (eds) 1998. *Perspectives on the Bird's Head of Irian Jaya, Indonesia: Proceedings of the Conference, Leiden, 13–17 October 1997*. Rodopi, Amsterdam; Atlanta. doi.org/10.1163/9789004652644.

Milsom, J., D. Masson, and G. Nicols 1992. Three trench endings in eastern Indonesia. *Marine Geology* 104(1–4):227–241. doi.org/10.1016/0025-3227(92)90099-4.

Moore, C. 2003. *New Guinea: Crossing boundaries and history*. University of Hawai'i Press, Honolulu. doi.org/10.2307/j.ctvsrfkh.

Moore, C.C. and A.K. Romney 1994. Material culture, geographic propinquity, and linguistic affiliation on the north coast of New Guinea: A reanalysis of Welsch, Terrell, and Nadolski (1992). *American Anthropologist* 96(2):370–392. doi.org/10.1525/aa.1994.96.2.02a00050.

Mote, O. and D. Rutherford 2001. From Irian Jaya to Papua: The limits of primordialism in Indonesia's troubled east. *Indonesia* (72):115–140. doi.org/10.2307/3351483.

Norman, K., C. Shipton, S. O'Connor, W. Malanali, P. Collins, R. Wood, W.M. Saktura, R.G. Roberts, and Z. Jacobs 2022. Human occupation of the Kimberley coast of northwest Australia 50,000 years ago. *Quaternary Science Reviews* 288:107577. doi.org/10.1016/j.quascirev.2022.107577.

O'Connor, S., K.P. Aplin, M. Spriggs, P. Veth, and L.K. Ayliffe 2002. From savannah to rainforest: Changing environments and human occupation at Liang Lembudu, Aru Islands, Maluku (Indonesia). In P. Kershaw, B. David, N. Tapper, D. Penny, and J. Brown (eds), *Bridging Wallace's Line: The environmental and cultural history and dynamics of the SE-Asian-Australian region*, pp. 279–306. Catena Verlag, Ämelgasse.

O'Connor, S., K. Aplin, K. Szabó, J. Pasveer, P. Veth, and M. Spriggs 2005. Liang Lemdubu: A Pleistocene cave site in the Aru Islands. In S. O'Connor, M. Spriggs, and P. Veth (eds), *The archaeology of the Aru Islands, Eastern Indonesia*, pp. 171–204. ANU ePress, Canberra.

O'Connor, S., A. McWilliam, J.N. Fenner, and S. Brockwell 2012. Examining the origin of fortifications in East Timor: Social and environmental factors. *Journal of Island and Coastal Archaeology* 7(2):200–218. doi.org/10.1080/15564894.2011.619245.

Ono, R., F. Aziz, A.A. Oktaviana, D. Prastiningtyas, M. Ririmasse, N. Iriyanto, I. Zesse, Y. Hisa, and M. Yoneda 2018. Development of regional maritime networks during the Early Metal Age in Northern Maluku Islands: A view from excavated glass ornaments and pottery variation. *Journal of Island and Coastal Archaeology* 13(1):90–108. doi.org/10.1080/15564894.2017.1395374.

Pasveer, J. 2005. Bone artefacts from Liang Lemdubu and Liang Nabulei Lisa, Aru Islands. In S. O'Connor, M. Spriggs, and P. Veth (eds), *The archaeology of the Aru Islands, Eastern Indonesia*, pp. 235–254. ANU ePress, Canberra.

Pasveer, J. 2007. Prehistoric human presence in Papua and adjacent areas. In A.J. Marshall and B.M. Beehler (eds), *The ecology of Papua*, pp. 121–133. Periplus, Singapore.

Pasveer, J.M. 2004. *The Djief hunters: 26,000 years of rainforest exploitation on the Bird's Head of Papua, Indonesia*. A.A. Balkema, Leiden. doi.org/10.1201/b17006.

Pasveer, J.M., S.J. Clarke, and G.H. Miller 2002. Late Pleistocene human occupation of inland rainforest, Bird's Head, Papua. *Archaeology in Oceania* 37(2):92–95. doi.org/10.1002/j.1834-4453.2002.tb00510.x.

Pawley, A. 2003. Locating Proto Oceanic. In M. Ross, A. Pawley, and M. Osmond (eds), *The lexicon of Proto Oceanic: The culture and environment of ancestral Oceanic society, 2: The physical environment*, pp. 17–34. Research School of Pacific and Asian Studies, The Australian National University, Canberra.

Pawley, A. and H. Hammarström 2018. The Trans New Guinea family. In B. Palmer (ed.), *The languages and linguistics of the New Guinea area: A comprehensive guide*, pp. 21–196. De Gruyter Mouton, Berlin; Boston. doi.org/10.1515/9783110295252-002.

Pedro, N., N. Brucato, V. Fernandes, M. André, L. Saag, W. Pomat, C. Besse, A. Boland, J.-F. Deleuze, C. Clarkson, H. Sudoyo, M. Metspalu, M. Stoneking, M.P. Cox, M. Leavesley, L. Pereira, and F.-X. Ricaut 2020. Papuan mitochondrial genomes and the settlement of Sahul. *Journal of Human Genetics* 65:875–887. doi.org/10.1038/s10038-020-0781-3.

Penders, C.L.M. 2002. *The West New Guinea debacle: Dutch decolonisation and Indonesia, 1945–1962*. Brill, Leiden. doi.org/10.1163/9789004487239.

Pétrequin, A.-M. and P. Pétrequin 2006. *Objets de Pouvoir en Nouvelle-Guinée: Catalogue de La Donation Anne-Marie et Pierre Pétrequin*. Musée d'Archéologie nationale de Saint-Germain-en-Laye, Paris.

Ploeg, A. 1966. Some comparative remarks about the Dani of Baliem Valley and the Dani at Bokondini. *Bijdragen tot de Taal-, Land- en Volkenkunde* 122(2):255–273. doi.org/10.1163/22134379-90002932.

Poulgrain, G. 1999. Delaying the 'discovery' of oil in West New Guinea. *Journal of Pacific History* 34(2):205–218. doi.org/10.1080/00223349908572903.

Pouwer, J. 1966. Towards a configurational approach to society and culture in New Guinea. *The Journal of the Polynesian Society* 75(3):267–86.

Pouwer, J. 1999. The colonisation, decolonisation and recolonisation of West New Guinea. *Journal of Pacific History* 34(2):157–179. doi.org/10.1080/00223349908572900.

Ratman, N. 1998. Geology of the Bird's Head, Irian Jaya, Indonesia. In J. Miedema, C. Odé, and R.A.C. Dam (eds), *Perspectives on the Bird's Head of Irian Jaya, Indonesia: Proceedings of the Conference, Leiden, 13–17 October 1997,* pp. 719–755. Rodopi, Amsterdam; Atlanta. doi.org/10.1163/ 9789004652644_036.

Roberts, J.M., C.C. Moore, and A.K. Romney 1995. Predicting similarity in material culture among New Guinea villages from propinquity and language: A log-linear approach. *Current Anthropology* 36(5):769– 788. doi.org/10.1086/204431.

Ronsumbre, A. 2020. *Ensiklopedia Suku Bangsa di Provinsi Papua Barat.* Penerbit Kepel Press, Yogyakarta.

Rottman, G.L. 2005. *Japanese army in World War II: The South Pacific and New Guinea, 1942–43.* Osprey Publishing, New York.

Rutherford, D. 2009. Sympathy, state building, and the experience of empire. *Cultural Anthropology* 24(1):1–32. doi.org/10.1111/j.1548-1360.2009.00025.x.

Sapin, F., M. Pubellier, J.-C. Ringenbach, and V. Bailly 2009. Alternating thin versus thick-skinned decollements, example in a fast tectonic setting: The Misool–Onin–Kumawa Ridge (West Papua). *Journal of Structural Geology* 31(4):444–459. doi.org/10.1016/j.jsg.2009.01.010.

Schiefenhövel, W. and M. Vanhaeren 2017. A window into Papua's past: Archaeological and anthropological status quo in the Star Mountains. *Papua* 9(2):119–160. doi.org/10.24832/papua.v9i2.211.

Shaw, B., J.H. Field, G.R. Summerhayes, S. Coxe, A.C.F. Coster, A. Ford, J. Haro, H. Arifeae, E. Hull, G. Jacobsen, R. Fullagar, E. Hayes, and L. Kealhofer 2020. Emergence of a Neolithic in highland New Guinea by 5000 to 4000 years ago. *Science Advances* 6(13):eaay4573. doi.org/10.1126/sciadv.aay4573.

Slama, M. and J. Munro (eds) 2015. *From 'Stone-Age' to 'Real-Time': Exploring Papuan temporalities, mobilities and religiosities.* ANU Press, Canberra. doi.org/10.22459/FSART.04.2015.

Slon, V., B. Viola, G. Renaud, M.-T. Gansauge, S. Benazzi, S. Sawyer, J.-J. Hublin, M.V. Shunkov, A.P. Derevianko, J. Kelso, K. Prüfer, M. Meyer, and S. Pääbo 2017. A fourth Denisovan individual. *Science Advances* 3(7):e1700186. doi.org/10.1126/sciadv.1700186.

Spriggs, M. 2012. Is the Neolithic spread in Island Southeast Asia really as confusing as the archaeologists (and some linguists) make it seem? In M.L. Tjoa-bonatz, A. Reinecke, and D. Bonatz (eds), *Crossing borders: Selected papers from the 13th International Conference of the European Association of Southeast Asian Archaeologists,* pp. 109–121. National University of Singapore Press, Singapore. doi.org/10.2307/ j.ctv1nthm4.15.

Summerhayes, G.R., M. Leavesley, A. Fairbairn, H. Mandui, J. Field, A. Ford, and R. Fullagar 2010. Human adaptation and plant use in Highland New Guinea 49,000 to 44,000 years ago. *Science* 330(6000):78–81. doi.org/10.1126/science.1193130.

Summerhayes, G.R., J.H. Field, B. Shaw, and D. Gaffney 2017. The archaeology of forest exploitation and change in the tropics during the Pleistocene: The case of Northern Sahul (Pleistocene New Guinea). *Quaternary International* 448:14–30. doi.org/10.1016/j.quaint.2016.04.023.

Swadling, P. 1996. *Plumes from Paradise: Trade cycles in outer Southeast Asia and their impact on New Guinea and nearby islands until 1920.* Papua New Guinea National Museum, Boroko.

Teixeira, J.C., G.S. Jacobs, C. Stringer, J. Tuke, G. Hudjashov, G.A. Purnomo, H. Sudoyo, M.P. Cox, R. Tobler, C.S.M. Turney, A. Cooper, and K.M. Helgen 2021. Widespread Denisovan ancestry in Island Southeast Asia but no evidence of substantial super-archaic hominin admixture. *Nature Ecology & Evolution* 5:616–624. doi.org/10.1038/s41559-021-01408-0.

Terrell, J.E. 2004. The 'sleeping giant' hypothesis and New Guinea's place in the prehistory of Greater Near Oceania. *World Archaeology* 36(4):601–609. doi.org/10.1080/0043824042000303782.

Timmer, J. 2007. A brief social and political history of Papua 1962–2005. In A.J. Marshall and B. Beehler (eds), *The ecology of Papua*, pp. 1124–1098. Periplus, Singapore.

Tsang, R., S. Katuk, S.K. May, P.S.C. Taçon, F.-X. Ricaut, and M.G. Leavesley 2022. Rock art and (re) production of narratives: A cassowary bone dagger stencil perspective from Auwim, East Sepik, Papua New Guinea. *Cambridge Archaeological Journal* 32(4):547–565. doi.org/10.1017/S0959774322000026.

Urwin, C., L. Lamb, R. Skelly, J.A. Bell, T. Beni, M. Leavesley, B. David, and H. Arifeae 2023. Rethinking agency in *hiri* exchange relationships on Papua New Guinea's south coast: Oral traditions and archaeology. *Journal of Anthropological Archaeology* 69:101484. doi.org/10.1016/j.jaa.2022.101484.

van der Kaars, S. 1995. Preliminary palynological results on the Pleistocene–Holocene transition, Seram Trench, offshore Irian Jaya, Indonesia. *Geologie en Mijnbouw* 74(3):285–286.

van der Kaars, W.A. 1991. Palynology of eastern Indonesian marine piston-cores: A Late Quaternary vegetational and climatic record for Australasia. *Palaeogeography, Palaeoclimatology, Palaeoecology* 85(3–4): 239–302. doi.org/10.1016/0031-0182(91)90163-L.

van der Veur, P.W. 1966. *Search for New Guinea's boundaries: From Torres Strait to the Pacific*. Australian National University Press, Canberra. doi.org/10.1007/978-94-015-3620-2.

Veth, P., S. O'Connor, M. Spriggs, W. Nayati, A. Jatmiko, and H. Mohammad 2005. The Ujir site: An early historic maritime settlement in northwestern Aru. In S. O'Connor, M. Spriggs, and P. Veth (eds), *The archaeology of the Aru Islands, Eastern Indonesia*, pp. 85–94. ANU ePress, Canberra.

Veys, F.W. 2018. Papua collections in the Netherlands: A story of exploration, research, missionization, and colonization. In L. Carreau, A. Clark, A. Jelinek, E. Lilje, and N. Thomas (eds), *Pacific presences: Oceanic art and European museums*, Vol. 1, pp. 127–164 Sidestone Press, Leiden.

Viartasiwi, N. 2018. The politics of history in West Papua—Indonesia conflict. *Asian Journal of Political Science* 26(1):141–159. doi.org/10.1080/02185377.2018.1445535.

Vlasblom, D. 2004. *Papoea: Een Geschiedenis*. Mets & Schilt, Amsterdam.

Voorhoeve, C. 1975. Central and Western Trans–New Guinea Phylum languages. In S.A. Wurm (ed.), *New Guinea area languages and language study, Vol. 1: Papuan languages and the New Guinea linguistic scene*. Pacific Linguistics, Research School of Pacific and Asian Studies, The Australian National University, Canberra.

Webster, D. 2013. Self-determination abandoned: The road to the New York Agreement on West New Guinea (Papua), 1960–62. *Indonesia* 95:9–24. doi.org/10.5728/indonesia.95.0009.

Welsch, R.L., J. Terrell, and J.A. Nadolski 1992. Language and culture on the north coast of New Guinea. *American Anthropologist* 94(3):568–600. doi.org/10.1525/aa.1992.94.3.02a00030.

Wichmann, A. 1909. *Nova Guinea. Uitkomsten Der Nederlandsche Nieuw-Guinea-Expeditie in 1903: Entdeckungsgeschichte von Neu-Guinea (Bis 1828)*. E.J. Brill, Leiden.

Wright, D., T. Denham, D. Shine, and M. Donohue 2013. An archaeological review of western New Guinea. *Journal of World Prehistory* 26(1):25–73. doi.org/10.1007/s10963-013-9063-8.

2

A historiography of research on West New Guinea's human past

Dylan Gaffney and Marlin Tolla

Abstract

This chapter is a historiography of research on West New Guinea's peoples and their social, biological, and material histories. It provides a synthesis of previous research undertaken on West New Guinea's human past, divided by chronological period, from Portuguese and Spanish voyages of discovery (1511–1606), Dutch economic expansion (1606–1795), European voyages of discovery and the emergence of the natural sciences (1767–1884), early ethnographic expeditions (1884–1945), the development of Netherlands New Guinea anthropology (1945–1963), and Indonesian-era archaeology and anthropology (1963–2022). Finally, the chapter reflects on the present state of cultural heritage legislation and practice in the region, which highlights how scholarship could productively engage Papuan communities in the future.

Abstrak

Bab ini menyajikan riwayat sejarah penelitian tentang kehidupan masyarakat yang berada di wilayah Papua bagian barat: sejarah sosial, biologi, dan budaya materi. Bab ini memaparkan sintesa dari penelitian sebelumnya yang dilakukan pada masa lalu di wilayah tersebut. Hal ini disajikan secara kronologis yang dimulai dengan awal kedatangan para pelancong berkebangsaan Portugis dan Spanyol (1511–1606), ekspansi ekonomi Belanda (1606–1795), pelayaran pertama yang dilakukan oleh bangsa Eropa dan kemunculan ilmu pengetahuan alam (1767–1884), ekspedisi awal etnografi (1884–1945), perkembangan antropologi Nugini-Belanda (1945–1963), dan perkembangan Ilmu arkeologi dan antropologi pada masa pemerintahan Indonesia (1963–2022). Pada bagian terakhir, tulisan ini mengulas peraturan dan praktek warisan budaya di wilayah tersebut serta menyoroti tentang pentingya pendidikan serta hal-hal yang mendukung proses tersebut sehingga menjadi prioritas masyarakat asli Papua dimasa yang akan datang.

Introduction

To situate the present state of human historical research on West New Guinea, we need to examine the ways in which anthropology, including subdisciplines like social anthropology, archaeology, material culture studies, and biological anthropology, as well as cognate fields like historical linguistics, have developed. Moreover, we need to understand how wider environmental, social, and political changes have shaped the types of questions that are asked about the region. Developing on Chapter 1, which provided an introduction to what we know about the environmental, cultural, and colonial histories of West New Guinea, this chapter explores how these events have shaped social and historical research from the mid-sixteenth century to the early twenty-first century. We subdivide these phases of documentation into the Portuguese and Spanish voyages of discovery (1511–1606), Dutch economic expansion (1606–1795), European voyages of discovery and the emergence of the natural sciences (1767–1884), early ethnographic expeditions (1884–1945), the development of Netherlands New Guinea anthropology (1945–1963), and Indonesian-era archaeology and anthropology (1963–2022). The chapter finally describes the present state of cultural heritage management in the area and provides some thoughts on future directions for human historical research in West New Guinea.

Iberian trade voyages: 1511–1606

Literature describing the people of West New Guinea began as a by-product of the Portuguese presence around Malukan Spice Islands in the early sixteenth century. Although Chinese merchant ships and east Indonesian fleets likely visited the offshore islands, the Bird's Head, and the Bomberai Peninsula earlier than the sixteenth century, there are no known written records describing these trips to New Guinea. The earliest European visits to the area were accidental and often described Papuans as savage and subhuman, establishing a racist myth that would persevere for several centuries (Wichmann 1909 provides an overview of European journeys from 1511–1606). In 1526, Jorge de Menezes, en route to take up the role as Portuguese governor of Maluku, was blown off course to 'Isla Versija',[1] which was either Warsia on the Bird's Head (Trotter 1884), the island of Waigeo (Hamy 1877, 8), or the island of Biak (Wichmann 1909, 15) (Figure 2.1). There, he waited out the monsoon season; it remains unclear whether he moored offshore or disembarked, and, if the latter, what interaction he had with locals. In 1537, the mutinous crew of Hernando de Grijalva's ship were wrecked and enslaved on an unnamed island around the north coast of New Guinea, and they provided a brief account of their experience to António Galvão, the Portuguese governor of Maluku who had ransomed them. The crew described their captors as cannibals, sorcerers, and heathens (Galvão 1944, 444–445). In 1538, Galvão sent João Fogaça to 'Ilhas dos Papuas' (the Papuan Islands, namely Raja Ampat or the Bird's Head) to enquire into Grijalva's ships and the potential for missionisation. Fogaça befriended the rajas of these islands and returned with provisions (Haga 1884, 8). This marked the start of a conceptual distinction between the peoples of the offshore islands (thought to be open to trading valuable commodities) and those of the mainland (who were thought to be more hostile). Writings by Father Marcos Prancudo in 1561, however, indicate that the Portuguese had limited knowledge of New Guinea east of Raja Ampat, despite half a century of occupation in Maluku (Wichmann 1909, 33).

---

1   Throughout this chapter, local language words are italicised and Papuan Malay or Indonesian words are underlined at first mention. Words from other languages (such as Dutch, Spanish, and French) are provided with single quote marks.

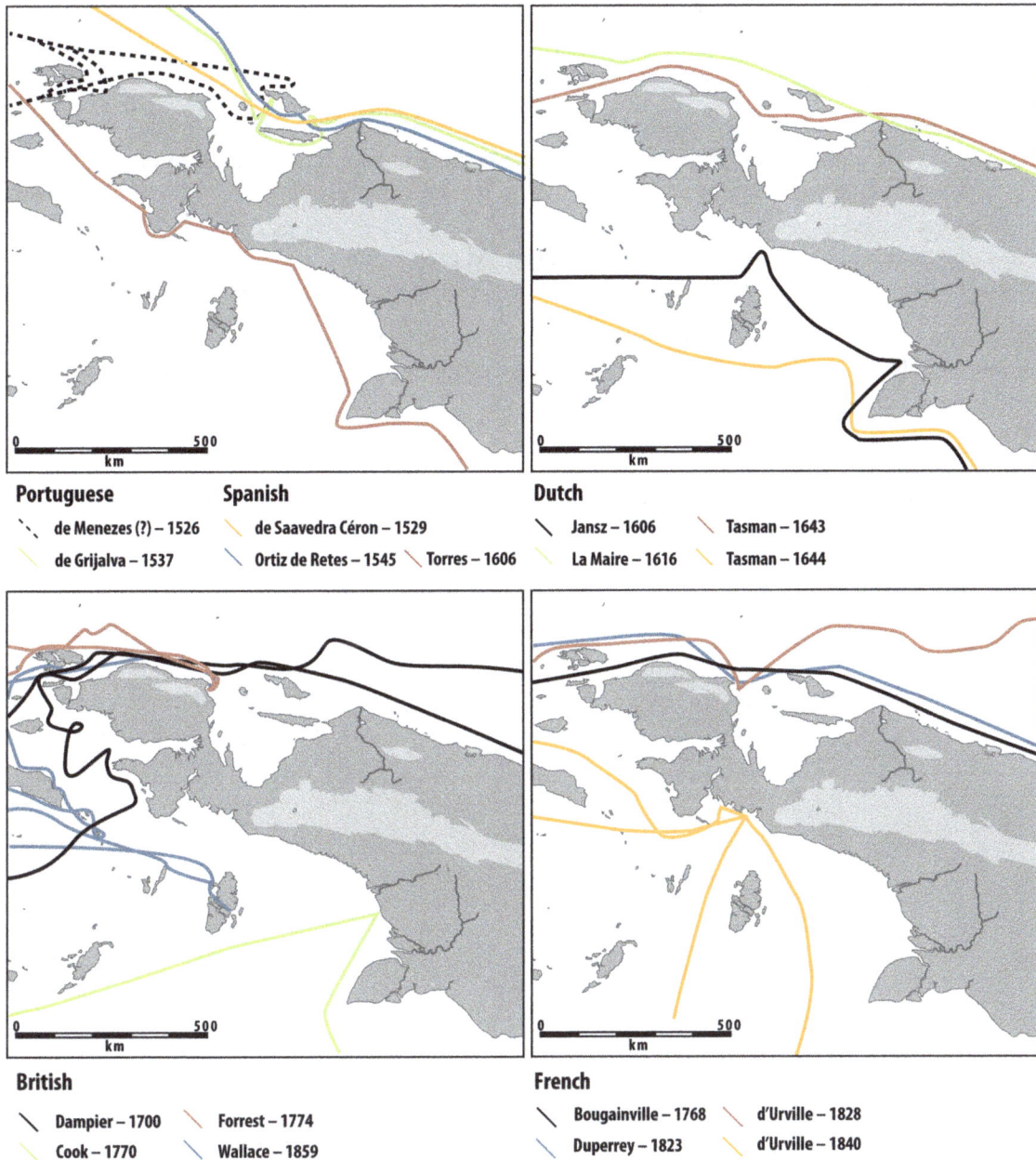

Figure 2.1: Approximate routes of a sample of early European voyages around West New Guinea.
Source: Dylan Gaffney.

Some of the earliest deliberate voyages to New Guinea stemmed from attempts to chart a safe seafaring route that could connect the Spanish colonies in the Americas with their outposts in Southeast Asia. For instance, in 1528–1529, Alvaro de Saavedra Cerón sailed from Tidore carrying three tons of cloves in two unsuccessful attempts to reach Mexico (Wright 1939). During the first attempt, his description of 'Islas de Oro' (Islands of Gold) while awaiting favourable winds helped to stimulate rumours that New Guinea was replete with gold. This was probably Cenderawasih Bay, where de Saavedra Cerón described the islanders primarily by physical type, but noted they possessed iron weapons (Douglas 2014, 59). On the second attempt, the voyage traversed a large stretch of the north coast of New Guinea, again describing the populations based on physical appearance (dark-skinned, curly haired, unclothed). These physical characteristics continued to be noted on future voyages, and seafarers often distinguished 'Papuans' with curly hair from those in Maluku with smooth hair.

Iberian encounters with locals were often mutually stand-offish, sometimes leading to cursory exchanges of commodities for food, and other times leading to murders, abductions of women, and the stealing of resources (such as on Torres's voyage through the Torres Strait). Numerous voyages involved exchanges of arrows and gunfire. For instance, the 1545 voyage of Yñigo Ortiz de Retez, to Cenderawasih Bay and the north coast was attacked several times and musket fire was returned, although there were also examples of peaceful trade (Wichmann 1909, 22–30).

By the end of the sixteenth century, the Spanish had developed a rough outline of life in the Raja Ampat Islands, the Bird's Head, and Cenderawasih Bay. Miguel Roxo de Brito provides the most detailed description, recounting his travels with the raja of Waigeo in 1581–1582, where they observed some Papuans with golden adornments, others who held large markets that sold slaves, and more still that wore textiles and venerated their ancestors' bones (Boxer and Manguin 1979; Roxo de Brito 2016). Torres provided a similarly detailed account of people along the south coast of New Guinea in 1606 (Hilder 1980).

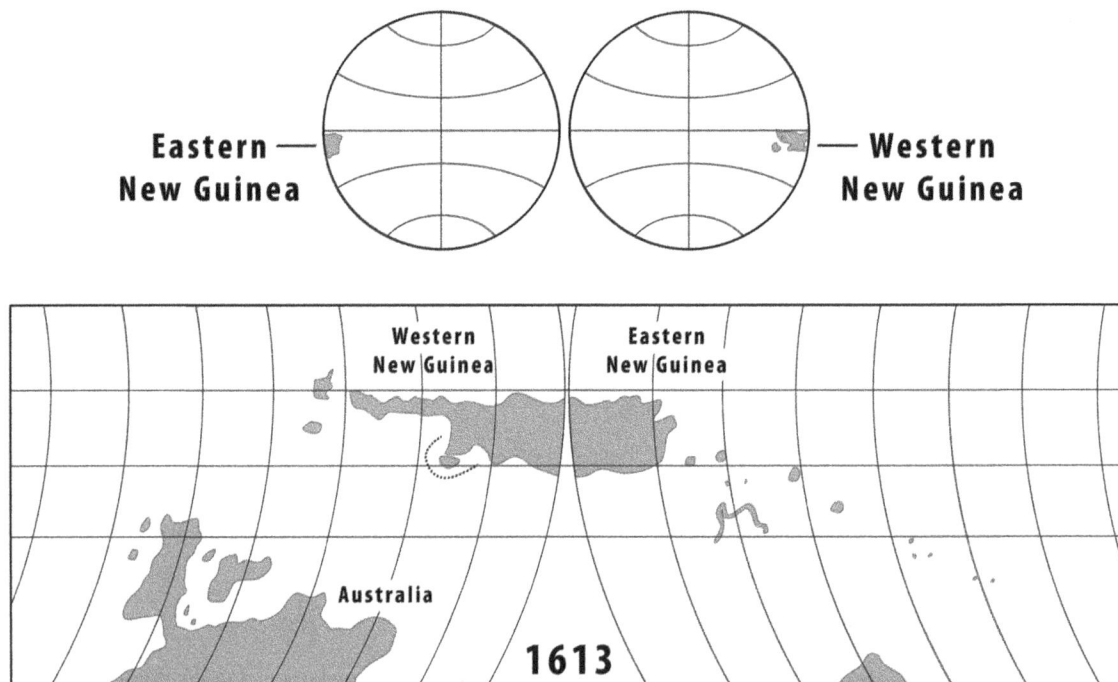

Figure 2.2: World map of 1613 by Emanuel Godinho de Erédia, a Portuguese-Bugis cartographer, showing New Guinea drawn at the extremity of the Asian and Pacific charts.
Source: Dylan Gaffney, redrawn from Hilder (1980, 138).

These explorations very slowly improved European knowledge of the region's geography. For instance, at the start of the sixteenth century, only the north-western coast of New Guinea had been charted. Until the early seventeenth century the Bird's Head was commonly thought to be one of the Papuan Islands, separated from New Guinea by Bintuni and Cenderawasih bays, and New Guinea itself was mistakenly connected with Australia. Furthermore, the conceptual separation of New Guinea into eastern and western halves traces back to these early explorations; some seafarers approached New Guinea from the west and others from the east, often considering the large island to separate the rich trading opportunities of Indonesia from the unexplored islands of the Pacific. As such, New Guinea quite literally lay at the edge of the maps of Asia and the Pacific until the late eighteenth century (Figure 2.2). For European voyagers, New Guinea acted as a barrier between these two worlds; perhaps unwittingly, however, explorations of West New Guinea were in fact serving to connect these two regions, linking together a gradually expanding horizon for trade and mobility.

Dutch economic expansion: 1606–1795

After the discovery of a shipping route between the Americas and the Philippines that bypassed New Guinea entirely, Spanish exploration of the island ceased. By the early seventeenth century, competing interests around the Spice Islands saw the 'Vereenigde Oostindische Compagnie' (Dutch East India Company, VOC) send fact-finding voyages to the western parts of New Guinea, with the hope of discovering resources and establishing trade relations. Voyages towards New Guinea also focused on intercepting Spanish ships laden with precious metals from the Americas (Wichmann 1909, 102). As a result, the Dutch made more headway in charting the geography of New Guinea than the Spanish had. As early as 1606, Willem Janszoon (Jansz) travelled along the south-west coast of New Guinea, in 1616 La Maire and Schouten sailed along the north coast, in 1623 Carstenszoon (Carstensz) noted the snow-capped peaks of the highlands, from 1643–1644 Abel Tasman explored both the north and south coasts, and in 1662–1663 Nicolaes Vinck described the Berau Gulf. Like the earlier Iberian voyages, initial contact with locals was usually marked by mutual apprehension, suspicion, and fear. Attempts to enter trading relations with Papuans were usually opportunistic, sometimes involving locals coming aboard to exchange glass beads, textiles, and red cloth (in the case of Schouten and Tasman's voyages), other times involving confrontation resulting in deaths on both sides (as in the case of Jansz's, Carstensz's, and Vinck's voyages). Although many of these early encounters involved trade, New Guinean objects do not seem to have reached the Netherlands, or at least did not hold such value as to have entered personal collections (Veys 2018). By way of peaceable exchanges, the Dutch began to regard mainlanders as inquisitive—with racist comparisons even drawn to monkeys—and through hostile relations the Dutch perpetuated Portuguese and Spanish characterisations that these people were frightening and cannibalistic (Wichmann 1909, 51, 67). Observations were typically marked by physical appearance, the use (or not) of iron, the major components of people's diet (fish, pig, sago, and the absence of grains), and the eagerness to trade or to be hostile.

The earliest writing that expresses an interest in the architecture and archaeology of West New Guinea comes from 1664, when Burgert Pietersz of the VOC described indigenous forts around Berau Gulf, used in defence against raids from Maluku (Galis 1957c). In 1678, Johannes Keyts, a VOC captain, guided by Laku the Seram-Laut leader, observed rock art on the west coast at Namatotte, south of Fakfak, when he travelled to West New Guinea to negotiate slave and massoi bark trade agreements with rajas around Onin (Heeres and Stapel 1934, 149–157). Unfortunately, this visit was generally forgotten and did not stimulate wide interest in the history of New Guinea.

Throughout the eighteenth century, the VOC's influence declined, and it eventually collapsed in 1795; however, throughout this period it had gathered information about the people and environment of West New Guinea, in so far as it cemented their influence in the spice trade and excluded competing European powers. During this time, the British and French also began to document the area, initially as forays to scout for natural resources (including spices that could be translocated to other colonies). In 1700, British navigator and privateer William Dampier travelled from Australia to New Guinea in search of new spice islands, recording large settlements of around 500 people and making early observations about linguistic affiliations along the coast (Dampier 1703). The British East India Company also made reconnaissance voyages to undermine Dutch control in the region, leading to early documentation in English. This included Thomas Forrest, in 1774–1775, covertly visiting the Raja Ampat Islands and Cenderawasih Bay with his Indonesian crew. Forrest (1969) described the political system of the rajas, the presence of stilted houses on the coast, treehouses in the interior, local politics and warfare, and Chinese–Papuan trade arrangements. Regarding the latter, there was a delayed system of trade involving iron, beads, sea cucumbers, tortoise, massoi, ambergris, pearls, bird-of-paradise, and slaves. Similarly, John McCluer, travelling on a British East India Company vessel, made two visits to the Bird's Head and the surrounding islands; from 1791–1792 he recorded nutmeg growing around Dore Bay leading to the establishment of Fort Coronation, and in 1794–1795 he retrieved the survivors of that failed settlement. Although written accounts of McCluer's voyages are not detailed, it is clear that the Fort Coronation settlers had been reliant on aid provided by local Papuans (Griffin 1990).

The French East India Company had similar designs for New Guinea and had successfully translocated nutmeg to their colonies in Mauritius in 1755 (Wichmann 1909, 214). In 1770 and 1772, Provoat made expeditions to Maluku where he met with envoys from the Raja Ampat Islands who were able to acquire nutmeg and cloves for him.

European voyages of discovery and natural science: 1767–1884

In the late eighteenth and early nineteenth centuries, European scientific societies commissioned voyages to the Pacific primarily as fact-finding missions. During this period, natural history was expanding to include the science of 'man', and naturalists like Georges Cuvier (1817, 99) and George Bennett (1834, 275) were trying to ascertain whether Papuans were related to Africans, having dispersed through South Asia or the Indian Ocean (Ballard 2008, 158; Starbuck 2016, 43). Many naval officers and their crews on these voyages—which included natural historians, geographers, and illustrators—described indigenous peoples, material culture, word lists, plants and animals, topographies, and settlement locations, with the express purpose of generating knowledge that would benefit the scientific and expansionist interests of their patrons.

In 1767, British naval officer Philip Carteret passed Mapia Atoll, both recording a map produced in chalk by Mapia Islanders who had come onboard to trade and taking a local into his company who became known as 'Joseph Freewill' (Wichmann 1909, 199). A few years later in 1770, during James Cook's first voyage, supported by the Royal Society to record the Transit of Venus, his crew landed in Asmat territory on the south-west coast of New Guinea where they exchanged spear throws with gunfire (Cook 1821, 235).

The French undertook competing voyages, beginning with that of Louis-Antoine de Bougainville who passed along the north coast in 1768. In 1794, Antoine Bruni d'Entrecasteaux and his crew had peaceful interactions with people on Waigeo and recorded notes on their culture (Labillardière 1800, 298). In 1818–1819, Louis de Freycinet also made favourable contact with people on the north coast of Waigeo, where local leaders—Srouane from Boni Island and Moro from the Ayu Islands—became regular dinner guests. De Freycinet was accompanied by his wife Rose, who circumnavigated the world disguised as a man and recorded in her diary a wide range of important ethnographic observations (de Freycinet 1996). Natural historians on the voyage, Quoy and Gaimard, also took skulls from an ossuary on nearby Rawak Island for phrenological study and even dug down below the surface to determine if the remains were related to a burial (Douglas

2014, 218). Louis-Isidore Duperrey's voyage in 1823 recorded settlements, stilt houses, and spirit houses, and collected ethnographic objects like *korwar* (wooden ancestor figurines) on Waigeo and the offshore islands of Cenderawasih Bay (Carreau 2018; Lesson 1839, 66–87). Dumont d'Urville passed north New Guinea in 1829 and was met in Cenderawasih Bay by large crowds wanting to trade. In a later excursion to south-west New Guinea in 1840, D'Urville recorded the relict foundations of Fort Du Bus, known locally as *Wama Runi* (d'Urville 1843, 141–144). During many of these French expeditions, Papuan leaders like Srouane and Moro carefully managed European activities at local villages and deliberately positioned themselves as interlocutors, actively toying with European preoccupations about indigenous curiosity, to acquire trade connections, knowledge, and political advantage (Starbuck 2016).

In 1825–1826, Dutch naval officer Dirk Hendrik Kolff scouted the south-west coast of New Guinea for British activity. This led to the first detailed description of south-west New Guinea's peoples (Kolff 1828). Kolff's mapping of the coast paved the way for the Triton Expedition of 1828, during which time the zoologist Salomon Müller showed an interest in material culture and made a small collection of clothing, tools, weapons, and ornaments that were transported to the Netherlands and later purchased by the Rijksmuseum van Oudheden (Museum of Antiquities) in Leiden (Veys 2018, 140). To our knowledge, these objects became the first New Guinean objects to enter a Dutch museum.

In 1850, an expedition to annex the north coast of New Guinea led by van den Dungen Gronovius, and involving an entourage of Malukan war canoes, resulted in a detailed account of the people of Cenderawasih Bay, produced by a lieutenant on the voyage, de Bruijn Kops (1850). Important English contributions included George Windsor Earl's translation of Kolff's monograph (Kolff and Earl 1840), and his *The Native Races of the Indian Archipelago: Papuans* (1853), which drew heavily from Kolff's and de Bruijn Kop's accounts (see Bruyns 2019). Although the latter book is essentially a racial categorisation of Papuans, preoccupied with comparing their physical characteristics with other ethnic groups that Europeans were increasingly encountering in the nineteenth century, the book also shows an interest in local customs such as scarification, septum piercing, and hair dyes, as well as types of material culture and comparative word lists. Like his contemporaries John Crawfurd and George Bennett, Earl was considered a foremost expert on New Guinea anthropology but had never visited the island himself (Ballard 2008).

The Protestant religion was brought to West New Guinea in 1855 by two German missionaries, Carl Wilhelm Ottow and Johann Gottlob Geissler, who established a mission on Mansinam at Dore Bay with the financial assistance of the Dutch committee 'De Christen Werkman' (Kamma 1977). There they met a handful of Europeans who had already begun to trade in the islands of the bay, including a merchant navy captain G.J. Fabritius and his family, who possessed some knowledge of the local languages (Pijnappel 1854). The missionaries wrote 'A brief survey of the land and people of the north-east coast of New Guinea' in German in 1857, which was later translated to Dutch and subsequently English (Ottow and Geissler 2010). Other missionaries penned extended works on the people of Cenderawasih Bay (Goudswaard 1863). A questionnaire sent to the mission in 1865 by the German Anthropological and Geographical Society was also completed by the missionaries Geissler, Jaesrich, and van Hasselt and detailed local languages, legends, religion, political organisation, land tenure, subsistence, recreation, cosmology, architecture, clothing, seafaring, trade, kinship, and so on (Gunson and Godschalk 2014). Although most missionary observations remain unpublished and untranslated, those documents that are available make clear that the missionaries had developed a working knowledge of local languages, which allowed them to interact more closely with locals— for instance, they were permitted to observe funerals and the production of ancestor figures.

In the mid-nineteenth century, the islands of New Guinea became a focus of natural history research. Alfred Russell Wallace developed his theory of evolution by travelling through the islands of Indonesia reaching West New Guinea with his Malay assistant Ali Wallace by 1859 (Wallace 1869), where he met with the missionaries Ottow and Geissler (Gunson and Godschalk 2014). His focus on the animals and plants of the region developed alongside an interest in the human population. Wallace illustrated market activity in the Aru Islands and the people and material culture of Cenderawasih Bay. He also drew a phenotypic boundary through Indonesia separating 'Malay' populations from 'Papuan' groups (Vetter 2006), which closely resembled his zoogeographic division between 'Oriental' and 'Australasian' animals now known as the Wallace Line (Ali and Heaney 2021). Other natural historians were to follow shortly after, including Germans Hermann von Rosenberg[2] (1878) in 1860, Heinrich Bernstein (1883) in 1863 and 1865, and Adolf Bernhard Meyer (1899) in 1873. Meyer, in particular, described the biological anthropology, languages, and customs of the people he worked with (Howes 2012). Conversely, the Italian Luigi Maria D'Albertis travelled up the Fly River in 1876 and 1877 (D'Albertis 1881), often taking everyday objects from houses, using guns and dynamite to intimidate and sometimes kill locals (Goode 1977).

Nicholai Miklouho-Maclay, a Russian polymath natural scientist and humanist, had been the first European anthropologist to live alongside New Guinean people for an extended period (near Madang in 1871, now in Papua New Guinea). He later spent time among the Kowiai people of Kaimana on the south-west coast in 1874, and wrote extensively about local customs, material culture, and language (Webster 1984). Although Miklouho-Maclay and his interlocuters still regarded each other with hesitation and sometimes fear (Kirksey 2010), his craniometric research in New Guinea, as well as his study of healthy intermarriages between Indonesians and Papuans, became crucial for overturning the concept of polygenism—the idea that different human groups represent different species (Levit and Hossfeld 2020).

Following in the footsteps of Keyts, it was in 1878 that Th. B. Léon travelled aboard the cargo steamer *Egeron* to visit villages and rock art around Arguni and the Onin Peninsula; this piqued public and intellectual interest in the history of West New Guinea (Dozy 1880). Léon also described marriage ceremonies, subsistence, locally grown spices and aromatics, religion, burials, and rock art hand stencils (although he mistook decorations on statues as Sanskrit inscriptions) and his visit led to a series of return visits by D.F. van Braam Morris in 1883 and H. Kühn in 1884. The combined evidence was even reported in the journal *Nature* (Metzger 1885).

Haga (1884), writing at the end of this period, provides a useful summary of the history of European activity in West New Guinea from the fourteenth to late nineteenth centuries. Similarly, Wichmann (1910) provides a history of nineteenth-century voyages to New Guinea. We finish this section in 1884, the year that the Dutch annexation of West New Guinea was recognised by competing colonial powers.

---

2   Von Rosenberg had been part of the Dutch-organised Etna Expedition, during which he met with A.R. Wallace at the mission on Mansinam Island. Some ethnographic objects were collected on that expedition, shipped to the 'Ethnographisch Museum Artis' in Amsterdam, now housed in the 'Tropenmuseum' (Veys 2018).

Early ethnographic expeditions: 1884–1945

As we have outlined in the preceding section, nineteenth-century scholars began to write ethnographic characterisations of West New Guinea by compiling traveller and missionary accounts. Natural scientists that spent several months living in nearby settlements developed an interest in the evolutionary history of Papuans and began to write accounts of people's customs, languages, biology, and material culture. Interest in the deep history of these groups remained limited but grew out of descriptions of coastal rock art sites. Following the international recognition that West New Guinea formed the eastern extent of the Dutch East Indies, the Netherlands began to organise larger expeditions to the island (see Wichmann 1912 for a history up to 1903). During this time, the myth of the primitive savage was increasingly replaced by one which asserted that Papuans were living in a state of nature, ready to receive conversion, study, and development aid (Pouwer 1999).

From 1887 to 1888, F.S.A. de Clercq, a civil servant in the Dutch East Indies, made four collecting trips to the north-west coast of New Guinea, at times travelling with local rajas (de Clercq 1893). De Clercq's work differed from his predecessors in that it was carefully detailed, describing life around the Raja Ampat Islands, Berau Gulf, Bintuni Bay, Cenderawasih Bay, the Mamberamo River delta, and Yos Sudarso Bay (Wichmann 1912, 426). A monograph of the material culture he collected was written up by 'Rijksmuseum voor Vulkenkunde' (now 'Wereldmuseum') curator J.D.E. Schmeltz (de Clercq and Schmeltz 1893). He also showed an interest in the region's past, visiting the historical seat of the raja on Waigeo and rock art sites around Misool and Onin.

In 1892, a Catholic mission was established on the south coast and administrative posts were created at Manokwari and Fakfak in 1898, Merauke in 1902, and Hollandia (now Jayapura) in 1910 (Pouwer 1999). The presence of staging posts around the coast paved the way for large-scale, multidisciplinary expeditions to record a wider array of local communities both along the coast and inland. As an aside, the results of many of these scientific expeditions can be found in the monograph series *Nova Guinea* (1909–1936). Most of the ethnographic objects collected during these expeditions were taken to the 'Rijks Ethnographisch Museum' (now Wereldmuseum) in Leiden, but some were diverted or returned to the museum of the 'Bataviaasch Genootschap van Kunsten en Wetenschappen' (Batavian Society for the Arts and Sciences; what is today the Museum Nasional Indonesia in Jakarta). Those objects still housed in the Netherlands are now searchable through the collective 'Nationaal Museum van Wereldculturen' (National Museum of World Cultures) online databases.

The first Dutch expedition to New Guinea—the North New Guinea Expedition—took place along the north coast in 1903 focusing on Cenderawasih Bay, Yos Sudarso Bay, and Lake Sentani (Figure 2.3). The venture was led by a German geologist from the University of Utrecht, Arthur Wichmann, and funded by the 'Maatschappij ter Bevordering van het Natuurkundig Onderzoek der Nederlandsche Koloniën' (Society for the Promotion of the Physics Research of the Dutch Colonies) primarily to investigate mineral resources in the region. However, ethnographic data from the expedition were subsequently published by the team's ethnologist: the retired military doctor turned biological anthropologist Gijsbertus Adrian van der Sande (1907). Two bronze axes and a bronze globular object from Asei, a village in eastern Lake Sentani, were first reported by van der Sande during this expedition and taken back to the Netherlands by the missionary G. Schneider. Rock engravings on Sösena Island, Lake Sentani, were also reported.

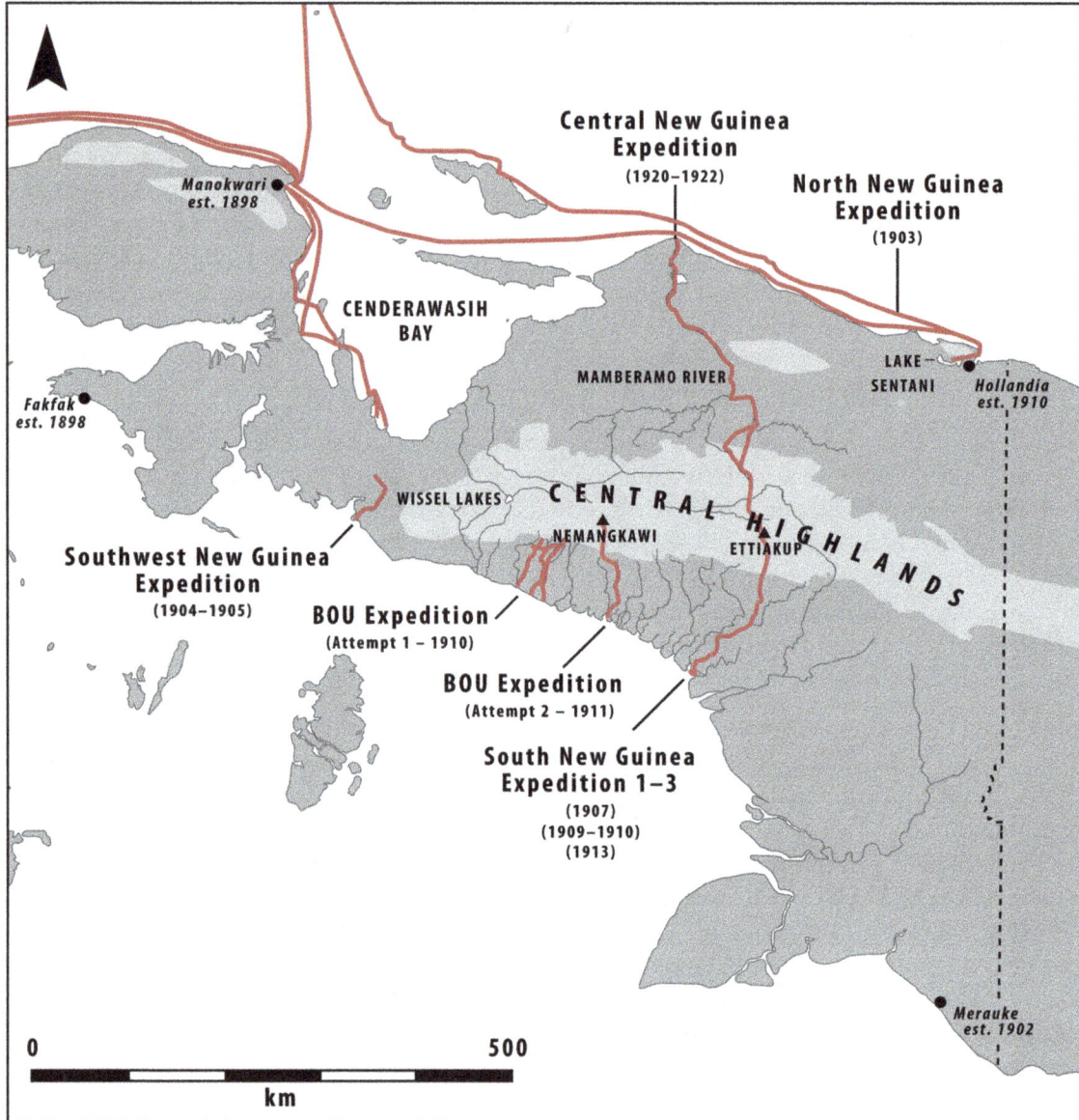

Figure 2.3: Routes of early expeditions to inland and highland ranges of West New Guinea.

Source: Dylan Gaffney, with information from Lorentz (1905), Seyne Kok and colleagues (1908), and Ploeg (1995).

In 1904–1905, the 'Koninklijk Nederlands Aardrijkskundig Genootschap' (Royal Dutch Geographic Society) organised the Southwest New Guinea Expedition, with the aim of recording the interior of West New Guinea for the first time, following the lowlands from Etna Bay on the Bird's Neck (Seyne Kok et al. 1908). The expedition leaders, Meyes and de Rochemont, were supported by scores of military personnel, convict labourers, and carriers from the Dutch East Indies. The expedition doctor, J.W.R. Koch, conducted ethnographic and biological anthropological research, which would form the data for his PhD at the University of Amsterdam (Koch 1908). The team collected hundreds of ethnographic objects and reached over 2000 m above sea level (asl), although not without the loss of numerous porters' lives (Brienen 2003).

Hendrikus Albertus Lorentz, a lawyer with an interest in biology, and a member of the North New Guinea Expedition, undertook two further journeys: the South New Guinea Expedition in 1907 and the Second South New Guinea Expedition in 1909–1910 (Lorentz 1913). These expeditions were accompanied by numerous labourers and soldiers but lacked a dedicated ethnologist (Ploeg 1995). The primary aim of these expeditions was to reach the central highlands for the first time via the south coast, following the Unir River[3] inland. The first expedition encountered mountain peoples: in one instance, hostilities ensued resulting in the death of a Papuan, for which Lorentz was severely reprimanded by the East Indies administration, but whose skeletal remains were retained and studied for biological anthropological purposes (Ploeg 1995). It was during the latter expedition that Lorentz and his team reached the perennial snowline of Ettiakup.[4] The leaders of this second expedition consciously attempted to maintain friendly interactions with the mountain people they encountered; they noted a population of about 200 'Pesegem'[5] people living in one valley system and spent three nights with them (Ploeg 1995). Fischer's (1923) *Ethnographica aus Sud- und Sudwest- Neu-Guinea* described Asmat and Mimika material culture collected by Lorentz during his expeditions.

The second expedition had been competing to reach the snowline before the British Ornithologists' Union Expeditions of 1909–1911 (Wollaston 1914, 1912). The Third South New Guinea Expedition of 1913 followed a similar route as the second and encountered the same mountain people who recalled the previous expedition members; this journey reached the summit of Ettiakup, and included military officer A. Franssen Herderschee, who carried out the ethnography, and medic G.M. Versteeg who recorded biological anthropological data (Ploeg 2022). Simultaneously, topographic mapping of many unrecorded areas was undertaken between 1907 and 1915 by large Dutch military detachments, which conducted opportunistic ethnographic and biological anthropological recording (Feuilletau de Bruyn 1947; Overweel 1998) and resulted in early documentation of the highland Mek people by 1910 (Godschalk 1999). Geological reconnaissance was also carried out both before and after World War I (WWI), primarily by the 'Kantoor voor het Mijnwezen in Nederlandsch-Indië' (Mining Office of the Dutch East Indies) (e.g. Loth 1924). The improved knowledge of New Guinea's terrain opened new possibilities for revisiting these areas for systematic fieldwork.

Perhaps the earliest long-term ethnographic research in West New Guinea was undertaken by the Swiss social anthropologist Paul Wirz, who spent 1916–1917 at Merauke with his wife Elizabeth Wirz, facilitated by missionaries there, to record the social lives, material culture, religion, and rituals of the Marind-anim (Wirz 1922a, 1922b). Many of the objects he collected during this period were donated to the 'Museum der Kulturen', Basel, and the 'Koloniaal Museum' (now Wereldmuseum), Amsterdam; other major contributions included his pioneering photography and films (Schmidt 1997). During his later work around Lake Sentani, he noted the presence of menhirs, potsherds, and possibly stone pestles or potters' anvils on the small islands within the lake (Wirz 1923).

The military physician, Hendricus Johannes Tobias Bijlmer, undertook some of the earliest systematic human biological research in West New Guinea. Bijlmer had been a member of the forward party of the 1920–1922 Central New Guinea Expedition that attempted to reach Ettiakup via the Mamberamo River on the north coast and encountered the Lani in the Toli Valley[6] (Bijlmer 1922). The follow-up party to this expedition included Paul Wirz, who became the first dedicated

---

3   Formerly the North River and later Lorentz River.

4   Mt Wilhelmina or Puncak Trikora.

5   Probably Dani people.

6   Formerly Swart Valley.

social anthropologist to take part in one of these large expeditions (Ploeg 1997). Other expeditions like the 1926 Dutch–American Central New Guinea Expedition led by Matthew Sterling and Willem Marius Docters van Leeuwen, in which Charles Le Roux acted as ethnologist, followed the same route and sought to study 'pygmy' communities (Taylor 2006). In 1935–1936, Bijlmer then led the Mimika Expedition to undertake anthropological work in the highlands proper, accompanied by Father Herman Tillemans, the administrator S. van der Goot, along with numerous East Indies field police and porters, and Papuans from Mimika (Bijlmer 1939). The expedition especially focused on the so-called 'Tapiro Pygmies' of the Wissel Lakes, who had been reported by the British Ornithologists' Union Expedition (Ballard 2000). At that time, investigations into people of short stature in New Guinea, Southeast Asia, and Africa were incorrectly preoccupied with determining if these groups represented a relict population from an early migration of Stone Age humans (Ballard 2006).

In 1936, Frits Julius Wissel flew over the interior of West New Guinea, noting canoes around what came to be known as the Wissel Lakes (now the Paniai Lakes). Jean Victor de Bruijn was a civil servant that worked from a newly opened outpost at Enarotali around the Wissel Lakes, which became the first permanent base from which to record details about the people in the highlands. The Wissel Lake and Nassau Mountain Expedition of 1939 was hosted at this outpost and the data published by the team leader Le Roux (1948–50), by then a curator at the Rijksmuseum voor Volkenkunde (now Wereldmuseum), Leiden. The expedition was stopped prematurely owing to the threat of world war; however, de Bruijn remained at Enarotali and, during 1942–1945, led Operation Oaktree, whereby he lived with Papuans in the interior while evading the Japanese military and provided intelligence to the Allies (Rhys 1947). Similarly, the Third Archibold Expedition of 1938–1939 to the Baliem Valley (Archibold et al. 1942) and Evelyn Cheesman's entomological work in Raja Ampat, Cenderawasih Bay, and the north coast of New Guinea (Cheesman 1949, 1940), associated with important ethnographic observations, were halted for the same reason (Cheesman 1943).

Missionary ethnographies were far smaller in scale than the large expeditions organised and funded by the colonial government and scientific societies, but some were of incredibly high quality for the time. Freerk C. Kamma, a protestant missionary, wrote about the oral traditions, mythology, and material culture of Cenderawasih Bay and the Raja Ampat Islands (e.g. Kamma 1948; Kamma and Kooijman 1973). His monograph on cargo cults (Kamma 1972), which developed from his PhD thesis at Leiden University (Kamma 1954), was one of the earliest dedicated works on this phenomenon in New Guinea. At the same time, G.J. Held was undertaking linguistic recording while employed by the 'Nederlands Bijbelgenootschap' (Dutch Bible Society) (Held 1947). Many early material culture traditions were recorded, and objects collected, by missionaries from the Utrecht Missionary Society, which operated from Manokwari, and the Catholic Mission, which operated from Merauke (Corbey and Weener 2015; Jaarsma 1993). Unfortunately, some missions were more interested in the mass destruction of material culture, the banning of customary traditions, and social conversion than they were any ethnographic endeavours (Corbey 2003).

After WWI, archaeological artefacts were reported more frequently, owing to the long-term presence of administrators and missionaries in the region. In 1930, one Dong Son bronze axe was presented to District Officer Halie by a local teacher from the village of Kwadeware, on Jonokom Island in Lake Sentani, which was then sent to the 'Koninklijk Instituut voor de Tropen' (Royal Tropical Institute) in Amsterdam. Around the same time, Protestant missionary G. Schneider (who sent the van der Sande objects to Europe) was gifted a further two bronze axes, a bell, a spearhead, and a scythe-like object from the same site, although these objects were lost when he died in WWII (Tichelman 1953). Another axe was in the possession of Reverend I.S. Kijne, given to him by Schneider, but this was also lost during the war years (Galis 1956). In 1935 at Sorong, a small bronze axe was recorded, but, according to van der Hoop who analysed the object, it was thought to be a Chinese rather than Dong Son type (Galis 1956). During WWII, George Agogino—at the time a radio operator for the Allies before becoming a celebrated Palaeoindian archaeologist—was tasked by Austrian anthropologist Robert Heine-Geldern with looking for archaeological objects while stationed in Hollandia. Agogino (1979) recorded bronze axes and green glass beads along the north coast of Lake Sentani and produced a report for Heine-Geldern.

The Frobenius Expedition initially led by Dr Ad. E. Jensen, and later by Dr H. Niggemeyer, visited Dutch New Guinea in 1937, for which Josef Röder described, and Albert Hahn painted, rock art from the Onin Peninsula between Kokas and Goras (Röder 1939). Their attention was turned to the rock art by Dutch missionaries and business owners living in Maluku (Röder 1959, 2). However, their aim was initially ethnographic, and they recorded folklore and material culture traditions too. During that visit, Dudumunir Cave was excavated by Röder on Arguni Island, spatially extending over several square metres and extending down 3.6 m (Röder 1940; van Benthem Jutting 1940). The publication of their research was delayed owing to WWII, with Hahn being conscripted and Röder moving to Bonn. The archaeological collections from Dudumunir Cave were destroyed during an air raid that hit the Frobenius Institute on 22 March 1944 (Röder 1959). Rock art images from the Röder expedition were exhibited in the Royal Tropical Institute, Amsterdam in 1954, and 'Museum voor Land- en Volkenkunde' (now Wereldmuseum), Rotterdam, in 1955 (Röder 1959, 4).

The development of Netherlands New Guinea anthropology: 1945–1963

We begin this section with the end of the Pacific War, the proclamation of Indonesian independence, and the return of the Dutch administration to West New Guinea. Prior to the war, expeditions to West New Guinea had been multidisciplinary and often included medical doctors performing the role of biological anthropologists and civil servants conducting ethnographic work (alongside hundreds of anonymous trekking specialists, porters, indentured labourers, and Papuan interpreters). Many of these expeditions sought to fill in the blanks on the map. Contemporary material culture had been collected on these trips but was often not the primary goal of the research. Archaeological material had been opportunistically recorded but only systematically investigated on one occasion (at Dudumunir Cave).

Dutch research in West New Guinea was substantially expedited after Indonesian independence was granted in 1949, when the Netherlands began to focus more resources on 'developing' its remaining territories. Although missionary scholarship continued during this period (Jaarsma 1993), social science was increasingly organised and centralised by the Netherlands New Guinea administration. Initially, research—including that on local customs, political systems, demography, language, and health—was often implemented with the strategic aim of assisting administrators to manage and develop their district. This research was written up as reports that would be reformulated as policy papers for the administration and for a yearly report for the United Nations (de Wolf and Jaarsma 1992; Jaarsma 1994, 1991). The 'Kantoor voor Bevolkingszaken' (Bureau for Native Affairs) was established in Hollandia in 1951 where colonial administrators were often trained as anthropologists, linguists, and demographers, and which increasingly hired university-trained social scientists (for bibliographies of this research, see Bureau for Native Affairs 1958; Galis 1962; Kooijman 1983; van Baal et al. 1984); much of these results were published in the journals *Nova*

Guinea (New Series: 1937–1966), *Tijdschrift Nieuw-Guinea* (1936–1956), and *Nieuw-Guinea Studien* (1957–1962). The proliferation of publicly available, Dutch-language information about the region's peoples is evident in Klein's three-volume edited collection *Nieuw-Guinea* (Klein 1954).

Although research in the mid-twentieth century was overseen by Dutch and sometimes other European scholars, their teams, and the administrative labour that supported them often came from New Guinea. After Indonesian independence, Papuans trained at the 'Opleidingsschool voor Inheemse Bestuursambtenaren' (School for Indigenous Administrators, OSIBA) in Hollandia from 1950–1962 and took up many of the administrative roles previously held by those from Maluku and further west (see oral histories presented in Visser 2012b). These Papuans often facilitated research and acted as interpreters for their Dutch colleagues in the civil service, speaking Biak as a lingua franca that would then be translated by a second interpreter into local languages (Visser 2012a).

Increased interest in long-term field ethnography was in part driven by Jan van Baal, who had written his PhD developing Wirz' data on the Marind-anim into a broader theoretical framework (van Baal 1934), and was 'Controleur' (assistant district commissioner) in Merauke in 1936–1938 before becoming governor of Dutch New Guinea between 1953–1958 (for an autobiography, see van Baal 1986, 1989). Prior to this time, anthropological research undertaken in Netherlands New Guinea was not usually taken seriously by either colonial administrators or international academics (Jaarsma 1994). However, with increasing support from the Bureau for Native Affairs under van Baal, numerous researchers conducted substantial field programs in the region: Pouwer (1955) undertook ethnographic work with the Mimika, van der Leeden (1956) with the Sarmi, Schoorl (1957) with the Muyu, and Boelaars (1958) with the Jaquj.

Other fields of anthropology saw renewed emphasis in the mid-twentieth century. A.W. Voors undertook detailed developmental biology work around Lake Sentani (Voors and Metselaar 1958), J.P. Kleiweg de Zwaan (1956) published a survey of biometric data from West New Guinea, and L.E. Nijenhuis and colleagues collected early blood group data from several survey locations (Nijenhuis 1961). P. Drabbe (1950), H.K. Cowan (1952), and J.C. Anceaux (1953), among several others, undertook pioneering linguistic work (see Voorhoeve 1975). During the late 1950s and 1960s, West New Guinea's social sciences began to contribute in important ways to global theory, especially through the work of van Baal, Pouwer, and van der Leeden.

Early surveys of West New Guinea art and design were compiled in the 1950s, based on large collections housed in ethnographic museums (e.g. Gerbrands 1951; Kooijman 1955). In 1961, the Harvard–Peabody Expedition to the Baliem Valley collected large numbers of art objects and included the filmmaker Robert Gardner who produced *Dead Birds* (1963), a film which furnished the international imagination about the interior of the island. The expedition was supported by the Rockefeller family and the Netherlands New Guinea administration; Michael Rockefeller, who was part of the expedition, later generated widespread international attention after his disappearance in the Asmat region three months after leaving Baliem. Adriaan Gerbrands, the deputy director of the Rijksmuseum voor Volkenkunde (now Wereldmuseum) in Leiden, who had already begun his own fieldwork on the south coast, produced important research on Asmat objects collected by Rockefeller (Gerbrands 1961).

Following the Pacific War, archaeology did not feature seriously in the Netherlands New Guinea research agenda. The publication of Alphonse Riesenfeld's *The Megalithic Culture of Melanesia* (1950)—a racial history that sought to establish when light- and dark-skinned people entered the region—did draw attention to Yos Sudarso Bay and Lake Sentani. However, the scant mention of West New Guinea in that volume demonstrates that the territory remained peripheral to the developing narrative of the Asia-Pacific's deep past. By contrast, systematic archaeological research during the 1950s–1960s in the Australian-administered Papua New Guinea would go on to revolutionise scholarship on the antiquity of the island and the wider region (Golson 2016; Summerhayes 2021).

At this time, interest in the archaeology of West New Guinea was localised and driven by individuals—often ethnographers who had spent a long time in New Guinea and developed a curiosity for local history. For instance, some incidental archaeological finds were made in areas formerly cleared by the Japanese, such as pottery-bearing middens around Hollandia that were excavated quickly but systematically by visiting American archaeologist Carl F. Miller, despite most of the material being lost before it could be analysed (Miller 1950).

Bronze, pottery, and megaliths from a grave mound called *Marweri Urang*, at Kwadeware in Sentani, were further reported by J.V. de Bruyn (1959, 1962), who investigated the area in 1958, undertaking a one-day excavation to 40 cm deep. Systematic excavations were not carried out owing to a lack of expertise; the administration banned fossicking and asked locals to help protect the site. De Bruyn notes that these sites were sacred and only the *ondoafi* (clan leader) could visit them. Perhaps owing to their experience as ethnographers, people like de Bruyn were relatively sensitive to local customs (de Bruyn mentions consulting the ondoafi that he might contact the group's ancestors before commencing work).

One colonial administrator—Klaas Wilhelm Galis—had a particular interest in the history of New Guinea's peoples. Galis had trained in Indology at Leiden, before becoming assistant district commissioner in Manokwari and Fakfak, and later an official in the Bureau for Native Affairs. He wrote his PhD based on his ethnographic work around Yos Sudarso Bay (Galis 1955) and was responsible for some of the earliest archaeological work around West New Guinea, undertaking rock art recording at Guwaimit Cave, Pinfelu Cave south of Hollandia (Galis 1957a, 1957b; see also Fairyo, this volume), and surveys of indigenous forts at Foe-oem on an island off the coast of the Onin Peninsula (Galis 1957c) and at Yembekaki on Batanta in the Raja Ampat Islands (Galis 1960; Galis and Kamma 1958; see also Gaffney et al., this volume). Galis also communicated with Gustav Heinrich Ralph von Koenigswald at the University of Utrecht—then considered a pre-eminent expert on Indonesian archaeology and palaeontology—sending New Guinea artefacts to him for analysis (von Koenigswald 1968).

Indonesian-era anthropology and archaeology: 1963–2022

This section starts in 1963, the date that West New Guinea was officially ceded to Indonesia. In this new period of Indonesian administration, and without access to the field, many Dutch scholars and government officials relocated to universities in the Netherlands and explored the available anthropological evidence at a theoretical and cross-comparative level (e.g. chapters in Ploeg 1970). Papuan civil servants and research assistants who had worked alongside the Dutch often remained in service; however, many were marginalised as Indonesian administrators moved to the region, their working lingua franca changed from Dutch and Biak to Bahasa Indonesia, and their reports were relayed from Jayapura to Jakarta (Visser 2012a). The continuity in social science and historical research between Dutch- and Indonesian-era administrations—and especially the role played by Papuans—remains unexplored.

The functions of the Bureau of Native Affairs, including the collection of ethnographic data and facilitation of research programs, were largely subsumed by the Departamen Pendidikan dan Kebudayaan (Department of Education and Culture) in Jakarta and Universitas Negeri Tjenderawasih (Bird-of-Paradise State University, now Universitas Cenderawasih) in Jayapura. Universitas Negeri Tjenderawasih was established in 1962 by a special presidential decree from Sukarno, initially teaching constitutional law and administration, and education (Wolfers 1969). The Abepura campus, which housed law and administration, was established in the former OSIBA headquarters, included 12 lecturers who had relocated from western Indonesia, and contained a research-only Institute of Anthropology. A museum to house ethnographic material culture, the Museum Loka Budaya (Cultural Centre Museum), was later opened at the university in 1970 with the support of the East–West Center at the University of Hawai'i and the Rockefeller Foundation. The Museum Kebudayaan dan Kemajuan Asmat (Museum of Asmat Culture and Development) in Agats was established in 1973 by the Catholic diocese. During this time, West New Guinea material culture was reformulated as a remote expression of a broader Indonesian collective.

In 1973, anthropology was named one of two key subjects in Universitas Cenderawasih's Pola Ilmiah Pokok (Primary Scientific Plan) because, alongside agriculture, it was considered to be key to the development of West New Guinea. Until 1981, the subject was taught out of a joint department for anthropology and linguistics as training in local languages was seen to go hand-in-hand with ethnographic observation. At this time, histories about the territory were usually written from outside West New Guinea and focused on biographies, memoirs, and government accounts, including autobiographies documenting political imprisonment by the Dutch (Ballard 1999).

Large research programs administered by the Department of Education and Culture included the Proyek Inventarisasi dan Dokumentasi Kebudayaan Daerah (Regional Cultural Inventory and Documentation Project), which grew from the Proyek Penelitian dan Pencatatan Kebudayaan Daerah (Irian Jaya Regional Cultural Research and Recording Project) (e.g. Suwondo and Yunus 1978), with the aim of recording the cultural diversity of the newly acquired territory as a way to make sense of the emerging nation-state, and in an attempt to preserve cultural elements that were thought to be at risk of disappearing. Much of this Indonesian-language research was published in 1972 in the journal *Irian: Bulletin of West Irian Development*, renamed shortly after as *Irian: Bulletin of Irian Jaya Development*. In 1981, the journal changed its focus from development to culture and language, resulting in a further name change to become *Irian: Bulletin of Irian Jaya*. By the late 1980s, the Irian Jaya Study Centre (IJSC) in Jayapura formed a home for research on the people of West New Guinea.

The 1970s–1980s saw the training of several prominent Papuan scholars, initially by Malcolm Walker who was part of the Fund of the United Nations for the Development of West Irian (FUNDWI) project, tasked with advising the new Rektor of Universitas Cenderawasih and providing teaching in the Institute of Anthropology at a time when funding was almost non-existent and Indonesian scrutiny of international academics was at its peak (Ballard 1998). These scholars especially included social anthropologists and linguists, although fewer human biologists and no archaeologists. One of these scholars was Johsz Mansoben who undertook work around Asmat and Raja Ampat before training for his PhD at Leiden University, compiling a comparative study of political systems across West New Guinea, which remains the most detailed description of the territory's broad-scale social and cultural patterns (Mansoben 1995). Another was Arnold Ap, curator at the Museum for Local Culture, ethnomusicologist, and founding member of the folk band Mambesak, who was later detained and shot by the military (Suryawan 2015). Ap had been central to bringing Papuans together to celebrate local culture and artistic expression. Sam Kapissa, a colleague and bandmate of

Ap (Figure 2.4), was an expert in Biak carving, using Dutch sources as well as his own knowledge of the island's ethnography to inform his work (Rutherford 2001). Don Flassy trained in linguistics in Java and the Netherlands, producing seminal studies on the languages of the Bird's Head and Bomberai Peninsula (e.g. Flassy 1981). An early example of local history (with a strong development focus) was produced in 1978 by F. and B. Mambrasar (1978), who wrote on the history of Kofiau Island in the Raja Ampat archipelago; in other areas, local historians have produced documents in Bahasa Indonesia and local languages too, although these are rarely available in published form (e.g. Mambrasar n.d.).

A small number of international expeditions were carried out in the 1960s–1980s. This included the Kyoto University West Irian Scientific Expedition of 1963–1964, in the Nassau Mountains (Kyoto University Biological Society 1977); however, the objectives were primarily zoological (Yamashina 1970). The Carstensz Glaciers Expeditions of 1971–1972 to record the environment of Nemangkawi also resulted in a provisional description of the people that moved around the mountains and involved sampling exposed sediments with archaeological remains at Mapala and Hamid rock shelters (Hope and Hope 1976). Mapala had been frequented by humans over 5000 years ago, providing the first evidence for very high-altitude hunting on New Guinea at about 4000 m asl. Additionally, a large German project among the Eipo of the Star Mountains, which began in 1974 and continued for several decades, focused on a wide range of anthropological topics including indigenous medicine, human ethology, and ethnomusicology (e.g. Schiefenhövel 1979). Ploeg (2004) provides an overview of the Eipo expeditions and describes how the anthropologists sometimes emphasised the 'simple' nature of Eipo material culture, but also acknowledged the creativity involved in making this simplicity work to their advantage.

Figure 2.4: Arnold Ap (left) and Sam Kapissa (right) with korwar figure.
Source: Constantinopel Ruhukail. Published courtesy of Museum Loka Budaya.

William G. Solheim and R.P. Soejono attempted to establish a systematic archaeological project on West New Guinea but met with difficulty for a variety of political reasons (Solheim 2006). Soejono completed a review of West New Guinea's archaeology at the time of the Indonesian takeover and, influenced by Riesenfeld, concluded that the island had received almost all its cultural influences from Indonesia to the west (Soejono 1963). Solheim, at first working independently of Soejono, initially obtained from German-Dutch archaeologist von Koenigswald several potsherds deriving from Yos Sudarso Bay and collected by Galis (Solheim 1958). He later became involved via the University of Hawai'i links to the Cultural Centre Museum and spent his sabbatical of 1975–1976 surveying the north coast of West New Guinea (Solheim 1978). Solheim, alongside Arnold Ap, made a visit to Padwa on Biak Island and recorded caves as well as *korwar* (wooden ancestor figurine) manufacture, and later visited Waigeo and Gag in the Raja Ampat Islands, noting burial caves and charred coconut shell eroding out of an exposed section (Solheim 1979). Owing to the rapid nature of these trips, however, the team was only able to describe above-ground details like rock art (Souza and Solheim 1976) and surface artefacts, many of which were collected for the Cultural Centre Museum. By contrast, Solheim's work at Makbon was more substantial and involved the excavation and description of archaeological pottery at a manufacturing site on the Bird's Head (Solheim 1998). Alongside Solheim, Mansoben and Ap were the first to undertake ethnographic observations of pottery making for the purposes of archaeological comparison in West New Guinea (Solheim and Ap 1977; Solheim and Mansoben 1977).

This tradition of using West New Guinea as a source for ethnoarchaeology has been followed, more extensively, by researchers in the 1980s–1990s. Ethnoarchaeological work was carried out most notably by Anne-Marie and Pierre Pétrequin, who described ceramic traditions and axe-adze making from 1984 to 2005 (Pétrequin and Pétrequin 1993, 1999, 2006). Collecting went alongside description, with these objects now stored, and in 2006–2008 exhibited, in the 'Musée d'Archéologie Nationale' (National Museum of Archaeology), Paris (Musée d'Archéologie Nationale 2006). The explicit drive behind this work was an ethnological comparison, especially between stilt houses around Lake Sentani and the Neolithic structures of the French Jura, based around lakeshores (Pétrequin et al. 2001, 2006; Pétrequin 1994). The Pétrequins' research followed on from the ethnographic and petrographic work of geoarchaeologist Erik Gonthier in the early 1980s around Lake Sentani and in the Baliem Valley (e.g. Gonthier and Schubnel 1981). From American universities, Bud Hampton (1999) undertook ethnographic work among Dani axe-adze makers between 1982 and 1993 for his PhD research, and in 1999 Dietrich Stout also conducted ethnographic work nearby, related to axe-adze making around the Ey River (Stout 2002).

Although some Dutch academic and missionary researchers continued to do important linguistic and anthropological data collection throughout the 1970s–1980s, these studies became increasingly rare (e.g. Van Enk and De Vries 1997; Voorhoeve 1971). Large-scale Dutch–Indonesian collaborations, however, did resume at the end of the twentieth century. The Upgrading of Irianese Scholars in the Field of Irian Jaya Studies (IRIS) program began in the 1980s, a collaboration between the Department of Languages and Cultures of Southeast Asia and Oceania (DSALCUL) at Leiden University, the IJSC in Jayapura, and the Lembaga Ilmu Pengetahuan Indonesia (Indonesian Institute of Sciences, LIPI) in Jakarta. From 1993 to 2001, 'Irian Jaya Studies: A Programme for Interdisciplinary Research' (ISIR) was initiated as part of this collaboration with the aim of generating new knowledge about West New Guinea using archival material in the Netherlands and Indonesia. To increase the impact of funding stemming from the Netherlands Foundation for the Advancement of Tropical Research (WOTRO), the initiative focused primarily on the Bird's Head region. This initiative published several proceedings, as well as the monographs *Studies in Irian Languages* (Reesink 1996, 2000), *Bird's Head Approaches* (Bartstra 1998), *Perspectives on the*

Bird's Head of Irian Jaya, Indonesia (Miedema et al. 1998), *One Head Many Faces* (Miedema and Reesink 2004), and the *Irian Jaya Source Materials* series. Introductions to these volumes expose the sometimes-conflicting agendas driving research in West New Guinea (Masinambow 1998), and tensions between international and Indonesian researchers; international researchers were interested in undertaking theoretical anthropological research to generate knowledge about the region and Indonesian academics wanted to conduct applied research with a focus on development, of a similar kind promoted under Dutch administration, such as agronomy, demography, and economics. What is missing from these discourses in the 1990s, however, is how international and Indonesian researchers interrelated with indigenous Papuan stakeholders, experts, and scholars.

Part of the ISIR's mandate was to investigate the cultural history of West New Guinea. As part of this project, a survey was undertaken in the interior of the Bird's Head in 1993, and in 1995 Johan Jelsma excavated Toé Cave and Juliette Pasveer excavated Kria Cave. These were the first systematic excavations in West New Guinea since Röder's work in Arguni Bay (Pasveer 2007, 2004; Pasveer et al. 2002). The radiocarbon dating of the Toé sequence pushed the evidence for human occupation in West New Guinea back to about 31,000–30,000 years ago, while Kria provided a sequence of intensive wallaby hunting when climates warmed in the Holocene. Wright and colleagues (2013) reviewed all previous archaeological research in West New Guinea and noted that these have remained the only two sites that have been published with chronostratigraphic sequences from this large region. Essentially the archaeology of West New Guinea has been built exclusively from these two sites for the past three decades, supplemented by palaeoecological data for forest burning obtained from the central highlands (Haberle et al. 1991, 2001).

New directions emerged in the early twenty-first century, following the end of the Suharto era in 1998 and the often-patchily implemented Special Autonomy law of 2001 (recently revised in 2021). Universitas Papua (University of Papua) was founded at Manokwari in 2000, developing out of an agricultural campus of Universitas Cenderawasih, which had in turn been the tropical agriculture research station operated by the Dutch (Wolfers 1969). The university now provides an opportunity for further education outside of Jayapura, providing subjects such as language and cultural studies, economics, and natural science. Both at Universitas Cenderawasih and Universitas Papua, a new generation of Papuan scholars are asking different types of questions of their own communities and those elsewhere in the region. For instance, Marlina Flassy, the first Papuan to become dean of the Faculty of Social and Political Sciences at Universitas Cenderawasih, has investigated the medical anthropology of disease around her home communities on the Bird's Head, and has used this information to provide recommendations for public health interventions (Flassy 2018, 2019). Others, like Benny Giay, continue to examine the role that religion and nonviolent action can play in peace processes (Giay 1995, 2005). Bernarda Meteray (2012) has researched the shifting history of Papuan national ideologies. Adolf Ronsumbre and Marlon Arthur Huwae have examined customary land ownership (Ronsumbre and Huwae 2022). Naffi Sanggenafa and Michael Howard have studied contemporary changes to society and material culture in the context of recent migrations into West New Guinea (Howard and Sanggenafa 2005). At the Cultural Centre Museum, curators and staff, such as Enrico Yori, undertake ethnographic and material culture research around West New Guinea, and those based at several newly established Balai Pelestarian Kebudayaan Wilayah (Regional Cultural Heritage Centres) support local customary practices and cultural events.

Balai Arkeologi Jayapura (Jayapura Centre of Archaeology) was established in 1996 and later renamed Balai Arkeologi Papua (Papua Centre of Archaeology). As an Indonesian government organisation funded by the Ministry of Education and Culture, the office was responsible for archaeological research in the West New Guinea region, initially carrying out small-scale archaeological surveys and test excavations throughout the 2000s. This fieldwork was mainly concentrated around the coast, with little undertaken in the highlands owing to military violence in many administrative areas and prohibitive costs in others. Later fieldwork conducted by the Papua Centre of Archaeology in the 2010s expanded on the initial period of research, with larger-scale excavations being undertaken especially around Lake Sentani, Jayapura, and the Bomberai Peninsula (see Djami 2020; Mene, this volume; Suroto, this volume). By 2020, preliminary reconnaissance surveys had covered about 25 per cent of the territory. In 2022 the research centre became part of the Badan Riset dan Inovasi Nasional (National Research and Innovation Agency, BRIN). At the Indonesia-wide level, the Organisation of Archaeology is divided into three research centres including Prehistoric and Historical Archaeology; Environmental, Maritime, and Sustainable Cultural Archaeology; and Archaeometry, with the intention being to bring regional centres of archaeology into a wider Indonesian national research framework.

Most archaeological studies so far have focused on documenting aspects of 'traditional' culture and examining evidence for the history of these practices. This research is still in the early stages of preliminary data gathering. Projects involving excavation have recovered hundreds to thousands of material findings like pottery and stone artefacts, which predispose publications to be primarily descriptive in nature. The archaeometric tools required to tackle emerging questions in archaeology are not available locally. This includes radiocarbon dating, which has been limited owing to funding shortages. Much of the Indonesian-language research produced within West New Guinea is now published in the archaeology journal *Papua: Jurnal Penelitian Arkeologi* and the anthropology journal *Cenderawasih: Jurnal Antropologi Papua*.

International anthropologists (usually operating as lone fieldworkers) are increasingly exploring the possible futures of West New Guinea, writing on topics such as the historicity of culture (Harple 2000), religious transformation (Timmer 2000), reproduction and morality (van Oosterhout 2002), health and stigma (Butt 2005), visual identities (Cookson 2008), mutable perceptions of otherness (Stasch 2009), intercultural encounters (de Hontheim 2011), nation-building (Rutherford 2012), resource extraction (Kirksey 2012), devolution of governance (Powell Davies 2021), and major ecological transformations (Chao 2022). The publication of large quantities of archival information and photographs is also reconceptualising the period of Dutch administration and missionisation (Corbey 2017, 2019). Basic linguistic data continue to be gathered and compiled into grammars and dictionaries, especially important given the growing number of endangered languages in the region (see Arnold, this volume). Large collaborative archaeological projects, although rare owing to a long period of exclusion in West New Guinea, are beginning to be undertaken involving teams from Europe, Australasia, Indonesia, and West New Guinea itself (e.g. Boesl et al. this volume; Gaffney et al. this volume).

We finish this section in 2022, the year that West New Guinea was subdivided into a series of smaller administrative provinces. The following section now uses these historiographical insights from 1511–2022 to generate ideas about future ways that research on the human histories of West New Guinea might be conducted.

Future prospects for the study of the human past in West New Guinea

The narrative so far has been overwhelmingly one of external observations on local subjects. The politics of this process are particularly palpable given the history of racialisation and violence, touched upon in the previous sections, which makes it clear that future research must reflect on and address these issues in practice. What is sorely needed now are narratives focused on the deep and ongoing histories of Papuans themselves. As Kusuma and colleagues (this volume) explain for their genetic work, and Arnold (this volume) describes for linguistics, mutualistic research producing knowledge for both researchers and local participants must be the minimal standard. Although social anthropological and some linguistic studies have involved extended fieldwork and return visits to communities, most archaeological and biological anthropological work has not yet built these ongoing commitments. In the future, research produced with Papuan involvement and leadership certainly has the capacity to challenge and rewrite our understanding of New Guinea's past in unforeseen and meaningful ways.

Scholars face a combination of challenges, however. These challenges include finding ways to genuinely engage local communities in research. Because there is substantial variation in how Papuans perceive their history and their heritage places, some communities are rightfully protective of their sites and stories about their past, whereas others are open to archaeological research. Outreach activities that explain clearly what archaeology (or a related discipline) aims to achieve, how the subject produces data, and how those data can be used to produce historical narratives, are one way to promote engagement. For instance, the Papua Centre of Archaeology undertook regular outreach activities around schools in Jayapura and Lake Sentani to describe what can be learned from heritage places, with booklets and field trip activities designed for pupils.

Several research projects administered by the Papua Centre of Archaeology also encountered issues about the legality of archaeological fieldwork. Under Indonesian law, a permit from both the local government and the landowner needs to be obtained prior to fieldwork. However, in several cases, fieldwork has been stopped owing to protests from the listed landowner's relatives. In many parts of West New Guinea, families are large and disparate, with land rights administered by clan leaders and councils of elders, meaning that a single representative cannot always grant legitimate access to places for survey and excavation. As such, the imposition of state-level administration of cultural heritage sites is often at odds with local political processes. As a minimal standard, all research should only proceed following community consultation to establish which groups hold authority to grant access to archaeological areas, and whether they want the work to be undertaken.

Lately, several steps have been implemented by local governments and their partner organisations to promote the protection of archaeological sites and heritage places. The Ministry of Education and Culture of Indonesia has designed programs to be delivered to indigenous Papuans in an attempt to preserve, celebrate, and promote cultural heritage based on locally specific knowledge and perceptions about historical places. Again, the programs aim to emphasise to young people the value of protecting heritage places. However, the growing number of institutions attempting to develop such heritage programs means that these initiatives are sometimes patchily implemented and with a variable long-term financial commitment to the communities or their heritage places. To improve this situation, there must be effective coordination between stakeholders at the community and government level as well as genuine appraisal of the interests of the local community in maintaining and managing their heritage landscapes.

Excavated material remains, and data produced about these remains, also need careful consideration. Currently, several collections are housed overseas (e.g. the Toé and Kria collections are based at The Australian National University) and the BRIN facilities in Jayapura provide the only dedicated space to house archaeological remains in West New Guinea. As such, material is often removed from local communities and stored elsewhere without attention given to the long-term preservation of these specimens, or whether storage outside of the local area is appropriate. Moreover, the illegal removal of antiquities from archaeological sites for sale on the private market is ongoing. Since the period of Dutch administration, and continuing today, archaeological and ethnographic material culture has been exported overseas for private sale, at times driven by the tourist sector. It is therefore important to increase awareness about the damage that this trade does to locally finite cultural objects. Alternative incomes might include the production and sale of replica objects or modern craft products.

Regarding ethnographic material culture, apart from the Cultural Centre Museum administered by Universitas Cenderawasih, and Museum Negeri Provinsi Papua (State Museum of Papua Province) in Jayapura, and the Museum of Asmat Culture and Development in Agats, provincial centres in West New Guinea do not have dedicated museums to conserve and display objects. Building capacity for such museums, including storage facilitates as well as specialist knowledge, would be one way to exhibit the cultural diversity that characterises New Guinea. In the three abovementioned museums, the conservation of their collections and the expansion of these collections with present-day material culture is crucial. The inclusion of archaeological material, as well as human, biological, and linguistic information in these museums would help to provide a historical context to the ethnographic artefacts on display, emphasising that New Guinea was a place of dramatic cultural change, rather than stasis (challenging Stone Age stereotypes which abound within Indonesia and internationally). Supporting such museum infrastructure would encourage requests for the repatriation of ethnographic and archaeological objects: although museums internationally, and especially in the Netherlands, are making their West New Guinea photographs, videos, and material objects available for online study, most early collections relating to the pre-Indonesian era remain overseas and beyond reach for Papuans.

Lastly, in terms of tertiary education, there has been systematic underinvestment in the facilities and specialist knowledge relating to West New Guinea's human past. For instance, in order to undertake archaeological research in West New Guinea, Indonesian law requires practitioners to hold a university degree in archaeology and obtain permission from a designated government institution (formerly the Papua Centre of Archaeology and currently BRIN). However, at the time of writing, there are no archaeology programs at Universitas Cenderawasih or Universitas Papua. Although some Papuan scholars have successfully trained in anthropology at Universitas Cenderawasih and later transitioned to archaeology, most researchers train in archaeology in western and central Indonesia—at Universitas Gadjah Mada and Universitas Indonesia in Java, Universitas Udayana in Bali, and Universitas Hasanuddin in Sulawesi—and relocate to Jayapura. For Papuans to participate in archaeological interpretation and cultural heritage preservation, communities and especially young people must have access to higher education, field experience, and laboratory facilities in West New Guinea itself.

Conclusion

Understanding the history of research on the human past in West New Guinea is important for contextualising research practice in the present and envisioning possible futures for scholarship. Chance encounters led to the first written description of Papuan people by Iberian mariners in the sixteenth century. These descriptions generally characterised Papuans based on their appearance and developed a series of racist misconceptions about the area that continued to characterise Dutch voyages around the island in the seventeenth and eighteenth centuries. During this time, a small number of mariners expressed an interest in the human history of New Guinea, recording rock art and local architecture. English and French voyages of discovery during the late eighteenth and early nineteenth centuries paid greater attention to describing local peoples and making small collections of ethnographic objects for museums. During the mid-nineteenth century, permanent Dutch outposts were established from which missionaries began to interact with Papuans across longer time periods. This period was characterised by a transition in the European imagination, which moved from describing Papuans as heathens and cannibals to noble savages. It also saw a small but growing interest in the history of New Guinea's peoples, with rock art sites revisited by several Dutch explorers.

At the start of the twentieth century, large-scale multidisciplinary scientific expeditions were sent by the Dutch administration along the coast and then into the interior, even reaching several groups of people living in the highlands. These expeditions resulted in a wealth of ethnographic, human biological, and linguistic data as well as the export of material culture to European museums on a colossal scale. Archaeological material was recorded opportunistically, the exception being a large-scale excavation by a German team around the Bomberai Peninsula. At this time, the deep history of West New Guinea's peoples remained a peripheral topic, except in so far as it could address the question of whether small-statured highland peoples represented a relict lineage of humanity. Following the Pacific War, ethnographic material from early expeditions was synthesised and began to contribute important insights to global anthropological theory, which stimulated further systematic recording across the territory. Chance archaeological discoveries were made by interested social anthropologists around West New Guinea, but these generally did not contribute to emerging narratives about 'Melanesian prehistory'.

Following the handover of West New Guinea to Indonesia in 1963, Dutch scholars lost access to the field and began to revisit the existing ethnographic evidence from afar. Tertiary institutions were established in Jayapura to support Indonesian scholars and, although the territory remained peripheral to the developing perception of national identity, some large-scale recording and documentation was undertaken to gather information about communities around West New Guinea. The latter twentieth century saw the training of several prominent Papuan anthropologists and linguists, although the deep human history of the region was strategically understudied. Today, although there are strong social anthropology and linguistics programs in West New Guinean universities, there are no opportunities for Papuan students to study archaeology or biological anthropology locally. The contentious recent history of the area brings the ethics of fieldwork in West New Guinea into sharp focus. Future research must actively address these concerns in practice by involving local communities in decision-making and provide opportunities for the mutual exchange of knowledge: generating capacity for archaeological research and cultural heritage management within West New Guinea will enable local people to guide and eventually lead such projects.

Acknowledgements

We thank Nicholas Thomas and Chris Ballard for their constructive feedback on a draft manuscript.

References

Agogino, G.A. 1979. Book review of 'Prehistory of the Eastern Highlands of New Guinea' by V. Watson and J.D. *Man* 14:756. doi.org/10.2307/2802163.

Ali, J.R. and L.R. Heaney 2021. Wallace's line, Wallacea, and associated divides and areas: History of a tortuous tangle of ideas and labels. *Biological Reviews* 96(3):922–942. doi.org/10.1111/brv.12683.

Anceaux, J.C. 1953. De huidige stand van het taalonderzoek op Nieuw-Guinea's Westhelft. *Bijdragen tot de Taal-, Land- en Volkenkunde* 109(3):231–248. doi.org/10.1163/22134379-90002404.

Archibold, R., A.L. Rand, and L.J. Brass 1942. Summary of the 1938–1939 New Guinea Expedition. *Bulletin of the American Museum of Natural History* 79(3):197–288.

Ballard, C. 1998. Malcolm Walker interview 1998. Interview transcript. Unpublished. On file with Chris Ballard, The Australian National University, Canberra.

Ballard, C. 1999. Blanks in the writing: Possible histories for West New Guinea. *Journal of Pacific History* 34(2):149–155. doi.org/10.1080/00223349908572899.

Ballard, C. 2000. Collecting Pygmies: The 'Tapiro' and the British Ornithologists' Union Expedition to Dutch New Guinea, 1910–1911. In M. O'Hanlon and R.L. Welsch (eds), *Hunting the gatherers: Ethnographic collectors, agents and agency in Melanesia, 1870s–1930s*, pp. 127–154. Berghahn Books, New York; Oxford. doi.org/10.1515/9780857456915-009.

Ballard, C. 2006. Strange alliance: Pygmies in the colonial imaginary. *World Archaeology* 38(1):133–151. doi.org/10.1080/00438240500510155.

Ballard, C. 2008. 'Oceanic Negroes': British anthropology of Papuans, 1820–1869. In B. Douglas and C. Ballard (eds), *Foreign bodies: Oceania and the science of race 1750–1940*, pp. 157–201. ANU ePress, Canberra. doi.org/10.22459/FB.11.2008.04.

Bartstra, G.-J. (ed.) 1998. *Bird's Head approaches: Irian Jaya studies—A programme for interdisciplinary research*. A.A. Balkema, Rotterdam.

Bennett, G. 1834. *Wanderings in New South Wales, Batavia, Pedir Coast, Singapore, and China: Being the journal of a naturalist in those countries during 1832, 1833, and 1834*. Richard Bentley, London. doi.org/10.5962/bhl.title.96943.

Bernstein, H.A. 1883. *Dagboek van Dr. H. A. Bernstein's Laatste Reis van Ternate Naar Nieuw-Guinea, Salawati En Batanta 17 October 1864 – 19 April 1865*. M. Nijhoff, 'S-Gravenhage.

Bijlmer, H.J.T. 1922. Met de centraal Nieuw-Guinee-expeditie, Ao 1920, naar een onbekenden volksstam in het hooggebergte. *Tijdschrift van het Koninklijk Nederlandsch Aardrijkskundig Genootschap* 39:156–183.

Bijlmer, H.J.T. 1939. Tapiro pygmies and Pania mountain-Papuans: Results of the anthropological Mimika Expedition in New-Guinea 1935–36. *Nova Guinea: New Series* 3:113–184.

Boelaars, J. 1958. *Papoea's Aan de Mappi*. De Fontein, Utrecht.

Boxer, C.R. and P. Manguin 1979. Miguel Roxo de Brito's narrative of his voyage to the Raja Empat (May 1581–1582). *Archipel* 18(1):175–194. doi.org/10.3406/arch.1979.1508.

Brienen, C.C. 2003. Zuidwest-Nieuw-Guinea 1904–1905. In A. Wentholt (ed.), *In Kaart Gebracht Met Kapmes En Kompas; Met Het Koninklijk Nederlandsch Aardrijkskundig Genootschap Op Expeditie Tussen 1873 En 1960*, pp. 63–71. ABP & KNAG, Heerlen.

Bruyns, W.F.J.M. 2019. The taking possession of part of New Guinea by the Dutch in 1828, and their contribution to the knowledge of the Arafura Sea. *The Great Circle* 41(1):38–59.

Bureau for Native Affairs 1958. Anthropological research in Netherlands New Guinea since 1950. *Oceania* 29(2):132–163. doi.org/10.1002/j.1834-4461.1958.tb02950.x.

Butt, L. 2005. 'Lipstick girls' and 'fallen women': AIDS and conspiratorial thinking in Papua, Indonesia. *Cultural Anthropology* 20(3):412–442. doi.org/10.1525/can.2005.20.3.412.

Carreau, L. 2018. Curiosity, revolution, science, and art: Pacific collections and French museums. In L. Carreau, A. Clark, A. Jelinek, E. Lilje, and N. Thomas (eds), *Pacific presences: Oceanic art and European museums*, Vol. 1, pp. 81–123. Sidestone Press, Leiden.

Chao, S. 2022. *In the shadow of the palms: More-than-human becomings in West Papua*. Duke University Press, Durham. doi.org/10.1515/9781478022855.

Cheesman, L.E. 1940. Two unexplored islands off Dutch New Guinea: Waigeu and Japen. *The Geographical Journal* 95(3):208–217. doi.org/10.2307/1788404.

Cheesman, L.E. 1943. Japanese operations in New Guinea. *The Geographical Journal* 101(3): 97–110. doi.org/10.2307/1788873.

Cheesman, L.E. 1949. *Six legged snakes in New Guinea*. Harrap, London.

Cook, J. 1821. *The three voyages of Captain James Cook round the world*. Longman, Hurst, Rees, Orme, and Brown, London. doi.org/10.5962/bhl.title.6760.

Cookson, M.B. 2008. Batik Irian: Imprints of Indonesian Papua. Unpublished PhD thesis. The Australian National University, Canberra.

Corbey, R. 2003. Destroying the graven image: Religious iconoclasm on the Christian frontier. *Anthropology Today* 19(4):10–14. doi.org/10.1111/1467-8322.00202.

Corbey, R. 2017. *Raja Ampat ritual art: Spirit priests and ancestor cults in New Guinea's far west*. C. Zwartenkot Art Books, Leiden.

Corbey, R. 2019. *Korwar: Northwest New Guinea ritual art according to missionary sources*. C. Zwartenkot Art Books, Leiden.

Corbey, R. and F.K. Weener 2015. Collecting while converting: Missionaries and ethnographics. *Journal of Art Historiography* 12(12):1–14.

Cowan, H.K. 1952. Een toontaal in Nederlands Nieuw-Guinea. *Tijdschrift Nieuw Guinea* 13: 55–60.

Cuvier, G. 1817. *Le Regne Animal Distribué D'après son Organisation, Pour Servir de Base à L'Histoire Naturelle des Animaux et D'introduction à L'Anatomie Comparé*, Tome 1. Imprimérie de A. Belin, Paris.

D'Albertis, L.M. 1881. *New Guinea: What I did and what I saw*. Sampson Low, Marston, Searle, & Rivington, London.

Dampier, W. 1703. *A voyage to New Holland, &c. in the year, 1699*. James Knapton, London. doi.org/10.5962/bhl.title.117049.

de Bruijn Kops, G.F. 1850. Bijdrage tot de Kennis der Noord- en Oostkusten van Nieuw Guinea. *Natuurkundig Tijdschrift voor Nederlandsch Indië* 1:163–292.

de Bruyn, J.V. 1959. New archaeological finds at Lake Sentani. *Nieuw-Guinea Studien* 3:1–8.

de Bruyn, J.V. 1962. New bronze finds at Kwadeware, Lake Sentani. *Nieuw-Guinea Studien* 6(1):61–62.

de Clercq, F.S.A. 1893. *De West- En Noordkust van Nederlandsch Nieuw-Guinea*. E.J. Brill, Leiden.

de Clercq, F.S.A. and J.D.E. Schmeltz 1893. *Ethnographische Beschrijving van de West- En Noordkust van Nederlandsch Nieuw-Guinea*. P.W.M. Trap, Leiden.

de Freycinet, R.M.P. 1996. *A woman of courage: The journal of Rose de Freycinet on her voyage around the world*. National Library of Australia, Canberra.

de Hontheim, A. 2011. *Devil chasers and art gatherers: Intercultural encounters with the Asmat.* E.M.E. (Éditions Modulaires Européennes) and InterCommunications, Fernelmont and Paris.

de Wolf, J.J. and S.R. Jaarsma 1992. Colonial ethnography: West New Guinea (1950–1962). *Bijdragen tot de Taal-, Land- en Volkenkunde* 148(1):103–124. doi.org/10.1163/22134379-90003170.

Djami, E.N.I. 2020. Megalitik Gunung Srobu dalam Konteks Budaya Melanesia. *Amerta* 38(2): 129–144. doi.org/10.24832/amt.v38i2.129-144.

Douglas, B. 2014. *Science, voyages, and encounters in Oceania, 1511–1850.* Palgrave MacMillan, Basingstoke. doi.org/10.1057/9781137305893.

Dozy, G.J. (ed.) 1880. *Aardrijkskundig Weekbald (Nieuwe Serie).* De Erven H. van Munster & Zoon, Amsterdam.

Drabbe, P. 1950. Talen en Dialecten van Zuid-West Nieuw-Guinea. *Anthropos* 45(4/6):545–574.

d'Urville, D. 1843. *Voyage Au Pôle Sud et Dans l'Océanie, Sur Les Corvettes 'l'Astrolabe' et 'La Zélée'.* Gide & Co, Paris.

Earl, G.W. 1853. *The native races of the Indian Archipelago: Papuans.* Hippolyte Bailliere, London. doi.org/10.5962/bhl.title.101733.

Feuilletau de Bruyn, W.K.H. 1947. *Pioniers in de Rimboe: Avonturen van Een Exploratie-Detachement in Zuidwest-Nieuw-Guinea.* Spaarnestad, Haarlem.

Fischer, H.W. 1923. Ethnographica aus Sud- und Sudwest- Neu-Guinea. *Nova Guinea* 7:37–144.

Flassy, D.A.L. 1981. *Struktur Bahasa Tehid.* Pusat Pembinaan dan Pengembangan Bahasa, Departemen Pendidikan dan Kebudayaan, Jakarta.

Flassy, M. 2018. Local knowledge, disease and healing in a Papua community. Unpublished PhD thesis. Faculty of Social Sciences, Georg-August University, Göttingen.

Flassy, M. 2019. *Local knowledge, disease and healing in a Papua community.* KSP Books, Istanbul.

Forrest, T. 1969. *A voyage to New Guinea and the Moluccas, 1774–1776.* Oxford University Press, Oxford.

Galis, K. 1956. Oudheidkundig onderzoek in Nederlands Nieuw-Guinea. *Bijdragen tot de Taal-, Land- en Volkenkunde* 112(3):271–284. doi.org/10.1163/22134379-90002318.

Galis, K.W. 1955. Papua's van de Humboldt-Baai: Bijdrage Tot Een Ethnografie. Unpublished PhD thesis. Universiteit Leiden, Leiden.

Galis, K.W. 1957a. De grotten van Jaand. *Nieuw Guinea Studien* 1:118–129.

Galis, K.W. 1957b. De Pinfeloe-Grot nabij Tainda. *Nieuw Guinea Studien* 1:118–129.

Galis, K.W. 1957c. Oude fortificatie ontdekt. *Nieuw Guinea Studien* 1:324–325.

Galis, K.W. 1960. Het fort te Jémbekaki, addendum. *Nieuw-Guinea Studien* 4:52–54.

Galis, K.W. 1962. *Bibliographie van Nederlands-Nieuw-Guinea.* Samengesteld door, Den Haag.

Galis, K.W. and F.C. Kamma 1958. Het fort te Jémbakaki. *Nieuw-Guinea Studien* 2:206–222.

Galvão, A. 1944. *Tratado Dos Descobrimentos.* Visconde de Legoa, da Academia Portuguesa da Historia, Porto.

Gardner, R. (dir.) 1963. *Dead birds.* Film. Film Study Center of the Peabody Museum at Harvard University.

Gerbrands, A.A. 1951. Kunststijlen in West Nieuw-Guinea. *Indonesië* 4:251–283.

Gerbrands, A.A. 1961. *The Asmat of New Guinea: The Michael C. Rockefeller collections, 1961.* Museum of Primitive Art, New York, NY.

Giay, B. 1995. *Zakheus Pakage and his communities: Indigenous religious discourse, socio-political resistance and ethnohistory of the Me of Irian Jaya.* VU University Press, Amsterdam.

Giay, B., 2005. West Papua peace zone: The role of the church in West Papua and local initiatives in the struggle for human rights. In G. ter Haar and J. Busuttil (eds), *Bridge or barrier,* pp. 202–224. Brill, Amsterdam. doi.org/10.1163/9789047405733_012.

Godschalk, J.A. 1999. A.C. de Kock's encounter with the 'Goliath Pygmies': The first ethnographic data from the Mek culture area in the Eastern Highlands of Irian Jaya. *Journal of Pacific History* 34(2):219–228. doi.org/10.1080/00223349908572904.

Golson, J. 2016. Susan Bulmer, an archaeological pioneer. *Archaeology in Oceania* 51:11–18. doi.org/10.1002/arco.5117.

Gonthier, E. and H.J. Schubnel 1981. Les derniers lapidaires du Néolithique de la vallée de la Baliem. *Revue de Gemmologie* 69:12–15.

Goode, J. 1977. *Rape of the fly: Explorations in New Guinea.* Nelson, Melbourne.

Goudswaard, A. 1863. *De Papoewa's van de Geelvinksbaai.* H.A.M. Roelants, Schiedam.

Griffin, A. 1990. London, Bengal, the China trade and the unfrequented extremities of Asia: The East India Company's settlement in New Guinea, 1793–95. *The British Library Journal* 16(2):151–173.

Gunson, N. and J. Godschalk 2014. Manuscript XXVIII: An early ethnography of the Geelvink Bay people, West New Guinea. *Journal of Pacific History* 49(1):95–121. doi.org/10.1080/00223344.2014.892236.

Haberle, S.G., G.S. Hope, and Y. DeFretes 1991. Environmental change in the Baliem Valley, Montane Irian Jaya, Republic of Indonesia. *Journal of Biogeography* 18(1):25–40. doi.org/10.2307/2845242.

Haberle, S.G., G.S. Hope, and S. van der Kaars 2001. Biomass burning in Indonesia and Papua New Guinea: Natural and human induced fire events in the fossil record. *Palaeogeography, Palaeoclimatology, Palaeoecology* 171(3–4):259–268. doi.org/10.1016/S0031-0182(01)00248-6.

Haga, A. 1884. *Nederlandsch Nieuw Guinea: Historische Bijdrage ±1500–1883.* W. Bruining & Co, Batavia.

Hampton, O.W. 1999. *Culture of stone: Sacred and profane uses of stone among the Dani.* Texas A&M University Press, College Station.

Hamy, E.-T. 1877. *Commentaires Sur Quelques Cartes Anciennes de La Nouvelle-Guinée : Pour Servir à l'histoire de La Découverte de Ce Pays Parles Navigateurs Espagnols (1528–1608).* Société de Géographie, Paris.

Harple, T. 2000. Controlling the dragon: An ethno-historical analysis of social engagement among the Kamoro of South-West New Guinea (Indonesian Papua/Irian Jaya). Unpublished PhD thesis. The Australian National University, Canberra.

Heeres, J.E. and F.W. Stapel 1934. Corpus Diplomaticum Neerlando-Indicum. Verzameling van politieke contracten en verdere verdragen door de Nederlanders in het Oosten gesloten, van privilegebrieven, aan hen verleend, enz. Derde deel (1676-1691). *Bijdragen tot de Taal-, Land- en Volkenkunde van Nederlandsch-Indië* 1:583–616.

Held, G.J. 1947. Het tijdsperspectief in de Geelvinkbaai-culturen. *Indonesië* 1:162–177.

Hilder, B. 1980. *The voyage of Torres: The discovery of the southern coastline of New Guinea and Torres Strait by Captain Luis Baez de Torres in 1606*. University of Queensland Press, St Lucia.

Hope, G.S. and J.H. Hope 1976. Man on Mt. Jaya. In G.S. Hope, J.A. Peterson, U. Radok, and I. Allison (eds), *The equatorial glaciers of New Guinea. Results of the 1971–1973 Australian Universities' Expeditions to Irian Jaya: Survey, glaciology, meteorology, biology and paleoenvironments*, pp. 225–238. A.A. Balkema, Rotterdam. doi.org/10.1201/9780203736777-11.

Howard, M.C. and N. Sanggenafa (eds) 2005. *Indigenous peoples and migrants of Northern Papua, Indonesia*. White Lotus, Bangkok.

Howes, H. 2012. 'Shrieking savages' and 'men of milder customs': Dr Adolf Bernhard Meyer in New Guinea, 1873. *Journal of Pacific History* 47(1):21–44. doi.org/10.1080/00223344.2011.653052.

Jaarsma, S.R. 1991. An ethnographer's tale: Ethnographic research in Netherlands (West) New Guinea (1950–1962). *Oceania* 62(2):128–146. doi.org/10.1002/j.1834-4461.1991.tb02384.x.

Jaarsma, S.R. 1993. 'More pastoral than academic …': Practice and purpose of missionary ethnographic research (West New Guinea, 1950–1962). *Anthropos* 88(1/3):109–133.

Jaarsma, S.R. 1994. 'Your work is of no use to us …': Administrative interests in ethnographic research (West New Guinea, 1950–1962). *The Journal of Pacific History* 29(2):153–171. doi.org/10.1080/00223349408572769.

Kamma, F.C. 1948. De verhouding tussen Tidore en de Papoese eilanden in legende en historie. *Indonesië* 1:536–559.

Kamma, F.C. 1954. De Messiaanse Koréri-Bewegingen in Het Biaks-Noemfoorse Cultuurgebied. Unpublished PhD thesis. Faculteit der Godgeleeidheid, Universiteit Leiden, Leiden.

Kamma, F.C. 1972. *Koreri: Messianic movements in the Biak-Numfor culture area*. Martinus Nijhoff, The Hague. doi.org/10.1007/978-94-015-0742-4.

Kamma, F.C. 1977. *'Dit Wonderlijke Werk': Het Probleem van de Communicatie Tussen Oost En West Gebaseerd Op de Ervaringen in Het Zendingswerk Op Nieuw-Guinea (Irian Jaya), 1855-1972: Een Socio-Missiologische Benadering*. Raad voor de Zending der Nederlandse Hervormde Kerk, Oegstgeest.

Kamma, F.C. and S. Kooijman 1973. *Romawa Forja, child of the fire: Iron working and the role of iron in West New Guinea (West Irian)*. E.J. Brill, Leiden. doi.org/10.1163/9789004545243.

Kirksey, E. 2010. Anthropology and colonial violence in West Papua. *Cultural Survival Quarterly* 26(3).

Kirksey, E. 2012. *Freedom in entangled worlds: West Papua and the architecture of global power*. Duke University Press, Durham. doi.org/10.1515/9780822394761.

Klein, W.C. (ed.), 1954. *Nieuw Guinea: De Ontwikkeling Op Economisch, Social En Cultureel Gebied, in Nederlands En Australisch Nieuw Guinea*. Staatsdrukkerij en Uitgeverijbedrijf, 's-Gravenhage.

Kleiweg de Zwaan, J.P. 1956. The Papuans of Dutch New Guinea, a physico-anthropological survey. *Antiquity and Survival* 1:321–343.

Koch, J.W.R. 1908. Bijdrage Tot de Anthropologie Der Bewoners van Zuidwest Nieuw-Guinea: Benevens Uitkomsten van Lichaamsmetingen Verricht Bij Javanen, Sumatranen, Baliërs En Sasaks. Unpublished PhD thesis. Faculteit der Geneeskunde, Universiteit van Amsterdam, Amsterdam.

Kolff, D.H. 1828. *Reize Door Den Zuidelijken Molukschen Archipel En Längs de Zuidwestkust van Nieuw Guinea: Gedaan Inde Jaren 1825 En 1826*. G.J.A. Beijerinck, Amsterdam.

Kolff, D.H. and G.W. Earl 1840. *Voyages of the Dutch brig of war* Dourga *through the southern and little-known parts of the Moluccan archipelago, and along the previously unknown southern coast of New Guinea, performed during the years 1825 & 1826.* James Madden & Co, London.

Kooijman, S. 1955. *De Kunst van Nieuw Guinea.* Servire, Den Haag.

Kooijman, S. 1983. The Netherlands and Oceania: a summary of research. *Bijdragen tot de Taal-, Land- en Volkenkunde* 139(2/3):199–246. doi.org/10.1163/22134379-90003442.

Kyoto University Biological Society 1977. ニューギニア中央高地 京都大学西イリアン学術探検隊報告 *1963–1964* [*New Guinea Central Highlands Kyoto University West Irian Scientific Expedition Report 1963–1964*]. Asahi Shimbun Company, Kyoto.

Labillardière, M. 1800. *Relation du Voyage à la Recherche de la Pérouse,* Tome 1. Deboffe, London.

Le Roux, C.C.F.M. 1948–50. *De Bergpapoea's van Nieuw-Guinea en Hun Woongebied.* E.J. Brill, Leiden.

Lesson, R.P. 1839. *Voyage Autour du Monde Entrepris par Ordre du Gouvernement sur La Corvette La Coquille,* Vol. 1. Gregoir, Wouters, & Co., Brussels. doi.org/10.5962/bhl.title.119917.

Levit, G.S. and U. Hossfeld 2020. Ernst Haeckel, Nikolai Miklucho-Maclay and the racial controversy over the Papuans. *Frontiers in Zoology* 17(1):1–20. doi.org/10.1186/s12983-020-00358-w.

Lorentz, H.A. 1905. *Eenige Maanden Onder de Papoea's.* Brill, Leiden.

Lorentz, H.A. 1913. *Zwarte Menschen-Witte Bergen: Verhaal van Den Tocht Naar Het Sneeuwgebergte van Nieuw-Guinea.* Brill, Leiden.

Loth, J.E. 1924. Verslag over de geologisch-mijnbouwkundige verkenning van West Nieuw-Guinee. *Jaarboek van het Mijnwezen in Nederlands-Indië* 53:114–146.

Mambrasar, A. n.d. Raja Ampat history. Oral history report. Unpublished. On file with Max Ammer, Kri Eco Resort, Kabupaten Raja Ampat.

Mambrasar, F. and B. Mambrasar 1978. Sejarah Kepulauan Kofiau. *Irian: Bulletin of Irian Jaya Development* 7(3):3–33.

Mansoben, J.R. 1995. *Sistem Politik Tradisional Di Irian Jaya.* LIPI-RUL, Leiden.

Masinambow, E.K.M. 1998. Anthropological fieldwork and international cooperation. In J. Miedema, C. Odé, and R.A.C. Dam (eds), *Perspectives on the Bird's Head of Irian Jaya, Indonesia: Proceedings of the Conference, Leiden, 13–17 October 1997,* pp. 27–31. Rodopi, Amsterdam; Atlanta. doi.org/10.1163/9789004652644_005.

Meteray, B. 2012. *Nasionalisme Ganda Orang Papua.* Penerbit Buku Kompas, Jakarta.

Metzger, E. 1885. Rock-pictures in New Guinea. *Nature* 31(806):527–528. doi.org/10.1038/031527b0.

Meyer, A.B. 1899. *The distribution of the Negritos in the Philippine Islands and elsewhere.* Stengel & Co, Dresden.

Miedema, J. and G. Reesink 2004. *One head, many faces: New perspectives on the Bird's Head Peninsula of New Guinea.* KITLV Press, Leiden. doi.org/10.1163/9789004454385_017.

Miedema, J., C. Odé, and R.A.C. Dam (eds) 1998. *Perspectives on the Bird's Head of Irian Jaya, Indonesia: Proceedings of the Conference, Leiden, 13–17 October 1997.* Rodopi, Amsterdam; Atlanta. doi.org/10.1163/9789004652644.

Miller, C.F. 1950. Pottery types from kitchen middens of Dutch New Guinea. In E.K. Reed and D.S. King (eds), *For the Dean: Essays in anthropology in honor of Bryan Cummings on his eighty-ninth birthday*, pp. 277–289. Hohokam Museum Association and Southwest Monuments Association, Tucson.

Musée d'Archéologie Nationale 2006. Objets de pouvoir en Nouvelle-Guinée. *Le Petit Journal des Grande Expositions* 394: 1–15.

Nijenhuis, L.E. 1961. Bloodgroup frequencies in the Netherlands, Curaçao, Surinam and New Guinea. Unpublished PhD thesis. Municipal University of Amsterdam, Amsterdam.

Ottow, C.W. and J.G. Geissler 2010. Geelvink Bay: Carl Wilhelm Ottow and Johann Gottlob Geissler, A brief survey of the land and people on the northeast coast of New Guinea (Mansinam, 29 January 1857). *White on black: Writings on Oceania* 1:1–61.

Overweel, J. 1998. 'A systematic activity': Military exploration in Western New Guinea, 1907–1915. In J. Miedema, C. Odé, and R.A.C. Dam (eds), *Perspectives on the Bird's Head of Irian Jaya, Indonesia: Proceedings of the Conference, Leiden, 13–17 October 1997*, pp. 455–478. Rodopi, Amsterdam; Atlanta. doi.org/10.1163/9789004652644_024.

Pasveer, J.M. 2004. *The Djief hunters: 26,000 years of rainforest exploitation on the Bird's Head of Papua, Indonesia*. A.A. Balkema, Leiden. doi.org/10.1201/b17006.

Pasveer, J.M. 2007. Prehistoric human presence in Papua and adjacent areas. In A.J. Marshall and B.M. Beehler (eds), *The ecology of Papua*, pp. 121–133. Periplus, Singapore.

Pasveer, J.M., S.J. Clarke, and G.H. Miller 2002. Late Pleistocene human occupation of inland rainforest, Bird's Head, Papua. *Archaeology in Oceania* 37(2):92–95. doi.org/10.1002/j.1834-4453.2002.tb00510.x.

Pétrequin, A.-M. and P. Pétrequin 1999. La poterie en Nouvelle-Guinée: savoir-faire et transmission des techniques. *Journal de la Société des Océanistes* 108(1):71–101. doi.org/10.3406/jso.1999.2080.

Pétrequin, A.-M. and P. Pétrequin 2006. *Objets de Pouvoir en Nouvelle-Guinée: Catalogue de La Donation Anne-Marie et Pierre Pétrequin*. Musée d'Archaéologie Nationale de Saint-Germain-en-Laye, Paris.

Pétrequin, P. 1994. De la Nouvelle-Guinée au néolithique du Jura: Le rôle de l'écologie et de l'ethno-archéologie pour comprendre l'évolution de la culture matérielle. In B. Latour and P. Lemonnier (eds), *De La Préhistoire Aux Missiles Balistiques: L'intelligence Sociale Des Techniques*, pp. 83–100. La Découverte, Paris. doi.org/10.3917/dec.latou.1994.01.0085.

Pétrequin, P. and A.-M. Pétrequin 1993. *Écologie d'un outil: la hache de pierre en Irian Jaya (Indonésie)*. CNRS, Paris.

Pétrequin, P., O. Weller, E. Gauthier, A. Dufraisse, and J.-F. Piningre 2001. Salt springs exploitation without pottery during Prehistory. From New Guinea to the French Jura. In S. Beyries and P. Pétrequin (eds), *Ethno-archaeology and its Transfers: Papers from a session held at the European Association of Archaeologists Fifth Annual Meeting in Bournemouth 1999*, pp. 37–65. British Archaeological Reports, Oxford.

Pétrequin, P., A.-M. Pétrequin, M.G.L. Errera, S. Cassen, and C. Croutsch 2006. Complexité technique et valorisation sociale: Haches polies de Nouvelle-Guinée et du Néolithique alpin. In L. Astruc, F. Bon, V. Léa, P.-Y. Milcent, and S. Philibert (eds), *Normes Techniques et Pratiques Sociales : De la Simplicité des Outillages Pré- et Protohistoriques*, pp. 417–431. APDCA, Antibes.

Pijnappel, J. 1854. Eenige bijzonderheden betreffende de Papoea's van de Geelvinksbaai van Nieuw-Guinea. *Bijdragen tot de Taal-, Land- en Volkenkunde* 2(1):371–383. doi.org/10.1163/22134379-90001189.

Ploeg, A. (ed.) 1970. *Land tenure in West Irian*. Research School of Pacific Studies, New Guinea Research Unit Committee, The Australian National University, Canberra.

Ploeg, A. 1995. First contact, in the highlands of Irian Jaya. *Journal of Pacific History* 30(2):227–239. doi.org/ 10.1080/00223349508572797.

Ploeg, A. 1997. Observations on the value of early ethnographic reports: Paul Wirz's research in the Toli Valley, Irian Jaya, in 1921. *Zeitschrift für Ethnologie* 122(2):209–228.

Ploeg, A. 2004. The German Eipo research project. *Journal de la Société des Océanistes* 118:35–79. doi.org/ 10.4000/jso.263.

Ploeg, A. 2022. The 'Third Expedition to South New Guinea': A review essay. *Journal of Pacific History* 57(1): 89–98. doi.org/10.1080/00223344.2021.1994855.

Pouwer, J. 1955. *Enkele Aspecten van de Mimika-Cultuur.* Staatsdrukkerij en Uitgeversbedrijf, 's-Gravenhage.

Pouwer, J. 1999. The colonisation, decolonisation and recolonisation of West New Guinea. *Journal of Pacific History* 34(2):157–179. doi.org/10.1080/00223349908572900.

Powell Davies, T. 2021. The three hearths: Custom, church and state as colliding orders of time and space in Asmat, Indonesian Papua. Unpublished PhD thesis. Department of Social Anthropology, University of Cambridge, Cambridge.

Reesink, G.P. (ed.) 1996. *Studies in Irian languages, Part 1.* Universitas Katolik Indonesia Atma Jaya, Jakarta.

Reesink, G.P. (ed.) 2000. *Studies in Irian languages, Part 2.* Universitas Katolik Indonesia Atma Jaya, Jakarta.

Rhys, L. 1947. *Jungle pimpernel: The story of a district officer in Central Netherlands New Guinea.* Hodder & Stoughton, London.

Riesenfeld, A. 1950. *The megalithic culture of Melanesia.* Brill, Leiden.

Röder, J. 1939. Rock-pictures and prehistoric times in Dutch New Guinea. *Man* 39:175–178. doi.org/ 10.2307/2792120.

Röder, J. 1940. Ergebnisse einer Probegrabung in der Höhle Dudumunir auf Arguni, MacCluergolf (Holländisch West-Neuguinea). *Nova Guinea* 4:1–11.

Röder, J. 1959. *Felsbilder und Vorgeschichte des MacCluer-Golfes West-Neuguinea.* L.C. Wittich, Darmstadt.

Ronsumbre, A. and M.A. Huwae 2022. Identity, power, myth contestation and land control in Manokwari, West Papua-Indonesia. *World Journal of Advanced Research and Reviews* 14(1):223–228. doi.org/10.30574/ wjarr.2022.14.1.0318.

Roxo de Brito, M. 2016. New Guinea. In G.B. Souza and J.S. Turley (eds), *The Boxer codex: Transcription and translation of an illustrated late sixteenth-century Spanish manuscript concerning the geography, ethnography and history of the Pacific, South-East Asia and East Asia,* pp. 503–524. Brill, Leiden.

Rutherford, D. 2001. Remembering Sam Kapissa. *Inside Indonesia: The peoples and cultures of Indonesia* 67 (July–September 2001).

Rutherford, D. 2012. *Laughing at Leviathan: Sovereignty and audience in West Papua.* University of Chicago Press, Chicago IL. doi.org/10.7208/chicago/9780226731995.001.0001.

Schiefenhövel, W. 1979. The Eipo—Members of the Mek group in the highlands of Irian Jaya. A short introduction. *Bulletin of Irian Jaya Development* 7:47–67.

Schmidt, A.E. 1997. In search of men of nature: Paul Wirz's photography in New Guinea, 1916–1955. *Pacific Studies* 20:16.

Schoorl, J.W. 1957. *Kultuur En Kultuurveranderingen in Het Moejoe-Gebied.* J.N. Voorhoeve, Den Haag.

Seyne Kok, J., N. Adriani, and G.P. Rouffaer (eds) 1908. *De Zuidwest Nieuw-Guinea-Expeditie 1904/5 van Het Kon. Ned. Aardrijkskundig Genootschap.* Brill, Leiden.

Soejono, R.P. 1963. Prehistori Irian Barat. In Koentjaraningrat and H.W. Bachtiar (eds), *Penduduk Irian Barat*, pp. 39–54. Penerbitan Universitas, Jakarta.

Solheim, W.G. 1958. Some potsherds from New Guinea. *The Journal of the Polynesian Society* 67(2):155–157.

Solheim, W.G. 1978. Archaeological survey, Irian Jaya. *Pacific Arts Newsletter* 6:1–5.

Solheim, W.G. 1979. Irian Jaya origins. *Australian Natural History* 19(10):24–27.

Solheim, W.G. 1998. Preliminary report on Makbon archaeology, the Bird's Head, Irian Jaya. In G.-J. Bartstra (ed.), *Bird's Head approaches: Irian Jaya studies—A programme for interdisciplinary research*, pp. 29–40. A.A. Balkema, Rotterdam.

Solheim, W.G. 2006. Soejono's efforts in starting archaeological research in Papua (Irian Jaya). In T. Simanjuntak, M. Hisyam, B. Prsetyo, and T.S. Nastiti (eds), *Archaeology: Indonesian perspective, RP Soejono's festschrift*, pp. 15–28. Indonesian Institute of Sciences, Jakarta.

Solheim, W.G. and A.C. Ap 1977. Pottery manufacture in Abar, Lake Sentani, Irian Jaya. *Irian: Bulletin of Irian Jaya Development* 6(1):52–70.

Solheim, W.G. and J. Mansoben 1977. Pottery manufacture in Mansinam, Manokwari, Irian Jaya. *Irian: Bulletin for Irian Jaya Development* 6(1):46–51.

Souza, C.R. and W. Solheim 1976. A new area of rock paintings in Irian Jaya, Indonesian New Guinea. In K.K. Chakravarty (ed.), *Rock-art of India: Paintings and engravings*, pp. 182–195. Arnold-Heinemann, New Delhi.

Starbuck, N. 2016. 'Race', intimacy and go-between in French-West Papuan encounters. In T. Shellam, M. Nugent, S. Konishi, and A. Cadzow (eds), *Brokers and boundaries: Colonial exploration in Indigenous territory*, pp. 39–60. ANU Press, Canberra. doi.org/10.22459/BB.04.2016.03.

Stasch, R. 2009. *Society of others: Kinship and mourning in a West Papuan place.* University of California Press, Oakland. doi.org/10.1525/9780520943322.

Stout, D. 2002. Skill and cognition in stone tool production: An ethnographic case study from Irian Jaya. *Current Anthropology* 43(5):693–722. doi.org/10.1086/342638.

Summerhayes, G.R. 2021. History of archaeology in Papua New Guinea: The early years up to 1960. In I. McNiven and B. David (eds), *The Oxford handbook of the archaeology of Indigenous Australia and New Guinea*, pp. 85–108. Oxford University Press, Oxford. doi.org/10.1093/oxfordhb/9780190095611. 013.3.

Suryawan, I.N. 2015. Singing for unity: Mambesak and the making of Papuan heritage. In S. Legene, B. Purwanto, and H.S. Nordholt (eds), *Sites, bodies and stories: Imagining Indonesian history*, pp. 199–209. NUS Press, Singapore. doi.org/10.2307/j.ctv1nth6b.14.

Suwondo, B. and A. Yunus (eds) 1978. *Cerita Rakyat Daerah Irian Jaya.* Departemen Pendidik dan Kebudayaan Proyek Inventarisasi dan Dokumentasi Kebudayaan Daerah, Jayapura.

Taylor, P.M. 2006. Introduction: Revisiting the Dutch and American New Guinea Expedition of 1926. In P.M. Taylor (ed.), *By aeroplane to Pygmyland: Revisiting the 1926 Dutch and American Expedition to New Guinea.* Smithsonian Institution Libraries, Digital Editions, Washington, DC.

Tichelman, G.L. 1953. Beroemd bronzen bijltje. *Oost en West* 46(5):14.

Timmer, J. 2000. *Living with intricate futures: Order and confusion in Imyan Worlds, Irian Jaya, Indonesia.* Centre for Pacific and Asian Studies, Nijmegen.

Trotter, C. 1884. New Guinea: A summary of our present knowledge with regard to the island. *Proceedings of the Royal Geographical Society and Monthly Record of Geography* 6(4):196. doi.org/10.2307/1800587.

van Baal, J. 1934. Godsdienst En Samenleving in Nederlandsch-Zuid-Nieuw-Guinea. Unpublished PhD thesis. Faculty of Law, Rijksuniversiteit te Leiden, Leiden.

van Baal, J. 1986. *Ontglipt verleden; Verhaal van mijn jaren in een wereld die voorbijging. I: Tot 1947, Indisch bestuursambtenaar in vrede en oorlog.* Wever, Franeker.

van Baal, J. 1989. *Ontglipt verleden; Verhaal van mijn jaren in een wereld die voorbijging; II: Leven in verandering.* Van Wijnen, Franeker.

van Baal, J., K.W. Galis, and K.P.H. Koentjaraningrat 1984. *West Irian: A bibliography.* Foris Publications, Dordrecht.

van Benthem Jutting, W.S. 1940. Molluskenschalen von prähistoriscchen Mahlzeitresten aus der Höhle Dudumunit in West Neuguinea. *Nova Guinea* 4:11–29.

van der Leeden, A.C. 1956. *Hoofdtrekken Der Sociale Struktuur in Het Westerlijke Binnenland van Sarmi.* Eduard Ijdo N.V, Leiden.

van der Sande, G.A.J. 1907. *Ethnography and anthropology. Nova Guinea resultats de L'Expedition Scientifique Neerlandaise a la Nouvelle-Guinee en 1903 sous les auspices de Arthur Wickmann, Vol. III.* EJ Brill, Leiden.

van Enk, G. and L. de Vries 1997. *The Korowai of Irian Jaya: Their language and cultural context.* Oxford University Press, Oxford. doi.org/10.1093/oso/9780195105513.001.0001.

van Oosterhout, D. 2002. *Landscapes of the body: Reproduction, fertility and morality in a Papuan society.* CNWS Publications, Leiden.

Vetter, J. 2006. Wallace's other line: Human biogeography and field practice in the eastern colonial tropics. *Journal of the History of Biology* 39:89–123. doi.org/10.1007/s10739-005-6543-4.

Veys, F.W. 2018. Papua collections in the Netherlands: A story of exploration, research, missionization, and colonization. In L. Carreau, A. Clark, A. Jelinek, E. Lilje, and N. Thomas (eds), *Pacific presences: Oceanic art and European museums*, Vol. 1, pp. 127–164. Sidestone Press, Leiden.

Visser, L. 2012a. The everyday life of Papuan civil servants 1950–1990. In L. Visser (ed.), *Governing New Guinea: An oral history of Papuan administrators, 1950–1990*, pp. 1–19. KITLV Press, Leiden. doi.org/10.1163/9789004260450_002.

Visser, L. (ed.) 2012b. *Governing New Guinea: An oral history of Papuan administrators, 1950–1990.* KITLV Press, Leiden. doi.org/10.26530/OAPEN_428891.

von Koenigswald, G.V. 1968. Classification of some stone tools from Java and New Guinea. In W.G. Solheim (ed.), *Anthropology at the Eighth Pacific Science Congress*, pp. 113–138. Social Science Research Institute, University of Hawai'i, Honolulu.

von Rosenberg, H. 1878. *Der Malayische Archipel.* Verlag von Gustav Weigel, Leipzig.

Voorhoeve, C. 1971. Miscellaneous notes on the languages of West Irian, New Guinea. *Papers in New Guinea Linguistics* 14:47–114.

Voorhoeve, C. 1975. A hundred years of Papuan linguistic research: Western New Guinea area. In S.A. Wurm (ed.), *New Guinea area languages and language study, Vol. 1: Papuan languages and the New Guinea linguistic scene*. Pacific Linguistics, The Australian National University, Canberra.

Voors, A.W. and D. Metselaar 1958. The reliability of dental age as a yard-stick to assess the unknown calendar age. *Tropical and Geographical Medicine* 10:175–180.

Wallace, A.R. 1869. *The Malay archipelago*. Macmillan and Co, London.

Webster, E.M. 1984. *The moon man: A biography of Nikolai Miklouho-Maclay*. University of California Press, Berkeley.

Wichmann, A. 1909. *Nova Guinea. Uitkomsten Der Nederlandsche Nieuw-Guinea-Expeditie in 1903: Entdeckungsgeschichte von Neu-Guinea (Bis 1828)*. E.J. Brill, Leiden.

Wichmann, A. 1910. *Nova Guinea. Uitkomsten Der Nederlandsche Nieuw-Guinea-Expeditie in 1903: Entdeckungsgeschichte von Neu-Guinea (1828 Bis 1885)*. E.J. Brill, Leiden.

Wichmann, A. 1912. *Nova Guinea. Uitkomsten Der Nederlandsche Nieuw-Guinea-Expeditie in 1903: Entdeckungsgeschichte von Neu-Guinea (1885 Bis 1903)*. E.J. Brill, Leiden.

Wirz, P. 1922a. *Die Marind-Anim von Holländisch-Süd-Neu-Guinea I. Band. Teil I. Die Materielle Kultur Der Marind-Anim*. L. Friedrichsen & Co, Hamburg. doi.org/10.1515/9783111322193.

Wirz, P. 1922b. *Die Marind-Anim von Holländisch-Süd-Neu-Guinea I. Band. Teil II. Die Religiösen Vorstellungen Und Die Mythen Der Marind-Anim, Sowie Die Herausbildung Der Totemistisch-Sozialen Gruppierungen*. L. Friedrichsen & Co, Hamburg. doi.org/10.1515/9783111588902.

Wirz, P. 1923. Dies und jenes über die Sentanier und die Geheimkulte im Norden von Neu-Guinea. *Tijdschrift voor Indische Taal-, Land- en Volkenkunde* 53:1–80.

Wolfers, E. 1969. EPW -21 West Irian I: The Bird of Paradise State University. Correspondence. Unpublished. Institute of Current World Affairs, Washington, DC.

Wollaston, A.F.R. 1912. *Pygmies & Papuans: The Stone Age to-day in Dutch New Guinea*. John Murray, London. doi.org/10.5962/bhl.title.21534.

Wollaston, A.F.R. 1914. An expedition to Dutch New Guinea. *The Geographical Journal* 43(3):248–268. doi.org/10.2307/1778612.

Wright, D., T. Denham, D. Shine, and M. Donohue 2013. An archaeological review of western New Guinea. *Journal of World Prehistory* 26(1):25–73. doi.org/10.1007/s10963-013-9063-8.

Wright, I.S. 1939. The first American voyage across the Pacific, 1527–1528: The voyage of Alvaro de Saavedra Cerón. *Geographical Review* 29(3):472–82. doi.org/10.2307/209886.

Yamashina, Y. 1970. 第1部 所内論文京都大学西イリアン科学調査隊採集ニュ ーギニア産鳥類標本について [Birds collected by Kyoto University West Irian Scientific Expedition, 1963–64, in the central highlands of West New Guinea]. *Journal of the Yamashina Institute for Ornithology* 6(1–2):1–15. doi.org/10.3312/jyio1952.6.1.

3

Language as a lens into the prehistory of West New Guinea

Laura Arnold

Abstract

With over 260 languages belonging to some 30 families and a further 18 language isolates, West New Guinea is one of the most linguistically diverse regions on the planet. Despite this diversity, many languages of the region share similarities in their vocabularies and structure. While some of these similarities can be explained by inheritance from a common ancestor, others are due to contact and borrowing between different language groups. By teasing apart the reasons underlying these similarities, the linguistic data can provide valuable insights into ancient population movements and contacts in the region. I begin with an overview of the language families of West New Guinea. A broad distinction can be made between languages belonging to the Austronesian family, and those belonging to the many unrelated 'Papuan' families. The Austronesian languages are relatively recent incomers to the area; speakers of an ancestor to many of these languages probably arrived in Cenderawasih Bay some 3500 years ago. The Papuan families, on the other hand, are endemic to New Guinea—at least some are probably descendants of languages spoken by the original colonisers of Sahul. Following this, I turn to the linguistic evidence for contact between different language groups, paying particular attention to the quantity and quality of this contact. The data show that West New Guinea has long been an area of complex and intense interactions between different language groups. In some cases, these were trading relationships, whereas in others contact was more prolonged, involving intermarriage between different communities. Similarly, the patterns of borrowing suggest that in some cases Austronesian groups were socio-politically dominant; in others, the dominant groups were Papuan. With the recent developments in archaeological and ethnographic studies in West New Guinea, now is the perfect time to take stock, and compare findings with scholars of parallel disciplines. The overview of linguistic research presented in this chapter provides just such a point of calibration, and as such contributes a valuable context to interpret the chapters in the rest of this volume.

Abstrak

Di wilayah Papua bagian barat atau Papua-Indonesia, terdapat lebih dari 260 bahasa yang tergolong dari 30 rumpun bahasa, dimana 18 bahasa diantaranya telah diidentifikasikan sebagai kelompok bahasa yang terisolasi. Walaupun terdapat beberapa kesamaan dalam kosakata dan struktur yang diperkirakan bersumber dari warisan nenek moyang yang sama, serta perolehan bahasa dari kontak dengan kelompok yang berbeda, wilayah Papua merupakan salah satu wilayah di dunia yang paling kaya dalam sisi keragaman bahasa. Hal inilah yang kemudian diuraikan dalam bab ini, terutama mengupas alasan-alasan yang mendasari kemiripan-kemiripan bahasa tersebut. Data linguistik yang dipaparkan dalam bab ini dimulai dengan tinjauan umum rumpun bahasa di wilayah Papua, dimana melalui hal ini diharapkan dapat memberikan wawasan yang berharga mengenai pergerakan manusia pada masa lalu serta kontak budaya yang terjadi di wilayah ini dengan kelompok yang berbeda. Perbedaan yang terdapat dalam bahasa yang ada kemudian menjadi landasan pembagian bahasa tersebut kedalam dua kelompok besar yaitu bahasa Austronesia dan kelompok bahasa Papua. Rumpun bahasa Austronesia merupakan kelompok imigran yang datang di wilayah ini melalui Teluk Cenderawasih sekitar 3500 tahun yang lalu. Sementara itu, rumpun bahasa Papua diperkirakan digunakan oleh penutur yang telah mendiami Papua sebelum penutur Austronesia ber-imigrasi ke daerah ini. Setidaknya beberapa bahasa yang terhimpun dalam kelompok bahasa Papua dituturkan oleh imigran yang mendiami Papua pada saat paparan Sahul masih terbentuk. Terkait dengan bukti linguistik yang menunjukkan adanya kontak budaya antar kedua kelompok bahasa yang berbeda, pemaparan selanjutnya yakni mengenai kuantitas dan kualitas dari kontak budaya tersebut. Berdasarkan data yang ada, maka diketahui bahwa pulau Papua telah lama menjadi wilayah bagi berbagai kelompok bahasa yang saling berinteraksi dan diperkirakan terjadi dalam situasi yang kompleks dan intensif. Kontak budaya antar kelompok penutur bahasa tersebut diperkirakan terjadi melalui perdagangan serta melalui perkawinan antar komunitas yang berbeda, dimana hal ini berimplikasi terhadap hubungan kontak yang sifatnya berkelanjutan. Terkait dengan pola peminjaman bahasa yang terjadi antar dua kelompok rumpun bahasa, maka diketahui bahwa rumpun Austronesia lebih dominan secara sosial-politik, sedangkan dalam kasus lain didominasi oleh rumpun bahasa Papua. Bab ini selanjutnya diisi dengan pemaparan data yang ada serta membandingkannya secara multidisiplin. Ulasan yang didasarkan pada data linguistik dalam bab ini sebagai data menjadi pembanding dimana diharapkan, data tersebut melengkapi topik – topik lainnya yang terdapat dalam buku ini.

Introduction

The aim of this chapter is to synthesise the current state of the art in linguistic research in West New Guinea, and show how the linguistic data can be used to peer into human prehistory in the region. In keeping with the rest of this volume, West New Guinea here refers to the regions today under Indonesian governance, divided into six provinces. Included in this territory are the Bird's Head Peninsula and nearby islands, Cenderawasih Bay, the Bomberai Peninsula, and Bird's Neck, running through into the bulk of mainland New Guinea as far as the border with Papua New Guinea (PNG). These post-colonial borders are of course artificial from a deep time perspective; where relevant, this discussion will therefore spill eastwards into PNG, and westwards into Island Southeast Asia (ISEA).

New Guinea is famously a region of great linguistic diversity: a bewildering patchwork of language families, ranging from tiny to vast. With upwards of 270 languages belonging to somewhere between 11 and 32 different families and many language isolates, West New Guinea is no exception. Despite this genealogical diversity, the languages of West New Guinea are often, in some ways, remarkably similar, particularly in terms of their grammatical structures. This genealogical diversity and structural similarity are two sides of the same coin: both have emerged, over many millennia, from linguistic ecologies frequently characterised by small and mobile language groups; extensive multilingualism in neighbouring languages through intermarriage and trade, facilitating vocabulary borrowing and grammatical convergence (Schapper 2020a); and local linguistic identities focused on the village or the clan, with speakers sometimes consciously introducing innovations into their language to distinguish themselves from neighbouring speech communities (Evans 2019).

A broad distinction is made in New Guinea linguistics between Austronesian and Papuan languages. 'Austronesian' is a genealogical term, referring to a group of languages that have demonstrably descended from a single common ancestor, widely agreed to have been spoken in Taiwan (Blust 2013). 'Papuan', however, is not a genealogical term, and refers to all of the languages spoken on New Guinea and nearby islands that are not Austronesian (shown in an alternate term, 'non-Austronesian', which is often used synonymously). The distribution of Austronesian and the various Papuan language families of West New Guinea, following the classifications in Hammarström and colleagues (2020), is given in Figure 3.1.

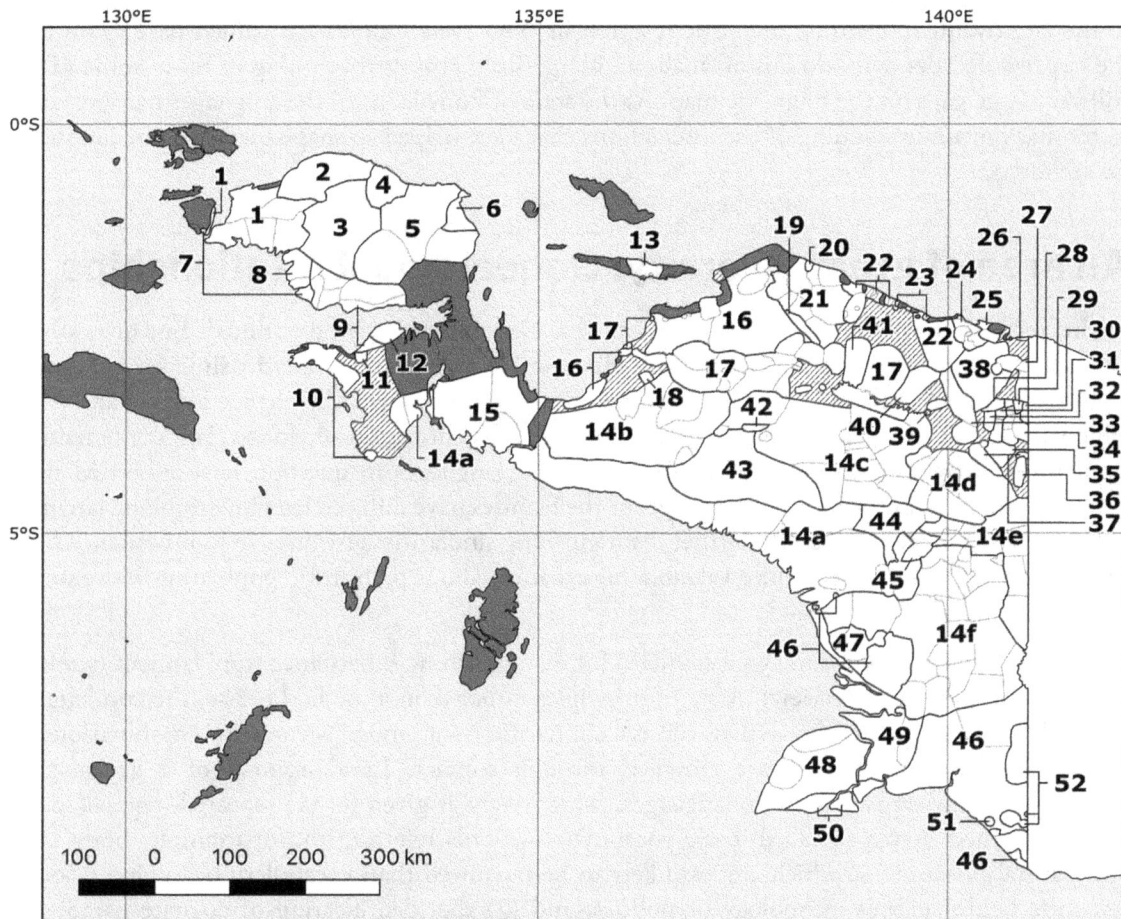

Figure 3.1: The language families of West New Guinea.

Hatched areas = uninhabited; dark grey = Austronesian; white = Papuan. Numbers mark the following Papuan families (* = isolate, † = potential member of Trans–New Guinea): 1. West Bird's Head, 2. Abun (*), 3. Maybrat (*), 4. Mpur (*), 5. East Bird's Head, 6. Hatam-Mansim, 7. Inanwatan, 8. Konda-Yahadian, 9. South Bird's Head, 10. West Bomberai (†), 11. Mor (*), 12. Sumuri/Tanahmerah (*), 13. Yapen, 14. Trans–New Guinea (a. Asmat-Kamoro, b. Paniai (Wissel) Lakes, c. Dani, d. Mek, e. Ok-Oksapmin, f. Greater Awyu), 15. Mairasic, 16. East Cenderawasih (Geelvink) Bay, 17. Lakes Plain, 18. Kehu (*) 19. Burmeso (*), 20. Massep (*), 21. Greater Kwerba, 22. Tor-Orya, 23. Mawes (*), 24. Nimboranic, 25. Sentanic, 26. Sko, 27. Border, 28. Molof (*), 29. Yabanda (*), 30. Senagi, 31. Namla-Tofanma, 32. Usku (*), 33. Kaure-Kosare, 34. Pauwasi, 35. Yetfa (*), 36. Kimki (*), 37. Lepki-Murkim-Kembra, 38. Elseng (*), 39. Kapori (*), 40. Sause (*), 41. Abinomn (*), 42. Dem (*), 43. Damal (*), 44. Somahai (†), 45. Bayono-Awbono, 46. Anim (†), 47. Kayagar (†), 48. Mombum-Koneraw, 49. Bulaka River, 50. Kolopom (†), 51. Marori (* or †), 52. Yam.

Source: Adapted from Arnold (2020), Eberhard and colleagues (2024), Evans and colleagues (2018), Kim (2006a, b), and Rumaropen (2005). Classifications follow Hammarström and colleagues (2020). Created using materials in Edwards (2023).

As discussed in Gaffney and Tolla (Chapter 1, this volume), the Indonesian half of New Guinea is understudied when compared with PNG. This observation holds for the languages of the area. Papuan and Austronesian languages are the most poorly documented on the planet: 48 per cent are represented by only a wordlist or less (Hammarström and Nordhoff 2012). In West New Guinea, the number rises further still to 54 per cent. This lack of documentation applies not only to the level of individual languages, but also to language families: of the 27 least-documented families in the world, nearly half are in West New Guinea (Hammarström 2010). Linguistic research in the area began in the late 1800s (e.g. de Clerq, Fabritius), carrying on into the early and mid-twentieth century (e.g. Anceaux, Cowan, Drabbe, Esser, Grace, Maan, Voorhoeve, and Wurm). After a slump in the late twentieth century, linguistic research in West New Guinea has gained pace again over the last few decades, with dozens of small- and large-scale projects beginning to fill in some of the still very large gaps on the linguistic map. As the state of knowledge of the languages has increased, so too has our understanding of the interactions that have helped to shape the linguistic landscape we see today.

An area of great diversity: Genealogical relationships

In this section, the genealogical groupings of West New Guinea will be outlined. But first, a brief word on methods in comparative linguistics. Historical linguists seek to identify similarities between languages, and sift out those which are coincidental—have occurred by chance alone—and those which are due to universal tendencies in language, such as onomatopoeic forms. For any remaining similarities, there are two potential explanations: the languages in question have inherited these features from a common ancestral language; or the features have diffused laterally from one language into another through contact. By further distinguishing similarities attributable to inheritance from those due to contact, we can infer valuable information about prehistoric population movements, lifestyles, and ecologies.

The comparative method is the gold standard for distinguishing inheritance from contact (see Ross 1995 for an accessible overview). A set of principles rather than a method per se, the comparative method operates on the basis that certain similarities—or, more accurately, combinations of similarities—are unlikely to have emerged through contact. In a proposal of a genealogical relationship between two or more languages, most weight is given to: (1) repeated, regular sound correspondences across so-called 'basic vocabulary'—words referring to, for example, body parts and natural phenomena, which are less likely to be borrowed than vocabulary belonging to other semantic fields, such as technology or politics; and (2) the identification of cognate paradigms, such as pronouns, or verbal morphemes marking subject or object, which are also unlikely to be borrowed.

A careful application of the comparative method can provide evidence for the homeland of a language group, in two ways. First, it is often possible to identify which features in each language or subbranch are innovative with respect to the ancestral language, and through this 'undo' the innovations to reconstruct the proto-language. This proto-language may give clues as to the original habitat of its speakers. For example, reconstructed proto-Austronesian vocabulary points to a homeland in a region that was seasonal, prone to earthquakes, and had flora and fauna typical of the Asian mainland (Blust 1984–85). A second method is by identifying the geographic region with the greatest genealogical diversity, defined by the number of first-order branches. All else being equal, the area with the highest genealogical diversity is likely to represent the original dispersal point, for the simple reason that there has been more time for the languages to diverge from each other. Nine of the 10 first-order branches of Austronesian are in Taiwan; coupled with the reconstructed evidence, this makes it almost certain this was the proto-Austronesian homeland.

Before we continue, two words of caution are in order. First, the comparative method can only be used to classify languages as long as evidence of genealogical relationship is still available. Given enough time, two related languages will change to the extent that any remaining signal of a genealogical relationship will be so weak that it is indistinguishable from chance similarity (Harrison 2003). Second, languages do not change at a constant rate. Language change may be faster in one language, and slower in another (compare the lexically innovative English with the more conservative Icelandic); and the rate of change fluctuates within a single language across time (for example, the rapid changes in English through contact with Norman French). Thus, while the comparative method can provide information on the relative order in which speech communities have diverged from each other, there is no widely accepted methodology to place absolute dates on these divergence events (Heggarty 2014). We therefore continue to rely on our archaeologist colleagues for their input—as, for example, in the correlation of proto-Oceanic with the development of Lapita culture in the Bismarck Archipelago around 3300 years ago (Pawley 2008).

The Papuan languages of West New Guinea

Papuan languages are endemic to New Guinea and nearby islands; they are likely to be descendants of the languages spoken by the original colonisers of Sahul. This huge time depth means any linguistic trace of the original genealogical groupings spoken by these colonisers has long been lost. Other factors have conspired to limit the efficacy of the comparative method in New Guinea: the aforementioned low levels of documentation; as well as, in places, unusually high levels of vocabulary replacement. While some have been sceptical about the possibility of classification and reconstruction in this context, recent efforts have seen the successful application of the comparative method to several Papuan families. However, the fact remains that many regions of New Guinea are characterised by extremely small language families—often with no more than two or three members—and language isolates, none of which can, at present, convincingly be shown to share a common ancestor with any other living language.

The major exception to this is Trans–New Guinea (TNG), a hypothesised macro-family of 300–500 languages. TNG dominates much of New Guinea, particularly the central cordillera. The TNG hypothesis has undergone several incarnations over the decades (for a full history, see Pawley 1998). One major proposal—made, among other places, in Wurm (1975)—included nearly all of the Papuan languages of New Guinea; however, this proposal was criticised for not adhering to the tenets of the comparative method (Haiman 1979). The TNG hypothesis was revived in the 1990s, with evidence from pronouns and reconstructed vocabulary putting it on firmer footing (Pawley 1998; Ross 2005). A recent and authoritative overview of TNG can be found in Pawley and Hammarström (2018).

While many genealogical groups can be uncontroversially assigned to TNG, the precise bounds of the family are still being debated. In West New Guinea, the following groupings are securely established as TNG (numbers refer to the map in Figure 3.1): Asmat–Kamoro (14a), Paniai (Wissel) Lakes (14b), Dani (14c), Mek (14d), Ok–Oksapmin (14e), and Greater Awyu (14f). Several other groups in West New Guinea are possibly classifiable as TNG, pending further investigation. The following groups are assigned to TNG by Pawley and Hammarström (2018), but not by the more conservative

Hammarström and colleagues (2020): West Bomberai (10); the little-known two-language family Somahai (44); Anim (46); Kayagar (47); Kolopom (50); and the critically endangered language Marori (51), a proposed family level isolate.

The precise origins and age of the TNG family is an open question. The diversity of the family suggests the branches have been diverging for some time, possibly 6000–10,000 years (Pawley and Hammarström 2018, 154). Pawley (2005) hypothesises that the TNG expansion was driven by agricultural developments in the Upper Wahgi Valley around 10,000 years ago, and Schapper (2017) presents preliminary lexical evidence suggesting that this agricultural package included sugarcane and bananas. Recent archaeological data, however, indicate that these agricultural developments were more gradual and regionally varied than previously assumed (Gaffney and Denham 2021), so the link with the TNG expansion remains unclear. Based on the current subgrouping of TNG, the homeland is tentatively placed in the east of the central highlands; however, the internal structure of TNG is very much a work in progress, so this must be taken as preliminary. If correct, the TNG languages spoken in West New Guinea would thus be westward migrations from this homeland.

Elsewhere in the region, we typically find small families and isolates. These are presumed to be remnants of the former diversity in New Guinea, prior to the TNG expansion. Summaries and typological overviews of the languages of the Bird's Head and its surrounds, the area between the central cordillera and the north coast, and the southern lowlands can be found in Holton and Klamer (2018), Foley (2018), and Evans and colleagues (2018), respectively.

The Papuan languages of the Bird's Head are the best documented in West New Guinea; as shown in Figure 3.1, several shallow genealogical groupings have been firmly established here (1–13, 15). There have been attempts to group these lower-level units into higher genealogical groupings. In particular, there have been several proposals of a 'West Papuan Phylum'. For example, Cowan (1957) groups nearly all of the Bird's Head languages together (1–5, 8–9), along with the family of Papuan languages spoken in North Halmahera; Voorhoeve (1987) proposes a similar grouping, but excludes the groups in the south-west of the Bird's Head (8–9); and Ross (2005) proposes that East Bird's Head (5) is related to Sentanic (25) and Burmeso (19), both spoken in north central New Guinea, and tentatively proposes that this group may be related to the West Papuan languages and Yapen (13), in a group he calls 'extended West Papuan'. In addition, South Bird's Head (9) was included in TNG by Wurm (1975). However, none of these proposals have yet been satisfactorily demonstrated by the comparative method. There is one promising proposal: West Bomberai (10) may be related to Timor–Alor–Pantar, a Papuan family spoken in the Lesser Sundas, in a family called 'Greater West Bomberai' (Schapper 2020b). Recall from above that West Bomberai is possibly a TNG group; if subsequent research shows this to be correct, the implication is that Timor–Alor–Pantar was a TNG expansion westwards from the New Guinea mainland.

Elsewhere in West New Guinea, the genealogical picture is more fragmented still; particularly in the area to the north of the Bintang Mountains and the south of Jayapura, where we find many very small families interspersed with several isolates (28–39). However, these languages are also the most under-documented of West New Guinea; further research may provide evidence for a genealogical relationship between at least some of these little-known languages.

Austronesian arrivals in West New Guinea

Compared with Papuan languages, the origin and dispersals of Austronesian languages are better understood. However, there are still many areas of debate—particularly regarding the higher-level subgrouping of the family and the mechanisms of spread. As mentioned above, the homeland of Austronesian languages was Taiwan, where there are at least nine first-order subbranches. All of the Austronesian languages spoken outside of Taiwan belong to the Malayo–Polynesian (MP) subbranch of Austronesian. Correlations between linguistic and archaeological data suggest that MP speakers migrated out of the Austronesian homeland of Taiwan and into the Philippines around 4500–4000 years ago (Bellwood 2007). From the Philippines, MP languages began to spread throughout ISEA and its surrounds, eventually reaching areas spanning more than half the globe, from Madagascar in the west to the far eastern reaches of the Pacific.

The conventional view of the higher-level subgroups of MP is given in Figure 3.2, following Blust (2009, 2013). The most relevant branches for this chapter are those under the Central–Eastern Malayo–Polynesian (CEMP) node (i.e. Central Malayo–Polynesian, CMP; South Halmahera–West New Guinea, SHWNG; and Oceanic), all of which are spoken eastwards of Sulawesi and central Sumbawa.

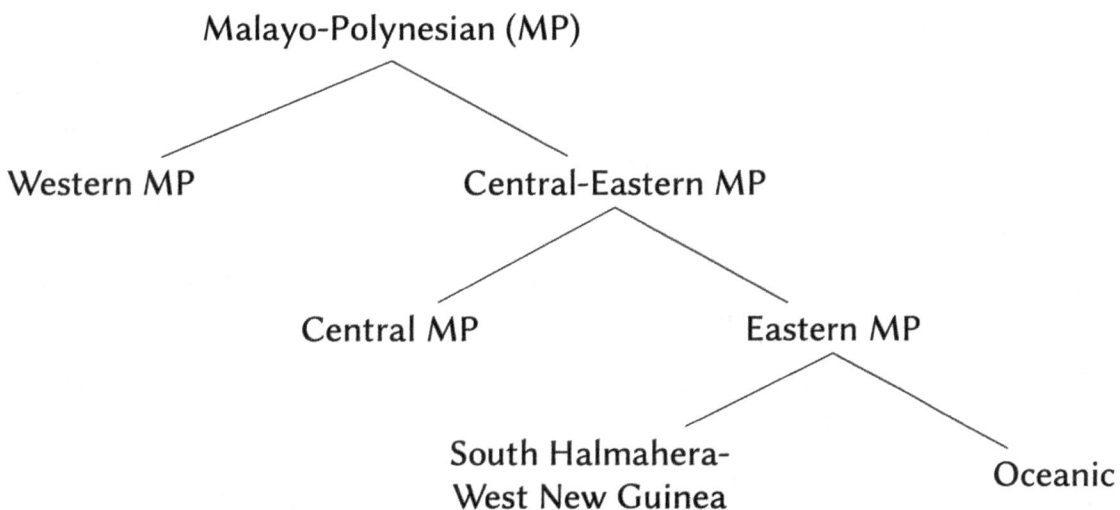

Figure 3.2: The standard view of Malayo–Polynesian higher-level groupings.
Source: Blust (2009, 2013).

The MP, SHWNG, and Oceanic nodes of Figure 3.2 are all uncontroversial, in that they are clearly defined by innovations. However, the validity of several nodes has been questioned. While outside the scope of this chapter, Western Malayo–Polynesian (WMP) is no longer generally accepted as a genealogical subgroup (Blust 2013, 31–32; Ross 1995); lower-level groups traditionally assigned to WMP are now considered to be first-order subgroups of MP (Smith 2017). More relevant to our discussion, both the CEMP and CMP nodes have been fiercely criticised (e.g. Donohue and Grimes 2008, and the rejoinder by Blust 2009). Eastern Malayo–Polynesian (EMP), as outlined by Blust (1978, 1983–84) has not received so much attention; while Ross et al. (2023, 40–46) question its validity, it has not yet been systematically investigated. However, at this stage, EMP is best seen as a working hypothesis, in that no convincing subgroup-defining phonological or morphological innovations have yet been proposed.

Taking the criticisms of WMP, CEMP, and CMP into consideration, Donohue and Denham (2010) present a 'rake-like' tree of higher-level Austronesian groupings; this tree, incorporating an agnostic position on EMP, is given in Figure 3.3. The implication of this subgrouping is that linguistic evidence cannot be brought to bear on the relative separation of each of the groups; the data are compatible either with an interpretation in which each group diverged from proto-MP independent of any other, or one in which there were fewer initial separations, but the time that each subgroup spent together before separating was too brief for any shared innovations to develop (cf. Klamer 2019).

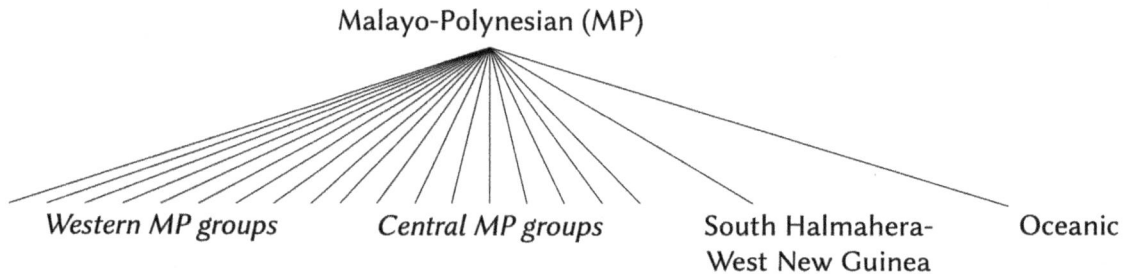

Figure 3.3: A rake-like view of Malayo–Polynesian higher-level groupings.
Source: After Donohue and Denham (2010), incorporating an agnostic position on EMP.

While Austronesian languages dominate ISEA to the west, they are only spoken in small, mainly coastal pockets in West New Guinea. The majority of Austronesian languages of the region belong to the SHWNG subbranch; SHWNG languages are spoken in Raja Ampat and on the coasts and islands of Cenderawasih Bay, as well as on Halmahera to the west. Besides SHWNG, languages traditionally classified as CMP are spoken on the Bomberai Peninsula; and there are two separate offshoots of Oceanic in the area—one on the north coast of central New Guinea in the region of Jayapura; and one on Mapia Island, off the north coast of the Bird's Head.

If the EMP hypothesis is correct, the first Austronesians likely arrived in West New Guinea around 3500–3300 years ago, possibly settling first in Cenderawasih Bay (Kamholz 2014; Spriggs 2010). From here, one group split off, heading eastwards towards what would become the proto-Oceanic homeland in the Bismarck Archipelago. Those EMP languages that remained in West New Guinea became the SHWNG subbranch.

The internal diversification and spread of SHWNG is now fairly well understood, thanks to the work of Kamholz (2014). From its homeland in southern Cenderawasih Bay, SHWNG is hypothesised to have split into seven primary branches. One group travelled back westwards along the north coast of the Bird's Head Peninsula, settling in Raja Ampat and Halmahera. Two more groups travelled eastwards along the coast, settling around the mouth of the Mamberamo. Three other groups remained in southern Cenderawasih Bay. A final group split into three: one group remained in southern Cenderawasih Bay; a second, the ancestors of the present-day Biakic languages, migrated first to the north-west, to Wandamen Bay, with speakers of the ancestor of Biak thence migrating to Biak and nearby islands; and the final group migrated to Yapen island and there diversified, with speakers of the ancestor of Wamesa subsequently migrating westwards to Wandamen Bay.

The Austronesian languages spoken further east along the coast, between Sarmi and Jayapura, are all Oceanic languages. It might reasonably be assumed that these languages represent an early offshoot, perhaps a group who broke off from the rest of the Oceanic travellers as they skimmed the north coast of New Guinea. The linguistic data, however, do not support this interpretation. In fact, the

Sarmi–Jayapura languages group are probably members of the North New Guinea linkage (Ross 1996). As the homeland of North New Guinea was in New Britain, this implies an east-to-west migration of this group to north-central New Guinea.

One more Oceanic language is (or was) spoken in West New Guinea—or, at least, in the administrative region of Papua Province: Mapia, of the Mapia Atoll, some 190 km north of Manokwari. Mapia belongs to the Micronesian branch of Oceanic, the homeland of which may have been Kosrae in central Micronesia (Jackson 1983; Marck 1994). Mapia is now extinct—the last speaker passed away in the 1990s. The atoll is now Biak-speaking, due to migrations presumably over the last few hundred years.

The Austronesian languages of the Bomberai Peninsula present a fairly complex picture. Blust (1993) recognised that those spoken in the west of Bomberai are not SHWNG; the most recent research shows that they can be subgrouped with the Austronesian languages of central Maluku, and thus represent an eastwards movement from there (Edwards and Grimes 2021; Grimes and Edwards submitted; Schapper and Zobel 2024).

Finally, to round out the picture, the last few hundred years have seen increasing influence from Austronesian languages originating from further west—particularly varieties of Malay, including the national language Indonesian. Malay may have been used as a trade language in coastal regions of West New Guinea for several centuries; a regional variety, Papuan Malay, began developing around 130 years ago (Kluge 2017). Both Papuan Malay and Indonesian have been spreading across West New Guinea in recent decades, often at the expense of the local vernaculars. This spread is partly due to substantial migration from further west in Indonesia, and has been facilitated by rapid modernisation, including increased formal education, developments in transportation and telecommunication infrastructure, and the influence of the media. The implications of this will be returned to below, in the conclusion to this chapter.

Areas of similarity: Contact

Above we maintained a strict division between Austronesian and Papuan languages and between the different Papuan families. However, this is far from the reality of the linguistic landscape of New Guinea: in many ways, languages of the different groups have converged in their vocabularies and grammatical structures, to the extent that genealogical descent may be heavily obscured by lateral transmission. This evidence points to sustained and intense contact across the region; while in most cases each language community was only in contact with other geographically proximal languages, taken together these contacts form intricate networks across the wider area, facilitating the transmission of linguistic features from one language into the next.

Given the right sociolinguistic circumstances, any type of linguistic material—vocabulary, phonological features, word order patterns, and so forth—can be transferred between languages. However, different kinds of contact situations typically have different linguistic outcomes. While these outcomes are extremely complex and difficult to predict, some generalisations can be made (see Ross 2013 and Thomason 2010 for overviews). In what follows, I will for expository purposes describe contact situations in which only two languages are involved. However, this is an oversimplification—particularly in New Guinea, where most contact has been multilateral, involving several different language communities.

Language contact implies there is some knowledge of the language of another speech community—this may be monodirectional (speakers of Language X know Language Y, but speakers of Y do not know X) or mutual (speakers of X know Y, and vice versa). The intensity of contact, defined in terms of duration of contact, and the level of language proficiency in the speech community, is one factor influencing what material is transferred between languages. In more casual contact scenarios, such as those of light trade or long-distance social or political influence, borrowed linguistic material tends to be limited to open-class vocabulary (such as nouns and verbs, particularly words referring to non-basic items or concepts such as technology, religion, or politics). As contact becomes more intense, more basic vocabulary may be borrowed, and deeper grammatical structures are affected—for example, there may be borrowing of words from closed vocabulary classes (such as conjunctions and pronouns), morphological borrowing, and syntactic restructuring.

The age at which speakers acquire their non-dominant language also affects contact outcomes. Preadolescents are known to acquire complex linguistic features—such as morphological irregularities, or complex combinations of sounds—more readily than adults (Kerswill 1996). Thus, if children are bilingual in both Language X and Language Y, they may import the more complex features from Y into X, and vice versa. This may occur, for example, where there is a high degree of intermarriage between different language communities, with children growing up fluent in the languages of both parents. In very intense contact situations, the lexicons of two languages may remain distinct, but the grammars radically converge, in a process Ross (2013) refers to as 'metatypy'; such convergence is cognitively economical, in that the more similar the grammars of two languages are, the less processing power is required by the bilingual speakers when switching between them. If, however, it is adults who are learning a second language, they may acquire Y less than perfectly, simplifying and regularising some of the more complex grammatical features of Y. If there is a large enough group of adult second language learners in a Y-dominant community—for example, where there are large numbers of speakers marrying into the community—this simplified version of Y may be passed down to the next generation. Finally, while the situations described so far may be quite stable, lasting for many generations, in some cases speakers may shift to another language very quickly, over the course of a generation or two—for example, when one community is conquered by another, and is forced to shift to the language of the incomers. Here the shifting community has no time to become proficient in their new language; the result is often radical simplification, as in the creation of pidgins and creoles.

I know of no studies in West New Guinea that point to simplification, radical or otherwise, of languages in contact. While Ross (2013) suggests this indicates that rapid linguistic shift due to warfare has been rare in the small-scale societies of Melanesia, the lack of attested simplification scenarios may simply be due to a lack of documentation. There is, however, ample data evidencing widespread early life multilingualism across the region, from deep time to the present day. Within West New Guinea, there have been several proposals for linguistic areas—geographic regions where multiple languages share structural features as a result of convergence (i.e. the shared features cannot be attributed to inheritance or chance similarity; Thomason 2000). Within a linguistic area, different features have different origins, and are transmitted via different vectors at different times, with varying geographic spread. The identification of a linguistic area thus implies the type of long-term multilingualism described above.

Northwest New Guinea (NWNG)—encompassing Raja Ampat, the Bird's Head and Neck, the Bomberai Peninsula, and Cenderawasih Bay—is the best-studied region of West New Guinea in terms of contact. Several recent studies suggest that this area itself constitutes a linguistic area. For example, Gil (2017) shows that many languages in NWNG use a single word to mean both 'do' and 'give'. He argues that this feature ultimately originated in certain kinds of verbal constructions in the Papuan languages of the Bird's Head, which spread into SHWNG very early on. Arnold (2023) traces the development of multiple inalienable paradigms around the Bird's Head, concluding that this feature likely originated in a contact zone involving the Papuan languages in the east of the Bird's Head and Biak; Biak then acted as a vector for the spread of this feature to nearby Austronesian languages. Gasser (2019) examines patterns of borrowed basic vocabulary for colours, flora, and fauna across NWNG. She notes that, while borrowing has occurred in both directions, most terms have been borrowed from Austronesian into Papuan languages, suggesting that Austronesian speakers were historically more culturally influential.

Within NWNG, more localised contact zones have been identified. Reesink (1998) discusses ancient Austronesian vocabulary in the Papuan languages of the Bird's Head. He concludes that this lexical evidence, coupled with some typically Austronesian morphosyntactic features of the languages, points to long-standing contact of the Papuan languages both with Austronesian, and with each other. The presence of tone in several SHWNG languages of Raja Ampat and Cenderawasih Bay has attracted a fair amount of attention: Arnold (2018) and Kamholz (2017) show that these tone systems have developed independently from each other (i.e. they were not inherited from a common ancestor). The evidence suggests that speakers were once bilingual in both a tonal Papuan language, and the formerly atonal SHWNG language, into which they imported tone, but, as there are no obvious tonal Papuan donors spoken near to these languages today, that speakers eventually abandoned their heritage Papuan language. Finally, linguistic correlates of the well-documented dominance of Tidore over NWNG include the distribution of a form *ma*, used to modify noun phrases and as a reflexive marker, across the region (Reesink 1998); and loanwords from Patipi, who operated as the Tidore vassals in Bomberai, into Inanwatan in the south of the Bird's Head, with whom they had trading relationships (de Vries 1996).

Outside of NWNG, there have been fewer studies of local language contacts. There are, however, some notable exceptions. Voorhoeve (2005) and van den Heuvel and Fedden (2014) look at contact between the TNG groups Awyu, Ok, and Asmat. The evidence here points to ancient contact between Awyu and Ok, and between Ok and Asmat; since the Asmat languages are today spoken in the southern lowlands, Voorhoeve infers that this contact occurred before this group migrated out of the highlands, where the Ok languages are still spoken. In southern New Guinea, Evans (2019) reports on some features shared by the Papuan families of the area; however, he also notes that these languages have not actually converged anywhere near as much as may be expected from the high levels of multilingualism in the area. Finally, in north-central New Guinea, Donohue and Crowther (2005) describe a mismatch between local oral histories, colonial records, and linguistic data: while the phonological convergence between the languages would normally point to long-term contact between the groups of the area, oral histories and written records show that the groups in the region have only very recently come into contact, in some cases as little as 50 years ago. These latter two studies thus urge caution when inferring contact prehistories from linguistic data alone.

West New Guinea also has links with the wider region, lying at the overlap of three large linguistic areas. Northwest New Guinea is itself a sub-area of linguistic Wallacea, an area which also includes Maluku and the Lesser Sundas (Schapper 2015). Northwest New Guinea also lies at the easternmost edge of the Mekong–Mamberamo macro-area, running from the Mekong in mainland Southeast Asia, across ISEA, terminating around the mouth of the Mamberamo (Gil 2015). Both Schapper and Gil argue that these linguistic areas are ancient, and that the features by which they are characterised were shared by the languages of the region before the arrival of Austronesian speakers; in particular, the distribution of features in Wallacea points to a pre-Austronesian maritime culture, in which there were strong links between the New Guinea mainland and ISEA, a view that is consistent with the archaeological record. Finally, West New Guinea is part of Linguistic Melanesia, which includes ISEA from the east of Sulawesi, all of New Guinea, and extends south-east into the Pacific as far as New Caledonia, Vanuatu, and Fiji (Schapper 2020a). Linguistic Melanesia is characterised by several features which pattern in 'concentric circles' clustering around the interior of mainland New Guinea, reflecting the convergence of Austronesian languages on Papuan norms and Papuan languages on Austronesian norms in the coastal and insular contact zones. Schapper emphasises the role of multiple borrowing events between neighbouring languages as the explanation for the observed distributions, with both convergence and divergence driven by linguistic ecologies of egalitarian multilingualism, in which communities are mutually bilingual with no major imbalance of power (François 2012).

Summary and looking forward

The linguistic data discussed in this chapter paint the following picture. Throughout much of the history of human habitation of New Guinea, language communities were generally small. Different relations likely held at different times between different groups: for example, extrapolating from ethnographic observations of Papuan groups at the time of first European contact (Roscoe 2014), hostile relations have likely always existed between at least some groups at least some of the time. However, the overall picture from the available linguistic evidence is one of convergence between different languages, often resulting in complexification, as speakers added features from Language Y into Language X and vice versa. This evidence suggests in many cases there were ecologies of small-scale and generally egalitarian multilingualism, with speakers fluent both in the language of their own community and those of other nearby groups with whom they had friendly relations.

Assuming that present-day observations of rapid vocabulary replacement held true historically, any evidence for the genealogical relationships of Papuan languages in deep time would have eroded very quickly, creating the patchwork of small language families and isolates still seen in some areas today. Some of this former genealogical diversity, particularly in the highlands, was then eradicated by the expansion of TNG languages sometime after 10,000 years ago, probably moving westwards from the eastern highlands. From around 3500 years ago, groups of Austronesian speakers began to arrive in the region, at different times and from different locations. The evidence suggests that, while Austronesian speakers had some cultural prestige, they did not dominate and overwhelm the Papuan speakers. Rather, they entered into the linguistic ecologies of their newfound neighbours: intermarrying, trading, and so forth. The most recent waves of Austronesian influence, primarily from Malay/Indonesian, have become the most threatening for the languages of West New Guinea, both Austronesian and Papuan: today, nearly 70 per cent are threatened to some degree, with around a third likely to become extinct in the next few generations.

As we move into the middle of the twenty-first century, the linguistic priorities are clear. While fantastic progress is being made, detailed research has yet to be carried out on more than half of the languages of West New Guinea. Focus in the first instance should therefore be on the documentation and description of these languages—particularly the little-known isolates and small language families, and particularly those languages most at risk of extinction. In part due to this lack of data, previous historical research has tended to take a 'top-down' approach, comparing languages at great time depths. As more data become available, focus can shift to 'bottom-up' work, which begins with a fine-grained study of the genealogical and contact relationships between languages at shallower time depths, before comparing these findings at deeper time depths. Besides providing further information on prehistoric population movements and contacts, which can then be compared with findings from colleagues in our sister disciplines, this research will inform how we think about language change more generally: some of the studies discussed above indicate that observations on language change from elsewhere in the world may not always hold true for New Guinea. For scholars of the Pacific, the languages of New Guinea still hold many secrets; we have only just begun to scratch the surface.

Acknowledgements

I am grateful to Owen Edwards, Emily Gasser, David Gil, Chuck Grimes, Harald Hammarström, Marian Klamer, and Eline Visser for providing feedback on earlier drafts of this chapter, as well as Antoinette Schapper for reviewer comments, and Dylan Gaffney for editorial comments; their input improved the clarity and broadened the scope of this work. All errors and misinterpretations are my own.

References

Arnold, L. 2018. A preliminary archaeology of tone in Raja Ampat. In A. Schapper (ed.), *Contact and substrate in the languages of Wallacea*, part 2, pp. 7–39. Special edition of *NUSA: Linguistic Studies of Indonesian and Other Languages in Indonesia* 64. doi.org/10.5281/zenodo.1450778.

Arnold, L. 2020. Four undocumented languages of Raja Ampat, West Papua, Indonesia. *Language Documentation and Description* 17:25–43. doi.org/10.25894/ldd95.

Arnold, L. 2023. Split Inalienable Coding in linguistic Wallacea: Typology, origins, spread. In E. Gasser and A. Schapper (eds), *Possession in the languages of Wallacea*, pp. 331–368. Special issue of *STUF: Language Typology and Universals* 76(3). doi.org/10.1515/stuf-2023-2013.

Blust, R. 1978. Eastern Malayo–Polynesian: A subgrouping argument. In S. Wurm and L. Carrington (eds), *Second International Conference on Austronesian Linguistics: Proceedings*, pp. 181–234. Pacific Linguistics C-61. Research School of Pacific and Asian Studies, The Australian National University, Canberra.

Blust, R. 1983–84. More on the position of the languages of eastern Indonesia. *Oceanic Linguistics* 22/23 (1/2):1–28.

Blust, R. 1984–85. The Austronesian homeland: A linguistic perspective. *Asian Perspectives* 26(1):45–67.

Blust, R. 1993. Central and Central–Eastern Malayo–Polynesian. *Oceanic Linguistics* 32(2):241–293. doi.org/10.2307/3623195.

Blust, R. 2009. The position of the languages of eastern Indonesia: A reply to Donohue and Grimes. *Oceanic Linguistics* 48(1):36–77. doi.org/10.1353/ol.0.0034.

Blust, R. 2013. *The Austronesian languages*. Research School of Pacific and Asian Studies, The Australian National University, Canberra.

Cowan, H.K.J. 1957. A large Papuan language phylum in West New Guinea. *Oceania* 28(2):159–166. doi.org/10.1002/j.1834-4461.1957.tb00736.x.

de Vries, L. 1996. Notes on the morphology of the Inanwatan language. *NUSA: Linguistic Studies of Languages in and around Indonesia* 40:97–127.

Donohue, M. and M. Crowther 2005. Meeting in the middle: Interaction in North-Central New Guinea. In A. Pawley, R. Attenborough, J. Golson, and R. Hide (eds), *Papuan pasts: Cultural, linguistic and biological histories of the Papuan-speaking peoples*, pp. 167–184. Pacific Linguistics 572. Research School of Pacific and Asian Studies, The Australian National University, Canberra.

Donohue, M. and T. Denham 2010. Farming and language in Island Southeast Asia: Reframing Austronesian history. *Current Anthropology* 51(2):223–256. doi.org/10.1086/650991.

Donohue, M. and C.E. Grimes 2008. Yet more on the position of the languages of Eastern Indonesia and East Timor. *Oceanic Linguistics* 47(1):114–158. doi.org/10.1353/ol.0.0008.

Eberhard, D.M., G.F. Simons, and C.D. Fennig (eds) 2024. *Ethnologue: Languages of the world*, 27th edition. SIL International, Dallas, Texas. Online resource: www.ethnologue.com (accessed 13 March 2024).

Edwards, O. 2023. *Linguistic-Map-Making: Guide for producing linguistic maps*. Online resource: github.com/OwenAmarasi/Linguistic-Map-Making (accessed 13 March 2024).

Edwards, O. and C.E. Grimes 2021. *Revising the classification of the Austronesian languages of eastern Indonesia and Timor-Leste*. Presentation given at the 15th International Conference on Austronesian Linguistics, 10 June.

Evans, N. 2019. Linguistic divergence under contact. In M. Cennamo and C. Fabrizio (eds), *Historical linguistics 2015: Selected papers from the 22nd International Conference on Historical Linguistics, Naples, 27–31 July 2015*, pp. 563–591. John Benjamins, Amsterdam/Philadelphia. doi.org/10.1075/cilt.348.26eva.

Evans, N., W. Arka, M. Carroll, Y.J. Choi, C. Döhler, V. Gast, E. Kashima, E. Mittag, B. Olsson, K. Quinn, D. Schokkin, P. Tama, C. van Tongeren, and J. Siegel 2018. The languages of Southern New Guinea. In B. Palmer (ed.), *The languages and linguistics of the New Guinea area: A comprehensive guide*, pp. 641–774. De Gruyter Mouton, Berlin/Boston. doi.org/10.1515/9783110295252-006.

Foley, W.A. 2018. The languages of Northwest New Guinea. In B. Palmer (ed.), *The languages and linguistics of the New Guinea area: A comprehensive guide*, pp. 433–568. De Gruyter Mouton, Berlin/Boston. doi.org/10.1515/9783110295252-004.

François, A. 2012. The dynamics of linguistic diversity: Egalitarian multilingualism and power imbalance among northern Vanuatu languages. *International Journal of the Sociology of Language* 214:85–110. doi.org/10.1515/ijsl-2012-0022.

Gaffney, D. and T. Denham 2021. The archaeology of social transformation in the New Guinea highlands. In I.J. McNiven and B. David (eds), *The Oxford handbook of the archaeology of Indigenous Australia and New Guinea*. Oxford University Press, Oxford. doi.org/10.1093/oxfordhb/9780190095611.013.31.

Gasser, E. 2019. Borrowed color and flora/fauna terminology in Northwest New Guinea. *Journal of Language Contact* 12(3):609–659. doi.org/10.1163/19552629-01203003.

Gil, D. 2015. The Mekong–Mamberamo linguistic area. In N.J. Enfield and B. Comrie (eds), *Languages of Mainland Southeast Asia: The state of the art*, pp. 266–354. Pacific Linguistics 649. De Gruyter Mouton, Berlin. doi.org/10.1515/9781501501685.

Gil, D. 2017. Roon ve, DO/GIVE coexpression, and language contact in Northwest New Guinea. In Antoinette Schapper (ed.), *Contact and substrate in the languages of Wallacea*, part 1, pp. 41–100. Special edition of *NUSA: Linguistic Studies of Indonesian and Other Languages in Indonesia* 62. doi.org/10.15026/89844.

Grimes, C.E. and O. Edwards submitted. *Wallacean subgroups: Unravelling the prehistory and classification of the Austronesian languages of Eastern Indonesia and Timor-Leste*.

Haiman, J. 1979. Review of Wurm, ed. 1975. *Language* 55(4):894–903. doi.org/10.2307/412750.

Hammarström, H. 2010. The status of the least documented language families in the world. *Language Documentation and Conservation* 4:177–212.

Hammarström, H. and S. Nordhoff 2012. The languages of Melanesia: Quantifying levels of coverage. In N. Evans and M. Klamer (eds), *Melanesian languages of the edge of Asia: Challenges for the 21st Century*, pp. 13–33. Special edition of *Language Documentation and Conservation* 5.

Hammarström, H., R. Forkel, M. Haspelmath, and S. Bank 2020. *Glottolog 4.3.* Max Planck Institute for the Science of Human History. Online database: glottolog.org (accessed 17 March 2021). doi.org/10.5281/zenodo.4061162.

Harrison, S.P. 2003. On the limits of the comparative method. In B.D. Joseph and R.D. Janda (eds), *The handbook of historical linguistics*, pp. 213–243. Blackwell, Malden. doi.org/10.1002/9781405166201.ch2.

Heggarty, P. 2014. Prehistory through language and archaeology. In C. Bowern and B. Evans (eds), *Routledge handbook of historical linguistics*, pp. 598–626. Routledge, London. doi.org/10.4324/9781315794013.ch28.

Holton, G. and M. Klamer 2018. The Papuan languages of East Nusantara and the Bird's Head. In B. Palmer (ed.), *The languages and linguistics of the New Guinea area: A comprehensive guide*, pp. 569–640. De Gruyter Mouton, Berlin/Boston. doi.org/10.1515/9783110295252-005.

Jackson, F.H. 1983. The internal and external relationships of the Trukic languages of Micronesia. Unpublished PhD thesis. Department of Linguistics, University of Hawai'i, Mānoa.

Kamholz, D. 2014. Austronesians in Papua: Diversification and change in South Halmahera–West New Guinea. Unpublished PhD thesis. Department of Linguistics, University of California, Berkeley.

Kamholz, D. 2017. Tone and language contact in southern Cenderawasih Bay. In A. Schapper (ed.), *Contact and substrate in the languages of Wallacea*, part 1, pp. 7–39. Special edition of *NUSA: Linguistic Studies of Indonesian and Other Languages in Indonesia* 62. doi.org/10.15026/89843.

Kerswill, P. 1996. Children, adolescents, and language change. *Language Variation and Change* 8(2):177–202. doi.org/10.1017/S0954394500001137.

Kim, S.H. 2006a. *Draft survey report on the Yetfa language of Papua, Indonesia.* Unpublished SIL manuscript.

Kim, S.H. 2006b. *Draft survey report on the Bgu language, the Kaptiau language and the Tarpia language of Papua, Indonesia.* Unpublished SIL manuscript.

Klamer, M. 2019. The dispersal of Austronesian languages in Island South East Asia: Current findings and debates. *Language and Linguistics Compass* 13(4):e12325. doi.org/10.1111/lnc3.12325.

Kluge, A. 2017. *A grammar of Papuan Malay.* Studies in Diversity Linguistics 11. Language Science Press, Berlin. doi.org/10.5281/zenodo.376415.

Marck, J.C. 1994. Proto-Micronesian terms for the physical environment. In A. Pawley and M. Ross (eds), *Austronesian terminologies: Continuity and change*, pp. 301–328. Pacific Linguistics C-127. Research School of Pacific and Asian Studies, The Australian National University, Canberra.

Pawley, A. 1998. The Trans New Guinea Phylum hypothesis: A reassessment. In J. Miedema, C. Odé, and R.A.C. Dam (eds), *Perspectives on the Bird's Head of Irian Jaya, Indonesia: Proceedings of the Conference, Leiden, 13–17 October 1997*, pp. 655–689. Rodopi, Amsterdam; Atlanta. doi.org/10.1163/9789004652644_034.

Pawley, A. 2005. The chequered career of the Trans New Guinea hypothesis. In A. Pawley, R. Attenborough, J. Golson, and R. Hide (eds), *Papuan pasts: Cultural, linguistic and biological histories of the Papuan-speaking peoples*, pp. 67–107. Pacific Linguistics 572. Research School of Pacific and Asian Studies, The Australian National University, Canberra.

Pawley, A. 2008. Where and when was Proto-Oceanic spoken? Archaeological and linguistic evidence. In Y.A. Lander and A.K. Ogloblin (eds), *Language and text in the Austronesian world: Studies in honour of Ülo Sirk*, pp. 47–71. Studies in Austronesian Linguistics 6. Lincom, Munich.

Pawley, A. and H. Hammarström 2018. The Trans New Guinea family. In B. Palmer (ed.), *The languages and linguistics of the New Guinea area: A comprehensive guide*, pp. 21–196. De Gruyter Mouton, Berlin/ Boston. doi.org/10.1515/9783110295252-002.

Reesink, G.P. 1998. The Bird's Head as a Sprachbund. In J. Miedema, C. Odé, and R.A.C. Dam (eds), *Perspectives on the Bird's Head of Irian Jaya, Indonesia: Proceedings of the Conference, Leiden, 13–17 October 1997*, pp. 603–642. Rodopi, Amsterdam/Atlanta. doi.org/10.1163/9789004652644_032.

Roscoe, P. 2014. Foragers and war in contact-era New Guinea. In M.W. Allen and T.L. Jones (eds), *Violence and warfare among hunter-gatherers*, pp. 223–240. Left Coast Press, Walnut Creek. doi.org/10.4324/ 9781315415970.

Ross, M. 1995. Some current issues in Austronesian linguistics. In D.T. Tryon (ed.), *Comparative Austronesian dictionary*, volume 1, pp. 45–120. Mouton de Gruyter, Berlin. doi.org/10.1515/9783110884012.1.45.

Ross, M. 1996. On the genetic affiliation of the Oceanic languages of Irian Jaya. *Oceanic Linguistics* 35(2): 258–271. doi.org/10.2307/3623174.

Ross, M. 2005. Pronouns as a preliminary diagnostic for grouping Papuan languages. In A. Pawley, R. Attenborough, J. Golson, and R. Hide (eds), *Papuan pasts: Cultural, linguistic and biological histories of the Papuan-speaking peoples*, pp. 15–66. Pacific Linguistics 572. Research School of Pacific and Asian Studies, The Australian National University, Canberra.

Ross, M. 2013. Diagnosing contact processes from their outcomes: The importance of life stages. *Journal of Language Contact* 6(1):5–47. doi.org/10.1163/19552629-006001002.

Ross, M., A. Pawley, and M. Osmond 2023. *The lexicon of Proto Oceanic: The culture and environment of ancestral Oceanic society. Volume 6—People: society*. School of Culture, History, and Language, College of Asia and the Pacific, The Australian National University, Canberra.

Rumaropen, B. 2005. *Draft laporan sosiolinguistik bahasa Poulle di kampung Molof dan Waley kabupaten Keerom, Papua, Indonesia*. Unpublished SIL manuscript.

Schapper, A. 2015. Wallacea, a linguistic area. *Archipel* 90:99–152. doi.org/10.4000/archipel.371.

Schapper, A. 2017. Farming and the Trans-New Guinea family: A consideration. In M. Robbeets and A. Savelyev (eds), *Language dispersal beyond farming*, pp. 155–181. John Benjamins, Amsterdam/ Philadelphia. doi.org/10.1075/z.215.07sch.

Schapper, A. 2020a. Linguistic Melanesia. In E. Adamou and Y. Matras (eds), *Routledge handbook of language contact*, pp. 480–502. Routledge, Abingdon. doi.org/10.4324/9781351109154-29.

Schapper, A. 2020b. Introduction. In A. Schapper (ed.), *The Papuan languages of Timor, Alor and Pantar: Sketch grammars*, volume III, pp. 1–52. Pacific Linguistics 660. De Gruyter Mouton, Boston/Berlin. doi.org/ 10.1515/9781501511158-001.

Schapper, A. and E. Zobel 2024. The classification of Irarutu and Koiwai: A new proposal. *Oceanic Linguistics*, 63(2). doi.org/10.1353/ol.2024.a935052.

Smith, A.D. 2017. The Western Malayo-Polynesian problem. *Oceanic Linguistics* 56(2):435–490. doi.org/ 10.1353/ol.2017.0021.

Spriggs, M. 2010. 'I was so much older then, I'm younger than that now': Why the dates keep changing for the spread of Austronesian languages. In J. Bowden, N.P. Himmelmann, and M. Ross (eds), *A Journey through Austronesian and Papuan linguistic and cultural space: Papers in honour of Andrew K. Pawley*, pp. 113–140. Pacific Linguistics 615. Research School of Pacific and Asian Studies, The Australian National University, Canberra.

Thomason, S. 2000. Linguistic areas and language history. In D.G. Gilbers, J. Nerbonne, and J. Schaeken (eds), *Languages in contact*, pp. 311–327. Special edition of *Studies in Slavic and General Linguistics* 28. doi.org/10.1163/9789004488472_030.

Thomason, S. 2010. Contact explanations in linguistics. In R. Hickey (ed.), *The handbook of language contact*, pp. 31–47. Blackwell, Oxford. doi.org/10.1002/9781444318159.ch1.

van den Heuvel, W. and S. Fedden 2014. Greater Awyu and Greater Ok: Inheritance or contact? *Oceanic Linguistics* 53(1):1–36. doi.org/10.1353/ol.2014.0008.

Voorhoeve, C.L. 1987. Worming one's way through New Guinea: The chase of the peripatetic pronouns. In D.C. Laycock and W. Winter (eds), *A world of language: Papers presented to Professor S. A. Wurm on his 65th Birthday*, pp. 709–727. Pacific Linguistics C-100. Research School of Pacific and Asian Studies, The Australian National University, Canberra.

Voorhoeve, C.L. 2005. Asmat-Kamoro, Awyu-Dumut and Ok: An enquiry into their linguistic relationships. In A. Pawley, R. Attenborough, J. Golson, and R. Hide (eds) *Papuan pasts: Cultural, linguistic and biological histories of the Papuan-speaking peoples*, pp. 145–166. Pacific Linguistics 572. Research School of Pacific and Asian Studies, The Australian National University, Canberra.

Wurm, S.A. (ed.) 1975. *New Guinea area languages and language study Vol 1: Papuan languages and the New Guinea linguistic scene*. Pacific Linguistics C-38. Department of Linguistics, Research School of Pacific Studies, The Australian National University, Canberra.

4

Deep histories in New Guinea: Insights from human genetics on regional demography and archaic introgression

Guy Jacobs, Pradiptajati Kusuma, and Robert Attenborough[1]

Abstract

In this, the first of three linked chapters oriented to human biology—specifically, genetics and genomics—we selectively review and synthesise aspects of research in the discipline that shed light on the deep histories of New Guinea's indigenous inhabitants. Since these histories predate modern boundaries, we draw on and integrate data from across the island, east as well as west, and relate them to the broader region. Anthropological genetic research over the past century has been crucially conditioned not only by conceptual advances but also—on an extraordinary scale recently—by technological ones. As a result, the literature available for our review is very much more informative than 30 years ago. Newton-like, it can provide insights not dreamed of then. We review two themes in particular here: first, the dispersals of *Homo sapiens* to Sahul and their ancient interactions with other hominin species, if not in New Guinea then en route there; and second, the deep connections of New Guinean populations with other populations in the region. On the second theme, we also present new analyses of ancient effective population size changes within, and splits between, regional populations, incorporating data on the Korowai of West New Guinea. Having noted some of the remarkable findings of recent years, we close by contemplating the prospect of many deep histories yet to be told in, and about, this extraordinarily diverse yet still under-researched island.

Abstrak

Dalam bab ini, yang merupakan seri pertama dari tiga bab terkait genetika manusia, kami secara selektif mengulas berbagai aspek penelitian dalam disiplin ilmu yang dapat memberikan informasi sejarah mendalam kependudukan asli di Papua. Karena sejarah ini mendahului batas-batas modern, kami mengintegrasikan data dari seluruh pulau Papua, baik Papua Barat dan Papua Nugini, untuk menganalisis dan menginterpretasi hasil lebih komprehensif. Penelitian genetika antropologi selama satu abad terakhir sangat dipengaruhi tidak hanya oleh perkembangan konseptual, tetapi juga oleh kemajuan

---

1   All authors contributed equally.

teknologi genomik yang pesat. Sebagai hasilnya, literatur yang tersedia untuk ulasan kami jauh lebih informatif daripada 30 tahun yang lalu. Pada bab ini, kami mengulas dua tema secara khusus: pertama, penyebaran Homo sapiens ke Sahul dan interaksi kuno mereka dengan spesies hominin lain; dan kedua, hubungan yang dalam antara populasi Papua Nugini dengan populasi lain di wilayah tersebut. Mengenai tema kedua, kami juga menyajikan analisis baru tentang perubahan ukuran populasi efektif pada, dan pemisahan antara, populasi regional, dengan menggabungkan data genom dari suku Korowai di Papua Barat. Kami menutup dengan merenungkan prospek penelitian untuk mempelajari lebih lanjut sejarah yang dalam yang belum diceritakan tentang pulau yang luar biasa beragam namun masih sedikit diteliti ini.

Introduction

New Guinea has a deep and complex history of human occupation, covered only shallowly by its written history, and patchily by its developing archaeological record. Human biology has contributions to make in posing and addressing fundamental questions about the island's deep human past. Here, in the first of three connected chapters, we selectively review evidence from human genetics and genomics, which recently have seen rapid and remarkable advances in laboratory and computational technology. Our focus here is on regional diversity and deep history: interactions of populations of our own species with other hominins in the region, and arrivals in New Guinea. Given this broad focus and the limited genetic data available for West New Guinea, including mainland Western New Guinea (WNG), we draw on evidence from the island as a whole, including eastern New Guinea (ENG)—that is, the mainland of Papua New Guinea (PNG).

The geography of the region sets the context for the biological understanding of its people. In broad terms, it must have been populated from Southeast Asia, across stretches of sea that were extensive at any phase of sea level variation. The earliest peoples would have encountered the single New Guinea–Australia–Tasmania landmass, Sahul. How they got there—the location and number of earliest landfalls—has been a focus of much debate, as have the genetic interrelationships of New Guineans and Australians before and after the drowning of the Sahul–Arafura shelf and the formation of the Torres Strait.

We open our perspective into the deep past by contemplating the diversity for which New Guinea is famous in our own day. Linguistic diversity is especially salient: New Guinea's indigenous languages number 850 or so, grouped into 18 or more not demonstrably interrelated families—in the same sense that Indo-European is a family—plus several isolates (Pawley and Hammarström 2017). The Austronesian family has an extensive distribution from Madagascar to Polynesia; but in New Guinea it has a limited and mostly coastal distribution, reflecting its relatively late arrival in the region. The other families, occupying the greater part of the interior as well as some coastal areas, are included, along with a few other families from eastern Indonesia and Near Oceania, in the negatively defined (i.e. non-Austronesian) 'Papuan' grouping. Indigenous Australian languages form the region's third main grouping.

In a prominent model based on classical genetic polymorphisms surveyed among extant populations, Kirk (1992) proposed three patterns, partly linked to linguistic diversity and corresponding to a broad chronological sequence. The first, reflecting the earliest peopling of Sahul, was represented by genetic markers shared by New Guineans and Indigenous Australians. The second, 'Proto-Papuan', represented by markers frequent in New Guinea including the interior, but not shared with Australians, was presumed to have arrived in or evolved in New Guinea after the drowning of the land bridge. The third, associated with the arrival of Austronesian-speaking peoples, was represented by markers absent from Australia and absent or rare in interior New Guinea, but more frequent along New Guinea's northern and south-eastern coasts, as well as elsewhere in the Pacific islands. Thirty years later we reconsider this model in the light of subsequent research. Here and in the next chapter we find that more modern data reinforce some but not all signals (see Figure 5.1 in Kusuma et al., this volume, for a summary of recent datasets).

Early peopling: Origins and routes

Genetic studies have provided insights into deep human history globally, long supporting an African origin followed by dispersal throughout the world (Cann et al. 1987). Genetic dates based on modern genomes confirm a shared non-African genetic bottleneck and indicate divergence between non-African and African populations in the range 150,000–40,000 years ago (Wang et al. 2020), while ancient DNA confirms early (Fu et al. 2014) though complex (Yang et al. 2017) divergence between west and east Eurasia by ~45,000 years ago. Dispersals reached Sahul at a very early date: at least, and potentially significantly before, ~50,000 years ago (Clarkson et al. 2017; O'Connell et al. 2018). There is evidence that they reached the highlands of ENG 49,000–44,000 years ago (Summerhayes et al. 2010).

Who were these early modern human migrants? The relationships between early *Homo sapiens* communities spreading out of Africa and the routes that they took have been the subject of considerable debate. From a genetic perspective, the relationships between non-African and African populations, as well as among different non-African populations, are seen as key. As modern genetic data have emerged, core questions include whether modern New Guineans derive from a dispersal through southern Eurasia separate to that which populated west Eurasia, or have ancestry from an early dispersal from Africa entirely separate from the 'classic' successful out-of-Africa wave contributing all other modern mainland Eurasian ancestry. While the former model is inherently stated in geographic terms, the latter focuses on the temporal layering of dispersals rather than explicitly on routes; they are not mutually exclusive. In a simple model with limited post-dispersal migration, the former would cause closer clustering among some subset of mainland or island Asian groups, while the latter would imply greater divergence between New Guinean populations and Africans than between Eurasians and Africans. Practically, both the (modern) genetic data, and genetic expectations given undoubted later gene flow and, as it happens, archaic introgression, are more complex, and interpretations will rely on integrating many sources of evidence.

Australian and New Guinean mitochondrial DNA (mtDNA) and Y-chromosomes sit deep in known out-of-Africa founder haplogroups (haplogroups M and N for mtDNA, and haplogroups C and F for the Y-chromosome, see Hudjashov et al. 2007), consistent with ancient origins from a single out-of-Africa migration but, depending on the diversity of the African source populations and detailed dispersal dynamics, not necessarily ruling out multiple migrations. Explicit phylogenetic model selection drawing on genotype data from ENG and regional samples supported a single-source dispersal from Africa followed by early separation between the ancestors of modern mainland Eurasian and New Guinean populations (Wollstein et al. 2010). Initial genotype data from Indigenous Australians of the Riverine region (McEvoy et al. 2010) confirmed the clustering of Australian and New Guinean populations, mimicking Kirk's first pattern and reflecting deep shared ancestry.

The first Indigenous Australian genome soon followed (Rasmussen et al. 2011), and argued for overall similar divergence between non-African (Australian, Asian, and European) and African groups. Internal non-African structure was detected, however, with closer clustering among mainland Eurasian groups than between these and the Indigenous Australian genome: the split date was estimated at 75,000–62,000 years ago, followed by later gene flow. Subsequent work, this time including a small sample of New Guinean full genomes, made a related argument, for an earlier divergence between New Guinean and African ancestry than between Eurasian and African ancestry. This is consistent with a minor contribution—at least 1.9 per cent—from an earlier and separate dispersal to Sahul, named 'xOOA', followed by later mixing (Pagani et al. 2016). The earlier divergence of New Guinean and African populations has been replicated in a recent whole-genome survey of New Guinean groups (Brucato et al. 2021), but not in a small sample of New Guinean genomes, physically phased so as to avoid certain methodological biases, from the Human Genome Diversity Project (Bergström et al. 2020). Detailed explicit demographic model fitting—by which we mean, a full description of the structured relationships, branching patterns, and effective population-size dynamics of the theoretical populations needed to yield data similar to sampled genomes—has been performed on a sample of Indigenous Australian and New Guinean genomes (Malaspinas et al. 2016). This found that a single-dispersal model was sufficient to describe the observed joint site frequency spectrum (jSFS), a conclusion supported by later analysis of certain allele-sharing signals (Wall 2017), with xOOA not required by genetic data or worsening the fit, respectively.

It appears, then, that there are multiple challenges, concerning both methodology and interpretation. Taking into account archaic introgression (discussed below) and the complexities of recent migration—between mainland Eurasian groups, between mainland Eurasia and Africa (Chen et al. 2020), and potentially during the Holocene from South Asia to Australia (Pugach et al. 2013)—will prove critical. Indeed, some models incorporating gene flow argue for a much earlier (>100,000 year old) initial separation of ancestral New Guinean populations from both the ancestral French and Han populations, followed by a major pulse of admixture around 20,000 years ago (Steinrücken et al. 2019), in contrast with more recent separation and limited contact as usually inferred. The possibility of ancient divergence is supported by a recent analysis that infers the location of shared ancestors using a large global sample of genomes, with some ancestors of modern New Guineans appearing to have lived in the region up to 140,000 years ago (Wohns et al. 2022). As the authors note, this date is long before archaeological evidence for human habitation of the island, and could rather reflect archaic introgression that is not shared with populations beyond New Guinea, or genetic structure that predates initial modern human migrations to the area. There are potential connections to the xOOA debate above with regard to this latter point, in that New Guinea–specific variation derived from a potentially structured African population would be expected to show common ancestry predating out-of-Africa dispersals, with those common ancestors themselves inferred as local to the island by this analysis. The deep relationship between ancient population size and the timing of genetic common ancestry also advises nuance when relating these within-genome signals to the timing of migration events.

Overall, the detailed interpretation of the 140,000-year-old date is clearly an open question. More broadly, given the range of results from different studies, we emphasise that model design and methodological assumptions can be critical. The challenges of interpretation given grand scales of time and space are significant, and the degree to which archaeological search will catch up with the more ancient genetic dates, or genetic methodology will catch up with the archaeological consensus, remains to be seen. Linked to the question of who dispersed to Sahul is the question of how they got there (reviewed also, among other topics of regional genetic demography, in Taufik et al. 2022). Their possible routes through Wallacea to Sahul—whether northerly via Sulawesi or southerly via

Timor—were modelled by Birdsell (1977), but have long proven hard to clarify. A recent analysis identifies the former as the simplest route, predicting the first footfall in Sahul to be in or near West New Guinea, possibly around what is today Misool Island (Kealy et al. 2018). However, modelling that explicitly attempts to fit the (sparse) distribution of archaeological finds argues for either a single southern dispersal ~50,000 years ago, or near-simultaneous northern and southern dispersals ~75,000 years ago (Bradshaw et al. 2021). The most recent mtDNA surveys—which show significant separation in the diversity of New Guinean and Indigenous Australian haplogroups— have been interpreted variously as supporting this dual-dispersal hypothesis (Pedro et al. 2020), and as being uninformative about initial dispersal routes (Purnomo et al. 2021). High-resolution Y-chromosome phylogeny incorporating samples spanning Island Southeast Asia (ISEA), New Guinea, and Australia (Karmin et al. 2022) argues for early diversification of extant deep lineages ~50,000 years ago, followed by a period of relative lineage stability 40,000–25,000 years ago, likely corresponding to significant population structure/limited contact between islands. More recent dynamics appear more complex, including significant lineage expansions—likely reflecting episodes of population growth—in New Guinea and Australia 15,000–10,000 years ago.

Genomic data (Malaspinas et al. 2016) support an ancient (~60,000 years ago) split between an Indigenous Australian/New Guinean ancestral clade and the ancestors of Eurasians, followed by ancient divergence (~40,000 years ago). Depending on the geographic model, the 60,000-year-old split date could point to a single dispersal to Sahul, though the deep 40,000-year-old divergence may equally be consistent with multiple dispersals. Drawing on a diverse dataset from New Guinea (especially ENG) and surrounding islands, a recent and extremely detailed investigation found that, while both single and dual dispersals can broadly fit Australian and New Guinean genetic diversity, a model with two dispersals is generally preferred. Specifically, the authors favour the northerly dispersal origin of New Guineans, potentially via the Moluccas, yet with evidence, based on available data, interpreted as supporting the earliest successful colonisation of New Guinea from the now-submerged Arafura Plain (Brucato et al. 2021). This study also supports greater migration connections in the post-colonisation phase between New Guinean communities and the broader region than usually believed.

As a final piece to the puzzle, we note evidence from non-human sources: *Helicobacter pylori* (Moodley et al. 2009) and Hepatitis B (Yuen et al. 2019). In the former case, the separation between a Sahul and Asian clade dating to 37,000–31,000 years ago supports a common origin of Sahulian populations, with New Guinean and Australian subtypes diverging 32,000–23,000 years ago, indicating a significant period of isolation. The Hepatitis B data focus on two strains, HBV/C4 (now endemic among Indigenous Australians) and HBV/C3 (now endemic in some Pacific Island populations). The deep common ancestor of HBV/C4 (67,000–36,000 years ago) coupled with the significant divergence of HBV/C3 and its absence from the Australian sample supported two origins, and hence two ancient colonisation waves.

Thus, while neither modelling nor modern genetic data have yet fully resolved the routes or timing of dispersal, progress is being made. Resolution may depend on further archaeological evidence or, especially, ancient DNA (aDNA). Surprisingly, modern human genomes, and especially those from New Guinea, include strong signals of archaic introgression from other *Homo* species (Green et al. 2010; Reich et al. 2010). This has implications for dispersals, population interactions, and adaptation in the region (Mathieson 2020; Slatkin and Racimo 2016).

Archaic introgression

In contrast to earlier models of our evolution, modern humans are now generally believed to have reproduced successfully with multiple divergent hominin groups, several and perhaps many times. Further, this genetic endowment was often subject to evolutionary selection, and makes important contributions to present-day phenotypic diversity.

The global story of archaic ancestry is well told (Gokcumen 2020). Inferences are variously based on comparing a target modern human group to a Neanderthal or other ancient hominin genome and/or to other *H. sapiens* populations, seeking excess similarity to the former and excess divergence from the latter. Based on these signals, African groups have very limited Neanderthal ancestry (Chen et al. 2020), while Eurasian populations are estimated to have about 2 per cent Neanderthal ancestry (Wall et al. 2013). Neanderthal ancestry in New Guinea (Figure 4.1) is high at 2.5–3 per cent, and may be marginally elevated relative to western and perhaps eastern Eurasian populations (Choin et al. 2021; Sankararaman et al. 2016). However, the history of the region appears more complex, and it is the rich history of admixture with the enigmatic Denisovans, a sister clade to Neanderthals identified from bone and teeth fragments in Siberia, that has drawn most attention (Meyer et al. 2012; Reich et al. 2010; Sawyer et al. 2015; Slon et al. 2018, 2017).

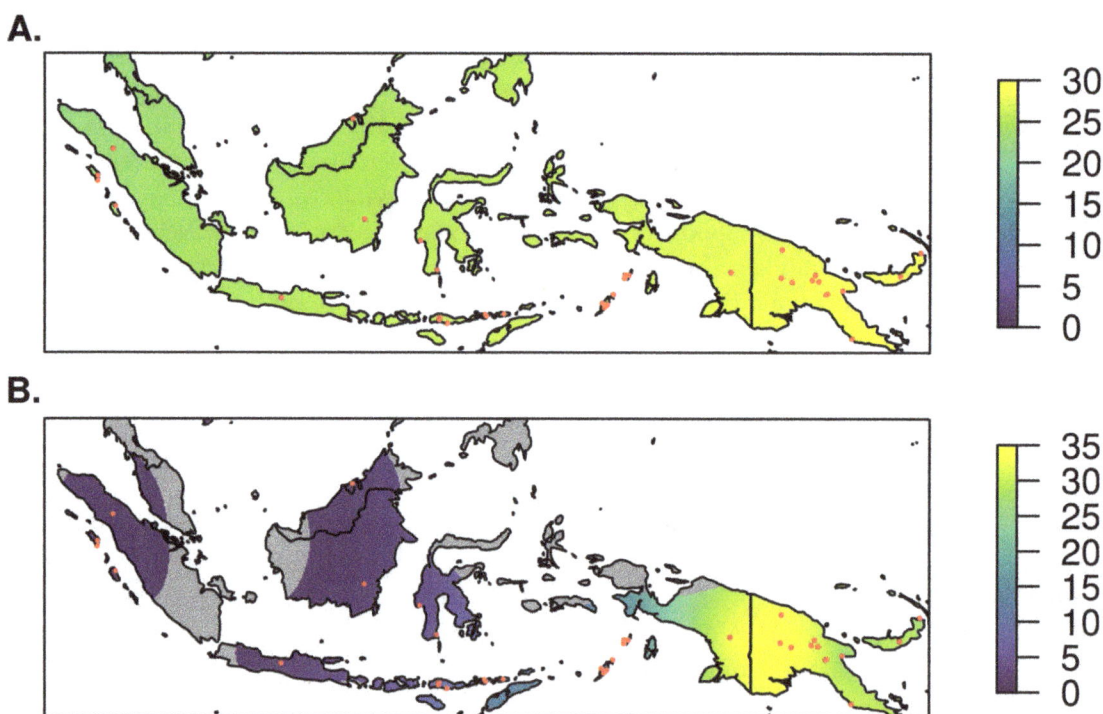

Figure 4.1: Spatial distribution of amount of Neanderthal (A) and Denisovan (B) introgression (in megabases, Mb), using the samples and algorithm described in Jacobs et al. (2019).

Notes: This approach seeks to extract archaic introgressed chunks in the genome and has higher sensitivity to detect Neanderthal than Denisovan chunks; the total Mb detected is below the total amount of introgression. Interpolation between data points (red) by spatial krigging; regions of low interpolation confidence based on this dataset (variance > 10Mb) are greyed out, including the Bird's Head region of WNG, for which data are currently unavailable and an impression of reducing Denisovan ancestry is potentially artefactual.

Source: The samples and algorithm described in Jacobs et al. (2019).

Denisovan ancestry in New Guinea is estimated at 4–6 per cent (Reich et al. 2011, 2010), apparently exceeded only by the indigenous Ayta Magbukon in the Philippines (Larena et al. 2021). These levels are considerably enriched relative to minor signals in East and South Asia (Mallick et al. 2016), and increase jointly with New Guinean ancestry across eastern Indonesia (Jacobs et al. 2019). This pattern—island populations thousands of miles away from Siberia showing greatest 'Denisovan' ancestry—is particularly compelling, leading to debate especially around when and where contact occurred. Have other populations become 'diluted' for Denisovan ancestry after shared ancestral introgression, did introgression occur through multiple independent events, or did Denisovan ancestry spread to mainland Eurasia through back-migration following local contact in present-day ISEA or New Guinea? And what does this mean for the genetic diversity of New Guinea groups?

In the absence of further aDNA (or potentially palaeoproteomic) data—whether *H. sapiens* or other hominin—from ISEA or New Guinea, these questions cannot yet be fully resolved. However, by extracting introgressed haplotypes from modern DNA and comparing these extracted introgressed haplotypes (EIHs) to the high-coverage Altai Denisovan genome (Meyer et al. 2012), it is possible to search for demographic complexity in the introgression process. A bimodal peak in East Asia (Browning et al. 2018) supports other evidence for two distinct source Denisovan populations there (Massilani et al. 2020), one closely related to the Altai Denisovan. Intriguingly, similar analysis in New Guinea focusing on very long introgressed haplotypes suggests two more divergent Denisovan-like sources, identified as D1 and D2, with D1 splitting from the Altai Denisovan 283,000 years ago (95 per cent CI 297,000–261,000 years ago) and D2 around 363,000 years ago (95 per cent CI 377,000–334,000 years ago) (Jacobs et al. 2019). Other modelling approaches support regional introgression complexity (Mondal et al. 2019), as does a recent analysis of Oceanian genetic data (Choin et al. 2021).

Three considerations support local introgression of D1, potentially in Wallacea or New Guinea itself. First, this composite signal appears strongest in New Guinea and Oceania (Jacobs et al. 2019). Second, D1 EIHs are longer than D2 EIHs, with length distributions suggesting introgression perhaps as recently as 30,000 years ago (though dates are highly debated, with the degree of signal sharing and split time of New Guinean and Australian populations relevant, e.g. Teixeira and Cooper 2019). Third, there is local geographic variation in the relative strength of the signals (Choin et al. 2021; Jacobs et al. 2019). Detailed interpretation is nevertheless complicated, with evidence from Oceanian genomes (Choin et al. 2021) supporting different timing of introgression processes. Ultimately, while further evidence is needed to resolve interpretation, the Denisovan clade is increasingly revealed as highly structured, and complexity in introgression signals is supported in New Guinea and the broader region.

There is as yet no genomic evidence regarding the likely island-dwarfed *Homo floresiensis* (on Flores possibly until ~50,000 years ago; Sutikna et al. 2016) or *Homo luzonensis* (on Luzon until 67,000–50,000 years ago; Détroit et al. 2019). The exact phylogenetic placement of these samples remains uncertain, and it is unclear what genetic signals would be expected from any admixture that did occur. Potentially of relevance, a recent survey (Teixeira et al. 2021) found no significant deeply divergent non-African haplotypes in ISEA or New Guinean groups. This suggests absence of introgression from the more deeply divergent *Homo erectus*, though inferences are made without *H. erectus* DNA to guide us and therefore inevitably await confirmation. This is despite the probable presence of late-surviving *H. erectus* in Java (Rizal et al. 2020; but also see Swisher et al. 1996).

What, then, have been the phenotypic and evolutionary impacts of ancient hominin admixture on the people of New Guinea? Elevated introgression is apparent in some genomic regions while others show depleted introgression (Vernot et al. 2016), consistent with positive selection (due to a fitness advantage of archaic introgressed variants relative to modern human variants) and purifying selection (due to a fitness disadvantage of archaic introgressed variants), respectively. This pattern is further supported by the depletion of archaic variants in conserved and regulatory regions (Sankararaman et al. 2016; Telis et al. 2020), and by findings that Neanderthal-introgressed variation in Europeans (among whom most genotype–phenotype association data are available) contributes to complex traits and disease (Dannemann and Kelso 2017; Simonti et al. 2016). Of particular interest, archaic introgression appears to have had an adaptive role impacting immunity, including in New Guinean populations (e.g. apparent Denisovan-origin human leukocyte antigen [HLA] genes [Abi-Rached et al. 2011]; *STAT2* from Neanderthals [Mendez et al. 2012]; and polygenic immune signals based on Bismarck Islander genomes [Gouy and Excoffier 2020]). An interesting and currently relevant example is a protective Neanderthal-inherited haplotype that is associated with a reduction in the risk of COVID-19 severe clinical manifestation when infected with the coronavirus SARS-CoV-2 (Zeberg and Pääbo 2020). The introgressed allele at the tag-SNP rs1156361, associated with protection, is at intermediate frequencies across Eurasia, but it is absent among the 45 WNG and ENG samples we analyse below. At present, information on the detailed functional impact of introgressed variation in New Guinea remains scarce. A notable exception concerns the Denisovan version of the *TNFAIP3* gene, involved in innate and adaptive immune response and believed to have been under positive selection (Gittelman et al. 2016). This is found at ~63 per cent frequency in a New Guinea and regional sample, and in 9/14 haplotypes among the Korowai of WNG (Jacobs et al. 2019). Investigations in mice of the functional impact of relevant Denisovan variants suggest that they may increase resistance to microbial pathogens (Zammit et al. 2019), hence potentially driving positive selection. Adaptively introgressed genes affecting other biological processes, in particular dietary metabolism, among New Guinean and regional populations have also been proposed (Gouy and Excoffier 2020; Jacobs et al. 2019).

More detailed work on the functional impact of archaic introgression in New Guinea is emerging. Analysis of correlations between archaic introgressed variants in New Guinea and chromatin states in different cell types reveals complex patterns, including overall enrichment in genomic regions functional in immune cells (Vespasiani et al. 2022). These patterns appear to result both from chromatin states and from, for instance, transcription factor binding site disruption, suggesting that these variants play a role in supporting the differential expression of immune genes. Meanwhile, additional direct evidence of Denisovan variants having regulatory effects is mounting, as investigated among the Korowai through whole-blood transcriptomic and DNA methylation analysis (Natri et al. 2022, 2020). These studies—which stand out in applying this multiomics approach to non-Eurasian populations—explore the cline in both New Guinean ancestry and Denisovan introgression across Indonesia to investigate both the patterns and evolutionary causes of regulatory differences. Notably, many differentially expressed genes were directly found to overlap Denisovan haplotype blocks, again including genes involved in immunity; and some of this Denisovan-ancestry-associated differential expression has been narrowed down to specific expression and methylation quantitative trait loci (QTLs), genetic variants with a detected impact on expression/methylation phenotypes.

To sum up, the exact timing and location of contact between modern humans and ancient hominins, and the relationship to the exodus from Africa and dispersals to Sahul, are still under debate. The broad signal of Neanderthal introgression in contemporary non-Africans may imply that the first human occupants of New Guinea already had at least some non-*sapiens* DNA, though with estimates of introgression timing generally in the range 55,000–25,000 years ago juxtaposed against the potentially ancient occupation of Sahul, other scenarios deserve consideration also. During and following introgression, many archaic variants were deleterious and purged by selection while others were positively selected, particularly immune-related genes in New Guinea. With this context in mind, our questions now turn to the genetic history of New Guinean populations in their regional context. Given the lack of focused demographic analysis on recent genome data including WNG, we present a mixture of new analyses and existing results.

New Guinea in regional context

Genetic data indicate deep shared ancestry among Sahulian populations, with more recent population divergence between New Guinea and Australia (Choin et al. 2021; Malaspinas et al. 2016). We now seek to assess the degree and timescale of population differentiation between a broader sample of New Guinean groups, including the Citak and Korowai from Mappi district of WNG (Jacobs et al. 2019; Natri et al. 2022) along with PNG samples and populations representing the regional (Malaspinas et al. 2016; Mallick et al. 2016) and global (The 1000 Genomes Project Consortium 2015) context.

To explore the relationship of New Guinean populations to those in East Asia and ISEA we used Principal Component Analysis (PCA). All WNG and PNG samples (here including a few Bougainville genomes) are grouped together relative to non–New Guineans (Figure 4.2A; purple circles). We replicate the known signal of a genetic cline between Asian and New Guinean ancestry over eastern Indonesia (Hudjashov et al. 2017; Xu et al. 2012), thought to reflect the Austronesian expansion; similar signals of Asian ancestry partially associated with Austronesian languages are known on the coast of ENG (Bergström et al. 2017). The PCA results are supported by ADMIXTURE analysis (Alexander et al. 2009) which seeks to detect genetic ancestral components and characterise individuals as combinations of these. Under the statistically preferred model (K = 3 ancestry components), we detect uniform shared ancestry among New Guinea groups, in contrast to the composite ancestry of available Indigenous Australian genomes from the Simons Genome Diversity Project (Figure 4.2B). Exploratory extension of the analysis to five ancestry components suggests that Indigenous Australians are related to South Asian and especially Onge (Andaman) groups (Pugach et al. 2013; though see Malaspinas et al. 2016).

We used SMC++ (Terhorst et al. 2017) to infer effective population size histories and split dates. For simplicity, this approach assumes a 'clean split' model, in which no gene flow occurs after populations split; post-split migration, as is likely to have occurred, will lead to underestimates of divergence time, such that our results represent lower bounds. Split dates between New Guinean groups and Indigenous Australians are inferred as ~37,000–32,000 years ago (Figure 4.2C–E). These dates are congruent with published split dates on the basis of different statistical approaches between ENG Highlands populations and Indigenous Australians of ~35,000 years ago (Malaspinas et al. 2016) and ~34,000 years ago (Steinrücken et al. 2019). The dates are also within the same range as the split date between New Guineans and Near Oceanians (Bismarck and Solomon islanders) of ~38,000–31,000 years ago (Choin et al. 2021).

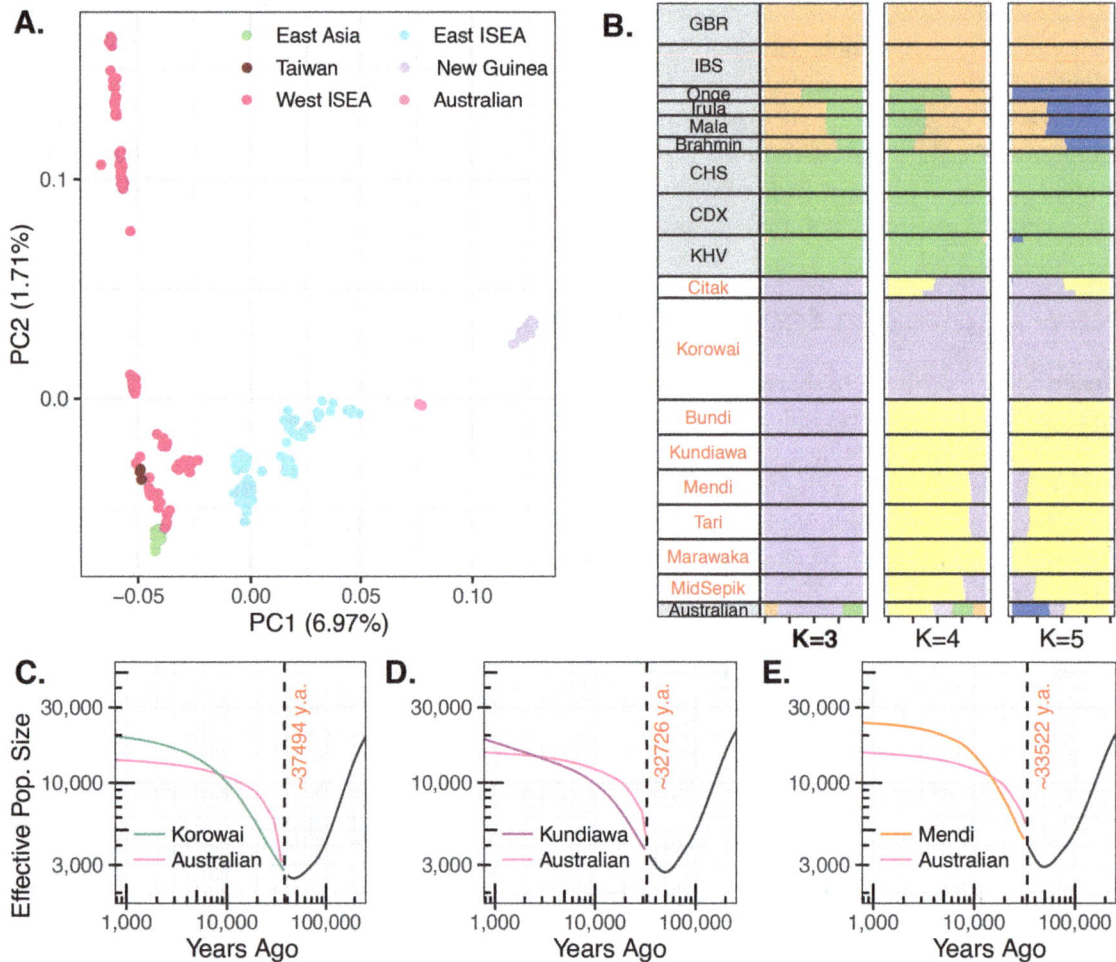

Figure 4.2: New Guinea population analysis.

(A) Principal Component Analysis (PCA) of New Guinea individuals in a regional context. (B) ADMIXTURE analysis (lowest cross-validation error — K = 3) of New Guinea groups and Indigenous Australians (Simons Genome Diversity Project), compared to Europeans (British (GBR), Iberian (IBS)), South Asians (Brahmin, Mala, Irula, Onge), East Asian populations (Southern Han Chinese (CHS), Chinese Dai (CDX), Kinh Vietnamese (KHV)). (C–E) Effective population size dynamics and population split times between Indigenous Australians and the Korowai, Kundiawa, and Mendi, respectively, as inferred by SMC++.

Source: Authors' analysis of data from Jacobs et al. (2019); Natri et al. (2022); Mallick et al. (2016); Malaspinas et al. (2016); and The 1000 Genomes Project Consortium (2015).

SMC++ also offers insight into population size dynamics, again, with modelling assumptions such as random mating. An effective population size is inferred; this ideally approximates to the number of reproductive individuals in a population, but for complex reasons, it underestimates the census population significantly (capturing perhaps only 10–20 per cent of the census, depending on assumptions; Palstra and Fraser 2012). Nonetheless, this approach can capture relative and comparative dynamics, such as recent population growth, or differences between groups. Our analysis detects a clear signal of ancestral population decline from at least 200,000 to 50,000 years ago, as observed among other non-African populations (Schiffels and Durbin 2014), likely reflecting serial out-of-Africa bottlenecks potentially coupled with population reduction or increasing subpopulation fragmentation within Africa. Population recovery precedes and continues through the split times identified above, likely corresponding to growth following initial dispersals. With the caution already mentioned, we note the relatively greater effective population size of the recent ancestors of New Guinean groups as compared to those of the Indigenous Australian sample.

In summary, the clustering of New Guinean and Indigenous Australian populations compared to East Asians (see above) and indeed global populations (Malaspinas et al. 2016; Mallick et al. 2016) supports shared ancestry between these regions; hence Kirk's first genetic signal. The second hypothesis—of an initially unified population history of Australia and New Guinea followed by the emergence or arrival of distinct local ancestry in New Guinea after the drowning of the land bridge—is more complex. Potentially asymmetric connections between New Guinea and Australia are proposed (Malaspinas et al. 2016), and similar levels of Denisovan ancestry especially in New Guinea and Australia argue for a significantly shared history. There is no evidence of a late pulse of pre-Austronesian Asian-related ancestry into New Guinea, nor of a recent burst of shared drift in New Guinea, in our results or others (Bergström et al. 2017; Malaspinas et al. 2016). Rather, divergence in the region likely built up over a considerable time, promoted by small population sizes and drift and moderated to some degree by migration. Kirk's third pattern, of ancestry signals in coastal New Guinea shared both to the west and with communities of the Pacific islands, is generally associated with the Austronesian expansion and strongly supported by recent genotyping and whole-genome surveys (Bergström et al. 2017; Brucato et al. 2021).

A note on future directions: Regional histories

Reflecting the current state of the debates, our discussion has, perhaps, highlighted more of the unknown than the known, regarding first dispersals, archaic introgression, and later regional connections. Despite this, the capacity of genomic analyses to infer deep evolutionary histories from relatively few and sparse samples has led to considerable progress—even if models involve rarely realistic hard population splits and pulses or constant streams of migration between groups. In just over a decade, researchers have started to tease apart New Guinean history beyond the simplest out-of-Africa dispersal models—assessing evidence of xOOA and post-dispersal contacts between regional populations, detecting and profiling the impact of our hominin relatives on the Denisovan clade, and revealing the signal of deep genetic structure within New Guinea. While answers lead to more questions, progress is rapid and tangible.

While more detailed regional sampling and more nuanced inference methods will continue to clarify regional demographic history, it is likely that aDNA will reveal the most detailed and potentially surprising results. The combination of technological advances, experience, and serendipity has allowed retrieval of ancient human DNA, and indeed sedimentary DNA, from challenging tropical environments, and we must hope for this for New Guinea also. Any aDNA or palaeoproteomics from non-*sapiens* hominins in the broader ISEA region would be of especial interest, if attainable. Human aDNA from Vanuatu and the wider region has already clarified ancestry associated with various stages of the Lapita culture (Posth et al. 2018; Skoglund et al. 2016), while the recent Leang Panninge genome from Sulawesi (Carlhoff et al. 2021) has revealed, perhaps surprisingly, early composite New Guinean and early Asian-related ancestry east of the Wallace Line >7000 years ago. Similar data from New Guinea and surrounding islands, or indeed from proposed dispersal routes, could be extremely informative for disentangling the demographic implications of the modern distribution of mainland and regional diversity. Given trends in DNA preservation and retrieval, it is probable that relatively more recent data will be available first in New Guinea, potentially but not necessarily from the cooler highlands. In such a culturally and linguistically dynamic environment, even relatively modern sequences could reveal much about early dispersals and contact with Austronesian-speaking groups, as well as social process and the demographic impact of agriculture—topics we discuss in the next chapter.

References

Abi-Rached, L., M.J. Jobin, S. Kulkarni, A. McWhinnie, K. Dalva, L. Gragert, F. Babrzadeh, B. Gharizadeh, M. Luo, F.A. Plummer, J. Kimani, M. Carrington, D. Middleton, R. Rajalingam, M. Beksac, S.G.E. Marsh, M. Maiers, L.A. Guethlein, S. Tavoularis, A.-M. Little, R.E. Green, P.J. Norman, and P. Parham 2011. The shaping of modern human immune systems by multiregional admixture with archaic humans. *Science* 334:89–94. doi.org/10.1126/science.1209202.

Alexander, D.H., J. Novembre, and K. Lange 2009. Fast model-based estimation of ancestry in unrelated individuals. *Genome Research* 19:1655–1664. doi.org/10.1101/gr.094052.109.

Bergström, A., S.J. Oppenheimer, A.J. Mentzer, K. Auckland, K. Robson, R. Attenborough, M.P. Alpers, G. Koki, W. Pomat, P. Siba, Y. Xue, M.S. Sandhu, and C. Tyler-Smith 2017. A Neolithic expansion, but strong genetic structure, in the independent history of New Guinea. *Science* 357:1160–1163. doi.org/10.1126/science.aan3842.

Bergström, A., S.A. McCarthy, R. Hui, M.A. Almarri, Q. Ayub, P. Danecek, Y. Chen, S. Felkel, P. Hallast, J. Kamm, H. Blanché, J.-F. Deleuze, H. Cann, S. Mallick, D. Reich, M.S. Sandhu, P. Skoglund, A. Scally, Y. Xue, R. Durbin, and C. Tyler-Smith 2020. Insights into human genetic variation and population history from 929 diverse genomes. *Science* 367:eaay5012. doi.org/10.1126/science.aay5012.

Birdsell, J.B. 1977. The recalibration of a paradigm for the first peopling of Greater Australia. In J. Allen, J. Golson, and R. Jones (eds), *Sunda and Sahul: Prehistoric studies in Southeast Asia, Melanesia, and Australia*, pp. 113–167. Academic Press, London.

Bradshaw, C.J.A., K. Norman, S. Ulm, A.N. Williams, C. Clarkson, J. Chadœuf, S.C. Lin, Z. Jacobs, R.G. Roberts, M.I. Bird, L.S. Weyrich, S.G. Haberle, S. O'Connor, B. Llamas, T.J. Cohen, T. Friedrich, P. Veth, M. Leavesley, and F. Saltré 2021. Stochastic models support rapid peopling of Late Pleistocene Sahul. *Nature Communications* 12:2440. doi.org/10.1038/s41467-021-21551-3.

Browning, S.R., B.L. Browning, Y. Zhou, S. Tucci, and J.M. Akey 2018. Analysis of human sequence data reveals two pulses of archaic Denisovan admixture. *Cell* 173:53–61.e9. doi.org/10.1016/j.cell.2018.02.031.

Brucato, N., M. André, R. Tsang, L. Saag, J. Kariwiga, K. Sesuki, T. Beni, W. Pomat, J. Muke, V. Meyer, A. Boland, J.-F. Deleuze, H. Sudoyo, M. Mondal, L. Pagani, I. Gallego Romero, M. Metspalu, M.P. Cox, M. Leavesley, and F.-X. Ricaut 2021. Papua New Guinean genomes reveal the complex settlement of North Sahul. *Molecular Biology and Evolution* 38:5107–5121. doi.org/10.1093/molbev/msab238.

Cann, R.L., M. Stoneking, and A.C. Wilson 1987. Mitochondrial DNA and human evolution. *Nature* 325: 31–36. doi.org/10.1038/325031a0.

Carlhoff, S., A. Duli, K. Nägele, M. Nur, L. Skov, I. Sumantri, A.A. Oktaviana, B. Hakim, B. Burhan, F. Ali Syahdar, D.P. McGahan, D. Bulbeck, Y.L. Perston, K. Newman, A.M. Saiful, M. Ririmasse, S. Chia, Hasanuddin, D.A.T. Pulubuhu, Suryatman, Supriadi, C. Jeong, B.M. Peter, K. Prüfer, A. Powell, J. Krause, C. Posth, and A. Brumm 2021. Genome of a middle Holocene hunter-gatherer from Wallacea. *Nature* 596:543–547. doi.org/10.1038/s41586-021-03823-6.

Chen, L., A.B. Wolf, W. Fu, L. Li, and J.M. Akey 2020. Identifying and interpreting apparent Neanderthal ancestry in African individuals. *Cell* 180:677–687.e16. doi.org/10.1016/j.cell.2020.01.012.

Choin, J., J. Mendoza-Revilla, L.R. Arauna, S. Cuadros-Espinoza, O. Cassar, M. Larena, A. Min-Shan Ko, C. Harmant, R. Laurent, P. Verdu, G. Laval, A. Boland, R. Olaso, J.-F. Deleuze, F. Valentin, Y.-C. Ko, M. Jakobsson, A. Gessain, L. Excoffier, M. Stoneking, E. Patin, and L. Quintana-Murci 2021. Genomic insights into population history and biological adaptation in Oceania. *Nature* 592:583–589. doi.org/10.1038/s41586-021-03236-5.

Clarkson, C., Z. Jacobs, B. Marwick, R. Fullagar, L. Wallis, M. Smith, R.G. Roberts, E. Hayes, K. Lowe, X. Carah, S.A. Florin, J. McNeil, D. Cox, L.J. Arnold, Q. Hua, J. Huntley, H.E.A. Brand, T. Manne, A. Fairbairn, J. Shulmeister, L. Lyle, M. Salinas, M. Page, K. Connell, G. Park, K. Norman, T. Murphy, and C. Pardoe 2017. Human occupation of northern Australia by 65,000 years ago. *Nature* 547:306–310. doi.org/10.1038/nature22968.

Dannemann, M. and J. Kelso 2017. The contribution of Neanderthals to phenotypic variation in modern humans. *American Journal of Human Genetics* 101:578–589. doi.org/10.1016/j.ajhg.2017.09.010.

Détroit, F., A.S. Mijares, J. Corny, G. Daver, C. Zanolli, E. Dizon, E. Robles, R. Grün, and P.J. Piper 2019. A new species of *Homo* from the Late Pleistocene of the Philippines. *Nature* 568:181–186. doi.org/10.1038/s41586-019-1067-9.

Fu, Q., H. Li, P. Moorjani, F. Jay, S.M. Slepchenko, A.A. Bondarev, P.L.F. Johnson, A. Aximu-Petri, K. Prüfer, C. de Filippo, M. Meyer, N. Zwyns, D.C. Salazar-García, Y.V. Kuzmin, S.G. Keates, P.A. Kosintsev, D.I. Razhev, M.P. Richards, N.V. Peristov, M. Lachmann, K. Douka, T.F.G. Higham, M. Slatkin, J.-J. Hublin, D. Reich, J. Kelso, T. Bence Viola, and S. Pääbo 2014. Genome sequence of a 45,000-year-old modern human from western Siberia. *Nature* 514:445–449. doi.org/10.1038/nature13810.

Gittelman, R.M., J.G. Schraiber, B. Vernot, C. Mikacenic, M.M. Wurfel, and J.M. Akey 2016. Archaic hominin admixture facilitated adaptation to Out-of-Africa environments. *Current Biology* 26:3375–3382. doi.org/10.1016/j.cub.2016.10.041.

Gokcumen, O. 2020. Archaic hominin introgression into modern human genomes. *American Journal of Physical Anthropology* 171:60–73. doi.org/10.1002/ajpa.23951.

Gouy, A., and L. Excoffier 2020. Polygenic patterns of adaptive introgression in modern humans are mainly shaped by response to pathogens. *Molecular Biology and Evolution* 37:1420–1433. doi.org/10.1093/molbev/msz306.

Green, R.E., J. Krause, A.W. Briggs, T. Maricic, U. Stenzel, M. Kircher, N. Patterson, H. Li, W. Zhai, M. Hsi-Yang Fritz, N.F. Hansen, E.Y. Durand, A.-S. Malaspinas, J.D. Jensen, T. Marques-Bonet, C. Alkan, K. Prüfer, M. Meyer, H.A. Burbano, J.M. Good, R. Schultz, A. Aximu-Petri, A. Butthof, B. Höber, B. Höffner, M. Siegemund, A. Weihmann, C. Nusbaum, E.S. Lander, C. Russ, N. Novod, J. Affourtit, M. Egholm, C. Verna, P. Rudan, D. Brajkovic, Ž. Kucan, I. Gušic, V.B. Doronichev, L.V. Golovanova, C. Lalueza-Fox, M. de la Rasilla, J. Fortea, A. Rosas, R.W. Schmitz, P.L.F. Johnson, E.E. Eichler, D. Falush, E. Birney, J.C. Mullikin, M. Slatkin, R. Nielsen, J. Kelso, M. Lachmann, D. Reich, and S. Pääbo 2010. A draft sequence of the Neandertal genome. *Science* 328:710–722. doi.org/10.1126/science.1188021.

Hudjashov, G., T. Kivisild, P.A. Underhill, P. Endicott, J.J. Sanchez, A.A. Lin, P. Shen, P. Oefner, C. Renfrew, R. Villems, and P. Forster 2007. Revealing the prehistoric settlement of Australia by Y chromosome and mtDNA analysis. *Proceedings of the National Academy of Sciences* 104:8726–8730. doi.org/10.1073/pnas.0702928104.

Hudjashov, G., T.M. Karafet, D.J. Lawson, S. Downey, O. Savina, H. Sudoyo, J.S. Lansing, M.F. Hammer, and M.P. Cox 2017. Complex patterns of admixture across the Indonesian archipelago. *Molecular Biology and Evolution* 34:2439–2452. doi.org/10.1093/molbev/msx196.

Jacobs, G.S., G. Hudjashov, L. Saag, P. Kusuma, C.C. Darusallam, D.J. Lawson, M. Mondal, L. Pagani, F.-X. Ricaut, M. Stoneking, M. Metspalu, H. Sudoyo, J.S. Lansing, and M.P. Cox 2019. Multiple deeply divergent Denisovan ancestries in Papuans. *Cell* 177:1010–1021.e32. doi.org/10.1016/j.cell.2019.02.035.

Karmin M., R. Flores, L. Saag, G. Hudjashov, N. Brucato, C. Crenna-Darusallam, M. Larena, P.L. Endicott, M. Jakobsson, J.S. Lansing, H. Sudoyo, M. Leavesley, M. Metspalu, F.-X. Ricaut, and M.P. Cox 2022. Episodes of diversification and isolation in Island Southeast Asian and Near Oceanian male lineages. *Molecular Biology and Evolution* 39(3):msac045. doi.org/10.1093/molbev/msac045.

Kealy, S., J. Louys, and S. O'Connor 2018. Least-cost pathway models indicate northern human dispersal from Sunda to Sahul. *Journal of Human Evolution* 125:59–70. doi.org/10.1016/j.jhevol.2018.10.003.

Kirk, R.L. 1992. Population origins in Papua New Guinea—A human biological overview. In R. Attenborough and M.P. Alpers (eds), *Human biology in Papua New Guinea: The small cosmos*, pp. 172–197. Research monographs on human population biology 10. Clarendon Press, Oxford. doi.org/10.1093/oso/9780198575146.003.0008.

Larena, M., J. McKenna, F. Sanchez-Quinto, C. Bernhardsson, C. Ebeo, R. Reyes, O. Casel, J.-Y. Huang, K. Pullupul Hagada, D. Guilay, J. Reyes, F. Pir Allian, V. Mori, L.S. Azarcon, A. Manera, C. Terando, L. Jamero Jr, G. Sireg, R. Manginsay-Tremedal, M. Shiela Labos, R.D. Vilar, A. Latiph, R. Linsahay Saway, E. Marte, P. Magbanua, A. Morales, I. Java, R. Reveche, B. Barrios, E. Burton, J.C. Salon, Ma. J. Tuazon Kels, A. Albano, R.B. Cruz-Angeles, E. Molanida, L. Granehäll, M. Vicente, H. Edlund, J.-H. Loo, J. Trejaut, S.Y.W. Ho, L. Reid, K. Lambeck, H. Malmström, C. Schlebusch, P. Endicott, and M. Jakobsson 2021. Philippine Ayta possess the highest level of Denisovan ancestry in the world. *Current Biology* 31:4219–4230. doi.org/10.1016/j.cub.2021.07.022.

Malaspinas, A.-S., M.C. Westaway, C. Muller, V.C. Sousa, O. Lao, I. Alves, A. Bergström, G. Athanasiadis, J.Y. Cheng, J.E. Crawford, T.H. Heupink, E. Macholdt, S. Peischl, S. Rasmussen, S. Schiffels, S. Subramanian, J.L. Wright, A. Albrechtsen, C. Barbieri, I. Dupanloup, A. Eriksson, A. Margaryan, I. Moltke, I. Pugach, T.S. Korneliussen, I.P. Levkivskyi, J.V. Moreno-Mayar, S. Ni, F. Racimo, M. Sikora, Y. Xue, F.A. Aghakhanian, N. Brucato, S. Brunak, P.F. Campos, W. Clark, S. Ellingvåg, G. Fourmile, P. Gerbault, D. Injie, G. Koki, M. Leavesley, B. Logan, A. Lynch, E.A. Matisoo-Smith, P.J. McAllister, A.J. Mentzer, M. Metspalu, A.B. Migliano, L. Murgha, M.E. Phipps, W. Pomat, D. Reynolds, F.-X. Ricaut, P. Siba, M.G. Thomas, T. Wales, C. Ma'run Wall, S.J. Oppenheimer, C. Tyler-Smith, R. Durbin, J. Dortch, A. Manica, M.H. Schierup, R.A. Foley, M. Mirazón Lahr, C. Bowern, J.D. Wall, T. Mailund, M. Stoneking, R. Nielsen, M.S. Sandhu, L. Excoffier, D.M. Lambert, and E. Willerslev 2016. A genomic history of Aboriginal Australia. *Nature* 538:207–214. doi.org/10.1038/nature18299.

Mallick, S., H. Li, M. Lipson, M. Gymrek, F. Racimo, M. Zhao, N. Chennagiri, S. Nordenfelt, A. Tandon, P. Skoglund, I. Lazaridis, S. Sankararaman, Q. Fu, N. Rohland, G. Renaud, Y. Erlich, T. Willems, C. Gallo, J.P. Spence, Y.S. Song, G. Poletti, F. Balloux, G. van Driem, P. de Knijff, I. Gallego Romero, A.R. Jha, D.M. Behar, C.M. Bravi, C. Capelli, T. Hervig, A. Moreno-Estrada, O.L. Posukh, E. Balanovska, O. Balanovsky, S. Karachanak-Yankova, H. Sahakyan, D. Toncheva, L. Yepiskoposyan, C. Tyler-Smith, Y. Xue, M. Syafiq Abdullah, A. Ruiz-Linares, C.M. Beall, A. Di Rienzo, C. Jeong, E.B. Starikovskaya, E. Metspalu, J. Parik, R. Villems, B.M. Henn, U. Hodoglugil, R. Mahley, A. Sajantila, G. Stamatoyannopoulos, J.T.S. Wee, R. Khusainova, E. Khusnutdinova, S. Litvinov, G. Ayodo, D. Comas, M.F. Hammer, T. Kivisild, W. Klitz, C.A. Winkler, D. Labuda, M. Bamshad, L.B. Jorde, S.A. Tishkoff, W.S. Watkins, M. Metspalu, S. Dryomov, R. Sukernik, L. Singh, K. Thangaraj, S. Pääbo, J. Kelso, N. Patterson, and D. Reich 2016. The Simons Genome Diversity Project: 300 genomes from 142 diverse populations. *Nature* 538:201–206. doi.org/10.1038/nature18964.

Massilani, D., L. Skov, M. Hajdinjak, B. Gunchinsuren, D. Tseveendorj, S. Yi, J. Lee, S. Nagel, B. Nickel, T. Devièse, T. Higham, M. Meyer, J. Kelso, B.M. Peter, and S. Pääbo 2020. Denisovan ancestry and population history of early East Asians. *Science* 370:579–583. doi.org/10.1126/science.abc1166.

Mathieson, I., 2020. Human adaptation over the past 40,000 years. *Current Opinion in Genetics and Development* 62: 97–104. doi.org/10.1016/j.gde.2020.06.003.

McEvoy, B.P., J.M. Lind, E.T. Wang, R.K. Moyzis, P.M. Visscher, S.M. van Holst Pellekaan, and A.N. Wilton 2010. Whole-genome genetic diversity in a sample of Australians with deep Aboriginal ancestry. *American Journal of Human Genetics* 87:297–305. doi.org/10.1016/j.ajhg.2010.07.008.

Mendez, F.L., J.C. Watkins, and M.F. Hammer. 2012. A haplotype at *STAT2* introgressed from neanderthals and serves as a candidate of positive selection in Papua New Guinea. *American Journal of Human Genetics* 91:265–274. doi.org/10.1016/j.ajhg.2012.06.015.

Meyer, M., M. Kircher, M.-T. Gansauge, H. Li, F. Racimo, S. Mallick, J.G. Schraiber, F. Jay, K. Prüfer, C. de Filippo, P.H. Sudmant, C. Alkan, Q. Fu, R. Do, N. Rohland, A. Tandon, M. Siebauer, R.E. Green, K. Bryc, A.W. Briggs, U. Stenzel, J. Dabney, J. Shendure, J. Kitzman, M.F. Hammer, M.V. Shunkov, A.P. Derevianko, N. Patterson, A.M. Andrés, E.E. Eichler, M. Slatkin, D. Reich, J. Kelso, and S. Pääbo 2012. A high-coverage genome sequence from an archaic Denisovan individual. *Science* 338: 222–226. doi.org/10.1126/science.1224344.

Mondal, M., J. Bertranpetit, and O. Lao 2019. Approximate Bayesian computation with deep learning supports a third archaic introgression in Asia and Oceania. *Nature Communications* 10:246. doi.org/10.1038/s41467-018-08089-7.

Moodley, Y., B. Linz, Y. Yamaoka, H.M. Windsor, S. Breurec, J.-Y. Wu, A. Maady, S. Bernhöft, J.-M. Thiberge, S. Phuanukoonnon, G. Jobb, P. Siba, D.Y. Graham, B.J. Marshall, and M. Achtman 2009. The peopling of the Pacific from a bacterial perspective. *Science* 323:527–530. doi.org/10.1126/science.1166083.

Natri, H.M., K.S. Bobowik, P. Kusuma, C.C. Darusallam, G.S. Jacobs, G. Hudjashov, J.S. Lansing, H. Sudoyo, N.E. Banovich, M.P. Cox, and I. Gallego Romero 2020. Genome-wide DNA methylation and gene expression patterns reflect genetic ancestry and environmental differences across the Indonesian archipelago. *PLoS Genetics* 16:e1008749. doi.org/10.1371/journal.pgen.1008749.

Natri, H.M., G. Hudjashov, G.S. Jacobs, P. Kusuma, L. Saag, C.C. Darusallam, M. Metspalu, H. Sudoyo, M.P. Cox, I. Gallego Romero, and N.E. Banovich 2022. Genetic architecture of gene regulation in Indonesian populations identifies QTLs associated with global and local ancestries. *American Journal of Human Genetics* 109:50–65. doi.org/10.1016/j.ajhg.2021.11.017.

O'Connell, J.F., J. Allen, M.A.J. Williams, A.N. Williams, C.S.M. Turney, N.A. Spooner, J. Kamminga, G. Brown, and A. Cooper 2018. When did *Homo sapiens* first reach Southeast Asia and Sahul? *Proceedings of the National Academy of Sciences* 115(34):8482–8490. doi.org/10.1073/pnas.1808385115.

Pagani, L., D.J. Lawson, E. Jagoda, A. Mörseburg, A. Eriksson, M. Mitt, F. Clemente, G. Hudjashov, M. DeGiorgio, L. Saag, J.D. Wall, A. Cardona, R. Mägi, M.A. Wilson Sayres, S. Kaewert, C. Inchley, C.L. Scheib, M. Järve, M. Karmin, G.S. Jacobs, T. Antao, F. Mircea Iliescu, A. Kushniarevich, Q. Ayub, C. Tyler-Smith, Y. Xue, B. Yunusbayev, K. Tambets, C. Basu Mallick, L. Saag, E. Pocheshkhova, G. Andriadze, C. Muller, M.C. Westaway, D.M. Lambert, G. Zoraqi, S. Turdikulova, D. Dalimova, Z. Sabitov, G.N.N. Sultana, J. Lachance, S. Tishkoff, K. Momynaliev, J. Isakova, L.D. Damba, M. Gubina, P. Nymadawa, I. Evseeva, L. Atramentova, O. Utevska, F.-X. Ricaut, N. Brucato, H. Sudoyo, T. Letellier, M.P. Cox, N.A. Barashkov, V. Škaro, L. Mulahasanovic', D. Primorac, H. Sahakyan, M. Mormina, C.A. Eichstaedt, D.V. Lichman, S. Abdullah, G. Chaubey, J.T.S. Wee, E. Mihailov, A. Karunas, S. Litvinov, R. Khusainova, N. Ekomasova, V. Akhmetova, I. Khidiyatova, D. Marjanović, L. Yepiskoposyan, D.M. Behar, E. Balanovska, A. Metspalu, M. Derenko, B. Malyarchuk, M. Voevoda, S.A. Fedorova, L.P. Osipova, M. Mirazón Lahr, P. Gerbault, M. Leavesley, A. Bamberg Migliano, M. Petraglia, O. Balanovsky, E.K. Khusnutdinova, E. Metspalu, M.G. Thomas, A. Manica, R. Nielsen, R. Villems, E. Willerslev, T. Kivisild, and M. Metspalu 2016. Genomic analyses inform on migration events during the peopling of Eurasia. *Nature* 538:238–242. doi.org/10.1038/nature19792.

Palstra, F.P. and D.J. Fraser 2012. Effective/census population size ratio estimation: a compendium and appraisal. *Ecology and Evolution* 2:2357–2365. doi.org/10.1002/ece3.329.

Pawley, A. and H. Hammarström 2017. The Trans New Guinea Family. In B. Palmer (ed.), *The languages and linguistics of the New Guinea area: A comprehensive guide,* pp. 21–196. De Gruyter Mouton, Berlin; Boston. doi.org/10.1515/9783110295252-002.

Pedro, N., N. Brucato, V. Fernandes, M. André, L. Saag, W. Pomat, C. Besse, A. Boland, J.-F. Deleuze, C. Clarkson, H. Sudoyo, M. Metspalu, M. Stoneking, M.P. Cox, M. Leavesley, L. Pereira, and F.-X. Ricaut 2020. Papuan mitochondrial genomes and the settlement of Sahul. *Journal of Human Genetics* 65:875–887. doi.org/10.1038/s10038-020-0781-3.

Posth, C., K. Nägele, H. Colleran, F. Valentin, S. Bedford, K.W. Kami, R. Shing, H. Buckley, R. Kinaston, M. Walworth, G.R. Clark, C. Reepmeyer, J. Flexner, T. Maric, J. Moser, J. Gresky, L. Kiko, K.J. Robson, K. Auckland, S.J. Oppenheimer, A.V.S. Hill, A.J. Mentzer, J. Zech, F. Petchey, P. Roberts, C. Jeong, R.D. Gray, J. Krause, and A. Powell 2018. Language continuity despite population replacement in Remote Oceania. *Nature Ecology and Evolution* 2:731–740. doi.org/10.1038/s41559-018-0498-2.

Pugach, I., F. Delfin, E. Gunnarsdóttir, M. Kayser, and M. Stoneking 2013. Genome-wide data substantiate Holocene gene flow from India to Australia. *Proceedings of the National Academy of Sciences* 110:1803–1808. doi.org/10.1073/pnas.1211927110.

Purnomo, G.A., K.J. Mitchell, S. O'Connor, S. Kealy, L. Taufik, S. Schiller, A. Rohrlach, A. Cooper, B. Llamas, H. Sudoyo, J.C. Teixeira, and R. Tobler 2021. Mitogenomes reveal two major influxes of Papuan ancestry across Wallacea following the Last Glacial Maximum and Austronesian contact. *Genes* 12:965. doi.org/10.3390/genes12070965.

Rasmussen, M., X. Guo, Y. Wang, K.E. Lohmueller, S. Rasmussen, A. Albrechtsen, L. Skotte, S. Lindgreen, M. Metspalu, T. Jombart, T. Kivisild, W. Zhai, A. Eriksson, A. Manica, L. Orlando, F.M. De La Vega, S. Tridico, E. Metspalu, K. Nielsen, M.C. Ávila-Arcos, J. Víctor Moreno-Mayar, C. Muller, J. Dortch, M.T.P. Gilbert, O. Lund, A. Wesolowska, M. Karmin, L.A. Weinert, B. Wang, J. Li, S. Tai, F. Xiao, T. Hanihara, G. van Driem, A.R. Jha, F.-X. Ricaut, P. de Knijff, A.B. Migliano, I. Gallego Romero, K. Kristiansen, D.M. Lambert, S. Brunak, P. Forster, B. Brinkmann, O. Nehlich, M. Bunce, M. Richards, R. Gupta, C.D. Bustamante, A. Krogh, R.A. Foley, M.M. Lahr, F. Balloux, T. Sicheritz-Pontén, R. Villems, R. Nielsen, J. Wang , and E. Willerslev 2011. An Aboriginal Australian genome reveals separate human dispersals into Asia. *Science* 334:94–98. doi.org/10.1126/science.1211177.

Reich, D., R.E. Green, M. Kircher, J. Krause, N. Patterson, E.Y. Durand, B. Viola, A. W. Briggs, U. Stenzel, P.L.F. Johnson, T. Maricic, J.M. Good, T. Marques-Bonet, C. Alkan, Q. Fu, S. Mallick, H. Li, M. Meyer, E.E. Eichler, M. Stoneking, M. Richards, S. Talamo, M.V. Shunkov, A.P. Derevianko, J.-J. Hublin, J. Kelso, M. Slatkin, and S. Pääbo 2010. Genetic history of an archaic hominin group from Denisova Cave in Siberia. *Nature* 468:1053–1060. doi.org/10.1038/nature09710.

Reich, D., N. Patterson, M. Kircher, F. Delfin, M.R. Nandineni, I. Pugach, A. Min-Shan Ko, Y.-C. Ko, T.A. Jinam, M.E. Phipps, N. Saitou, A. Wollstein, M. Kayser, S. Pääbo, and M. Stoneking 2011. Denisova admixture and the first modern human dispersals into Southeast Asia and Oceania. *American Journal of Human Genetics* 89:516–528. doi.org/10.1016/j.ajhg.2011.09.005.

Rizal, Y., K.E. Westaway, Y. Zaim, G.D. van den Bergh, E.A. Bettis III, M.J. Morwood, O.F. Huffman, R. Grün, R. Joannes-Boyau, R.M. Bailey, Sidarto, M.C. Westaway, I. Kurniawan, M.W. Moore, M. Storey, F. Aziz, Suminto, J.-x. Zhao, Aswan, M.E. Sipola, R. Larick, J.-P. Zonneveld, R. Scott, S. Putt, and R. L. Ciochon 2020. Last appearance of *Homo erectus* at Ngandong, Java, 117,000–108,000 years ago. *Nature* 577:381–385. doi.org/10.1038/s41586-019-1863-2.

Sankararaman, S., S. Mallick, N. Patterson, and D. Reich 2016. The combined landscape of Denisovan and Neanderthal ancestry in present-day humans. *Current Biology* 26:1241–1247. doi.org/10.1016/j.cub.2016.03.037.

Sawyer, S., G. Renaud, B. Viola, J.-J. Hublin, M.-T. Gansauge, M.V. Shunkov, A.P. Derevianko, K. Prüfer, J. Kelso, and S. Pääbo 2015. Nuclear and mitochondrial DNA sequences from two Denisovan individuals. *Proceedings of the National Academy of Sciences* 112:15696–15700. doi.org/10.1073/pnas.1519905112.

Schiffels, S. and R. Durbin 2014. Inferring human population size and separation history from multiple genome sequences. *Nature Genetics* 46:919–925. doi.org/10.1038/ng.3015.

Simonti, C.N., B. Vernot, L. Bastarache, E. Bottinger, D.S. Carrell, R.L. Chisholm, D.R. Crosslin, S.J. Hebbring, G.P. Jarvik, I.J. Kullo, R. Li, J. Pathak, M.D. Ritchie, D.M. Roden, S.S. Verma, G. Tromp, J.D. Prato, W.S. Bush, J.M. Akey, J.C. Denny, and J.A. Capra 2016. The phenotypic legacy of admixture between modern humans and Neandertals. *Science* 351:737–741. doi.org/10.1126/science.aad2149.

Skoglund, P., C. Posth, K. Sirak, M. Spriggs, F. Valentin, S. Bedford, G.R. Clark, C. Reepmeyer, F. Petchey, D. Fernandes, Q. Fu, E. Harney, M. Lipson, S. Mallick, M. Novak, N. Rohland, K. Stewardson, S. Abdullah, M.P. Cox, F.R. Friedlaender, J.S. Friedlaender, T. Kivisild, G. Koki, P. Kusuma, D.A. Merriwether, F.-X. Ricaut, J.T.S. Wee, N. Patterson, J. Krause, R. Pinhasi, and D. Reich 2016. Genomic insights into the peopling of the Southwest Pacific. *Nature* 538:510–513. doi.org/10.1038/nature19844.

Slatkin, M. and F. Racimo 2016. Ancient DNA and human history. *Proceedings of the National Academy of Sciences* 113:6380–6387. doi.org/10.1073/pnas.1524306113.

Slon, V., B. Viola, G. Renaud, M.-T. Gansauge, S. Benazzi, S. Sawyer, J.-J. Hublin, M.V. Shunkov, A.P. Derevianko, J. Kelso, K. Prüfer, M. Meyer, and S. Pääbo 2017. A fourth Denisovan individual. *Science Advances* 3(7):e1700186. doi.org/10.1126/sciadv.1700186.

Slon, V., F. Mafessoni, B. Vernot, C. de Filippo, S. Grote, B. Viola, M. Hajdinjak, S. Peyrégne, S. Nagel, S. Brown, K. Douka, T. Higham, M.B. Kozlikin, M.V. Shunkov, A.P. Derevianko, J. Kelso, M. Meyer, K. Prüfer, and S. Pääbo 2018. The genome of the offspring of a Neanderthal mother and a Denisovan father. *Nature* 561:113–116. doi.org/10.1038/s41586-018-0455-x.

Steinrücken, M., J. Kamm, J.P. Spence, and Y.S. Song 2019. Inference of complex population histories using whole-genome sequences from multiple populations. *Proceedings of the National Academy of Sciences* 116:17115–17120. doi.org/10.1073/pnas.1905060116.

Summerhayes, G.R., M. Leavesley, A. Fairbairn, H. Mandui, J. Field, A. Ford, and R. Fullagar 2010. Human adaptation and plant use in highland New Guinea 49,000 to 44,000 years ago. *Science* 330(6000):78–81. doi.org/10.1126/science.1193130.

Sutikna, T., M.W. Tocheri, M.J. Morwood, E. Wahyu Saptomo, Jatmiko, R. Due Awe, S. Wasisto, K.E. Westaway, M. Aubert, B. Li, J.-x. Zhao, M. Storey, B.V. Alloway, M.W. Morley, H.J.M. Meijer, G.D. van den Bergh, R. Grün, A. Dosseto, A. Brumm, W.L. Jungers, and R.G. Roberts 2016. Revised stratigraphy and chronology for *Homo floresiensis* at Liang Bua in Indonesia. *Nature* 532:366–369. doi.org/10.1038/nature17179.

Swisher, C.C., W.J. Rink, S.C. Antón, H.P. Schwarcz, G.H. Curtis, A. Suprijo, and Widiasmoro 1996. Latest *Homo erectus* of Java: Potential contemporaneity with *Homo sapiens* in Southeast Asia. *Science* 274:1870–1874. doi.org/10.1126/science.274.5294.1870.

Taufik, L., J.C. Teixeira, B. Llamas, H. Sudoyo, R. Tobler, and G.A. Purnomo 2022. Human genetic research in Wallacea and Sahul: Recent findings and future prospects. *Genes* 13:2373. doi.org/10.3390/genes13122373.

Teixeira, J.C. and A. Cooper 2019. Using hominin introgression to trace modern human dispersals. *Proceedings of the National Academy of Sciences* 116:15327–15332. doi.org/10.1073/pnas.1904824116.

Teixeira, J.C., G.S. Jacobs, C. Stringer, J. Tuke, G. Hudjashov, G.A. Purnomo, H. Sudoyo, M.P. Cox, R. Tobler, C.S.M. Turney, A. Cooper, and K.M. Helgen 2021. Widespread Denisovan ancestry in Island Southeast Asia but no evidence of substantial super-archaic hominin admixture. *Nature Ecology & Evolution* 5:616–624. doi.org/10.1038/s41559-021-01408-0.

Telis, N., R. Aguilar, and K. Harris 2020. Selection against archaic hominin genetic variation in regulatory regions. *Nature Ecology and Evolution* 4:1558–1566. doi.org/10.1038/s41559-020-01284-0.

Terhorst, J., J.A. Kamm, and Y.S. Song 2017. Robust and scalable inference of population history from hundreds of unphased whole genomes. *Nature Genetics* 49:303–309. doi.org/10.1038/ng.3748.

The 1000 Genomes Project Consortium 2015. A global reference for human genetic variation. *Nature.* 526:68–74. doi.org/10.1038/nature15393.

Vernot, B., S. Tucci, J. Kelso, J.G. Schraiber, A.B. Wolf, R.M. Gittelman, M. Dannemann, S. Grote, R.C. McCoy, H. Norton, L.B. Scheinfeldt, D.A. Merriwether, G. Koki, J.S. Friedlaender, J. Wakefield, S. Pääbo , and J.M. Akey 2016. Excavating Neandertal and Denisovan DNA from the genomes of Melanesian individuals. *Science* 352:235–239. doi.org/10.1126/science.aad9416.

Vespasiani, D.M., G.S. Jacobs, L.E. Cook, N. Brucato, M. Leavesley, C. Kinipi, F.-X. Ricaut, M.P. Cox, and I. Gallego Romero 2022. Denisovan introgression has shaped the immune system of present-day Papuans. *PLoS Genetics* 18:e1010470. doi.org/10.1371/journal.pgen.1010470.

Wall, J.D. 2017. Inferring human demographic histories of non-African populations from patterns of allele sharing. *American Journal of Human Genetics* 100:766–772. doi.org/10.1016/j.ajhg.2017.04.002.

Wall, J.D., M.A. Yang, F. Jay, S.K. Kim, E.Y. Durand, L.S. Stevison, C. Gignoux, A. Woerner, M.F. Hammer, and M. Slatkin 2013. Higher levels of Neanderthal ancestry in East Asians than in Europeans. *Genetics* 194:199–209. doi.org/10.1534/genetics.112.148213.

Wang, K., I. Mathieson, J. O'Connell, and S. Schiffels 2020. Tracking human population structure through time from whole genome sequences. *PLoS Genetics* 16:e1008552. doi.org/10.1371/journal.pgen.1008552.

Wohns, A.W., Y. Wong, B. Jeffrey, A. Akbari, S. Mallick, R. Pinhasi, N. Patterson, D. Reich, J. Kelleher, and G. McVean 2022. A unified genealogy of modern and ancient genomes. *Science* 375:eabi8264. doi.org/10.1126/science.abi8264.

Wollstein, A., O. Lao, C. Becker, S. Brauer, R.J. Trent, P. Nürnberg, M. Stoneking, and M. Kayse 2010. Demographic history of Oceania inferred from genome-wide data. *Current Biology* 20:1983–1992. doi.org/10.1016/j.cub.2010.10.040.

Xu, S., I. Pugach, M. Stoneking, M. Kayser, L. Jin, and the HUGO Pan-Asian SNP Consortium 2012. Genetic dating indicates that the Asian–Papuan admixture through Eastern Indonesia corresponds to the Austronesian expansion. *Proceedings of the National Academy of Sciences* 109:4574–4579. doi.org/10.1073/pnas.1118892109.

Yang, M.A., X. Gao, C. Theunert, H. Tong, A. Aximu-Petri, B. Nickel, M. Slatkin, M. Meyer, S. Pääbo, J. Kelso, and Q. Fu 2017. 40,000-year-old individual from Asia provides insight into early population structure in Eurasia. *Current Biology* 27:3202–3208.e9. doi.org/10.1016/j.cub.2017.09.030.

Yuen, L.K.W., M. Littlejohn, S. Duchêne, R. Edwards, S. Bukulatjpi, P. Binks, K. Jackson, J. Davies, J.S. Davis, S.Y.C. Tong, and S. Locarnini 2019. Tracing ancient human migrations into Sahul using Hepatitis B virus genomes. *Molecular Biology and Evolution* 36:942–954. doi.org/10.1093/molbev/msz021.

Zammit, N.W., O.M. Siggs, P.E. Gray, K. Horikawa, D.B. Langley, S.N. Walters, S.R. Daley, C. Loetsch, J. Warren, J.Y. Yap, D. Cultrone, A. Russell, E.K. Malle, J.E. Villanueva, M.J. Cowley, V. Gayevskiy, M.E. Dinger, R. Brink, D. Zahra, G. Chaudhri, G. Karupiah, B. Whittle, C. Roots, E. Bertram, M. Yamada, Y. Jeelall, A. Enders, B.E. Clifton, P.D. Mabbitt, C.J. Jackson, S.R. Watson, C.N. Jenne, L.L. Lanier, T. Wiltshire, M.H. Spitzer, G.P. Nolan, F. Schmitz, A. Aderem, B.T. Porebski, A.M. Buckle, D.W. Abbott, J.B. Ziegler, M.E. Craig, P. Benitez-Aguirre, J. Teo, S.G. Tangye, C. King, M. Wong, M.P. Cox, W. Phung, J. Tang, W. Sandoval, I.E. Wertz, D. Christ, C.C. Goodnow, and S.T. Grey 2019. Denisovan, modern human and mouse *TNFAIP3* alleles tune A20 phosphorylation and immunity. *Nature Immunology* 20:1299–1310. doi.org/10.1038/s41590-019-0492-0.

Zeberg, H. and S. Pääbo 2020. The major genetic risk factor for severe COVID-19 is inherited from Neanderthals. *Nature* 587:610–612. doi.org/10.1038/s41586-020-2818-3.

5

Deep histories in New Guinea: Insights from human genetics on local demography and social processes

Pradiptajati Kusuma, Guy Jacobs, and Robert Attenborough[1]

Abstract

In this, the second of three linked chapters oriented to human biology—specifically, genetics and genomics—we selectively review and synthesise aspects of research in the discipline that shed light on the deep histories of New Guinea's indigenous inhabitants. At >800,000 km², the island is accounted the world's second-largest, and its physiographical and ecological variety is extreme; its human inhabitants are likewise diverse in culture and language, and far from uniform in biology. Here we focus on this human biological variation and its implications for New Guinea's deep histories. Since these histories predate modern boundaries, we draw on and integrate data from across the island. As with the broader canvas of our first chapter, so also here, the literature available for our review—conditioned as it is by extraordinary technical advances in genetics and genomics—is very much more informative than it would have been 30 years ago. We begin by looking, cautiously, through the lens of the ethnographic and linguistic present. We then review existing literature selectively, and with an emphasis on research since 1990. This takes us from the era of classical polymorphisms, through uniparental markers, to the present genomic age. We explore the interrelationships of selected language groups across western and eastern New Guinea and between highlands and lowlands in some fresh analyses, exploring the implications for 'split times' between groups, their population size dynamics over time, and their environmentally and socially structured demographic processes. We also discuss the still unresolved extent to which genetic and linguistic variation may mirror each other. As with our first chapter, we close by contemplating the prospect of many deep histories yet to be told in, and about, this extraordinarily diverse yet still under-researched island.

---

1   All authors contributed equally.

Abstrak

Dalam bab ini, yang merupakan seri kedua dari tiga bab yang saling terkait mengenai genetika, kami secara selektif mengulas sejarah demografi populasi Papua dari sudut pandang penelitian genetika manusia. Wilayah Papua memiliki luas lebih dari 800.000 km², yang merupakan pulau terbesar kedua di dunia. Keragaman geografis dan ekologi di Papua sangat tinggi. Budaya dan bahasa pada populasi-populasi manusia di Papua pun sangat beragam, baik itu di Papua dan Papua Nugini. Namun, sejarah demografi di Papua lebih tua dibanding batas-batas geopolitik modern, sehingga kami mengumpulkan, mengintegrasikan, dan menganalisi data genetika populasi di Papua Barat dan Papua Nugini. Kami memulai bab ini melalui lensa etnografis dan linguistik populasi modern. Kemudian kami melanjutkan dengan mengulas literatur penelitian genetika sejak tahun 1990-an, yaitu era polimorfisme klasik penanda uniparental, hingga penelitian genomik modern saat ini. Kami mengeksplorasi hubungan antara kelompok populasi di Papua bagian barat dan timur, serta populasi yang tinggal di dataran tinggi dan rendah. Kami melakukan analisis baru untuk i) mengestimasi "waktu pemisahan" antarkelompok populasi, ii) mengamati dinamika ukuran populasi dari waktu ke waktu, dan iii) menyimpulkan proses sejarah demografis terstruktur berdasarkan kondisi geografis dan sosial. Kami juga mendiskusikan sejauh mana variasi genetik dan linguistik dapat menyimpulkan hal yang sama terkait keragaman genetik populasi di Papua. Di akhir bab ini, kami menutup dengan merenungkan tentang banyaknya informasi sejarah populasi Papua yang belum dapat kami ulas karena keterbatasan data akibat sedikitnya publikasi hasil penelitian terkait populasi Papua, terutama di Papua Barat.

Introduction

The island of New Guinea is often discussed as a hub of cultural diversity, as most clearly represented by the many hundreds of local languages spoken by the population. The question of how this variation arose and is maintained remains open—a complex and fascinating function of ecological, social, and historical factors. While ethnographic work can inform our understanding of cultural behaviour in recent and perhaps more ancient times, and while close study of available archaeological data and linguistics can inform on deeper histories, the genetic record offers different and distinctive insights into the human past. The local patterns of human genetic variation reflect an intricate, island-wide family tree, describing histories of movements, interactions, and population dynamics. In this chapter, we introduce genetic data in their ecological, historical, and ethnographic context, and ask what can be and has been learned about social and historical processes within the island of New Guinea. In keeping with this volume, we focus wherever possible on West New Guinea and its peoples, specifically the mainland of western New Guinea (WNG). In many cases, however, the take-home messages from genetics and genomics about New Guinea's deep past are not closely location-specific. The territorial divisions imposed on New Guinea in the nineteenth century by the Netherlands, Germany, and Britain have thrown long shadows over subsequent developments, including subsequent research (see Gaffney and Tolla, Chapter 2, this volume), but are not fundamentally relevant to understanding the deep past. With this in mind, we shall not hesitate to include evidence from investigations conducted in Papua New Guinea (PNG), particularly the mainland of eastern New Guinea (ENG), as relevant to our story.

From ethnographic present to deep past

All the evidence on which this chapter is based derives from what we loosely call the 'ethnographic present' (hereafter, the present). It originates from biological samples (from living people) and contextual data collected in the past six decades or so—the blink of an eye, relative to evolutionary time depth. It is because human population genetic change is relatively slow that we can make inferences about the deep past. But to what extent can these inferences be guided by present-day contexts?

New Guinea's environments range from small islands, peninsulas and coasts, inland lowland swamps, lakes, and riverine systems to highlands fringes and true highlands—cloudy, seasonally rainy in some parts, perennially rainy in others. This diversity of tropical environment and climate types is broadly similar across west and east, though in the west the mountains are higher and the swamps larger (Beehler 2007; Gressitt 1982). In the east the indigenous human population is, on recent estimates, perhaps two to three times larger. As the early hunter-gatherer inhabitants populated the island, they entered a range of ecozones affecting their diversity, adaptation, and differentiation. These environments have changed over the tens of millennia under consideration, in large part associated with changing climate. The land connection with Australia (see Jacobs et al., this volume), at its most extensive around 21,000 years ago, was finally inundated around 8000 years ago; an inland sea in the Sepik–Ramu basin was at its maximum 7000–6000 years ago and did not become a floodplain until around 4000 years ago; and parts of the Digul–Fly southern lowlands were inundated, perhaps peaking around 6000 years ago (Swadling and Hide 2005). The people themselves brought environmental impacts, including through fire, faunal change, and plant manipulation (Hope and Haberle 2005), with root crops cultivated from around 10,000 years ago (Denham et al. 2017a). South American sweet potatoes were introduced only circa AD 1700 (Ballard et al. 2005; Bayliss-Smith et al. 2017), but as a staple crop have acquired great nutritional and demographic significance. On occasion there would have been earthquakes, tsunamis, and volcanic eruptions (Swadling and Hide 2005). Plainly, New Guinea as we see it today is not exactly as its first human arrivals would have seen it. That said, there is much in today's physiography, tropical climate, and phenology that would be broadly comparable, particularly at lower elevations (see Attenborough et al., this volume).

By the time European outsiders began to describe New Guinea's people and their societies, especially from the mid-nineteenth to mid-twentieth centuries, most parts of the island were at least sparsely populated. There were hunter-gatherers, hunter-horticulturalists, and fishers, as well as fully committed horticulturalists; the carbohydrate staples of many people were root crops or sago; aquatic resources were important to many coastal and riverine groups (Roscoe 2002, 2005). There was also great variety in sociocultural and sociodemographic systems.

An extensive demographic survey of WNG in 1961, under Dutch administration, gave quantitative evidence of the small scale of traditional social life: 97 per cent of settlements had fewer than 500 inhabitants; 77 per cent of the population lived in such settlements, 50 per cent in settlements of 75–300 inhabitants (Groenewegen and van den Kaa 1964, Tables IX and X). Mean settlement size overall was 159 (Table VIII). No comparably extensive survey of ENG exists for the period, but Forge (1972) assembled data from a variety of sources suggesting settlement size in the 70–300 range, with a mean of 170.

In both datasets, an ecological influence is suggested by smaller settlements in interior, tuber-dependent settings than in ones by coasts, rivers, and lakes (Groenewegen and van den Kaa 1964, Table X). Forge also noted the consistent egalitarianism (lack of status ascribed at birth, other than gender roles) in tuber-dependent societies, which he linked to pressures of resource ecology and warfare but also to social dynamics becoming less manageable with the increasing size of egalitarian[2] settlements.

New Guinea communities, as they were in former times, are sometimes described as isolated from one another, but that is an exaggeration. Trade routes provide evidence of long-term connections between communities (Hughes 1977). Probably more important for gene flow are indications of marital mobility. While New Guinea societies vary greatly, many of them might traditionally have recognised themselves in the statement by Mae Enga people of highland ENG: 'We marry the people we fight!' (Meggitt 1965, 101). Enmities, even in pre-colonial times, did not entirely prevent marriage or movement across communities and even language boundaries (often made more permeable by bilingualism). Littlewood (1972) estimated migration rates between 'village complexes' in the Eastern Highlands of PNG, which vary widely, mostly between 4 per cent and 52 per cent, and gene flow between language groups between 1 per cent and 24 per cent, concluding that 'demographic clustering' and linguistic barriers slowed but did not block gene flow. Other quantitative studies in PNG, among the Bundi people of the highlands fringes of Madang Province (Malcolm et al. 1971), in two widely separated rural lowland populations (Serjeantson et al. 1983), and on Karkar Island (Boyce et al. 1978; Harrison et al. 1974), present a similar picture. Geographic displacement and the marriage of 'strangers' are also common among the Korowai, although many of those marriages are interlocal only by a kilometre or so (Stasch 2009, 175 ff.; R. Stasch pers. comm.). Thus, high inter-community migration rates traditionally linked community to community in New Guinea. These rates greatly exceed the (random) migration required to limit genetic divergence between populations, albeit at varying spatial scales (Wright 1931). Certainly 'semi-isolated' would be a better description than 'isolated'.

Despite great diversity in many respects, then, New Guinea's traditional communities in the ethnographic present, both west and east, present certain fairly consistent social and demographic features: small scale and egalitarian social dynamics in most cases, semi-isolation but with some inter-community gene flow. We would be rash to project this ethnographic present too confidently back into a millennia-long deep past (see Hiscock [2007] for Australia). But we agree with Roscoe (2005) that it should be a question of how rather than whether we draw on the ethnographic present for insights into the deep past.

Diversity within New Guinea

The New Guinea literature, across many disciplines, stresses the internal diversity for which the island and its inhabitants are famous. The paradigm case is linguistic diversity. At the level of language families, New Guinea is six times more diverse than pre-Columbian Europe (Pawley 2005), with some 850 indigenous languages, grouped into at least 18 language families plus several isolates (Pawley and Hammarström 2017). Language group membership (rather than, say, location or polity) has been found to be a sound and analytically coherent basis for defining specific New Guinea groups for genetic characterisation (e.g. Harley 2006).

---

2   In the sense followed by Forge, see above; see also discussion by Moreau (2020).

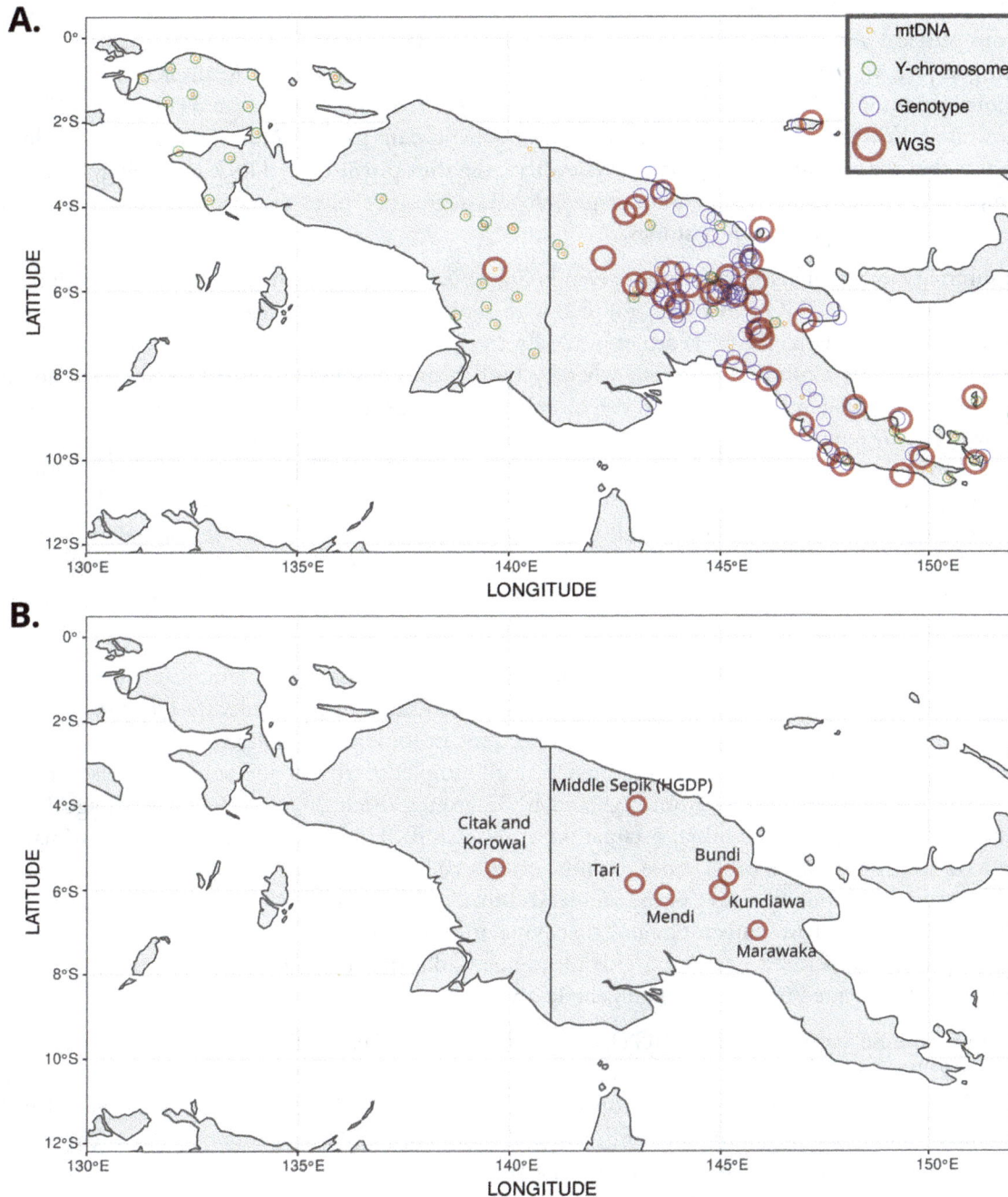

Figure 5.1: Summary of available modern data.

Notes: (A) Location of published genetic data from the island of New Guinea, excluding classical genetic markers and some lower resolution data (e.g. ENG mtDNA restriction mapping from Stoneking et al. 1990; ENG Y-chromosome SNPs [single-nucleotide polymorphisms] and autosomal STRs [short tandem repeats] from Harley 2006). In contrast to ENG, WNG diversity is hardly represented in genotype or whole-genome sequencing (WGS) datasets, but has been studied more extensively using uniparental markers (mtDNA and Y-chromosome). (B) Map of WNG and ENG whole-genome samples analysed in this chapter.

Sources: Tommaseo-Ponzetta et al. (2002); Kayser et al. (2003); Harley (2006); Mona et al. (2007); Tommaseo-Ponzetta et al. (2007); van Oven et al. (2014); Mallick et al. (2016); Malaspinas et al. (2016); Bergström et al. (2017); Jacobs et al. (2019); Pedro et al. (2020); Purnomo et al. (2021); Brucato et al. (2021), with some nearby sites merged for clarity.

Outsiders' research interest in the peoples of WNG dates back many decades, with a trajectory from physical anthropology to classical genetic markers (blood groups including human leukocyte antigen [HLA], red cell enzymes, serum proteins) to modern sequencing. Examples of significant contributions include those of Nijenhuis and colleagues (1966) and Gajdusek and colleagues (1978), as well as Keats (1977) who combined classical genetic data from WNG and ENG to produce results that are still intelligible today. As elsewhere, the shift provided by DNA technology through uniparental, genotyping, and genome sequencing have greatly refined our scope for inferring deep regional and local population histories.

A summary of available modern data is given in Figure 5.1A. Analyses confirm: (i) the closely linked genetic history of WNG and ENG, coupled with some genetic divergence on the Y-chromosome especially (Kayser et al. 2003; Pedro et al. 2020; Purnomo et al. 2021; Tommaseo-Ponzetta et al. 2013, 2002); (ii) a composite pattern whereby both Y-chromosome and mtDNA (mitochondrial DNA) haplotypes tend to be of local origin rather than imported from Asia, with the former also showing vastly reduced population diversity (Kayser et al. [2003]; also see below); (iii) a signal, albeit varied, of more Asian mtDNA haplotypes in the linguistically mixed (Austronesian and Papuan[3] language families) Bird's Head region of WNG (Tommaseo-Ponzetta et al. 2007) as well as some coastal regions of ENG (Bergström et al. 2017; Redd et al. 1995; Redd and Stoneking 1999); (iv) signals of Y-chromosome expansions hypothetically associated with the Trans–New Guinean language family and agriculture in the highlands, despite very few Asian Y-chromosome haplogroups (Mona et al. 2007).

Genotype data are available for ENG (Bergström et al. 2017) and have been remarkably informative. Analyses reveal the signal of Austronesian expansion–associated Asian admixture into lowland and especially coastal ENG groups (reaching >50 per cent in some communities). Genetic split times between populations have also been estimated, with sampled northern and southern coastal ENG populations dated as splitting from highland ENG groups about 20,000–10,000 years ago (thus significantly postdating the initial occupation of the island). Highland ENG groups are estimated to have split from one another more recently, often <10,000 years ago, during a period associated with increasing population sizes in the highlands broadly synchronous with, and possibly linked to, the emergence of plant cultivation; and that population divergence is generally high and strongly geographically structured between highland groups, indicating that populations were sufficiently small and fragmented to generate high genetic divergence.

Whole-genome data from both WNG (Jacobs et al. 2019; Natri et al. 2022) and ENG (Bergström et al. 2017; Bergström et al. 2020; Brucato et al. 2021; Malaspinas et al. 2016) are available. Especially detailed analyses have recently been contributed by Brucato and colleagues (2021), who placed southeast coastal samples at the root of ENG genetic diversity, potentially identifying ancient plains now under the Arafura Sea as an early entry point. The internal clustering of samples suggests that settlement of the highlands followed multiple waves, from ENG's eastern foothills to its eastern highlands and from its southern lowlands to its western highlands, potentially along major rivers. This model may apply to the dispersals to the highlands of New Guinea as a whole, though at present no samples from highland WNG are available to confirm this hypothesis. After a period of dynamism, significant isolation between highland and lowland populations is inferred between 20,000 and 3000 years ago—driving the divergence observed in this and other datasets.

---

3   Although other chapters in this book use 'Papuan' to denote indigenous inhabitants of West New Guinea, conforming to local usage, we reserve 'Papuan' for this linguistic sense (see also Arnold, this volume), elaborated below. For this reason, we use 'New Guinean' to refer to the people of the whole island, whereas some genetic publications use 'Papuan'.

While the limited WNG data (from the Korowai and Citak, of the inland lowland riverine plains, not far from the centre of the island) appear genetically connected to southern lowland populations of ENG (Brucato et al. 2021), no detailed analysis focusing on their relationships is presently available. We therefore here extend our analysis (building on Jacobs et al., this volume) to assess the degree and timescales of population differentiation among these WNG groups, and their level of inbreeding relative to the highland ENG (group/language: Bundi/Gende, Mendi/Angal, Marawaka/Angan, Tari/Hela, and Kundiawa/Simbu) genomes (Malaspinas et al. 2016), and the inferred Middle Sepik samples from the Human Genome Diversity Panel (HGDP) (Bergström et al. 2017; Mallick et al. 2016) (see Figure 5.1B).

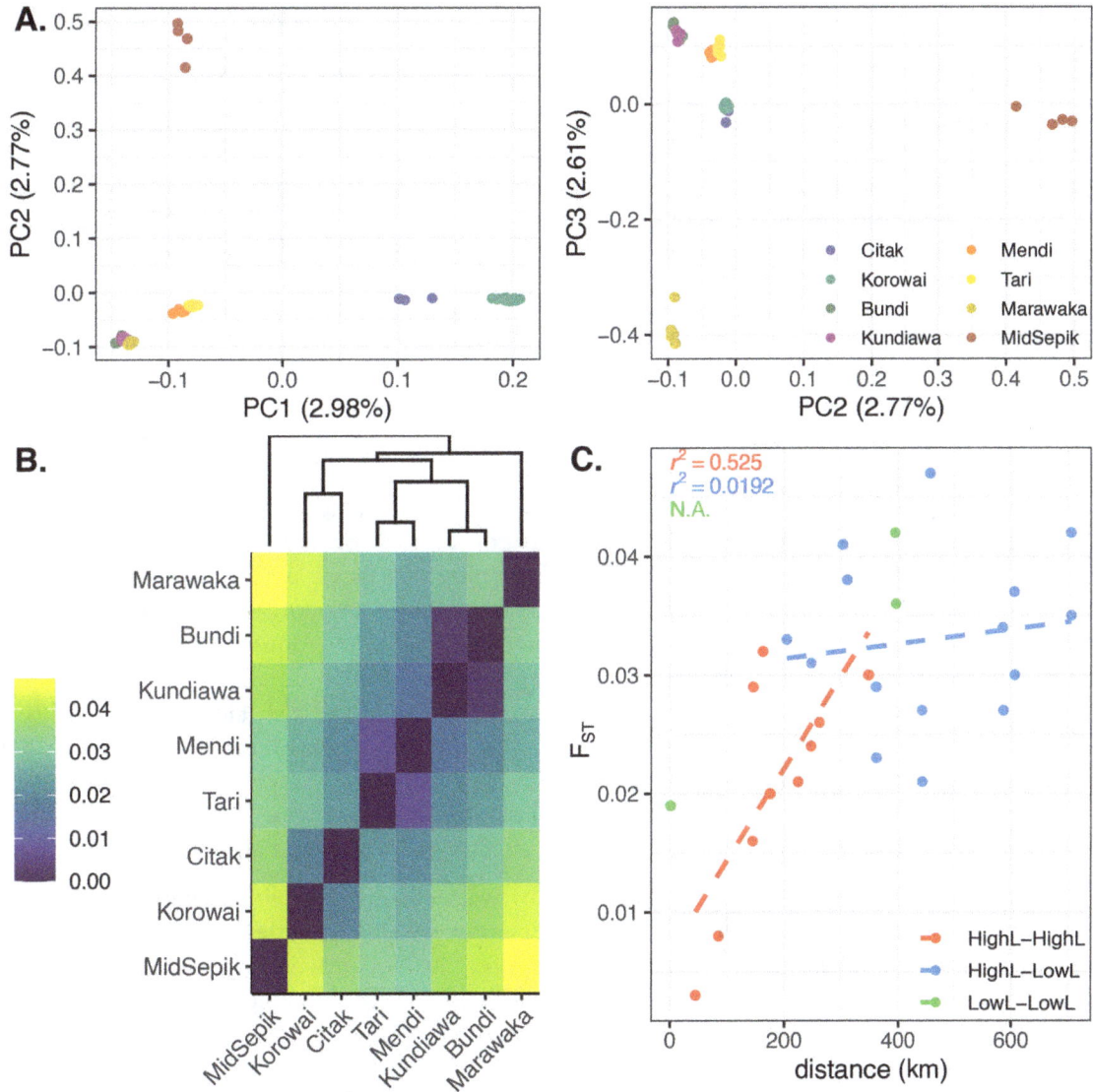

Figure 5.2: New Guinea population analysis.

Notes: (A) Principal Component Analysis (PCA) of New Guinea individuals. (B) Hierarchical clustering (UPGMA method) of pairwise F_{ST} values. (C) Correlation between interpopulation geographical distance and F_{ST} values.

Source: Authors' analysis of data from Malaspinas et al. (2016), Mallick et al. (2016), Jacobs et al. (2019), and Natri et al. (2022).

Despite the homogeneity of these New Guinean populations relative to non–New Guineans and their lack of modern East Asian ancestry (see Jacobs et al. this volume, Figure 4.2A, B), a clear differentiation is detected by Principal Component Analysis (PCA; see Figure 5.2A, B). PC1 distinguishes the lowland WNG groups from all ENG groups. PC2—explaining almost as much variance as PC1, 2.77 per cent compared to 2.98 per cent—differentiates the Middle Sepik group from the highland ENG and the WNG groups, while PC3 (2.61 per cent) separates Marawaka from other ENG groups. This picture—of certain ENG communities showing a similar degree of genetic divergence as the WNG–ENG comparison—is mirrored in hierarchical clustering based on genetic distance (F_{ST}), which identifies Middle Sepik, Marawaka, and the WNG populations as deeply branching groups (Figure 5.2B). Neighbouring populations also cluster (Korowai and Citak are from samples generally <5 km apart; Bundi and Kundiawa are from Simbu and Madang Provinces, ~45 km apart; Mendi and Tari are from Hela/Southern Highlands provinces, ~85 km apart), and we qualitatively replicate analyses from Bergström and colleagues (2017) showing a stronger isolation-by-distance signal among highland groups than between highland/lowland pairs and suggestive of environmentally structured demographic processes (Figure 5.2C). The WNG groups, Korowai and Citak, separate on the PCA and show relatively high F_{ST} differentiation, suggesting that relevant social practices in the swampy lowlands of WNG (which may have included taboos on Korowai men marrying Citak women, but not the reverse; as well as raiding upriver, particularly by the Citak [R. Stasch pers. comm.]) can be as much of a barrier for gene flow as the topography and customs of the highlands.

To further investigate recent shared ancestry, we analyse chunks of the genome that are 'identical by descent' (IBD) between pairs of individuals (Figure 5.3A–D). Chunk length is expressed in centi-Morgans (cM), and longer shared chunks reflect more recent common ancestors while shorter chunks reflect ancient shared ancestry (Thompson 2013). In a European context, blocks longer than 2 cM rarely reflect common ancestors older than 4000 years ago (Ralph and Coop 2013), and blocks longer than 4 cM tend to arise from ancestors 1000–500 years ago; these estimates should be interpreted qualitatively because IBD chunk length depends on the detailed demography of populations. Using RefinedIBD (Browning and Browning 2013), we detect the most numerous and longest shared IBD blocks between individuals from the same population (Figure 5.3C, D). Geographic proximity plays a major role in IBD sharing across populations, and we observe long-shared IBD chunks between nearby population pairs (Figure 5.3D), in agreement with the F_{ST} analysis (Figure 5.2B). All communities share shorter IBD chunks (>2 cM, Figure 5.3A), with the Middle Sepik more isolated at the 4 cM threshold. Overall, IBD chunks indicate that populations share some recent ancestors (here, likely <4000 years ago, and often <1000 years ago) as might be expected given an ethnographic context of 'semi-isolation' at local scales. For a population-scale inference capturing group split dates we turn again to SMC++ (Terhorst et al. 2017).

To sample clusters across the F_{ST} tree (Figure 5.2B) we focus on the split times and population dynamics of the Korowai, Kundiawa, and Mendi samples. SMC++ infers a split between the highland ENG groups (Kundiawa and Mendi) at around 10,700 years ago, in general agreement with genotype-based inference (Bergström et al. 2017). Given the proximity of these populations (~145 km), the split date offers some context to interpreting the steep gradient of F_{ST} with geographic distance among highland ENG populations (Figure 5.2C). The date corresponds approximately with the origins of cultivation in the highlands (Denham et al. 2017a), and with climatic amelioration (see Attenborough et al., this volume). The split between the WNG lowland Korowai and highland ENG groups is inferred as ~21,000 years ago, broadly comparable to previously inferred splits between the Middle Sepik group and some ENG highland populations (Bergström et al. 2017). We detect population growth beginning ~50,000 years ago and extending through both population splits and over the beginnings of cultivation before stabilising, generally consistent with the regional reconstructions (see Jacobs et al., this volume, Figure 4.2C–E).

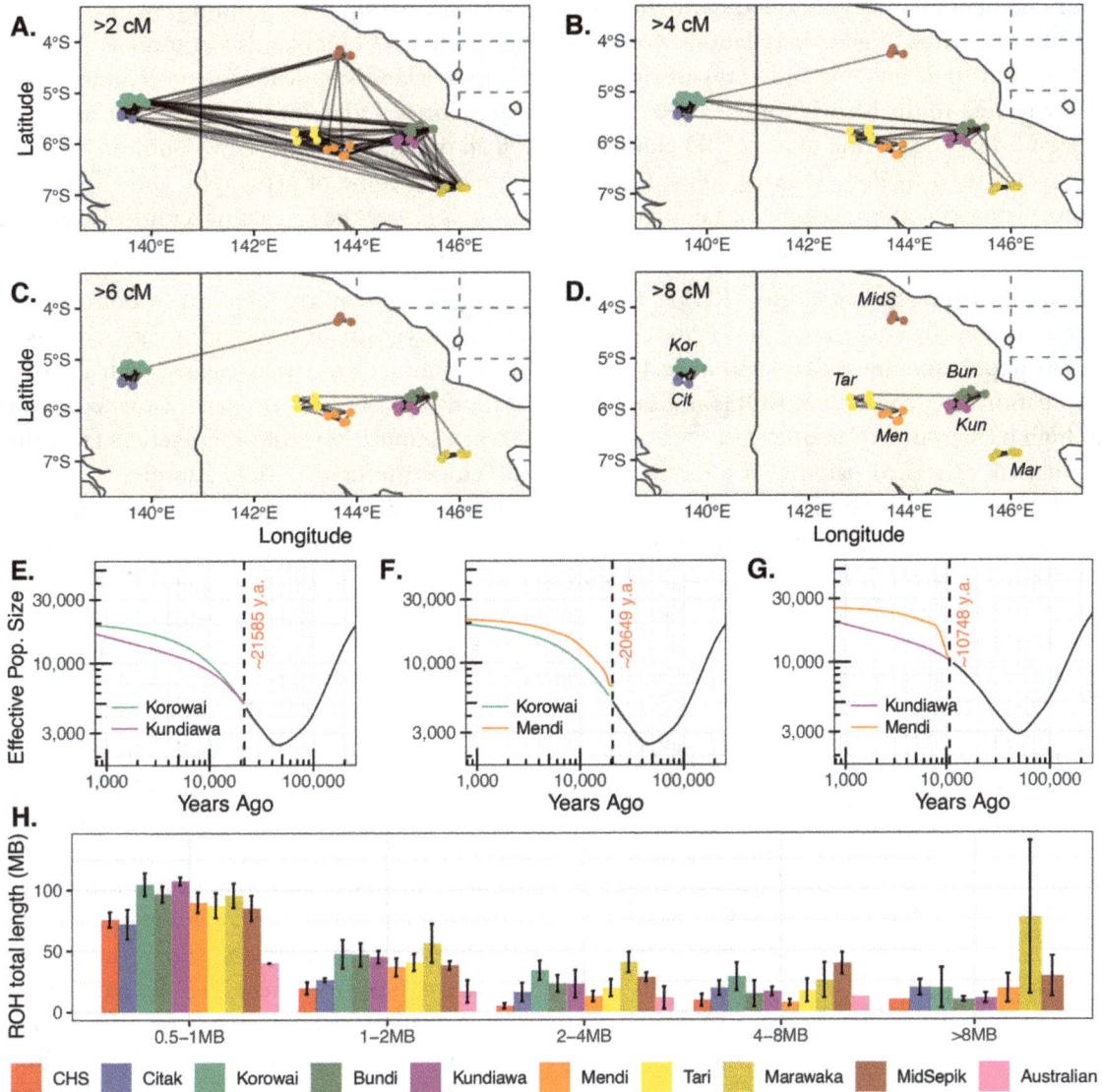

Figure 5.3: New Guinean genome analysis.

Notes: (A–D) Pairwise interindividual identical-by-descent (IBD) analysis, with >2 cM, >4 cM, >6 cM, and >8 cM thresholds, respectively, as inferred by RefinedIBD. The circles represent individuals in approximate locations as the positions are jittered to avoid overlap. (E–G) Effective population size dynamics and population split times intra-New Guineans, between Korowai and Kundiawa, Korowai and Mendi, and Kundiawa and Mendi, respectively, as inferred by SMC++. (H) Average total length of runs of homozygosity (with standard deviation bars) in different ROH fragment thresholds. CHS (Han Chinese, 1000 Genomes Project Consortium 2015) and two Indigenous Australian samples (Mallick et al. 2016) are included for qualitative comparison.

Source: Authors' analysis of data from Malaspinas et al. (2016), Mallick et al. (2016), Jacobs et al. (2019), and Natri et al. (2022).

Our demographic analyses, then, show considerable structure within New Guinea (Figure 5.2A, B), reflecting a signal of genetic isolation-by-distance within the ENG highlands but more ambiguous patterns in highland–lowland comparisons and lowland–lowland population pairs (Figure 5.2C), likely related to the island's complex geography. This has not excluded limited migration, as clearly evidenced by the sharing of long IBD chunks between all population pairs. New Guinean diversity is characterised by deep internal splits, likely a combined outcome of geography and subsistence history, moderated by generally local migration. We now consider the impact of semi-isolation and marriage practices more broadly on internal community genetic diversity.

We used runs of homozygosity (ROHs; chunks of the genome that are identical in both parents due to recent shared ancestry, and detected as a run of homozygosity in the child) to assess levels of recent population inbreeding/drift in each group. Greater homozygosity is associated with a smaller population size; and longer ROHs indicate closer relationships between the parents, whether due to high background relatedness between all individuals in a population, cultural practices favouring endogamy or related parents, or a recent bottleneck (Pemberton et al. 2012). Samples from both WNG and ENG have higher total ROH than an outbred comparison group, the Han Chinese (CHS, Figure 5.3H), in support of previous work (Kirin et al. 2010). Excess ROH was particularly apparent for larger 1–8 megabase (MB) fragments, indicating generally high genetic relatedness between parents. The longest ROHs are observed in the Marawaka group, suggestive of greater isolation or founder events. There is no clear distinction between New Guinean populations from the highlands and lowlands, or from ENG and WNG.

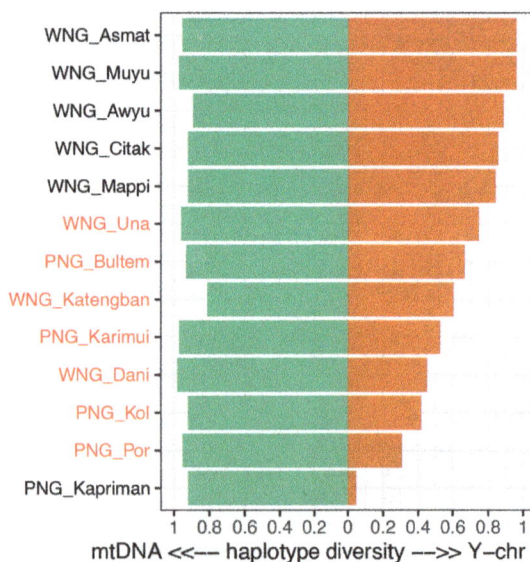

Figure 5.4: Y-chromosome (orange) and mtDNA (green) haplotype diversity of highland (red) and lowland (black) groups in WNG and ENG.

Source: Data from Harley (2006) and Tommaseo-Ponzetta et al. (2002).

A more striking pattern is apparent in the mtDNA and Y-chromosome data, which are widely available from both WNG and ENG populations (Figure 5.4). These uniparental markers are inherited through the maternal and paternal lines, respectively, and hence show sex-biased demographic signatures that can be used to infer cultural practices such as patrilocality and matrilocality (Lansing et al. 2017; Oota et al. 2001; Seielstad et al. 1998). Results from WNG (Kayser et al. 2003; Tommaseo-Ponzetta et al. 2002) and ENG (Harley 2006) show a general pattern of consistently high mtDNA diversity coupled with similar or reduced Y-chromosome diversity within communities (Kayser et al. 2003). Such a signal can be explained by patrilocality (leading, for example, local men to share recent ancestry through the patriline but to have non-local and hence genetically more different mothers) and/or highly skewed reproductive success in males (Chung et al. 2019), whether due to polygyny or male-specific mortality caused by violence or warfare. All Papuan-speaking populations in New Guinea in the present are, broadly speaking, patrilocal. Furthermore, polygyny has historically been widely practised, if not overly commonly, in the region (Gardner and Weiner 1992); warfare has also been historically prevalent (Heider 1997). In general, such cultural practices will tend to increase local genetic drift on the Y-chromosome, reducing intragroup Y-chromosome diversity relative to mtDNA diversity and increasing Y-chromosome divergence between groups. As expected with excess drift affecting the Y-chromosome, low within-group diversity is coupled with high between-group divergence—Y-chromosome genetic distance between groups (calculated as R_{ST} value) correlates positively with geographical distance (measured in days of walking required to travel between groups); and, to no surprise, mtDNA genetic distance (calculated as F_{ST} value) does not show such a correlation (Mona et al. 2013).

Differing mutation rates between loci make direct diversity comparisons challenging. However, relatively speaking, within-group Y-chromosome diversity is especially low compared to mtDNA diversity in highland WNG and ENG populations, in contrast to WNG lowland groups. It is not clear whether this pattern holds for ENG as there is only one lowland sample—the highly patrilocal Kapriman (Kumagai 1998), located just south of the Sepik river, who have extremely low Y-chromosome diversity. When discussing the difference between highland and lowland WNG mtDNA and Y-chromosome diversity, Kayser and colleagues (2003) consider the impact of patrilocality, polygyny, and warfare. They also assess evidence for population expansion, potentially associated with cultivation in the highlands, from mtDNA and Y-chromosome diversity. The question is which of these histories or practices differ between lowland and highland groups, and the answer is not simple. For example, both lowland and highland groups are patrilocal. Both can be polygynous (Tommaseo-Ponzetta [1986] recorded 27 per cent of Citak men as living with multiple wives). Both have historically engaged in warfare, though we have no evidence as to the scale or interpopulation variation of resulting mortality. And while population expansion might be expected to be associated with extensive cultivation, as argued by Bergström and colleagues (2017), our analyses do not clearly distinguish the population size dynamics of the Korowai from the highland ENG Kundiawa and Mendi (Figure 5.3D–F). While it is possible that ancestral Korowai may have migrated from the highlands or elsewhere, as suggested for some other New Guinean peoples, there is no indication of that in Korowai oral histories (R. Stasch pers. comm.). Furthermore, Kayser and colleagues (2003) find complex signals, with statistical evidence of population expansion strongly impacting the Y-chromosome but less consistent for the mtDNA, and variously present in horticultural and sago-gathering groups. The signal, then, is intriguing, but unresolved.

From a genetics perspective, the interaction of processes, particularly population growth coupled with marriage practices, is important, with the potential for synergistic impacts on diversity (Chung et al. 2019). Imbalances between mtDNA and Y-chromosome divergence between communities can also be informative. Kayser and colleagues (2003) report sex biases in migration based on mtDNA and Y-chromosome diversity, arguing that migration from the highlands to the lowlands has tended to be male-biased, a point that could be enriched by demographic and ethnographic study.

Genetic and linguistic diversity

The relevance of New Guinea's astonishing and radical linguistic diversity goes beyond its convenience for identifying populations. It is echoed by diversity in broader cultural respects (for the west, see Gregerson 1997; Knauft 1993; Miedema and Reesink 2004; Strathern 1995; Szalay 1999; Weiner 1988). And the question arises whether linguistic and cultural diversity correlate with genetic diversity, and if so, what this may imply for deep population histories.

The enormously long time for which New Guinea has been populated is probably the most important factor permitting the development of inter-group diversity at all levels. Rates of language splitting known for Europe are more than sufficient to produce New Guinea's linguistic diversity (Foley 1986, 9). Difficult, often rugged terrain, as well as suspicion of neighbours, may have played parts in maintaining diversity of all kinds among groups; as may the role of language as a badge of identity. At a genetic level, mutation, the strong drift characteristic of small communities, and potentially natural selection (see Attenborough et al., this volume) will have accentuated inter-group diversity, though marital mobility will have moderated it.

At a regional scale, Serjeantson and colleagues (1983) investigated the relationships between linguistic difference (quantified lexicostatistically), genetic difference (derived from classical genetic polymorphisms), and linear geographic distance in one sub-province of Madang Province, PNG. They found that genetic diversity was more dependent on distance than on language cognates. Lee and colleagues (2010), analysing mitochondrial DNA, also inferred language barriers to gene flow in ENG to be weak. But at a broader scale, Harley (Harley 2006; Harley et al. 2005), analysing Y-chromosome diversity among 32 non-contiguously distributed ENG populations, found the diversity of short tandem repeats on the Y-chromosome (Y-STR) to be distributed almost language-group-specifically; mtDNA haplotype diversity much less so.

In New Guinea, language groups and language families vary greatly in number of speakers and territorial distribution. Might the distributional disparities be partly explicable through a process like that postulated by Bellwood (2001): a past expansion of dominant groups, driven in some cases by an agricultural demography, taking their linguistic and genetic heritages with them? Local linguistic affiliations can change without expansive migration, facilitated by bi- and multilingualism (Foley 1986, 29–30), but Bellwood's argument is intended to apply on a large geographical scale and to whole language families.

One Papuan language family, Trans–New Guinea (TNG), has a geographical distribution much greater than any other, extending across much of the interior and some coastal areas (Pawley and Hammarström 2017). The Kuk archaeological site in the Wahgi valley, ENG highlands, the classical location for evidence for early, independently innovated, New Guinea plant cultivation, lies in a now TNG-speaking area—somewhere one could plausibly imagine as central to a TNG diffusion. Denham and colleagues (2017a) put the first phase of cultivation at Kuk 10,000 years ago. Pawley (1998, 684–685) had earlier pointed out that most TNG subgroups are centred in the highlands, and estimated that their diversity is consistent with dispersal across the highlands 'at least 5000 years ago and possibly considerably earlier'. Might tuber cultivation practices be 'the cultural advantage that allowed TNG speakers to spread over a large part of New Guinea' (Attenborough 2010; Pawley 2005, 1998, 684)? Might this involve the movement of people as well as the dispersal of language families, crops, and cultivation practices? Mona and colleagues (2007) viewed most Y-chromosome haplotypes as local in origin but identified two as 'suggestive markers for the TNG expansion', proposing that genetic diversity 'intersect[s] with' (p 2546) the TNG hypothesis.

Meanwhile, Bergström and colleagues (2017) find that TNG-speaking highlanders are more genetically similar to Sepik–Ramu-speaking northern lowlanders than to TNG-speaking southern lowlanders, implying that profound linguistic divergence does not necessarily translate to more extreme genetic divergence. Nonetheless, they find support for demographic expansion among TNG language family–speaking populations over the last 10,000 years consistent with an agricultural expansion. Consistent with this, stone mortars and pestles associated with past or present taro cultivation, dated between 8000 and 3000 years ago, have a wide distribution in New Guinea, especially in the highlands, suggestive of extensive exchange networks (Swadling 2005; Swadling

2019). Similarly, major developments in highlands crop cultivation were unambiguously underway by 8000–4000 years ago, including at Kuk (Phase 2, 7000–6500 years ago: Denham et al. 2017b) and still more so at Waim, Jimi valley (5000–4000 years ago), where there are strong signs of demographic and sociocultural changes of the kind classically associated with 'Neolithic' transitions elsewhere in the world (Shaw et al. 2020). But it is early days yet, when even the most thorough genetic studies are based on sampling only a handful of the island's 850 language groups.

A note on future directions: Local diversity

As discussed, the demographic history and social practices underlying rich human biological variation within New Guinea are complex. Much remains unknown—the detailed relationship between languages, technology, geography, and genes; the sociocultural processes structuring diversity; and the impacts of these interactions on local variation and health, for example.

Resolving these questions is not simple, and more genetic data are required, critically with the consent and close involvement of local communities, and with benefit-sharing as a guiding principle. The novelty of our analyses above shows how little is known about even genetic relationships between WNG and ENG populations. More detailed genomic surveys of WNG especially are sorely needed, particularly involving more people and communities, and with suitable engagement to understand relevant local questions and offer rich ethnographic, phenotypic, and health insights. A focus on some key regions could especially help address long-standing anthropological questions (for example, the highland fringes to revive and resolve discussions about highland/lowland demographic interactions; or the complex Bird's Head region or little-sampled south of WNG). Inevitably and appropriately, computational methods and simulation will form the major analytical tool for hypothesis testing and data interpretation. Ancient DNA analysis from nearby islands has proven extremely informative about ancient demography especially, and we expect similar developments in New Guinea—with the potential to address social questions when larger numbers of samples are available especially.

Finally, genetic data are extremely deficient if nothing is known about the individuals and communities providing it. Detailed linguistic and social information is critical in a region as diverse as New Guinea; or archaeological information in the case of ancient DNA. Biological annotation will further enable us to build hypotheses about the evolutionary and functional role of variation—important themes that we address in the coming chapter. In sum, despite some fascinating research, we have barely started to document genomic diversity in WNG, let alone profile ancient and more recent drivers of local variation. Progress requires care and time—community engagement to collect genetic data sensitively and ensure rich and representative involvement of New Guinean people, as well as national and international collaboration between geneticists, anthropologists, linguists, and archaeologists.

References

Attenborough, R. 2010. Genes, languages and agriculture in New Guinea population prehistory. In J. Bowden, N.P. Himmelmann, and M. Ross (eds), *A journey through Austronesian and Papuan linguistic and cultural space: Papers in honour of Andrew Pawley*, pp. 59–78. Pacific Linguistics. The Australian National University, Canberra.

Ballard, C., P. Brown, R.M. Bourke, and T. Harwood (eds.) 2005. *The sweet potato in Oceania: A reappraisal.* Ethnology Monographs 19; Oceania Monographs 56. University of Pittsburgh and University of Sydney.

Bayliss-Smith, T., J. Golson, and P. Hughes 2017. Phase 6: Impact of the sweet potato on swamp landuse, pig rearing and exchange relations. In J. Golson, T. Denham, P. Hughes, P. Swadling, and J. Muke (eds), *Ten thousand years of cultivation at Kuk Swamp in the Highlands of Papua New Guinea,* pp. 297–323. Terra Australis 46. ANU Press, Canberra. doi.org/10.22459/TA46.07.2017.16.

Beehler, B.M. 2007. Introduction to Papua. In B.M. Beehler and A.J. Marshall (eds), *The ecology of Indonesian Papua Part One.* The Ecology of Indonesia Series. Periplus Editions, Singapore.

Bellwood, P. 2001. Early agriculturalist population diasporas? Farming, languages, and genes. *Annual Review of Anthropology* 30:181–207. doi.org/10.1146/annurev.anthro.30.1.181.

Bergström, A., S.J. Oppenheimer, A.J. Mentzer, K. Auckland, K. Robson, R. Attenborough, M.P. Alpers, G. Koki, W. Pomat, P. Siba, Y. Xue, M.S. Sandhu, and C. Tyler-Smith 2017. A Neolithic expansion, but strong genetic structure, in the independent history of New Guinea. *Science* 357:1160–1163. doi.org/10.1126/science.aan3842.

Bergström, A., S.A. McCarthy, R. Hui, M.A. Almarri, Q. Ayub, P. Danecek, Y. Chen, S. Felkel, P. Hallast, J. Kamm, H. Blanché, J.-F. Deleuze, H. Cann, S. Mallick, D. Reich, M.S. Sandhu, P. Skoglund, A. Scally, Y. Xue, R. Durbin, and C. Tyler-Smith 2020. Insights into human genetic variation and population history from 929 diverse genomes. *Science* 367:eaay5012. doi.org/10.1126/science.aay5012.

Boyce, A.J., G.A. Harrison, C.M. Platt, R.W. Hornabrook, S. Serjeantson, R.L. Kirk, and P.B. Booth 1978. Migration and genetic diversity in an island population: Karkar, Papua New Guinea. *Proceedings of the Royal Society B: Biological Sciences* 202:269–295. doi.org/10.1098/rspb.1978.0067.

Browning, B.L. and S.R Browning 2013. Improving the accuracy and efficiency of identity-by-descent detection in population data. *Genetics* 194:459–471. doi.org/10.1534/genetics.113.150029.

Brucato, N., M. André, R. Tsang, L. Saag, J. Kariwiga, K. Sesuki, T. Beni, W. Pomat, J. Muke, V. Meyer, A. Boland, J.-F. Deleuze, H. Sudoyo, M. Mondal, L. Pagani, I. Gallego Romero, M. Metspalu, M.P. Cox, M. Leavesley, and F.-X. Ricaut 2021. Papua New Guinean genomes reveal the complex settlement of North Sahul. *Molecular Biology and Evolution* 38:5107–5121. doi.org/10.1093/molbev/msab238.

Chung, N.N., G.S. Jacobs, H. Sudoyo, S.G. Malik, L.Y. Chew, J.S. Lansing, and M.P. Cox 2019. Sex-linked genetic diversity originates from persistent sociocultural processes at microgeographic scales. *Royal Society Open Science* 6:190733. doi.org/10.1098/rsos.190733.

Denham, T., J. Golson, and P. Hughes 2017a. Phase 1: The case for 10,000-year-old agriculture at Kuk. In J. Golson, T. Denham, P. Hughes, P. Swadling, and J. Muke (eds), *Ten thousand years of cultivation at Kuk Swamp in the Highlands of Papua New Guinea*, pp. 187–200. Terra Australis 46. ANU Press, Canberra. doi.org/10.22459/TA46.07.2017.11.

Denham, T., J. Golson, and P. Hughes 2017b. Phase 2: Mounded cultivation during the mid Holocene. In J. Golson, T. Denham, P. Hughes, P. Swadling, and J. Muke (eds), *Ten thousand years of cultivation at Kuk Swamp in the Highlands of Papua New Guinea*, pp. 201–220. Terra Australis 46. ANU Press, Canberra. doi.org/10.22459/TA46.07.2017.12.

Foley, W.A. 1986. *The Papuan languages of New Guinea.* Cambridge University Press, Cambridge.

Forge, A. 1972. Normative factors in the settlement size of Neolithic cultivators (New Guinea). In P.J. Ucko, R. Tringham, and G.W. Dimbleby (eds), *Man, settlement and urbanism*, pp. 363–376. Duckworth, London.

Gajdusek, D.C., W.C. Leyshon, R.L. Kirk, N.M. Blake, B. Keats, and E.M. McDermid 1978. Genetic differentiation among populations in Western New Guinea. *American Journal of Physical Anthropology* 48:47–63. doi.org/10.1002/ajpa.1330480109.

Gardner, D.S. and J.F. Weiner 1992. Social anthropology in Papua New Guinea. In R. Attenborough and M.P. Alpers (eds), *Human biology in Papua New Guinea: The small cosmos*, pp. 119–135. Clarendon Press, Oxford. doi.org/10.1093/oso/9780198575146.003.0005.

Gregerson, M. 1997. *Kinship and social organization in Irian Jaya: A glimpse of seven systems.* Cendrawasih University and Summer Institute of Linguistics, Jayapura & Dallas.

Gressitt, J.L. 1982. General introduction. In J.L. Gressitt (ed.), *Biogeography and ecology of New Guinea: Part one–seven*, pp. 3–13. Monographiae Biologicae. Springer Netherlands, Dordrecht. doi.org/10.1007/978-94-009-8632-9_1.

Groenewegen, K. and D.J. van den Kaa 1964. *Resultaten van het Demografisch Onderzoek Westelijk Nieuw-Guinea: 1, Nieuw-Guinea als Gebied voor Demografische Onderzoekingen.* Government Printing and Publishing Office, The Hague.

Harley, N.L. 2006. Patterns of genetic variation in peoples of mainland Papua New Guinea: Studies of Y-chromosome, mitochondrial and autosomal genome diversity in Papuan-speaking populations. PhD thesis. College of Medicine and Health Sciences, The Australian National University, Canberra.

Harley, N.L., R. Attenborough, M.P. Alpers, C. Mgone, K. Bhatia, and S. Easteal 2005. The importance of social structure for patterns of human genetic diversity: Y-chromosome and mitochondrial genome variation in Papuan-speaking people of mainland Papua New Guinea. In A. Pawley, R. Attenborough, J. Golson, and R. Hide (eds), *Papuan pasts: Cultural, linguistic and biological histories of the Papuan-speaking peoples.* pp. 729–756. Pacific Linguistics 572. Research School of Pacific and Asian Studies, The Australian National University, Canberra.

Harrison, G.A., R.W. Hiorns and A.J. Boyce 1974. Movement, relatedness and the genetic structure of the population of Karkar Island. *Philosophical Transactions of the Royal Society B: Biological Sciences* 268:241–249. doi.org/10.1098/rstb.1974.0027.

Heider, K.G. 1997. *Grand Valley Dani: Peaceful warriors,* 3rd ed. Case Studies in Cultural Anthropology. Holt, Rinehart & Winston, New York.

Hiscock, P. 2007. *Archaeology of ancient Australia,* 1st ed. Routledge, London. doi.org/10.4324/9780203448359.

Hope, G.S. and S.G. Haberle 2005. The history of the human landscapes of New Guinea. In A. Pawley, R. Attenborough, J. Golson, and R. Hide (eds), *Papuan pasts: Cultural, linguistic and biological histories of the Papuan-speaking peoples,* pp. 541–554. Pacific Linguistics 572. Research School of Pacific and Asian Studies, The Australian National University, Canberra.

Hughes, I. 1977. *New Guinea Stone Age trade: The geography and ecology of traffic in the interior.* Terra Australis 3. Department of Prehistory, Research School of Pacific Studies, The Australian National University, Canberra.

Jacobs, G.S., G. Hudjashov, L. Saag, P. Kusuma, C.C. Darusallam, D.J. Lawson, M. Mondal, L. Pagani, F.-X. Ricaut, M. Stoneking, M. Metspalu, H. Sudoyo, J.S. Lansing, and M.P. Cox 2019. Multiple deeply divergent Denisovan ancestries in Papuans. *Cell* 177:1010–1021.e32. doi.org/10.1016/j.cell.2019.02.035.

Kayser, M., S. Brauer, G. Weiss, W. Schiefenhövel, P. Underhill, P. Shen, P. Oefner, M. Tommaseo-Ponzetta, and M. Stoneking 2003. Reduced Y-chromosome, but not mitochondrial DNA, diversity in human populations from West New Guinea. *American Journal of Human Genetics* 72:281–302. doi.org/10.1086/346065.

Keats, B. 1977. Genetic structure of the indigenous populations in Australia and New Guinea. *Journal of Human Evolution* 6:319–339. doi.org/10.1016/S0047-2484(77)80002-X.

Kirin, M., R. McQuillan, C.S. Franklin, H. Campbell, P.M. McKeigue, and J.F. Wilson 2010. Genomic runs of homozygosity record population history and consanguinity. *PLoS ONE* 5:e13996. doi.org/10.1371/journal.pone.0013996.

Knauft, B.M. 1993. *South Coast New Guinea cultures: History, comparison, dialectic.* Cambridge University Press, Cambridge. doi.org/10.1017/CBO9780511621741.

Kumagai, K. 1998. Migration and shifting settlement patterns among the Kapriman people of East Sepik Province, Papua New Guinea. In S. Yoshida and Y. Toyoda (eds), *Fringe area of Highlands in Papua New Guinea,* pp. 43–60. Senri Ethnological Studies. National Museum of Ethnology, Osaka.

Lansing, J.S., C. Abundo, G.S. Jacobs, E.G. Guillot, S. Thurner, S.S. Downey, L.Y. Chew, T. Bhattacharya, N.N. Chung, H. Sudoyo, and M.P. Cox 2017. Kinship structures create persistent channels for language transmission. *Proceedings of the National Academy of Sciences* 114:12910–12915. doi.org/10.1073/pnas.1706416114.

Lee, E.J., G. Koki, and D.A. Merriwether 2010. Characterization of population structure from the mitochondrial DNA vis-à-vis language and geography in Papua New Guinea. *American Journal of Physical Anthropology* 142:613–624. doi.org/10.1002/ajpa.21284.

Littlewood, R.A. 1972. *Physical anthropology of the Eastern Highlands of New Guinea.* Anthropological Studies in the Eastern Highlands of New Guinea. University of Washington Press, Seattle.

Malaspinas, A.-S., M.C. Westaway, C. Muller, V.C. Sousa, O. Lao, I. Alves, A. Bergström, G. Athanasiadis, J.Y. Cheng, J.E. Crawford, T.H. Heupink, E. Macholdt, S. Peischl, S. Rasmussen, S. Schiffels, S. Subramanian, J.L. Wright, A. Albrechtsen, C. Barbieri, I. Dupanloup, A. Eriksson, A. Margaryan, I. Moltke, I. Pugach, T.S. Korneliussen, I.P. Levkivskyi, J.V. Moreno-Mayar, S. Ni, F. Racimo, M. Sikora, Y. Xue, F.A. Aghakhanian, N. Brucato, S. Brunak, P.F. Campos, W. Clark, S. Ellingvåg, G. Fourmile, P. Gerbault, D. Injie, G. Koki, M. Leavesley, B. Logan, A. Lynch, E.A. Matisoo-Smith, P.J. McAllister, A.J. Mentzer, M. Metspalu, A.B. Migliano, L. Murgha, M.E. Phipps, W. Pomat, D. Reynolds, F.-X. Ricaut, P. Siba, M.G. Thomas, T. Wales, C. Ma'run Wall, S.J. Oppenheimer, C. Tyler-Smith, R. Durbin, J. Dortch, A. Manica, M.H. Schierup, R.A. Foley, M. Mirazón Lahr, C. Bowern, J.D. Wall, T. Mailund, M. Stoneking, R. Nielsen, M.S. Sandhu, L. Excoffier, D.M. Lambert, and E. Willerslev 2016. A genomic history of Aboriginal Australia. *Nature* 538:207–214. doi.org/10.1038/nature18299.

Malcolm, L.A., P.B. Booth, and L.L. Cavalli-Sforza 1971. Intermarriage patterns and blood group gene frequencies of the Bundi people of the New Guinea Highlands. *Human Biology* 43:187–199.

Mallick, S., H. Li, M. Lipson, M. Gymrek, F. Racimo, M. Zhao, N. Chennagiri, S. Nordenfelt, A. Tandon, P. Skoglund, I. Lazaridis, S. Sankararaman, Q. Fu, N. Rohland, G. Renaud, Y. Erlich, T. Willems, C. Gallo, J.P. Spence, Y.S. Song, G. Poletti, F. Balloux, G. van Driem, P. de Knijff, I. Gallego Romero, A.R. Jha, D.M. Behar, C.M. Bravi, C. Capelli, T. Hervig, A. Moreno-Estrada, O.L. Posukh, E. Balanovska, O. Balanovsky, S. Karachanak-Yankova, H. Sahakyan, D. Toncheva, L. Yepiskoposyan, C. Tyler-Smith, Y. Xue, M. Syafiq Abdullah, A. Ruiz-Linares, C.M. Beall, A. Di Rienzo, C. Jeong, E.B. Starikovskaya, E. Metspalu, J. Parik, R. Villems, B.M. Henn, U. Hodoglugil, R. Mahley, A. Sajantila, G. Stamatoyannopoulos, J.T.S. Wee, R. Khusainova, E. Khusnutdinova, S. Litvinov, G. Ayodo, D. Comas, M.F. Hammer, T. Kivisild, W. Klitz, C.A. Winkler, D. Labuda, M. Bamshad, L.B. Jorde, S.A. Tishkoff, W.S. Watkins, M. Metspalu, S. Dryomov, R. Sukernik, L. Singh, K. Thangaraj, S. Pääbo, J. Kelso, N. Patterson, and D. Reich 2016. The Simons Genome Diversity Project: 300 genomes from 142 diverse populations. *Nature* 538:201–206. doi.org/10.1038/nature18964.

Meggitt, M.J. 1965. *The lineage system of the Mae-Enga of New Guinea.* Barnes & Noble, New York.

Miedema, J. and G. Reesink 2004. *One head, many faces: New perspectives on the Bird's Head Peninsula and Beyond.* In G. Reesink *One Head, Many Faces:New Perspectives on the Bird's Head Peninsula of New Guinea,* p. 173. KITLV Press, Leiden. doi.org/10.1163/9789004454385_017.

Mona, S., M. Tommaseo-Ponzetta, S. Brauer, H. Sudoyo, S. Marzuki, and M. Kayser 2007. Patterns of Y-chromosome diversity intersect with the Trans–New Guinea hypothesis. *Molecular Biology and Evolution* 24:2546–2555. doi.org/10.1093/molbev/msm187.

Mona, S., E. Mordret, M. Veuille, and M. Tommaseo-Ponzetta 2013. Investigating sex-specific dynamics using uniparental markers: West New Guinea as a case study. *Ecology and Evolution* 3:2647–2660. doi.org/10.1002/ece3.660.

Moreau, L. 2020. Social inequality without farming: What we can learn from how foraging societies shape(d) social inequality? In L. Moreau (ed.) *Social inequality before farming? Multidisciplinary approaches to the study of social organization in prehistoric and ethnographic hunter-gatherer-fisher societies,* pp. 1–18. McDonald Institute Monographs, University of Cambridge. doi.org/10.17863/CAM.60627.

Natri, H.M., G. Hudjashov, G.S. Jacobs, P. Kusuma, L. Saag, C.C. Darusallam, M. Metspalu, H. Sudoyo, M.P. Cox, I. Gallego Romero, and N.E. Banovich 2022. Genetic architecture of gene regulation in Indonesian populations identifies QTLs associated with global and local ancestries. *American Journal of Human Genetics* 109:50–65. doi.org/10.1016/j.ajhg.2021.11.017.

Nijenhuis, L.E., A.C. van der Gugten, H. den Butter, and J.W. Doeland 1966. Blood group frequencies in Northern West New Guinea (West Irian). *American Journal of Human Genetics* 18:39–56.

Oota, H., W. Settheetham-Ishida, D. Tiwawech, T. Ishida, and M. Stoneking 2001. Human mtDNA and Y-chromosome variation is correlated with matrilocal versus patrilocal residence. *Nature Genetics* 29:20–21. doi.org/10.1038/ng711.

Pawley, A. 1998. The Trans New Guinea Phylum hypothesis: A reassessment. In J. Miedema, C. Odé, and R.A.C. Dam (eds), *Perspectives on the Bird's Head of Irian Jaya, Indonesia: Proceedings of the Conference, Leiden, 13–17 October 1997,* pp. 655–689. Rodopi, Amsterdam; Atlanta. doi.org/10.1163/9789004652644_034.

Pawley, A. 2005. Introduction to the chapters on historical linguistics. In A. Pawley, R. Attenborough, J. Golson, and R. Hide (eds), *Papuan pasts: Cultural, linguistic and biological histories of the Papuan-speaking peoples,* pp. 1–14. Pacific Linguistics 572. Research School of Pacific and Asian Studies, The Australian National University, Canberra.

Pawley, A. and H. Hammarström 2017. The Trans New Guinea Family. In B. Palmer (ed.), *The languages and linguistics of the New Guinea area: A comprehensive guide,* pp. 21–196. De Gruyter Mouton, Berlin; Boston. doi.org/10.1515/9783110295252-002.

Pedro, N., N. Brucato, V. Fernandes, M. André, L. Saag, W. Pomat, C. Besse, A. Boland, J.-F. Deleuze, C. Clarkson, H. Sudoyo, M. Metspalu, M. Stoneking, M.P. Cox, M. Leavesley, L. Pereira, and F.-X. Ricaut 2020. Papuan mitochondrial genomes and the settlement of Sahul. *Journal of Human Genetics* 65:875–887. doi.org/10.1038/s10038-020-0781-3.

Pemberton, T.J., D. Absher, M.W. Feldman, R.M. Myers, N.A. Rosenberg, and J.Z. Li 2012. Genomic patterns of homozygosity in worldwide human populations. *American Journal of Human Genetics* 91: 275–292. doi.org/10.1016/j.ajhg.2012.06.014.

Purnomo, G.A., K.J. Mitchell, S. O'Connor, S. Kealy, L. Taufik, S. Schiller, A. Rohrlach, A. Cooper, B. Llamas, H. Sudoyo, J.C. Teixeira, and R. Tobler 2021. Mitogenomes reveal two major influxes of Papuan ancestry across Wallacea following the Last Glacial Maximum and Austronesian contact. *Genes* 12:965. doi.org/10.3390/genes12070965.

Ralph, P. and G. Coop 2013. The geography of recent genetic ancestry across Europe. *PLoS Biology* 11:e1001555. doi.org/10.1371/journal.pbio.1001555.

Redd, A.J., and M. Stoneking 1999. Peopling of Sahul: mtDNA variation in aboriginal Australian and Papua New Guinean populations. *American Journal of Human Genetics* 65:808–828. doi.org/10.1086/302533.

Redd, A.J., N. Takezaki, S.T. Sherry, S.T. McGarvey, A.S.M. Sofro, and M. Stoneking 1995. Evolutionary history of the COII/tRNALys intergenic 9 base pair deletion in human mitochondrial DNAs from the Pacific. *Molecular Biology and Evolution* 12:604–615. doi.org/10.1093/oxfordjournals.molbev.a040240.

Roscoe, P. 2002. The hunters and gatherers of New Guinea. *Current Anthropology* 43(1):153–162. doi.org/10.1086/338289.

Roscoe, P. 2005. Foraging, ethnographic analogy, and Papuan pasts: Contemporary models for the Sepik–Ramu past. In A. Pawley, R. Attenborough, J. Golson, and R. Hide (eds), *Papuan pasts: Cultural, linguistic and biological histories of the Papuan-speaking peoples,* pp. 555–584. Pacific Linguistics 572. Research School of Pacific and Asian Studies, The Australian National University, Canberra.

Seielstad, M.T., E. Minch and L.L. Cavalli-Sforza 1998. Genetic evidence for a higher female migration rate in humans. *Nature Genetics* 20:278–280. doi.org/10.1038/3088.

Serjeantson, S.W., R.L. Kirk, and P.B. Booth 1983. Linguistic and genetic differentiation in New Guinea. *Journal of Human Evolution* 12:77–92. doi.org/10.1016/S0047-2484(83)80014-1.

Shaw, B., J.H. Field, G.R. Summerhayes, S. Coxe, A.C.F. Coster, A. Ford, J. Haro, H. Arifeae, E. Hull, G. Jacobsen, R. Fullagar, E. Hayes, and L. Kealhofer 2020. Emergence of a Neolithic in highland New Guinea by 5000 to 4000 years ago. *Science Advances* 6(13):eaay4573. doi.org/10.1126/sciadv.aay4573.

Stasch, R. 2009. *Society of others: Kinship and mourning in a West Papuan place.* University of California Press, Oakland. doi.org/10.1525/9780520943322.

Stoneking, M., L.B. Jorde, K. Bhatia, and A.C. Wilson 1990. Geographic variation in human mitochondrial DNA from Papua New Guinea. *Genetics* 124(3):717–733. doi.org/10.1093/genetics/124.3.717.

Strathern, A.J. 1995. *Migration and transformations: Regional perspectives on New Guinea.* ASAO Monograph. University of Pittsburgh Press, Pittsburgh.

Swadling, P. 2005. The Huon Gulf and its hinterlands: A long-term view of Coastal–Highlands interactions. In C. Gross, H.D. Lyons, and D.A. Counts (eds), *A polymath anthropologist: Essays in honour of Ann Chowning,* pp. 1–14. Auckland Research in Anthropology and Linguistics Monograph No. 6. Department of Anthropology, University of Auckland.

Swadling, P. 2019. *Plumes from Paradise: Trade cycles in outer Southeast Asia and their impact on New Guinea and nearby islands until 1920.* Sydney University Press, Sydney. doi.org/10.2307/j.ctv10vkzrf.

Swadling, P., and R. Hide 2005. Changing landscape and social interaction: Looking at agricultural history from a Sepik–Ramu perspective. In A. Pawley, R. Attenborough, J. Golson, and R. Hide (eds), *Papuan pasts: Cultural, linguistic and biological histories of the Papuan-speaking peoples,* pp. 289–328. Pacific Linguistics 572. Research School of Pacific and Asian Studies, The Australian National University, Canberra.

Szalay, A. 1999. Maokop: The Montane cultures of Central Irian Jaya: Environment, society, and history in Highland West New Guinea. PhD thesis. Department of Anthropology, University of Sydney, Sydney.

Terhorst, J., J.A. Kamm, and Y.S. Song 2017. Robust and scalable inference of population history from hundreds of unphased whole genomes. *Nature Genetics* 49:303–309. doi.org/10.1038/ng.3748.

The 1000 Genomes Project Consortium 2015. A global reference for human genetic variation. *Nature*. 526:68–74. doi.org/10.1038/nature15393.

Thompson, E.A. 2013. Identity by descent: Variation in meiosis, across genomes, and in populations. *Genetics* 194:301–326. doi.org/10.1534/genetics.112.148825.

Tommaseo-Ponzetta, M. 1986. Gli Asmat della Nuova Guinea. In Centro Studi e Ricerche Ligabue (ed.), *Indonesia, La Grande Derive Etnica*. Erizzo, Venezia.

Tommaseo-Ponzetta, M., M. Attimonelli, M. De Robertis, F. Tanzariello, and C. Saccone 2002. Mitochondrial DNA variability of West New Guinea populations. *American Journal of Physical Anthropology* 117:49–67. doi.org/10.1002/ajpa.10010.

Tommaseo-Ponzetta, M., M. Cascione, M. Attimonelli, Y. Syukriani, A.S. Noer, H. Sudoyo, and S. Marzuki 2007. Mitochondrial DNA M and N haplogroups in WNG Populations. In E. Indriati (ed.), *Recent advances on Southeast Asian paleoanthropology and archaeology*, pp. 207–215. Laboratory of Bioanthropology and Paleoanthropology, Faculty of Medicine, Gadjah Mada University, Yogyakarta, Indonesia.

Tommaseo-Ponzetta, M., S. Mona, F. Calabrese, G. Konrad, E. Vacca, and M. Attimonelli 2013. Mountain pygmies of Western New Guinea: A morphological and molecular approach. *Human Biology* 85:285–308. doi.org/10.3378/027.085.0314.

van Oven, M., A. Van Geystelen, M. Kayser, R. Decorte, and M.H. Larmuseau 2014. Seeing the wood for the trees: A minimal reference phylogeny for the human Y chromosome. *Human Mutation* 35(2):187–191. doi.org/10.1002/humu.22468.

Weiner, J.F. (ed.) 1988. *Mountain Papuans: Historical and comparative perspectives from New Guinea fringe highlands societies*. University of Michigan Press, Ann Arbor. doi.org/10.3998/mpub.9552.

Wright, S. 1931. Evolution in Mendelian populations. *Genetics* 16:97–159. doi.org/10.1093/genetics/16.2.97.

6

Deep histories in New Guinea: Insights from genetics on human adaptation to malaria and diverse environments

Robert Attenborough, Guy Jacobs, and Pradiptajati Kusuma[1]

Abstract

In this, the third of three linked chapters oriented to human biology—specifically, genetics and genomics—in New Guinea, we change focus from investigating ancestry to investigating adaptation. Given the slow rate of evolutionary adaptation, prevalent genes adaptive to particular environmental pressures indicate probable exposure to those pressures for many past generations. Indeed, they suggest that such pressures were—maybe still are—life-and-death matters. We begin this chapter by sketching the present and past range of environments that characterise New Guinea and may exert pressures on human survival and reproduction. Our main example—it could hardly be otherwise—is malaria. We review a number of the 'antimalarial' alleles prevalent in New Guinea. We present simple models designed to provide qualitative insights into the time depth of these adaptations and hence of malaria itself on the island. No other example matches malaria, but we review existing evidence surrounding some other pressures—prion disease, solar radiation, altitude, diet—as well as some health implications of New Guinean genetic variation more broadly.

Abstrak

Dalam bab ini, seri ketiga dari tiga bab terkait genetika manusia, kami mengubah fokus dari menyelidiki asal-usul manusia menjadi menyelidiki jejak adaptasi manusia di Papua. Mengingat laju evolusi adaptasi yang lambat, gen-gen yang umumnya beradaptasi terhadap tekanan lingkungan dan penyakit menunjukkan kemungkinan paparan terhadap tekanan tersebut sejak lama, bergenerasi-generasi yang lalu. Tekanan lingkungan dan penyakit tersebut merupakan masalah hidup-dan-mati bagi populasi manusia saat itu, hingga sekarang. Kami memulai bab ini dengan menggambarkan kondisi tekanan lingkungan dan penyakit pada saat ini dan pada masa lalu di wilayah Papua, yang dimungkinkan memberikan tekanan terhadap kelangsungan hidup dan reproduksi manusia. Contoh utama kami adalah malaria. Kami mengulas sejumlah alel, atau penanda genetik, "anti-malaria" yang umum di

---

1   All authors contributed equally.

populasi Papua. Kami menyajikan beberapa permodelan sederhana yang dirancang untuk memberikan wawasan kualitatif tentang waktu dari proses adaptasi terhadap malaria di Papua. Tidak ada contoh lain yang sepadan dengan malaria, tetapi kami meninjau bukti-bukti yang ada mengenai beberapa tekanan lain—penyakit prion, radiasi matahari, ketinggian, pola makan—serta beberapa implikasi kesehatan dari variasi genetik populasi Papua secara lebih luas.

Introduction

Genetics and genomics offer increasingly powerful methods for gaining insights into the biological ancestries and deep pasts of human populations everywhere. Elsewhere, we discuss both New Guinea populations' relationships to other populations in the wider region, including introgression from other hominin species (Jacobs et al., this volume), and the geography of human genetic diversity within the island, together with its implied population dynamics over time (Kusuma et al., this volume)—viewing the genetic heritage of today's New Guineans largely as guidance as to their ancestry, interrelationships, and past demography. Only in passing do we pay attention in those chapters to such adaptive evolution (adaptive introgression included) as may have assisted New Guinean populations to survive—and in many cases thrive—in the challenging environments faced for millennia by their ancestors. Yet that is a crucial topic, and it is the focus of our present chapter. Our questions are: what can we deduce from New Guineans' genomes as to their biological adaptation to their and their ancestors' environments? And what are the functional implications of their present-day genetic variation?

We begin by sketching some of New Guinea's past and present environmental challenges, physical and biotic, to human life. We then review selected genetic traits of New Guineans that appear adaptive to those challenges. The latter include dietary regimes and infectious agents, above all malaria. We present some simple models that attempt to put an order of magnitude on the timescales of exposure and genetic adaptation to malaria. Finally, we review a few suggestive indications of other possible adaptations, and discuss a few other prevalent and potentially significant alleles.

The contexts of environmental adaptation for ancestral New Guineans

New Guinea is a 'small cosmos': an extraordinary diversity of environments contained within one island of 808,512 km². Many features of the landscape, climate, and biota are very different from those of the Wallacean world that first and many subsequent arrivals on the island would have come from. Populating it for the first time would have amounted not to spreading out into blank space or a uniform habitat, but to encountering contrasting and novel obstacles, hazards, and threats to survival—as well as remarkable opportunities. For subsequent arrivals, the human inhabitants already there, and their environmental impacts, may have posed challenges too.

Threats to human survival and reproductive success vary strongly with the island's geography, especially its altitudinal variation. A large complex spine of rugged mountains, exceeding 3000 m in places, runs between the Bird's Head and the islands of Milne Bay. Within this cordillera are wide, fertile intramontane ('highlands') valleys with floors between 1500 and 1600 m above sea level (asl). Around the cordillera are the 'highlands fringes', steeply dissected regions of moderate altitude (600–1500 m asl). Major rivers and their gorges drain the highlands and fringes into the extensive lowlands, which, before reaching the coasts, encompass lesser mountain ranges, volcanoes, plateaux, forests, plains, and swamps; and here the rivers become massive and meandering (Allen 1992; Ward and Lea 1970).

Nowadays, the largest and densest non-urban human populations are in the highlands, with some lowland areas, especially the Sepik basin, also quite densely inhabited. Estimates for pre-colonial Papua New Guinea (PNG) are relatively similar: dense human populations amounting to 40 per cent of the total were concentrated in the highlands, with few other parts as densely populated, and the fringes particularly sparsely (Parkinson 1974; Riley 1983; Ward and Lea 1970). Consistent with the earlier arguments of Bulmer and Bulmer (1964), Parkinson saw the fringes as keeping lowlands and highlands populations all but apart.

The New Guinea island today has a range of rainy, cloudy, often hot environments characteristic of the humid tropics, with patterns of seasonality varying locally. Altitude moderates average temperature, which is reduced by, for example, ~10 °C at ~2000 m asl (Allen 1992). The Holocene climate broadly resembled today's, but earlier periods were cooler. Globally, no earlier period since the Eemian interglacial ~120,000 years ago quite matches Holocene warmth, and the same appears true for New Guinea. Somewhat cooler temperatures and lower rainfall prevailed since that interglacial, though sometimes with rapid fluctuations. Contrasts with the present day were most marked during the stadials which peaked around 60,000, 40,000, and 20,000 years ago. During the last of those stadials, the highland valleys were on average 7 °C cooler than today, with more extensive subalpine grasslands and glaciation, and a lower tree line at 2200 m asl (Gaffney and Denham 2021; Haberle 1993; Hope and Haberle 2005). Hope and Tulip (1994) estimated that before 8500 years ago a site 780 m asl may have been some 4.5 °C below its present mean temperature, with a greater reduction of perhaps 5.5 °C occurring at higher altitudes. This is in keeping with estimates from the wider region, with temperatures ranging between 4 and 7 °C (Hope et al. 2004; van der Kaars et al. 2000) or even 7 to 9 °C (Hunt et al. 2012) below present ones. Both subalpine and lowland grasslands became more extensive during cooler periods than they are now, and the tree line retreated as montane forest expanded downslope. Nonetheless, typically equatorial rainforest persisted in the lowlands throughout the cooler phases, with temperature changes there being slighter (Hope et al. 2004; Hope and Haberle 2005). Early peopling even of the highlands must have taken place through those still warm and humid lowlands, where everything and everybody was biodegradable. There was, then, plenty of opportunity, over 50,000 years or more, for natural selection in situ to have had impacts on New Guinea's human population; or rather, on its numerous semi-isolated, semi-interconnected, small sub-populations. Indeed, recent analysis of the time depth of potentially adaptive variation in the region detects enrichment of allelic origins during the early colonisation period, >50,000 years ago (Brucato et al. 2022). What might have been the agents of selection acting on these genetic variants?

New Guinea's rich biota include plenty of potentially and actually pathogenic microorganisms, including helminths, protozoa, fungi, bacteria, and viruses, and many arthropods capable of acting as vectors. So infectious disease looms large. Altitude may affect human biology directly via hypoxia, although most New Guinea 'Highlands' populations live at only moderate altitudes. Despite cloudiness, New Guinea also receives intense solar radiation and tropical humid heat. And while earlier New Guineans were hunter-gatherers and ate a varied diet (Gaffney et al. 2021; Sutton et al. 2009), plant cultivation, along with increasing population density and forest clearance, would have made for a less varied diet, and most likely a starchier one—which is not to deny a starchy component in hunter-gatherer diets. We have insufficient space to discuss all the plausible selective agents, or the most striking functional variants prevalent in New Guinean people's genomes. In any case, some are insufficiently researched. We have chosen a few to enlarge on below. Pride of place goes to malaria.

Malaria

It would be hard to overstate the burden that malaria must have imposed on lowland New Guinea's early peoples, whether they brought it to the island with them, or—especially—if it only struck them with full force after they had settled there. A readily transmitted disease with high mortality, especially among children and non-immune adults, would surely have wreaked havoc and inspired fear—suspicions of sorcery too, maybe—in an insufficiently protected population.

Malaria remains a major health burden, in both West New Guinea, including the western New Guinea (WNG) mainland (Devine et al. 2017; Kenangalem et al. 2019; Pava et al. 2016), and in PNG, including the eastern New Guinea (ENG) mainland (Alpers 2018; Cattani 1992; Kattenberg et al. 2020; Müller et al. 2003). In the lowlands, it is endemic, often hyperendemic, even holoendemic. The highlands fringes are also highly malarial. Before 1930, the central highlands were probably largely free of endemic malaria, except in low-lying and swampy areas (Riley and Lehmann 1992), though that is not the case now (Müller et al. 2002). Malaria transmission decreases in approximate correlation with mean annual temperature and thus altitude. In New Guinea nowadays malaria becomes unstable and more epidemic around 1300–1600 m asl, and ceases above 1700–1800 m asl (Müller et al. 2003). The malaria parasite, *Plasmodium*, depends on environmental temperature—minimally 16 °C for *P. vivax*, 18 °C for *P. falciparum* (Bruce-Chwatt 1987)—during the portion of its life cycle that takes place in the *Anopheles* mosquito.

The outsider science of New Guinea malaria began early in the colonial period (Spencer 1994). Robert Koch observed it in 1899–1900, in the then German New Guinea (Attenborough 2007; Ewers 1972a, 1972b). Other observations followed, including in Dutch New Guinea (e.g. Metselaar 1956). But this is 'shallow history'. With mean annual temperatures ~20 °C at 1500 m asl recently (Allen 1992) but ~7 °C lower during stadial periods, it seems clear that highland populations were essentially malaria-free during stadials, probably right through the Pleistocene, quite likely through the Holocene too, and up to 1930s. In the lowlands, however, climate and ecology would, as discussed above, have been such as to favour malaria transmission throughout.

According to Trájer's (2022, Table 1) modelling, the ENG highlands endemic-malaria-free zone would have reduced greatly in extent between the Last Glacial Maximum and the Mid-Holocene Period, with its lower altitudinal border rising by 300–425 m, but it would not have changed greatly between then and 1960–1990. Trájer finds a consistent difference between *P. vivax* and *P. falciparum*, whereby the altitudinal border lay 325–450 m lower for *P. falciparum* at all three periods. He draws attention to the fact—a suggestive one, albeit one potentially subject to the patchy distribution of archaeological fieldwork to date—that all 16 of the Mid-Holocene ENG Neolithic archaeological sites listed by Shaw and colleagues (2020) are in areas modelled to be *falciparum*-free or low-risk for *falciparum* at the time. By contrast, these sites are not generally in *vivax*-free areas, though they are not far from those areas.

One indication of malaria's antiquity in New Guinea lies in Riley's (1983) argument that it was the most important determinant of pre-colonial population distribution in PNG; which one might extend to New Guinea as a whole. Consistent with this, a 'population sink' model (references in Attenborough et al. [1997]) envisages a long-term process of population growth in the highlands leading to expansion into the fringes where they encounter arthropod-borne diseases such as malaria and cannot thrive, their populations remaining sparse and subject to high mortality.

Once parasite, vector, and host were all present in New Guinea, three interacting sets of populations, ecologies, and genomics would have been involved: those of various species of the single-celled protozoan *Plasmodium*, various species of the *Anopheles* mosquito, and the human hosts.

The pathogens: *Plasmodium*

The many species of *Plasmodium* parasitise many vertebrate hosts, but only five species regularly parasitise humans. Of these, four cause significant disease in New Guinea (Müller et al. 2007). We focus on the two most problematic and best-researched, *P. falciparum* and *P. vivax*. *P. falciparum*, as its complications cause the most dangerous disease, often fatal, especially for non-immunes including children. *P. vivax*, the most widespread species outside Sub-Saharan Africa, causes a relapsing disease, less often directly fatal but less benign than once thought, owing especially to impacts on children and patients with comorbidities (Douglas et al. 2014; Price et al. 2007). *P. vivax* appears well adapted to survival and replication in the spleens of chronically, even if asymptomatically, infected hosts (Kho et al. 2021). Both species are abundant in New Guinea now, with *P. falciparum* appearing to gain ground lately (Attenborough 2007; Müller et al. 2005).

The evolutionary histories of both species have been controversial (Hume et al. 2003; Joy et al. 2003). *P. falciparum* appears to have originated in Africa, as a zoonosis from western gorillas (Liu et al. 2010; Loy et al. 2017; Otto et al. 2018; Su et al. 2020; York 2018). It has strikingly low genetic diversity. Loy and colleagues (2017, 91) argue that 'the observed level of genetic diversity in *P. falciparum* could have readily accumulated within the past 10,000 years', that the zoonotic transfer probably took place within that period, and that a bottleneck at the point of transfer probably accounts for the present low diversity. Otto and colleagues (2018, 4), however, put the date at 60,000–40,000 years ago, but still 'significantly later than the evolution of the first modern humans and their spread throughout Africa'. They also infer a numerical decline in *P. falciparum* from around 11,000 years ago, reaching a bottleneck around 5000 years ago, which they link to a farming-related expansion of the African human population, with consequent selection pressure on *Anopheles* to specialise in human hosts.

Regarding *P. falciparum*'s arrival date in New Guinea, we might best turn to Joy and colleagues' (2003) tentative but broadly compatible estimate of a rapid expansion ~19,000–13,000 years ago. Speculatively, one might ask whether the mass human movements enforced by rising sea levels 21,000–8000 years ago (Chappell 2005) might have provided an engine for this expansion. The implication that *P. falciparum*'s arrival would have been many millennia after the earliest peopling of the island fits, intriguingly, with Groube's (1993, 2000) thinking. The genetic diversity of *P. falciparum* in New Guinea is high compared with other regions, but variably so, related probably to high transmission intensity in relatively isolated human and vector populations (Schultz et al. 2010).

That *P. vivax* also originated in Africa now appears broadly (Hupalo et al. 2016; Kissinger 2016; Liu et al. 2014) though not universally (Rougeron et al. 2020) agreed. Putatively, a non-host-specific *P. vivax* ancestor circulated among western and eastern gorillas, chimpanzees (but not bonobos), and humans, until the human-specific strains emerged from within the radiation of ape strains. As a result of a bottleneck, human *P. vivax* is less diverse than ape *P. vivax*. Even so, global *P. falciparum* is less diverse than global human *P. vivax* or indeed any of the main *P. vivax* regional populations. This strongly, but qualitatively, suggests much greater antiquity for *P. vivax*.

A New Guinea grouping of *P. vivax* is the most divergent within the Old World cluster, suggesting long isolation there (Hupalo et al. 2016; Kissinger 2016; Pearson et al. 2016). Some arguments about New Guinea's prehistory (Clark and Kelly 1993; Leclerc et al. 2004) have implied that *P. vivax* too may have arrived relatively late. But very probably it—and likely *P. malariae* and *P. ovale* too— reached New Guinea well before *P. falciparum*, possibly with the first human inhabitants.

In short, lowland New Guineans may or may not have always had to live with and die from malaria; but it does now seem probable that they were not subject to *P. falciparum* malaria until relatively late in their prehistory.

The vectors: *Anopheles*

When taking a blood meal from human (or other vertebrate) sources, infected female mosquitoes of the genus *Anopheles* may inject the *Plasmodium* parasites into their bloodstream. Of the hundreds of *Anopheles* species globally, New Guinea has ~27 primary, secondary, and possible malaria vector species (Attenborough 2015; Beebe et al. 2013). *Anopheles* mosquitoes have inhabited New Guinea for very much longer than human beings, drawing their blood meals from native fauna. There would thus have been a potential for human malaria transmission as soon as the people and the parasites joined the mosquitoes in New Guinea, albeit with possible needs for the parasites to adapt to carriage by the local vectors, and for the vectors to become anthropophilic. One species, *A. punctulatus*, is now a primary vector, well suited to environments around human habitations. From its relatively low genetic diversity, it appears to have undergone rapid recent population growth and dispersal in New Guinea, following a bottleneck (Seah et al. 2013), at an unknown date for which 30,000 years might be a reasonable estimate (N. Beebe pers. comm. 2021).

The hosts: New Guinean people

Malaria has been the pre-eminent cause of childhood mortality in many parts of the world for much of the past 5000 years, and its known impact on the human genome is similarly pre-eminent (Boyce et al. 1995; Flint et al. 1993). Its propensity to cause heavy and early mortality is among Kariuki and Williams's (2020) reasons for describing malaria as 'the strongest force for selective pressure on the human genome yet described'. Host genetic factors modulate the risk and severity of infections. Around one-third of worldwide variability in the risk of severe and complicated malaria can be attributed to host genetic variants (Kariuki and Williams 2020; Williams 2016). From the abundance of such variants in the genomes of indigenous New Guineans we seek here to draw inferences about malaria's history among their forebears.

The most classical genetic host factor, sickle-cell haemoglobin, does not occur indigenously in New Guinea (Lavu et al. 2002), but several other 'genetic antimalarial' (Diamond 1989) variants do. Just as, in New Guinea's most intensely endemic areas, malaria is as severe as anywhere in Africa (Cattani 1992), so also, the island's range of associated genetic variants rivals or exceeds that seen elsewhere. That these genetic variants are not at 100 per cent frequency suggests either an incomplete selective sweep or, demonstrably in most cases, a counterbalancing biological cost to malaria resistance.

Even just one of these variants at substantial frequency, associated with malaria resistance, would suffice to establish a deep timescale for endemic malaria in ancestral populations. The multiplicity of these variants not only provides corroboration, but also enables us to explore timescales with more nuance. First, we outline here the best-supported adaptations to malaria among New Guineans. A fuller review, still valid in most respects, is provided by Serjeantson and colleagues (1992). Williams (2016) provides an even more up-to-date global review.

Table 6.1: Summary overview of alleles considered to confer relative resistance to malaria among New Guineans.

Locus	Resistance-associated alleles	Heterozygous condition	Homozygous condition	Lowland allele frequencies^	Highland allele frequencies	Considered resistant to	Key citations
HBB, Chr.11	β-thalassaemia point mutations	Malaria-resistant	Severe genetic anaemia	Average of 8 Provinces: 2.27% Range: 0–17.28%§	Average of 4 Provinces: 0.27% Range: 0–0.54%§	P. falciparum at least	Serjeantson et al. (1992)
HBA1 & HBA2, i.e. duplicated, Chr.16	α-thalassaemia single deletions	Malaria-resistant with 1 deletion	Mild to severe anaemia with >1 deletion	Average: **39%** Northern: **68%** Southern: 22% Eastern: 38%	Average: **4%** Range: 2–5%	Severe malaria, especially due to P. falciparum*	Flint et al. (1986); Nurfitriani et al. (2014); Serjeantson et al. (1992)
G6PD, X Chr.	G6PD enzyme deficiency (G6PDd)	Malaria-resistant (females only)	Benign under most conditions; drug sensitivities	West Papua Province: 4.8% Biak, Papua: **4%** Bagaiserwar, Papua: 1% Wor, Papua: 33% E. Sepik: **20.2%** Range: 0–53%#	Absent in many groups	P. falciparum at least	Kawulur et al. (2020); Prins et al. (1963); Yoshida et al. (1973); Beck et al. (1994); Yenchitsomanus et al. (1986); Serjeantson et al. (1992); Howes et al. (2012, 2013); Pava et al. (2016)
SLC4A1, Chr.17	SE Asian ovalocytosis deletion	Malaria-resistant; usually asymptomatic	Usually lethal in utero	ENG lowlands average: 7.5% Range: 0–17.6% Wosera, E. Sepik: 0–0.05% Liksul, Madang Province: 7.4% Coastal Madang Province: **17.6%** Sentani: **3.8%** Biak: **2%**	Goroka, E. Highlands: 0%	P. falciparum, P. vivax, P. malariae, P. knowlesi	Mgone et al. (1996); Patel et al. (2004); Serjeantson et al. (1992)
GYPC, Chr.2	Gerbich-negative allele	No known effect	Malaria-resistant	ENG northern lowlands average: ~30% Absent from southern lowlands Wosera, E. Sepik Province: **46.5%** Liksul, Madang Province: **17.6%**	Absent	P. falciparum and/or P. vivax	Booth et al. (1972a, 1972b, 1972c); Serjeantson (1989); not confirmed by Patel et al. (2001, 2004); Tavul et al. (2008)
DARC, Chr.1	Duffy-negative allele FY*A^Null	No known effect	Malaria-resistant	Wosera, E. Sepik: 2.2% Dreikikir, E. Sepik: 0%	Unknown	P. vivax	Zimmerman et al. (1999, 2013)
ABO blood group, Chr.9	O allele (i.e. A and B negative)	No known effect	Malaria-resistant	Polymorphic in both lowlands and highlands but not yet analysed by altitude		Severe and complicated malaria	Cavalli-Sforza et al. (1994); Mourant (1978); Williams (2016)

Notes: Bold frequencies correspond to those used in Figure 6.1.

§ Estimated from heterozygote frequencies; for original findings see papers cited.

* Putatively, reduced resistance to *P. vivax* improves resistance to *P. falciparum* via cross-immunity.

Allele frequency generally (except Kawalur et al. 2020) determined as % of (hemizygous) males affected.

∧ Allele frequency in some cases refers to the cumulative frequency of multiple variants associated with malaria resistance.

Source: Authors' summary.

In Table 6.1 we summarise salient features of seven of the genetic variants that occur polymorphically in New Guinea: α- and β-thalassaemia (deficiencies in production of α- and β-globin chains, respectively), deficiency of the key red blood cell enzyme glucose-6-phosphate dehydrogenase (G6PD), Hereditary (Southeast Asian) Ovalocytosis (SAO), Gerbich-negative blood group (unique to New Guinea), Duffy-negative blood group, and O blood group (in the ABO system). These vary in their genetic bases (dominant/intermediate/recessive expression; sex-linked inheritance; duplication). Most of these variants, at least, have arisen multiple times, potentially even within New Guinea, by independent mutation. Geographically, their distribution within New Guinea co-varies broadly with present or past malaria endemicity—as is also true of most of the six variants that occur beyond New Guinea. That is, in both cases, wherever these genetic variants occur at a notable frequency in the indigenous population, malaria is or has been endemic. The converse is not always true.

We cannot enlarge here on the varied biological mechanisms by which the alleles in question confer the degree of protection that they do, nor on the nature and strength of the evidence for that. But in general, this protection is only relative: in most cases, it reduces risk and/or severity. What is most frequently conferred is relative protection from severe and/or complicated malaria—most often caused by *P. falciparum*—while detectable protection from lighter malarial infections may be less, or none. In the paradoxical case of α-thalassaemia, the benefit is thought to flow from an actual increase in susceptibility to *P. vivax*, and hence improved cross-immunity to *P. falciparum* (Maitland et al. 1997; Williams et al. 1996). The Duffy-negative blood group, best known from Africa, is different from the others in that its benefit is strong but relates specifically to *P. vivax*. Although the ABO blood group has long been investigated in relation to malaria, including in New Guinea (Mourant 1978), O is a more recent addition to the list of well-supported, malaria-resistant phenotypes. We note the likely existence of other polymorphisms and mechanisms in New Guinea beyond this list (e.g. CR1 [Cockburn et al. 2003]).

Bioarchaeological evidence has shown thalassaemia (both α and β) to have been present and potentially a major health burden in mainland SE Asia ~7000 years ago (Vlok et al. 2021). This is millennia before the local transition to agriculture, in contrast to the 'Livingstone hypothesis' (reviewed by e.g. Durham 1991), whereby malaria was not an important disease before agriculture.

Models

How deep is malaria's antiquity in the New Guinea lowlands? A minimum estimate is provided by asking a different question: how long would it take for malaria-adapted variants to rise to the frequencies observed today? This can be modelled, subject to assumptions. For sickle cell, past models (summarised in Attenborough 2007) have arrived at estimates generally in the range of a few thousand years, mostly 1000 to 4500 years. The implication is an origin potentially as recent as 4500–1000 years ago, but this does not rule out a more ancient rise followed by equilibrium (which, for sickle-cell, now appears more plausible: Esoh and Wonkam 2021).

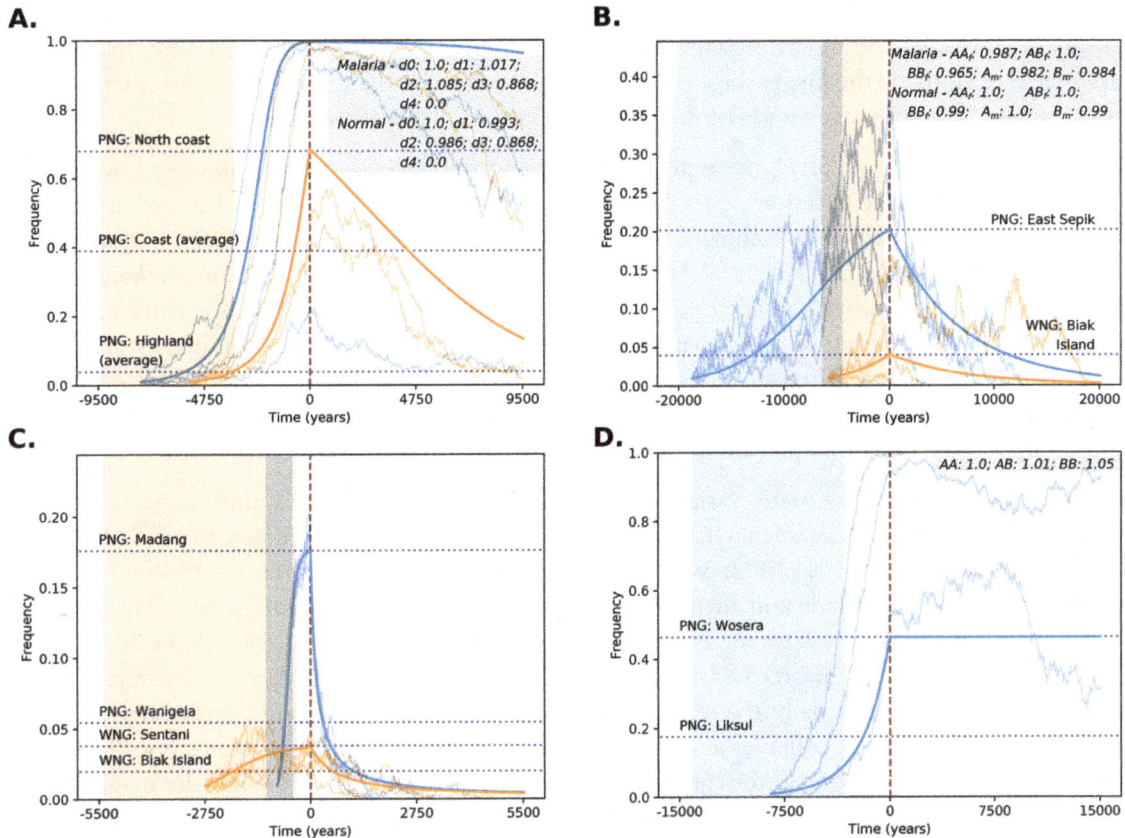

Figure 6.1: Allele frequency dynamics under representative selection regimes for principal malaria adaptations in New Guinea.

Notes: These plots attempt to model the impact of natural selection on the frequency over time of alleles causing malaria resistance, with implications for the time depth of malaria-driven selection. Initial frequency of the positively selected allele is 0.01 in each plot; generation time is 25 years. The allele frequency is tracked during a period of malaria selection, followed by the relaxation of selection at Year 0. Modelled fitness regimes are as shown above or described in the main text. Shaded regions correspond to the 2.5th to 97.5th percentile range of first passage times to the corresponding observed frequency (not fully shown in (B)), with example finite-population size traces from the modelled initial conditions also shown (both diploid N = 1500). (A) α-thalassaemia: frequency of single deletion -α allele with fitnesses of d(0) to d(4) deletions indicated, introductions 7600 years ago and 5500 years ago; (B) G6PD deficiency: frequency of a G6PDd haplotype, *B*, with selection on females (subscript *f*) and males (subscript *m*) indicated assuming equal prevalence of cerebral malaria and anaemia, introductions at 18,750 and 5750 years ago; (C) Southeast Asian Ovalocytosis: frequency of the SAO-causing deletion, with selection (AA: 1 − s; AB: 1; BB: 0) calculated based on frequencies reported by Mgone et al. (1996) and assuming equilibrium with s = p/(1−p), introductions at 2750 and 875 years ago; (D) Gerbich-negative: frequency of the Gerbich-negative GYPC exon 3 deletion, assessing the implications of strong selection with introduction at 8475 years ago.

Sources: (A) Hedrick (2011a) and Flint et al. (1986); (B) Clarke et al. (2017), Beck et al. (1994), and Prins et al. (1963); (C) Mgone et al. (1996); (D) Patel et al. (2004).

We model the frequency changes of α-thalassaemia, G6PDd, Southeast Asian Ovalocytosis, and Gerbich-negative blood group in New Guinea (Figure 6.1; frequencies from Table 6.1). For simplicity, these models ignore drift and migration, generally assume constant selection regimes over time and space, assume a 1 per cent initial frequency of alleles, and ignore interactions between different polymorphisms, although we also simulate some finite-population size (diploid N = 1500) iterations by incorporating a binomial (or multinomial) random sampling step on allele frequencies to represent the potential impact of genetic drift. The intention is qualitative insight—into the time that selection takes to bring malaria-protective alleles up to high frequency in malarial areas, and then to drive them down in non-malarial areas. This decay is relevant if highlanders' ancestors were once malaria-adapted, having moved slowly through the lowlands. Finally, we used the finite-population size model to simulate the first passage time to reach key allele frequencies in New Guinea, providing approximate minimum age ranges of the onset of selection (1000 iterations).

For α-thalassemia (Figure 6.1A), we replicate and extend the frequency traces presented by Hedrick (2011a), using the same selection values (rescaled). Notably, the high frequency observed in northern lowland New Guinea can be achieved under strong selection within around 5500 years (finite simulations: mean 5275; 2.5th to 97.5th percentile range: 3425–9401). The time taken to reach lower frequencies of other coastal zones is correspondingly reduced. We include a trace showing the trajectory to near fixation to emphasise both the limited additional time required (around 2500 more years) and the predicted slow decline in frequency in the absence of malarial selection. This might argue that, had selection been acting for considerably longer than 5000 years, we would expect to see even higher frequencies, under the restrictive assumption of our model.

G6PDd can be caused by many variants on the G6PD gene. In New Guinea alone, at least 24 variants are known, with deficiency ranging between the severe Mediterranean and milder African levels (Chockkalingam et al. 1982; Wagner et al. 1996; Yenchitsomanus et al. 1986). We model selection on a single variant and include a representation of X-linked inheritance (Figure 6.1B). With no recent fitness estimates for New Guinea, we draw on work in Africa (Clarke et al. 2017). This suggests differential protective/susceptibility effects for cerebral malaria and severe malarial anaemia. We weighted equally the selection pressure from each condition, noting that both are prevalent in New Guinea (Allen et al. 1996). We included limited selection against G6PDd in the absence of malarial pressures (pre-reproductive mortality of 1 per cent), though the magnitude of such selection is unknown. Under these assumptions, high frequencies of G6PDd-causative variants in East Sepik (Beck et al. 1994) imply a long selection timeframe, potentially >15,000–20,000 years (finite simulations: mean 13,100; 2.5th to 97.5th percentile range: 4349–32,308). For WNG, survey data mainly from the north-east indicate wide local variation in frequencies (Prins et al. 1963). While allele frequencies may be lower than in East Sepik (Table 6.1), these are nevertheless consistent with selection over at least 5000 years. The probable limited selection against G6PDd in non-malarial zones implies slow relaxation to the very low frequencies observed in the highlands, such that G6PDd may have been rare, if present at all, in founding highland populations.

Interestingly, our age estimates based on the observed frequency and present-day mortality (Clarke et al. 2017) are significantly older than models drawing on observed frequency and haplotype diversity, which support the origins of several G6PDd haplotypes in the last 5000–10,000 years (Hedrick 2011b). These methods—not yet applied to New Guinean genetic variation—co-infer fitness with allele origin time, and tend to assume simpler fitness models than that implemented here; further work is required.

For SAO (Figure 6.1C), because homozygous embryos are generally inviable, strong selection is required to maintain high frequencies. Therefore, unlike our other examples, higher frequencies necessarily indicate stronger selection, and thus a more recent minimum bound on local allele age. For example, for Madang (deletion allele frequency p = 17.6 per cent) our models indicate a minimum time to reach the observed frequency of around 875 years (finite simulations: mean 702; 2.5th to 97.5th percentile range: 450–1150) whereas for Sentani (p = 3.8 per cent) the value is around 2750 years (finite simulations: mean 1974; 2.5th to 97.5th percentile range: 375–5376). Conversely, the frequency decay in the absence of malaria is rapid—observing SAO strongly suggests ongoing malarial mortality. Given p = 17.6 per cent (Table 6.1), inferred from an SAO frequency in Madang of 35.2 per cent (Mgone et al. 1996), pre-reproductive mortality from malaria among non-

SAO individuals of p(1–p) ~ 21 per cent (Dobzhansky 1972) is implied. This assumes equilibrium, and that the 35.2 per cent observation follows malaria selection. To maintain an SAO frequency of 35 per cent at birth (i.e. before malaria selection), a higher mortality of 27 per cent would be required. While Mgone and colleagues do not detect a clear trend of SAO frequency increasing with age cohorts (expected given strong selection), and while a separate Madang sample from Genton and colleagues (1995) supports lower mortality of around 9 per cent, the recent and ongoing human cost of malaria, and its impact on genes, is clear. From an epidemiological perspective, a fine-scale map of SAO prevalence could be a useful (if approximate) tool for understanding largely unknown local disease pressures over the last couple of thousand years.

Finally, we consider the Gerbich-negative blood group (Figure 6.1D). Very little is known about the degree of protection offered. While Serjeantson (1989) reports that it may reduce infection of *P. falciparum* and/or *P. vivax* by about 70 per cent, other studies have not found associations (Patel et al. 2001; Tavul et al. 2008). The condition is recessive (Booth and McLoughlin 1972; also see Reid et al. 1987), though the exact selection regime and selection coefficients for the various genotypes in malarial and non-malarial zones are unknown. We apply an example selection model with strong positive selection on the homozygote but including weak positive selection on the heterozygote— noting only that the high frequency observed in Wosera (Patel et al. 2004), for example, may imply long-term (e.g. >8000 years) selection under this model. Finite-population size simulations indicate wide bounds on first-passage time to 46.5 per cent (mean: 6758; 2.5th to 97.5th percentile range: 3123–14,110). The time depth is interesting given the absence of Gerbich-negative in the highlands, perhaps implying a post-highland/lowland population divergence origin of the allele, or unknown selection against the homozygote, or both.

Our models are simplifications and can only offer qualitative information on the history of selection at these loci. Nevertheless, observed frequencies are not independent of the selection process, and it is likely that certain general conclusions hold. In particular, SAO is informative about recent and ongoing selection processes, while the high frequency of several variants implies selection from malaria over millennia. Indeed, for G6PDd and α-thalassemia, selection regimes were modelled using regions with high current mortality, which may overestimate mortality given potentially reduced malaria prevalence in a past of lower population densities. Whether this tendency to underestimate antiquity counterbalances the effect of (random) genetic drift to high frequencies leading to cases of age overestimation is unclear. Ultimately, further genetic analysis, ideally including ancient DNA, is needed to understand past selection for malaria resistance, though models are consistent with pressures over several and perhaps many thousands of years.

Adaptation and diversity beyond malaria

The biological diversity and, where known, history of evolutionary adaptation among New Guineans is not limited to malaria. Table 6.2 considers the impact of environments (altitude and UV exposure), disease (kuru), and diet (low protein nutrition, lactose tolerance, and dietary starch). Each of these pressures is complex in different ways and, generally, knowledge of genetic adaptation is limited.

Table 6.2: Selected environmental pressures in New Guinea and related phenotypic/genetic variation.

Environmental pressure	Phenotypic variation	Genetic variation and evidence for selection
Altitude	Various: lung capacity in children, though potentially environmental (Anderson et al. 1978); stature, lung capacity, and haemoglobin concentration (André et al. 2021). Some mountain groups are especially short-statured, with potential links to growth hormone-binding protein (Baumann et al. 1991) or iodine-deficient environments and thyroid hormone (Tommaseo-Ponzetta et al. 2013).	Not yet known in New Guinea, though HLA haplotypes have been suggested as under altitude-related selection in ENG (Smith et al. 1994).
UV exposure	Variable melanin index (MI), particularly between mainland New Guinea and some islands e.g. Bougainville (Norton et al. 2006); reddish skin phenotype (Bearup 1936) with a proposed autosomal recessive factor (Walsh 1971) but likely complex genetic architecture (Littlewood 1972).	*OCA2* pigmentation-associated allele shows high differentiation between mainland NG and Bougainville (Lao et al. 2007); association of *TYRP1* variation with blond hair in the Solomon Islands (Kenny et al. 2012) but not in Bougainville (Norton et al. 2016) suggesting regional complexity; shared pigmentation-associated loci with Africans in *MFSD11*, *TMEM138*, *DDB1*, and *HERC2* (Crawford et al. 2017); signals of selection in Asian indigenous populations on 'basal Asian' ancestry, including e.g. archaic introgression potentially pigmentation-related *MTHFD1* (Deng et al. 2022).
Kuru prion disease due to ritual cannibalism	Prion disease resistance.	Multiple loci at the *PRNP* locus: heterozygote resistance to prion disease from M129V (Cervenáková et al. 1998) and genotype frequency changes through time among the Fore people affected by kuru (Mead et al. 2008); also resistance from *PRNP* M127V (Mead et al. 2009). GWAS potentially identifies additional loci. Genome-wide selection statistics vary (Quinn 2020).
Classically dietary lactose; though unlikely in New Guinea	Lactase persistence at up to 15% frequency in New Guinea (Jenkins et al. 1981).	Not yet known, especially given no history of dairying in New Guinea. Established lactase persistence alleles (rs41525747, rs4988235, rs41380347, rs869051967, rs145946881) are, as expected, absent in the New Guinean sample from Jacobs and colleagues (2019).
Low-protein diet, particularly in the highlands (Norgan et al. 1974; Ulijaszek 1992)	Healthy resilience to low protein intake.	Not known. Potentially microbiome-related adaptation (Greenhill et al. 2015).
High-starch diet	Globally, variation in amylase gene copy numbers has been associated with variation in dietary starch intake. Some traditional foods in New Guinea are high in starch (e.g. sago, sweet potato, other tubers).	Very limited information on amylase gene copy numbers; see text.

Note: HLA: human leukocyte antigen.

Source: Authors' summary.

Altitude

While altitude has an important effect in structuring malarial zones, high altitude also brings the physiological challenge of hypoxia. Most highland New Guinea populations live below the conventional 2500 m asl cut-off for high-altitude studies (Pawson and Jest 1978), though habitation ranges up to 2700 in some places (André et al. 2021). Some human biological correlates of altitude have been observed (Anderson et al. 1978; André et al. 2021), but any genetic component to these has yet to be confirmed.

Ultra-violet radiation

Skin pigmentation is under strong selection in global populations (Quillen et al. 2019), and several loci show patterns of regional variation and/or association consistent with past selection, though investigation in mainland New Guinea remains limited. A range of biological and cultural effects are probable (Harvey 1985; Norton et al. 2006; Walsh 1964). Research on shared and unique signals of selection in genome-wide surveys (Deng et al. 2022) has argued for pigmentation (and other) selection in the so-called 'basal Asian ancestry' of New Guineans, presumed by parsimony to have a dark skin tone. Ongoing surveys in both ENG (Morez et al. 2018) and WNG will shed light both on the distribution of skin pigmentation variation and the genetic factors driving it.

Prion disease

The kuru epidemic among the Fore of the PNG Eastern Highlands (reviewed in Alpers 1992) drew attention to the occurrence of transmissible prion disease in humans, with multiple genetic variants at the *PRNP* locus found to associate with susceptibility. These show some local signals of selection (Mead et al. 2009, 2008; Quinn 2020). Diversity in *PRNP* worldwide has led to suggestions of widespread ancient prion disease, perhaps driven by cannibalism (Mead et al. 2003). It is not known how common the consumption of human flesh was in New Guinea's deep past.

Diet

While diet has been a driver of genetic adaptation in humans, signals in New Guinea are limited. Recent selection scan work has identified variation in the genes *RARB*, *KCMB2*, and *POR* with potential dietary connections, respectively, to intestinal adaptive immunity in response to diet, a folic acid and methionine-rich diet, and polyphenol metabolism (Brucato et al. 2022). 'Classic' dietary signals have also been studied to some extent. Lactase persistence into adulthood—a globally recurrent adaptation to dairying traditions and drinking unprocessed milk—occurs at surprisingly high frequencies in New Guinea, up to 15 per cent, with inheritance consistent with a dominant genetic cause (Jenkins et al. 1981). It is not known whether this reflects drift on background genetic variation, an adaptation unrelated to dairy—for example, supporting the hydrolysis of phlorizin in plant foods, a hypothesised explanation for high lactase persistence in the Hadza (Ranciaro et al. 2014)—or a non-genetic factor such as the microbiome. Another widely discussed dietary adaptation is high amylase copy number potentially reflecting short (Perry et al. 2007) or longer-term (Inchley et al. 2016) adaptation to high-starch diets—potentially relevant in New Guinea given traditional consumption of sago and tubers. Just six individuals are included in the global study of Inchley and colleagues (2016), all identified as Haplotype E and with *AMY1* copy numbers (6–7) in line with the global average though potentially slightly elevated *AMY2A* copies (average 2.5). Twelve of the 18 tag-SNPs used by that team are known for the 56 New Guinean individuals in Jacobs and colleagues (2019), with the others potentially present but excluded during bioinformatic processing steps. These 12 define five different haplotypes, with the most common (26/56) consistent with

Haplotype E, though direct investigation of copy numbers is needed. Finally, the diet of healthy New Guineans is unusually low in protein (Norgan et al. 1974; Ulijaszek 1992), particularly among highlanders who have in recent centuries relied heavily on sweet potato. Recent literature has started to consider the gut microbiome in PNG (Greenhill et al. 2015; Martínez et al. 2015), including potential dietary drivers and the possibility that microbes, rather than adaptations in the human genome itself, might support health in the context of food intakes that would usually be considered protein-deficient.

Genetic variation of unknown adaptive significance with phenotypic consequences

Our discussion has focused on selection pressures. However, genetic variation with a more ambiguous evolutionary history can also have important present-day phenotypic effects. And malaria-resistance alleles can have health impacts beyond disease when they are homozygous—such as G6PDd potentially causing acute haemolysis on treatment with quinine-derived antimalarials. Before concluding, we briefly summarise, in Table 6.3, variation with known phenotypic effects but with unknown or speculative selection pressures.

Table 6.3: Selected genetic variation in New Guinea with potential health and drug associations.

Gene	New Guinea alleles	Associations
Apolipoprotein E	Allele ApoE 4 is at globally high frequency in New Guinea (e.g. 49% among the Huli)	Lipid profiles (Abondio et al. 2019); Alzheimer's Disease (Sadigh-Eteghad et al. 2012); malaria risk (Aucan et al. 2004) and/or protection (Fujioka et al. 2013); life history trade-offs (Abondio et al. 2019).
G6PD	High G6PDd frequency in the lowlands	Malaria resistance, but also risk of acute haemolysis on treatment with quinine-derived antimalarials.
CYP2B6	Allele 516G>T *6 is at globally high frequency in PNG (Andriguetti et al. 2021)	Efavirenz (HIV) and other drug metabolism, including artemisinin (antimalarial).
AHRR	AHRR variant Pro185Ala at high frequency in East Sepik	Regulates CYP1A2 inducibility, with potential cancer risk consequences for betel chewing, given role of this enzyme in DNA adduct formation (Cavaco et al. 2013). CYP1A2 also involved in drug metabolism, including efavirenz.
CYP2C19	Loss of function variants *2 and *3 at high frequency in ENG (Hsu et al. 2008)	Poor metaboliser phenotype for various drugs, including proguanil (antimalarial).
CYP2D6	High genetic variation and heterozygosity in PNG (von Ahsen et al. 2010)	High rate of CYP2D6 ultra-rapid metabolisers, including primaquine (antimalarial).

Source: Authors' summary.

We firstly emphasise the complex case of Apolipoprotein E ancestral isoform ApoE 4, common in some populations in New Guinea (Abondio et al. 2019). Phenotypic impacts are varied—from lipid profiles, to immune responses, malaria risk, and extremely strong association with Alzheimer's Disease (Sadigh-Eteghad et al. 2012). Which combination of phenotypic impacts, if any, maintained ApoE 4 at high frequency in part of New Guinea is not clear, but the potential for important impacts on contemporary and indeed past health is strong. We secondly draw attention to pharmacogenetic variation. In this context, we note that archaic introgression (reviewed in Jacobs et al., this volume) has had an outsized effect on immunity (Gouy and Excoffier 2020; Vespasiani et al. 2022), with some functional investigation (Natri et al. 2022; Zammit et al. 2019). While the extent to which pharmacogenetic variation has been under natural selection in New Guinea remains an open question, extending existing work to better understand local variation in drug response, particularly given the high diversity and genetic differentiation between New Guinean populations, is an important health focus given the high infectious disease load.

Future directions: Research and application

The biological diversity of present-day New Guinean peoples reflects the outcome of demography, selection, and their interactions, all in a local environmental and social context. This diversity is important for the insights it can provide into the challenges people faced, from the first arrivals to present-day inhabitants. Our focus on malaria reflects its major historic and ongoing health burden, as well as available research. For other phenotypes, genetic variants and the exact extent of selective pressures are often unknown. In drawing attention to biological variation that is not yet well characterised we hope that this chapter inspires future research.

What steps would be needed to meet this research challenge? The call for more (community-supported) genomic sampling, with carefully collected phenotype and health data, is clearly a prerequisite. Sample sizes suitable for selection scans are easily reached, though interpretation is challenging without strong prior hypotheses and functional validation. Local—rather than European-ancestry—genome-wide association studies would also help, but these require large samples, focused questions, and simple genetic architecture to anticipate success, especially given local population structure. Combined epidemiological and genetic surveys are also needed. Recently, targeted studies investigating population variation in gene regulation and epigenetics (Natri et al. 2020, 2022), including in a medical context (Bobowik et al. 2021), have emerged from the region. Such methods can help to elucidate the impact and, potentially, the evolutionary history of genetic variation. Finally, we note that human biology is an emergent phenomenon, based not only on our genetic variation and development, but also on our community biology. Given especially the broad range of diets and environments in New Guinea, we look forward to developments in microbiome analysis (Greenhill et al. 2015; Martínez et al. 2015). Modelling, extending the approach taken here, may also be useful when connecting present-day variation to the evolutionary past.

The scale of this challenge is considerable, and the path may be a slow one. But steps will be made. We look forward to new results that both clarify regional evolutionary history, including the extent to which biology has constrained and enabled occupation and lifeways in New Guinea, and, especially, that support local health outcomes.

Acknowledgements

The writing of our three chapters was greatly assisted by advice from and discussion with Michael Alpers, Nigel Beebe, Tom Burkot, Chris Hunt, Robin Hide, Deirdre Joy, Andrew Pawley, Ric Price, Rupert Stasch, Tom Williams, and especially Dylan Gaffney, which we gratefully acknowledge. Any remaining errors are our own responsibility.

References

Abondio, P., M. Sazzini, P. Garagnani, A. Boattini, D. Monti, C. Franceschi, D. Luiselli, and C. Giuliani 2019. The genetic variability of *APOE* in different human populations and its implications for longevity. *Genes* 10:E222. doi.org/10.3390/genes10030222.

Allen, B.J. 1992. The geography of Papua New Guinea. In R. Attenborough and M.P. Alpers (eds), *Human biology in Papua New Guinea: The small cosmos,* pp. 36–66. Clarendon Press, Oxford. doi.org/10.1093/oso/9780198575146.003.0002.

Allen, S.J., A. O'Donnell, N.D. Alexander, and J.B. Clegg 1996. Severe malaria in children in Papua New Guinea. *QJM Monthly Journal of the Association of Physicians* 89:779–788. doi.org/10.1093/qjmed/89.10.779.

Alpers, M.P. 1992. Kuru. In R. Attenborough and M.P. Alpers (eds), *Human biology in Papua New Guinea: The small cosmos,* pp. 313–334. Clarendon Press, Oxford. doi.org/10.1093/oso/9780198575146.003.0016.

Alpers, M.P. 2018. Personal reflections on malaria after 40 years of the Malaria Research Program at the Papua New Guinea Institute of Medical Research. *PNG Medical Journal* 61:3–14.

Anderson, H.R., J.A. Anderson, H.O.M. King, and J.E. Cotes 1978. Variations in the lung size of children in Papua New Guinea: genetic and environmental factors. *Annals of Human Biology* 5:209–218. doi.org/10.1080/03014467800002831.

André, M., N. Brucato, S. Plutniak, J. Kariwiga, J. Muke, A. Morez, M. Leavesley, M. Mondal, and F.-X. Ricaut 2021. Phenotypic differences between highlanders and lowlanders in Papua New Guinea. *PLoS ONE* 16:e0253921. doi.org/10.1371/journal.pone.0253921.

Andriguetti, N.B., H.K. van Schalkwyk, D.T. Barratt, J. Tucci, P. Pumuye, and A.A. Somogyi 2021. Large variability in plasma efavirenz concentration in Papua New Guinea HIV/AIDS patients associated with high frequency of *CYP2B6* 516T allele. *Clinical and Translational Science* 14: 2521–2531. doi.org/10.1111/cts.13120.

Attenborough, R. 2007. Health changes in Papua New Guinea: From adaptation to double jeopardy? In R. Ohtsuka and S.J. Ulijaszek (eds), *Health change in the Asia-Pacific region,* pp. 254–302. Cambridge Studies in Biological and Evolutionary Anthropology. Cambridge University Press, Cambridge. doi.org/10.1017/CBO9780511542510.012.

Attenborough, R. 2015. What are species and why does it matter? Anopheline taxonomy and the transmission of malaria. In A.M. Behie and M.F. Oxenham (eds), *Taxonomic tapestries: The threads of evolutionary, behavioural and conservation research,* pp. 129–152. ANU Press, Canberra. doi.org/10.22459/TT.05.2015.07.

Attenborough, R.D., T.R. Burkot, and D.S. Gardner 1997. Altitude and the risk of bites from mosquitoes infected with malaria and filariasis among the Mianmin people of Papua New Guinea. *Transactions of the Royal Society of Tropical Medicine and Hygiene* 91:8–10. doi.org/10.1016/S0035-9203(97)90373-4.

Aucan, C., A.J. Walley, and A.V.S. Hill 2004. Common apolipoprotein E polymorphisms and risk of clinical malaria in the Gambia. *Journal of Medical Genetics* 41:21–24. doi.org/10.1136/jmg.2003.011981.

Baumann, G., M.A. Shaw, R.C. Brumbaugh, and J. Schwartz 1991. Short stature and decreased serum growth hormone-binding protein in the Mountain Ok people of Papua New Guinea. *The Journal of Clinical Endocrinology & Metabolism* 72:1346–1349. doi.org/10.1210/jcem-72-6-1346.

Bearup, A.J. 1936. The Ramu and Wahgi Valleys of New Guinea. *Australian Geographer* 3:3–14. doi.org/10.1080/00049183608702160.

Beck, H.P., I. Felger, S. Kabintik, L. Tavul, B. Genton, N. Alexander, K.K. Bhatia, F. Al-Yaman, J. Hii, and M. Alpers 1994. Assessment of the humoral and cell-mediated immunity against the *Plasmodium falciparum* vaccine candidates circumsporozoite protein and SPf66 in adults living in highly endemic malarious areas of Papua New Guinea. *American Journal of Tropical Medicine and Hygiene* 51(3):356–364. doi.org/10.4269/ajtmh.1994.51.356.

Beebe, N.W., T.L. Russell, T.R. Burkot, N.F. Lobo, and R.D. Cooper 2013. The systematics and bionomics of malaria vectors in the Southwest Pacific. In S. Manguin (ed.), Anopheles *Mosquitoes*. IntechOpen, New York. doi.org/10.5772/55999.

Bobowik, K., D. Syafruddin, C.C. Darusallam, H. Sudoyo, C. Wells, and I. Gallego Romero 2021. Transcriptomic profiles of *Plasmodium falciparum* and *Plasmodium vivax*-infected individuals in Indonesia. *bioRxiv* 2021.01.07.425684. doi.org/10.1101/2021.01.07.425684.

Booth, P.B. and K. McLoughlin 1972. The Gerbich blood group system, especially in Melanesians. *Vox Sanguinis* 22(1):73–84. doi.org/10.1111/j.1423-0410.1972.tb03968.x.

Booth, P.B., K. McLoughlin, R.W. Hornabrook, A. Macgregor, and L.A. Malcolm 1972a. The Gerbich blood group system in New Guinea. II. The Morobe District and North Papuan Coast. *Human Biology in Oceania* 1:259–266.

Booth, P.B., K. McLoughlin, R.W. Hornabrook, and A. Macgregor 1972b. The Gerbich blood group system in New Guinea. III. The Madang District, the Highlands, the New Guinea Islands and the South Papuan Coast. *Human Biology in Oceania* 1:267–272.

Booth, P.B., L. Wark, K. McLoughlin, and R. Spark 1972c. The Gerbich blood group system in New Guinea. I. The Sepik District. *Human Biology in Oceania* 1:215–222.

Boyce, A.J., R.M. Harding, and J.J. Martinson 1995. Population genetics of the α-globin complex in Oceania. In A.J. Boyce and V. Reynolds (eds), *Human populations: Diversity and adaptation,* pp. 217–232. Oxford University Press, Oxford. doi.org/10.1093/oso/9780198522942.003.0012.

Brucato, N., M. André, G. Hudjashov, M. Mondal, M.P. Cox, M. Leavesley, and F.-X. Ricaut 2022. Chronology of natural selection in Oceanian genomes. *iScience* 25(7):104583. doi.org/10.1016/j.isci.2022.104583.

Bruce-Chwatt, L.J. 1987. Malaria and its control: Present situation and future prospects. *Annual Review of Public Health* 8:75–110. doi.org/10.1146/annurev.pu.08.050187.000451.

Bulmer, S.E. and R.N.H. Bulmer 1964. The prehistory of the Australian New Guinea Highlands. *American Anthropologist* 66(4):39–76.

Cattani, J.A. 1992. The epidemiology of malaria in Papua New Guinea. In R. Attenborough and M.P. Alpers (eds), *Human biology in Papua New Guinea: The small cosmos*, pp. 302–312. Clarendon Press, Oxford. doi.org/10.1093/oso/9780198575146.003.0015.

Cavaco, I., F.W. Hombhanje, J.P. Gil, and A. Kaneko 2013. Frequency of the functionally relevant aryl hydrocarbon receptor repressor (AhRR) Pro185Ala SNP in Papua New Guinea. *Drug Metabolism and Pharmacokinetics* 28:519–521. doi.org/10.2133/dmpk.dmpk-13-sc-035.

Cavalli-Sforza, L.L., P. Menozzi, and A. Piazza 1994. *The history and geography of human genes*. Princeton University Press, Princeton.

Cervenáková, L., L.G. Goldfarb, R. Garruto, H.-S. Lee, D.C. Gajdusek, and P. Brown 1998. Phenotype-genotype studies in kuru: Implications for new variant Creutzfeldt–Jakob disease. *Proceedings of the National Academy of Sciences* 95:13239–13241. doi.org/10.1073/pnas.95.22.13239.

Chappell, J. 2005. Geographic changes of coastal lowlands in the Papuan past. In A. Pawley, R. Attenborough, J. Golson, and R. Hide (eds), *Papuan pasts: Cultural, linguistic and biological histories of the Papuan-speaking peoples.* pp. 525–540. Pacific Linguistics 572. Research School of Pacific and Asian Studies, The Australian National University, Canberra.

Chockkalingam, K., P.G. Board, and G.T. Nurse 1982. Glucose-6-phosphate dehydrogenase deficiency in Papua New Guinea. The description of 13 new variants. *Human Genetics* 60:189–192. doi.org/10.1007/BF00569710.

Clark, J.T., and K.M. Kelly 1993. Human genetics, paleoenvironments, and malaria: Relationships and implications for the settlement of Oceania. *American Anthropologist* 95:612–630. doi.org/10.1525/aa.1993.95.3.02a00040.

Clarke, G.M., K. Rockett, K. Kivinen, C. Hubbart, A.E. Jeffreys, K. Rowlands, M. Jallow, D.J. Conway, K.A. Bojang, M. Pinder, S. Usen, F. Sisay-Joof, G. Sirugo, O. Toure, M.A. Thera, S. Konate, S. Sissoko, A. Niangaly, B. Poudiougou, V.D. Mangano, E.C. Bougouma, S.B. Sirima, D. Modiano, L.N. Amenga-Etego, A. Ghansah, K.A. Koram, M.D. Wilson, A. Enimil, J. Evans, O.K. Amodu, S. Olaniyan, T. Apinjoh, R. Mugri, A. Ndi, C.M. Ndila, S. Uyoga, A. Macharia, N. Peshu, T.N. Williams, A. Manjurano, N. Sepúlveda, T.G. Clark, E. Riley, C. Drakeley, H. Reyburn, V. Nyirongo, D. Kachala, M. Molyneux, S.J. Dunstan, N.H. Phu, N.N. Quyen, C.Q. Thai, T.T. Hien, L. Manning, M. Laman, P. Siba, H. Karunajeewa, S. Allen, A. Allen, T.M.E. Davis, P. Michon, I. Mueller, S.F. Molloy, S. Campino, A. Kerasidou, V.J. Cornelius, L. Hart, S.S. Shah, G. Band, C.C.A. Spencer, T. Agbenyega, E. Achidi, O.K. Doumbo, J. Farrar, K. Marsh, T. Taylor, D.P. Kwiatkowski, and MalariaGEN Consortium 2017. Characterisation of the opposing effects of G6PD deficiency on cerebral malaria and severe malarial anaemia. *eLife* 6:e15085. doi.org/10.7554/eLife.15085.

Cockburn, I.A., M.J. Mackinnon, A. O'Donnell, S.J. Allen, J.M. Moulds, M. Baisor, M. Bockarie, J.C. Reeder, and J.A. Rowe 2003. A human complement receptor 1 polymorphism that reduces *Plasmodium falciparum* rosetting confers protection against severe malaria. *Proceedings of the National Academy of Sciences* 101(1):272–277. doi.org/10.1073/pnas.0305306101.

Crawford, N.G., D.E. Kelly, M.E.B. Hansen, M.H. Beltrame, S. Fan, S.L. Bowman, E. Jewett, A. Ranciaro, S. Thompson, Y. Lo, S.P. Pfeifer, J.D. Jensen, M.C. Campbell, W. Beggs, F. Hormozdiari, S.W. Mpoloka, G.G. Mokone, T. Nyambo, D.W. Meskel, G. Belay, J. Haut, NISC Comparative Sequencing Program, H. Rothschild, L. Zon, Y. Zhou, M.A. Kovacs, M. Xu, T. Zhang, K. Bishop, J. Sinclair, C. Rivas, E. Elliot, J. Choi, S.A. Li, B. Hicks, S. Burgess, C. Abnet, D.E. Watkins-Chow, E. Oceana, Y.S. Song, E. Eskin, K.M. Brown, M.S. Marks, S.K. Loftus, W.J. Pavan, M. Yeager, S. Chanock, and S.A. Tishkoff 2017. Loci associated with skin pigmentation identified in African populations. *Science* 358:eaan8433. doi.org/10.1126/science.aan8433.

Deng, L., Y. Pan, Y. Wang, H. Chen, K. Yuan, S. Chen, D. Lu, Y. Lu, S.S. Mokhtar, T.A. Rahman, B.-P. Hoh, and S. Xu 2022. Genetic connections and convergent evolution of tropical Indigenous peoples in Asia. *Molecular Biology and Evolution* 39:msab361. doi.org/10.1093/molbev/msab361.

Devine, A., E. Kenangalem, F.H. Burdam, N.M. Anstey, J.R. Poespoprodjo, R.N. Price, and S. Yeung 2017. Treatment-seeking behavior after the implementation of a unified policy of Dihydroartemisinin-Piperaquine for the treatment of uncomplicated malaria in Papua, Indonesia. *American Journal of Tropical Medicine and Hygiene* 98:543–550. doi.org/10.4269/ajtmh.17-0680.

Diamond, J. 1989. Blood, genes and malaria. *Natural History* 8–18.

Dobzhansky, T. 1972. Natural selection in mankind. In G.A. Harrison and A.J. Boyce (eds), *The structure of human populations*, pp. 213–233. Clarendon Press, Oxford.

Douglas, N.M., G.J. Pontororing, D.A. Lampah, T.W. Yeo, E. Kenangalem, J.R. Poespoprodjo, A.P. Ralph, M.J. Bangs, P. Sugiarto, N.M. Anstey, and R.N. Price 2014. Mortality attributable to *Plasmodium vivax* malaria: A clinical audit from Papua, Indonesia. *BMC Medicine* 12:217. doi.org/10.1186/s12916-014-0217-z.

Durham, W.H. 1991. *Coevolution: Genes, culture, and human diversity*. Stanford University Press, Stanford. doi.org/10.1515/9781503621534.

Esoh, K. and A. Wonkam 2021. Evolutionary history of sickle-cell mutation: Implications for global genetic medicine. *Human Molecular Genetics* 30(2):R119–R128. doi.org/10.1093/hmg/ddab004.

Ewers, W. 1972a. Robert Koch, his work in New Guinea, and his contribution to malariology. *PNG Medical Journal* 15:117–124.

Ewers, W. 1972b. Malaria in the early years of German New Guinea. *Journal of the Papua New Guinea Society* 6:3–30.

Flint, J., A.V.S. Hill, D.K. Bowden, S.J. Oppenheimer, P.R. Sill, S.W. Serjeantson, J. Bana-Koiri, K. Bhatia, M.P. Alpers, A.J. Boyce, D.J. Weatherall, and J.B. Clegg 1986. High frequencies of α-thalassaemia are the result of natural selection by malaria. *Nature* 321:744–750. doi.org/10.1038/321744a0.

Flint, J., R.M. Harding, J.B. Clegg, and A.J. Boyce 1993. Why are some genetic diseases common? Distinguishing selection from other processes by molecular analysis of globin gene variants. *Human Genetics* 91:91–117. doi.org/10.1007/BF00222709.

Fujioka, H., C.F. Phelix, R.P. Friedland, X. Zhu, E.A. Perry, R.J. Castellani, and G. Perry 2013. Apolipoprotein E4 prevents growth of malaria at the intraerythrocyte stage: Implications for differences in racial susceptibility to Alzheimer's disease. *Journal of Health Care for the Poor and Underserved* 24:70–78. doi.org/10.1353/hpu.2014.0009.

Gaffney, D. and T. Denham 2021. The archaeology of social transformation in the New Guinea highlands. In I.J. McNiven and B. David (eds), *The Oxford handbook of the archaeology of Indigenous Australia and New Guinea*. Oxford University Press, Oxford. doi.org/10.1093/oxfordhb/9780190095611.013.31.

Gaffney, D., G.R. Summerhayes, S. Luu, J. Menzies, K. Douglass, M. Spitzer, and S. Bulmer 2021. Small game hunting in montane rainforests: Specialised capture and broad spectrum foraging in the Late Pleistocene to Holocene New Guinea Highlands. *Quaternary Science Reviews* 253:106742. doi.org/10.1016/j.quascirev.2020.106742.

Genton, B., F. Al-Yaman, C.S. Mgone, N. Alexander, M.M. Paniu, M.P. Alpers, and D. Mokela 1995. Ovalocytosis and cerebral malaria. *Nature* 378:564–565. doi.org/10.1038/378564a0.

Gouy, A. and L. Excoffier 2020. Polygenic patterns of adaptive introgression in modern humans are mainly shaped by response to pathogens. *Molecular Biology and Evolution* 37:1420–1433. doi.org/10.1093/molbev/msz306.

Greenhill, A.R., H. Tsuji, K. Ogata, K. Natsuhara, A. Morita, K. Soli, J.-A. Larkins, K. Tadokoro, S. Odani, J. Baba, Y. Naito, E. Tomitsuka, K. Nomoto, P.M. Siba, P.F. Horwood, and M. Umezaki 2015. Characterization of the gut microbiota of Papua New Guineans using reverse transcription quantitative PCR. *PLoS ONE* 10:e0117427. doi.org/10.1371/journal.pone.0117427.

Groube, L.M. 1993. Contradictions and malaria in Melanesian and Australian prehistory. In M. Spriggs, D.E. Yen, W. Ambrose, R. Jones, A. Thorne, and A. Andrews (eds), *A community of culture: The people and prehistory of the Pacific*, pp. 164-186. Department of Prehistory, Research School of Pacific Studies, The Australian National University, Canberra.

Groube, L.M. 2000. *Plasmodium falciparum*: The African Genesis. In A. Anderson and T. Murray (eds), *Australian archaeologist: Collected papers in honour of Jim Allen.* pp. 131–144. Coombs Academic Publishing, The Australian National University, Canberra.

Haberle, S.G. 1993. Pleistocene vegetation change and early human occupation of a tropical mountainous environment. In M.A. Smith, M. Spriggs, and B. Fankhauser (eds), *Sahul in review: Pleistocene archaeology in Australia, New Guinea and Island Melanesia*, pp. 109–122. Department of Prehistory, The Australian National University, Canberra.

Harvey, R.G. 1985. Ecological factors in skin color variation among Papua New Guineans. *American Journal of Physical Anthropology* 66:407–416. doi.org/10.1002/ajpa.1330660409.

Hedrick, P.W. 2011a. Selection and mutation for α thalassemia in nonmalarial and malarial environments. *Annals of Human Genetics* 75:468–474. doi.org/10.1111/j.1469-1809.2011.00653.x.

Hedrick, P.W. 2011b. Population genetics of malaria resistance in humans. *Heredity* 107:283–304. doi.org/10.1038/hdy.2011.16.

Hope, G.S. and S.G. Haberle 2005. The history of the human landscapes of New Guinea. In A. Pawley, R. Attenborough, J. Golson, and R. Hide (eds), *Papuan pasts: Cultural, linguistic and biological histories of the Papuan-speaking peoples*, pp. 541–554. Pacific Linguistics 572. Research School of Pacific and Asian Studies, The Australian National University, Canberra.

Hope, G. and J. Tulip 1994. A long vegetation history from lowland Irian Jaya, Indonesia. *Palaeogeography, Palaeoclimatology, Palaeoecology* 109:385–398. doi.org/10.1016/0031-0182(94)90187-2.

Hope, G., A.P. Kershaw, S. van der Kaars, S. Xiangjun, P.-M. Liew, L.E. Heusser, H. Takahara, M. McGlone, N. Miyoshi, and P.T. Moss 2004. History of vegetation and habitat change in the Austral-Asian region. *Quaternary International* 118–119:103–126. doi.org/10.1016/S1040-6182(03)00133-2.

Howes, R.E., F.B. Piel, A.P. Patil, O.A. Nyangiri, P.W. Gething, M. Dewi, M.M. Hogg, K.E. Battle, C.D. Padilla, J.K. Baird, and S.I. Hay 2012. G6PD deficiency prevalence and estimates of affected populations in malaria endemic countries: A geostatistical model-based map. *PLoS Medicine* 9(11):p.e1001339. doi.org/10.1371/journal.pmed.1001339.

Howes, R.E., M. Dewi, F.B. Piel, W.M. Monteiro, K.E. Battle, J.P. Messina, A. Sakuntabhai, A.W. Satyagraha, T.N. Williams, J.K. Baird, and S.I. Hay 2013. Spatial distribution of G6PD deficiency variants across malaria-endemic regions. *Malaria Journal* 12:418. doi.org/10.1186/1475-2875-12-418.

Hsu, H.-L., K.J. Woad, D.G. Woodfield, and N.A. Helsby 2008. A high incidence of polymorphic *CYP2C19* variants in archival blood samples from Papua New Guinea. *Human Genomics* 3:17–23. doi.org/10.1186/1479-7364-3-1-17.

Hume, J.C.C., E.J. Lyons, and K.P. Day 2003. Malaria in antiquity: A genetics perspective. *World Archaeology* 35:180–192. doi.org/10.1080/0043824032000111362.

Hunt, C.O., D.D. Gilbertson, and G. Rushworth 2012. A 50,000-year record of late Pleistocene tropical vegetation and human impact in lowland Borneo. *Quaternary Science Reviews* 37:61–80. doi.org/10.1016/j.quascirev.2012.01.014.

Hupalo, D.N., Z. Luo, A. Melnikov, P.L. Sutton, P. Rogov, A. Escalante, A.F. Vallejo, S. Herrera, M. Arévalo-Herrera, Q. Fan, Y. Wang, L. Cui, C.M. Lucas, S. Durand, J.F. Sanchez, G.C. Baldeviano, A.G. Lescano, M. Laman, C. Barnadas, A. Barry, I. Mueller, J.W. Kazura, A. Eapen, D. Kanagaraj, N. Valecha, M.U. Ferreira, W. Roobsoong, W. Nguitragool, J. Sattabonkot, D. Gamboa, M. Kosek, J.M. Vinetz, L. González-Cerón, B.W. Birren, D.E. Neafsey, and J.M. Carlton2016. Population genomics studies identify signatures of global dispersal and drug resistance in *Plasmodium vivax*. *Nature Genetics* 48:953–958. doi.org/10.1038/ng.3588.

Inchley, C.E., C.D.A. Larbey, N.A.A. Shwan, L. Pagani, L. Saag, T. Antão, G. Jacobs, G. Hudjashov, E. Metspalu, M. Mitt, C.A. Eichstaedt, B. Malyarchuk, M. Derenko, J. Wee, S. Abdullah, F.-X. Ricaut, M. Mormina, R. Mägi, R. Villems, M. Metspalu, M.K. Jones, J.A.L. Armour, and T. Kivisild 2016. Selective sweep on human amylase genes postdates the split with Neanderthals. *Scientific Reports* 6:37198. doi.org/10.1038/srep37198.

Jacobs, G.S., G. Hudjashov, L. Saag, P. Kusuma, C.C. Darusallam, D.J. Lawson, M. Mondal, L. Pagani, F.-X. Ricaut, M. Stoneking, M. Metspalu, H. Sudoyo, J.S. Lansing, and M.P. Cox 2019. Multiple deeply divergent Denisovan ancestries in Papuans. *Cell* 177:1010–1021.e32. doi.org/10.1016/j.cell.2019.02.035.

Jenkins, T., S.F. Gibney, G.T. Nurse, and R.J.A. Penketh 1981. Persistent high intestinal lactase activity in Papua New Guinea. Lactose absorption curves in two populations. *Annals of Human Biology* 8:447–451. doi.org/10.1080/03014468100005271.

Joy, D.A., X. Feng, J. Mu, T. Furuya, K. Chotivanich, A. U. Krettli, M. Ho, A. Wang, N.J. White, E. Suh, P. Beerli, and X.-z. Su 2003. Early origin and recent expansion of *Plasmodium falciparum*. *Science* 300: 318–321. doi.org/10.1126/science.1081449.

Kariuki, S.N. and T.N. Williams 2020. Human genetics and malaria resistance. *Human Genetics* 139:801–811. doi.org/10.1007/s00439-020-02142-6.

Kattenberg, J.H., D.L. Gumal, M. Ome-Kaius, B. Kiniboro, M. Philip, S. Jally, B. Kasian, N. Sambale, P.M. Siba, S. Karl, A.E. Barry, I. Felger, J.W. Kazura, I. Mueller, and L.J. Robinson 2020. The epidemiology of *Plasmodium falciparum* and *Plasmodium vivax* in East Sepik Province, Papua New Guinea, pre- and post-implementation of national malaria control efforts. *Malaria Journal* 19:198. doi.org/10.1186/s12936-020-03265-x.

Kawulur, H.S.I., H. Krismawati, and C. Imaniar 2020. Screening of glucose-6-phosphate dehydrogenase (G6PD) deficiency in two high endemic malaria populations, West Papua province and North Moluccas. *AIP Conference Proceedings* 2260:040014. doi.org/10.1063/5.0017808.

Kenangalem, E., J.R. Poespoprodjo, N.M. Douglas, F.H. Burdam, K. Gdeumana, F. Chalfein, Prayoga, F. Thio, A. Devine, J. Marfurt, G. Waramori, S. Yeung, R. Noviyanti, P. Penttinen, M.J. Bangs, P. Sugiarto, J.A. Simpson, Y. Soenarto, N.M. Anstey, and R.N. Price 2019. Malaria morbidity and mortality following introduction of a universal policy of artemisinin-based treatment for malaria in Papua, Indonesia: A longitudinal surveillance study. *PloS Medicine* 16:e1002815. doi.org/10.1371/journal.pmed.1002815.

Kenny, E.E., N.J. Timpson, M. Sikora, M.-C. Yee, A. Moreno-Estrada, C. Eng, S. Huntsman, E.G. Burchard, M. Stoneking, C.D. Bustamante, and S. Myles 2012. Melanesian blond hair is caused by an amino acid change in *TYRP1*. *Science* 336:554–554. doi.org/10.1126/science.1217849.

Kho, S., L. Qotrunnada, L. Leonardo, B. Andries, P.A.I. Wardani, A. Fricot, B. Henry, D. Hardy, N.I. Margyaningsih, D. Apriyanti, A.M. Puspitasari, P. Prayoga, L. Trianty, E. Kenangalem, F. Chretien, I. Safeukui, H.A. del Portillo, C. Fernandez-Becerra, E. Meibalan, M. Marti, R.N. Price, T. Woodberry, P.A. Ndour, B.M. Russell, T.W. Yeo, G. Minigo, R. Noviyanti, J.R. Poespoprodjo, N.C. Siregar, P.A. Buffet, and N.M. Anstey2021. Hidden biomass of intact malaria parasites in the human spleen. *New England Journal of Medicine* 384:2067–2069. doi.org/10.1056/NEJMc2023884.

Kissinger, J.C. 2016. An unsettling picture emerges from population genomic studies of *Plasmodium vivax*. *Nature Genetics* 48:825–826. doi.org/10.1038/ng.3630.

Lao, O., J.M. de Gruijter, K. van Duijn, A. Navarro, and M. Kayser 2007. Signatures of positive selection in genes associated with human skin pigmentation as revealed from analyses of single nucleotide polymorphisms. *Annals of Human Genetics* 71:354–369. doi.org/10.1111/j.1469-1809.2006.00341.x.

Lavu, E.K., G. Oswyn, and J.D. Vince 2002. Sickle-cell/β+-thalassaemia in a Papua New Guinean: the first reported case of the sickle gene in Papua New Guinea. *The Medical Journal of Australia* 176:70–71. doi.org/10.5694/j.1326-5377.2002.tb04288.x.

Leclerc, M.C., P. Durand, C. Gauthier, S. Patot, N. Billotte, M. Menegon, C. Severini, F.J. Ayala, and F. Renaud 2004. Meager genetic variability of the human malaria agent *Plasmodium vivax*. *Proceedings of the National Academy of Sciences* 101:14455–14460. doi.org/10.1073/pnas.0405186101.

Littlewood, R.A. 1972. *Physical anthropology of the Eastern Highlands of New Guinea*. Anthropological Studies in the Eastern Highlands of New Guinea. University of Washington Press, Seattle.

Liu, W., Y. Li, K.S. Shaw, G.H. Learn, L.J. Plenderleith, J.A. Malenke, S.A. Sundararaman, M.A. Ramirez, P.A. Crystal, A.G. Smith, F. Bibollet-Ruche, A. Ayouba, S. Locatelli, A. Esteban, F. Mouacha, E. Guichet, C. Butel, S. Ahuka-Mundeke, B.-I. Inogwabini, J.-B.N. Ndjango, S. Speede, C.M. Sanz, D.B. Morgan, M.K. Gonder, P.J. Kranzusch, P.D. Walsh, A.V. Georgiev, M.N. Muller, A.K. Piel, F.A. Stewart, M.L. Wilson, A.E. Pusey, L. Cui, Z. Wang, A. Färnert, C.J. Sutherland, D. Nolder, J.A. Hart, T.B. Hart, P. Bertolani, A. Gillis, M. LeBreton, B. Tafon, J. Kiyang, C.F. Djoko, B.S. Schneider, N.D. Wolfe, E. Mpoudi-Ngole, E. Delaporte, R. Carter, R.L. Culleton, G.M. Shaw, J.C. Rayner, M. Peeters, B.H. Hahn, and P.M. Sharp 2014. African origin of the malaria parasite *Plasmodium vivax*. *Nature Communications* 5:3346. doi.org/10.1038/ncomms4346.

Liu, W., Y. Li, G.H. Learn, R.S. Rudicell, J.D. Robertson, B.F. Keele, J.-B.N. Ndjango, C.M. Sanz, D.B. Morgan, S. Locatelli, M.K. Gonder, P.J. Kranzusch, P.D. Walsh, E. Delaporte, E. Mpoudi-Ngole, A.V. Georgiev, M.N. Muller, G.M. Shaw, M. Peeters, P.M. Sharp, J.C. Rayner, and B.H. Hahn 2010. Origin of the human malaria parasite *Plasmodium falciparum* in gorillas. *Nature* 467:420–425. doi.org/10.1038/nature09442.

Loy, D.E., W. Liu, Y. Li, G.H. Learn, L.J. Plenderleith, S.A. Sundararaman, P.M. Sharp, and B.H. Hahn 2017. Out of Africa: Origins and evolution of the human malaria parasites *Plasmodium falciparum* and *Plasmodium vivax*. *International Journal of Parasitology* 47:87–97. doi.org/10.1016/j.ijpara.2016.05.008.

Maitland, K., T.N. Williams and C.I. Newbold 1997. *Plasmodium vivax* and *P. falciparum*: Biological interactions and the possibility of cross-species immunity. *Parasitology Today* 13:227–231. doi.org/10.1016/s0169-4758(97)01061-2.

Martínez, I., J.C. Stegen, M.X. Maldonado-Gómez, A.M. Eren, P.M. Siba, A.R. Greenhill, and J. Walter 2015. The gut microbiota of rural Papua New Guineans: Composition, diversity patterns, and ecological processes. *Cell Reports* 11:527–538. doi.org/10/3vh.

Mead, S., M.P.H. Stumpf, J. Whitfield, J.A. Beck, M. Poulter, T. Campbell, J.B. Uphill, D. Goldstein, M. Alpers, E.M.C. Fisher, and J. Collinge 2003. Balancing selection at the prion protein gene consistent with prehistoric kurulike epidemics. *Science* 300:640–643. doi.org/10.1126/science.1083320.

Mead, S., J. Whitfield, M. Poulter, P. Shah, J. Uphill, J. Beck, T. Campbell, H. Al-Dujaily, H. Hummerich, M.P. Alpers, and J. Collinge 2008. Genetic susceptibility, evolution and the kuru epidemic. *Philosophical Transactions of the Royal Society B* 363:3741–3746. doi.org/10.1098/rstb.2008.0087.

Mead, S., J. Whitfield, M. Poulter, P. Shah, J. Uphill, T. Campbell, H. Al-Dujaily, H. Hummerich, J. Beck, C.A. Mein, C. Verzilli, J. Whittaker, M.P. Alpers, and J. Collinge 2009. A novel protective prion protein variant that colocalizes with kuru exposure. *The New England Journal of Medicine* 361:2056–2065. doi.org/10.1056/NEJMoa0809716.

Metselaar, D. 1956. Spleens and holoendemic malaria in West New Guinea. *Bulletin of the World Health Organization* 15:635–649.

Mgone, C.S., G. Koki, M.M. Paniu, J. Kono, K.K. Bhatia, B. Genton, N.D.E. Alexander, and M.P. Alpers 1996. Occurrence of the erythrocyte band 3 (AE1) gene deletion in relation to malaria endemicity in Papua New Guinea. *Transactions of the Royal Society of Tropical Medicine and Hygiene* 90:228–231. doi.org/10.1016/S0035-9203(96)90223-0.

Morez, A., N. Brucato, K. Susaki, R. Tsang, J. Kariwiga, L. Saag, J. Muke, K. Miampa, A. Kuaso, T. Kivisild, M. Metspalu, W. Pomat, M. Leavesley, and F.-X. Ricaut 2018. Population adaptation in Papua New Guinea. *The e XVIII International Union for Prehistoric and Protohistoric Sciences Congress*, Jun 2018, PARIS, France. hal-01865793.

Mourant, A.E. 1978. *Blood groups and diseases: A study of associations of diseases with blood groups and other polymorphisms,* 1st edition. Oxford University Press, Oxford.

Müller, I., J. Taime, E. Ibam, J. Kundi, M. Lagog, M. Bockarie, and J.C. Reeder et al. 2002. Complex patterns of malaria epidemiology in the highlands region of Papua New Guinea. *PNG Medical Journal* 45:200–205.

Müller, I., M. Bockarie, M. Alpers, and T. Smith 2003. The epidemiology of malaria in Papua New Guinea. *Trends in Parasitology* 19:253–259. doi.org/10.1016/S1471-4922(03)00091-6.

Müller, I., J. Tulloch, J. Marfurt, R. Hide, and J.C. Reeder 2005. Malaria control in Papua New Guinea results in complex epidemiological changes. *PNG Medical Journal* 48:151–157.

Müller, I., P.A. Zimmerman, and J.C. Reeder 2007. *Plasmodium malariae* and *Plasmodium ovale*—The 'bashful' malaria parasites. *Trends in Parasitology* 23:278–283. doi.org/10.1016/j.pt.2007.04.009.

Natri, H.M., K.S. Bobowik, P. Kusuma, C.C. Darusallam, G.S. Jacobs, G. Hudjashov, J.S. Lansing, H. Sudoyo, N.E. Banovich, M.P. Cox, and I. Gallego Romero 2020. Genome-wide DNA methylation and gene expression patterns reflect genetic ancestry and environmental differences across the Indonesian archipelago. *PLoS Genetics* 16:e1008749. doi.org/10.1371/journal.pgen.1008749.

Natri, H.M., G. Hudjashov, G.S. Jacobs, P. Kusuma, L. Saag, C.C. Darusallam, M. Metspalu, H. Sudoyo, M.P. Cox, I. Gallego Romero, and N.E. Banovich 2022. Genetic architecture of gene regulation in Indonesian populations identifies QTLs associated with global and local ancestries. *American Journal of Human Genetics* 109:50–65. doi.org/10.1016/j.ajhg.2021.11.017.

Norgan, N.G., A. Ferro-Luzzi, and J.V. Durnin 1974. The energy and nutrient intake and the energy expenditure of 204 New Guinean adults. *Philosophical Transactions of the Royal Society B: Biological Sciences* 268:309–348. doi.org/10.1098/rstb.1974.0033.

Norton, H.L., J.S. Friedlaender, D.A. Merriwether, G. Koki, C.S. Mgone, and M.D. Shriver 2006. Skin and hair pigmentation variation in Island Melanesia. *American Journal of Biological Anthropology* 130:254–268. doi.org/10.1002/ajpa.20343.

Norton, H.L., M. Hanna, E. Werren, and J. Friedlaender 2016. The rs387907171 SNP in *TYRP1* is not associated with blond hair color on the Island of Bougainville. *American Journal of Human Biology* 28:431–435. doi.org/10.1002/ajhb.22795.

Nurfitriani, R., A. Abinawanto, R. Noviyanti, L. Trianti, and I.M. Nainggolan 2014. Detection of Papua New Guinea Thalassemia Alpha mutation in Gayo, Sumba, Ternate, and Timika populations. *Makara Journal of Sciences* 183138:47–51. doi.org/10.7454/mss.v18i2.3138.

Otto, T.D., A. Gilabert, T. Crellen, U. Böhme, C. Arnathau, M. Sanders, S.O. Oyola, A.P. Okouga, L. Boundenga, E. Willaume, B. Ngoubangoye, N.D. Moukodoum, C. Paupy, P. Durand, V. Rougeron, B. Ollomo, F. Renaud, C. Newbold, M. Berriman, and F. Prugnolle 2018. Genomes of all known members of a *Plasmodium* subgenus reveal paths to virulent human malaria. *Nature Microbiology* 3:687–697. doi.org/10.1038/s41564-018-0162-2.

Parkinson, A.D. 1974. Malaria in Papua New Guinea 1973. *PNG Medical Journal* 17:22–30.

Patel, S.S., R.K. Mehlotra, W. Kastens, C.S. Mgone, J.W. Kazura, and P.A. Zimmerman 2001. The association of the glycophorin C exon 3 deletion with ovalocytosis and malaria susceptibility in the Wosera, Papua New Guinea. Blood 98:3489–3491. doi.org/10.1182/blood.v98.12.3489.

Patel, S.S., C.L. King, C.S. Mgone, J.W. Kazura, and P.A. Zimmerman 2004. Glycophorin C (Gerbich antigen blood group) and band 3 polymorphisms in two malaria holoendemic regions of Papua New Guinea. *American Journal of Hematology* 75:1–5. doi.org/10.1002/ajh.10448.

Pava, Z., F.H. Burdam, I. Handayuni, L. Trianty, R.A.S. Utami, Y.K. Tirta, E. Kenangalem, D. Lampah, A. Kusuma, G. Wirjanata, S. Kho, J.A. Simpson, S. Auburn, N.M. Douglas, R. Noviyanti, N.M. Anstey, J.R. Poespoprodjo, J. Marfurt, and R.N. Price 2016. Submicroscopic and asymptomatic *Plasmodium* parasitaemia associated with significant risk of anaemia in Papua, Indonesia. *PLoS ONE* 11:e0165340. doi.org/10.1371/journal.pone.0165340.

Pawson, I.G. and C. Jest 1978. The high-altitude areas of the world and their cultures. In P.T. Baker (ed), *The biology of high-altitude peoples,* pp. 17–46. Cambridge University Press, Cambridge.

Pearson, R.D., R. Amato, S. Auburn, O. Miotto, J. Almagro-Garcia, C. Amaratunga, S. Suon, S. Mao, R. Noviyanti, H. Trimarsanto, J. Marfurt, N.M. Anstey, T. William, M.F. Boni, C. Dolecek, H.T. Tran, N.J. White, P. Michon, P. Siba, L. Tavul, G. Harrison, A. Barry, I. Mueller, M.U. Ferreira, N. Karunaweera, M. Randrianarivelojosia, Q. Gao, C. Hubbart, L. Hart, B. Jeffery, E. Drury, D. Mead, M. Kekre, S. Campino, M. Manske, V.J. Cornelius, B. MacInnis, K.A. Rockett, A. Miles, J.C. Rayner, R.M. Fairhurst, F. Nosten, R.N. Price, and D.P. Kwiatkowski 2016. Genomic analysis of local variation and recent evolution in *Plasmodium vivax. Nature Genetics* 48:959–964. doi.org/10.1038/ng.3599.

Perry, G.H., N.J. Dominy, K.G. Claw, A.S. Lee, H. Fiegler, R. Redon, J. Werner, F.A. Villanea, J.L. Mountain, R. Misra, N.P. Carter, C. Lee, and A.C. Stone 2007. Diet and the evolution of human amylase gene copy number variation. *Nature Genetics* 39:1256–1260. doi.org/10.1038/ng2123.

Price, R.N., E. Tjitra, C.A. Guerra, S. Yeung, N.J. White, and N.M. Anstey 2007. *Vivax* malaria: Neglected and not benign. *American Journal of Tropical Medicine and Hygiene* 77:79–87. doi.org/10.4269/ajtmh.2007.77.79.

Prins, H.K., J.A. Loos, and J.H. Meuwissen 1963. Glucose-6-phosphate dehydrogenase (G6PD) deficiency in West New Guinea. *Tropical and Geographical Medicine* 15:361–370.

Quillen, E.E., H.L. Norton, E.J. Parra, F. Lona-Durazo, K.C. Ang, F.M. Illiescu, L.N. Pearson, M.D. Shriver, T. Lasisi, O. Gokcumen, I. Starr, Y.-L. Lin, A.R. Martin, and N.G. Jablonski 2019. Shades of complexity: New perspectives on the evolution and genetic architecture of human skin. *American Journal of Physical Anthropology* 168:4–26. doi.org/10.1002/ajpa.23737.

Quinn, L.J. 2020. Genetic study of kuru. PhD thesis. MRC Prion Unit, Institute of Prion Diseases, University College London, London.

Ranciaro, A., M.C. Campbell, J.B. Hirbo, A. Ranciaro, M.C. Campbell, J.B. Hirbo, W.-Y. Ko, A. Froment, P. Anagnostou, M.J. Kotze, M. Ibrahim, T. Nyambo, S.A. Omar, and S.A. Tishkoff 2014. Genetic origins of lactase persistence and the spread of pastoralism in Africa. *American Journal of Human Genetics* 94:496–510. doi.org/10.1016/j.ajhg.2014.02.009.

Reid, M.E., C. Sullivan, M. Taylor, and D.J. Anstee 1987. Inheritance of human-erythrocyte Gerbich blood group antigens. *American Journal of Human Genetics* 41:1117–1123.

Riley, I.D. 1983. Population change and distribution in Papua New Guinea: An epidemiological approach. *Journal of Human Evolution* 12:125–132. doi.org/10.1016/S0047-2484(83)80017-7.

Riley, I.D. and D. Lehmann 1992. The demography of Papua New Guinea: Migration, fertility and mortality patterns. In R. Attenborough and M.P. Alpers (eds), *Human biology in Papua New Guinea: The small cosmos*, pp. 67–92. Clarendon Press, Oxford. doi.org/10.1093/oso/9780198575146.003.0003.

Rougeron, V., E. Elguero, C. Arnathau, B. Acuña Hidalgo, P. Durand, S. Houze, A. Berry, S. Zakeri, R. Haque, M.S. Alam, F. Nosten, C. Severini, T.G. Woldearegai, B. Mordmüller, P.G. Kremsner, L. González-Cerón, G. Fontecha, D. Gamboa, L. Musset, E. Legrand, O. Noya, T. Pumpaibool, P. Harnyuttanakorn, K.M. Lekweiry, M.M. Albsheer, M.M.A. Hamid, A.O.M.S. Boukary, J.-F. Trape, F. Renaud, and F. Prugnolle 2020. Human *Plasmodium vivax* diversity, population structure and evolutionary origin. *PLoS Neglected Tropical Diseases* 14:e0008072. doi.org/10.1371/journal.pntd.0008072.

Sadigh-Eteghad, S., M. Talebi, and M. Farhoudi 2012. Association of apolipoprotein E epsilon 4 allele with sporadic late onset Alzheimer's disease: A meta-analysis. *Neurosciences Journal* 17:321–326.

Schultz, L., J. Wapling, I. Mueller, P.O. Ntsuke, N. Senn, J. Nale, B. Kiniboro, C.O. Buckee, L. Tavul, P.M. Siba, J.C. Reeder, and A.E. Barry 2010. Multilocus haplotypes reveal variable levels of diversity and population structure of *Plasmodium falciparum* in Papua New Guinea, a region of intense perennial transmission. *Malaria Journal* 9:336. doi.org/10.1186/1475-2875-9-336.

Seah, I.M., L. Ambrose, R.D. Cooper, and N.W. Beebe 2013. Multilocus population genetic analysis of the Southwest Pacific malaria vector *Anopheles punctulatus*. *International Journal of Parasitology* 43:825–835. doi.org/10.1016/j.ijpara.2013.05.004.

Serjeantson, S.W. 1989. A selective advantage for the Gerbich-negative phenotype in malarious areas of Papua New Guinea. *PNG Medical Journal* 32:5–9.

Serjeantson, S.W., P.G. Board, and K. Bhatia 1992. Population genetics in Papua New Guinea: A perspective in human evolution. In R. Attenborough and M.P. Alpers (eds), *Human biology in Papua New Guinea: The small cosmos*, pp. 198–233. Clarendon Press, Oxford. doi.org/10.1093/oso/9780198575146.003.0009.

Shaw, B., J.H. Field, G.R. Summerhayes, S. Coxe, A.C.F. Coster, A. Ford, J. Haro, H. Arifeae, E. Hull, G. Jacobsen, R. Fullagar, E. Hayes, and L. Kealhofer 2020. Emergence of a Neolithic in highland New Guinea by 5000 to 4000 years ago. *Science Advances* 6(13):eaay4573. doi.org/10.1126/sciadv.aay4573.

Smith, T., K. Bhatia, M. Prasad, G. Koki, and M. Alpers 1994. Altitude, language, and class I HLA allele frequencies in Papua New Guinea. *American Journal of Physical Anthropology* 95:155–168. doi.org/10.1002/ajpa.1330950204.

Spencer, M. 1994. *Malaria, the Australian experience, 1843–1991*. Australian College of Tropical Medicine, Townsville, Australia.

Su, X.-Z., C. Zhang, and D.A. Joy 2020. Host–malaria parasite interactions and impacts on mutual evolution. *Frontiers in Cellular and Infection Microbiology* 10:587933. doi.org/10.3389/fcimb.2020.587933.

Sutton, A., M.-J. Mountain, K. Aplin, S. Bulmer, and T. Denham 2009. Archaeozoological records for the highlands of New Guinea: a review of current evidence. *Australian Archaeology* 69(1):41–58. doi.org/10.1080/03122417.2009.11681900.

Tavul, L., I. Mueller, L. Rare, E. Lin, P.A. Zimmerman, J. Reeder, P. Siba, and P. Michon 2008. Glycophorin C delta(exon3) is not associated with protection against severe anaemia in Papua New Guinea. *PNG Medical Journal* 51:149–154.

Tommaseo-Ponzetta, M., S. Mona, F. Calabrese, G. Konrad, E. Vacca, and M. Attimonelli 2013. Mountain pygmies of Western New Guinea: A morphological and molecular approach. *Human Biology* 85:285–308. doi.org/10.3378/027.085.0314.

Trájer, A.J. 2022. Late Quaternary changes in malaria-free areas in Papua New Guinea and the future perspectives. *Quaternary International* 628:28–43. doi.org/10.1016/j.quaint.2022.04.003.

Ulijaszek, S.J. 1992. Dietary and nutrient intakes of 25 Ningerum (New Guinea) adult males at two times of the year. *American Journal of Human Biology* 4:469–479. doi.org/10.1002/ajhb.1310040406.

van der Kaars, S., X. Wang, P. Kershaw, F. Guichard, and D.A. Setiabudi 2000. A Late Quaternary palaeoecological record from the Banda Sea, Indonesia: patterns of vegetation, climate and biomass burning in Indonesia and northern Australia. *Palaeogeography, Palaeoclimatology, Palaeoecology* 155:135–153. doi.org/10.1016/S0031-0182(99)00098-X.

Vespasiani, D.M., G.S. Jacobs, L.E. Cook, N. Brucato, M. Leavesley, C. Kinipi, F.-X. Ricaut, M.P. Cox, and I. Gallego Romero 2022. Denisovan introgression has shaped the immune system of present-day Papuans. *PLoS Genetics* 18:e1010470. doi.org/10.1371/journal.pgen.1010470.

Vlok, M., H.R. Buckley, J.J. Miszkiewicz, M.M. Walker, K. Domett, A. Willis, H.H. Trinh, T.T. Minh, M.H.T. Nguyen, L.C. Nguyen, H. Matsumura, T. Wang, H.T. Nghia, and M.F. Oxenham 2021. Forager and farmer evolutionary adaptations to malaria evidenced by 7000 years of thalassemia in Southeast Asia. *Scientific Reports* 11:5677. doi.org/10.1038/s41598-021-83978-4.

von Ahsen, N., M. Tzvetkov, H.A. Karunajeewa, S. Gomorrai, A. Ura, J. Brockmöller, T.M.E. Davis, I. Mueller, K. F.Ilett, and M. Oellerich 2010. *CYP2D6* and *CYP2C19* in Papua New Guinea: High frequency of previously uncharacterized CYP2D6 alleles and heterozygote excess. *International Journal of Molecular Epidemiology and Genetics* 1:310–319.

Wagner, G., K. Bhatia, and P. Board 1996. Glucose-6-phosphate dehydrogenase deficiency mutations in Papua New Guinea. *Human Biology* 68:383–394.

Walsh, R.J. 1964. Variation in the melanin content of the skin of New Guinea natives at different ages. *Journal of Investigative Dermatology* 42:261–265. doi.org/10.1038/jid.1964.59.

Walsh, R.J. 1971. A distinctive pigment of the skin in New Guinea indigenes. *Annals of Human Genetics* 34:379–388. doi.org/10.1111/j.1469-1809.1971.tb00250.x.

Ward, R.G. and D.A.M. Lea (eds) 1970. *An atlas of Papua and New Guinea*. Department of Geography, University of Papua and New Guinea/Collins-Longman, Port Moresby.

Williams, T.N. 2016. Host genetics. In D. Gaur, C.E. Chitnis, and V.S. Chauhan (eds), *Advances in malaria research*, pp. 465–494. John Wiley & Sons, Ltd, New Jersey. doi.org/10.1002/9781118493816.ch17.

Williams, T.N., K. Maitland, S. Bennett, M. Ganczakowski, T.E.A. Peto, C.I. Newbold, D.K. Bowden, D.J. Weatherall, and J.B. Clegg 1996. High incidence of malaria in α-thalassaemic children. *Nature* 383:522–525. doi.org/10.1038/383522a0.

Yenchitsomanus, P., K.M. Summers, C. Chockkalingam, and P.G. Board 1986. Characterization of G6PD deficiency and thalassaemia in Papua New Guinea. *PNG Medical Journal* 29:53–58.

York, A. 2018. On the origin of *Plasmodium falciparum*. *Nature Review Microbiology* 16:393. doi.org/10.1038/s41579-018-0038-8.

Yoshida, A., E.R. Giblett, and L.A. Malcolm 1973. Heterogeneous distribution of glucose-6-phosphate dehydrogenase variants with enzyme deficiency in the Markham Valley Area of New Guinea. *Annals of Human Genetics* 37(2):145–150. doi.org/10.1111/j.1469-1809.1973.tb01822.x.

Zammit, N.W., O.M. Siggs, P.E. Gray, K. Horikawa, D.B. Langley, S.N. Walters, S.R. Daley, C. Loetsch, J. Warren, J.Y. Yap, D. Cultrone, A. Russell, E.K. Malle, J.E. Villanueva, M.J. Cowley, V. Gayevskiy, M.E. Dinger, R. Brink, D. Zahra, G. Chaudhri, G. Karupiah, B. Whittle, C. Roots, E. Bertram, M. Yamada, Y. Jeelall, A. Enders, B.E. Clifton, P.D. Mabbitt, C.J. Jackson, S.R. Watson, C.N. Jenne, L.L. Lanier, T. Wiltshire, M.H. Spitzer, G.P. Nolan, F. Schmitz, A. Aderem, B.T. Porebski, A.M. Buckle, D.W. Abbott, J.B. Ziegler, M.E. Craig, P. Benitez-Aguirre, J. Teo, S.G. Tangye, C. King, M. Wong, M.P. Cox, W. Phung, J. Tang, W. Sandoval, I.E. Wertz, D. Christ, C.C. Goodnow, and S.T. Grey 2019. Denisovan, modern human and mouse *TNFAIP3* alleles tune A20 phosphorylation and immunity. *Nature Immunology* 20:1299–1310. doi.org/10.1038/s41590-019-0492-0.

Zimmerman, P.A., I. Woolley, G.L. Masinde, S.M. Miller, D.T. McNamara, F. Hazlett, C.S. Mgone, M.P. Alpers, B. Genton, B.A. Boatin, and J.W. Kazura 1999. Emergence of *FY*A*null* in a *Plasmodium vivax*-endemic region of Papua New Guinea. *Proceedings of the National Academy of Sciences* 96:13973–13977. doi.org/10.1073/pnas.96.24.13973.

Zimmerman, P.A., M.U. Ferreira, R.E. Howes, and O. Mercereau-Puijalon 2013. Red blood cell polymorphism and susceptibility to *Plasmodium vivax*. *Advances in Parasitology* 81:27–76. doi.org/10.1016/B978-0-12-407826-0.00002-3.

7

A submerged landscape at the entrance of Sahul

Fabian Boesl, Shinatria Adhityatama, and Alexander F. Wall

Abstract

It is still unclear when and how people reached Sahul, the former landmass including Australia and New Guinea. The Bird's Head of West New Guinea, Indonesia, is considered to be a likely entrance point from a northern route. But, despite being an important stepping stone, not much research has been done in the area. Misool, now a part of the Raja Ampat Islands, is a key location for people arriving from the west. As part of the Sahul Shelf, it was connected to New Guinea during lower sea level stands and only became an island when sea levels rose. Under these conditions, Misool underwent numerous environmental changes over the last glacial cycle. However, there is still a huge knowledge gap in and around Misool, especially with regard to palaeoenvironmental studies of ecological and anthropogenic change. Here we synthesise the research in this area so far. We present a first detailed reconstruction of potential sea level fluctuations and propose how coastlines could have looked during the likely periods of human colonisation. We investigate the circumstances under which people could have interacted with this highly dynamic landscape. Furthermore, we propose potential research prospects for future expeditions.

Abstrak

Masih belum jelas kapan dan bagaimana manusia mencapai Sahul yang merupakan daratan yang menghubungkan Australia dan Papua Nugini. Wilayah kepala burung, yang saat ini masuk dalam wilayah administrasi Provinsi Papua Barat daya, kemungkinan merupakan pintu gerbang masuknya imigran pertama ke wilayah ini dari arah rute utara. Meskipun merupakan batu loncatan yang penting dalam proses migrasi, penelitian di wilayah Kepala burung selama ini masih sangat terbatas dilakukan. Pulau Misool yang berada dalam wilayah Kepulauan Raja Ampat, merupakan salah satu jalur migrasi manusia pada masa lalu terutama yang datang dari jalur barat. Misool yang saat ini terpisah dari pulau besar Papua, pada masa paparan Sahul masih terbentuk, pulau ini masih terhubung atau berada satu daratan dengan wilayah Papua. Setelah berakhirnya masa glasial, Misool mengalami perubahan lingkungan yang cukup signifikan. Untuk itu, dalam bab ini pembahasan mengenai pulau Misool disajikan terutama yang berkaitan dengan potensi fluktuasi permukaan laut serta merekonstruksi garis pantai yang kemungkinan nampak selama ekspansi manusia di pulau tersebut. Hal ini dilakukan sebagai langkah awal untuk menjembatani kesenjangan data serta pengetahuan mengenai pulau ini, terutama yang berkaitan dengan studi paleo-lingkungan yang berhubungan dengan perubahan ekologi dan antropogenik. Beberapa point seperti prospek penelitian serta adanya potensi ekspedisi ilmiah dilakukan pada masa yang akan datang disajikan pada bagian akhir dari bab ini.

Introduction

There is ample evidence that ancient people migrating through Australasia had to cross the sea on several occasions, but the exact circumstances are still unknown (Allen and O'Connell 2020; Bird et al. 2019). It has been demonstrated that the founding population of modern humans would have reached Sahul intentionally rather than by accident (Bradshaw et al. 2019). Birdsell (1977) proposed two possible pathways for modern human dispersal from Sunda (the Pleistocene landmass consisting of Sumatra, Borneo, Java, and Bali) to Sahul (the Pleistocene continent comprising the islands of Australia, New Guinea, and Tasmania) known as the northern and southern routes, respectively (see Figure 7.1). However, to date, such a model is only poorly constrained with regards to where and under which circumstances the first anatomically modern humans (AMH) crossed the sea and in what proportion people used the proposed routes on their initial journey into Sahul. To better understand modern humans' expansion into this part of the world and their potential challenges, it is pivotal to study changing landscapes over time (see Harff et al. 2016).

Misool and the surrounding Misool Shelf to the west of Wallacea were once connected to the mainland of northern Sahul. AMH could have landed in Misool or on the exposed shelf area when coming from Seram, the latter of which is considered as one of the possible stepping stones into today's Australia and New Guinea (Kealy et al. 2018). Here we assess from an archaeological and palaeoenvironmental perspective what is known about this region in the vicinity of West New Guinea and we summarise under what circumstances people could have migrated through this part of the world during the last glacial cycle. In addition, we review sea level high and low stands, and show how Pleistocene palaeo-shorelines could have formed very different land surfaces when compared to the Holocene.

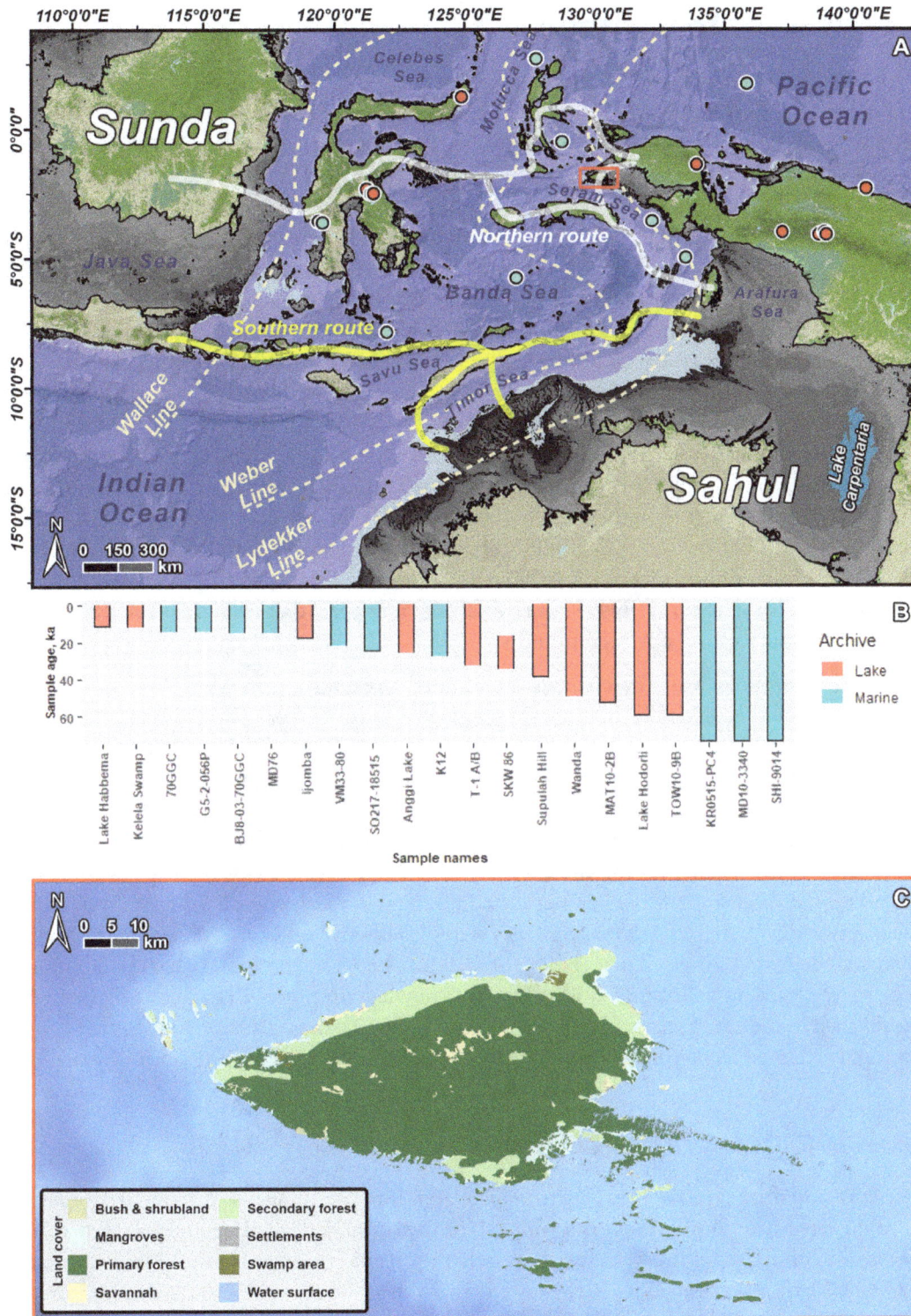

Figure 7.1: Misool overview.

Notes: (A) Location of Misool along the northern migration route proposed by Birdsell (1977). Palaeoenvironmental archives in region spanning into the Late Pleistocene are marked as red (lacustrine) and turquoise (marine); (B) All published, pre-Holocene palaeoenvironmental archives in the region from 3°N–7°S and 118°E–141°E sorted from west to east; (C) Overview of modern environments in Misool.

Sources: ESA (2017) and GEBCO Compilation Group (2020).

Early seafarers in Wallacea

It is difficult to reconstruct the exact routes that AMH migrated through Wallacea (Figure 7.1) in order to reach the Sahul Shelf. Both environmental history and the timing of the first people's arrival need further clarification. However, the Wallacea region has increasingly become the focus of archaeological research after the discovery of *Homo floresiensis* in Flores. The skeletal remains of the so-called Hobbit at Liang Bua were dated to around 100,000–60,000 years ago and this finding confirmed that archaic humans had crossed the sea much earlier than previously thought. AMH, on the other hand, are believed to have arrived on Flores ~46,000 years ago (Sutikna et al. 2018). Although evidence of modern humans passing through Wallacea is scarce, recent research shows that *Homo sapiens* inhabited South Sulawesi at least 45,000 years ago (Aubert et al. 2019; Brumm et al. 2021) and Central Sulawesi around 30,000 years ago (Ono et al. 2020), while occupation in North Maluku (closer to Misool) dates to around 35,000 years ago (Bellwood 2019). Moving to the southern route, besides Flores, modern humans have been traced back to Timor, where they have settled since at least 44,000 years ago (Shipton et al. 2019), while another close by site in Alor shows human occupation around 40,000 years ago (Kealy et al. 2020). These ages leave a considerable gap between the initial human migration through Wallacea and the oldest sites in New Guinea (49,000–43,000 years ago) and Australia (65,000–59,300 years ago) (Clarkson et al. 2017; Summerhayes et al. 2010). As there is more evidence for archaeological sites in Australia dating back further than 50,000 years old (see Roberts et al. 1994; Veth et al. 2017), it appears that evidence of AMH's initial migration through Wallacea has not been found yet.

Regardless of the chronological discrepancies mentioned previously, several archaeological sites in Wallacea have shown evidence of how AMH interacted with the sea. For example, Kealy and colleagues (2020) proposed that people in Alor were dependent on seafood as their main protein source during the Late Pleistocene. There is evidence of deep-sea fishing in Timor going back to 42,000 years ago, which suggests that the early inhabitants of Wallacea were highly developed seafarers catching pelagic fish (O'Connor et al. 2011). Isotope studies on fossil teeth of both islands confirm that people first adapted to marine environments around 42,000–39,000 years ago before shifting to terrestrial food sources (Roberts et al. 2020). Edible marine shells (*Turbo* spp.), which date back to between 39,000 and 34,000 years ago, were also discovered in an archaeological context on Gebe Island (Bellwood 2019). An exchange of obsidian between the islands Kisar, Timor, and Alor can be traced back to at least 15,000 years ago, showing that inter-island connections were already established in the Late Pleistocene (Reepmeyer et al. 2019). In conclusion, we see that people have been highly adapted to marine environments and resources for tens of thousands of years.

Archaeological evidence in and around Misool

There are many potential migration routes from Wallacea into Sahul and it is likely that modern humans would have used multiple entry points (Norman et al. 2018). If people arrived in the Misool Shelf area coming from the west, it seems likely they would have settled in Seram beforehand (see Figure 7.1). Kealy and colleagues (2018) suggest that this is the most likely scenario for modern humans coming into Sahul when looking at least-cost pathway modelling. Recent research by the Pusat Penelitian Arkeologi Nasional (Indonesian National Research Centre for Archaeology, ARKENAS)[1] on the northern coast of Seram has found stone artefacts with Palaeolithic characteristics, but there are no available dating results so far (Jatmiko and Mujabuddawat 2016). This discovery brings new

---

1   Now part of Badan Riset dan Inovasi Nasional (BRIN).

insights to the region, as Palaeolithic stone artefacts are generally very rarely found in other parts of Wallacea, except Sulawesi and Flores. In addition, Seram has several rock art sites that were reported by Röder (1959), ARKENAS, and University of Washington, USA (Oktaviana et al. 2018). Further north-west of Misool and Seram, Obi is another key island where ongoing research discovered evidence for human occupation around ~18,000 years ago (Shipton et al. 2020). Thus, it seems likely that these islands could potentially provide evidence for Late Pleistocene occupation, which in turn could reduce the gap between sites in Wallacea and Sahul.

In particular, Misool is situated in a strategic position on the north-west edge of Sahul and on the migration route for AMH from Wallacea to Sahul. Misool has numerous archaeological sites, predominantly rock art sites which were first reported by Chazine (2011). Since 2014, ARKENAS has carried out an extensive survey campaign in Misool and the Raja Ampat region in order to identify and document the potential sites for modern human occupation (Sulistyarto et al. 2014; Adhityatama 2017). Over 50 rock art sites have been identified, consisting of various figurative images that are dominated by aquatic fauna such as fish, marine mammals, turtles, and jellyfish, as well as some hand stencils (Adhityatama 2017; Oktaviana et al. 2018). Many themes of the rock art in Misool show similarities to the ones in Seram (Oktaviana et al. 2018), but they differ considerably from other sites in Borneo and Sulawesi (except hand stencils), which are dominated by terrestrial fauna (Aubert et al. 2019; Brumm et al. 2021). The unique images of Misool's rock art most likely reflect the adaptation of inhabitants to local marine resources. However, due to its uniqueness, some archaeologists believe that Misool's rock art is likely related to Austronesian cultures (Ballard 1992; Leihitu and Permana 2019; Pasaribu et al. 2020). Furthermore, similarity with the rock art in East Seram raises the suspicion that the Misool rock art culture may have originated from the west (for example in Seram). Even so, the lack of dating results keeps the origins unresolved.

Apart from rock art, many caves and rock shelters can be found in Misool and the small islands in its vicinity. This includes both terrestrial and underwater caves. One excavated site is Gua Putri Termenung (GPT; see Figures 7.1 and 7.2), which is a limestone cave that indicates residential activity in the Late Pleistocene. During sea level low stands, this island was part of the exposed shelf area connected to western mainland New Guinea, and we interpret that this cave was actively used as a habitation because traces of human activities (e.g. food consumption and stone tools) were found during excavations conducted by ARKENAS in 2018 (Oktaviana et al. 2018) and by ARKENAS and the Centre of Excellence for Australian Biodiversity and Heritage (CABAH) in 2019. Analyses are still ongoing and results will be published soon.

Besides that, there are other sites to be excavated in the future. There is Korwa Cave, an underwater cave that was once dry before marine transgression (indicated by speleothems) and could have been occupied by modern humans in the Late Pleistocene (Adhityatama and Yarista 2019). Another cave called Liang Farlon on the mainland of Misool has extensive fire marks on the walls and ceiling which may indicate occupation over a longer time frame. There are no published dates for archaeological sites in Misool yet, but two cave sites at Ayamaru on the Bird's Head have been dated to around 30,000 years old (Clarke et al. 2007; Pasveer et al. 2002). So far, those ^{14}C dates are the oldest reported in West New Guinea and as Misool was connected to the Bird's Head at this time, it is likely that new research could produce similar or even older ages compared to those in Ayamaru.

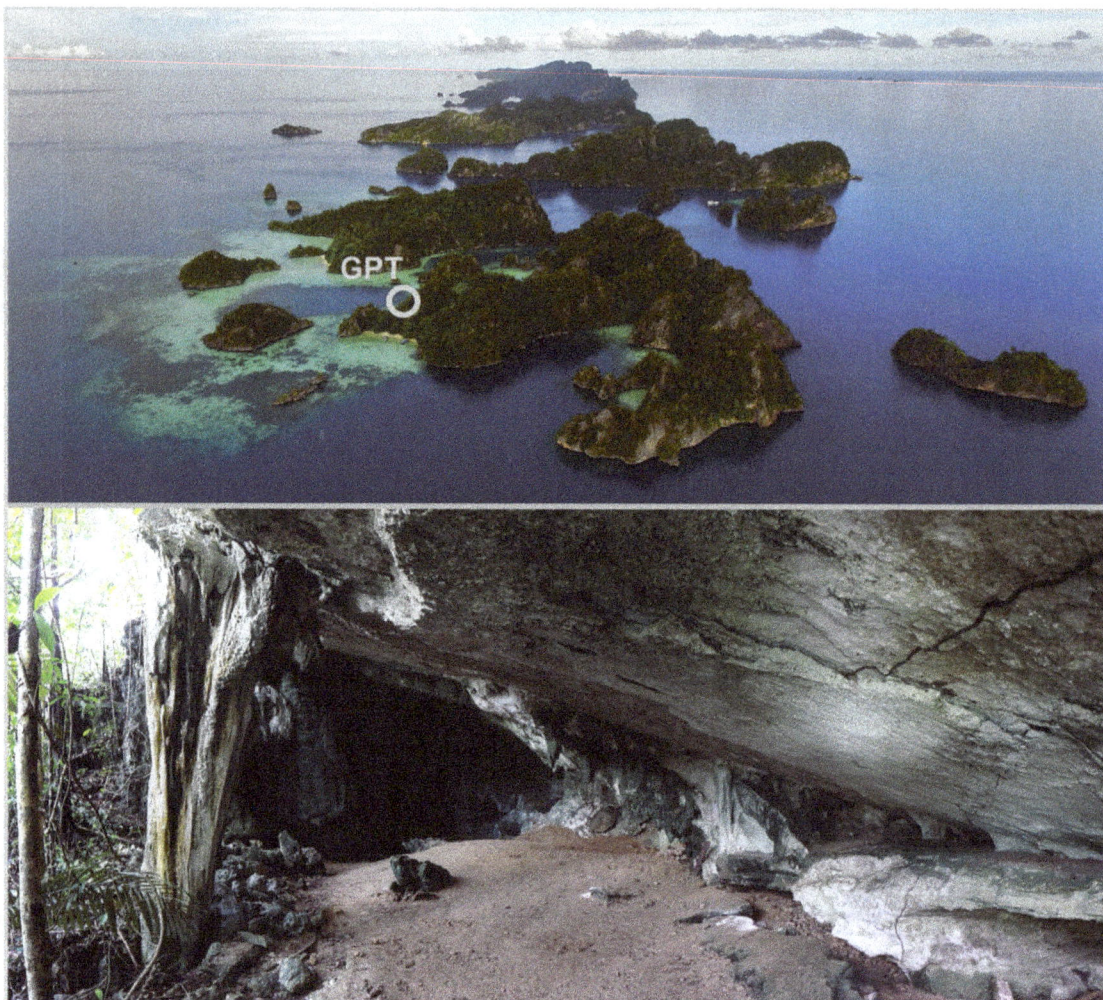

Figure 7.2: Overview of location of Gua Putra Termenung (GPT), currently the only excavated archaeological site in Misool.

Note: The bottom half shows the cave chamber, which was potentially inhabited during the Late Pleistocene.

Source: Both images were taken and processed by Fabian Boesl.

Modern environments on Misool Island

Misool Island is situated at c. 1.85°S, just south of the equator, and is part of tropical Australasia. It is a small island, approximately 80 km across and 40 km north to south, with a maximum elevation of just 561 m. It lies within the Indo-Pacific Warm Pool, the warmest part of the global ocean, which has a minimum sea surface temperature (SST) of 28 °C and is the primary moisture source for the region's monsoon systems (De Deckker 2016). The intertropical convergence zone (ITCZ), where the extremely high-altitude clouds that deliver the monsoon's rain form, passes over Misool in the summer and winter, yet the island receives abundant rainfall year-round. Thus, there is little monsoonal signature (Beck et al. 2018). Conversely, the El Niño Southern Oscillation (ENSO) plays an outsized role on the island (Takeuchi 2003). These environmental factors produce relatively little seasonal climatic variation there, but El Niño droughts and La Niña floods can cause great inter-annual variation. These environmental factors at play in Misool cause tropical rainforest to be dominant there—much of it intact primary forest—while also supporting patches of shrub- and grassland. Deforestation, however, is slowly degrading its remaining pristine ecosystems (Hansen et al. 2013).

Misool's geology is generally younger Quaternary alluvial, and littoral sediment appears in the north and proceeds southward through each older geologic time period in turn to Triassic sedimentary rocks in the very south (Rusmana et al. 1983). Occasional layers of volcanic tuffs are found throughout the sequence, while a portion of the south-west of the island is thought to be much older Devonian slate, argillite, and quartzite (Hasibuan 1990). Most areas exhibit poor soil development, possibly limiting species richness relative to the Bird's Head (Takeuchi 2003).

Misool's most dominant ecosystem type is the primary lowland rainforest (see Figure 7.1C). These forests are often dense but stunted tangles of woody vegetation. In the few areas of deep soil, however, like those along flood plains of larger rivers and the valleys of the karst islets to the south-east, are tall forests with well-developed canopy structures. North of the centre of the island and smattered westward there are a few areas of rare savannah, comprising a variety of grasses and tea-trees, which Takeuchi (2003) notes appears to experience regular burning. This ecosystem is similar to the savannah found on mainland New Guinea, which Hope and Tulip (1994) suggest has persisted throughout their 60,000-year record and is thus likely to be naturally occurring. When reflecting on what is and is not known about Misool's environmental history, however, it is important to recognise that human influence is especially difficult to reconstruct without local records.

Palaeoenvironmental records from the region

While the Mesozoic geology and palaeontology of Misool have been described (Hasibuan 1990 and references therein), no Quaternary palaeoenvironmental records have been published from the island. Such records from nearby islands and seas, however, can give us an idea of how Misool may have changed over time. This section briefly covers the published records from the region and what they tell us about past environmental change, broken into marine isotope stages (MIS) (Lisiecki and Raymo 2005).

Long-term changes in rainfall in the Indo-Pacific are thought to be controlled to a large extent by changes in sea level/exposure of land area (DiNezio and Tierney 2013). Palaeoenvironmental records show a general cooling and lowering of sea level in the region from MIS 4 (74,000–59,000 years ago) through MIS 2 (24,000–14,000 years ago) (Barmawidjaja et al. 1993). Many records also show drying during this time (Van der Kaars and Dam 1995; Reeves et al. 2013), but some show greater or fluctuating precipitation (Shiau et al. 2011; De Deckker et al. 2019). Similarly, patterns in the amount of burning on landscapes in the region are complex. Burning is also a significant environmental factor in the Indo-Pacific and is controlled to a large degree by the amount of rainfall (Mooney et al. 2011). See Figure 7.1A and B for the locations of palaeoenvironmental records mentioned in the following section. As illustrated by the complex natural histories of sites throughout the region, local environments are the result of a huge array of drivers from glacial dynamics in the Arctic to the bedrock underfoot, thus there is no substitute for local data (Pico et al. 2020).

MIS 4: 74,000–59,000 years ago

MIS 4 is of particular interest here because it is the earliest stage that very likely predates human migration to Sahul. While the timing of this arrival is debated, as described previously, there is broad consensus that it fell between 65,000 and 48,000 years ago (O'Connell et al. 2018; Clarkson et al. 2017), thus the early part of MIS 4 at least should represent a pre-arrival landscape on Sahul and therefore Misool.

During this time, the region, and the planet generally, was much cooler, and the sea level may have been as much as 100 m lower (De Deckker et al. 2019). Thus, as during much of its deep history, Misool would have been a highland area and westernmost tip of the Bird's Head, and not an island at all (see Figure 7.3).

Pollen data from the Banda Sea (core SHI-9014) suggest that in the region overall, and perhaps in Misool as well, more open forests were dominant. Dang and colleagues (2015) argue that rainfall in Halmahera (marine core MD10-3340) was quite high at the beginning of MIS 4 but rapidly decreased to very low by 59,000 years ago. If, however, Misool's rainfall was closely linked to ENSO—as it is today—special attention should be given to records associated with that phenomenon. Zhao and colleagues (2019) and Jia and colleagues (2018) found that, though SSTs were cooler overall, the temperature difference between the warmer western Pacific and cooler eastern Pacific was similar to today, implying the configuration of ENSO was generally similar as well. It is difficult, therefore, to judge whether Misool would have had rainfall at levels lower than or similar to today.

The potential for human activity on the landscape in the latter part of this record is another complicating factor, as they (if present) likely would have influenced burning regimes, and thereby vegetation, on the island. Mooney and colleagues (2011) compiled a wide range of charcoal records from the Australasian region from 80,000 years ago. They found burning trends over tens of thousands of years tended to follow broader precipitation changes and were, like rainfall, generally depleted relative to today, though the Banda Sea record is an exception, containing more charcoal during MIS 4 than today (Kershaw et al. 2003). On a finer, centennial to millennial timescale, peaks in charcoal often coincided with Dansgaard–Oeschger (D–O) events. The causes of D–O events are little understood, but in the Northern Hemisphere, they are periods of rapid warming followed by slow cooling, while they present as less pronounced, slower warming followed by slow cooling in the Southern Hemisphere. The data from Australasia are consistent with worldwide data, suggesting increased burning during D–O events (Daniau et al. 2010). It is worth reiterating, however, that these patterns in Misool are not necessarily in lockstep with the rest of the region.

MIS 3: 59,000–24,000 years ago

The region was warmer overall during MIS 3 than during the preceding or following stage, though temperatures fluctuated significantly. Warming was rapid in early MIS 3, though never reaching today's temperatures, and then it slowly cooled for the majority of the stage. Sea levels rose, though it is unclear whether inundation separated Misool from the Bird's Head at any point (see Figure 7.3). Rainfall may have also followed a similar pattern; a record in the Halmahera Sea suggests precipitation increased rapidly around 59,000 years ago and then slowly decreased until 30,000 years ago (Dang et al. 2015). Farther afield, lake records from Sulawesi show rainfall levels similar to today for much of MIS 3, but then decreasing significantly by the end of the stage (Pico et al. 2020). Proxies for ENSO support this interpretation, as the temperature difference between the western and eastern Pacific increased, creating overall conditions similar to today's La Niña at the onset of MIS 3, and then decreasing towards the end of the period creating an ENSO configuration more similar to today (Jia et al. 2018; Zhao et al. 2019). Van der Kaars and colleagues (2000) use the Banda Sea record to highlight a dramatic reduction in climax rainforest species (i.e. species which only become common in a well-established, stable rainforest), an increase in disturbance flora (i.e. species that are able to rapidly establish themselves after a disturbance such as a forest fire has cleared an area), and increased amounts of charcoal at 37,000 years ago. These, they argue, are the result of anthropogenic alteration of the landscapes in the region. The regional charcoal record, however, shows a general but unsteady increase until a peak at 38,000 years ago, which they argue is coincident with a D–O event rather than implicating human activity, followed by a gradual decline (Mooney et al. 2011).

MIS 2: 24,000–14,000 years ago

MIS 2 begins with a marked cooling. Despite the ubiquitous drop in temperature, most records from the region suggest an increase in precipitation right at the onset of this stage (Reeves et al. 2013). As temperatures continued to decline over the first few thousand years, precipitation began to dry up, particularly in lowland areas of tropical Australasia. This culminates in the Last Glacial Maximum (LGM), defined in various ways by different authors, but describing the coldest and driest interval of the last glacial cycle, with the lowest sea level and a greatly diminished (or perhaps absent) monsoon at around 20,000 years ago. Nevertheless, the greatest temperature drops are recorded in the highlands of the region while SST may have only changed one or two degrees (Barrows et al. 2011). Thus, temperature changes on low-lying Misool may have been less dramatic than suggested by records from elevated records on nearby landmasses.

There are several palaeoenvironmental records near Misool that extend to this stage. Haberle and colleagues (2001) produced a terrestrial charcoal record compilation more narrowly focused on Indonesia and Papua New Guinea than that of Mooney and colleagues (2011). Only two of their records, which are from Papua New Guinea, reach back to 20,000–17,000 years ago, but they show unexpectedly low charcoal abundances from 20,000–17,000 years ago (contradicting the Banda Sea record [Kershaw et al. 2003]); they suggest that low temperatures may have improved soil moisture retention, countering the reduction in rainfall. As Hope (1998) points out, humans were likely burning the landscape since at least 32,500 years ago, thus it is possible their changing use of the landscape in response to changing temperatures is a driving force of charcoal accumulation. Temperatures rose from about 17,000 years ago and charcoal became more abundant for the rest of the stage. These interpretations are generally compatible with the larger-scale compilation of Mooney and colleagues (2011).

Grasslands and open savannahs were more widespread in tropical Australasia during MIS 2, while mangroves were very rare, possibly including on Misool (Kershaw et al. 2003). Montane forests were found at much lower elevations, while lowland forests generally shrank; some authors describe much of the then-exposed Sunda shelf as a savannah corridor (Wurster and Bird 2016). On the other hand, the earlier-mentioned records are primarily from areas with greater relief and more monsoonal rainfall than Misool. There is evidence that Misool may have been relatively wet at this time, perhaps even wetter than it is today. ENSO's neutral phase would have been similar to very strong La Niña-like conditions today, probably resulting in increased rainfall from that source (Jia et al. 2018; Zhao et al. 2019). Furthermore, colder temperatures in the tropics caused the ITCZ not to migrate as far south as today and thus remain closer to Misool during Austral summers (Denniston et al. 2017), perhaps increasing the proportion of monsoonal rainfall delivered to Misool. Lower temperatures and lower sea levels, however, would have countered this to some degree by decreasing overall monsoonal rainfall.

Close to the end of MIS 2, around 14,500 years ago, the warming trend that followed the LGM abruptly reversed in the Southern Hemisphere. This Antarctic Cold Reversal lasted approximately just a few thousand years and is thought to be related to a huge volume of ice melting and suddenly being dumped into the ocean, though the source and teleconnection are unsettled (Pedro et al. 2016), after which warming resumed. These events are thought to be related to the slightly later Younger Dryas cooling event in the Northern Hemisphere.

MIS 1: 14,000 years ago – today

By 14,000 years ago and the onset of MIS 1, warming accelerated and sea level rose quickly. Misool rapidly became an island separated from the Bird's Head. Precipitation was also generally increasing in the region as large swathes of Sunda and Sahul were inundated, resulting in more ocean surface area from which rain could form. This transgression allowed for the formation of large areas of mangroves in southern New Guinea (Grindrod et al. 1999), while increased rainfall caused forests to expand in New Guinean highlands (Haberle et al. 2001; Barrows et al. 2011). Notably, climax rainforest species did not recover to the extent they had in previous warm stages. These processes continued without dramatic change 11,700 years ago, but the end of the Younger Dryas in the Northern Hemisphere demarks the onset of the end of the Pleistocene and onset of the Holocene and thus the official shift from glacial to interglacial.

Approximately at 6000 years ago, temperatures and sea level stabilised, both at levels slightly higher than today. The monsoon reinitiated and/or significantly strengthened and rainfall in at least the southern reaches of tropical Australasia was higher than today as well (Reeves et al. 2013). By 5000 years ago, these factors reached levels very similar to today; the monsoon had weakened somewhat, ENSO strengthened, and temperature and sea level decreased slightly. Meanwhile, charcoal levels throughout the region had unprecedented spikes at various times during MIS 2 up until the most recent few centuries, thought to be caused by human modification of the landscape (Haberle et al. 2001). Humans have become an increasingly major driver of environmental change, adding further complexity and interest to the environmental story. The many wetlands, fossil corals, and other untapped palaeoenvironmental archives on Misool may contain records preserving lost chapters of this story.

Global sea level changes during the last glacial cycle

Arguably the most important variable when looking at drowned landscapes are absolute and relative sea level changes. While the first term describes global (eustatic) rise and fall due to changing ice volumes around the poles and thermal expansion/contraction of water, the latter takes regional factors like tectonics into account. Similar to the climatic development on Earth, one can simplify global sea level change from a decline at the end of the last interglacial maximum (MIS 5e) at 6–11 m above present (Turney et al. 2020) to the lowest stand during the LGM (MIS 2). However, it should be noted that sea levels are always oscillating and never really stand still in a geological timeframe. The exact frequencies and magnitudes of marine transgression and regression phases in the Late Pleistocene are still debated, even in the last glacial cycle since MIS 5e. In addition to MIS 2, another major low stand in this period occurred in MIS 4. MIS 3, on the other hand, was characterised by a fluctuating higher sea level, but still below modern values (see Lambeck and Chappell 2001; Murray-Wallace and Woodroffe 2014).

Despite the fact that the underlying records are site-specific, all global sea level curves generally follow the glacio-eustatic trend (Murray-Wallace and Woodroffe 2014; cf. Grant et al. 2012; Lambeck and Chappell 2001; Waelbroeck et al. 2002). Therefore, they are generally in line with each other on a larger timescale. However, as Table 7.1 shows, there are differences in how pronounced sea level high and low stands are. Furthermore, the exact timing and magnitude of those is still debated and uncertainties remain, especially during MIS 3.

Table 7.1: Sea level curves and stands for peak MIS 4 and high stand MIS 3 in metres beyond present sea level (bpsl).

Study	Low stand MIS 4 (65,000 years ago)	High stand MIS 3 (52,000 years ago)	Location of proxy
Grant et al. (2012)	c. 100 m	c. 60 m	Red Sea
Lambeck and Chappell (2001)	c. 85 m	c. 53 m	Huon Peninsula, PNG
Waelbroeck et al. (2002)	c. 85 m	c. 40 m (53,000 years ago) / c. 35 m (59,000 years ago)	North Atlantic, Southern Indian Ocean, Equatorial Pacific Ocean

Source: See sources cited throughout the table.

Studies on the formerly exposed continental shelves in tropical Australasia due to lower sea level stands usually decide to use a curve which is supposed to be the most appropriate for the study site (cf. Bird et al. 2018; De Deckker et al. 2019; Kealy et al. 2017). Here we assess how different sea level curves and values would change the story for Misool and the Misool Shelf, which is part of the north-western Sahul Shelf.

Implications for the Misool Shelf

The lack of local studies in Raja Ampat and West New Guinea makes it difficult to ground-truth global sea level curves. However, when looking at the low stands during MIS 4 and MIS 2, a higher or lower sea level value does not substantially affect palaeocoastline reconstructions (see Figure 7.3). While the sea level curve published by Lambeck and Chappell (2001) shows a low stand at 85 m bpsl during MIS 4, there is other literature suggesting an even deeper drop down to 100 m bpsl (De Deckker et al. 2019; Grant et al. 2012). While an uncertainty of 15 m seems imprecise, it appears to be negligible in this area and time frame. The same applies to the even more pronounced sea level drop during MIS 2. As the shelf area surrounding Misool is relatively shallow, most of it is exposed when sea levels drop under the region's shelf break of approximately 50 m bpsl (Pico et al. 2020). When sea levels drop further underneath the shelf break, new land exposure during marine regression decreases as the slope increases. That leaves MIS 3 as a major period of interest because the sea level fluctuated around the shelf break. Because of that, it is unclear if Misool became an island or remained connected to the mainland at this time. Some sources suggest a higher sea level, above the shelf break (Chappell 2002; Shackleton 2000), while a newer modelling study even suggests that the sea level rose above 40 m bpsl in MIS 3 (Pico et al. 2020). Other data and studies contradict this, on the other hand (i.e. Grant et al. 2012).

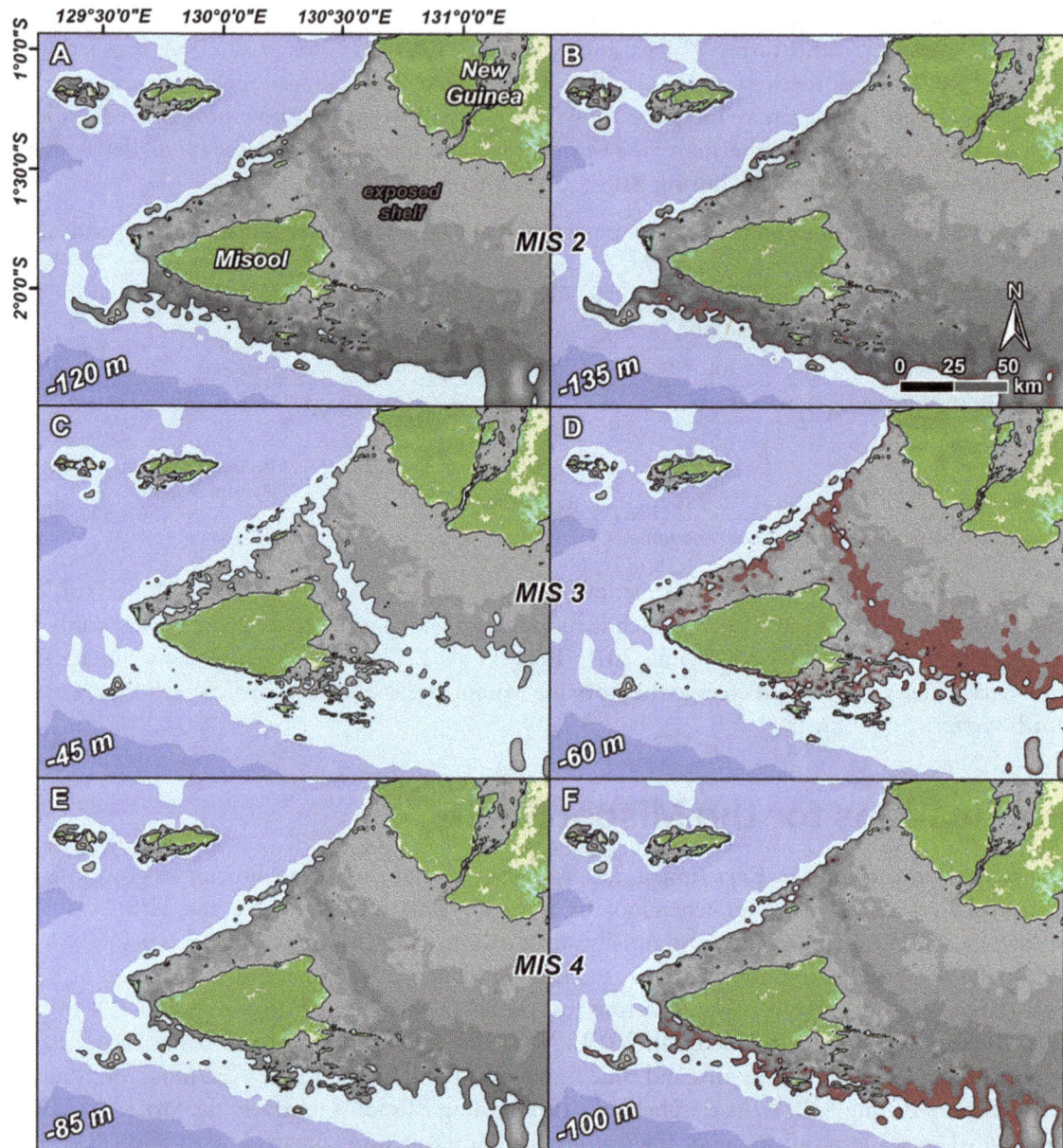

Figure 7.3: Bathymetric data in combination with a range of different values for sea level high and low stands taken from literature (see Table 7.1).

Notes: Exposed area due to lower estimates highlighted in red: (A) and (B) show the exposed shelf at respectively 120 and 135 m bpsl during the LGM; (C) and (D) show the exposed shelf at respectively 45 and 60 m bpsl when sea level peaked during MIS 3; (E) and (F) show the exposed shelf during the MIS 4 low stand at respectively 85 and 100 m bpsl.

Sources: ESA (2017); GEBCO Compilation Group (2020).

Pedoja and colleagues (2014) published an extensive review of sea level high stands inferred from palaeo-shorelines all over the globe. Elevated MIS 3 coastlines are only preserved above present sea level where uplifting rates are very high, and therefore relatively seldom. Such examples in former Sahul can be found in Biak, eastern Indonesia or the Huon Peninsula, Papua New Guinea (Chappel 2002; Tjia et al. 1974). Several high stands during MIS 3 left uplifted coral terraces behind. Chappell (2002) describes six distinct high stands between 60,000 and 30,000 years ago at the Huon Peninsula with a peak at 52,000 years ago, when sea level went up to 45 m bpsl. These data are also incorporated into the sea level curve proposed by Lambeck and Chappell (2001). Another sea level reconstruction approach by modelling was published by Pico and colleagues (2020) with a focus on the Sunda and Sahul Shelf during MIS 3 as well. The authors stress how recent research suggests that the sea level rose even above 40 m bpsl, drowning large areas of the continental shelf during this time. However, there are still many uncertainties regarding the exact timing and local manifestation of this transgression. According to Pedoja and colleagues (2018), many unstudied Pleistocene shorelines remain in eastern Indonesia, for example in Seram or Halmahera. Even in the north of Misool, elevated coral terraces seem to be present but remain unstudied (Sapin et al. 2009). These are potential opportunities to better understand sea level dynamics and tectonic processes in this area over time.

Nevertheless, the presence of uplifted palaeo-shorelines indicates local tectonic processes. These have to be taken into account when studying coastline changes in the past. Misool lies within one of the most complex tectonic areas on Earth. The Misool Shelf is part of the Bird's Head (micro-) Plate, which is subducted under the Banda Sea Plate in the south (Bird 2003). This convergence zone had a critical role in the evolution of an anticline, which uplifted Misool Island from the rest of the shelf (Sapin et al. 2009). On the other side, large parts of the shelf area around Misool belong to the Salawati basin and it is poorly understood to what account it is tectonically active on a relatively recent geological timescale (Gold et al. 2017). Another important feature is the Sorong Fault zone, which runs north of Misool but is regarded as inactive in relatively recent geological times (Watkinson and Hall 2017). However, it is even possible that Misool (as an anticline) behaves differently than the shelf area surrounding it. Because of this complexity, it is currently impossible to apply any tectonic correction on a bathymetric dataset for the time frame of interest.

Another variable is to what extent the drowned shelf area is modified by modern (Holocene) sedimentation. At least in the case of the nearby Sunda shelf, there seems to be only a negligible Holocene sediment cover (Hanebuth et al. 2011). However, there are no studies on how thick a recent sediment layer could be above the Misool Shelf. However, information could be locally available since several corporate coring expeditions were conducted in the context of oil and gas exploitation (e.g. Kingston 1988).

Using the Gulf of Carpentaria as an analogue

Pico and colleagues (2020) point out that the shelf break of the Sunda and Sahul Shelf both are c. 50 m bpsl. Therefore, the area is substantially flooded when the ocean rises above this threshold. One way to infer potential exposure of the Misool Shelf is by comparing it to an adequate analogue. The Gulf of Carpentaria seems well suited, due to its nearby geographic location and the Arafura sill. The latter is a barrier for marine inundation events at 53 m bpsl during lower sea level stands (Reeves et al. 2008). In addition, the Gulf of Carpentaria is regarded as tectonically stable (Lewis et al. 2013). Therefore, the Misool Shelf would have possibly undergone similar fluctuations. It would have started to become flooded around the same sea level height as the Gulf and would be entirely disconnected from mainland western New Guinea if the Gulf reached almost full marine conditions (see Figure 7.4). However, Reeves and colleagues (2008) point out that sediment cores from the Gulf of Carpentaria only show a minor marine incursion during MIS 3. Hence, that suggests that the sea level reached the elevation of the Arafura Sill, but without substantially exceeding it. In terms of chronology, these datasets are in line with the sea level curve produced by Lambeck and Chappell (2001), connoting that this minor flooding event occurred around 52,000 years ago.

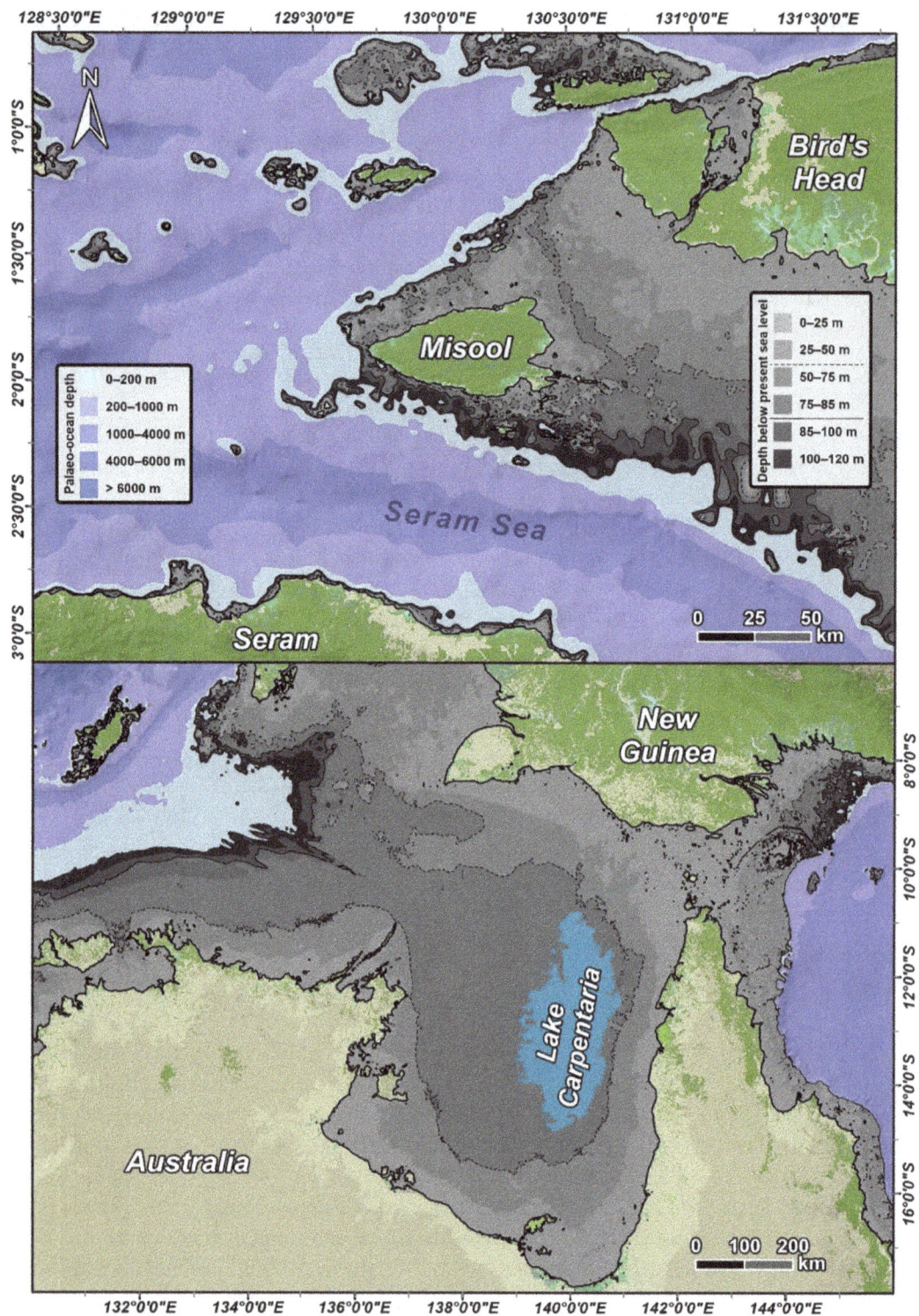

Figure 7.4: Bathymetric data showing that Misool Island would be almost entirely disconnected from mainland New Guinea when the sea level rose above 50 m bpsl (dashed line) and flooded the Gulf of Carpentaria.

Note: As there is no sedimentological evidence for such an event during MIS 3 so far, it appears that Misool potentially stayed connected to the Bird's Head.

Sources: ESA (2017) and GEBCO Compilation Group (2020).

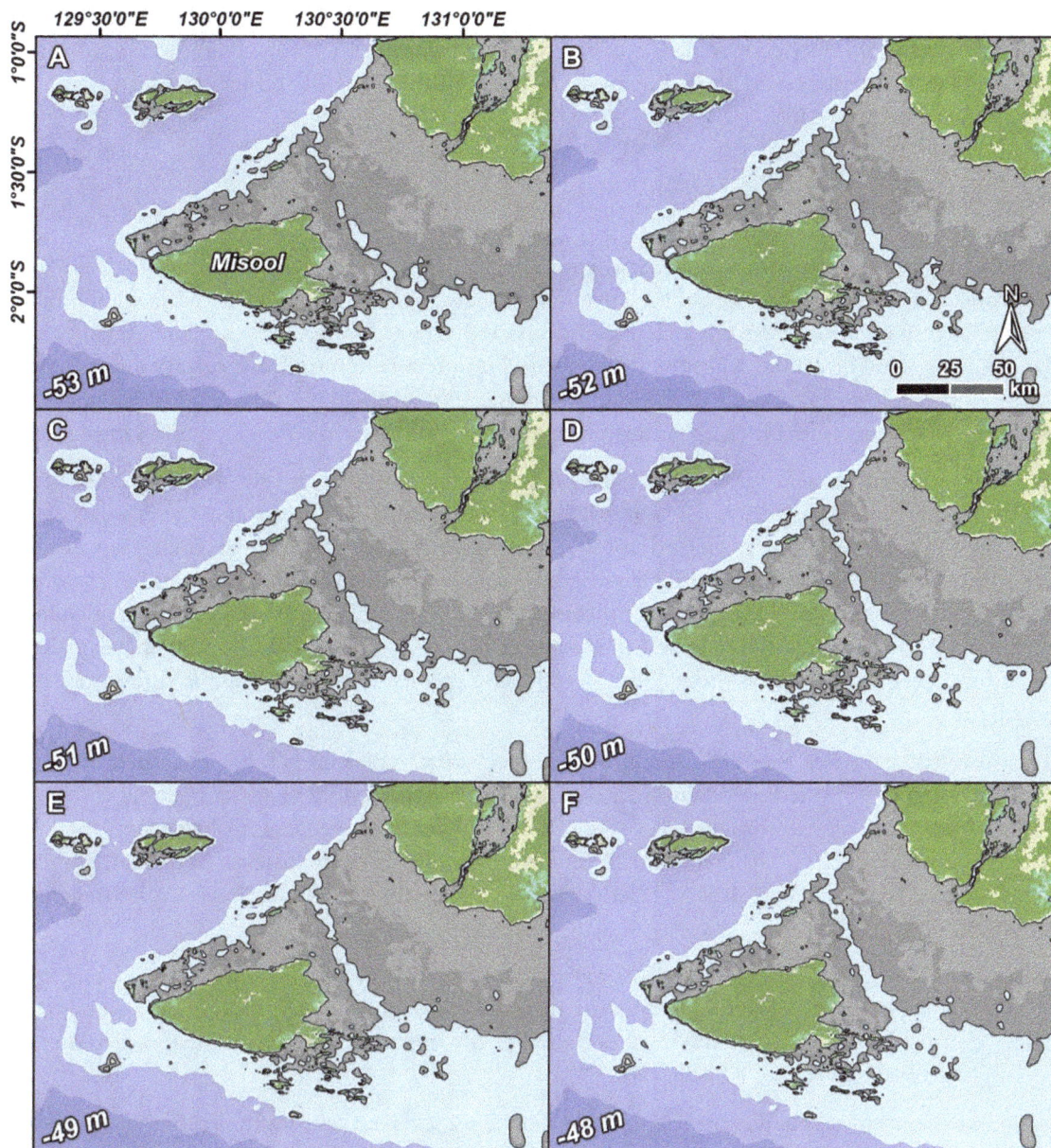

Figure 7.5: Misool disconnecting from the Bird's Head due to sea level transgression between 53 m and 48 m bpsl.

Notes: Misool Island and the exposed shelf area at: (A) 53 m bpsl; (B) 52 m bpsl; (C) 51 m bpsl; (D) 50 m bpsl; (E) 49 m bpsl; (F) 48 m bpsl. While Misool is still largely connected to the mainland of New Guinea at 53 m bpsl, it fully disconnects when the sea level rises above 48 m bpsl.

Sources: ESA (2017) and GEBCO Compilation Group (2020).

As Figure 7.5 shows, Misool would only start to disconnect from the Bird's Head when the sea level reached 53 m bpsl in MIS 3, after the previous drop in MIS 4. Moreover, it would only become an isolated island if marine transgression reached and exceeded a height of 48 m bpsl. From this perspective, it does not seem possible to unambiguously determine if it was an island based on the available data. When comparing the Misool Shelf to the sedimentological record of the Gulf of Carpentaria, it appears that Misool would have retained some sort of connection to New Guinea during MIS 3. But as mentioned previously, when reviewing literature, there are compelling arguments for higher sea level high stands during MIS 3. Therefore, it seems to be impossible to determine if the Misool Shelf stayed fully exposed or not during MIS 3. However, marine sediments from the Salawati basin could show potential drying and drowning of the sea floor, if not eroded while exposed during MIS 2.

Conclusion

We hope this chapter has shown how many gaps remain in the archaeological and geological record in the area. The remoteness of Misool relative to archaeological hubs in Jakarta and Jayapura makes it very challenging to organise research expeditions, as access is limited and the journey expensive. The environmental history of Misool and the Bird's Head can be inferred to a certain amount from nearby studies. However, because of the highly dynamic environmental processes, this will not make up for the lack of well-documented palaeoenvironmental and archaeological sites and samples.

No palaeoenvironmental records from Misool have yet been published. Our understanding of the island's environmental history is currently based on its present condition and the history of the region at large. Yet we know the island's present environment sets it apart from the region in some ways, thus local records are crucial for any but the vaguest reconstructions. We can be reasonably confident that Misool was cooler during most of the last 74,000 years, yet even the signs of changes in much-reduced precipitation are at times uncertain. Vegetation and fire are intimately tied to the human experience and, without local records, any reconstruction of these is little more than speculation.

This shows that further research expeditions are necessary, which target, for example, the main island of Misool to find sediment sinks. As wetlands have the potential to sustain people with water and food, this is where we would expect archaeological remains as well. Locals have confirmed that there are caves near Lake Tip in the northern centre of Misool, which never have been surveyed by researchers. Unfortunately, it is hard to get funding to explore such locations despite their huge potential.

As we are looking at a submerged landscape around Misool, we also think that many archaeological records are underwater nowadays. Because of that, and the nature of the karstic environment, we believe that marine archaeology has huge potential to discover new sites in the area, if dive sites are carefully selected.

It also has been shown that the application of different sea level curves produces different outcomes. Therefore, one should consider very carefully which data set to use and, if possible, compare it to other datasets and regional sea level indicators. The north shore of Misool contains several Pleistocene coral terraces, which could potentially help to understand the tectonic and eustatic history of Misool, if well-perservered coral can be found and dated. But as the tectonic setting in the region is one the most complex in the world, it is difficult to account for all factors like vertical movement and Holocene sedimentation.

In the near future, we hope to publish the first results from GPT and to put the first excavated, potentially Pleistocene archaeological site on the map. In addition, we hope that geochemical analysis will further shine a light on what kind of environment our early ancestors would have found when migrating through this nowadays submerged landscape at the entrance of Sahul.

References

Adhityatama, S. 2017. Silang Budaya: Kebinekaan di Pulau Misool, Papua Barat. In B. Prasetyo (ed.), *Kebinekaan Nusantara: Dalam Sudut Pandang Arkeologi* 41. Buku Obor, Jakarta.

Adhityatama, S. and A.S. Yarista 2019. Potensi arkeologi lanskap bawah air Indonesia. *Kalpataru* 28(1):55–71. doi.org/10.24832/kpt.v28i1.505.

Allen, J. and J.F. O'Connell 2020. A different paradigm for the initial colonisation of Sahul. *Archaeology in Oceania* 55(1):1–14. doi.org/10.1002/arco.5207.

Aubert, M., R. Lebe, A.A. Oktaviana, M. Tang, B. Burhan, Hamrullah, A. Jusdi, Abdullah, B. Hakim, J.-X. Zhao, I.M. Geria, P.H. Sulistyarto, R. Sardi, and A. Brumm 2019. Earliest hunting scene in prehistoric art. *Nature* 576:442–445. doi.org/10.1038/s41586-019-1806-y.

Ballard, C. 1992. Painted rock art sites in western Melanesia: Locational evidence for an 'Austronesian' tradition. In J. McDonald and I.P. Haskovec (eds), *State of the art: Regional art studies in Australia and Melanesia*, pp. 94–106. Occasional AURA Publication Number 6. Australian Rock Art Research Association, Melbourne.

Barmawidjaja, B.M., E.J. Rohling, W.A. van der Kaars, C.V. Grazzini, and W.J. Zachariasse 1993. Glacial conditions in the northern Molucca Sea region (Indonesia). *Palaeogeography, Palaeoclimatology, Palaeoecology* 101(1–2):147–167. doi.org/10.1016/0031-0182(93)90157-E.

Barrows, T.T., G.S. Hope, M.L. Prentice, L.K. Fifield, and S.G. Tims 2011. Late Pleistocene glaciation of the Mt Giluwe volcano, Papua New Guinea. *Quaternary Science Reviews* 30(19–20):2676–2689. doi.org/10.1016/j.quascirev.2011.05.022.

Beck, H.E., N.E. Zimmermann, T.R. McVicar, N. Vergopolan, A. Berg, and E.F. Wood 2018. Present and future Köppen-Geiger climate classification maps at 1-km resolution. *Scientific Data* 5:180214. doi.org/10.1038/sdata.2018.214.

Bellwood, P. 2019. The northern Spice Islands in prehistory, from 40,000 years ago to the recent past. In P. Bellwood (ed.), *The Spice Islands in prehistory: Archaeology in the Northern Moluccas, Indonesia*, pp. 211–221. ANU Press, Canberra. doi.org/10.22459/TA50.2019.13.

Bird, M.I., R.J. Beaman, S.A. Condie, A. Cooper, S. Ulm, and P. Veth 2018. Palaeogeography and voyage modelling indicates early human colonization of Australia was likely from Timor-Roti. *Quaternary Science Reviews* 191:431–439. doi.org/10.1016/j.quascirev.2018.04.027.

Bird, M.I., S.A. Condie, S. O'Connor, D. O'Grady, C. Reepmeyer, S. Ulm, M. Zega, F. Saltré, and C.J.A. Bradshaw 2019. Early human settlement of Sahul was not an accident. *Scientific Reports* 9:8220. doi.org/10.1038/s41598-019-42946-9.

Bird, P. 2003. An updated digital model of plate boundaries. *Geochemistry, Geophysics, Geosystems* 4(3):1027. doi.org/10.1029/2001GC000252.

Birdsell, J.B. 1977. The recalibration of a paradigm for the first peopling of Greater Australia. In J. Allen, J. Golson, and R. Jones (eds), *Sunda and Sahul: Prehistoric studies in Southeast Asia, Melanesia, and Australia*, pp. 113–167. Academic Press, London.

Bradshaw, C.J.A, S. Ulm, A.N. Williams, M.I. Bird, R.G. Roberts, Z. Jacobs, F. Laviano, L.S. Weyrich, T. Friedrich, K. Norman, and F. Saltré 2019. Minimum founding populations for the first peopling of Sahul. *Nature Ecology & Evolution* 3:1057–1063. doi.org/10.1038/s41559-019-0902-6.

Brumm, A., A.A. Oktaviana, B. Burhan, B. Hakim, R. Lebe, J. Zhao, P.H. Sulistyarto, M. Ririmasse, S. Adhityatama, I. Sumantri, and M. Aubert 2021. Oldest cave art found in Sulawesi. *Science Advances* 7(3):eabd4648. doi.org/10.1126/sciadv.abd4648.

Chappell, J. 2002. Sea level changes forced ice breakouts in the Last Glacial cycle: new results from coral terraces. *Quaternary Science Reviews* 21(10):1229–1240. doi.org/10.1016/S0277-3791(01)00141-X.

Chazine, J. 2011. New survey of painted panels of Northwest Papua: A precise identification of their location parameters and some insight into their function. In E. Anati (ed.), *Art and communication in pre-literate societies. XXIV Valcamonica Symposium,* pp. 106–113. Jaca Book, Milan.

Clarke, S.J., G.H. Miller, C.V. Murray-Wallace, B. David, and J.M. Pasveer 2007. The geochronological potential of isoleucine epimerisation in cassowary and megapode eggshells from archaeological sites. *Journal of Archaeological Science* 34(7):1051–1063. doi.org/10.1016/j.jas.2006.09.020.

Clarkson, C., Z. Jacobs, B. Marwick, R. Fullagar, L. Wallis, M. Smith, R.G. Roberts, E. Hayes, K. Lowe, X. Carah, S.A. Florin, J. McNeil, D. Cox, L.J. Arnold, Q. Hua, J. Huntley, H.E.A. Brand, T. Manne, A. Fairbairn, J. Shulmeister, L. Lyle, M. Salinas, M. Page, K. Connell, G. Park, K. Norman, T. Murphy, and C. Pardoe 2017. Human occupation of northern Australia by 65,000 years ago. *Nature* 547:306–310. doi.org/10.1038/nature22968.

Dang, H., Z. Jian, C. Kissel, and F. Bassinot 2015. Precessional changes in the western equatorial Pacific Hydroclimate: A 240 kyr marine record from the Halmahera Sea, East Indonesia. *Geochemistry, Geophysics, Geosystems* 16(1):148–164. doi.org/10.1002/2014gc005550.

Daniau, A.L., S.P. Harrison, and P.J. Bartlein 2010. Fire regimes during the Last Glacial. *Quaternary Science Reviews* 29(21–22):2918–2930. doi.org/10.1016/j.quascirev.2009.11.008.

De Deckker, P. 2016. The Indo-Pacific Warm Pool: Critical to world oceanography and world climate. *Geoscience Letters* 3:20. doi.org/10.1186/s40562-016-0054-3.

De Deckker, P., L.J. Arnold, S. van der Kaars, G. Bayon, J.W. Stuut, K. Perner, R. Lopes dos Santos, R. Uemura, and M. Demuro 2019. Marine Isotope Stage 4 in Australasia: A full glacial culminating 65,000 years ago—Global connections and implications for human dispersal. *Quaternary Science Reviews* 204:187–207. doi.org/10.1016/j.quascirev.2018.11.017.

Denniston, R.F., Y. Asmerom, V.J. Polyak, A.D. Wanamaker Jr., C.C. Ummenhofer, W.F. Humphreys, J. Cugley, D. Woods, and S. Lucker 2017. Decoupling of monsoon activity across the northern and southern Indo-Pacific during the Late Glacial. *Quaternary Science Reviews* 176:101–105. doi.org/10.1016/j.quascirev.2017.09.014.

DiNezio, P.N. and J.E. Tierney 2013. The effect of sea level on glacial Indo-Pacific climate. *Nature Geoscience* 6:485–491. doi.org/10.1038/ngeo1823.

ESA 2017. Land Cover CCI Product User Guide Version 2.0. Technical report available at: maps.elie.ucl.ac.be/CCI/viewer/download/ESACCI-LC-Ph2-PUGv2_2.0.pdf. (accessed 13 March 2024).

GEBCO Compilation Group 2020. GEBCO_2020 Grid [published data library]. doi.org/10.5285/a29c5465-b138-234d-e053-6c86abc040b9.

Gold, D.P., P.M. Burgess, and M.K. BouDagher-Fadel 2017. Carbonate drowning successions of the Bird's Head, Indonesia. *Facies* 63:25. doi.org/10.1007/s10347-017-0506-z.

Grant, K.M., E.J. Rohling, M. Bar-Matthews, A. Ayalon, M. Medina-Elizade, C. Bronk Ramsey, C. Satow, and A.P. Roberts 2012. Rapid coupling between ice volume and polar temperature over the past 150,000 years. *Nature* 491:744–747. doi.org/10.1038/nature11593.

Grindrod, J., P. Moss, and S. van der Kaars 1999. Late Quaternary cycles of mangrove development and decline on the north Australian continental shelf. *Journal of Quaternary Science* 14(5):465–470. doi.org/10.1002/(SICI)1099-1417(199908)14:5<465::AID-JQS473>3.0.CO;2-E.

Haberle, S.G., G.S. Hope, and S. van der Kaars 2001. Biomass burning in Indonesia and Papua New Guinea: Natural and human induced fire events in the fossil record. *Palaeogeography, Palaeoclimatology, Palaeoecology* 171(3):259–268. doi.org/10.1016/S0031-0182(01)00248-6.

Hanebuth, T.J.J., H.K. Voris, Y. Yokoyama, Y. Saito, and J. Okuno 2011. Formation and fate of sedimentary depocentres on Southeast Asia's Sunda Shelf over the past sea-level cycle and biogeographic implications. *Earth-Science Reviews* 104(1–3):92–110. doi.org/10.1016/j.earscirev.2010.09.006.

Hansen, M.C., P.V. Potapov, R. Moore, M. Hancher, S.A. Turubanova, A. Tyukavina, D. Thau, S.V. Stehman, S.J. Goetz, T.R. Loveland, A. Kommareddy, A. Egorov, L. Chini, C.O. Justice, J.R.G. Townshend 2013. High-resolution global maps of 21st-century forest cover change. *Science* 342(6160):850–853. doi.org/10.1126/science.1244693.

Harff, J., G. Bailey, and F. Lüth (eds) 2016. *Geology and archaeology: Submerged landscapes of the continental shelf.* Special Publications 411. Geological Society, London. doi.org/10.1144/SP411.13.

Hasibuan, F. 1990. Mesozoic stratigraphy and paleontology of Misool archipelago, Indonesia. Unpublished PhD thesis. Department of Geology, University of Auckland, Auckland.

Hope, G. 1998. Early fire and forest change in the Baliem Valley, Irian Jaya, Indonesia. *Journal of Biogeography* 25(3):453–461. doi.org/10.1046/j.1365-2699.1998.2530453.x.

Hope, G., and J. Tulip 1994. A long vegetation history from lowland Irian Jaya, Indonesia. *Palaeogeography, Palaeoclimatology, Palaeoecology* 109:385–398. doi.org/10.1016/0031-0182(94)90187-2.

Jatmiko, and M.A. Mujabuddawat 2016. Jejak budaya Paleolitik di Pulau Seram: Kajian migrasi manusia awal di wilayah Indonesia timur. *Kapata Arkeologi* 12(1):71–78. doi.org/10.24832/kapata.v12i1.324.

Jia, Q., T. Li, Z. Xiong, S. Steinke, F. Jiang, F. Chang, and B. Qin 2018. Hydrological variability in the western tropical Pacific over the past 700 kyr and its linkage to Northern Hemisphere climatic change. *Palaeogeography, Palaeoclimatology, Palaeoecology* 493:44–54. doi.org/10.1016/j.palaeo.2017.12.039.

Kealy, S., J. Louys, and S. O'Connor 2017. Reconstructing palaeogeography and inter-island visibility in the Wallacean Archipelago during the likely period of Sahul colonization, 65–45000 years ago. *Archaeological Prospection* 24(3):259–272. doi.org/10.1002/arp.1570.

Kealy, S., J. Louys, and S. O'Connor 2018. Least-cost pathway models indicate northern human dispersal from Sunda to Sahul. *Journal of Human Evolution* 125:59–70. doi.org/10.1016/j.jhevol.2018.10.003.

Kealy, S., S. O'Connor, Mahirta, D.M. Sari, C. Shipton, M.C. Langley, C. Boulanger, H.A.F. Kaharudin, E.P.B.G.G. Patridina, M.A. Algifary, A. Irfan, P. Beaumont, N. Jankowski, S. Hawkins, and J. Louys 2020. Forty-thousand years of maritime subsistence near a changing shoreline on Alor Island (Indonesia). *Quaternary Science Reviews* 249:106599. doi.org/10.1016/j.quascirev.2020.106599.

Kershaw, A.P., S. Van der Kaars, and P.T. Moss 2003. Late Quaternary Milankovitch-scale climatic change and variability and its impact on monsoonal Australasia. *Marine Geology* 201(1):81–95. doi.org/10.1016/S0025-3227(03)00210-X.

Kingston, J. 1988. Undiscovered petroleum resources of Indonesia. Open-file report. United States Department of the Interior Geological Survey, Washington, DC. doi.org/10.3133/ofr88379.

Lambeck, K. and J. Chappell 2001. Sea level change through the Last Glacial Cycle. *Science* 292(5517):679–686. doi.org/10.1126/science.1059549.

Leihitu, I. and R.C.E. Permana 2019. A reflection of painting tradition and culture of the Austronesian based on the rock art in Misool, Raja Ampat, West Papua. *Journal of Southeast Asian Studies* 24(1):220–242. doi.org/10.22452/jati.vol24no1.10.

Lewis, S.E., C.R. Sloss, C.V. Murray-Wallace, C.D. Woodroffe, and S.G. Smithers 2013. Post-glacial sea-level changes around the Australian margin: A review. *Quaternary Science Reviews* 74:115–138. doi.org/10.1016/j.quascirev.2012.09.006.

Lisiecki, L.E. and M.E. Raymo 2005. A Pliocene–Pleistocene stack of 57 globally distributed benthic δ^{18}O records. *Paleoceanography and Paleoclimatology* 20(1):PA1003. doi.org/10.1029/2004PA001071.

Mooney, S.D., S.P. Harrison, P.J. Bartlein, A.-L. Daniau, J. Stevenson, K.C. Brownlie, S. Buckman, M. Cupper, J. Luly, M. Black, E. Colhoun, D. D'Costa, J. Dodson, S. Haberle, G.S. Hope, P. Kershaw, C. Kenyon, M. McKenzie, and N. Williams 2011. Late Quaternary fire regimes of Australasia. *Quaternary Science Reviews* 30(1–2):28–46. doi.org/10.1016/j.quascirev.2010.10.010.

Murray-Wallace, C.V. and C.D. Woodroffe 2014. *Quaternary sea-level changes: A global perspective.* Cambridge University Press, Cambridge. doi.org/10.1017/CBO9781139024440.

Norman, K., J. Inglis, C. Clarkson, J.T. Faith, J. Shulmeister, and D. Harris 2018. An early colonisation pathway into northwest Australia 70–60,000 years ago. *Quaternary Science Reviews* 180:229–239. doi.org/10.1016/j.quascirev.2017.11.023.

O'Connell, J.F., J. Allen, M.A.J. Williams, A.N. Williams, C.S.M. Turney, N.A. Spooner, J. Kamminga, G. Brown, and A. Cooper 2018. When did *Homo sapiens* first reach Southeast Asia and Sahul? *Proceedings of the National Academy of Sciences* 115(34):8482–8490. doi.org/10.1073/pnas.1808385115.

O'Connor, S., R. Ono, and C. Clarkson. 2011. Pelagic fishing at 42,000 years before the present and the maritime skills of modern humans. *Science* 334(6059):1117–1121. doi.org/10.1126/science.1207703.

Oktaviana, A.A., P.V. Lape, and M.N. Ririmasse. 2018. Recent rock art research on East Seram, Maluku: A key site in the rock art of West Papua and South East Maluku. *Kapata Arkeologi* 14(2):135–144. doi.org/10.24832/kapata.v14i2.534.

Ono, R., R. Fuentes, A. Pawlik, H.O. Sofian, Sriwigati, N. Aziz, N. Alamsyah, and M. Yoneda 2020. Island migration and foraging behaviour by anatomically modern humans during the late Pleistocene to Holocene in Wallacea: New evidence from Central Sulawesi, Indonesia. *Quaternary International* 554:90–106. doi.org/10.1016/j.quaint.2020.03.054.

Pasaribu, Y.A., M.O. Rahim, and F. Latief 2020. Konteks budaya motif binatang pada seni cadas prasejarah Misool, Raja Ampat, Papua Barat. *Amerta* 38(1):1–16. doi.org/10.24832/amt.v38i1.1-16.

Pasveer, J.M., S.J. Clarke, and G.H. Miller 2002. Late Pleistocene human occupation of inland rainforest, Bird's Head, Papua. *Archaeology in Oceania* 37(2):92–95. doi.org/10.1002/j.1834-4453.2002.tb00510.x.

Pedoja, K., L. Husson, M.E. Johnson, D. Melnick, C. Witt, S. Pochat, M. Nexer, B. Delcaillau, T. Pinegina, Y. Poprawski, C. Authemayou, M. Elliot, V. Regard, and F. Garestier 2014. Coastal staircase sequences reflecting sea-level oscillations and tectonic uplift during the Quaternary and Neogene. *Earth-Science Reviews* 132:13–38. doi.org/10.1016/j.earscirev.2014.01.007.

Pedoja, K., L. Husson, A. Bezos, A.-M. Pastier, A.M. Imran, C. Arias-Ruiz, A.-C. Sarr, M. Elliot, E. Pons-Branchu, M. Nexer, V. Regard, A. Hafidz, X. Robert, L. Benoit, B. Delcaillau, C. Authemayou, C. Dumoulin, and G. Choblet 2018. On the long-lasting sequences of coral reef terraces from SE Sulawesi (Indonesia): Distribution, formation, and global significance. *Quaternary Science Reviews* 188:37–57. doi.org/10.1016/j.quascirev.2018.03.033.

Pedro, J.B., H.C. Bostock, C.M. Bitz, F. He, M.J. Vandergoes, E.J. Steig, B.M. Chase, C.E. Krause, S.O. Rasmussen, B.R. Markle, and G. Cortese 2016. The spatial extent and dynamics of the Antarctic Cold Reversal. *Nature Geoscience* 9(1):51–55. doi.org/10.1038/ngeo2580.

Pico, T., D. McGee, J. Russell, and J.X. Mitrovica 2020. Recent constraints on MIS 3 sea level support role of continental shelf exposure as a control on Indo-Pacific hydroclimate. *Paleoceanography and Paleoclimatology* 32:e2020PA003998. doi.org/10.1029/2020PA003998.

Reepmeyer, C., S. O'Connor, S. Kealy, Mahirta, and T. Maloney 2019. Kisar, a small island participant in an extensive maritime obsidian network in the Wallacean Archipelago. *Archaeological Research in Asia* 19:100139. doi.org/10.1016/j.ara.2019.100139.

Reeves, J.M., A.R. Chivas, A. García, S. Holt, M.J.J. Couapel, B.G. Jones, D.I. Cendón, and F. Fink 2008. The sedimentary record of palaeoenvironments and sea-level change in the Gulf of Carpentaria, Australia, through the last glacial cycle. *Quaternary International* 183(1):3–22. doi.org/10.1016/j.quaint.2007.11.019.

Reeves, J.M., H.C. Bostock, L.K. Ayliffe, T.T. Barrows, P. De Deckker, L.S. Devriendt, G.B. Dunbar, R.N. Drysdale, K.E. Fitzsimmons, M.K. Gagan, M.L. Griffith, S.G. Haberle, J.D. Jansen, C. Krause, S. Lewis, H.V. McGregor, S.D. Mooney, P. Moss, G.C. Nanson, A. Purcell, and S. van der Kaars 2013. Palaeoenvironmental change in tropical Australasia over the last 30,000 years—a synthesis by the OZ-INTIMATE group. *Quaternary Science Reviews* 74:97–114. doi.org/10.1016/j.quascirev.2012.11.027.

Roberts, P., J. Louys, J. Zech, C. Shipton, S. Kealy, S. Samper Carro, S. Hawkins, C. Boulanger, S. Marzo, B. Fiedler, N. Boivin, Mahirta, K. Aplin, and S. O'Connor 2020. Isotopic evidence for initial coastal colonization and subsequent diversification in the human occupation of Wallacea. *Nature Communications* 11(1):2068. doi.org/10.1038/s41467-020-15969-4.

Roberts, R.G., R. Jones, N.A. Spooner, M.J. Head, A.S. Murray, and M.A. Smith 1994. The human colonisation of Australia: optical dates of 53,000 and 60,000 years bracket human arrival at Deaf Adder Gorge, Northern Territory. *Quaternary Science Reviews* 13(5–7):575–585. doi.org/10.1016/0277-3791(94)90080-9.

Röder, J. 1959. *Felsbilder und Vorgeschichte des MacCluer-Golfes West-Neuguinea.* L.C. Wittich, Darmstadt.

Rusmana, E. and U. Hartono 1983. Geologic map of Misool quadrangle, scale 1:250.000. Open file report. Geological Research and Development Centre, Bandung.

Sapin, F., M. Pubellier, J.-C. Ringenbach, and V. Bailly 2009. Alternating thin versus thick-skinned decollements, example in a fast tectonic setting: The Misool–Onin–Kumawa Ridge (West Papua). *Journal of Structural Geology* 31(4):444–459. doi.org/10.1016/j.jsg.2009.01.010.

Shackleton, N.J. 2000. The 100,000-year Ice-Age cycle identified and found to lag temperature, carbon dioxide, and orbital eccentricity. *Science* 289:1897–1902. doi.org/10.1126/science.289.5486.1897.

Shiau, L.-J., M.-T. Chen, S.C. Clemens, C.-A. Huh, M. Yamamoto, and Y. Yokoyama 2011. Warm pool hydrological and terrestrial variability near southern Papua New Guinea over the past 50k. *Geophysical Research Letters* 38(8):L00F01. doi.org/10.1029/2010GL045309.

Shipton, C., S. O'Connor, N. Jankowski, J. O'Connor-Veth, T. Maloney, S. Kealy, and C. Boulanger 2019. A new 44,000-year sequence from Asitau Kuru (Jerimalai), Timor-Leste, indicates long-term continuity in human behaviour. *Archaeological and Anthropological Sciences* 11(10):5717–5741. doi.org/10.1007/s12520-019-00840-5.

Shipton, C., S. O'Connor, S. Kealy, Mahirta, I.N. Syarqiyah, N. Alamsyah, and M. Ririmasse 2020. Early ground axe technology in Wallacea: The first excavations on Obi Island. PLoS ONE 15(8):e0236719. doi.org/10.1371/journal.pone.0236719.

Sulistyarto, P.H., A.A. Oktaviana, S. Adhityatama, A.S. Ramadhan, A.P. Ariadi, I. Mahmud, and Y. Prameswari 2014. *Penelitian Arkeologi: Maritim Hunian Prasejarah dan Lukisan Cadas di Kepulauan Misool, Kabupaten Raja Ampat, Provinsi Papua Barat*. Laboran Penclitian Arkeologi, Jakarta.

Summerhayes, G.R., M. Leavesley, A. Fairbairn, H. Mandui, J. Field, A. Ford, and R. Fullagar 2010. Human adaptation and plant use in highland New Guinea 49,000 to 44,000 years ago. *Science* 330(6000):78–81. doi.org/10.1126/science.1193130.

Sutikna, T., M.W. Tocheri, J.T. Faith, Jatmiko, R. Due Awe, H.J.M. Meijer, E. Wahyu Saptomo, R.G. Roberts 2018. The spatio-temporal distribution of archaeological and faunal finds at Liang Bua (Flores, Indonesia) in light of the revised chronology for Homo floresiensis. *Journal of Human Evolution* 124:52–74. doi.org/10.1016/j.jhevol.2018.07.001.

Takeuchi, W. 2003. An ecological summary of the Raja Ampat vegetation. In R. Donnelly, D. Neville, and P.J. Mous (eds), *Report on a rapid ecological assessment of the Raja Ampat Islands, Papua, Eastern Indonesia held October 30 – November 22, 2002*. The Nature Conservancy—Southeast Asia Center for Marine Protected Areas, Bali.

Tjia, H.D., S. Fujii, K. Kigoshi, and A. Sugimura 1974. Late Quaternary uplift in eastern Indonesia. In R. Green (ed.), *Recent crustal movements and associated seismic and volcanic activity*, pp. 427–433. Special issue of *Tectonophysics* 23(4). doi.org/10.1016/0040-1951(74)90079-1.

Turney, C.S.M., R.T. Jones, N.P. McKay, E. Van Sebille, Z.A. Thomas, C.-D. Hillenbrand, and C.J. Fogwill 2020. A global mean sea surface temperature dataset for the Last Interglacial (129–116 ka) and contribution of thermal expansion to sea level change. *Earth System Science Data* 12:3341–3356. doi.org/10.5194/essd-12-3341-2020.

van der Kaars, S., and M.A.C. Dam 1995. A 135,000-year record of vegetational and climatic change from the Bandung area, West-Java, Indonesia. *Palaeogeography, Palaeoclimatology, Palaeoecology* 117(1):55–72. doi.org/10.1016/0031-0182(94)00121-N.

van der Kaars, S., X. Wang, P. Kershaw, F. Guichard, and D.A. Setiabudi 2000. A Late Quaternary palaeoecological record from the Banda Sea, Indonesia: Patterns of vegetation, climate and biomass burning in Indonesia and northern Australia. *Palaeogeography, Palaeoclimatology, Palaeoecology* 155(1):135–153. doi.org/10.1016/S0031-0182(99)00098-X.

Veth, P., I. Ward, T. Manne, S. Ulm, K. Ditchfield, J. Dortch, F. Hook, F. Petchey, A. Hogg, D. Questiaux, M. Demuro, L. Arnold, N. Spooner, V. Levchenko, J. Skippington, C. Byrne, M. Basgall, D. Zeanah, D. Belton, P. Helmholz, S. Bajkan, R. Bailey, C. Placzek, and P. Kendrick 2017. Early human occupation of a maritime desert, Barrow Island, North-West Australia. *Quaternary Science Review* 168:19–29. doi.org/10.1016/j.quascirev.2017.05.002.

Waelbroeck, C., L. Labeyrie, E. Michel, J.C. Duplessy, J.F. McManus, K. Lambeck, E. Balbon, and M. Labracherie 2002. Sea-level and deep water temperature changes derived from benthic foraminifera isotopic records. *Quaternary Science Reviews* 21:295–305. doi.org/10.1016/S0277-3791(01)00101-9.

Watkinson, I.M. and R. Hall 2017. Fault systems of the eastern Indonesia triple junction: Evaluation of Quaternary activity and implications for seismic hazards. In P.R. Cummins, and I. Meilano (eds), *Geohazards in Indonesia: Earth science for disaster risk reduction*, pp. 71–120. Special Publications 441. Geological Society, London. doi.org/10.1144/SP441.8.

Wurster, C.M. and M.I. Bird 2016. Barriers and bridges: early human dispersals in equatorial SE Asia. In J. Harff, G. Bailey, and F. Lüth (eds), *Geology and archaeology: Submerged landscapes of the continental shelf*, pp. 235–250. Special Publications 411. Geological Society, London. doi.org/10.1144/SP411.2.

Zhao, D., S. Wan, Z. Song, X. Gong, L. Zhai, X. Shi, and A. Li 2019. Asynchronous variation in the Quaternary East Asian winter monsoon associated with the tropical Pacific ENSO-like system. *Geophysical Research Letters* 46(12):6955–6963. doi.org/10.1029/2019GL083033.

8

First footsteps across the Lydekker Line: An archaeological survey in the northern Raja Ampat Islands

Dylan Gaffney, Daud Tanudirjo, Zubair Mas'ud, Erlin Novita Idje Djami, Abdul Razak Matcap, and Tristan Russell

Abstract

This chapter describes an archaeological survey conducted in the northern Raja Ampat Islands, West New Guinea. These islands border a key biogeographic transitional zone known as Lydekker's Line, representing the north-western edge of the Australasian faunal zone. Raja Ampat therefore marks a critical ecological transition for any humans that moved between island Wallacea and continental Sahul in the Late Pleistocene, or New Guinea during the Holocene. Moreover, the islands were key locations articulating trade and migrations between Southeast Asia and the Pacific in the recent, and perhaps more distant, past. Despite these factors, the archipelago suffers from an almost complete lack of archaeological research. The chapter therefore summarises regional environmental conditions and the history of colonial Dutch and Indonesian research in the area (largely unpublished or reported in Dutch and Indonesian), before describing new survey results from the Raja Ampat Archaeological Project, presenting 125 previously unrecorded sites including recent pre-colonial and historical sites, burial caves, rock art panels, pottery-bearing sites, caves, and rock-shelters.

Abstrak

Topik yang dibahas dalam bab ini adalah menyangkut hasil survei arkeologi yang dilakukan di kepulauan Raja Ampat bagian utara. Pulau – pulau yang terdapat di wilayah ini berbatasan langsung dengan zona transisi yang dikenal dengan Garis Lydekker, dimana zona ini mewakili tepi barat laut sebaran fauna Australasia. Berdasarkan keletakannya, kepulauan Raja Ampat diperkirakan merupakan zona transisi ekologis yang penting dalam proses migrasi manusia antara pulau yang berada di wilayah Wallacea dan Sahul pada akhir pleistosen. Selain itu, Raja Ampat juga diperkirakan memiliki peranan besar pada manusia prasejarah di Papua secara khusus pada masa Holosen. Selain itu, pulau-pulau yang berada dalam wilayah tersebut diperkirakan merupakan kawasan yang mengartikulasikan proses perdagangan dan migrasi antara Asia Tenggara dan Pasifik di masa lalu bahkan mungkin mencapai wilayah yang lebih luas lagi. Kendati demikian, data ilmiah mengenai potensi yang ada terutama dari sisi arkeologi sangat minim ditemukan karena kurangnya penelitian arkeologi yang dilakukan selama ini. Oleh karena itu, sebagai langkah awal, bab ini menyajikan rangkuman kondisi lingkungan serta memaparkan hasil penelitian yang pernah dilakukan terutama oleh peneliti berkebangsaan Belanda dan juga peneliti dari Indonesia. Hasil penelitian tersebut, sebagian besar tidak dipublikasikan baik dalam bahasa Belanda maupun Indonesia. Adapun hasil penelitian terbaru dari kepulauan Raja Ampat yang juga diuraikan dalam bab ini adalah berupa, 125 situs arkeologi, situs pra-kolonial, gua-gua penguburan, lukisan cadas, situs pemukiman yang ditandai dengan gerabah, alat batu, dan lain-lain.

Introduction

The Raja Ampat Islands—consisting of four main isles (Waigeo, Batanta, Salawati, and Misool) along with hundreds of other smaller islands, karsts, and reefs—are located at the western edge of Southwest Papua Province, today administered by Indonesia (Figure 8.1). The archipelago is superbly situated to address several pertinent questions about how different maritime groups crossed back and forth across a major biogeographical transition to populate island rainforests and newfound continents, prompting diverse responses to these new and challenging environments. This transition is known as the Lydekker Line, which separates the mainland New Guinea–Australian fauna, and the edge of the Sahul Plate, from the islands of Wallacea. Despite their potential, the islands suffer from an almost complete lack of archaeological fieldwork. Therefore, they are often ignored from interpretations seeking to track the migration of humans into the Pacific for the first time in the Late Pleistocene, and subsequent population movements throughout the Holocene record. As Raymond Corbey (2017) notes for the anthropology of the area—and this equally applies to the archaeology—the Raja Ampat Islands are often left to the Southeast Asian specialists by Pacific researchers, and vice versa.

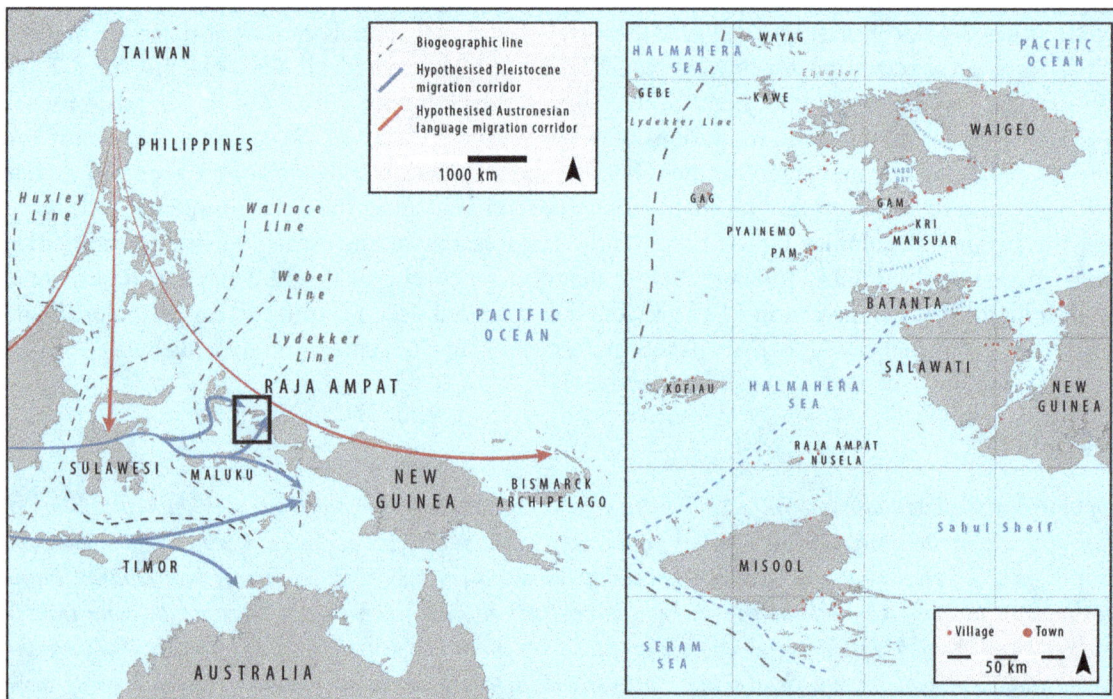

Figure 8.1: The Raja Ampat Islands in the circum–New Guinea region, showing major hypothesised dispersal corridors and biogeographic divisions.

Source: Dylan Gaffney.

In particular, Raja Ampat is perfectly placed to address current debates on the timing and nature of the Southern Dispersal out of Africa and into Sahul by coastally adapted and seafaring *Homo sapiens*. Recent GIS (geographic information system) modelling studies based on up-to-date bathymetry and interisland visibility suggest Raja Ampat would have been a key area along the Birdsell Northern Route (Birdsell 1977), facilitating the dispersal of *Homo sapiens* across Wallacea and into northern Sahul for the first time (Kealy et al. 2018; Norman et al. 2018). Wright and colleagues (2013) reviewed all previous archaeological research in West New Guinea, noting that only two sites—Toé Cave and Kria Cave in the interior of the Bird's Head Peninsula (Pasveer 2004)—provide robust chronostratigraphic sequences for this route, dating the earliest known human occupation to about 30,000 years ago, just before the Last Glacial Maximum (LGM) but substantially after the initial colonisation of Sahul. Although several research projects in Timor and north-west Australia continue to push back the timing of the southern colonisation route and associated maritime technologies, few archaeologists are focusing on this northern route.

Moreover, the area is well placed to address the migration of Austronesian-speaking, pottery-producing cultures from Asia to the Pacific. Based on linguistic evidence, the nearby Bird's Head and Cenderawasih Bay area have long been posited as the source of immediately pre-Lapita peoples before they migrated to the Bismarck Archipelago (Blust 1984–85; Pawley and Ross 1993). Currently, the nature of Lapita dispersals in Near and Remote Oceania is debated, with one group of scholars supporting a fast-track model, whereby highly mobile Austronesian speakers moved through Island Southeast Asia and the Pacific, initially with little admixture but later substantial interactions, innovations, and integrations (Spriggs et al. 2019), while another group supports gradual technological and language dispersals through established social networks along a west to east cline (Specht et al. 2014). Other themes of interest involve the Late Pleistocene and Early–Mid-Holocene transfer of crops (e.g. banana), animals (e.g. marsupials), and material culture (e.g. obsidian stemmed tools) from New Guinea into its surrounding islands, and vice versa (Barton and Denham 2011; Summerhayes 2007); the emergence of a widespread rock art complex with common features spanning from West New Guinea and eastern Wallacea to Remote Oceania (Arifin and Delanghe 2004; Ballard 1992); the Late Holocene development of globalising trade and exchange networks, especially the introduction of bronze axes, iron, and the origins of the spice trade (Ono et al. 2018; Swadling 1996); and recent pre-colonial and ethnographic movements of different linguistic groups from Maluku, New Guinea, Southeast Asia, China, and Europe, which can be documented in the archaeological, linguistic, and oral history records (Arnold 2017, 2018).

In this chapter, we take the first tentative footsteps across the Lydekker Line into the Raja Ampat Islands—as the ancestors of the Pacific did—with the aim of addressing these gaps in the record. The chapter presents new survey results from the Raja Ampat Archaeological Project, the first systematic archaeological program in the island group (see Gaffney 2021). The survey focuses on the largest island in the archipelago, Waigeo, along with several smaller islands and reefs in the Waigeo area and off the north coast of Batanta Island.

The northern Raja Ampat Islands

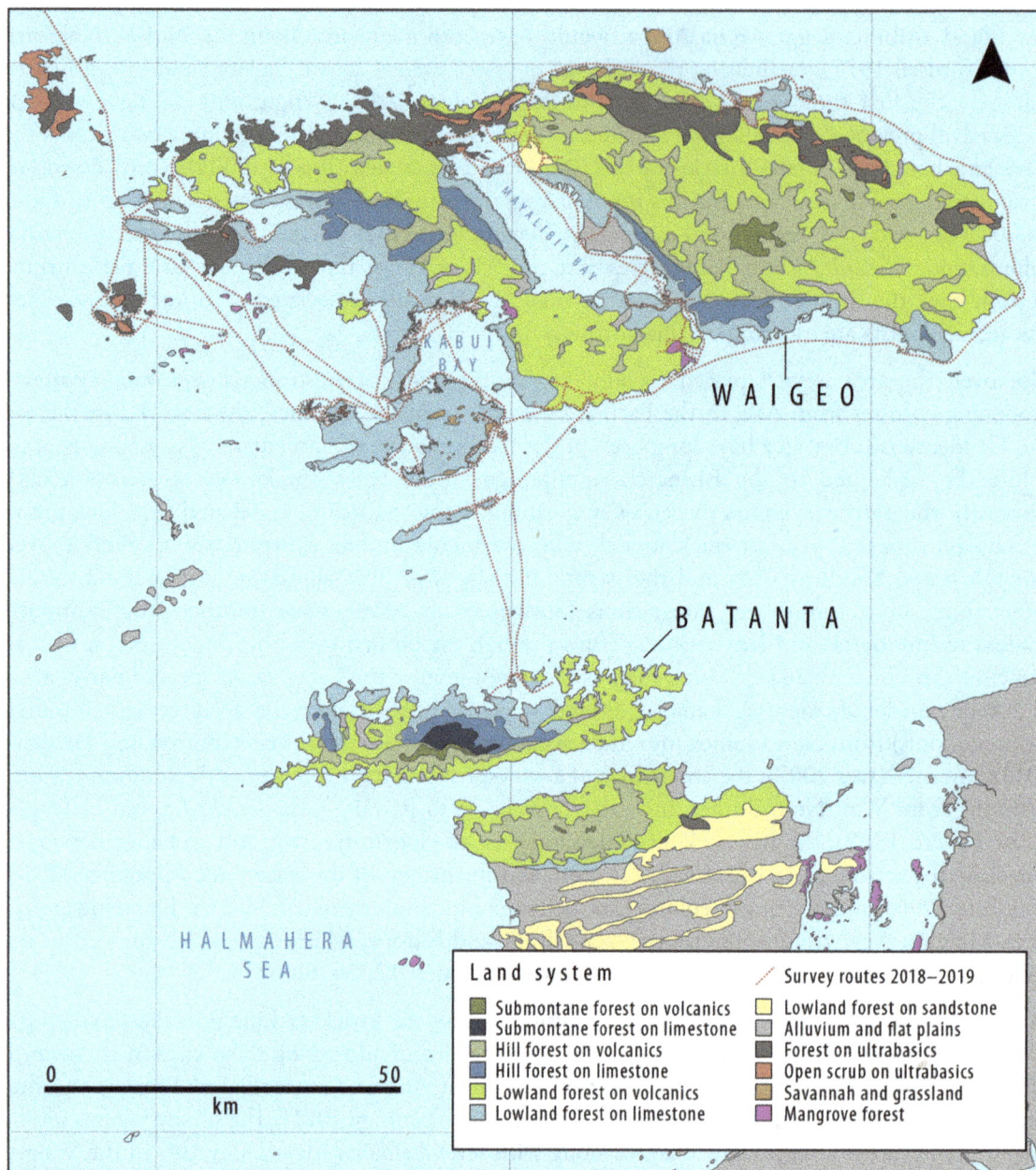

Figure 8.2: Major landforms in the northern Raja Ampat Islands and routes of the reconnaissance survey undertaken in 2018–2019.

Source: Dylan Gaffney, with base map redrawn from Webb (2005).

Several environmental zones characterise the northern Raja Ampat Islands because of their underlying geological diversity (Charlton et al. 1991; Supriatna et al. 1995; Figure 8.2). These include dense lowland rainforests, rugged karst, exposed metal-rich hills, volcanic peaks around 1000 m above sea level (asl), small-scale coconut and sago plantations, and abundant coral reefs (Bird and Ongkosongo 1980). In fact, Raja Ampat lies at the heart of the coral triangle and is the most bio-diverse marine environment on the planet, with a high abundance of reef fishes, sharks and rays, sea cucumbers, shellfish, crustaceans, sea turtles, saltwater crocodiles, sea birds, and marine mammals (Donnelly et al. 2003; McKenna et al. 2002; Natsir and Subkhan 2016). The land supports a diverse array of vegetational zones including lowland tropical forests, swamps, karst, submontane forests, and occasional grasslands, which in turn support a limited number of small- to medium-bodied forest birds, marsupials, rodents, bats, and reptiles. Evergreen tropical forests are sustained by stable year-round temperatures and relatively abundant rainfall even in the drier months of June to July. Spatial variation in rainfall, in combination with the underlying geology and land systems, mean that the islands likely presented past human populations with a range of vegetational areas, variably productive for foraging and cropping. For instance, lowland forests on karst limestones between 0–300 m asl tend to seasonally produce abundant fruits, but also absorb groundwater, meaning that soils are thin and prone to drought stress (Webb 2005, 16). Forest fires around these karst forests and ultrabasic scrublands would have been regular, particularly during glacial and stadial periods. Only at around 600–700 m asl on the highest peaks such as Mt Nok on Waigeo does lowland tropical forest give way to submontane forest including ferns, brush, acacia, orchids, and mosses (Cheesman 1949, 71). This is a result of the high mountains being very close to the ocean, resulting in submontane vegetation occurring at lower altitudes than it would on the New Guinea mainland (Webb 2005, 13). Unfortunately, no palaeoenvironmental research has been undertaken in the islands to reconstruct vegetational histories or provide evidence for anthropogenic forest management in the past.

Previous archaeological work

Based on the limited available historical and ethnographic information (e.g. Cheesman 1949; Remijsen 2001), the recent settlement of northern Raja Ampat seems to have been small-scale but highly dynamic, involving speakers of numerous languages that shifted their home bases relatively frequently, even into the twentieth century. Archaeological evidence is therefore essential to examine the nature of settlement at the millennial scale, and to provide clarification about how settlement practices shifted throughout these insular rainforest environments since initial occupation in the Late Pleistocene and into the Holocene.

No systematic archaeological surveys, excavations, or radiocarbon determinations have been published from the Raja Ampat Islands. Previous attempts to set up archaeological programs in West New Guinea by Solheim and Soejono were met with difficulty for a variety of political reasons (Solheim 2006), although throughout the twentieth century, a handful of European colonial officers and archaeologists unsystematically visited some islands, providing patchy evidence for locations of past settlement (see also Gaffney and Tolla, Chapter 2, this volume).

At Yenbekaki on the north coast of Batanta Island, F.C. Kamma, a missionary turned ethnographer, reported a 'fort' with a number of ceramics in 1937. According to oral tradition, the Yenbekaki[1] hillfort was the home of Manarmakeri. This fort remains undated but it probably predates the initial Biak settlement of the north Batanta coast during the nineteenth century, instead relating to the expansion of Tidorese influence, perhaps being used as a stopover for Tidorese envoys (Maryone 2010), the guerrilla leader Prince Nuku (Galis and Kamma 1958; see Widjojo 2009), or, given the fear of Tidorese hongi[2] raids and Dutch control (Swadling 1996, 112), it may have been a local Olon/Batta response to increased violence in the seventeenth and eighteenth centuries.

---

1   Named in Biak for its 'high sand' at the beach. Also known as *Layn ni kot* in Batta language; 'Jèmbekaki' in the Dutch orthography; sometimes spelled Yembekaki in English/Indonesian. Not to be confused with a present-day Biak settlement of the same name on the eastern coast of Waigeo.

2   Throughout this chapter, local language words are italicised and Papuan Malay or Indonesian words are underlined at first mention. Words from other languages (such as Dutch) are provided with single quote marks.

Figure 8.3: A selection of potsherds recovered by Galis and Kamma from Yenbekaki, north Batanta Island.

Notes: (A)–(B) coil-ware with finger impressions; (C)–(D) bowls with direct rims and red-slip; (E) possible stand for ceramic oven; (F) painted incurving unrestricted rim; (G) incurving restricted globular vessel; (H) pedestal for red-slipped pot; (I)–(J) face appliqué decoration; (K) carved and punctate decoration (Makbon ware); (L) incised base.

Source: Photos by Jasmijn Ouwendijk; illustrations by Dylan Gaffney; Courtesy of Museum Volkenkunde, cat # RV-09-243; RV-3510-1 — RV-3510-1173.

Twenty years later, Kamma returned to Yenbekaki with K.W. Galis, a colonial ethnologist for the 'Kantoor voor Bevolkingszaken' (Bureau of Native Affairs), to record the site. The fortification walls were built from coral, around 75 m long, 6–7.60 m in breadth, and 1.20–1.52 m high. Pottery densely littered the surface within the walls and was eroding down the hillsides (Galis and Kamma 1958). Having reanalysed the Yenbekaki collections now accessioned at the 'Wereldmuseum' (Figure 8.3), the pottery (n = 1256) is dominated by globular pots, dishes, and bowls, many of which are characteristic of the last few centuries before the present. Many of the globular pots are coarsely tempered and thick-bodied with possible slip or burnish surface treatments. Most of the bowls/dishes are decorated with carving and triangular punctation (n = 237), identical to flaring bowls/dishes excavated at Makbon, just north of Sorong on the Bird's Head (Solheim 1998a). Some of the carved sherds also preserve ornamental appliqué figures with human faces and arms (n = 9). Galis (1960) noted that one small ceramic cup in the form of a human face has similarities to ceramic figures from the Karama River area of Sulawesi. Incised bases (n = 8) characteristic of central Maluku are also present (see Latinis and Stark 2003). Rarer rim forms include a single thin-bodied painted sherd characteristic of pottery from southern Maluku (see Veth et al. 2005). The collection also includes several notched lip vessel sherds with light incision (n = 30), paddle-impressed sherds (n = 11), fingernail-impressed sherds (n = 2), appliqué spiral decorated sherds (n = 17), ceramic handles (n = 44), a pedestal base (n = 1), rectilinear sago oven fragments (n = 17), Chinese/European glazed earthenware and stoneware (n = 118), stone objects possibly being manuports or sling stones (n = 16), and a single stone or glass bead.

Around the same time, in June 1956 Deputy Officer E.A. Polansky and medical doctor L.C. Binsber came across a 'Biak cemetery', at Bukorsawai, 15 minutes' sailing from Asoker (now Asukweri) in north Waigeo (Anon. 1957). Allegedly these were the bones of Sawai people who came from Patani in south-east Halmahera and were lured there by Biak men Pasrif and Fakok. The cemetery was located at the bottom of a large triangular space:[3] this contained two 1.25 m-long crates made from iron and wood in the shape of a large fish. A third crate was in the same style but had since decayed. These were filled with 14 skulls and some post-cranial bones in secondary burial contexts. A square ceramic sago oven, divided into four compartments, was also found nearby, along with two *korwar* ancestor figures (Corbey 2017). One year later, Controller R. Stephan visited three rock art sites: one on a cliff to the east of Asoker village[4] (Galis 1964). These paintings were faded and no description was provided. Souza and Solheim (1976) and Nitihaminoto (1980) visited what they assumed to be the same site, which was locally known as *Sapormerek* (painted cape), and located at the edge of a river or on the coast.

In 1975, Solheim (1998b) visited Gag Island, noting a charcoal lens with coconut shells several metres deep in an exposed section cut for a new landing strip. On Me Island, just north-west of Saleo, west Waigeo, he also recorded a small shrine with carved wooden images and an old bronze gong, along with a triton shell and human skullcap (Solheim 1979). In Waigeo's Kabui Bay, a burial cave was noted with skeletons, a wooden platform decorated with *mon* figures, wooden chests, coffins, porcelain, and stoneware (Figure 8.4), although many of the grave offerings had been stolen several months beforehand by Sumatran traders from Sorong.[5] Solheim put in a small shovel pit there but this 'did not amount to much' (Solheim 1998b, 66); however, his team did collect some recent ceramic sherds and a wooden altar for the Cultural Centre Museum at Universitas Cenderawasih, and a mon[6] figure was collected at another unspecified cave (Solheim 1978).

---

3   This site has been relocated and recorded as WAI-40.

4   This site has been relocated and recorded as WAI-63.

5   This site has been relocated and recorded as WAI-24.

6   Solheim misidentifies this object as a korwar figure.

Figure 8.4: Secondary burial offerings from the Waigeo area, collected by Bill Solheim in 1975.

Notes: (A) wooden platform from Monfeu cave; (B)–(C) details of carved mon figures on wooden platform; (D) mon figure from unspecified cave site.

Source: Photographs by Dylan Gaffney, courtesy of the Cultural Centre Museum, University of Cenderawasih, Jayapura, 2018.

Indonesian researchers are increasingly beginning to turn their attention to southern Raja Ampat and there have recently been small research projects based around south-east Misool, run by the Pusat Penelitian Arkeologi Nasional (Indonesian National Research Centre for Archaeology, ARKENAS) (Adhityatama and Yarista 2019), and the Balai Arkeologi Papua (Papua Centre of Archaeology) (Balai Arkeologi Jayapura 2012; Fairyo 2010), both of which are now part of Badan Riset dan Inovasi Nasional (BRIN). These projects have focused on an area of impressive rock art in the karst archipelago around Tomolol and at Limalas, first reported by de Clercq (1893) and later by Chazine (2009, 2011, 2014), Sulistyarto (2014), and Nasruddin (2015). These rock paintings depict hand stencils, animals, and anthropomorphs, and are part of a larger rock art complex, stretching from eastern Wallacea into West New Guinea and the Pacific (Arifin and Delanghe 2004; Röder 1939, 1959). Most recently, the Centre of Excellence for Australian Biodiversity and Heritage has undertaken a survey and excavation on Misool in collaboration with ARKENAS (Boesl et al., this volume). Raja Ampat is also host to a number of World War II (WWII) wrecks and marine archaeological sites, which have been recorded by ARKENAS (Dillenia et al. 2016), and on Salawati, at the Dezh Mountain site, and Doom Island, between Salawati and New Guinea, historical artefacts and structures relate to Japanese imperial occupation (Fairyo 2014; Sukandar 2012a, 2013). There have only been occasional visits by members of the Papuan Archaeology Centre to the northern Raja Ampat Islands, resulting in a small database of sites, most of which are very recent (e.g. Mahmud 2013; Sukandar 2012b), and of limited potential for excavation (Table 8.1), although Zubair Mas'ud has undertaken test pitting at several cave sites (see Gaffney 2021).

Table 8.1: Sites previously recorded in northern Raja Ampat.

Island	District	Bahasa name/description	English name	Location	Description
Waigeo	Distrik Tiplol Mayalibit	Bentabon (piring sejarah)	Bentabon (historical plate)	Kabilol village	Stone plates marking the birthplace of the Louw clan.
	Distrik Teluk Mayalibit	Kuburan tua bersejarah	Historic burial	Lopintol village	Grave of the first settler from Ternate, Danu Arif Syafudin, and his daughter, who taught Islam. Grave is over 100 years old.
		Bangku duduk raja	King's seat	Mumes village	The 'King's Seat', where the Raja of Waigeo resided.
		Gong (Korois)	Gong	Mumes village	Gong used by watch-people to call the villagers.
		Batu yang berbentuk "alat kelamin laki-laki"	Stone phallus	Warsambin village	Stone with ritual significance, giving childless people offspring if they touch it.
	Distrik Waigeo Utara	Patung batu	Stone statue	Kabare village	Describes the story of ancestral family murders.
	Distrik Supnin	Goa tengkorak	Skull cave	Rauki village	Stores the human remains of people who died from murder and disease in the past.
	Distrik Waigeo Selatan	Goa makam bersejarah	Historical burial cave	Wawiyai village	Human remains and all those people's possessions placed in a wooden coffin in the shape of a boat.
		Situs Kali Raja	Site of the Kali Raja	Wawiyai village	The origin place of the Raja Ampat groups, up a river that is the ancestral area of the Mayalibit Bay groups. The site comprises a building (un-walled house) in which the king's 'egg' and other items are stored.
		Batu Pensil (Pulau Belo)	Pencil Rock	Wawiyai village	Story related to this place: an old man was sailing near the island but suddenly the enemy came, so the man loosened his tethers and sailed off without having time to pull up the anchor, which later turned to stone.
		Bukit aiba	Aiba hill	Wawiyai village	An old grave, where the wife of Kurabesi is buried.
		Kawasan cagar budaya Pianemo	Pianemo cultural heritage area	Pianemo Islands	Karst cliff considered to be of heritage value due to its beauty and geological significance.
	Distrik Waigeo Barat	Kawasan cagar budaya Wayag	Wayag cultural heritage area	Wayag Islands	Karst cliff considered to be of heritage value due to its beauty and geological significance.

Island	District	Bahasa name/description	English name	Location	Description
Batanta	Distrik Batanta Utara	Benteng Yenbekaki	Yenbekaki fort	Arefi village	Large stone buildings that resemble a fort.
		Gereja tua (Eben-Haezer)	Old church	Arefi village	Church built during Japanese era and not maintained.
		Rumah peninggalan pdt. Yan Mamoribo	Heritage house	Arefi village	Former home of the first gospel-bearer in Raja Ampat.
		Puing pesawat dibawah air luat	Submerged aircraft wreck	Wai Island	Plane which crashed during the Japanese occupation.
		Telaga doreombon	–	Dayan Island	Named 'dolphin lake' due to large numbers in the area.
		Museum Dayan	Dayan Museum	Dayan Island	Storage place of historical artefacts.
		Goa Tafare dan Goa Paniki	Cuscus Cave and Bat Cave	Yensawai village	Cave with two chambers, one with a lot of cuscus and another with a lot of bats.
	Distrik Batanta Selatan	Batu perahu layar (Pat Wagle)	Sailboat stone	Yenanas village	Story suggests in ancient times a sailboat was turned upside down and became a rock due to exposure to waves and saltwater.

Source: Papua Centre of Archaeology (translated from Indonesian).

Archaeological survey and site distributions

The Raja Ampat Archaeological Project undertook about two months of dedicated site survey around Waigeo, Batanta, and their outlying islands during 2018 with ad hoc site visits made in 2019 during the excavation season. Owing to high-density forest cover on most of these islands, the survey was selective and targeted specific geological and topographic areas. These areas included (1) limestone karst on the coast and in the interior with potential caves, rock-shelters, and rock paintings, (2) beach flats and raised terraces around the coast, which could yield ceramic deposits from the Mid- and Late Holocene, and (3) flat spaces and ridge lines in the interior, with potential for open settlements. All ground surveys were undertaken with Raja Ampat landowners, whose knowledge of the local environment and access to different parts of the forest guided where sites were recorded. Within the wider context of our survey strategy, sites of archaeological and oral historical importance were also opportunistically recorded when Raja Ampat guides knew the location of these sites.

In total, 125 sites were recorded in the survey database (Appendix A). The recorded sites predominantly include caves and rock-shelters (n = 62), and secondary burial caves (n = 22), which are common in the Miocene Waigeo Limestone karst around Waigeo Island in Mayalibit Bay, Kabui Bay, near Kabare, Waisai, and Selpele, and on Gam Island. In these limestone areas, we also recorded nine rock art sites, known locally but previously unpublished. Recent beach middens, clay and stone quarries, historical sites, and artefact scatters are represented in smaller numbers. Furthermore, because the northern Raja Ampat Islands are so densely rainforested, with little evidence for major anthropogenic clearance, open sites were difficult to locate. In the following sections, we collate the major categories of archaeological sites and illustrate their distributions throughout the islands.

Recent historical sites and sacred locations

Several sites provide clarification about recent colonisation processes within the last five centuries (Figure 8.5). These sites are primarily restricted to very small offshore islands, located on low-lying Quaternary sand and coral formations, or in hilly areas among former gardens and open villages, suggesting recent migrations spread along the south coast of Waigeo, around Gam, Manyaifun, and north Batanta. Most historical sites recorded in Table 8.2 are found within the Biak language area and relate to their movements around the offshore Raja Ampat Islands in the last few centuries, as recorded in oral traditions.

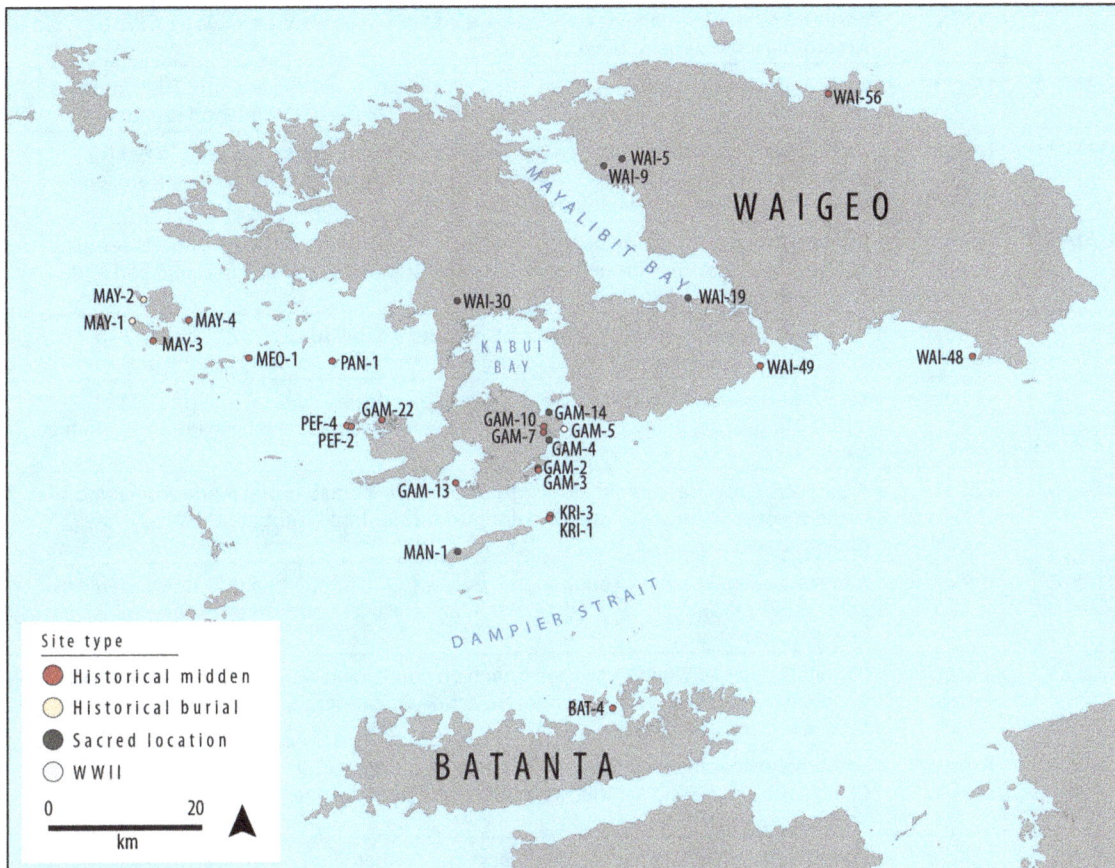

Figure 8.5: Location of recent historical and sacred sites on Waigeo, Gam, and surrounding islands.
Source: Dylan Gaffney.

Table 8.2: Summary of historical sites recorded in the Raja Ampat Archaeological Project database.

Site code	Type	Site description
WAI-48	Midden	Small beach flat on Memyai Island, with c. 20 m stretch of midden, containing plentiful shell, and a few ceramics (European/Chinese glazed wares and local earthen sago ovens and globular pots).
WAI-49	Midden	Small beach flat with shallow historical shell midden under topsoil (*Tridacna* sp., *Cypraea* sp., other gastropods and bivalves), some artefactual and recent ceramics including painted glazed plate (possibly mid-twentieth century).

Site code	Type	Site description
WAI-56	Artefact scatter	Flat area, c. 5 m away from steep limestone karst cliff, running east–west and looking down onto Rainkan river and north coast of Waigeo. Defensive position and small cave to south contains fresh water. Ground surface covered with shells, earthenware, porcelain, and stone and shell tools. Stories about the site suggest it is a recent Ambel habitation site. After Biak speakers moved to the area these groups fled north into what is now Micronesia.
GAM-5	WWII	Batu Lima (five offshore limestone rocks). A concrete survey marker is constructed on top, with kanji script on two sides. Built during WWII when Japanese forces occupied Raja Ampat.
GAM-7	Artefact scatter	In hills about 1.5 km inland from Raswan village, east Gam. Former garden and settlement area containing earthenware and glazed ceramics, including bottle from Amsterdam and a metal bowl.
GAM-10	Cave	Cave approximately 30 m west of Alfred Wallace recreation hut site. This contains one complete green glass bottle, and half a sago oven with pedestal stand.
GAM-13	Midden	Old village site at south-east entrance to Gaman Bay. Beach flat with long strip of historical midden (European/Chinese pottery, brown glazed earthenware, and unglazed earthenware, shell), and a grave.
GAM-22	Findspot	Former Ombrap village on north-west Gam. In use until the mid-twentieth century but now used as pearl farm. One findspot of Chinese/European ceramic and mid-twentieth-century cemetery.
PEF-2	Midden	Yenmaret beach on south Pef Island. Contains a small mound with *Tridacna* sp. midden and Chinese/European ceramics, along with scatters of pottery, metal, and shell.
PEF-4	Midden	Yenikwaen beach on south Pef Island. Long beach with several mounds, exposed midden in the beach flats, and surface Chinese/European pottery dating to the last century.
MAY-1	Burial	A burial at Taukapaya, west Manyaifun Island. This small burial made from concrete in the shape of a house is said to belong to former inhabitants of the area. Now damaged and looted for Maluku plates.
MAY-2	Burial	A burial at Tau Beach on Kodor Island. Bones found on the beach flat reburied with coral grave markers. Now used as place for offerings (modern coins, ceramics, metal bowls, *Tridacna* sp.).
MAY-3	'Former village'	Old village site at Yenmangkwaen beach on south-east Manyaifun Island. Used before people moved to Manyaifun village. No artefacts present on surface but a well is said to date to time of occupation.
MAY-4	Artefact scatter	Yentamako beach on small island north-east of Manyaifun. Contains a few Dutch and Chinese ceramics and earthenware plate and bowl fragments among *Tridacna* sp. shells.
MEO-1	Midden	Yefkabu Island, where a memorial marks the former village that was first to receive the Bible in 1941. One Chinese/European ceramic surface find and strip of shell midden in the exposed beach flat.
PAN-1	'Former village'	Mututru Island, adjacent to Paniki Island. Said to be village site before people moved to Ombrap. They established a wooden church here. Some flaked lithics on surface (possibly for ring making) and a cemetery.
KRI-1	Artefact scatter	The Papua Diving helipad and hanger area, which has recently been cleared. The small natural valley contains numerous Chinese/European ceramics and gastropod shell, marking former gardens or settlements.
KRI-3	Artefact scatter	Papua Diving resort area. A small pile of Chinese/European ceramics and *Tridacna* and gastropod shell on the surface suggests a former village area.
BAT-4	Midden	On Yu Island, c. 2 km north of Batanta and c. 1 km east of Birie Island. An old village with a grave made from a bush turkey nest. Nearby midden contains shell, sago oven sherds, Chinese/European ceramics.

Source: Raja Ampat Archaeological Project database.

Figure 8.6: Recent sites relating to the migration of Biak speakers to Raja Ampat.

Notes: (A) house burial on Manyaifun Island (MAY-1); (B) monument to first Christians at Yefkabu Island (MEO-1); (C) view of Mututru Island (PAN-1); (D) former site of Besir village (GAM-13) with midden eroding from beach flat and rock overhang on the north side. Scale 20 cm intervals.

Source: Photographs by Dylan Gaffney, 2018.

At MEO-1 on Yefkabu, a monument notes the former village was the first place in the area to receive the Bible in 1941, and sparse glazed ceramics indicate recent habitation (Figure 8.6). At PAN-1 on Mututru Island near Paniki Island, there is a memorial to the first church constructed out of bush material, along with a cemetery dating to the mid-twentieth century. At the same time, oral traditions suggest these groups used two sites on the south coast of Pef Island (PEF-2 and PEF-4), which contain small middens of glazed ceramics and shells. These groups then moved to the Ombrap village site (GAM-22) on Gam Island.

GAM-13 represents the largest historical site recorded—one of the former Besir settlements that was first occupied by Biak speakers from Arborek before they formed a new village in the mid-twentieth century. It is situated on a small island just off the south-east coast of Gam, concealed in a small bay 1.5 km north-west of Kapisawar village. The site consists of a c. 50-meter-long strip of beach midden containing Chinese/European glazed ceramics, earthenware, and shells. The beach flat is flanked by rock overhangs in the north and south, and an uplifted fringing reef in the west which makes the space very sheltered and protected.

Further north, GAM-3 is located on a large island[7] off the east coast of Gam, at Nyandebas beach. The Nyandebas beach flats are now used as sweet potato gardens, and a c. 10 × 10 m area contains earthenware and rare glazed sherds. We test-pitted this site in early 2019, revealing a shallow stratigraphy with charcoal, shell, and ceramics present in the top layer only, likely related to habitation within the last century (Gaffney et al. 2024a).

Around Manyaifun Island, two unique graves (MAY-1 and MAY-2) are said to belong to a pre-Biak people. One of these graves is in the form of a concrete house burial, and similar house burials made of organic materials called *no* have been described from Iesbi Island in Fafak Bay (Cheesman 1949, 107). The first Biak settlement in the area at Yenmangkwaen (MAY-3) is still known on south Manyaifun Island. On MAY-4, on the beach of a small island to the north-east of Manyaifun, ceramics are said to derive from a stilted village of the Dimara clan before they relocated in WWII.

At BAT-4 site on Yu Island, just north of Batanta, an alleged grave was found when local children discovered Maluku plates eroding from a brush turkey nest. A Biak leader of the Marino clan is said to be interred inside. The area also contains a beach midden of ceramics and shells, with old garden soils eroding down the cliff behind. People probably lived here while collecting black potting clay at BAT-3, 20 m to the west (see Gaffney and Tanudirjo 2019). It is unclear when this site was first occupied, in relation to modern Arefi and Yensawai, and the archaeologically recorded Yenbekaki hillfort (Galis and Kamma 1958).

One historical site also relates to European occupation. A reconstruction of Wallace's (1869, Ch. 36) campsite while he was collecting bird-of-paradise specimens near the northern Besir village has been produced by local guides for ecotourism. The location chosen was based on knowledge passed down by elders and could only be an approximation. However, a nearby cave (GAM-10) known as Jangkrik for all of the cricket-like insects covering the walls, contains historical artefacts dating to the mid–late nineteenth century. This may, indeed, indicate that this was the place where Wallace was based for about six months.

A number of geological formations have also been incorporated into local oral traditions relating to the origin stories of the Ma'ya and Ambel speakers. The Kali Raja site (WAI-30) is an important place, known throughout Raja Ampat. It is here, at a building complex c. 4 km up the Wawage (Dusun) River, that a small stone is venerated as the egg of an unhatched raja. This stone is one of six that provide the origin story for Raja Ampat. The Kali Raja stone is enshrined in highly prized ceramic and metal plates and a mosquito net shroud, housed in an open-walled house. To see the egg itself and change the 'clothes' of the Kali Raja, one must spend a week at the site cooking and making offerings, an opportunity that only occurs about every five years. This place is said to be the origin place for all of the Ma'ya-speaking groups, who later dispersed around Raja Ampat.

Caves and crevices (Table 8.3) are variously feared for containing malignant spirits (WAI-9), venerated as places where spirit princesses frequent (GAM-2), or consulted for good fortune while hunting when they contain benevolent princesses (WAI-5). On a limestone escarpment near Asukweri in north Waigeo there is a cave (WAI-64) containing a naga (serpent) head while giant octopodes are thought to inhabit other caves like GAM-30. Some formations, such as large, exposed speleothems resembling phalluses at the entrance to Mayalibit Bay (WAI-19), are used to bring fertility, whereby locals will go to pay an offering and take away a piece of the stone. Other areas are remembered

---

7   This island is marked as part of Gam on topographic maps because extensive mangrove areas appear to connect the two at the northern end, but one can pass through the mangroves into a large saltwater bay between the island and Gam itself, known as *Dore Dor* (the bay inside).

for their practical functions, such as storage places for bride wealth, where valuable objects could be hidden away from family members (GAM-4), or where old bamboo was left after being used to clean the infirm as a way of removing things associated with the sick from the village (GAM-14).

Table 8.3: Important sacred sites around northern Raja Ampat.

Site code	Language area	Site description
WAI-5	Ambel	Two small crevices containing princesses Lorina and Mariska.
WAI-9	Ambel	Set of small crevices containing *gin*.
WAI-19	Ambel	Phallic-shaped rocks used to increase fertility.
WAI-30	Ma'ya	Kali Raja egg-stone. Said to be an unhatched king of Raja Ampat.
GAM-2	Biak	Cave filled with water. Offerings left for princesses who bathe here.
GAM-4	Biak	Small cave used as storage for bride price valuables.
GAM-14	Biak	Small cave with stacks of bamboo used to wash sick people.
MAN-1	Biak	Limestone overhangs produce sounds of hourglass drumming at night.

Note: Most sites recorded in the database have their own stories attached; the sites in this table are of limited to no archaeological potential but are very significant to local groups.

Source: Raja Ampat Archaeological Project database.

Burial caves

Although modern Christian and Muslim cemeteries are situated close to villages, burial sites established before the early twentieth century were situated on offshore islands where houses of the dead were constructed (Cheesman 1949, 107), or in shelters and caves (Corbey 2017). This had the dual function of (1) removing the ancestral spirits from the space of the living, and (2) preventing physical remains from being exhumed by pigs and dogs, especially given the thin soils that overlie hard limestone bedrock in many coastal areas. Similar burial caves, involving the conservation of ancestral bones (especially skulls) away from the village, are commonly associated with pottery-making, Austronesian-speaking communities throughout Island Southeast Asia and the Pacific (e.g. Bedford and Spriggs 2007; Shaw 2014; Valentin and Sand 2008).

Twenty-two secondary burial locations were recorded around Waigeo, Gam, and Pef (Figure 8.7), which share locational attributes, being near modern or colonial-period village sites, and in hidden caves, rock overhangs, and crevices. This distribution may reflect looting which has removed bones and associated grave goods from the most conspicuous sites. Antique Maluku plates are stolen because they can be used for bride wealth, and some looters will even spend their time digging for complete vessels. Their positioning on coastal cliffs and caves with steep runoff into the sea also means that many original remains have been lost to erosion and wave action. Many of these sites are associated with human bones, animal bones, shells, and ceramics (Table 8.4). Those sites that continue to be maintained, or have taken on sacred or magical properties, often contain more recent offerings such as modern Indonesian coins or glazed ceramics. The best-surviving burial shelter recorded is Kalep Minet (WAI-24) on the north-west coast of Wayef Island, just south-west of Wawiyai village in Kabui Bay. This may be the same site visited by Solheim in 1975 (Solheim 1998b). It contains the remains of several individuals, along with associated grave goods, including Dutch and Chinese ceramics, and even a wooden canoe hull.

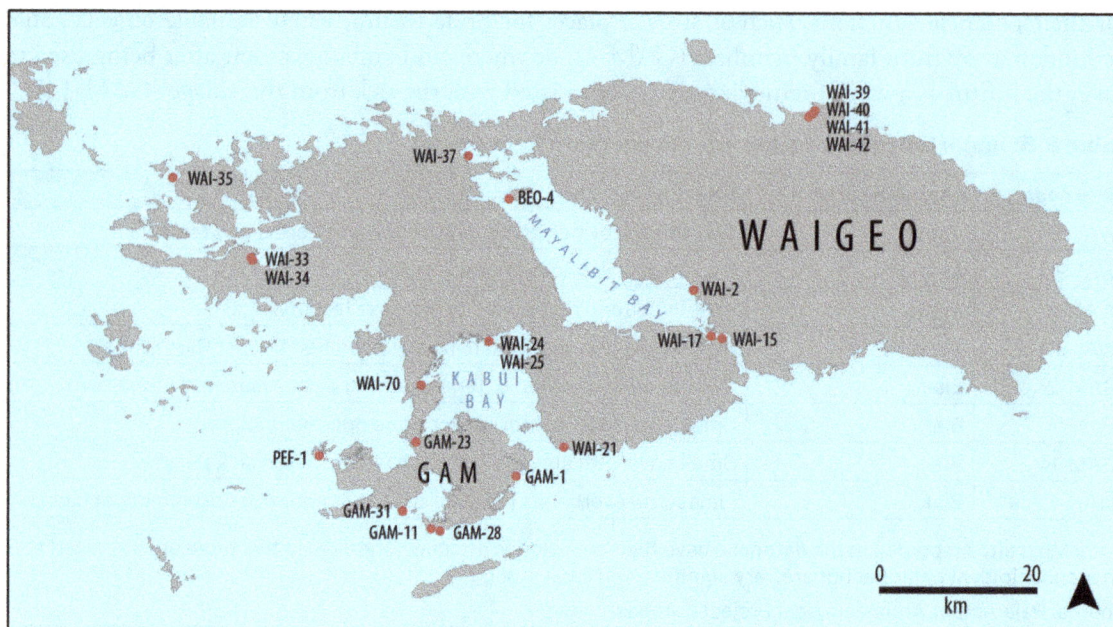

Figure 8.7: Distribution of secondary burial caves/shelters recorded around Waigeo and Gam.

Source: Dylan Gaffney.

Table 8.4: Secondary burials recorded in Waigeo and Gam area along with associated material culture.

Site code	Type	Language area	Contents
WAI-2	Overhang	Ambel	Human long bones and pelvises; one large and two small glazed bowls.
WAI-15	Cave	Ambel	Human bone; shell; pottery (earthenware).
WAI-17	Cave	Ambel	Two human bones.
WAI-21	Cave	Biak	Dog long bones and skull.
WAI-24	Overhang	Ma'ya	Numerous human long bones and skulls; Chinese/European bowls, plates, and teapots; wooden altars.
WAI-25	Crevices	Ma'ya	Human long bones and skulls; modern coins; pig skull.
WAI-33	Cave	Ma'ya	Four human skulls; broken Maluku plate.
WAI-34	Ledge	Ma'ya	Human bones (one skull, long bones) covered by Maluku plate; three bowl fragments.
WAI-35	Boulder	Ma'ya	No material remaining.
WAI-37	Overhang	Ambel	Numerous human long bones; plates (mid-twentieth century).
WAI-39	Ledge	Ambel	One human femur and smaller bones.
WAI-40	Overhang	Ambel	Twelve human skulls arranged in 3 × 4 and long bones, pelvises, and ribs; three plate fragments (two large Maluku plates and a Chinese plate).
WAI-41	Crevice	Ambel	Wooden coffins containing bones.
WAI-42	Cave	Ambel	Human long bones and skull fragments; ceramic sherds; possible stone artefacts. Dolphin and dugong (?) shaped wooden coffins with recent burial offerings including sago oven fragments.
WAI-70	Shelter	Ma'ya	Five cranial fragments (five individuals said to be Ma'ya ancestors): one occipital bone/foramen magnum, one complete cranium, one near complete cranium, one occipital/temporal fragment; shells.

Site code	Type	Language area	Contents
BEO-4	Overhang	Ambel	Human long bones and skulls; animal bones; shells (incl. pearl shell); large brown glazed and Chinese ceramics.
GAM-1	Crevice	Biak	Human bones; dog skull; modern ceramics and glass
GAM-11	Overhang	Biak	Human rib and long bones; Chinese glazed ceramics; shells.
GAM-23	Shelter	Biak	Human skulls and long bones, arranged neatly.
GAM-28	Overhang	Biak	Three human skulls, two femora, a humerus, and a pelvis.
GAM-31	Crevice	Biak	Human skull and shells.
PEF-1	Overhang	Biak	One human skull, humerus, fibula, and two ribs.

Source: Raja Ampat Archaeological Project database.

The taphonomy on the bones, and the different types of associated material culture, suggest these locations were used at different times in the recent past, perhaps over a period of several hundred years. For instance, Tanjung Aris Cave (WAI-15) at the entrance to Mayalibit Bay contains only earthenware pottery sherds, associated with human bones and shells, possibly implying it predates the widespread use of glazed import ceramics from Maluku, China, and Europe. To investigate the chronology of secondary burials around the northern Raja Ampat Islands, with the permission of clan owners, we carefully extracted three charcoal samples from an eroding section at Aput lo (WAI-33), a shelter inside Aljui Bay, western Waigeo. This site contained several human crania above an exposed section of interleaved charcoal and clay lenses, with thin deposits of shell, fish, and mammal bone midden, along with possible quartz stone tools. Radiocarbon dating indicates that this midden was produced within the last five centuries before the present and was used in at least two separate periods (Table 8.5).

Table 8.5: Radiocarbon dating results at Aput lo burial shelter (WAI-33).

Lab code	Site	Depth	Material	D(13C)	% modern	CRA*	Cal. years BP (2σ)
Beta-506675	WAI-33	80 mm	Charcoal	–26.7	95.50±0.36	370±30 BP	399–316 cal. BP (43.1%) 500–422 cal. BP (52.3%)
Beta-506676	WAI-33	150 mm	Charcoal	–29.4	95.86±0.36	340±30 BP	476–312 cal. BP (95.4%)
Beta-506677	WAI-33	300 mm	Charcoal	–24.7	93.03±0.35	580±30 BP	567–532 cal. BP (30.9%) 646–585 cal. BP (64.6%)

Note: * Conventional radiocarbon age (BP)

Source: Authors' summary, calibrated using IntCal 20 (Reimer et al. 2020).

Rock art sites

The rock art of northern Raja Ampat can be subdivided into two technical traditions: an earlier tradition using red and yellow pigments, and a later one using white pigment (Figure 8.8). Red-yellow rock art was recorded at three sites around western Waigeo. All three sites share locational attributes; they are positioned on coastal cliffs, several metres above the present-day sea level. This may be a preservation issue, with storm surges washing away all but the highest paintings. However, it may also suggest that they were produced by canoe-going populations in the Mid- to Late Holocene when the isostatic sea level high stand was several metres above today's level. Currently, no radiometric dating has been undertaken on rock art from the area.

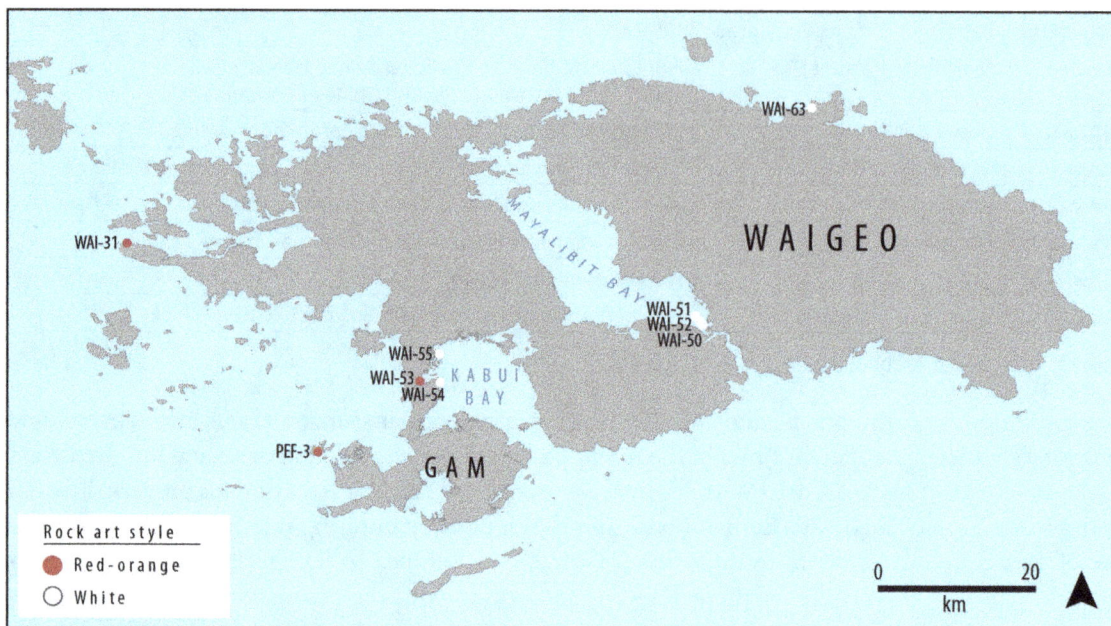

Figure 8.8: Newly recorded rock art sites around Waigeo and Pef, showing presence of red and white technical traditions.

Source: Dylan Gaffney.

PEF-3, known as Brambaem (hand stencil) in Biak, is located on the south-east edge of a small bay formed by Pef Island. The paintings—all negative hand stencils produced by blowing red pigment onto the hand—are located in two alcoves. One alcove is about 10 m up the cliff face containing two hand stencils (one right and one left hand) along with faded areas of pigment above them. Another painting, about 3 m up the cliff, contains a single right handprint. Further north, WAI-31 is located just under a kilometre north-east of Selpele village. This area is known as Lentagin in the local Kawe Ma'ya dialect and consists of a large limestone cliff face about 50 m high and 100 m long, facing east onto the Halmahera Sea. A single gallery, about 10 m long, is located 5–7 m above the high-tide mark, and includes red and yellow pigment negative hand stencils, anthropomorphs, geometrics, tallies, and zoomorphs (possibly fish). In Kabui Bay, *Mon Ake* (WAI-53), as it is known in the Wauyai dialect of Ma'ya, comprises a single red anthropomorph with one hand raised and another pointing down, and a geometric to the top left. Given the name of the site and the positioning of the figure's arms, the art may have links with the mon ancestor belief system (see Corbey 2017).

Similar red pigment rock art designs have been recorded throughout West New Guinea and eastern Indonesia. Hand stencils are present throughout Indonesia on Borneo, Sulawesi, Timor, and West New Guinea, while similar fish, anthropomorphic, and geometric designs are noted in the Berau Gulf (Galis 1957; Röder 1939) and on Misool (Nasruddin 2015). Ballard (1992) suggested these kinds of paintings co-occur with Austronesian languages, making the art complex a potential signature of early Proto-Eastern Malayo–Polynesian or Proto-South Halmahera–West New Guinea–speaking groups during the Late Holocene (similar rock art has been subsequently dated to c. 2500 years old in New Caledonia, Sand et al. 2006).

A second white pigment tradition appears to be more recent and occurs east of the red-yellow tradition, along the western flank of Kabui Bay, in the entrance to Mayalibit Bay, and on the north coast of Waigeo. Like the red-yellow tradition, the white rock art is exclusively situated along coastal limestone karst; however, the art is located only a few metres above modern mean sea level and could have been painted from canoes at high tide within the last few centuries. Stories relating to these paintings—primarily consisting of geometrics, animals, and people on canoes and sailboats— indicate that they were produced at a time of contact, and conflict, between local Ambel/Ma'ya groups and newcomers to the area, possibly those clans arriving from Biak and Maluku, as well as long-distance merchants.

Earthenware ceramic sites

Earthenware pottery sites predating the introduction of Chinese and European glazed ceramics are rare in the area due to dense forest cover. Four prospective sites were recorded around north Waigeo, Mayalibit Bay, Friwen Island, and on Birie Island off the north coast of Batanta (Figure 8.9). All of these sites represent small artefact scatters but have the potential for subsurface investigations to establish the initial timing of Late Holocene ceramic occupation in the islands.

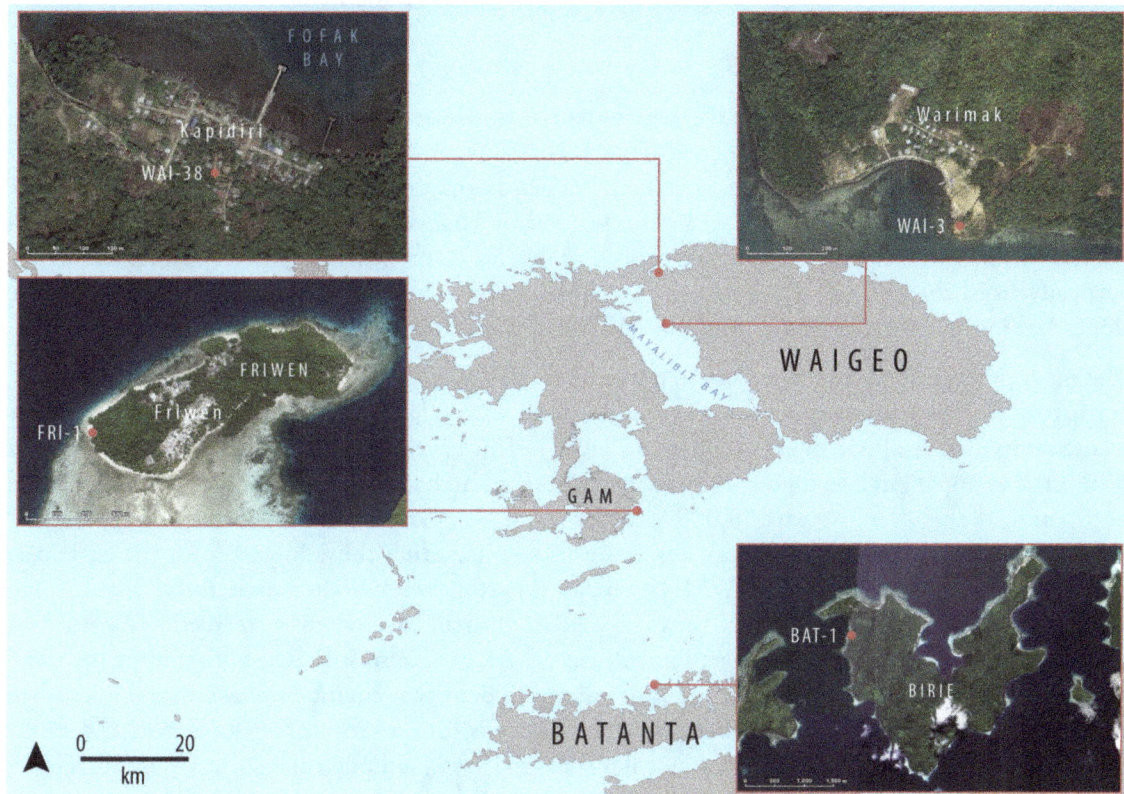

Figure 8.9: Earthenware sites recorded around Waigeo, Gam, and Batanta.
Source: Dylan Gaffney, satellite imagery from DigitalGlobe 2020.

At Kapidiri village, on the north coast of Waigeo, WAI-38 sits on an elevated terrace approximately 10 m asl and 100 m from the present shoreline, comprising a small, mounded area with numerous plain earthenware sherds eroding out of the northern side. Kapidiri overlooks the naturally sheltered Fofak Bay, which protects the area from strong winds that pass along the north coast of Waigeo. This would likely have been selected as a haven for canoes passing through the area, as it was for a number of early European sailing ships. Within Mayalibit Bay at Warimak village, WAI-3 is similarly positioned on the spur of an elevated ridgeline (c. 20 m asl) at the south end of the modern village. A handful of plain earthenware sherds and a possible red chert artefact were recovered from the surface, eroding out of a thin clay layer. A single-rim sherd found at the base of a cliff on Friwen

Island (FRI-1) off the east coast of Gam derives from a globular pot with an everted rim. This probably washed down the cliff from above; however, we were not able to locate the source of the erosion. These three sites are well suited to future investigation, being situated in ideal locations to investigate the Mid- to Late Holocene occupation when the eustatic sea level was several metres higher than today.

Lastly, one ceramic site, BAT-1, was recorded at Kris Iba beach on the north-west coast of Birie Island, just north of Batanta. This beach is now the area of a homestay and the beach flats have been recently modified and flattened to allow for bush hut construction. The slope behind the beach was possibly an old gardening area and loose brown soil is eroding downslope. Earthenware ceramics were found scattered along the beach in the homestay area, possibly eroding from the hill behind, or having been turned over in recent landscaping activities. The ceramics include plain globular pots, sago oven fragments, and carved sherds similar to those found at Yenbekaki fort on Batanta (Galis and Kamma 1958) and on the Bird's Head Peninsula at Makbon (Solheim 1998a).

Caves and rock-shelters

Cave and rock-shelter sites provide the best potential to preserve archaeological deposits dating to the Late Pleistocene and Early Holocene (Figure 8.10). Around Mayalibit Bay, 15 cave and shelter sites were recorded primarily in the limestone Waigeo Formation, although WAI-11 occurs in the Mayalibit Formation (Charlton et al. 1991), formed by large volcanic boulders. The limestone of Mayalibit Bay is several hundred metres thick in some areas, producing steep cliff faces, which rise vertically from the ground. These areas, now close to the coast, would have been located on the slopes leading towards the former Mayalibit Valley or Mayalibit Lake during the Pleistocene.

The most prospective cave site recorded, named Mololo (WAI-1) at the entrance to Mayalibit Bay, consists of an open and well-lit outer chamber, along with a large and dark inner chamber, home to a colony of several bat species (Figure 8.11A–B). This cave was excavated in late 2018 as part of the Raja Ampat Archaeological Project, producing an archaeological sequence spanning several occupation events over the past 50,000 years or more (see Gaffney 2021; Gaffney et al. 2024b). Other sites are suitable for small-scale test excavations, including those inland from the east coast of Mayalibit Bay, such as Kakit (WAI-4) a large limestone rock-shelter used today for sleeping while hunting in the interior, and Nikanyak (WAI-7), a small bat cave up a steep cliff face used for hunting. Inland from Kalitoko village, Banyok Pap (WAI-13) is also still used for bat hunting; it has a small but accessible entrance, opening into a dry and light first chamber with a flat, undisturbed deposit. On Beo Island, a steep limestone cliff face leads into a series of rock-shelters and caves. BEO-2 rock-shelter, in particular, contains flat sheltered areas, although the surface deposit is loose and indicates high-energy movement of sediment downslope during periods of rain.

On the north coast of Waigeo around Kabare there is an outcrop of Waigeo Formation limestone, where 19 caves and shelters were recorded, many of which had marine shell midden on the surface indicating their use in the recent past. The largest of these caves, Manwen Bokor (WAI-42), was excavated in early 2019 (see Gaffney and Tanudirjo 2024). At the western tip of Waigeo, one cave was recorded in the Aljui Bay area, on the north coast of the Selpele Peninsula. Monboto (WAI-32) is now completely filled with water with no archaeological potential for excavation; it would have been a large, sheltered space in the Pleistocene. A series of rock-shelters and caves (WAI-26–WAI-28) were also recorded on the south-eastern side of Waisai Bay, up a steep karst slope. WAI-28, in particular, includes dry and flat overhangs with substantial shell midden on the surface, along with a large cave, which would have once formed an excellent shelter but is now covered with fallen boulders.

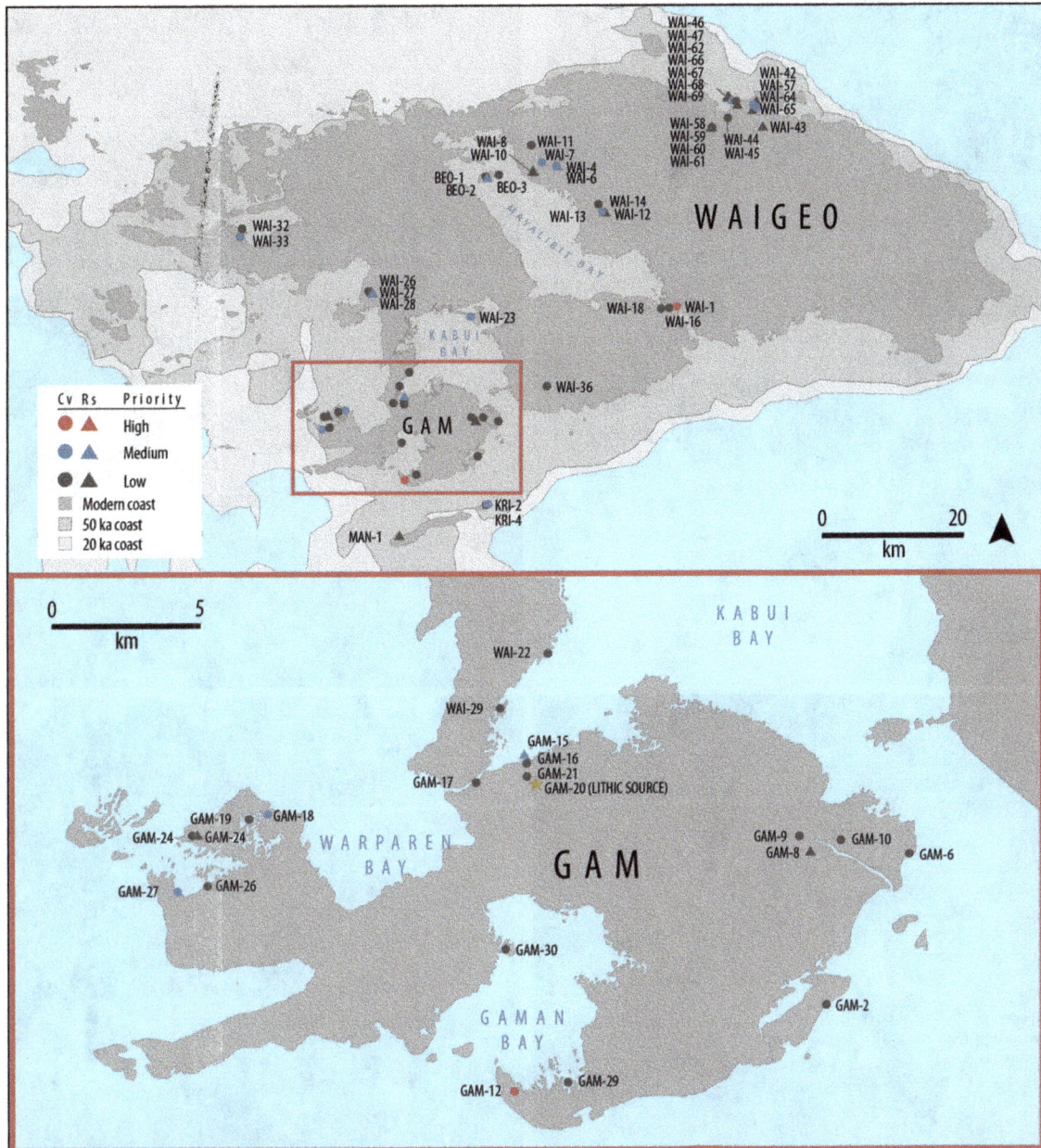

Figure 8.10: Distribution of cave and rock-shelter sites recorded around Waigeo and Gam, coded by their priority for archaeological excavation.

Source: Dylan Gaffney.

Figure 8.11: Cave sites recorded during survey.

Notes: (A) WAI-1 (Mololo) entrance; (B) WAI-1 (Mololo) dark inner chamber; (C) GAM-12 (Kapisawar) outer chamber; (D) WAI-33 (Aput lo) showing eroding lenses of charcoal and shell (sampled for radiocarbon dating).

Source: Dylan Gaffney.

The entirety of Gam Island is also situated on Waigeo Formation limestone, but the rock is different to that around Waigeo, primarily composed of uplifted coral, usually forming small caves and crevices with razor-sharp coralline edges. Most of these are of low potential for large-scale occupation. However, Kapisawar Cave (GAM-12) lies c. 14 m above modern sea level and contains two chambers and a small entrance (1.5 m wide, 4 m high; Figure 8.11c). Excavations at this site were undertaken in early 2019 (Gaffney 2021). GAM-15, GAM-18, and GAM-27 represent cave and shelter sites with surface shell midden or possible stone artefacts, and so warrant test excavations, but may be disturbed due to their surface topography and proximity to the sea.

Conclusion

This chapter has presented a reconnaissance survey from the northern Raja Ampat Islands. The results demonstrate that the northern Raja Ampats contain abundant archaeological sites and this allows some broad statements about earlier periods of settlement to be made. Caves and rock-shelters are common in the Waigeo Formation limestone and some have good prospects for providing evidence of Late Pleistocene and Holocene frequentation. Until about 8000 years ago, many of the recorded sites would have been deep in the lowland rainforested interior of Waigeo and Gam. Open sites containing earthenware ceramics are rare, but some are well placed for investigating the Late Holocene dispersal of Austronesian languages around eastern Wallacea and West New Guinea, immediately prior to Lapita occupation in the Bismarck Archipelago. Red-yellow pigment rock art was likely produced around the area at a similar time. More recently, white pigment rock art, secondary burial shelters, and shell middens provide evidence for a coastally focused settlement pattern as many groups were pulled towards globalising material culture networks connecting Wallacea, China, Europe, and New Guinea.

This study has taken the first steps towards redressing major gaps in our knowledge about human movements from Wallacea, across the Lydekker Line, into the rainforested islands of northern Raja Ampat. It is in this region that we can uniquely examine human behavioural responses to small island rainforests as they crossed into the Australasian faunal zone as well as the livelihoods that people created for themselves as they reshaped these ecologies over the longue durée. The sites recorded in the northern Raja Ampat Islands study area lay the foundation for exploring these topics through ongoing systematic excavation and survey.

Acknowledgements

Supriyanto Hadi, Harry Octavianus Sofian, and Shinatria Adhityatama provided valuable guidance on the parameters of the Raja Ampat Archaeological Project. Arif Prabowo at The Nature Conservancy (TNC) in Sorong provided useful regional advice and contacts. We thank the people of Warimak, Waifoi, Go, Kabilol, Kalitoko, Lopintol, Warsambin, Saporkren, Kapidiri, Kabare, Asukweri, Kalisadi, Andei, Bonsayor, Beo, Waisai, Wawiyai, Raswan, Yenbeser, Friwen, Kri, Yenbuba, Kurkapa, Yenbekwan, Yenwaupnor, Sawinggrai, Kapisawar, Kabui, Selpele, Saleo, Manyaifun, and Mutus for their hospitality and assistance during the work. On Waigeo, Wolter Gaman, Alfred Gaman, and Pak Solomon were invaluable guides and friends around Mayalibit Bay and the north coast. Martin Makusi, Tobias Mambrasar, Yahya Mambrasar, and Obed Makusi were excellent guides around Gam, western Waigeo, and the offshore islands. Max Ammer at Kri very kindly provided accommodation and a loan of a speedboat to Mansuar. In Waisai, Iin and family provided helpful use of their 4 × 4 and accommodation. Laura Arnold at Edinburgh provided local contacts and linguistic information. Raymond Corbey at Leiden provided local contacts and ethnographic insights. Jasmijn Ouwendijk assisted with Dutch translations. Cyprian Broodbank, Graeme Barker, and Glenn Summerhayes provided valuable guidance and feedback on the research design. The survey was supported by a National Geographic Early Career Grant, a University of Cambridge Humanities and Social Sciences Fieldwork Grant, and Gates Cambridge.

References

Adhityatama, S. and A.S. Yarista 2019. Potensi arkeologi landskap bawah air Indonesia. *Kalpataru* 28(1):55–71. doi.org/10.24832/kpt.v28i1.505.

Anon. 1957. Interessante vondst op het eiland Waigeo. *Nieuw-Guinea Studien* 1:59.

Arifin, K. and P. Delanghe 2004. *Rock art in West Papua*. UNESCO, Paris.

Arnold, L. 2017. Grammar of Ambel: An Austronesian language of Raja Ampat, West New Guinea. Unpublished PhD thesis. Department of Linguistics, University of Edinburgh, Edinburgh.

Arnold, L. 2018. The past inside the present: A glimpse into the deep history of Waigeo. *The blog of the Foundation for Endangered Languages*. www.ogmios.org/blog/the-past-inside-the-present-a-glimpse-into-the-deep-history-of-waigeo-by-laura-arnold/ (accessed 1 February 2020).

Balai Arkeologi Jayapura 2012. Penelitian Pusat Peradaban Pantai Barat Papua: Asal – Usul, Perkembangan dan Interaksi Percampuran Penutur Austronesia dan Austromelanesid. Field report. Unpublished. Balai Arkeologi Jayapura, Jayapura.

Ballard, C. 1992. Painted rock art sites in western Melanesia: Locational evidence for an 'Austronesian' tradition. In J. McDonald and I.P. Haskovec (eds), *State of the art: Regional art studies in Australia and Melanesia*, pp. 94–105. Occasional AURA Publication Number 6. Australian Rock Art Research Association, Melbourne.

Barton, H. and T.P. Denham 2011. Prehistoric vegeculture and social life in Island Southeast Asia and Melanesia. In G. Barker and M. Janowaski (eds), *Why cultivate? Anthropological and archaeological approaches to foraging–farming transitions in Southeast Asia*, pp. 17–25. McDonald Institute of Archaeology Research, Cambridge.

Bedford, S. and M. Spriggs 2007. Birds on the rim: A unique Lapita carinated vessel in its wider context. *Archaeology in Oceania* 42(1):12–21. doi.org/10.1002/j.1834-4453.2007.tb00010.x.

Bird, E.C.F. and O.S. Ongkosongo 1980. *Environmental changes on the coasts of Indonesia*. United Nations University Press, Tokyo.

Birdsell, J.B. 1977. The recalibration of a paradigm for the first peopling of Greater Australia. In J. Allen, J. Golson, and R. Jones (eds), *Sunda and Sahul: Prehistoric studies in Southeast Asia, Melanesia, and Australia*, pp. 113–167. Academic Press, London.

Blust, R. 1984–85. The Austronesian homeland: A linguistic perspective. *Asian Perspectives* 26(1):45–67.

Charlton, T.R., R. Hall, and E. Partoyo 1991. The geology and tectonic evolution of Waigeo Island, NE Indonesia. *Journal of Southeast Asian Earth Sciences* 6(3–4):289–297. doi.org/10.1016/0743-9547(91)90074-8.

Chazine, J.-M. 2009. The location of new paintings in the east of the archipelago (Misool) and identification of the generic parameters of their presence. *International Newsletter of Rock Art* 55:12–17.

Chazine, J.-M. 2011. New survey of painted panels of Northwest Papua: A precise identification of their location parameters and some insight into their function. In E. Anati (ed.), *Art and communication in pre-literate societies. XXIV Valcamonica Symposium,* pp. 106–113. Jaca Book, Milan.

Chazine, J.-M. 2014. Island Southeast Asia: Rock art. In C. Smith (ed.), *Encyclopedia of global archaeology,* pp. 4096–4105. Springer, New York. doi.org/10.1007/978-1-4419-0465-2_1908.

Cheesman, E. 1949. *Six legged snakes in New Guinea.* Harrap, London.

Corbey, R., 2017. *Raja Ampat ritual art: Spirit priests and ancestor cults in New Guinea's far west.* C. Zwartenkot Art Books, Leiden.

de Clercq, F.S.A. 1893. *Ethnographische Beschrijving van de West- En Noordkust van Nederlandsch Nieuw-Guinea.* P.W.M. Trap, Leiden.

Dillenia, I., R. Troa, and E. Triarso 2016. In situ preservation of marine archaeological remains based on geodynamic conditions, Raja Ampat, Indonesia. *Conservation and Management of Archaeological Sites* 18(1–3):364–371. doi.org/10.1080/13505033.2016.1182775.

Donnelly, R., D. Neville, and P.J. Mous 2003. *Report on a Rapid Ecological Assessment of the Raja Ampat Islands, Papua, Eastern Indonesia held October 30 – November 22, 2002.* The Nature Conservancy, Sanur.

Fairyo, K. 2010. Jejak migrasi penghuni pulau Misool. *Papua* 2(2):85–92.

Fairyo, K. 2014. Kajian situs Gunung Dezh di Pulau Salawati. *Papua* 6(2):187–193. doi.org/10.24832/papua. v6i2.32.

Gaffney, D. 2021. Human behavioural dynamics in island rainforests: Evidence from the Raja Ampat Islands, West Papua. Unpublished PhD thesis. Department of Archaeology, University of Cambridge, Cambridge.

Gaffney, D. and D. Tanudirjo 2019. Sago oven pottery production in the Raja Ampat Islands of the far western Pacific. *Journal of Pacific Archaeology* 10(2):63–72.

Gaffney, D. and D. Tanudirjo 2024. Late Holocene potting traditions in the far western Pacific: Evidence from the Raja Ampat Islands, 3500–1000 BP. In B. Shaw, A. Ford, and D. Gaffney (eds), *Forty years in the South Seas: Studies in the archaeology of Papua New Guinea and the Western Pacific.* ANU Press, Canberra.

Gaffney, D., D. Tanudirjo, L. Arnold, W. Gaman, T. Russell, E.N.I. Djami, and A.R. Macap 2024a. Five centuries of settlement dynamics and mobility in the northern Raja Ampat Islands of West Papua. *Journal of Pacific History.* doi.org/10.1080/00223344.2024.2328015.

Gaffney, D., D. Tanudirjo, E.N.I. Djami, Z. Mas'ud, A.R. Macap, T. Russell, M. Dailom, Y. Ray, T. Higham, F. Bradshaw, F. Petchey, S.A. Florin, P. Roberts, M. Lucas, M. Tromp, K. Greig, H. Xhauflair, A. Montenegro, R. Hall, C. Boulanger, R. Ono, A. Oertle, D. Scholz, M. Spitzer, K. Szabo, I. Bertelli, E. Ribechini, and S. Heberle 2024b. Human dispersal and plant processing in the Pacific 55,000–50,000 years ago. *Antiquity* 98(400):885–904. doi.org/10.15184/aqy.2024.83.

Galis, K.W. 1957. De grotten van Jaand. *Nieuw Guinea Studien* 1:118–129.

Galis, K.W. 1960. Het fort te Jémbekaki, addendum. *Nieuw-Guinea Studien* 4:52–54.

Galis, K.W. 1964. Recent oudheidkundig nieuws uit westelijk Nieuw-Guinea. *Bijdragen tot de Taal-, Land- en Volkenkunde* 2:245–274. doi.org/10.1163/22134379-90002992.

Galis, K.W. and F.C. Kamma 1958. Het fort te Jémbakaki. *Nieuw-Guinea Studien* 2:206–222.

Kealy, S., J. Louys, and S. O'Connor 2018. Least-cost pathway models indicate northern human dispersal from Sunda to Sahul. *Journal of Human Evolution* 125:59–70. doi.org/10.1016/j.jhevol.2018.10.003.

Latinis, K. and K. Stark 2003. Roasted dirt: Assessing earthenware assemblages from sites in Central Maluku, Indonesia. In J. Miksic (ed.), *Earthenware in Southeast Asia*, pp. 103–135. Singapore University Press, Singapore.

Mahmud, M.I. 2013. Akulturasi budaya lokal dan konsepsi Islam di situs Kali Raja, Raja Ampat. *Papua* 5(1): 59–75.

Maryone, R. 2010. Migrasi Orang Biak ke Pulau Batanta Kampung Arefi Kabupaten Raja Ampat. *Papua* 2(2):75–84.

McKenna, S.A., G.R. Allen, and S. Suryadi 2002. *A Marine Rapid Assessment of the Raja Ampat Islands, Papua Province, Indonesia*. Conservation International, Washington, D.C.

Nasruddin 2015. Membaca dan menafsirkan temuan gambar prasejarah di Pulau Misool Raja Ampat, Papua Barat. *Sangkhakala* 18(2):150–168.

Natsir, S.M. and M. Subkhan 2016. Benthic foraminifera in South Waigeo waters, Raja Ampat, West Papua. *Bulletin of the Marine Geology* 27(1):1–6.

Nitihaminoto, G. 1980. Sebuah catatan tambahan tentang prehistori Irian Jaya. *Penerbitan Balai Arkeologi* 1(1):3–23. doi.org/10.30883/jba.v1i1.273.

Norman, K., J. Inglis, C. Clarkson, J.T. Faith, J. Shulmeister, and D. Harris 2018. An early colonisation pathway into northwest Australia 70–60,000 years ago. *Quaternary Science Reviews* 180:229–239. doi.org/10.1016/j.quascirev.2017.11.023.

Ono, R., A.A. Oktaviana, M. Ririmasse, M. Takenaka, C. Katagiri, and M. Yoneda 2018. Early Metal Age interactions in Island Southeast Asia and Oceania: jar burials from Aru Manara, northern Moluccas. *Antiquity* 92(364):1023–1039. doi.org/10.15184/aqy.2018.113.

Pasveer, J.M. 2004. *The Djief hunters: 26,000 years of rainforest exploitation on the Bird's Head of Papua, Indonesia*. A.A. Balkema, Leiden. doi.org/10.1201/b17006.

Pawley, A. and M. Ross 1993. Austronesian historical linguistics and culture history. *Annual Review of Anthropology* 22:425–459. doi.org/10.1146/annurev.anthro.22.1.425.

Reimer, P.J., W.E.N. Austin, E. Bard, A. Bayliss, P.G. Blackwell, C. Bronk Ramsey, M. Butzin, H. Cheng, R.L. Edwards, M. Friedrich, P.M. Grootes, T.P. Guilderson, I. Hajdas, T.J. Heaton, A.G. Hogg, K.A. Hughen, B. Kromer, S.W. Manning, R. Muscheler, J.G. Palmer, C. Pearson, J. Van Der Plicht, R.W. Reimer, D.A. Richards, E.M. Scott, J.R. Southon, C.S.M. Turney, L. Wacker, F. Adolphi, U. Büntgen, M. Capano, S.M. Fahrni, A. Fogtmann-Schulz, R. Friedrich, P. Köhler, S. Kudsk, F. Miyake, J. Olsen, F. Reinig, M. Sakamoto, A. Sookdeo, and S. Talamo 2020. The IntCal20 Northern Hemisphere radiocarbon age calibration curve (0–55 cal kBP). *Radiocarbon* 62(4):725–757. doi.org/10.1017/RDC.2020.41.

Remijsen, A.C.L. 2001. *Word-prosodic systems of Raja Ampat languages*. LOT, Utrecht.

Röder, J. 1939. Rock-pictures and prehistoric times in Dutch New Guinea. *Man* 39:175–178. doi.org/10.2307/2792120.

Röder, J. 1959. *Felsbilder und Vorgeschichte des MacCluer-Golfes West-Neuguinea*. L.C. Wittich, Darmstadt.

Sand, C., H. Valladas, H. Cachier, N. Tisnérat-Laborde, M. Arnold, J. Bolé, and A. Ouetcho 2006. Oceanic rock art: First direct dating of prehistoric stencils and paintings from New Caledonia (Southern Melanesia). *Antiquity* 80(309):523–529. doi.org/10.1017/S0003598X0009400X.

Shaw, B. 2014. The archaeology of Rossel Island, Massim, Papua New Guinea: Towards a prehistory of the Louisiade Archipelago. Unpublished PhD thesis. Department of Archaeology, The Australian National University, Canberra.

Solheim, W.G. 1978. Archaeological survey, Irian Jaya. *Pacific Arts Newsletter* 6:1–5.

Solheim, W.G. 1979. Irian Jaya origins. *Australian Natural History* 19(10):24–27.

Solheim, W.G. 1998a. Preliminary report on Makbon archaeology, the Bird's Head, Irian Jaya. In G.-J. Bartstra (ed.), *Bird's Head approaches: Irian Jaya studies—A programme for interdisciplinary research*, pp. 29–40. A.A. Balkema, Rotterdam.

Solheim, W.G. 1998b. The University of Hawai'i archaeological programme in Eastern Indonesia. In M.J. Klokke and T. Bruijn (eds), *Southeast Asian archaeology, 1996: Proceedings of the 6th International Conference of the European Association of Southeast Asian Archaeologists, Leiden 2–6 September 1996*, pp. 61–73. Centre for South-East Asian Studies, Hull.

Solheim, W.G. 2006. Soejono's efforts in starting archaeological research in Papua (Irian Jaya). In T. Simanjuntak, M. Hisyam, B. Prsetyo, and T.S. Nastiti (eds), *Archaeology: Indonesian perspective, RP Soejono's Festschrift*, pp. 15–28. Indonesian Institute of Sciences, Jakarta.

Souza, C.R. and W. Solheim 1976. A new area of rock paintings in Irian Jaya, Indonesian New Guinea. In K.K. Chakravarty (ed.), *Rock-art of India: Paintings and engravings*, pp. 182–195. Arnold-Heinemann, New Delhi.

Specht, J., T. Denham, J. Goff, and J.E. Terrell 2014. Deconstructing the Lapita Cultural Complex in the Bismarck Archipelago. *Journal of Archaeological Research* 22(2):89–140. doi.org/10.1007/s10814-013-9070-4.

Spriggs, M., F. Valentin, S. Bedford, R. Pinhasi, P. Skoglund, D. Reich, and M. Lipson 2019. Revisiting ancient DNA insights into the human history of the Pacific Islands. *Archaeology in Oceania* 54(1):53–56. doi.org/10.1002/arco.5180.

Sukandar, S.C. 2012a. Tinggalan kolonial di pulau Doom. *Papua* 4(1):29–41.

Sukandar, S.C. 2012b. Aspek-aspek revitalisasi kawasan situs Kali Raja kabupatuen Raja Ampat. *Papua* 4(2): 67–78.

Sukandar, S.C. 2013. Bangunan pertahanan (Louvrak) Jepang di Pulau Doom. *Papua* 5(1):101–10.

Sulistyarto, P.H. 2014. *Penelitian Arkeologi Maritim Hunian Prasejarah Dan Lukisan Cadas Di Kepulauan Misool, Kabupaten Raja Ampat, Provinsi Papua Barat*. Pusat Arkeologi Nasional, Jakarta.

Summerhayes, G.R. 2007. Island Melanesian pasts: A view from archaeology. In J.S. Friedlaender (ed.), *Population genetics, linguistics, and culture history in the Southwest Pacific*, pp. 10–35. Oxford University Press, Oxford. doi.org/10.1093/acprof:oso/9780195300307.003.0002.

Supriatna, S., A.S. Hakim, and T. Apandi 1995. *Geologic map of Waigeo, 1:250,000*. Geological Research and Development Centre, Bandung.

Swadling, P. 1996. *Plumes from Paradise: Trade cycles in outer Southeast Asia and their impact on New Guinea and nearby islands until 1920*. Papua New Guinea National Museum, Boroko.

Valentin, F. and C. Sand 2008. Prehistoric burials from New Caledonia (southern Melanesia): A review. *Journal of Austronesian Studies* 2(1):1–30.

Veth, P., M. Spriggs, S. O'Connor, and A.D. Saleh 2005. Wangil midden: A late prehistoric site, with remarks on ethnographic pottery making. In S. O'Connor, M. Spriggs, and P. Veth (eds), *The archaeology of the Aru Islands, Eastern Indonesia*, pp. 95–124. ANU E Press, Canberra.

Wallace, A.R. 1869. *The Malay archipelago*. Macmillan and Co, London.

Webb, C.O. 2005. *A report to The Nature Conservancy: Vegetation of the Raja Ampat Island, Papua, Indonesia.* The Nature Conservancy, Sorong.

Widjojo, M. 2009. *The revolt of Prince Nuku: Cross-cultural alliance-making in Maluku, c.1780–1810.* Brill, Leiden. doi.org/10.1163/ej.9789004172012.i-280.

Wright, D., T. Denham, D. Shine, and M. Donohue 2013. An archaeological review of western New Guinea. *Journal of World Prehistory* 26(1):25–73. doi.org/10.1007/s10963-013-9063-8.

Appendix: Sites recorded in the Raja Ampat Archaeological Project database (2018–2019)

Island	Code	Local name (language)	Administrative district	Site type
Waigeo	WAI-1	Mololo (Ambel)	Distrik Teluk Mayalibit	Cave
	WAI-2	Mete kabum (Ambel)	Distrik Teluk Mayalibit	Burial cave/shelter
	WAI-3	Warimak (Ambel)	Distrik Tiplol Mayalibit	Artefact scatter
	WAI-4	Kakit (Ambel)	Distrik Tiplol Mayalibit	Rock-shelter
	WAI-5	Kanawbin hey (Ambel)	Distrik Tiplol Mayalibit	Oral history
	WAI-6	Abiap (Ambel)	Distrik Tiplol Mayalibit	Cave
	WAI-7	Nikanyak (Ambel)	Distrik Tiplol Mayalibit	Cave
	WAI-8	Mungawam (Ambel)	Distrik Tiplol Mayalibit	Rock-shelter
	WAI-9	Abiap Tamolo (Ambel)	Distrik Tiplol Mayalibit	Oral history
	WAI-10	Abiap Minki (Ambel)	Distrik Tiplol Mayalibit	Rock-shelter
	WAI-11	Abiap Mungwai (Ambel)	Distrik Tiplol Mayalibit	Cave
	WAI-12	–	Distrik Teluk Mayalibit	Rock-shelter
	WAI-13	Banyok pap (Ambel)	Distrik Teluk Mayalibit	Cave
	WAI-14	Wekakaba papup (Ambel)	Distrik Teluk Mayalibit	Cave
	WAI-15	Tanjung Aris (Indonesia)	Distrik Teluk Mayalibit	Burial cave/shelter
	WAI-16	Alip pelli (Ambel)	Distrik Teluk Mayalibit	Cave
	WAI-17	Manfaya (Ambel)	Distrik Teluk Mayalibit	Burial cave/shelter
	WAI-18	Muliale (Ambel)	Distrik Teluk Mayalibit	Cave
	WAI-19	Batu alat kelami (Indo.)	Distrik Teluk Mayalibit	Oral history
	WAI-20	–	Distrik Tiplol Mayalibit	Quarry
	WAI-21	Goa Lestar (Indonesia)	Distrik Waigeo Selatan	Burial cave/shelter
	WAI-22	Goa Raja Ampat (Indo.)	Distrik Waigeo Selatan	Cave
	WAI-23	Kalep kafni (Ma'ya)	Distrik Waigeo Selatan	Cave
	WAI-24	Kalep minet (Ma'ya)	Distrik Waigeo Selatan	Burial cave/shelter
	WAI-25	Fayef (Ma'ya)	Distrik Waigeo Selatan	Burial cave/shelter
	WAI-26	Waramkan (Biak?)	Distrik Waigeo Barat	Cave
	WAI-27	Waramkan (Biak?)	Distrik Waigeo Barat	Rock-shelter
	WAI-28	Waramkan (Biak?)	Distrik Waigeo Barat	Rock-shelter
	WAI-29	Nerbaken (Biak)	Distrik Waigeo Selatan	Cave
	WAI-30	Kali Raja (Indonesia)	Distrik Waigeo Selatan	Oral history

Island	Code	Local name (language)	Administrative district	Site type
Waigeo	WAI-31	Lentagin (Ma'ya)	Distrik Waigeo Barat	Rock art
	WAI-32	Monboto (Ma'ya)	Distrik Waigeo Barat	Cave
	WAI-33	Aput lo (Ma'ya)	Distrik Waigeo Barat	Combination
	WAI-34	Aput lo (Ma'ya)	Distrik Waigeo Barat	Burial cave/shelter
	WAI-35	Yefriui (Ma'ya)	Distrik Waigeo Barat	Burial cave/shelter
	WAI-36	Abiap Muden (Ambel)	Distrik Waigeo Selatan	Cave
	WAI-37	Ili Pap (Ambel)	Distrik Tiplol Mayalibit	Burial cave/shelter
	WAI-38	Gunung Kapidiri (Indo.)	Distrik Supnin	Artefact scatter
	WAI-39	Derepas Fwar (Ambel)	Distrik Waigeo Utara	Burial cave/shelter
	WAI-40	Sawai bokor (Ambel)	Distrik Waigeo Utara	Burial cave/shelter
	WAI-41	Abai ombon (Ambel)	Distrik Waigeo Utara	Burial cave/shelter
	WAI-42	Manwen bokor (Ambel)	Distrik Waigeo Utara	Combination
	WAI-43	Frai Kai (Ambel)	Distrik Waigeo Utara	Rock-shelter
	WAI-44	Abiap Mankwai (Ambel)	Distrik Waigeo Utara	Cave
	WAI-45	Abiap Mankwai Minki (A.)	Distrik Waigeo Utara	Cave
	WAI-46	Abiap Anday (Ambel)	Distrik Waigeo Utara	Cave
	WAI-47	Anday (Ambel)	Distrik Waigeo Utara	Rock-shelter
	WAI-48	Memyai (Biak?)	Distrik Waigeo Timur	Midden
	WAI-49	Nyanakrur (Ambel)	Distrik Teluk Mayalibit	Midden
	WAI-50	Yé ha (Ambel)	Distrik Teluk Mayalibit	Rock art
	WAI-51	Yé lal (Ambel)	Distrik Teluk Mayalibit	Rock art
	WAI-52	Yé mampiar (Ambel)	Distrik Teluk Mayalibit	Rock art
	WAI-53	Mon Ake (Ma'ya)	Distrik Waigeo Selatan	Rock art
	WAI-54	Mlelen Popo (Ma'ya)	Distrik Waigeo Selatan	Rock art
	WAI-55	Fafag (Ma'ya)	Distrik Waigeo Selatan	Rock art
	WAI-56	Abai Ombon (Biak)	Distrik Waigeo Utara	Artefact scatter
	WAI-57	Abai Ombon (Biak)	Distrik Waigeo Utara	Rock-shelter
	WAI-58	Abiap Puyauw (Ambel)	Distrik Waigeo Utara	Rock-shelter
	WAI-59	Abiap Puyauw (Ambel)	Distrik Waigeo Utara	Cave
	WAI-60	Abiap Puyauw (Ambel)	Distrik Waigeo Utara	Rock-shelter
	WAI-61	Abiap Kasiau (Ambel)	Distrik Waigeo Utara	Cave
	WAI-62	Masin bekrai (Biak)	Distrik Waigeo Utara	Rock-shelter
	WAI-63	–	Distrik Waigeo Utara	Rock art
	WAI-64	Manum Bakor (Biak)	Distrik Waigeo Utara	Cave
	WAI-65	–	Distrik Waigeo Utara	Rock-shelter
	WAI-66	Gunung Anday (Indo.)	Distrik Waigeo Utara	Rock-shelter
	WAI-67	Gunung Anday (Indo.)	Distrik Waigeo Utara	Rock-shelter
	WAI-68	Gunung Anday (Indo.)	Distrik Waigeo Utara	Rock-shelter
	WAI-69	Gunung Anday (Indo.)	Distrik Waigeo Utara	Rock-shelter
	WAI-70	Sembama (Ma'ya)	Distrik Waigeo Selatan	Burial cave/shelter

Island	Code	Local name (language)	Administrative district	Site type
Beo	BEO-1	Arilap (?) (Ma'ya)	Distrik Tiplol Mayalibit	Cave
	BEO-2	–	Distrik Tiplol Mayalibit	Rock-shelter
	BEO-3	Goa Sriti (Indonesia)	Distrik Tiplol Mayalibit	Cave
	BEO-4	Alig Galana (Ma'ya)	Distrik Tiplol Mayalibit	Burial cave/shelter
Gam	GAM-1	Yenbainus (Biak)	Distrik Waigeo Selatan	Burial cave/shelter
	GAM-2	Wartoren (Biak)	Distrik Waigeo Selatan	Cave
	GAM-3	Nyandebas (Biak)	Distrik Waigeo Selatan	Artefact scatter
	GAM-4	Ayau Karamram (Biak)	Distrik Waigeo Selatan	Cave
	GAM-5	Batu Lima (Indonesia)	Distrik Waigeo Selatan	WWII
	GAM-6	–	Distrik Waigeo Selatan	Cave
	GAM-7	–	Distrik Waigeo Selatan	Artefact scatter
	GAM-8	–	Distrik Waigeo Selatan	Rock-shelter
	GAM-9	Warwiki (Biak)	Distrik Waigeo Selatan	Cave
	GAM-10	Jangkrik (Biak)	Distrik Waigeo Selatan	Cave
	GAM-11	–	Distrik Meos Mansar	Burial cave/shelter
	GAM-12	–	Distrik Meos Mansar	Cave
	GAM-13	Kampung Tua (Indonesia)	Distrik Meos Mansar	Midden
	GAM-14	Tapor Inkasowi (Biak)	Distrik Waigeo Selatan	Oral history
	GAM-15	Warikaf (Biak)	Distrik Waigeo Selatan	Rock-shelter
	GAM-16	Goa Warikaf (Indonesia)	Distrik Waigeo Selatan	Cave
	GAM-17	Goa Paniki (Indonesia)	Distrik Waigeo Selatan	Cave
	GAM-18	Ayau Tubmodor (Biak)	Distrik Meos Mansar	Cave
	GAM-19	Ayau Tubmodor (Biak)	Distrik Meos Mansar	Cave
	GAM-20	Warasun (Biak)	Distrik Waigeo Selatan	Quarry
	GAM-21	Warikaf (Biak)	Distrik Waigeo Selatan	Cave
	GAM-22	Ombrap (Biak)	Distrik Meos Mansar	Find spot
	GAM-23	Tasiran (Biak)	Distrik Waigeo Selatan	Burial cave/shelter
	GAM-24	Dore Imbarbau (Biak)	Distrik Meos Mansar	Cave
	GAM-25	Dore Imbarbau (Biak)	Distrik Meos Mansar	Rock-shelter
	GAM-26	Dore Bao (Biak)	Distrik Meos Mansar	Cave
	GAM-27	Dore Bao (Biak)	Distrik Meos Mansar	Cave
	GAM-28	Topenmor (Biak)	Distrik Meos Mansar	Burial cave/shelter
	GAM-29	Ayau Mangwai (Biak)	Distrik Meos Mansar	Cave
	GAM-30	Meostray (Biak)	Distrik Meos Mansar	Cave
	GAM-31	Tapor Pandera (Biak)	Distrik Meos Mansar	Burial cave/shelter
Pef	PEF-1	Yenmakraek (Biak)	Distrik Meos Mansar	Burial cave/shelter
	PEF-2	Yenmaret (Biak)	Distrik Meos Mansar	Midden
	PEF-3	Brambaem (Biak)	Distrik Meos Mansar	Rock art
	PEF-4	Yenikwaen (Biak)	Distrik Meos Mansar	Midden

Island	Code	Local name (language)	Administrative district	Site type
Kri	KRI-1	Papua Diving helipad	Distrik Meos Mansar	Artefact scatter
	KRI-2	Papua Diving resort	Distrik Meos Mansar	Cave
	KRI-3	Papua Diving resort	Distrik Meos Mansar	Artefact scatter
	KRI-4	Papua Diving resort	Distrik Meos Mansar	Cave
Mansuar	MAN-1	Waiafel (Biak)	Distrik Meos Mansar	Rock-shelter
Yefkabu	MEO-1	Yefkabu (Biak)	Distrik Waigeo Barat	Midden
Paniki	PAN-1	Mututru (Biak)	Distrik Waigeo Barat	Oral history
Friwen	FRI-1	–	Distrik Waigeo Selatan	Find spot
Manyaifun	MAY-1	Taukapaya (Biak)	Distrik Waigeo Barat Kepulauan	Burial
	MAY-2	Kodor (Biak)	Distrik Waigeo Barat Kepulauan	Burial
	MAY-3	Yenmangkwaen (Biak)	Distrik Waigeo Barat Kepulauan	Oral history
	MAY-4	Yentamako (Biak)	Distrik Waigeo Barat Kepulauan	Artefact scatter
Batanta	BAT-1	Kris Iba (Biak)	Distrik Batanta Utara	Artefact scatter
	BAT-2	Sapor Ides (Biak)	Distrik Batanta Utara	Quarry
	BAT-3	Yu (Biak)	Distrik Batanta Utara	Quarry
	BAT-4	Yu (Biak)	Distrik Batanta Utara	Midden

Source: Raja Ampat Archaeological Project database.

9

Last Glacial Maximum to Late Holocene occupation on the Bomberai Peninsula: Preliminary results of archaeological research at Andarewa Cave, Fakfak Regency, West Papua Province

Bau Mene, Adi Dian Setiawan, and Dylan Gaffney

Abstract

This chapter reports preliminary excavation and artefactual evidence from Andarewa Cave, located in Fakfak Regency, on the Bomberai Peninsula. This area would have been a key thoroughfare between the Bird's Head of New Guinea and the rest of Sahul during the Pleistocene period. From 2018 to 2021, two 2 × 2 m units were excavated on the north side of the cave mouth. Excavated material at Andarewa included pottery, shells, stone tools, bone points and jewellery, red and yellow ochre, charcoal, and other ecofacts. Radiocarbon dating of charcoal indicates the site was occupied as early as the Last Glacial Maximum (LGM), 26,327–25,900 years ago. This makes Andarewa contemporary with Toé Cave on the Bird's Head of New Guinea, and the second oldest site known from the West New Guinea mainland region. The lithic analysis demonstrates that flaking of local sedimentary stone was expedient, focused on the production of small flakes and scrapers, some of which were retouched, although an igneous stone was imported from further afield. Bone artefact analysis demonstrates that bone points, characteristic of West New Guinea and north-eastern Wallacea, are represented at the site, and pig, dog, crocodile, and fish bone jewellery all date to the Late Holocene. Archaeological excavations are ongoing at Andarewa and sterile deposits are yet to be reached: future research will shed light on the antiquity of human occupation around this part of New Guinea.

Abstrak

Pada bagian ini, pemaparan tentang penelitian yang dilakukan di situs Gua Andarewa diuraikan beserta dengan bukti artefak dari situs tersebut. Gua Andarewa adalah salah satu gua prasejarah yang secara administrasi terletak di kabupaten Fakfak, di semenanjung Bomberai. Berdasarkan keletakannya, daerah ini merupakan jalur utama yang menghubungkan Kepala Burung dan seluruh dataran pada masa pleistosen. Kegiatan ekskavasi di situs ini telah dilakukan sejak tahun 2018–2021 dimana dua unit kotak ekskavasi berhasil dibuka dengan ukuran 2 × 2 m di sisi utara mulut gua. Adapun bukti arkeologi yang didapatkan pada situs Andarewa adalah gerabah, kerang, alat batu, tulang dan perhiasan, okker merah dan kuning, arang dan ekofak. Adapun hasil pertanggalan radiokarbon pada temuan arang di situs ini mengindikasikan tentang adanya kependudukan manusia sejak masa Glasial Maksimum Terakhir (LGM) yaitu 26.327–25.900 tahun yang lalu. Hal ini menjadikan situs Andarewa sebagai situs tertua kedua yang diketahui dari wilayah Papua. Adapun hasil yang didapatkan pada analisis alat litik menunjukkan adanya pemangkasan yang sempurna dilakukan pada batu jenis sedimen lokal. Alat batu seperti alat serpih, scrapers merupakan alat litik yang paling umum ditemukan dimana beberapa diantaranya telah mengalami pengerjaan ulang. Dari hasil analisis terhadap artefak tulang seperti tulang babi, buaya, dan ikan yang ditemukan pada situs ini, maka diketahui bahwa alat tersebut memperlihatkan ciri-ciri alat tulang yang selama ini sangat umum ditemukan di wilayah Papua dan juga ditemukan di wilayah Wallacea bagian timur. Ciri-ciri alat tulang tersebut diperkirakan berkembang pada masa akhir Holosen. Penggalian arkeologi pada situs ini masih belum selesai dilakukan sehingga diharapkan pada masa yang akan datang semakin banyak fakta baru yang ditemukan pada situs ini.

Introduction

Human occupation of West New Guinea during the Last Glacial Maximum (LGM) has previously been reported at Toé Cave, with initial frequentation at that site established by radiocarbon dating of cassowary eggshells to be about 30,700–29,900 years ago (Pasveer 2004). At that time, people were hunters and gatherers, frequenting the lowland rainforests of Ayamaru Plateau in the interior of the Bird's Head Peninsula. Further afield, in the Aru Islands that were once connected to New Guinea as part of the Pleistocene continent of Sahul, occupation at Liang Lemdubu occurred approximately 28,000–25,000 years ago (O'Connor et al. 2005). However, little is known about the distribution and nature of human occupation at this time, and no recent systematic archaeology has been undertaken on the Bomberai Peninsula, which formed a thoroughfare between the Bird's Head and the rest of Sahul. The first archaeological study around Bomberai was conducted by J.J. Röder in 1937. Röder (1939, 1959) excavated Dudumunir Cave on the island of Arguni, where he recovered flakes and pottery sherds; unfortunately, the collections were lost and have not therefore been reported in detail or radiometrically dated. This chapter is the first description of Pleistocene occupation around the Bomberai Peninsula of West New Guinea, presenting the preliminary results of excavations, radiocarbon dating, and lithic and bone artefact analyses at Andarewa Cave, about 25 km south-east of Dudumunir Cave (Figure 9.1). The aim of the analyses is to determine the timing of occupation, the type of stone tool and bone technology, and the nature of human societies that occupied the site.

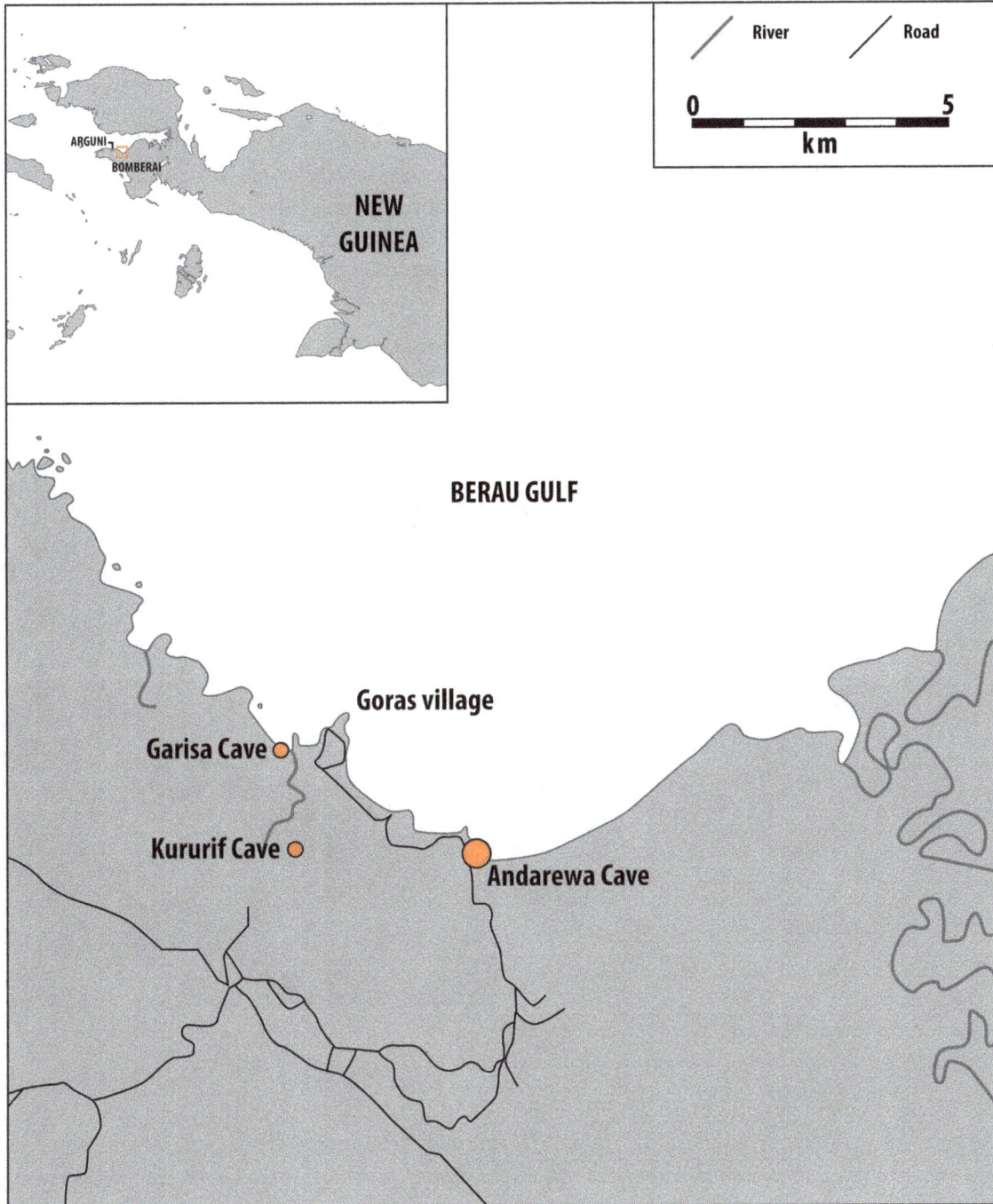

Figure 9.1: The location of Andarewa Cave, Fakfak Regency.

Source: Dylan Gaffney.

The Berau Gulf prehistoric archaeology project

Archaeological research relating to the prehistoric human occupation of the Berau Gulf was undertaken by <u>Balai Arkeologi Papua</u>[1] (Papua Centre of Archaeology) in 2018 in several areas of Fakfak Regency, including around the districts of Arguni, Goras, and Mbahamdandara. Renewed excavation was carried out in Dudumunir Cave, which successfully unearthed pig mandibles and other bones, fish bones, crab claws, marsupial bones, and human remains. Artefacts encountered during excavation included bone tools, stone flakes, possible stone points, ochre, stone axes, shell rings, shell jewellery, and pottery fragments. The Dudumunir material will be the focus of future analysis and reporting.

Figure 9.2: Andarewa Cave.

Notes: a) entrance route to cave; b) cave exterior; c) excavation; d) deep excavation with shoring.

Source: Photographs by Bau Mene.

Andarewa Cave (S 02° 48'11.7" E 132° 43'32.8") is located in the Goras Village area, Mbahamdandara District, Fakfak Regency, at 35 m above sea level (Figure 9.2). This site can be reached by using a boat to access the cave entrance, about 20 minutes from Goras. The cave looks over Berau Gulf to the north, mangrove forests in the east, and karst hills in the south, while to the west is Ugar Village. This cave was first identified in 2009 by a research team from the Papua Centre of Archaeology during a survey around the Goras area. In 2018, 1 × 1 m test pits were excavated in the cave, followed by more substantial excavation in 2019 on the north side of the cave mouth. Two different 2 × 2 m excavations were opened, ADR/FF/KT1 and ADR/FF/KT2, following 10 cm spits and using dry sieves. In 2021, the excavations were continued, and further survey was carried out in the area surrounding Andarewa Cave, where rock paintings were found on the cave walls in the form of

---

1   Bahasa Indonesia words are underlined at first mention.

black pigment suns, abstract designs, geometrics, lizards, and fish. These paintings are located on the north side of the cave site, facing the beach. The images are arranged from the left to the right with a distance of 2–3 m between one another, while the average height from the ground to the images varies between 1 and 3 m from the ground. Excavated material at Andarewa included pottery, shells, stone tools, bone jewellery, ochre (red and yellow), charcoal, and other ecofacts.

Excavation results 2018–2021

The two 2 × 2 m excavations (ADR/FF/KT1 and ADR/FF/KT2) opened during the 2018–2021 seasons at Andarewa will be described briefly (Figure 9.3). The chronology of the Andarewa site will also be reported, having been established with radiocarbon dating of charcoal samples from multiple sediment contexts. All radiocarbon dates were pretreated with standard acid/base/acid at Beta Analytic. The broad archaeological findings will then be described before examining the lithic and bone artefact material.

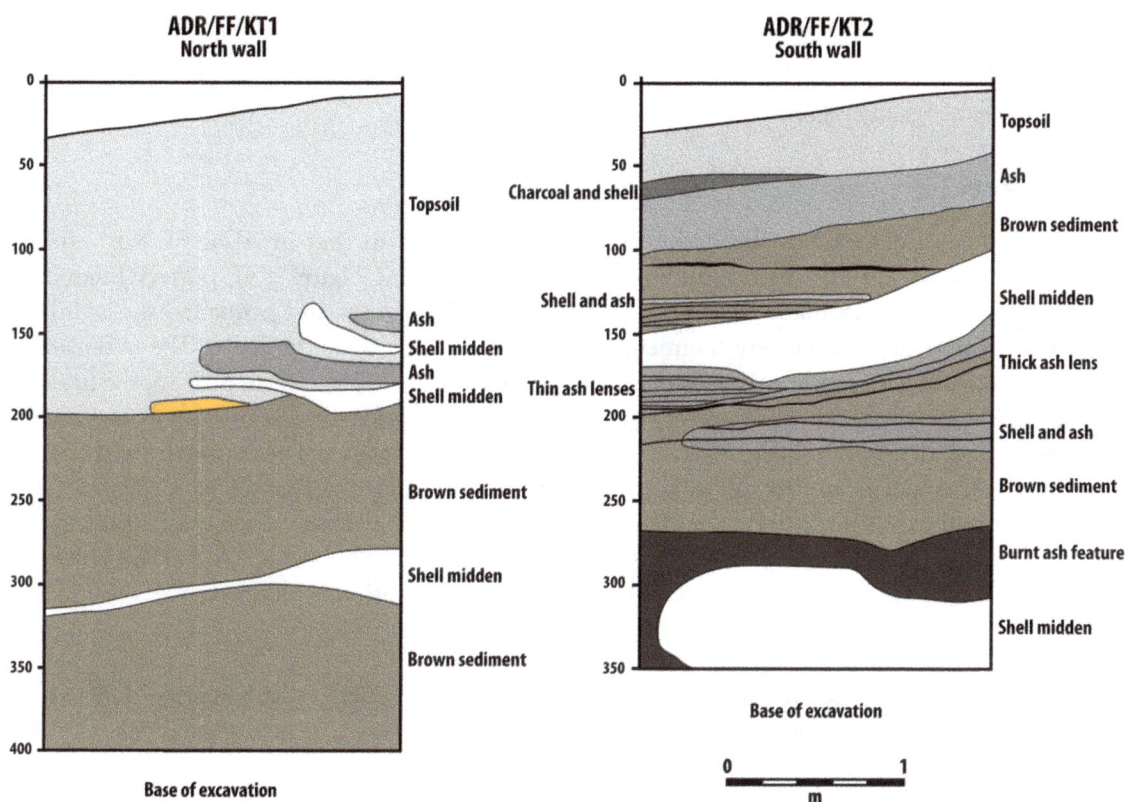

Figure 9.3: Stratigraphy of ADR/FF/KT1 and ADR/FF/KT2, incomplete and not yet at bedrock.
Source: Image by Dylan Gaffney, adapted from illustration by Bau Mene.

ADR/FF/KT1

The upper spits, Spits 1 to 24 (10 cm to 250 cm from datum level; see Figure 9.3), were dominated by midden shells, associated with pottery fragments (both decorated and plain), stone axe fragments, bone tools, bone, and bone jewellery in the form of rings and necklace pendants. Some shell and bone fragments were burned, indicating fires were used at the site. Charcoal was also found mixed with the burned shell. Radiocarbon dating indicates that the pottery postdates 5286–4970 years old

(Table 9.1). By Spit 29, the deposits were dominated by shells, alongside lithics, bones, and charcoal. By Spit 36, which dates to 9124–8784 years ago, stone flakes were more commonly encountered than above, alongside shell, mammal and fish bones, and charcoal. By Spit 39, which similarly dates to the Early Holocene, shells were less common but flakes were still abundant, alongside ochre, animal bones, and charcoal. By Spit 45, dating to the Terminal Pleistocene 12,024–11,818 years ago, archaeological material was less dense, including animal bones, lithics, and charcoal. In Spit 53, dating to the LGM at 26,302–25,926 years ago, animal bone was dense, alongside abundant ochre (red and yellow), scattered charcoal, and less frequent lithics. Bedrock was not reached and further excavation is required to reach culturally sterile layers.

Table 9.1: Radiocarbon results from Andarewa ADR/FF/KT1.

Lab code	Spit	Depth cm	Material	Radiocarbon age	d13C	Calibrated date (95.4%)
Beta-562599	29	290–300	Charcoal	4460±30 BP	−29.1	5286–4970 cal. BP
Beta-562600	36	360–370	Charcoal	8080±30 BP	−31.8	9124–8784 cal. BP
Beta-543746	39	390–400	Charcoal	8890±30 BP	−26.5	10,175–9900 cal. BP
Beta-543747	45	450–460	Charcoal	10,240±30 BP	−24.5	12,024–11,818 cal. BP
Beta-609186	53	530–540	Charcoal	21,870±80 BP	−24.5	26,302–25,926 cal. BP

Source: Authors' summary, calibrated using OxCal 4.1 with IntCal20.

ADR/FF/KT2

The archaeological material in this excavation was very similar to that in ADR/FF/KT1. In the upper spits, Spits 1–23 (10 cm to 230 cm from datum level; see Figure 9.3), pottery fragments, bone fragments, jewellery made from fish bones in the form of rings and pendants, shells, lithics, and charcoal were present. Pottery fragments in Spit 23 were particularly dense. The radiocarbon dating results indicate items in this spit are 1520–1358 years old (Table 9.2). In Spit 26, the findings included shells and charcoal, while pottery fragments were few in number. At this depth, three stone axes were found. In Spit 29, shells, shell artefacts, bone tools, and charcoal were present, and pottery was infrequent. Dates from this spit indicate pottery in the region is at least 2096–1182 years old. By Spit 39, pottery was not present, but shells, bone points, shell artefacts, crabs, mammal and fish bones, and stone artefacts were present. This spit dates to the Early Holocene, 7922–7700 years old. As at ADR/FF/KT1, bedrock was not reached, and further excavation is planned.

Table 9.2: Radiocarbon results from Andarewa ADR/FF/KT2.

Lab code	Spit	Depth cm	Material	Radiocarbon age	d13C	Calibrated date (95.4%)
Beta-562596	23	230–240	Charcoal	1580±30 BP	−25.0	1530–1394 cal. BP
Beta-562597	26	260–270	Charcoal	2030±30 BP	−24.7	2096–1182 cal. BP
Beta-562598	29	290–300	Charcoal	2030±30 BP	−26.6	2096–1182 cal. BP
Beta-609185	39	390–400	Charcoal	6970±30 BP	−27.1	7922–7700 cal. BP

Source: Authors' summary, calibrated using OxCal 4.1 with IntCal20.

Lithic technology at Andarewa Cave

Overall, 3697 stone artefacts were recovered from the two excavations. In both excavations, lithics were discovered in almost every spit. Several types of artefacts were present in the assemblages: flakes, cores, and stone axes. About 14 per cent of the lithics have so far been analysed (n = 530), having been randomly selected to provide a summary and qualitative description of the technology; the sample described here includes 516 flakes, seven cores, and seven axes.

Flakes

In the flake assemblage, 382 are complete, 77 are broken, and 57 have been designated as scrapers. Most flakes were made from a fine-grained sedimentary stone (reddish-brown, light brown, brown, grey, light grey, black, and white), although a small number were created from limestone and igneous rock. Most are regular in shape (Figure 9.4): the smallest intact flake measures 18.74 mm long, 30.47 mm wide, and 5.34 mm thick, and weighs 2.53 grams; the largest flake is 76.97 mm long, 23.85 mm wide, and 10.01 mm thick, and weighs 12.62 grams.

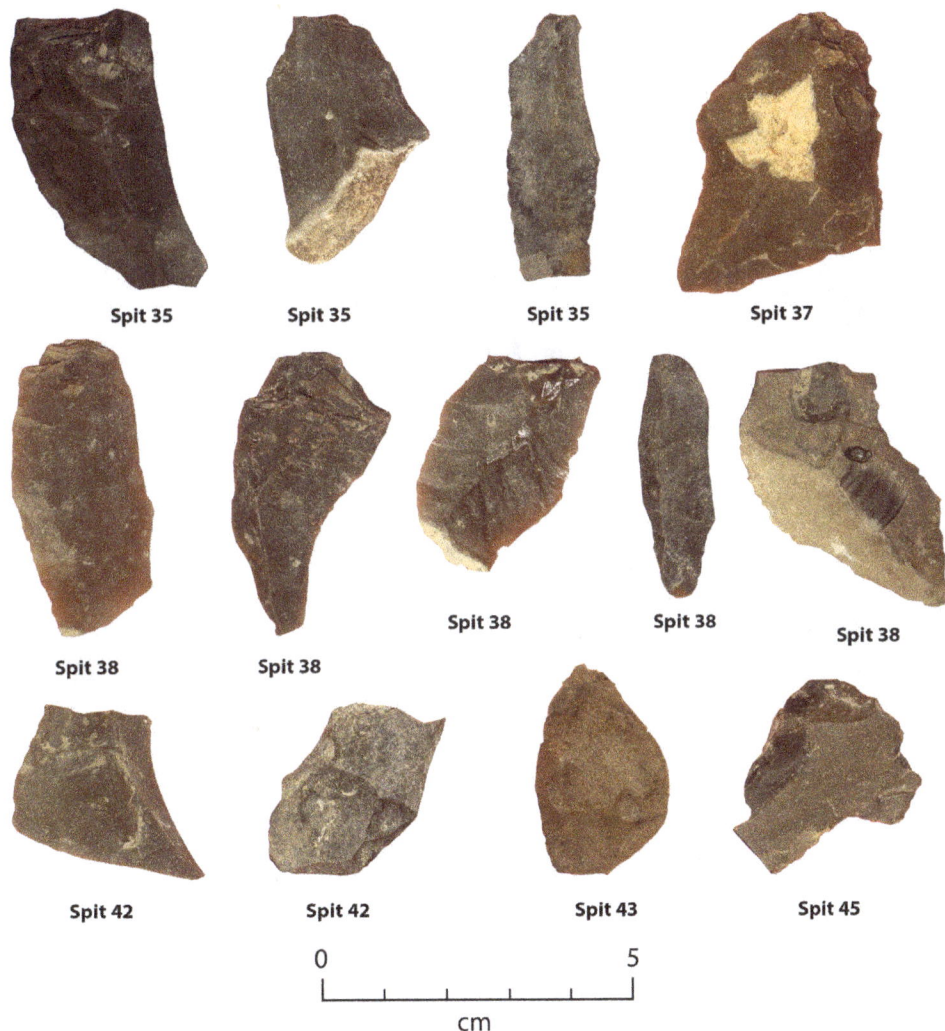

Figure 9.4: Flakes excavated from ADR/FF/KT1, Andarewa Cave.

Source: Image by Bau Mene and Dylan Gaffney.

Generally, flakes were made from cores using free-hand direct percussion. Flakes frequently have scars on the dorsal surface, indicating former flake removal in a unidirectional manner, or occasional platform preparation for future flaking. A small number of flakes retain scars initiated from various directions indicating multidirectional flake removals and core rotation. Of the complete flakes, 46 per cent have plain platforms, 17 per cent have faceted platforms, 34 per cent have crushed platforms, and 3 per cent are cortical. Many flakes are crushed at the proximal end indicating repeated attempts at flake removal from small cores. Discolouration and potlidding on some artefacts indicate they were exposed to fire, whether as part of the flaking process, or after discard and mixing with hearths at the site.

Blades were uncommon and not systematically produced. Eighteen flakes were retouched or shaped on the lateral and distal edges of the flake. Twenty-eight expanding flakes with retouched and utilised edges were designated scrapers and all of these are made of sedimentary stone. Scraper size from Andarewa varied: the smallest is 25.25 mm long, 29.55 mm wide, 5.02 mm thick, and 2.41 grams; the largest is 85.58 mm long, 38.45 mm wide, 9.41 mm thick, and 26.86 grams.

Cores

All seven cores were made on sedimentary stone and recovered from ADR/FF/KT2, Spit 26, at a depth of 270 cm (Figure 9.5). The average size is 58.14 mm by 39.43 mm and 48.38 grams in weight. The cores have both single and multiple striking platforms, with many cores having been rotated. The platform size is variable, with an average width of 25.88 mm.

Figure 9.5: Flake cores from Andarewa Cave.
Note: Top: shows core with unidirectional flake detachments from platform. Bottom: shows core with bifacial shaping around margin producing scars on dorsal surface.
Source: Image by Bau Mene.

Axes

Seven flaked stone axe preforms were found in Late Holocene contexts at the Andarewa excavations (Figure 9.6; Table 9.3). These include one limestone artefact recorded in ADR/FF/KT1, Spit 13. This limestone is a 3 on the Mohs Hardness Scale. Fine-grained sedimentary pieces were recorded in ADR/FF/KT2, from Spits 8, 26, and 27. This rock has a hardness of 5. These artefacts were associated with marine shells and earthenware pottery fragments. Those recorded in ADR/FF/KT2, Spit 26, were also associated with animal bones and bone jewellery. In general, stone axe production was carried out with longitudinal flaking, with primary flakes detached lengthways, followed by unifacial and bifacial shaping.

Figure 9.6: Axe preform from Andarewa Cave, ADR/FF/KT1, Spit 13.

Source: Image by Bau Mene and Dylan Gaffney.

Table 9.3: Stone axes recorded at Andarewa Cave.

XU	Spit	Length (mm)	Width (mm)	Thickness (mm)	Raw material	Associated archaeological material
ADR/FF/KT1	13	110	38	25	Limestone	Pottery, shell
ADR/FF/KT2	8	95	31	26	Sedimentary	Pottery, shell, bone jewellery
ADR/FF/KT2	26	60	30	14	Sedimentary	Pottery, shell, bone jewellery
ADR/FF/KT2	26	78	23	20	Sedimentary	Pottery, shell, bone jewellery
ADR/FF/KT2	26	70	33	16	Sedimentary	Pottery, shell, bone jewellery
ADR/FF/KT2	27	75	43	30	Sedimentary	Pottery, shell, bones
ADR/FF/KT2	27	94	31	21	Sedimentary	Pottery, shell, bones

Source: Authors' summary.

Bone artefacts at Andarewa Cave

Microscopic analysis was performed on bone artefacts to examine marks left by forming, working, and finishing techniques. This also allowed for a provisional taxonomic analysis of the kinds of animals used as raw materials. Each artefact was classified based on its shape and interpretations made about intended functions.

Pig tusks

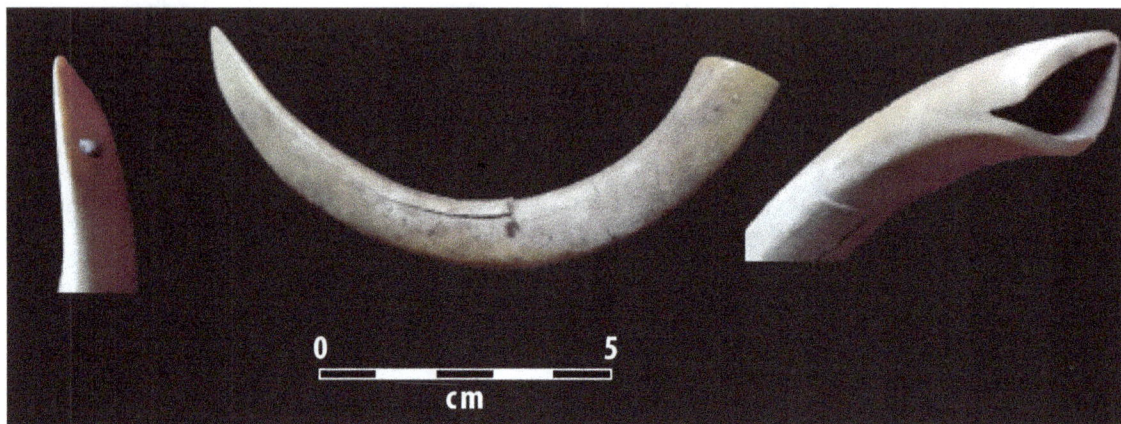

Figure 9.7: Pig tusk artefact from Andarewa, ADR/FF/KT2, Spit 7.
Source: Image by Adi Dian Setiawan.

The *Sus* sp. tusk in Figure 9.7 measures 10.5 cm by 1 cm and was recovered from ADR/FF/KT2, Spit 7, dating to sometime after 1530–1394 years ago. One hole is present at the distal end of the tusk, made by perforation. It has also undergone grinding and sharpening at the distal and proximal ends to make it smoother, sharper, and shinier. Pig tusks are commonly used as septum ornaments around the interior of New Guinea, often denoting prestige or personal preferences, sometimes used in ceremonies or other events. However, the perforation at one end of the tusk may indicate it was tied to other objects as a pendant, necklace, or string bag decoration.

Dog teeth

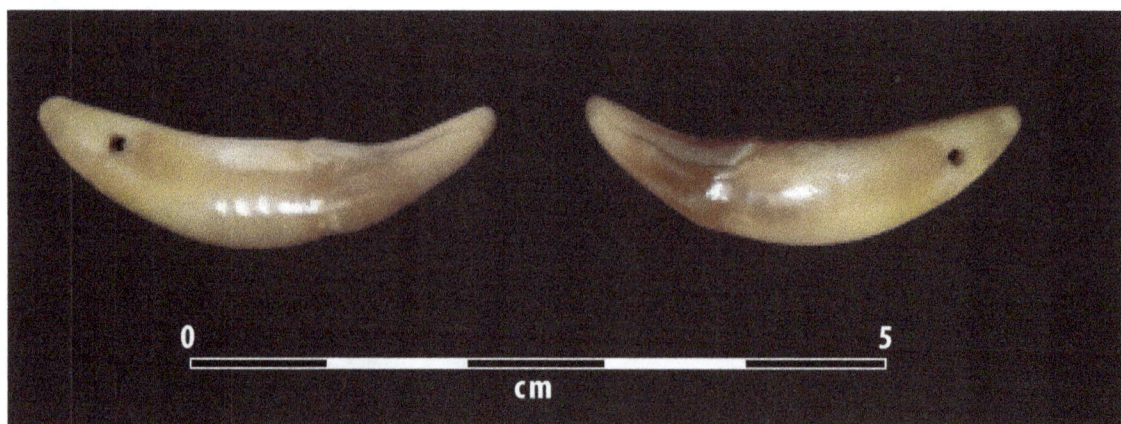

Figure 9.8: Dog canine tooth artefact from Andarewa, ADR/FF/KT2, Spit 6.
Source: Image by Adi Dian Setiawan.

The *Canis* sp. canine tooth in Figure 9.8 measures 3.3 cm long and 1 cm wide, and was excavated in ADR/FF/KT2, Spit 6, again dating to after 1530–1394 years ago. The tooth was also perforated in the proximal end and appears to belong to a dog-tooth necklace, common in some parts of coastal New Guinea.

Crocodile teeth

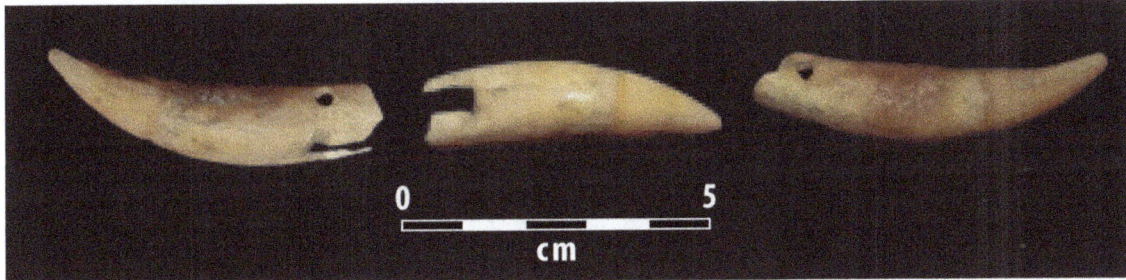

Figure 9.9: Crocodile tooth artefact from Andarewa, surface of ADR/FF/KT1.
Source: Image by Adi Dian Setiawan.

The crocodile (Crocodylidae) tooth in Figure 9.9 was found on the surface of ADR/FF/KT1, and measures 5 cm long and 1.3 cm wide, again with a perforation at the proximal end.

Fish bone

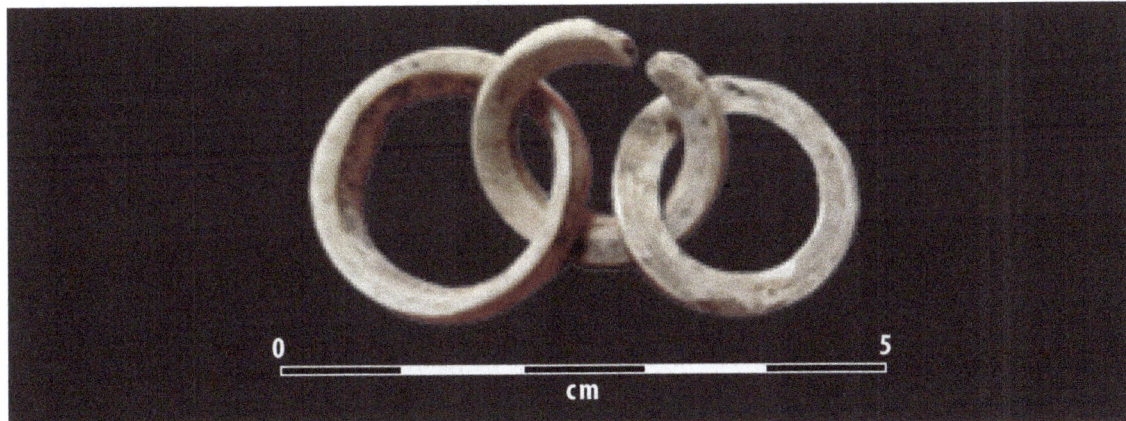

Figure 9.10: Three links in a fish vertebra chain necklace from Andarewa, ADR/FF/KT/1, Spit 8.
Source: Image by Adi Dian Setiawan.

Figure 9.10 shows three links in a necklace excavated as a series of objects from ADR/FF/KT1, Spit 8, and dating sometime after 5286–4970 years ago (Mene 2019, 26). The three chain links are 4.5 cm long, and each link is 2.2 cm wide and 2 mm thick. The object is made from large fish vertebrae that were widened manually to enlarge the foramina, and later polished.

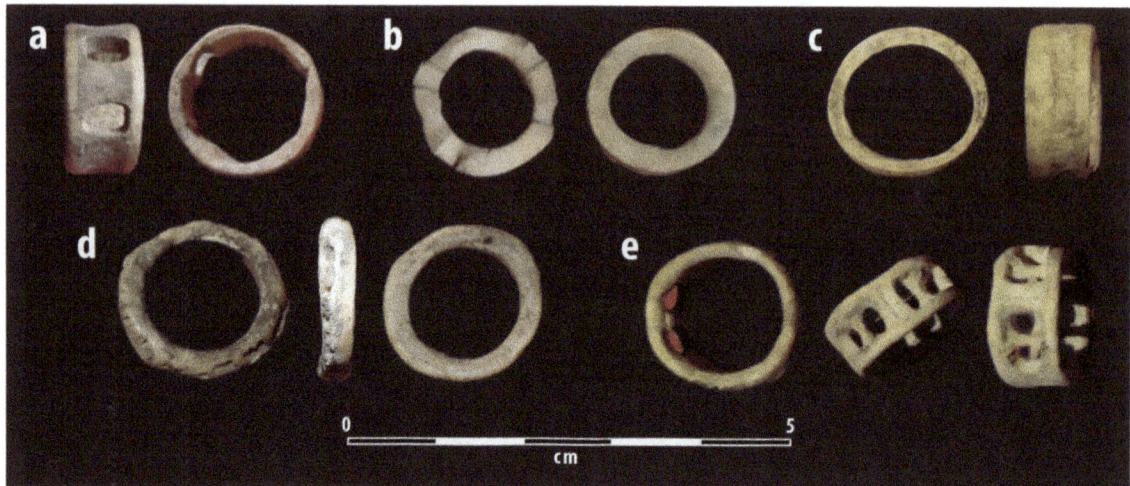

Figure 9.11: Fish vertebrae artefacts from Andarewa.

Source: Image by Adi Dian Setiawan.

The artefact in Figure 9.11a is made of a shark or ray (Chondrichthyes) vertebra. It was perforated in two parts to form the decoration, with scraping and polish on the outside. Abrasion marks on the inner surface are irregular indicating partial polishing or usewear. The fish vertebra jewellery in Figure 9.11b was found in ADR/FF/KT2, Spit 23, dating by association to 1530–1394 years old. It is 1.4 cm long, and 0.2 cm wide. It has four concave-shaped perforations on one side and it has subsequently been polished to flatten both the interior and exterior sides. The fish vertebra artefact in Figure 9.11c was excavated in ADR/FF/KT2, Spit 11, and has a length of 1.4 cm and a width of 0.5 cm. The object has a decorative V shape on the outside, formed by perforation followed by grinding and polishing techniques. The object may have been used as a ring or as part of a necklace or pendant.

The fish vertebra in Figure 9.11d was found in ADR/FF/KT2, Spit 13, and is 2.2 cm in diameter and 2 mm thick. It has been finished with a polishing technique on one side only. Based on the shape and size it is possible that this ring was part of a necklace in the same design as the three-link chain necklace (see Figure 9.10). The object in Figure 9.11e was recovered from the same spit in ADR/FF/KT2. This fish vertebra has a diameter of 2.2 cm with a thickness of 0.6 cm and several holes perforating the surface, likely made for decoration. The vertebra was subsequently polished.

Discussion

The 2018–2021 excavations at Andarewa provide a provisional sequence of cave use from the LGM through to the Late Holocene. From the small sample of lithics analysed in this chapter, the technology (the type of raw material and flaking process) was generally consistent across the spits. However, more intensive lithic analyses and statistical tests of the whole assemblage are required to verify this assertion.

The raw material of the stone tools from the Andarewa site is dominated by a fine-grained sedimentary, and the cortex material seems to derive from cobbles. The site sits on the edge of two geological zones: the Ogar Limestone to the west with reef limestone, minor chalk, and thin shale, and a Quaternary alluvium to the east. About 2 km to the south-west are outcrops of the Onin Limestone, which contains fine-grained limestone and minor argillaceous limestones and marlstones. The Waya River about 10 km to the south of the site flows through the Onin Limestone zone and, upon reconnaissance survey, was found to contain secondary deposits of flakable marlstone and limestone. It is likely that the sedimentary stone at Andarewa is the same marlstone, which can appear similar to chert but is derived from carbonate rather than siliceous mineral grains. Given the wide range of sedimentary stone colours recorded in the lithic assemblage, it is possible that other varieties of marl/chert were also imported into the site from a wider area. Igneous rock and limestone were also used as raw materials; the former would need to be imported from much further afield such as on the Bird's Neck or northern Bird's Head, while the latter may be local to Andarewa Cave or the underlying geological zone.

The high flake-to-core ratio (74:1), the general lack of cortex on the platforms and dorsal surface, and the high frequency of facetted and crushed platforms suggest the stone was in middle–late stages of reduction. Most cortical pieces had been removed offsite before cores were transported to the site for reduction. The cores at the site were nearing the point of exhaustion, which further supports the idea that raw material was obtained outside of the immediate area.

The association of stone axes with pottery, alongside Late Holocene radiocarbon dates ranging sometime between 2000 and 1000 years old, indicate that axe manufacture marked a recent shift in technology. This is despite the presence of stone axes from Wallacea and New Guinea in Early Holocene contexts (Gaffney et al. 2015; Shipton et al. 2020). Whether the change at Andarewa marks the influx of new communities bringing distinct stone tool-making practices (such as ancestors of what are now North Bomberai Austronesian speakers, or the West Bomberai non-Austronesian speakers; see Usher and Schapper 2021) or a shift in site use towards more intensive forest clearance and maintenance, needs to be resolved with further research. The preferential use of sedimentary stone (probably marlstone but possibly imported chert) rather than limestone for axes likely relates to the greater hardness and durability of the raw material.

Personal bone and tooth ornaments have been used around New Guinea since the Late Pleistocene (Langley et al. 2019; Leavesly 2007); however, no evidence for such objects have yet been recorded in Pleistocene layers at Andarewa. The bone artefacts at Andarewa all date to the Late Holocene, probably 1530–1394 years ago and thereafter. They are diverse in raw materials, form, and production techniques. The pig tusk may have been used as a male nose ornament perforating the septum, as practised ethnographically, or as part of a multicomponent object or body decoration. The dog and crocodile teeth seem to have been used as pendants, given the placement of the perforation at the proximal end, perhaps arranged along with many others to form a necklace like those known ethnographically from around the New Guinea coast. Some of the fish vertebrae appear to have formed a long necklace with multiple rings. It is also possible these vertebrae were hung individually as pendants, or used as finger rings, although no ethnographic examples for the latter are known from New Guinea (Tolla 2016, 9).

Conclusion

So far, the research conducted at Andarewa Cave on the Bomberai Peninsula between 2018 and 2021 has produced thousands of artefacts consisting of flaked stone tools, ochre, earthenware pottery fragments, bone tools and jewellery, and shell tools, alongside ecofacts like animal bone fragments, plant remains, shell midden, and charcoal, attesting to the hunting and gathering activities of the cave occupants. Much of this material is under current analysis and awaits publication. Provisional radiocarbon dating presented here demonstrates that human occupation recurred from the LGM, about 26,000 years ago, through to the Late Holocene, about 1400 years ago. Further excavation is planned to extend these sequences to bedrock and determine the initial timing of frequentation.

Based on the analysis of stone artefacts from Andarewa, tools are dominated by (probably local) fine-grained sedimentary flakes and cores, scrapers, and stone axes made by unifacial and bifacial hard-hammer percussion. Unlike some other sites in eastern Indonesia and in New Guinea, stone axes at Andarewa are associated only with pottery-bearing contexts dating to the last two millennia before the present. Bone jewellery was also produced in the Late Holocene, made from animals deriving from the marine and estuarine environments that characterise the site today, as well as from domestic animals.

Acknowledgments

We thank the communities of Goras and the Andarewa area for their support during fieldwork.

References

Gaffney, D., A. Ford, and G.R. Summerhayes 2015. Crossing the Pleistocene–Holocene transition in the New Guinea Highlands: Evidence from the lithic assemblage of Kiowa rockshelter. *Journal of Anthropological Archaeology* 39:223–246. doi.org/10.1016/j.jaa.2015.04.006.

Langley, M.C., C. Clarkson, and S. Ulm 2019. Symbolic expression in Pleistocene Sahul, Sunda, and Wallacea. *Quaternary Science Reviews* 221:105883. doi.org/10.1016/j.quascirev.2019.105883.

Leavesley, M.G. 2007. A shark-tooth ornament from Pleistocene Sahul. *Antiquity* 81(312):308–315. doi.org/10.1017/S0003598X00095193.

Mene, B. 2019. Okupasi Hunian Prasejarah di Teluk Berau Kabupaten Fakfak Papua Barat. Research report to Balai Arkeologi Papua. Unpublished. Kementerian Pendidikan dan Kebudayaan, Badan Penelitian dan Pengembangan, Pusat Penelitian Arkeologi Nasional, Jayapura.

O'Connor, S., K. Aplin, K. Szabó, J. Pasveer, P. Veth, and M. Spriggs 2005. Liang Lemdubu: A Pleistocene cave site in the Aru Islands. In S. O'Connor, M. Spriggs, and P. Veth (eds), *The archaeology of the Aru Islands, Eastern Indonesia*, pp. 171–204. ANU E Press, Canberra.

Pasveer, J.M. 2004. *The Djief hunters: 26,000 years of rainforest exploitation on the Bird's Head of Papua, Indonesia*. A.A. Balkema, Leiden. doi.org/10.1201/b17006.

Röder, J. 1939. Rock-pictures and prehistoric times in Dutch New Guinea. *Man* 39:175–178. doi.org/10.2307/2792120.

Röder, J. 1959. *Felsbilder und Vorgeschichte des MacCluer-Golfes West-Neuguinea*. L.C. Wittich, Darmstadt.

Shipton, C., S. O'Connor, S. Kealy, Mahirta, I.N. Syarqiyah, N. Alamsyah, and M. Ririmasse 2020. Early ground axe technology in Wallacea: The first excavations on Obi Island. *PLoS ONE* 15(8):e0236719. doi.org/10.1371/journal.pone.0236719.

Tolla, M. 2016. Kebhinekaan Budaya Papua: Perspektiv Arkeologi Prasejarah. Research report to Balai Arkeologi Papua. Unpublished. Kementerian Pendidikan dan Kebudayaan, Badan Penelitian dan Pengembangan, Pusat Penelitian Arkeologi Nasional, Jayapura.

Usher, T. and A. Schapper 2021. The Greater West Bomberai language family. *Oceanic Linguistics* 61(1): 469–527. doi.org/10.1353/ol.2022.0004.

10

Late Holocene human diets in the lowlands of West New Guinea: The isotopic evidence

Marlin Tolla, Patrick Roberts, Mary Lucas, Dominik Bonatz, and Cosimo Posth

Abstract

Over the course of the last 10 years, the Balai Arkeologi Papua (Papua Centre of Archaeology) archaeological program has undertaken fieldwork and multidisciplinary analyses to explore human behaviour during the Holocene in West New Guinea—a somewhat neglected part of the world. Despite the fact that humans made it to the tropical forests of New Guinea 45,000 years ago, and the island is also home to some of the earliest experiments in tropical cultivation, relatively little is known about how human diet and subsistence changed from the Pleistocene and into the Holocene in different parts of the island. Stable isotope analysis has emerged as a powerful tool for exploring dietary reliance on different aspects of tropical landscapes in the Pacific region, from dense tropical forests to coastal foodstuffs. Here, we present interim radiocarbon results from five archaeological sites in the lowland region of Papua and Papua Barat Province, Indonesia, as well as preliminary stable isotope data from human tooth enamel and bones from these same localities. We discuss the implications of our data for exploring trends in human diets and economies in this part of the tropics and highlight areas for future work.

Abstrak

Dalam kurun waktu 10 tahun terakhir, Balai Arkeologi Papua yang sekarang tergabung dalam Badan Riset dan Inovasi Nasional (BRIN) telah melakukan penelitian arkeologi di beberapa tempat di wilayah Papua. Berbagai pendekatan multidisipliner telah diterapkan untuk mengeksplorasi perilaku manusia selama masa Holosen di wilayah ini. Terlepas dari kenyataan bahwa Homo sapiens telah berhasil mencapai wilayah tropis Papua sejak 45.000 tahun yang lalu, pengetahuan mengenai pola makan serta adaptasi manusia dari masa Pleistosen hingga masa Holosen sangat terbatas diketahui di pulau ini. Analisis Isotope stabil telah berkembang dalam beberapa tahun ini dimana metode ini sangat pesat digunakan terutama untuk mengeksplorasi pola makanan serta tingkah laku manusia dalam suatu lingkungan mulai dari lingkungan laut, air tawar hingga hutan hujan tropis. Dalam bab ini, hasil awal/sementara radiokarbon yang telah didapatkan dari lima situs arkeologi di wilayah dataran rendah Papua beserta dengan hasil analisis isotop stabil berupa kolagen dan enamel apatite terhadap tulang pada lima situs arkeologi diuraikan. Pola diet manusia pada kelima situs tersebut dipaparkan berdasarkan hasil isotop stabil serta menekankan area-area yang kiranya perlu diteliti di masa yang akan datang.

Introduction

Near Oceania has been a critical region for the global recognition that, contrary to popular stereotypes (Bailey et al. 1989), tropical forests were rapidly inhabited by early members of our species (Roberts and Petraglia 2015) and also represent early sites of human experimentation with cultivation (Roberts 2019, 119–147). Human presence in the New Guinea Highlands has been documented as early as 45,000 years ago in the form of waisted axes and charred pandanus nutshells (Summerhayes et al. 2010, 2017). Meanwhile, microbotanical and archaeological evidence from Kuk Swamp in the Highlands provides some of the earliest indications of the human cultivation of tropical crops, including taro, yam, and banana, potentially as early as 9000 years ago (Denham et al. 2003). Despite these findings, however, studies of subsistence adaptation and diet in different parts of New Guinea over the course of the Late Pleistocene and Holocene have been relatively limited, with some local exceptions (e.g. Gaffney et al. 2021; Roberts et al. 2017; Sutton et al. 2009). This is problematic, especially as New Guinea and its inhabitants were to play a major role in shaping how people and economies moved through Near Oceania and out into the Pacific, and in the dispersal of various things—bananas, marsupials, languages, and genetics—westwards into Island Southeast Asia (Denham and Donohue 2009; Spriggs 1997, 53–54; Yen 1996).

One of the main problems has been the relative lack of directly dated archaeological sites from the lowlands of New Guinea, and a lack of applications of state-of-the-art scientific approaches being undertaken in West New Guinea (Indonesian Papua). Similarly, a lack of preservation, or systematic analysis, of archaeobotanical and archaeozoological remains from sites has made it difficult to reconstruct how past humans lived. Stable isotope analysis of human bone collagen also enables direct insights into overall dietary reliance on different types of foodstuffs. Although application to the osteoarchaeological record of the tropics has been limited, particularly for bone collagen that has often not been preserved, a growing number of studies have begun to demonstrate the efficacy of this approach for studying past tropical adaptations of our species. For example, stable carbon isotope analysis of Late Pleistocene human tooth enamel in Sri Lanka and Timor-Leste has demonstrated the clear reliance of our species on tropical forests (Roberts et al. 2015) and coastal foodstuffs (Roberts et al. 2020), respectively, as it moved into these parts of the world. Meanwhile, stable carbon and nitrogen isotope analysis of bone collagen in the Amazon Basin has revealed the diverse contributions made by incoming crops (maize), local crops (manioc), and wild plants and animals to the diets of different populations during the Middle and Late Holocene (Hermenegildo et al. 2017).

Nevertheless, despite the critical position of the New Guinea landmass in debates of early human tropical adaptations (Summerhayes et al. 2017), the origins of farming in the tropics (Golson 1985, 1989, 1991), and the interaction of indigenous and arriving forms of food production during the so-called Lapita expansion (Shaw et al. 2022), and despite the use of stable isotope approaches in Papua New Guinea (e.g. Kinaston et al. 2013, 2015; Roberts et al. 2022; Shaw et al. 2009, 2010, 2011), stable isotope analysis is yet to be applied to the osteoarchaeological record of West New Guinea. Here, we apply stable carbon and nitrogen isotope analysis to human bone collagen and enamel apatite in order to provide preliminary detail about the diets of humans that lived at the newly recorded sites of Yomokho 1, Srobu, Namatota, Mamorikotey, and Karas in Indonesian Papua.

The osteological specimens, spanning a period of c. 3400 to c. 110 years ago, offer the possibility of reconstructing how human economies and diets changed over a critical portion of the Holocene that witnessed significant human movements and the arrival of novel plants and animals to the New Guinea landmass (Ahmed et al. 2020; Powell 1976; Yen 1971, 1973).

Stable isotope research in the lowland tropics

Stable isotope analysis has long been used to reconstruct past human diets (Lee-Thorp 2008). Stable carbon (δ^{13}C) and nitrogen (δ^{15}N) analysis of bone collagen is one of the more common approaches in this regard. The dominant source of variation in δ^{13}C in land-based ecosystems is the distinction between C$_3$ plants and C$_4$ plants, which discriminate against the heavier isotope ^{13}C to differing extents during photosynthesis. C$_3$ plants, which dominate tropical forest environments, as well as domesticates such as yams, have δ^{13}C values between –35‰ and –19‰. Meanwhile, C$_4$ plants, which dominate tropical savannah ecosystems, have a δ^{13}C range between –13‰ and –8‰ (Calvin and Benson 1948; Hatch and Slack 1966). C$_3$ plants growing under a closed canopy have even lower δ^{13}C due to low light and recycled CO_2 (van der Merwe and Medina 1991). The δ^{13}C distinctions between plants are visible in the tissues of their consumers with a known fractionation effect (Ambrose and Norr 1993); the δ^{15}N of bone collagen provides information relating to the trophic level of consumers, being elevated c. 3–5‰ with each step in a food chain (O'Connell et al. 2012). Longer food chain lengths in aquatic systems mean that aquatic resources tend to also have higher δ^{15}N values. While marine resources tend to show both higher δ^{15}N and δ^{13}C, due to a different source of carbon in marine systems, δ^{13}C in freshwater habitats is far less predictable (Schoeninger and DeNiro 1984). Marine foods and their consumers have more positive δ^{13}C values because of the many trophic levels for marine fauna, which increases the ratios from level to level, in both nitrogen and carbon, resulting in δ^{13}C values similar to C$_4$ plants such as maize (Tykot 2016, 137). Thus, human collagen δ^{13}C and δ^{15}N can be used to discern varying reliance on different food groups in tropical environments.

Bone collagen has often been the tissue of choice for bioarchaeological investigations of diet and ecology using stable isotope analysis, due to the ability of stable nitrogen and carbon isotope analysis to provide resolution into trophic position as well as food sources (Schoeninger and Moore 1992). Moreover, when sampled from long bones and ribs, stable isotope analysis of bone collagen provides the longest averaged 'adult' signature of an individual diet due to the continuous nature of bone turnover (Hedges et al. 2007). Besides bones, collagen can also be found in dentine, which comprises 25–30 per cent of this organic compound (see Açil et al. 2005). Nevertheless, collagen in bone and dentine is typically poorly preserved in tropical contexts or is often of insufficient quality for it to be extracted, meaning that the stable isotopic analysis of tooth enamel provides an important alternative. The apatite of tooth enamel has few substitutions, low distortion, and larger crystals (LeGeros 1991), making it more resistant to post-mortem diagenetic degradation (Lee-Thorp 2008; Lee-Thorp et al. 1989). Furthermore, unlike bone collagen, the isotopic values will record a 'whole-diet' sequence for the period of enamel formation, a period that will vary depending on species and tooth sampled (Passey et al. 2005).

Stable carbon isotope (δ^{13}C) analysis of tooth enamel bioapatite has also been shown to reliably record the varying consumption of C3 and C4 resources (i.e. the plants and their consumers) which, in the tropics, often provide some indication of the type of environment (woody versus grassland) (Lee-Thorp and van der Merwe 1987; Levin et al. 2008). Within C3 ecosystems, the 'canopy effect' leads to lower δ^{13}C in organisms consuming resources under dense forest canopy than those feeding in more open areas (van der Merwe and Medina 1991). The consumption of marine resources can lead to $\delta^{13}C$ values similar to marine consumers (Kusaka et al. 2010), while freshwater resources can have highly variable $\delta^{13}C$. Overall, in pre-nineteenth-century diets, tooth enamel with $\delta^{13}C$ lower than –14‰ represents a reliance on closed canopy forest, while average values for 100 per cent C3 and C4 reliance are about –12‰ and 0‰ (Lee-Thorp et al. 1989; Levin et al. 2008). Compared to collagen carbon, the carbonate ions in enamel apatite are isotopically heavier, as high as +12 to +13‰ for free-ranging herbivores, as opposed to +5‰ for collagen.

Stable oxygen isotope ($\delta^{18}O$) analysis of tooth enamel primarily reflects the $\delta^{18}O$ of imbibed water, both from drinking and food (Luz et al. 1984; Luz and Kolodny 1985). Climatic (e.g. aridity, precipitation) and geographical (e.g. altitude, continental effect) impacts on $\delta^{18}O$ mean that it has been used as a proxy for both environmental conditions and palaeomobility (Longinelli 1984; Quade et al. 1995); in the altitude effect, the typical gradients are –0.15 to –0.5 ‰ per 100 m for $\delta^{18}O$, and –1.5 to –4 ‰ per 100 m for deuterium. However, physiological and behavioural variables have been shown to influence how faunal enamel $\delta^{18}O$ responds to changes in evaporative potential (Levin et al. 2006), with the $\delta^{18}O$ obligate drinkers (i.e. animals), like humans, that need to drink to get enough water, being less sensitive to local climatic changes.

Unlike bone collagen, enamel typically forms during childhood/the juvenile years, meaning that $\delta^{13}C$ and $\delta^{18}O$ values will record a period of time during early life (Longinelli 1984; Luz et al. 1984; Luz and Kolodny 1985). Oxygen isotope measurements are expressed in terms of a difference in the proportion of the heavier ^{18}O isotope relative to an international standard known as Vienna Standard Mean Ocean Water. The difference, $\delta^{18}O_{VSMOW}$, is expressed in units of parts per thousand (‰).

Bone collagen $\delta^{13}C$ primarily reflects the protein portions of the diet (Ambrose and Norr 1993; Fahy et al. 2017; Hedges et al. 2007). This means that low-protein plant portions of the diet can be under-represented. The $\delta^{13}C$ and $\delta^{15}N$ can also vary based on climatic factors such as evaporative potential and temperature, making an associated local baseline of faunal values important for interpreting human dietary signals (Cormie and Schwarcz 1996). Together, these isotopic methodologies offer the possibility of gaining direct insights into different human adaptations and reliance on different resource types in West New Guinea across space and time.

Four different human tooth types, including incisors, canines, premolars, and molars, form across different developmental periods (Hillson 2003), with their different processes of mineralisation providing different insights into past diets and environmental conditions (Dupras 2007; Longinelli 1984; Luz et al. 1984; Luz and Kolodny 1985; Wright and Schwarcz 1998). The anterior teeth (incisors and canines) provide information about the average record of water and food consumption during the late stage of pregnancy or early childhood. In contrast, the permanent molar tooth (posterior) as a late-erupting tooth provides information about an individual's geographic origin during childhood. The start and complete formation process of each tooth are tightly correlated with the first introduction of water sources or foods to individuals (Wright and Schwarcz 1998; Dupras 2007) since water is present in the form of mineral calcium phosphates as the element almost entirely composing the enamel tissue of the tooth (Hillson 2003, 217). For example, in humans, the first molar enamel mineralises between birth and three years of age while the third molars mineralise between seven and 13 years (Hillson 2003; AlQahtani et al. 2010). As a result, at least some of the first molar enamel forms prior to weaning, meaning that it is possible that $\delta^{18}O$ values from this tooth will reflect milk obtained from the mother rather than water or other food sources (Wright and Schwarcz 1998).

West New Guinea sites and archaeological materials

The materials for stable isotope analysis in this study were derived from 10 samples of human bone encountered during excavation at five different archaeological sites (Figure 10.1) spanning from c. 3400 to c. 110 years ago (Table 10.1). Due to the fragmentary nature of human skeletons from the five sites in this study, it was a challenge to identify whether the human remains were from the same or different individuals. However, the human remains were encountered in different sedimentary contexts and were found associated with different cultural materials, leading to the assumption that the human remains from each site were from different individuals.

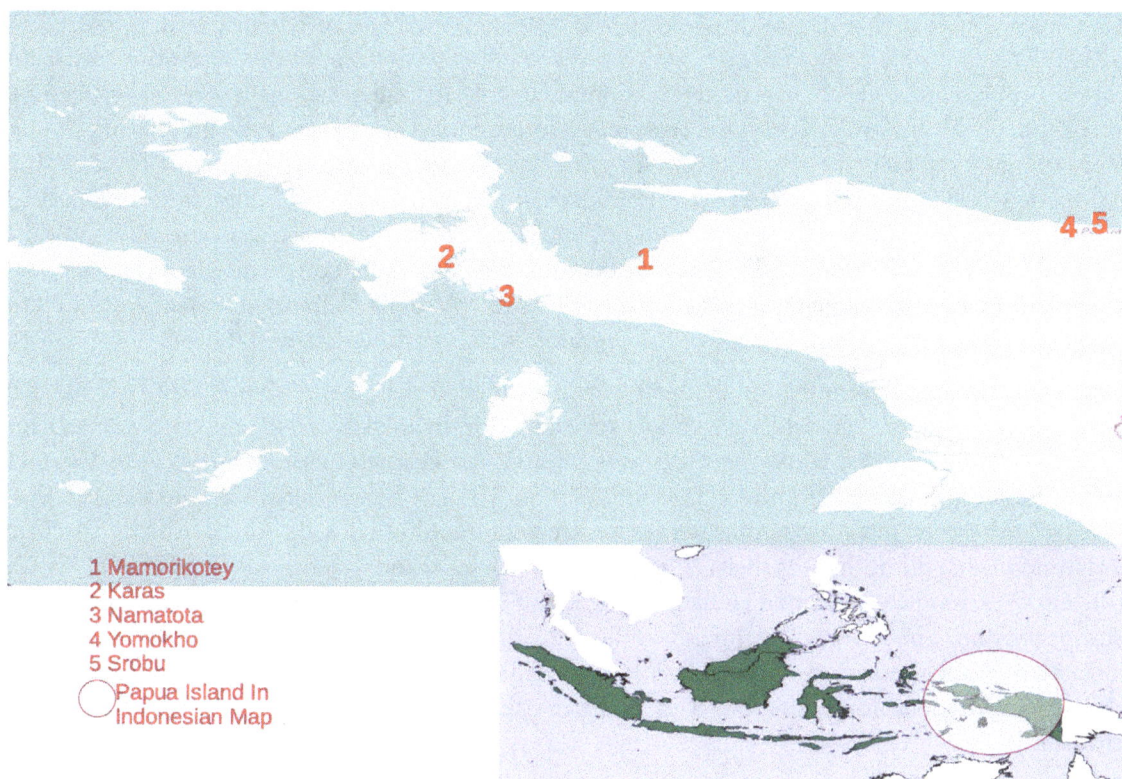

Figure 10.1: Map of sites involved in isotope analysis.
Source: Marlin Tolla 2021.

Table 10.1: Preliminary radiocarbon results from five West New Guinea sites.

Site	Available C14	Sample type	Calibrated date (2σ)	Source
Karas	3400 BP	Charcoal	–	Suroto et al. (2012); Mas'ud (2013)
Yomokho	2590±120 BP	Charcoal	2933–2353 cal. BP	Suroto (2016)
Mamorikotey	2520±50 BP	Charcoal	2749–2426 cal. BP	Current study (IHME-3995)
Srobu	1720±30 BP	Charcoal	1700–1539 cal. BP	Djami et al. (2019)
Namatota	110±40 BP	Charcoal	275–8 cal. BP	Current study (IHME-3994)

Note: Calibrations produced using OxCal 4.4.
Source: See sources cited throughout the table.

Karas

Karas is a cave site situated in Arguni District in the Kaimana Regency, Papua Barat Province, Indonesia (S 3.306583°; E 133.750556°). The site is situated about 45 m above sea level (asl) on a hill in the Arguni Bay area. Rock art with various paintings of figures such as anthropomorphs, fish, geometrics, circles, pyramids, grids, and unidentified paintings were found on the cave walls (Mas'ud 2013). A research team from the Balai Arkeologi Papua[1] (Papua Centre of Archaeology) excavated this site in 2012 and 2013. Three excavation boxes were opened in the same sector of the site: GKQ1 (I6), GKQI (F5), and GKQ1 (F6). Each box was excavated to a different depth, depending on the amount of archaeological material encountered, and digging was stopped when there were limited archaeological findings in the deepest spits. Human remains were recovered in GKQ1 (F6), in the flat part of the cave, which extended to 150 cm deep. In this excavation, at 10 cm until 40 cm from the surface, the matrix was dominated by light grey sediment with a silty texture. At a depth of 40 cm until 60 cm, the sediment became mixed with shell fragments. From 70 cm deep, the grey sediment became a sandy silt with several small limestone fragments present. The archaeological findings in this layer were dominated by marine shell, fish bones, and unidentified animal bones. Various archaeological findings, such as human skeletons, were found at Spit 12 (120 cm); pottery fragments, shells, and ecofacts consisting of animal bones and plant remains were discovered in several sediment layers (Suroto et al. 2012). A single charcoal fragment from 70 cm below the surface from box GKQ1 (F6) has produced a radiocarbon date of 3400 BP.

Minimally, two different human individuals were identified in the excavation box GKQ1 (F6). Two upper second incisors (left and right) were assigned to individual Krs/649; one was selected for collagen isotope analysis, while the other was selected for enamel apatite analysis. The Krs/649 specimens were excavated from a soft, sandy loam at 104 cm below the surface, associated with charcoal, fish bones, nut shells, animal bones, two fragments of human long bones, seashells (Arcidae and Veneridae), and freshwater shells (Littorinidae, Naticidae, and Terebridae) (Suroto et al. 2012, 17). Another sample of a human phalange assigned to individual Krs/638 was selected for collagen isotope analysis. The Krs/638 specimen was unearthed from a dark grey, soft and moist sandy loam at 120 cm from the surface. The archaeological findings associated with the Krs/638 consisted of nut shells, human long bones, as well as marine and freshwater molluscs (Arcidae, Veneridae, Littorinidae).

---

1   Bahasa Indonesia words are underlined at first mention.

Yomokho 1

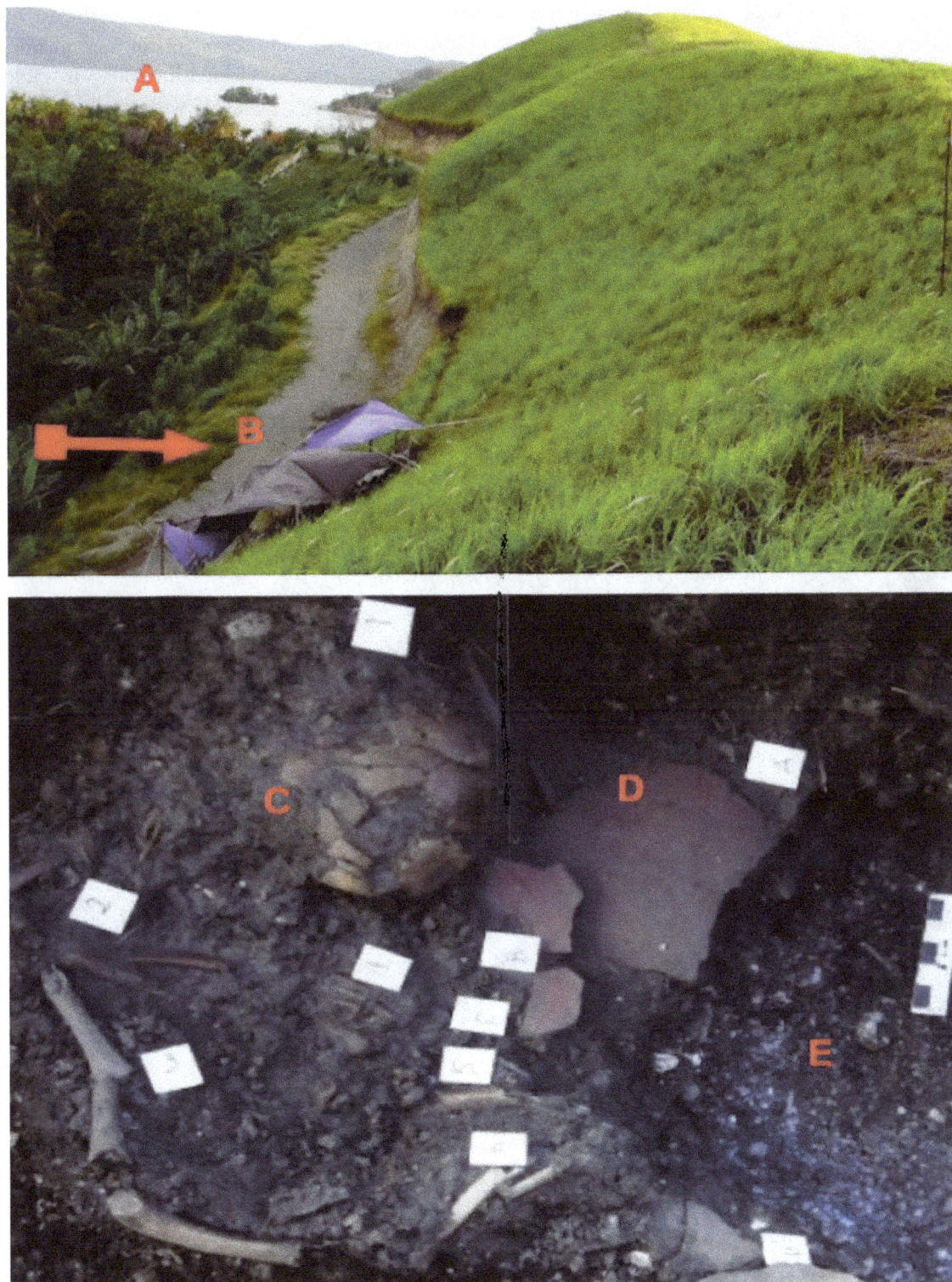

Figure 10.2: Yomokho 1.

Notes: (A) Lake Sentani; (B) the excavation box; (C) human cranial fragments; (D) ceramic vessel fragment.
Source: Photos by Balai Arkeologi Papua.

Yomokho 1 is an open site along a hill on the north coast of Lake Sentani in Jayapura Regency (S 2.598717°; E 140.574647°) (Figure 10.2; see also Suroto, this volume). At this site, two excavation boxes were opened. The first was opened on the top of the hill, to the north-east of the second box. The human remains sampled for isotopic analysis were found in the second unit and included Ymk/1-R (radius) and Ymk/2-P (phalange), which were selected for collagen stable isotope analysis. Ymk/1-R was found at 54 cm below the surface associated with molluscs and pottery fragments. The sediment associated with this depth was dark brown in colour with grain size ranging between 2 and 0.02 mm, reflecting sandy loam. Ymk/2-P was found associated with pottery fragments at 135 cm depth, in a sediment with grain size ranging from 0.02 to 0.002 mm. One radiocarbon determination is available for this site, based on charcoal that dates to 2590±120 BP (Suroto 2016, 1). The charcoal was found in the same spit as Ymk/2-P, providing an approximate age for the specimen. No radiocarbon dating has yet been obtained for the upper spits associated with Ymk/1-R, but it can be assumed that this specimen postdates 2590±120 BP.

Mamorikotey

Figure 10.3: Excavation units at Mamorikotey.

Notes: upper left: MMK/ktk1; upper right: MMK/ktk2; lower left: MMK/ktk3; lower right: screening during excavation.

Source: Photos by Balai Arkeologi Papua.

Mamorikotey (Figure 10.3) is an open site on Kapotar Island, Nabire Regency (S 3.073667°; E 135.590278°). It is in a hilly area, at 75 m asl, and about 20–30 m horizontally from the shoreline. At present, this site is overgrown by grasses and trees growing around 6–10 m in height. Three square-metre excavation boxes were opened on the site, given the names MMK1, MMK2, and MMK3, and excavated following 10 cm spits. Fragmentary human remains were found in all three excavations. MMK1 is located 18 m south-west from MMK2, while MMK3 is located 15 m east of MMK1. Two teeth from the Mamorikotey site, including a lower premolar (MMK_333) and lower molar (MMK_419), from two different humans were selected for enamel apatite analysis in this study.

The lower premolar (MMK_333) was found in MMK3 at 25 cm depth. The sediment associated with this depth was dark brown, wet, and fine in texture. The findings associated with MMK_333 include human incisors, pottery fragments, shells, marsupial teeth, seeds, the femur of a pig, molar teeth, fish bones and teeth, and several unidentified animal bones. A charcoal sample was radiocarbon dated to 2520±50 BP (IHME-3995) from MMK3 at a depth of 115 cm, providing a maximum possible age for MMK_333. The charcoal was found associated with marine shells and pig bones. The lower molar (MMK_419) was found in MMK1, at 35 cm from the surface. The sediment associated with this depth was dark brown, moist and fine in texture with a pH of 7. No radiocarbon dates have yet been obtained from the MMK1 excavation unit, but the lower molar likely postdates 2520±50 BP.

Srobu

Srobu is an open site located on a steep peninsula in Youtefa Bay, Abepura District, Jayapura, Papua Province (S 2.617937°; E 140.703464°). The site sits at about 85 m asl and covers around 20,059 m² of the peninsula. The archaeological materials covering the surface of the site include small megaliths, stone tools, human remains, pestles and mortars, pottery fragments, and a huge array of seashells (Djami 2015; Djami et al. 2016, 2017, 2018, 2019; Mene 2014).

Three bones from two different individuals have been selected for stable isotope analysis, including one upper canine selected for collagen analysis, and an upper canine and third molar selected for enamel apatite analysis. Srb_20 was found in unit B2S1, at 50 cm from the surface. It was found associated with animal bones, thousands of bivalve and gastropod shells, pottery sherds and so on. The soil was smooth in texture, and very friable when excavated. In contrast, Srb_413 was found 110 cm from the surface. At this depth, the soil was grey-black in colour, with a smooth texture, loose when excavated. The material encountered at this depth consisted of thousands of shells, as well as pottery fragments, and several stone tools (Djami et al. 2017). The available radiocarbon date from this site is 1720±30 BP, from a charcoal sample from another excavation unit (i.e. not from B2S1). Therefore, it is likely that the human remains used for isotope analysis in this study are Late Holocene, but it is difficult to speculate further about their precise age, pending further radiocarbon analyses from B2S1.

Namatota

Namatota is an open site located in the Namatota District, in the Kaimana Regency of Papua Barat Province, on the southern coast of the Bird's Neck (S 3.779007°; E 133.885388°). Irregular limestone karst landscapes generally characterise Kaimana. One square metre test pit was opened at this site, where archaeological material was recovered from 1 to 100 cm from the datum level. These remains included pottery fragments, several marsupial mandible fragments, pig molars, and shells. Two samples of human long bones, including an ulna and fibula, from two different individuals were selected for collagen stable isotope analysis. Specimen NMT/1-U (ulna) was encountered at 48 cm from the surface, while the NMT/2-F (fibula) was unearthed at 81 cm from the surface. The radiocarbon dating analysis of a charcoal sample from a depth of 76 cm presents a date of 110±40 BP (IHME-3994). This suggests that the human specimens selected for isotope analysis are very recent.

Isotope research methods

All samples selected for bone collagen and enamel apatite analysis were prepared and processed at the Department of Archaeology, Max Planck Institute for the Science of Human History, Jena, Germany. For the bone collagen specimens, the pretreatment method is as follows. After cleaning the sample's surface with a sandblaster, roughly 1 g of the sample was drilled from the original sample, weighed, and put into a test tube. 10 ml of 0.5 M HCl (hydrochloric acid) was then added to the sample. The sample was covered with aluminium foil and put in the fridge for 48 hours. After that, the 0.5 M HCl was decanted and replaced with new 0.5 M HCl until the sample was completely demineralised. After demineralisation, the sample was rinsed three times with ultra-pure water before 10 mL of a pH3 HCl solution was added to the sample. The sample was then put on a heat block at 70 °C for 48 hours. After that, the sample was filtered using an Ezee filter and transferred to a freeze dryer safe plastic tube with a known weight. The tube was covered with parafilm and transferred to the freezer overnight. The sample was then freeze-dried for 24 hours. The tube and sample weight were subtracted from the weight of the empty tube to calculate the sample weight and the collagen yield. 1.0 mg of collagen was then weighed into tin capsules for analysis in duplicate. $\delta^{13}C$ and $\delta^{15}N$ ratios were measured using a Thermo Scientific Flash 2000 Elemental Analyzer coupled to a Thermo Delta V Advantage Isotope Ratio Mass Spectrometer. Values were reported as the ratio of the heavier isotope to the lighter isotope ($^{13}C/^{12}C$ or $^{15}N/^{14}N$) as δ values in parts per mill (‰) relative to international standards—Vienna Peedee Belemnite (VPDB) for $\delta^{13}C$ and atmospheric N_2 (AIR) for $\delta^{15}N$. The results were calibrated against international standards (IAEA-CH-6: $\delta^{13}C$ = −10.80 ± 0.47‰, IAEA-N-2: $\delta^{15}N$ = 20.3 ± 0.2‰, and USGS40: $\delta^{13}C$ = −26.38 ± 0.042‰, $\delta^{15}N$ = 4.5 ± 0.1‰). Machine error was determined using repeat measurements of a laboratory standard (fish gelatine: $\delta^{13}C$ = ~ −15.1‰, $\delta^{15}N$ = ~14.3‰). Based on replicate analyses, machine error is ±0.2‰ for $\delta^{13}C$ and ±0.2‰ for $\delta^{15}N$. Overall measurement precision was studied through the measurement of repeats of fish gelatine (n = 80, ±0.2‰ for $\delta^{13}C$ and ±0.2‰ for $\delta^{15}N$).

The enamel apatite samples in this study were extracted from human teeth with no decay or teeth modification, an essential prerequisite for suitable stable isotopic analysis (Meier-Augenstein 2018, 353; Meier-Augenstein and Schimmelmann 2018). The enamel pretreatment method is as follows. After the tooth's surface was cleaned using a sandblaster, approximately 10 mg of enamel powder was drilled from the enamel surface onto a piece of aluminium foil. The sample was weighed and then carefully transferred to a labelled micro-centrifuge tube. Then approximately 1 ml of 1 per cent bleach solution was added to the sample for 60 minutes and the sample was agitated periodically. The tube was then centrifuged to separate the supernatant from the sample, and the supernatant was decanted. The sample was rinsed three times with ultra-pure water. After the last rinse was removed, approximately 1 ml of 0.1 M acetic acid was added to the sample for 10 minutes. The sample was then centrifuged and rinsed a further three times with ultra-pure water. After the water from the last rinse was removed, the sample tube was covered with parafilm and put into the freezer overnight. The sample was then put into a freeze dryer for four hours or until the sample was completely dry.

After this, roughly 3 mg of the sample was weighed into a borosilicate vial. Following the addition of 100 per cent phosphoric acid, $\delta^{13}C$ and $\delta^{18}O$ of the gases evolved were measured using a Thermo Gas Bench 2 connected to a Thermo Delta V Advantage Mass Spectrometer. $\delta^{13}C$ and $\delta^{18}O$ results were compared against international standards (IAEA-603: $\delta^{13}C$ = 2.5; $\delta^{18}O$ = −2.4; IAEA-CO-8: $\delta^{13}C$ = −5.8; $\delta^{18}O$ = −22.7; and USGS44: $\delta^{13}C$ = −42.2) and in-house standard (MERCK: $\delta^{13}C$ = −41.3; $\delta^{18}O$ = −14.4). Replicate analysis of the MERCK standards suggested that machine measurement error was c. ±0.1‰ for $\delta^{13}C$ and ±0.2‰ for $\delta^{18}O$. Overall measurement precision was studied through the measurement of repeat extracts from a bovid tooth enamel standard (n = 20, ±0.2‰ for $\delta^{13}C$; ±0.3‰ for $\delta^{15}N$).

Results

Human bone collagen δ¹³C$_{col}$ and δ¹⁵N$_{col}$

The bone samples from Yomokho 1, Srobu, and Namatota overall yielded C:N ratios between 2.9 and 3.6 and collagen yields of over 1 per cent, suggesting collagen of suitable quality was preserved (DeNiro 1985). The collagen yields from the site of Karas were lower, with one sample (Krs/649) dropping below the 1 per cent cut-off. This sample should be treated with caution, although both Krs/649 and Krs/638 yielded C:N ratios within the expected 2.9–3.6 range (DeNiro 1985).

The isotope bone collagen δ¹³C$_{col}$ values from the seven specimens yielded a range between –25.6‰ to –16.5‰ (Table 10.2). The lowest δ¹³C$_{col}$ values were found in the two individuals from Karas (Krs/638 with –24.6‰ and Krs/649 with –25.6‰), followed by Yomokho 1 (Ymk/1-R with –20.5‰ and Ymk/2-P with –21.2‰). Slightly higher δ¹³C$_{col}$ values were measured for the specimens from the Namatota site (–20.00‰ in NMT/2-F, and –16.5‰ for NMT/1) and the individual from the Srobu site (Srb_20 is –18.5‰).

The measured δ¹⁵N$_{col}$ from the seven samples ranged from 14.01‰ to 4.30‰. The highest δ¹⁵N$_{col}$ value was measured for the individual from Srobu (14.0‰), followed by the Yomokho 1 specimens (Ymk/2-P: 12.9‰, Ymk/1-R: 12.6‰). Stable isotope δ¹⁵N$_{col}$ from Namatota were 11.5‰ for NMT/1-U and 9.9‰ for NMT/2-F. Finally, the two individuals measured from the Karas site showed the lowest δ¹⁵N$_{col}$ of 7.7‰ (Krs/649) and 4.3‰ (Krs/638).

Table 10.2: The results of bone collagen stable isotopes from the five sites in this study.

Sample	Element	δ15N/14N‰ (AIR)				δ13C/12C‰ (PDB)			
		Test A	Test B	Average	St dev	Test A	Test B	Average	St dev
Ymk/2-P	Phalanges	12.82	12.90	12.86	0.055	–21.27	–21.11	–21.19	0.113
Ymk/1-R	Radius	12.58	12.59	12.59	0.003	–20.53	–20.38	–20.45	0.102
NMT/1-U	Ulna	11.42	11.56	11.49	0.099	–16.51	–16.49	–16.50	0.01
NMT/2-F	Fibula	9.92	9.90	9.91	0.017	–19.98	–19.92	–19.95	0.05
Srb_20	Upper canine	14.01	14.01	14.01	0.004	–18.48	–18.43	–18.46	0.03
Krs/649	Upper second incisor	7.66	7.82	7.74	0.112	–25.68	–25.52	–25.60	0.11
Krs/638	Phalanges	4.43	4.16	4.30	0.193	–24.37	–24.9	–24.63	0.38

Source: Marlin Tolla 2021.

Enamel apatite: Carbon isotope (δ¹³C$_{apat}$) and oxygen isotope (δ¹⁸O$_{apat}$)

Carbon isotope ratios δ¹³C$_{apat}$ from five specimens from three sites—Karas, Srobu, and Mamorikotey—range from –13.5‰ to –10.8‰ (Table 10.3). The lowest values are from Mamorikotey: MMK_333 is –13.1‰ and MMK_419 (lower molar) is –13.5 ‰. Slightly higher values derive from Karas—Krs/649 (upper second incisor) is –12.3‰—and Srobu: Srb_413 (third molar) is –12.4‰ and Srb_20 (upper canine) is –10.8‰. The oxygen isotope ratios δ¹⁸O$_{apat}$ for Mamorikotey were also highest: MMK_333 (lower premolar) is –8.2‰ and MMK_419 (lower molar) is –6.9‰. Karas and Srobu have comparable δ¹⁸O$_{apat}$: Krs/649 (upper second incisor) is –5.6‰, Srb_20 (upper canine) is –5.0 ‰, while Srb_413 is –5.5‰. As mentioned above, each tooth provides insight into the uptake of water and food at different stages of development (Table 10.4).

Table 10.3: The results of enamel apatite stable isotopes from the five sites in this study.

Sample name	Tooth	norm 13C	St dev	norm 18O	St dev
KRS/649	Upper second incisor	–12.3	0.2	–5.6	0.1
Srb_20	Upper canine	–10.8	0.3	–5.0	0.1
Srb_413	Third molar	–12.4	0.2	–5.5	0.1
MMK_333	Lower premolar	–13.1	0.2	–8.2	0.1
MMK_419	Lower molar	–13.5	0.1	–6.9	0.1

Source: Marlin Tolla 2021.

Table 10.4: Mineralisation of human permanent enamel tooth.

Sample name	Tooth name	Crown mineralisation start	Crown mineralisation end
KRS/649	Upper second incisor	10–12 months	3.3–5.9 years
Srb_20	Upper canine	4–5 months	4.0–5.8 years
Srb_413	Third molar	7–10 years	12–13.7 years
MMK_333	Lower first premolar	18–24 months	5–7 years

Source: After Schweissing (2004).

Discussion

One of the key ingredients in the human diet is protein; it contains about 30 per cent of the caloric energy needed by humans to live, and is found in nitrogen and carbon in human bone collagen (Draper 1977, 311; see also Ambrose and Norr 1993). Most tissues, including collagen $\delta^{15}N$, are enriched by ~3‰ relative to the diet, which will be passed up with each step at a trophic level, depending on the types of food intake by consumers (Minagawa and Wada 1984). Stable isotope nitrogen ($\delta^{15}N$) values were obtained from the seven individual specimens from four archaeological sites (Yomokho, Srobu, Karas, and Namatota), presenting a range of values between 4.16‰ to 14.01‰. These isotope ratios represent three different foci of past diets: marine and terrestrial (herbivore, carnivore, and omnivore) and plant protein consumption. $\delta^{13}C_{col}$ ranged between –16.50‰ and –25.60‰, and all except NMT/1-U are typical of C_3 diet intake.

Enamel apatite carbon isotope values obtained from five individuals range from –13.5‰ to –10.8‰, which are notably higher than the range obtained from collagen. The different value of carbon isotopes in collagen and enamel apatite is caused by the dietary carbon that reflects dietary protein in collagen, while the carbon in enamel apatite represents the whole diet (Ambrose and Norr 1993). Human enamel is one tissue that reflects the oxygen signal of drinking water, which is composed of chemical bonds that oxygen makes in crystalline apatite (Bryant et al. 1996, 397). The oxygen derived from drinking water is incorporated into human tooth enamel obtained from nearby water sources/natural water (Prowse et al. 2019, 135; White et al. 1998).

The ecology of New Guinea is diverse, from mangroves, swamps, and lowland rainforests to montane forests and alpine grasslands (Petocz 1989, 23). The five sites in this study are surrounded by several ecological zones, from the sea to closed-canopy forests; this means that both terrestrial and marine resources could be used as food. The ecofacts and material culture unearthed from the five sites in this study provide supplementary information about human behaviour concerning diet preference and this information will now be synthesised with the isotopic results, site by site (Figure 10.4).

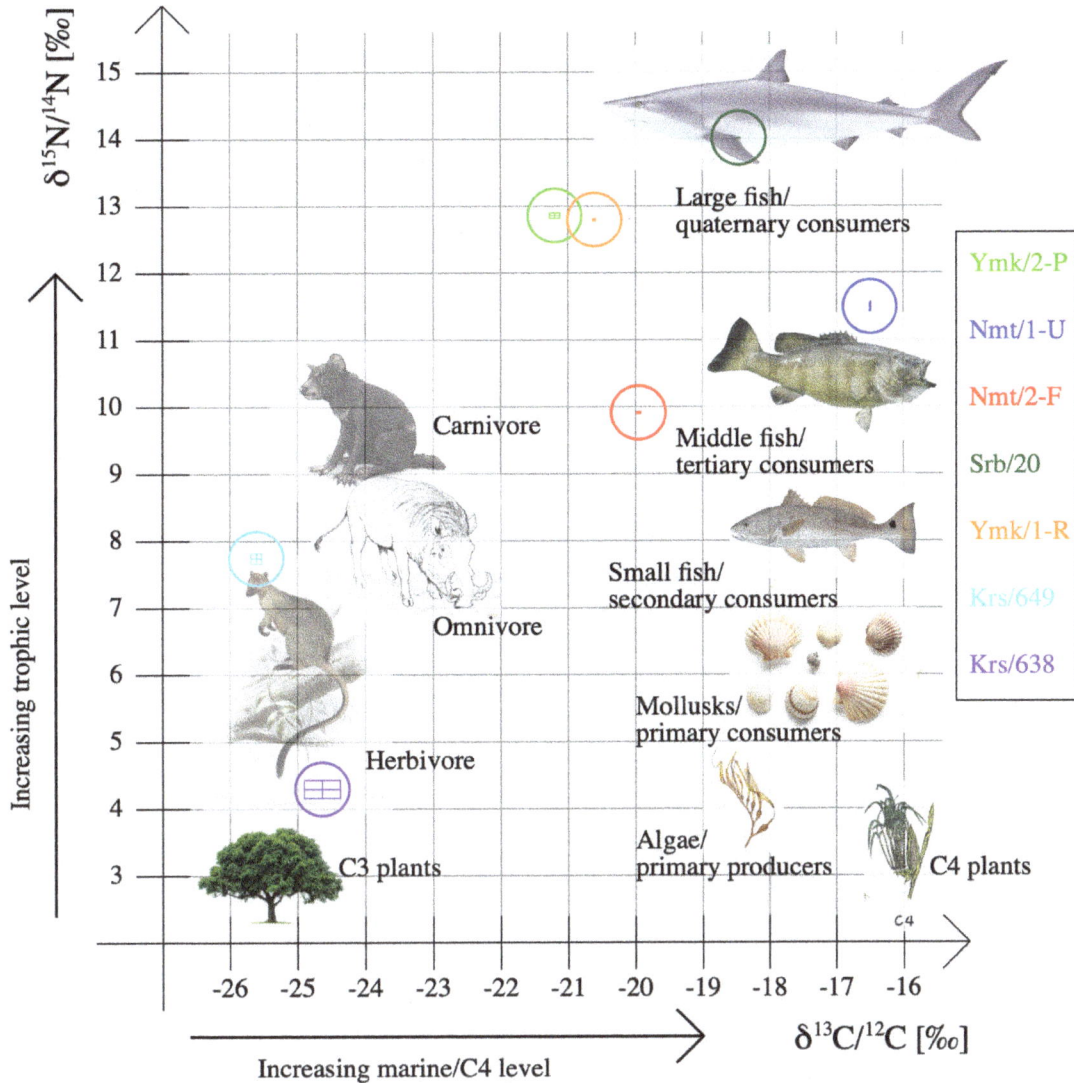

Figure 10.4: Typical isotope δ¹³C and δ¹⁵N values of key ecological resources compared with results from seven human bone collagen samples analysed in this study.

Notes: Yomokho 1 samples are abbreviated: YMK/1-R and YMK/2-P; the Namatota site samples: NMT/1-U and NMT/2-F; the Srobu sample: Srb/20; Karas site: Krs/638 and Krs/649.

Source: Marlin Tolla 2021.

Karas (≥3400 BP)

The collagen δ¹⁵N ratio for Krs/649 tentatively signifies an intermediate range of protein in the diet and suggests the person was consuming terrestrial foods including herbivores (Figure 10.4). For individual Krs/638, the ratio of collagen δ¹⁵N is substantially lower and provides stronger evidence for a reliance on herbivores. However, it should be noted that the low values could also be the result of secondary diagenesis owing to physical and chemical taphonomic alteration. This process leads to the microstructure of bone tissue degrading, which may affect isotope results.

For Krs/649, a collagen $\delta^{13}C$ ratio of –25.68‰ indicates C3 plant consumption. The $\delta^{13}C$ obtained from enamel apatite from Krs/649 is 12.3‰, which further suggests C_3 plants were consumed during childhood. Furthermore, the $\delta^{18}O$ value from the upper second incisor of Krs/649 is –5.6‰ (Figure 10.5) and, considering the process of mineralisation began between 10 and 12 months and was complete by 3.3–5.9 years, the values are in part reflective of the mother's breastmilk. Because human incisors mineralise in very early childhood, the $\delta^{18}O$ is expected to be enriched by the breastfeeding process, up to 0.7 to 2.69 $\delta^{18}O$, or one trophic level (Katzenberg 2008, 430; White et al. 1998). In the future, this assumption may need to be supported by the stable isotope analysis of animal bone from this site to provide an environmental baseline.

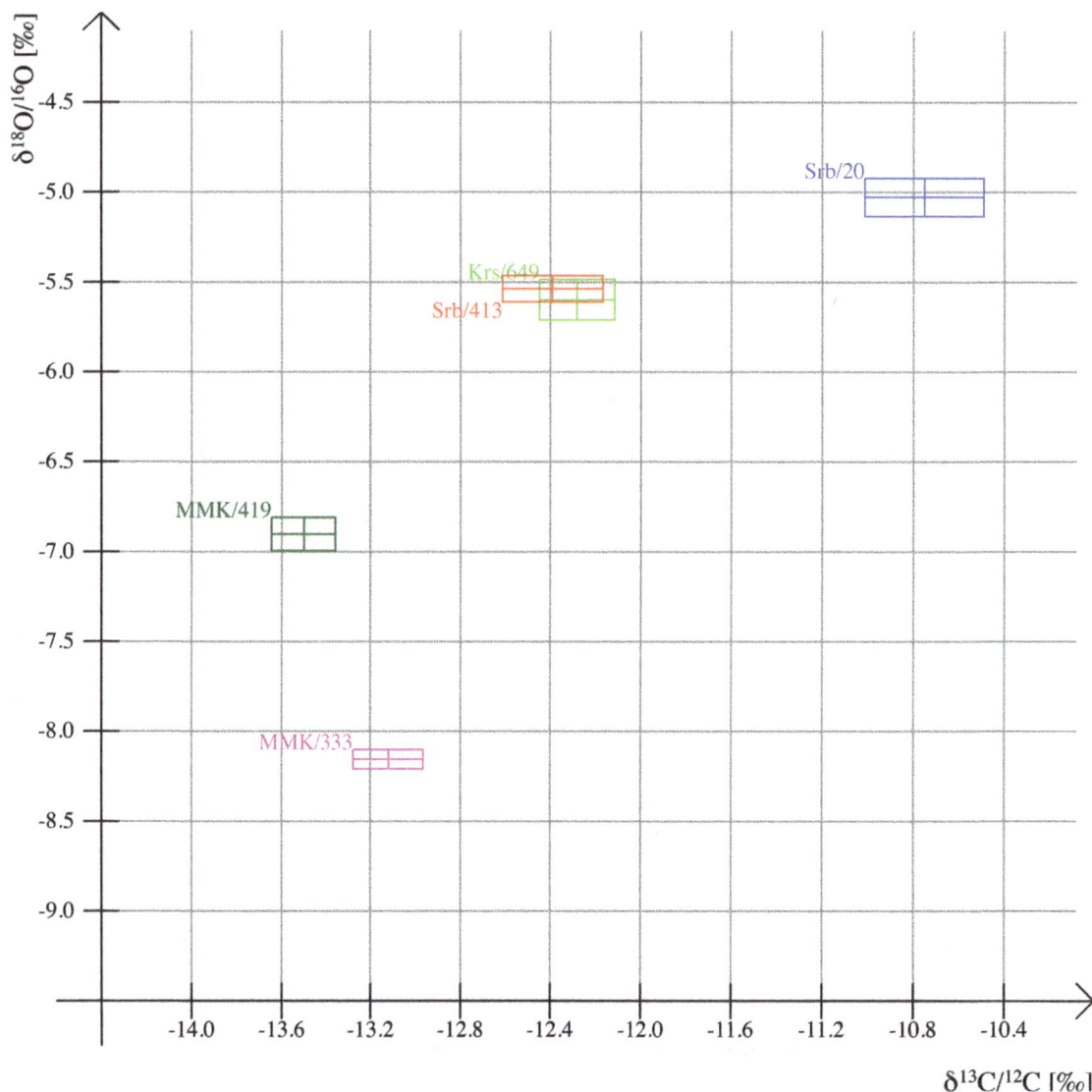

Figure 10.5: Isotope enamel apatite results on human teeth from four sites in this study.

Notes: The Srobu specimens are abbreviated: Srb/20 and Srb/413; the Karas specimen: Krs/649; the Mamorikotey specimens: MMK/333 and MMK/419.

Source: Marlin Tolla 2021.

The Karas site is surrounded today by lowland plains, interspersed with several small and large rivers that flow through the area. The ecofacts associated the human remains in the Karas site consist of nuts/seeds, seashells, freshwater shellfish, and marsupial and unidentified fauna bones (Suroto et al. 2012). These findings support the idea that the Karas occupants were primarily collecting plants and hunting herbivores in the surrounding forests.

Yomokho 1 (≤2590 BP)

The collagen $\delta^{15}N$ results for both Ymk/2-P and Ymk/1-R suggest the individuals were consuming piscivorous fish, while the collage $\delta^{13}C$ value indicates that C3 plants were also eaten (Figure 10.4). In New Guinea, piscivorous fishes are commonly found in marine, estuarine, and freshwater settings and are variable in size (Juanes et al. 2002, 267). However, given the site is on the northern shoreline of Lake Sentani, consumption of freshwater species may be the most parsimonious explanation.

Mamorikotey (≤2530 BP)

Based on the enamel apatite $\delta^{13}C$ ratio for the two Mamorikotey specimens, −13.5 ‰ to −13.1‰, it is likely that C_3 plants were a key part of the diet during childhood (Figure 10.5). The ratio of $\delta^{18}O$ was lower in the premolar (MMK_333) at −8.2‰, compared to the third molar (MMK_419) at −6.9 ‰. This may provide evidence about different types of water consumption at different times during development. Since the proportion of water obtained from breastmilk in premolar teeth is more enriched in $\delta^{18}O$ than drinking water, the amount of isotopic oxygen in early mineralising teeth such as premolars will be heavier than in late mineralising teeth like the third molar (Wright and Schwarcz 1998). The $\delta^{18}O$ enriched in mother's milk can be up to 2.69‰ (Katzenberg 2008, 430), and this enrichment can be between 0.7 and 1‰ in the enamel of breastfeeding infants. These values also correspond to the global distribution of $\delta^{18}O$ provided by the International Atomic Energy Agency that range from −2 to −10 for the Southern Hemisphere zone, which includes Papua. It is possible that the MMK_333 individual did not spend their early years around Mamorikotey, which lies at 75 m asl, and grew up in slightly higher elevations. Low altitudes are associated with positive $\delta^{18}O$ values, and the MMK_333 values are substantially lower than the results from individuals at similarly situated sites like Srobu (85 m asl).

Srobu (≤1720 BP)

The collagen $\delta^{15}N$ value for Srb/20 is 14.01‰, which implies a mixed diet of terrestrial omnivorous–herbivorous animals. The intermediate to high collagen $\delta^{13}C$ value of −18.46‰, corresponds to marine fish consumption (Nash et al. 2012; Trites 2019, 589). The combination of a high $\delta^{15}N$ and $\delta^{13}C/^{12}C$ values is strong evidence for marine food consumption because of the long food chain involved, which also supported by the high $\delta^{13}C$ in the enamel apatite. The results cannot yet be used to determine whether the individual was primarily eating C_3 or C_4 plants.

The enamel apatite $\delta^{13}C$ value of the Srb/413 third molar is −12.4‰. Based on these results, the diet consumed by the Srb/413 individual during childhood was based on C_3 plants from open woodland or perhaps C_3 grains. The significant consumption of terrestrial meat, marine fish, and C_3 plants is supported by the ecofacts found at the site, which consist of marine shell and fish, marsupials, pig bones, fragmentary animal bones of unidentified species, and several plant remains like nuts (Djami et al. 2016, 2017). Presently, the environment around Srobu consists of different ecological niches, including closed habitats (forest), shrublands, and the estuarine and coral reef seashore, representing different economic opportunities for people in the past. The zooarchaeological evidence demonstrates that humans exploited terrestrial, arboreal, and aquatic habitats. The macrobotanical remains further indicate that forest plants correspond with the C_3 values.

Namatota (c. 110 BP)

According to the bone collagen analysis from the Namatota site, the $\delta^{15}N$ for individual NMT/1-U is 11.56‰, while the $\delta^{13}C$ is –16.50‰, which suggests the consumption of marine food resources in the upper ranges of the food chain, for example middle- to large-sized fish. The collagen results for individual NMT/2-F—a $\delta^{15}N$ of 9.91‰ and $\delta^{13}C$ of 19.95‰—implies slightly less fish and more terrestrial foods were consumed. The differences between the two specimens indicates slight variation between individual diets, but a common reliance on fish.

Conclusion

Based on the study of bone collagen and enamel apatite stable isotopes from the five Late Holocene sites in this study—Karas, Yomokho 1, Mamorikotey, Srobu, and Namatota—the diet of lowland Papuan people in the past relied on a wide range of terrestrial and coastal foraging activities. The parts of West New Guinea where the sites are located are characterised by variable ecological zones, but primarily include coastal fringes and lowland rainforests, which offer marine resources and lowland C_3 plants and herbivores. Fittingly, this chapter has demonstrated that lowlanders were primarily focused on rainforest and aquatic resources to maintain their subsistence needs. However, there are some limitations in studying the ecological and palaeodietary patterns in this region, owing to differing preservation levels of the osteoarchaeological remains, caused by high humidity, heat, and climatic fluctuation. This posed challenges for providing clear interpretations of the collagen results, for instance in the two samples from Karas. In the future, it is hoped that methodological and technological advances in tropical isotope studies will provide better clarity. Moreover, the ecofacts from these five sites, including the terrestrial and marine fauna, and the botanical remains, need to be analysed both to identify species presence—and by extension, the types of habitats that foragers were frequenting—and to provide a stable isotope environmental benchmark to compare to the human remains. Finally, refined radiocarbon dating programs at these sites will perhaps allow us to build lowland subsistence strategies into a detailed chronological framework, to explore how people's diets changed in different parts of West New Guinea during the past four millennia of human history.

Acknowledgments

We thank the indigenous Papuans as the owners of the land where the excavations were performed and for their permission for archaeological fieldwork on their land, including Ondoafi (leader of the Pulau Asei Besar—Sentani). We thank the community of Nafri, Jayapura, who occupied the area of Abe Pantai where the Srobu site is located, and the community of Biakers in this area. We further thank the indigenous Papuans in District Arguni Bawah, including Enos, Frans, and Herman; the clan members of Aronggear and Aritahanu including Bapak Decky Aritanahu and family, Bapak Petrus Imburi, and all the indigenous Papuan community who live in Kepulauan Moora—Nabire Regency. Finally, we acknowledge the Local Government of Papua and Papua Barat Province, including Dinas Kebudayaan Jayapura, Bapak Elvis Kabey. We thank Hari Suroto and Erlin Djami for their permission to analyse the human remains from Yomokho, Srobu, and Karas sites for isotope analysis in this study. Last but not least, we extend our gratitude to the anonymous reviewer of this paper.

References

Açil, Y., A.E. Mobasseri, Warnke, H. Patrick, H. Terheyden, J. Wiltfang, and I. Springer 2005. Detection of mature collagen in human dental enamel. *Calcified Tissue International* 76:121–126. doi.org/10.1007/s00223-004-0122-0.

Ahmed, I., P.J. Lockhart, E.M.G. Agoo, K.W. Naing, D.V. Nguyen, D.K. Medhi, and P.J. Matthews 2020. Evolutionary origins of taro (*Colocasia esculenta*) in Southeast Asia. *Ecology and Evolution* 10(23):13530–13543. doi.org/10.1002/ece3.6958.

AlQahtani, S.J., M.P. Hector, and H.M. Liversidge 2010. The London atlas of human tooth development and eruption. *American Journal of Physical Anthropology* 142:481–490. doi.org/10.1002/ajpa.21258.

Ambrose, S.H. and L. Norr 1993. Experimental evidence for the relationship of the carbon isotope ratios of whole diet and dietary protein to those of bone collagen and carbonate. In J.B. Lambert and G. Grupe (eds), *Prehistoric human bone: Archaeology at the molecular level*, pp. 1–37. Springer-Verlag, Berlin. doi.org/10.1007/978-3-662-02894-0_1.

Bailey, R.C., G. Head, M. Jenike, B. Owen, and R. Rectman 1989. Hunting and gathering in tropical rainforests: Is it possible? *American Anthropologists* 91:59–82. doi.org/10.1525/aa.1989.91.1.02a00040.

Bryant, J.D., P.L. Koch, P.N. Froelich, W.J. Showers, and B.J. Genna 1996. Oxygen isotope partitioning between phosphate and carbonate in mammalian apatite. *Geochimica et Cosmochimica Acta* 60:5145–5148. doi.org/10.1016/S0016-7037(96)00308-0.

Calvin M. and A.A. Benson 1948. The patch of carbon in photosynthesis. *Science* 107:476–480. doi.org/10.1126/science.107.2784.476.

Cormie, A.B. and H.P. Schwarcz 1996. Effects of climate on deer bone δ15N and δ13C: Lack of precipitation effects on δ15N for animals consuming low amounts of C4 plants. *Geochimica et Cosmochimica Acta* 60(21):4161–4166. doi.org/10.1016/S0016-7037(96)00251-7.

Denham, T.P and M. Donohue 2009. Pre-Austronesian dispersal of banana cultivars west from New Guinea: Linguistic relics from eastern Indonesia. *Archaeology in Oceania* 44(1): 18–28. doi.org/10.1002/j.1834-4453.2009.tb00041.x.

Denham, T.P., S.G. Haberle, C. Lentfer, R. Fullagar, J. Field, M. Therin, N. Porch, and B. Winsborough 2003. Origins of agriculture at Kuk Swamp in the Highlands of New Guinea. *Science* 301:189–193. doi.org/10.1126/science.1085255.

DeNiro, M.J. 1985. Postmortem preservation and alteration of *in vivo* bone collagen isotope ratios in relation to palaeodietary reconstruction. *Nature* 317(6040):806–809. doi.org/10.1038/317806a0.

Djami, E. 2015. Penelitian terpadu di situs Srobu, Kelurahan Abe pantai—Distrik Abepura, Jayapura. Balai Arkeologi, Jayapura. Research report. Unpublished. Balai Arkeologi Papua, Jayapura.

Djami, E., H. Suroto, Z. Mas'ud, B. Mene, and K.M. Marani 2016. Rekonstruksi Bangunan Megalitik di Situs Srobu Kelurahan Abepantai—Distrik Abepura, Jayapura. Research report. Unpublished. Balai Arkeologi Papua, Jayapura.

Djami, E., H. Suroto, S.M. Kawer, B. Mene, K.M. Marani, and Konstantina 2017. Pola Spasial Situs Srobu Kelurahan Abepantai—Distrik Abepura, Jayapura. Research report. Unpublished. Balai Arkeologi Papua, Jayapura.

Djami, E., H. Suroto, S.M. Kawer, B. Mene, and K.M. Marani 2018. Pola Spasial Situs Srobu, Bagian II, Kelurahan Abepantai—Distrik Abepura, Jayapura. Research report. Unpublished. Balai Arkeologi Papua, Jayapura.

Djami, E., D.A. Tanudirjo, T. Koesbardiati, S.M. Kawer, T. Ngaderman, A.D. Setiawan, H.T. Siagian, and A. Bauw 2019. Akulturasi Budaya Austronesia—Australomelanesid di Situs Srobu Kelurahan Abepantai —Distrik Abepura, Jayapura. Research report. Unpublished. Balai Arkeologi Papua, Jayapura.

Draper, H.H. 1977. The aboriginal Eskimo diet in modern perspective. *American Anthropologist* 79:309–316. doi.org/10.1525/aa.1977.79.2.02a00070.

Dupras, T.L. 2007. Reconstruction infant weaning histories at Roman period Kellis, Egypt using stable isotope analysis of dentition. *American Journal of Physical Anthropology* 134:63–74. doi.org/10.1002/ajpa.20639.

Fahy E., C. Deter, R. Pitfield, J.J. Miszkiewicz, and P. Mahoney 2017. Bone deep: Variation in stable isotope ratios and histomorphometric measurements of bone remodelling within adult humans. *Journal of Archaeological Science* 87:10–16. doi.org/10.1016/j.jas.2017.09.009.

Gaffney, D., G.R. Summerhayes, S. Luu, J. Menzies, K. Douglass, M. Spitzer, and S. Bulmer 2021. Small game hunting in montane rainforests: Specialised capture and broad spectrum foraging in the Late Pleistocene to Holocene New Guinea Highlands. *Quaternary Science Reviews* 253:106742. doi.org/10.1016/j.quascirev. 2020.106742.

Golson, J. 1985. Agricultural origins in Southeast Asia: A view from the east. In N. Misra and P. Bellwood (eds), *Recent advances in Indo-Pacific prehistory*, pp. 307–314. E.J. Bill, Leiden. doi.org/10.1163/ 9789004644472_046.

Golson, J. 1989. The origins and development of New Guinea agriculture. In D.R. Harris and G.C. Hillman (eds), *Foraging and farming: The evolution of plant exploitation*, pp. 678–687. Unwin Hyman, Boston.

Golson, J. 1991. The New Guinea Highlands on the eve of agriculture. *Bulletin of the Indo-Pacific Prehistory Association* 11:82–91.

Hatch, M.D. and C.R. Slack 1966. Photosynthesis by sugarcane leaves: A new carboxylaton reaction and the pathway of sugar formation. *Biochemical Journal* 101:103–111. doi.org/10.1042/bj1010103.

Hedges, R.E.M., J.G. Clement, C.D.L. Thomas, and T.C. O'Connell 2007. Collagen turnover in the adult femoral mid-shaft: Modeled from anthropogenic radiocarbon tracer measurements. *American Journal of Physical Anthropology* 133(2):808–816. doi.org/10.1002/ajpa.20598.

Hermenegildo, T., T.C. O'Connell, V.L. Guapindaia, and E.G. Neves 2017. New evidence for subsistence strategies of late pre-colonial societies of the mouth of the Amazon based on carbon and nitrogen isotopic data. *Quaternary International* 448:139–149. doi.org/10.1016/j.quaint.2017.03.003.

Hillson, S. 2003. *Dental anthropology.* Cambridge University Press, Cambridge.

Juanes, F., J.A. Buckel, and F.S. Scharf 2002. Feeding ecology of piscivorous fishes. In P.J.B. Hart and J.D. Reynolds (eds), *Handbook of fish biology and fisheries*, Vol. 1, pp. 267–279. Blackwell, Oxford. doi.org/ 10.1002/9780470693803.ch12.

Katzenberg, M.A. 2008. Stable isotope analysis: A tool for studying past diet, demography, and life history. In M.A. Katzenberg and S.R. Saunders (eds), *Biological anthropology of the human skeleton*, pp. 305–327. John Wiley and Sons, New York. doi.org/10.1002/9780470245842.ch13.

Kinaston, R., H. Buckley, A. Gray, B. Shaw, and H. Mandui 2013. Exploring subsistence and cultural complexes on the south coast of Papua New Guinea using palaeodietary analyses. *Journal of Archaeological Science* 40(2):904–913. doi.org/10.1016/j.jas.2012.09.002.

Kinaston, R.L., D. Anson, P. Petchey, R. Walter, K. Robb, and H. Buckley 2015. Lapita diet and subsistence strategies on Watom Island, Papua New Guinea: New stable isotope evidence from humans and animals. *American Journal of Physical Anthropology* 157(1):30–41. doi.org/10.1002/ajpa.22685.

Kusaka, S., F. Hyodo T. Yumoto, and M. Nakatsukasa 2010. Carbon and nitrogen stable isotope analysis on the diet of Jomon populations from two coastal regions of Japan. *Journal of Archaeological Science* 37:1968–1977. doi.org/10.1016/j.jas.2010.03.002.

Lee-Thorp, J.A. 2008. On isotopes and old bones. *Archaeometry* 50:925–950. doi.org/10.1111/j.1475-4754. 2008.00441.x.

Lee-Thorp, J.A, and N.J. van der Merwe 1987. Carbon isotope analysis of fossil bone apatite. *South African Journal of Science* 83:712–715.

Lee-Thorp, J.A., J.C. Sealy, and N.J. van der Merwe 1989. Stable carbon isotope ratio differences between bone collagen and bone apatite, and their relationship to diet. *Journal of Archaeological Science* 16:585–599. doi.org/10.1016/0305-4403(89)90024-1.

LeGeros, R.Z. 1991. *Calcium phosphates in oral biology and medicine.* Monographs in Oral Science 15. Karger, Basel.

Levin, N.E., T.E. Cerling, B.H. Passey, J.M. Harris, and J.R. Ehleringer 2006. A stable isotope aridity index for terrestrial environments. *Proceedings of the National Academy of Science* 103(30):11201–11205. doi.org/ 10.1073/pnas.0604719103.

Levin, N.E., S.W. Simpson, J. Quade, T.E. Cerling, and S.R. Frost. 2008. Herbivore enamel carbon isotopic composition and the environmental context of *Ardipithecus* at Gona, Ethiopia. In J. Quade and J.G. Wynn (eds), *The geology of early humans in the Horn of Africa*, pp. 215–234. Geological Society of American Special Paper 446. Geological Society of America, Boulder, Colorado. doi.org/10.1130/2008.2446(10).

Longinelli, A. 1984. Oxygen isotopes in mammal bone phosphate: A new tool for paleohydrological and paleoclimatological research. *Geochimica et Cosmochimica Acta* 48(2):385–390. doi.org/10.1016/0016-7037(84)90259-X.

Luz, B., Y. Kolodny, and M. Horowitz 1984. Fractionation of oxygen isotopes between mammalian bone-phosphate and environmental drinking water. *Geochimica et Cosmochimica Acta* 48(8):1689–1693. doi.org/ 10.1016/0016-7037(84)90338-7.

Luz, B. and Y. Kolodny 1985. Oxygen isotope variations in phosphate of biogenic apatites, IV: Mammal teeth and bones. *Earth and Planetary Science Letters* 75(1):2936. doi.org/10.1016/0012-821X(85)90047-0.

Mas'ud. Z. 2013. Ekskavasi di Situs Karas, Bagian II. Research report. Unpublished. Balai Arkeologi Papua, Jayapura.

Meier-Augenstein, W. 2018. *Stable isotope forensics: An introduction to the forensic application of stable isotope analysis.* Wiley, Chichester. doi.org/10.1002/9780470688762.

Meier-Augenstein, W. and A. Schimmelmann 2018. A guide for proper utilisation of stable isotope reference materials. *Isotopes in Environmental and Health Studies* 55(2):113–128. doi.org/10.1080/10256016.2018. 1538137.

Mene, B. 2014. Eksplorasi arkeologi di situs Srobu, Abepantai-Kecamatan Abepura, Jayapura. Research report. Unpublished. Balai Arkeologi Papua, Jayapura.

Minagawa, M. and E. Wada 1984. Stepwise enrichment of ^{15}N along food chains: Further evidence and the relation between δ^{15}N and animal age. *Geochimica et Cosmochimica Acta* 48:1135–1140. doi.org/10.1016/0016-7037(84)90204-7.

Nash, S.H., A. Bersamin, A.R. Kristal, S.E. Hopkins, R.S. Church, R.L. Pasker, B.R. Luick, G.V. Mohatt, B.B. Boyer, and D.M. O'Brien 2012. Stable nitrogen and carbon isotope ratios indicate traditional and market food intake in an indigenous circumpolar population. *Journal of Nutrition* 142(1):84–90. doi.org/10.3945/jn.111.147595.

O'Connell, T.C., C.J. Kneale, N. Tasevska, and G.G.C. Kuhnle 2012. The diet–body offset in human nitrogen isotopic values: A controlled dietary study. *American Journal of Physical Anthropology* 149:426–434. doi.org/10.1002/ajpa.22140.

Passey, B.H., T.E. Cerling, G.T. Schuster, T.F. Robinson, B.L. Roeder, and S.K. Krueger. 2005. Inverse methods for estimating primary input signals from time-averaged isotope profiles. *Geochimica et Cosmochimica Acta* 69(16):4101–4116. doi.org/10.1016/j.gca.2004.12.002.

Petocz, R.G. 1989. *Conservation and development in Irian Jaya: A strategy for rational resource utilization.* E.J. Brill, Leiden. doi.org/10.1163/9789004642973.

Powell, J.M. 1976. Ethnobotany. In K. Paijmans (ed.), *New Guinea vegetation*, pp. 106–183. CSIRO and Australian National University Press, Canberra.

Prowse, T., R. Stark, and M. Emery 2019. Stable isotope analysis and human migration in the ancient Mediterranean and Near East. In J. Yoo, A. Zerbini, and C. Barron (eds), *Migration and migrant identities in the Near East from Antiquity to the Middle Ages*, pp. 125–152. Routledge, London. doi.org/10.4324/9781351254762-8.

Quade, J., J.M.L. Cater, T.P. Ojha, J. Adam, and T.M. Harrison 1995. Late Miocene environmental change in Nepal and the Northern Indian Subcontinent: Stable isotopic evidence from spaleosols. *Geological Society American Bulletin* 107(12):1381–1397. doi.org/10.1130/0016-7606(1995)107<1381:LMECIN>2.3.CO;2.

Roberts, P. 2019. *Tropical forests in prehistory, history, and modernity.* Oxford University Press, Oxford. doi.org/10.1093/oso/9780198818496.001.0001.

Roberts, P., N. Perera, O. Wedage, S. Deraniyagala, J. Perera S. Eregama, A. Gledhill, M.D. Petraglia, and J.A. Lee-Thorp 2015. Direct evidence for human reliance on rainforest resources in late Pleistocene Sri Lanka. *Science* 347:1246–1249. doi.org/10.1126/science.aaa1230.

Roberts, P. and M. Petraglia 2015. Pleistocene rainforests: Barriers or attractive environments for early human foragers? *World Archaeology* 47(5):718–739. doi.org/10.1080/00438243.2015.1073119.

Roberts, P., D. Gaffney, J. Lee-Thorp, and G. Summerhayes 2017. Persistent tropical foraging in the highlands of terminal Pleistocene/Holocene New Guinea. *Nature Ecology & Evolution* 1(3):0044. doi.org/10.1038/s41559-016-0044.

Roberts, P., J. Louys, J. Zech, C. Shipton, S. Kealy, S. Samper Carro, S. Hawkins, C. Boulanger, S. Marzo, B. Fiedler, N. Boivin, Mahirta, K. Aplin, and S. O'Connor 2020. Isotopic evidence for initial coastal colonization and subsequent diversification in the human occupation of Wallacea. *Nature Communications* 11(1):2068. doi.org/10.1038/s41467-020-15969-4.

Roberts, P., K. Douka, M. Tromp, S. Bedford, S. Hawkins, L. Bouffandeau, J. Ilgner, M. Lucas, S. Marzo, R. Hamilton, W. Ambrose, D. Bulbeck, S. Luu, R. Shing, C. Gosden, G.R. Summerhayes, and M. Spriggs 2022. Fossils, fish and tropical forests: Prehistoric human adaptations on the island frontiers of Oceania. *Philosophical Transactions of the Royal Society B* 377(1849):20200495. doi.org/10.1098/rstb.2020.0495.

Schoeninger, M.J and M.J. DeNiro 1984. Nitrogen and carbon isotopic composition of bone collagen from marine and terrestrial animals. *Geochemica et Cosmochimica Acta* 48:625–639. doi.org/10.1016/0016-7037(84)90091-7.

Schoeninger, M.J and K. Moore 1992. Bone stable isotope studies in archaeology. *Journal of World Prehistory* 6:247–296. doi.org/10.1007/BF00975551.

Schweissing, M.M. 2004. *Strontium-Isotopeanalyse (87Sr/86Sr). Eine archäometrische Applikation zur Klärung anthropologisher und archäologischer Fragestellungen in Bezug auf Migration und Handel.* Munchner Geologische Hefte, A 31, Munchen.

Shaw, B.J., G.R. Summerhayes, H.R. Buckley, and J.A. Baker 2009. The use of strontium isotopes as an indicator of migration in human and pig Lapita populations in the Bismarck Archipelago, Papua New Guinea. *Journal of Archaeological Science* 36(4):1079–1091. doi.org/10.1016/j.jas.2008.12.010.

Shaw, B., H. Buckley, G.R. Summerhayes, D. Anson, S. Garling, F. Valentin, H. Mandui, C. Stirling, and M. Reid 2010. Migration and mobility at the Late Lapita site of Reber–Rakival (SAC), Watom Island using isotope and trace element analysis: A new insight into Lapita interaction in the Bismarck Archipelago. *Journal of Archaeological Science* 37(3):605–613. doi.org/10.1016/j.jas.2009.10.025.

Shaw, B., H. Buckley, G.R. Summerhayes, C. Stirling, and M. Reid 2011. Prehistoric migration at Nebira, south coast of Papua New Guinea: New insights into interaction using isotope and trace element concentration analyses. *Journal of Anthropological Archaeology* 30(3):344–358. doi.org/10.1016/j.jaa.2011.05.004.

Shaw, B., S. Hawkins, L. Becerra-Valdivia, C.S. Turney, S. Coxe, V. Kewibu, J. Haro, K. Miamba, M. Leclerc, M. Spriggs, and K. Privat 2022. Frontier Lapita interaction with resident Papuan populations set the stage for initial peopling of the Pacific. *Nature Ecology & Evolution* 6:802–812. doi.org/10.1038/s41559-022-01735-w.

Spriggs, M. 1997. *The Island Melanesians.* Blackwell Publishers, Oxford.

Summerhayes, G.R., M. Leavesley, A. Fairbairn, H. Mandui, J. Field, A. Ford, and R. Fullager 2010. Human adaptation and plant use in highland New Guinea 49,000 to 44,000 years ago. *Science* 330(6000):78–81. doi.org/10.1126/science.1193130.

Summerhayes, G.R., J.H. Field, B. Shaw, and D. Gaffney 2017. The archaeology of forest exploitation and change in the tropics during the Pleistocene: The case of Northern Sahul (Pleistocene New Guinea). *Quaternary International* 448:14–30. doi.org/10.1016/j.quaint.2016.04.023.

Suroto, H. 2016. Budaya Austronesia di kawasan Danau Sentani (Austronesian culture in the Lake Sentani Area). *Papua* 8(2):121–128. doi.org/10.24832/papua.v8i2.182.

Suroto, H., E.N.I. Djami, and K. Fairyo 2012. Ekskavasi di Situs Karas. Research report. Unpublished. Balai Arkeologi Papua, Jayapura.

Sutton, A., M.-J. Mountain, K. Aplin, S. Bulmer, and T. Denham 2009. Archaeozoological records for the highlands of New Guinea: A review of current evidence. *Australian Archaeology* 69(1):41–58. doi.org/10.1080/03122417.2009.11681900.

Trites, A.W. 2019. Marine mammal trophic levels and trophic interactions. In J.K. Cochran, H.J. Bokuniewicz, and P.L. Yager (eds), *Encyclopedia of ocean sciences, Volume 1: Marine biogeochemistry.* 3rd edition, pp. 589–594. Elsevier, Amsterdam. doi.org/10.1016/B978-0-12-409548-9.11618-5.

Tykot, R.H. 2016. Isotope analyses and the histories of maize. In J.E. Staller, R.H. Tykot, B.F. Benz (eds), *Histories of maize in Mesoamerica: Multidisciplinary approaches*, pp. 130–141. Routledge, New York.

van der Merwe, N.J. and E. Medina 1991. The canopy effect, carbon isotope ratios and foodwebs in Amazonia. *Journal of Archaeological Science* 18(3):249–259. doi.org/10.1016/0305-4403(91)90064-V.

White, C.D., M.W. Spence, H.L.Q. Stuart-Williams, and H.P. Schwarcz 1998. Oxygen isotopes and the identification of geographical origins: The valley of Oaxaca versus the valley of Mexico. *Journal of Archaeological Science* 25(7):643–655. doi.org/10.1006/jasc.1997.0259.

Wright L.E. and H.P. Schwarcz 1998. Stable carbon and oxygen isotopes in human tooth enamel: Identifying breastfeeding and weaning in prehistory. *American Journal of Physical Anthropology* 106:1–18.

Yen, D.E. 1971. The development of agriculture in Oceania. In R.C. Green and M. Kelly (eds), *Studies in Oceanic culture history*, Vol. 2, pp. 1–12. Pacific Anthropological Records No. 12. Bernice P. Bishop Museum, Honolulu.

Yen, D.E. 1973. The origins of Oceanic agriculture. *Archaeology and Physical Anthropology in Oceania* 8:68–85.

Yen, D.E.,1996. Melanesian arboriculture: Historical perspectives with emphasis on the genus Canarium. In M.L. Stevens, R.M. Bourke, and B.R. Evans (eds), *South Pacific indigenous nuts*, pp. 36–44. Australian Centre for International Agricultural Research, Canberra.

11

Rock art from caves in the Keerom Regency, Papua Province

Klementin Fairyo
Translated by Marlin Tolla and Dylan Gaffney

Abstract

The rock paintings of Keerom Regency have not been previously researched. The purpose of this study is to describe the different forms of rock paintings in Keerom, near the border between Indonesia and Papua New Guinea, in relation to their social function and current meaning to the indigenous people who inhabit the surrounding area. A literature review and interviews with local stakeholders supplement the morphological and pictorial analyses of each painting site. The results of this analysis show that rock paintings in Keerom Regency consist of both figurative and non-figurative motifs, especially at the sites of Web and Kibay. The present meaning of these rock paintings to the local people in the Keerom Regency is tightly connected with religion and social communication. For the indigenous people in this area, the rock paintings are symbols of identity and important cultural elements that are used to preserve social boundaries and territory.

Abstrak

Tulisan dalam bab ini mengangkat topik lukisan cadas yang terdapat di dinding gua Web dan Kibay di Kabupaten Keerom, di wilayah perbatasan antara Indonesia dan Papua New Guinea. Tujuan dari penelitian ini adalah untuk mendeskripsikan berbagai lukisan cadas di Kabupaten tersebut yang belum pernah diteliti sebelumnya. Studi literatur dan wawancara dilakukan untuk mengetahui arti penting motif figuratif dan non-figuratif lukisan bagi masyarakat adat. Hasil yang didapatkan menunjukkan adanya fungsi keagamaan dan sebagai komunikasi sosial, simbol identitas kesukuan, serta sebagai elemen budaya dalam kaitannya dengan kepemilikan sebuah wilayah dan tanda batasan sosial antar suku yang berbeda.

Introduction

Rock art in Papua Province has been recorded on cave walls, cliffs, and large boulders. The rock art has been produced using several techniques including painting, scratching, stamping, spraying, and engraving, which were applied in accordance with the imagination and cultural concepts of the makers (Arifin 1992). In many parts of Indonesia, rock paintings were created by prehistoric hunter-gatherer groups since the Late Pleistocene, and are found in the most remote areas of Sumatra, Borneo, Sulawesi, Timor, and Maluku (e.g. Aubert et al. 2007, 2014, 2018; Notosusanto and Poesponegoro 1993). In Papua New Guinea, rock art may be related to Pleistocene hunter-gatherers as well as more recent cultivators and traders in the Late Holocene (e.g. Lamb et al. 2021; Tsang et al. 2020). The chronology, cultural associations, and symbolic meaning of rock art in West New Guinea (Indonesian Papua), however, remain almost totally unknown, despite some recording being undertaken in Papua Barat Province and the Baliem Valley (e.g. Arifin and Delanghe 2004; Ballard 2005). Among modern people in West New Guinea, rock art is generally connected to important ceremonies including burial rites, fertility rituals, and initiations, and may also be related to shamanism. According to van Baal (1971), cited in Arifin (1992), rock art produced by prehistoric people was similarly based on supernatural experiences that were believed to influence and protect human life. This chapter examines rock art in Keerom Regency, Papua Province, for the first time. In the first instance, the research describes the rock art sites and their associated motifs and explores their symbolic meaning for present-day inhabitants, with implications for the prehistoric past.

Rock art in Papua Province and Keerom Regency

As noted by Gaffney and Tolla (Chapter 2, this volume), the first description of rock paintings in Papua was made in the seventeenth century by European explorers. In 1678, Johannes Keyts, a Dutch merchant sailor, discovered rock paintings with various motifs on the cliffs of the Bird's Head of New Guinea (Arifin and Delanghe 2004, 49). Subsequently, rock paintings have also been found in Fakfak, Kaimana, Misool, Roon Island, Jayapura, Sentani, Keerom Regency, and Wamena by Dutch, German, American, and Indonesian scholars, and later by the Balai Arkeologi Papua[1] (Papua Centre of Archaeology).

In Keerom Regency, at the border between Indonesia and Papua New Guinea, rock art was first reported by Galis in 1957, who found paintings in Gumamit Cave and Pinfelu, located 75 km south of Jayapura. The rock paintings in these two caves consisted of images like lizards and abstract motifs (Galis 1957; see also Arifin 1992). Later, Koyafi (1976) reported rock paintings that he found in the Web and Yaffi areas, but he provided no further information in his report. Other information about rock paintings in Keerom Regency was obtained from Dian Wellip, an anthropologist from Universitas Cenderawasih. He confirmed that there are rock paintings covering the caves walls in Yuruf and Web districts of Keerom Regency. Based on these reports, in 2011 the Papua Centre of Archaeology undertook an archaeological survey in Web District, which located rock paintings scattered around the cliffs of caves in this area, including at Yadumblu Cave, Kwarpei, Kubiyam, and Gumumblu (Fairyo 2011). The motifs of the rock paintings were similar to those reported by Galis in the Gumamit and Pinfelu caves, consisting of lizards, suns, masks, hourglass drums, human footprints, spirals, abstracts, and geometrics. At the present time, similar motifs like drums, lizards, and spirals are still used as symbols for decorating traditional clothes in this area.

---

1   Bahasa Indonesia words are underlined at first mention. Local language words are italicised.

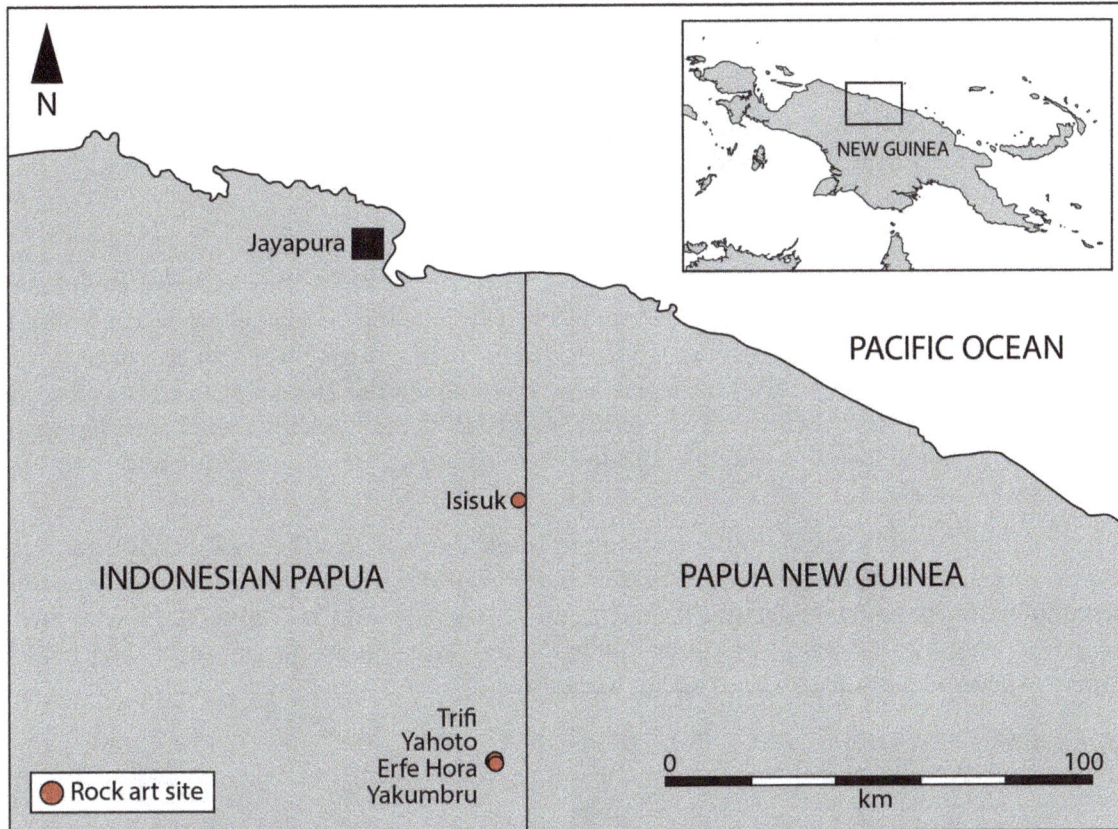

Figure 11.1: The distribution of caves with rock paintings known in Keerom Regency, Papua.

Source: Dylan Gaffney.

New information about unrecorded rock paintings in Web District and East Arso District came to light during interviews with local people in 2016 (Figure 11.1). Based on this information, a renewed survey was conducted in these areas and rock paintings were found on cave walls near Kibay village, East Arso District, and Yuruf village, Web District. The results of the 2016 survey of these rock art sites will now be described and discussed in relation to the painted designs and the meaning ascribed by indigenous people to those symbols, many of which are today used in cultural activities.

New descriptions of rock art in Keerom

Method of analysis

In this study, two different approaches were used to study the rock paintings. A semiotic approach was used to interpret the meaning and the function of the rock paintings in the prehistoric past (e.g. Conkey 2001). In addition, the ethnographical approach (following Tanudirjo 2009) was used to provide explanations about the rock painting designs through the interpretation provided by the indigenous people in this area. Data recording included morphological analysis, technological analysis, and pictorial recording methods.

Identification and classification of rock paintings

The distribution of the rock paintings in Kibay village and Yuruf village can be seen on the map in Figure 11.1. The rock paintings around Kibay village include Isisuk site, and around Yuruf village include Erfe Hora, Trifi, Yahoto, and Yakumbru caves.

Isisuk

The Isisuk site is located at South 03° 04'01.7" and East 140° 59'01.8". This rock-shelter and cave site faces east in the Kibay village area, Eastern Arso District. Rock paintings are situated on the shelter walls, which are 17 m high and 15 m wide. Today, the site is owned by the Kuntui and Psakor clans and the caves are used by people who travel around this area between Kibay village to the border of Papua New Guinea and vice versa. As such, more recent pictures and names of people using the site are also found on the cliffs. In addition to paintings, animal bones and teeth were also found on the cave floor.

Based on the form and shape of the rock painting at Isisuk, the images can be classified into figurative and non-figurative designs. In addition, several images were difficult to identify because of natural degradation. In the figurative group, the images consist of hands and feet (Figure 11.2), while non-figurative images consist of one spiral, one geometric, and three abstract images. All of these images appear to have been painted by hand using charcoal.

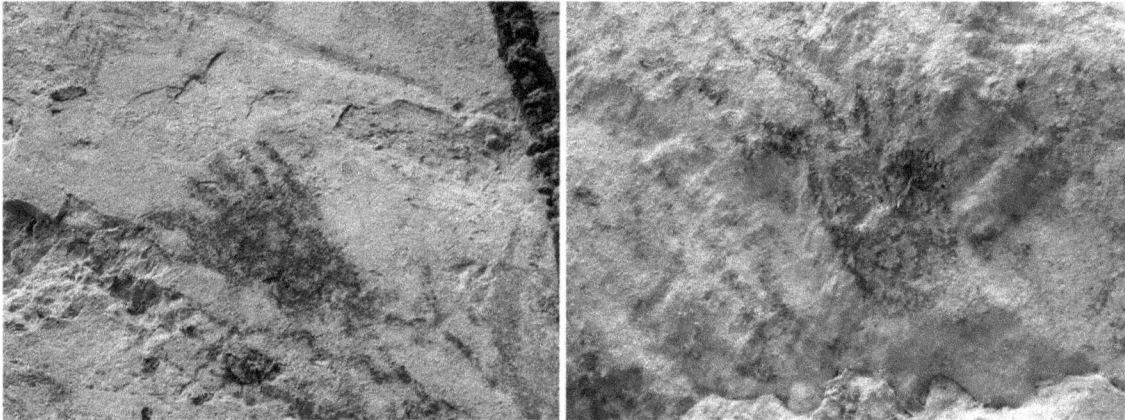

Figure 11.2: Images of human feet, Isisuk Cave.
Source: Photo by Klementin Fairyo.

Erfe Hora

The Erfe Hora Cave is located in the area of Watai clan; it is located at South 03° 34'55.8" and East 140° 55'27.4" in the Yuruf village area. This cave is formed from limestone 30 m high by 15 m wide, facing a north-east direction. Rock paintings found on the cave wall are all non-figurative forms (Figure 11.3), although some of the motifs could not be identified. Eight types of non-figurative designs were recognised, which consist of lines and abstract images, formed irregularly on the cave walls.

Figure 11.3: Rock paintings at Erfe Hora Cave.

Source: Photo by Klementin Fairyo.

Trifi

The Trifi site is located at South 03° 34'55.8" and East 140° 55'27.4" in the Yuruf village area, in the territory of Sumel clans. The cave is formed from limestone; it is 3 m in height, and 21 m in width, and the length from the end of the chamber to the cave entrance is 13 m. Rock paintings were found on the cave walls, ceilings, and crevices and consist of figurative, non-figurative, and unidentified designs. The figurative objects consist of lizards, turtles, fish, string bags, and flowers, while 41 non-figurative images have been identified consisting of circles, lines, suns, spirals, and abstract designs (Figure 11.4).

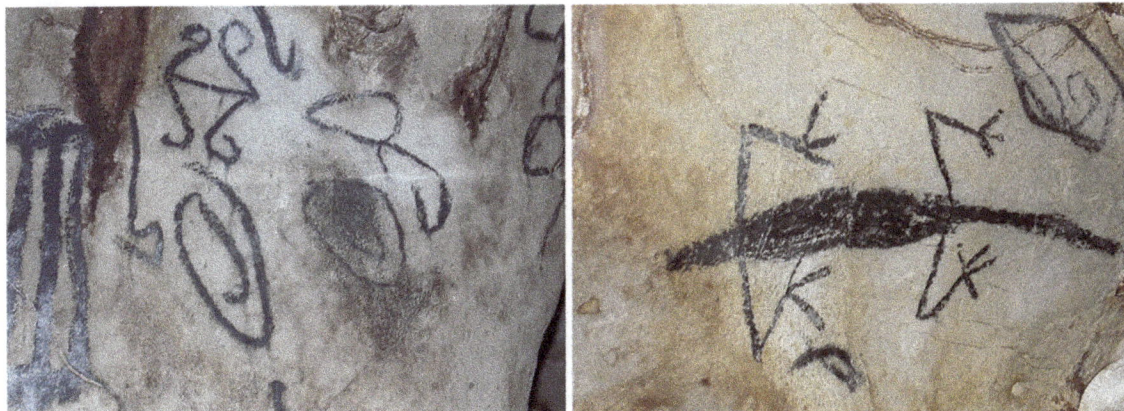

Figure 11.4: Rock paintings at Trifi Cave.

Notes: Left, non-figurative designs; right, figurative designs.

Source: Photo by Klementin Fairyo.

Yakumbru

This cave (also known as Bandi) faces south and is located at South 03° 34'48.4" and East 140° 55'37.0", 315 m from Erfe Horo. The length of the chamber from the cave entrance is 3 m. Again, rock paintings include figurative and non-figurative designs. The figurative designs are snake-like, while the non-figurative design is a circle (Figure 11.5).

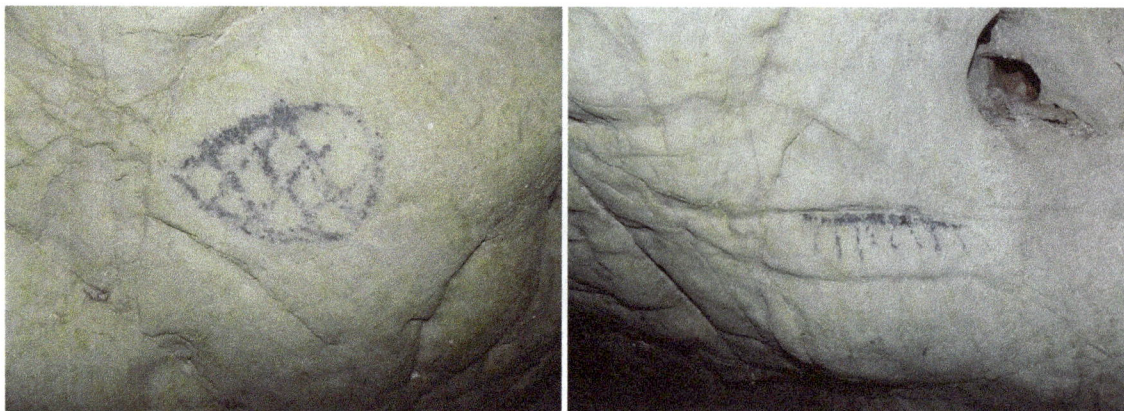

Figure 11.5: The rock paintings in Yakumbru Cave.

Source: Photo by Klementin Fairyo.

Yahoto

Yahoto Cave is formed from limestone, at South 03° 34'44.1" and East 140° 55'53.7", facing a north-eastern direction. The site is 620 m from Yakumbru. There are three irregular chambers in this cave, where both figurative and non-figurative images have been painted (Figure 11.6). The figurative images include human feet, hands, faces, string bags, and lizards made with black pigment, while 18 non-figurative images consist of circles, abstracts, and pig bones made from black and red pigment. The material used for colouring the red images may be made from laterite stone, found in the river nearby this site.

Figure 11.6: Red and black rock paintings at the Yahoto Cave.

Source: Photo by Klementin Fairyo.

Meaning and function of rock painting images

The following descriptions of meaning and function ascribed to the Keerom rock paintings derive from interviews with local stakeholders. This provides a modern interpretation of the rock art symbolism in the area that may, or may not, be similar to the meaning given to the art in the archaeological past. Where possible, common meanings ascribed to similar designs from other parts of West New Guinea are also mentioned.

Human foot

The motif of the human foot at Isisuk and Yahoto caves may indicate that people had travelled long distances by foot through valleys and mountains before reaching the shelters. These footprints may indicate the first people to pass through the area, or the ancestors who made the rock paintings, were 'walkers' (Fairyo 2013). In addition, the meaning of the handprint is likened to 'protective hands', namely the spirits of the ancestors placing their hands on the cave walls as a protection for their descendants (see also Röder 1939 in Arifin 1992).

Animal motifs

The fish image at Trifi Cave may be a sign requesting the ancestors to provide maximum results while the artists were fishing. Alternatively, it is possible that the design is a warning for others not to consume fish. Moreover, the fish image may have been used totemically to denote clan affiliations. The image of the turtle at Trifi Cave and the snake at Yakumbru Cave may be symbols of healing and might have been created by a sick person. If in their dreams the design appeared in the form of an animal or tree in a certain place, then the meaning of the dream would be interpreted that an inhabitant or spirit from that place was causing the illness. So as not to be forgotten, the design would be painted on the cave wall to show that there is a powerful spirit in that environment. The lizard paintings in Trifi Cave and Yahoto Cave may be symbols of fertility and healing. The image of a lizard on the cave walls often symbolised a promise to the ancestors to bless the garden and associated activities so that they could reap maximum results (Fairyo 2013).

Figure 11.7: Headdresses worn in the Yuruf and Kibay areas using symbols similar to those depicted in local rock art.

Source: Photo by Klementin Fairyo.

These lizard, fish, turtle, and spiral images are still used today by indigenous people in the Web District in the *Heru* ceremony as a form of respect for the symbols of the rock paintings. In the Heru ceremony, these images are painted on sago palm leaves, which are later used together with bird-of-paradise feathers as a headdress (Figure 11.7). Today, the decoration is a sign of liberation from the attachment to bad spirits, as well as a sign of respect for good spirits that are found in lizards, turtles, or fish, and which bring human prosperity and recovery from sickness.

Spiral images

The spiral design that is found at Trifi and Yahoto caves may symbolise fertility. The spiral symbols that exist throughout the human body, animals, plants, minerals, and the universe are the signs of the human life course that is constantly evolving. More broadly, this symbol is used to remind humans of the outer and inner evolution of all living things and to maintain balance and concentration of the human mind.

String bags

The knotted-net image that is found in the Trifi and Yahoto cave is rectangular in shape and contains three to four longitudinal lines. For Papuans, <u>noken</u> (string bags) are a symbol of both fertility and death (see Kanem, this volume). In daily life, string bags are used to transport babies while the mother moves from place to place. Besides that, string bags are also used as an accessory for women while performing traditional dances. Furthermore, in the contemporary culture of the people who live around these two sites, the meaning of string bags implies weaving together to achieve life's goals.

Circles

For the Yuruf groups who inhabit the area of Trifi Cave, the 'circle dot' image is a sign of land ownership.

Arrowhead image

For the groups who live around Isisuk Cave, the arrowhead image symbolises peace and is also a sign of aspiration for success in hunting activities.

The role of rock painting among the Yuruf and Kibay peoples

Based on the ethnographical study of the rock paintings in Keerom Regency, it can be determined that most of these images symbolise the cultural activities of the Yuruf and Kibay; whether these same meanings were given to the paintings as they were being produced, or if they are reinterpretations ascribed to existing art at the sites, the painted images are active participants in Yuruf and Kibay lives. The religious meanings of the art are tightly correlated to the worship of the ancestors. The Yuruf and Kibay peoples, as well as other groups in West New Guinea, have connections with an invisible world, in which anthropomorphic imagery plays an important role that strengthens the kinship to, and veneration of, the ancestors. These symbols are closely related to religion because they act as self-identity markers and materialise certain strengths (Geertz 1992). Moreover, rock art is a mode of communication, and it symbolises people's expression and connects them to the supernatural powers that surround them. These supernatural powers can help people protect their way of life on Earth. The social meanings contained in the rock painting of the Yuruf and Kibay also symbolise cooperation and brotherhood with other groups of people in their wider community. Both Yuruf and Kibay peoples have attachments to certain values and norms in their traditions that continue to be practised in their lives today.

For the Yuruf and Kibay, the rock paintings at Isisuk, Erfe Hora, Trifi, Yakumbru, and Yahoto are a legacy of their ancestors. According to the information gathered from my Yuruf and Kibay informants, their ancestors painted the images on the cave walls in the hope that they would succeed in their daily activities such as hunting and gathering animals and plants for food. The images came to their ancestors in dreams, and, after that, were painted on the cave walls. Besides that, the rock painting designs are the manifestation of supernatural powers that occupy areas around the caves.

Conclusion

The forms of rock paintings that are found in the Keerom Regency consist of figurative and non-figurative images such as human feet, human hands, human faces, lizards, fish, turtles, suns, spirals, circles, string bags, pig bones, arrowheads, and abstract designs. These rock paintings are the manifestation of ancestral people's cultural actions that represent their values in life. The existence of these rock paintings represents a bridge, connecting humans and supernatural powers around them, which are expected to protect human life. The meaning of the rock paintings to Yuruf and Kibay peoples today include fertility, healing, and death, and the images can be a mode of communication with supernatural powers, as well as markers of clan affiliation and territory. These meanings are still celebrated today and represent the identity of the indigenous people in Keerom Regency, as well as the defence of their territories. The images of the rock paintings are still found in Yuruf and Kibay peoples' cultural traditions, as can be seen in the ornaments that are used in the Heru dance ceremony. This chapter has provided provisional information about how rock art is interconnected with broader social and cosmological processes in Keerom—it is clear that more detailed analysis and ethnographical recording would provide an even richer story about the meaning that local people attach to rock art, as well as any possible connections between Keerom rock art and other art traditions around West New Guinea and Papua New Guinea.

References

Arifin, K. 1992. Lukisan Batu Karang di Indonesia Suatu Evaluasi Hasil Penelitian. Lembaga Penelitian Universitas, Depok.

Arifin, K. and P. Delanghe 2004. *Rock Art in West Papua*. UNESCO, Paris.

Aubert, M., S. O'Connor, M. McCulloch, G. Mortimer, A. Watchman, and M. Richer-LaFlèche 2007. Uranium-series dating rock art in East Timor. *Journal of Archaeological Science* 34(6):991–996. doi.org/10.1016/j.jas.2006.09.017.

Aubert, M., A. Brumm, M. Ramli, T. Sutikna, E.W. Saptomo, B. Hakim, M.J. Morwood, G.D. van den Bergh, L. Kinsley, and A. Dosseto 2014. Pleistocene cave art from Sulawesi, Indonesia. *Nature* 514(7521): 223–227. doi.org/10.1038/nature13422.

Aubert, M., P. Setiawan, A.A. Oktaviana, A. Brumm, P.H. Sulistyarto, E.W. Saptomo, B. Istiawan, T.A. Ma'rifat, V.N. Wahyuono, F.T. Atmoko, J.-X. Zhao, J. Huntley, P.S.C. Taçon, D.L. Howard, and H.E.A. Brand 2018. Palaeolithic cave art in Borneo. *Nature* 564(7735):254–257. doi.org/10.1038/s41586-018-0679-9.

Ballard, C. 2005. Rock art in West Papua. *Archaeology in Oceania* 40(2):78–80.

Conkey, M.W. 2001. Structural and semiotic approaches. In D. Whitley (ed.), *Handbook of rock art research*, pp. 273–310. Altamira Press, Walnut Creek.

Fairyo, K. 2011. Penelitian Arkeologi Prasejarah di Distrik Web, Kabupaten Keerom. Research report. Unpublished. Balai Arkeologi Jayapura, Jayapura.

Fairyo, K. 2013. Makna Simbol Lukisan dalam Gua Pada Aktifitas Budaya Orang Web di Kampung Yuruf Distrik Web Kabupaten Keerom. Research report. Unpublished. Universitas Cenderawasih, Jayapura.

Galis, K.W. 1957. *Ethnografische Notities over Het Senggi-Gebied*. Gouvernement van Nederlands Nieuw-Guinea, Kantoor voor Bevelkingszaken, Hollandia.

Geertz, C. 1992. *Kebudayaan dan Agama*. Kanisius, Yogyakarta.

Koyafi, A. 1976. Rite Heru dan Penggemblengannya dalam Liturgi Paskah pada Orang Dra Di Amgotro/ Keerom. STTK thesis. Anthropology Institute, Universitas Cenderawasih, Abepura.

Lamb, L., B. Barker, M. Leavesley, M. Aubert, A. Fairbairn, and T. Manne 2021. Rock engravings and occupation sites in the Mount Bosavi Region, Papua New Guinea: Implications for our understanding of the human presence in the Southern Highlands. *Archaeology in Oceania* 56(3):304–321. doi.org/10.1002/ arco.5247.

Notosusanto N. and D.M. Poesponegoro 1993. *Sejarah Nasional Indonesia I*. Balai Pustaka, Jakarta.

Röder, J. 1939. Rock-pictures and prehistoric times in Dutch New Guinea. *Man* 39:175–78. doi.org/10.2307/ 2792120.

Tanudirjo, D.A. 2009. Memikirkan kembali etnoarkeologi. *Papua* 1(2):3–15.

Tsang, R., W. Pleiber, J. Kariwiga, S. Plutniak, H. Forestier, P.S.C. Taçon, F.-X. Ricaut, and M.G. Leavesley 2020. Rock art and long-distance prehistoric exchange behavior: A case study from Auwim, East Sepik, Papua New Guinea. *Journal of Island and Coastal Archaeology* 17(3):432–444. doi.org/10.1080/1556489 4.2020.1834472.

van Baal, J. 1971. *Symbols for communication: An introduction to the anthropological study of religion*. Van Gorcum, Assen.

12

Prehistoric sites in the western Lake Sentani area, Papua Province

Hari Suroto
Translated by Marlin Tolla and Dylan Gaffney

Abstract

The purpose of this study is to determine the factors underlying the selection of settlement locations, and the human activities supporting settlements, in the western Lake Sentani region. The chapter presents new field data, material analyses, and interpretations. The results show that the key variables underlying prehistoric residential site selection in western Sentani related to the lake itself in providing productive land for foraging and cultivation and a reliable freshwater source. Based on artefactual, ecofactual, and environmental information, the modes of human subsistence supporting these settlements included terrestrial hunting, fishing, the collecting of shellfish, and the gathering of sago. In addition, based on the findings of marine shells at the western Sentani sites, either the mobility range of Sentani groups connected them to the northern coastline of New Guinea, or people obtained shells by trade with coastal communities.

Abstrak

Tulisan ini menyajikan beberapa situs pemukiman prasejarah di wilayah danau Sentani bagian barat serta mengulas faktor-faktor yang mendasari persebarannya. Berdasarkan data artefaktual, ekofak, dan lingkungan yang di dapatkan dilapangan, pemilihan lokasi pemukiman oleh suku-suku yang berdiam di wilayah tersebut didasarkan pada beberapa fungsi yang bersifat praktis. Hal ini terdiri dari lahan produktif yang dapat diandalkan untuk pemenuhan kebutuhan pangan serta memiliki sumber air tawar yang berlimpah yang dapat mendukung kehidupan keseharian. Lahan yang subur inilah yang merupakan rumah bagi hewan dan tumbuhan untuk hidup yang selanjutnya merupakan sumber bahan makanan bagi manusia prasejarah pada masa lalu. Hal ini tercermin dari ekofak dan artefak yang ditemukan, dimana diketahui bahwa, aktifivitas yang dilakukan pada masa lalu erat kaitannya dengan kegiatan perburuan binatang darat, penangkapan ikan, pengumpulan kerang serta pengumpulan sagu. Selain itu, dari bukti arkeologi yang ada, diketahui bahwa adanya mobilitas yang ramai terjadi melalui perdagangan antara pendukung situs di wilayah Sentani bagian barat dengan manusia prasejarah yang mendiami daerah pesisir utara Papua yang ditandai dengan kerang laut yang ditemukan pada situs-situs di kawasan ini.

Introduction

This chapter uses archaeological evidence recently generated by the Balai Arkeologi Papua[1] (Papua Centre of Archaeology) to examine the nature of prehistoric settlement in the western part of Lake Sentani (Figures 12.1–12.2), located in Jayapura Regency on the north coast of West New Guinea (East 140°21'–140°50' and South 2°31'–2°41'). This lake covers approximately 9360 ha, making it the largest lake in Papua Province, and is located at an altitude of 75 m above sea level (asl), with islands scattered throughout the body of water. In terms of morphology, Lake Sentani extends 26.5 km from east to west, with a minimal width of 0.5–2 km around the Simproto (Simbara) Strait, and a maximal width of 10 km in the eastern part of the lake and 5 km in the west (Lukman and Fauzi 1991).

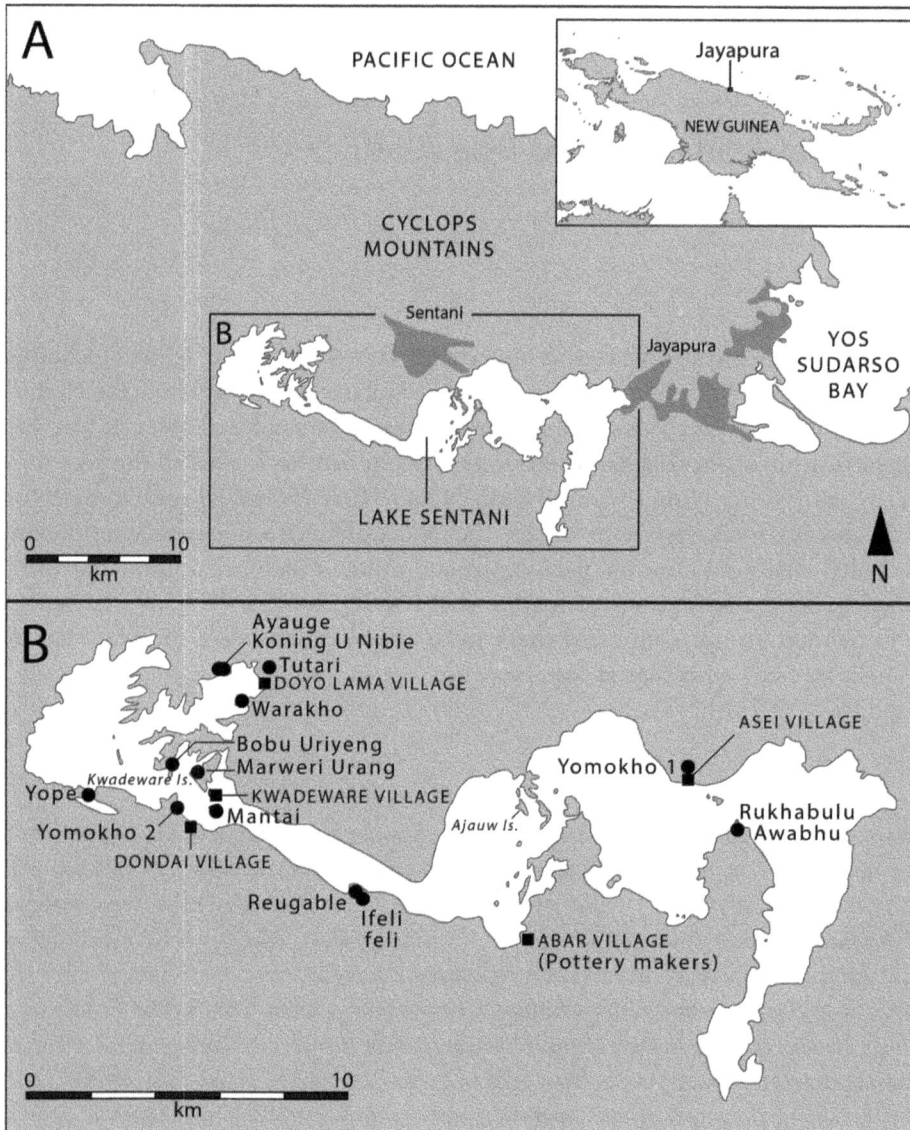

Figure 12.1: Map of Lake Sentani showing locations mentioned in the text.

Source: Map by Dylan Gaffney.

---

1   Bahasa Indonesia words are underlined and local language words are italicised at first mention. Other languages (e.g. French) are provided with single quote marks.

Figure 12.2: Western Lake Sentani.

Notes: (A) view over the lake; (B) stilt houses on the lake.

Source: Photos by Hari Suroto.

The indigenous people who occupy the Lake Sentani area speak the Sentani language, which is divided into three different dialects: *Rali bu* is spoken by the people inhabiting the eastern part of the lake. *Nolu bu* is spoken by Sentanians living around the central part of the lake. *Wai bu* is spoken around the western part of the lake (Mansoben 1995, 192). According to Sentani oral traditions, their ancestors came from the Sepik area of Papua New Guinea (Revassy 1989). During their initial arrival at Lake Sentani, these ancestors settled in three places: Yomokho Hill,[2] Ajauw Island, and Kwadeware Island. They later expanded and settled the shore and other islands of Lake Sentani (Dwiastoro 2009, 11).

Early archaeological research was conducted in 1979 in the Lake Sentani area by Pusat Penelitian Arkeologi Nasional (Indonesian National Research Centre for Archaeology, ARKENAS) in collaboration with a team from the Papua Centre of Archaeology (then called Balai Arkeologi Jayapura, Jayapura Centre of Archaeology). During this research, surveys were performed around the Tutari megalithic site to locate metal axes and glass beads corresponding to the wide distribution of these finds encountered by the local people around this site (Zaim and Haroen 1979). In 1994 and 1995, ARKENAS again conducted research at the Tutari megalithic site. Excavations were carried out by opening five boxes in the area where menhirs were standing, while another was implemented around a stone-ring complex. No artefacts or ecofacts were found in the excavation. The conclusion drawn from this excavation was that the Tutari megaliths primarily functioned as a ceremonial centre for the religion of local groups in the past (Prasetyo 2001, 43).

In 2010, a team from the Papua Centre of Archaeology conducted a survey in the Lake Sentani area for another research project: 'The Exploration of Prehistoric Archaeology in the Lake Sentani Area'. During the survey, several archaeological sites were found, consisting of both open sites and caves. The open sites include Yomokho 1, Marweri Urang, and Mantai, while three caves encountered around the lake shores comprised Rukhabulu Awabhu, Reugable, and Ifeli-feli. The research team also successfully collected data about glass beads, earthenware, stone bracelets, and bronze axes found by the local people around these sites (Balai Arkeologi Jayapura 2010). From 2011 to 2012, then continued in 2018, the Papua Centre of Archaeology focused its research on the eastern part of Lake Sentani by conducting excavations at the Yomokho 1 site. The aim of the excavation was to uncover early prehistoric settlements and their chronology (Suroto et al. 2011, 2012; radiocarbon dates and ceramic analyses will be the feature of future publications). From this excavation, it was concluded that settlements were built on the hilltop and the slopes of the Yomokho 1 site. In 2018, the Papua Centre of Archaeology further excavated one square metre at the top of the hill at Tutari, where

2   Yomokho 1 archaeological site.

pottery fragments were found in several sediment layers. In 2019, the Papua Centre of Archaeology's team conducted additional research with the project 'Early Prehistoric Settlement in the Western Part of Lake Sentani'. The team encountered pottery fragments, bronze axes, stone engravings, and stone mortars at two different open sites: Bobu Uriyeng and the Koning U Nibie site in this survey (Suroto 2019). Other sites surveyed included Warakho, Ayauge, and Yope, and another site, Yomokho 2,[3] was excavated. The following sections draw particularly from these archaeological sites excavated by the Papua Centre of Archaeology in the western part of Lake Sentani, providing a synthesis of key results and running interpretations about prehistoric occupation in the region.

Prehistoric sites around western Lake Sentani

Administratively, Lake Sentani's western part is in the Waibu District, Jayapura Regency, Papua Province, Indonesia. The eight archaeological sites were included in the Papua Centre of Archaeology fieldwork from 2018 to 2019, including Yomokho 2, the Tutari megalithic site, Warokho, Bobu Uriyeng, Yope, Koning U Nibie, and Ayauge. These seven sites are open sites distributed near the village neighbourhoods of Doyo Lama, Kwadeware, and Dondai.

Yomokho 2 site

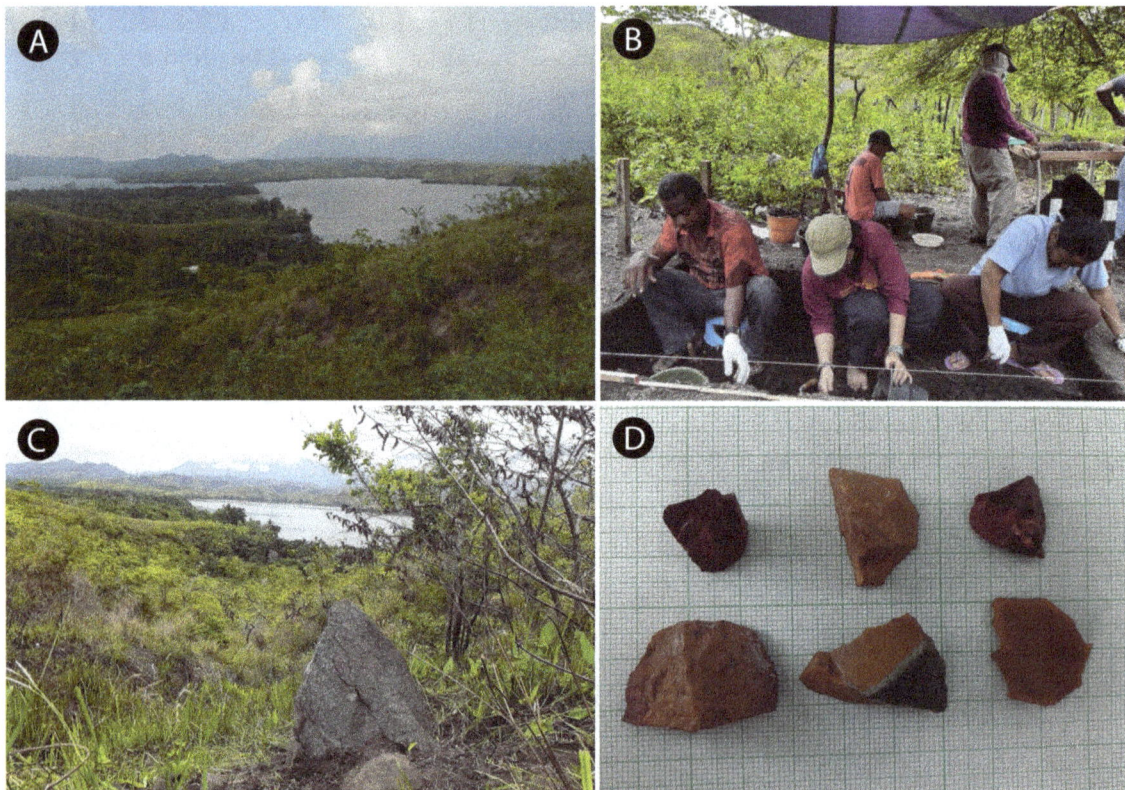

Figure 12.3: Yomokho 2 archaeological site.
Notes: (A) view of ridgeline; (B) excavations at Yomokho 2; (C) menhir from Yomokho 2; (D) flakes from Yomokho 2.
Source: Photos by Hari Suroto.

---

3   Around Lake Sentani, there are two archaeological sites named Yomokho. Yomokho 1, as it is labelled in Figure 12.1, is situated in the Asei village area and was excavated in 2011, 2012, and 2018. Yomokho 2, described in detail in this chapter, is located in the Dondai village area and was excavated by the Papua Centre of Archaeology in 2019.

Figure 12.4: Ceramics from Yomokho 2.

Source: Photos by Hari Suroto, compiled by Dylan Gaffney.

Yomokho 2 is an open site located near the western end of Dondai village. The hill is overgrown with weeds and guava trees and the flat area at the base of the hill near Lake Sentani is covered with mango trees and used as a cow shed (Figure 12.3). Pottery fragments were found distributed around almost all parts of this site; the hilltop ridgelines, on the hill slope, and in the flat areas at the base of the hill, with the eastern side of the hill being most densely covered (Figure 12.4). Freshwater shells (Thiaridae) and marine shells (Veneridae and Arcidae) associated with human bones were found in the eastern and southern hillsides. Stone sago pounders, stone axes, and stone net weights were also found distributed on the ground surface at this site. On the eastern side of Yomokho Hill, there is a megalith structure, which by its shape appears to be a dolmen with a large flat horizontal capstone or 'table'. The dolmen is oriented north–south (length 110 cm, width 58 cm, and thickness 10 cm), made from the peridotite stone, primarily found in the Cyclops Mountains, about 12 km north of the Dondai village area. A menhir was also found on the south-east slopes of Yomokho 2 hill (Figure 12.3C). This menhir is an unworked block of peridotite igneous rock, set upright, standing

100 cm high, 80 cm wide, and 20 cm thick. Furthermore, a stone arrangement extends roughly 3 m high from the base of the hill slope; it likely served as a staircase to climb the hill in prehistoric times. The upright menhirs and stone pathway at the site may have been used as a medium for worshipping ancestral spirits, as indicated by local groups regarding the Tutari megalithic site.

Two 2 × 1 m excavations were carried out at the base of the hill, following 10 cm spits. One excavation YMK/STN/KT1 was placed in a flat area that appeared undisturbed, near-surface finds of pottery. The site was excavated to about 150 cm below the surface and the final spit was reduced to 1 × 1 m (Spit 15). The upper layers were dry, coarse black soil, which graded into brownish-black clayey sediment towards the base of the deposit (Table 12.1). Pottery and bone were recorded down to Spit 13, about 130 cm deep. Charcoal samples from Spit 6 and Spit 12 at the excavation were dated at The Australian National University's Radiocarbon Laboratory, facilitated by Hsiao-chun Hung, and demonstrate that occupation occurred sometime between about 1300 to 300 years ago (Table 12.2; note that a pig tooth from Spit 11 provided no yield).

Table 12.1: Spit descriptions from YMK/STN/KT1 at Yomokho 2.

Spit	Depth below surface	Sediment description	Material
1	0–10 cm	Black, dense, dry sediment with roots and coarse texture.	Pottery, bone
2	10–20 cm	Black, dense, moist sediment mixed with limestone fragments, with roots. Coarse texture.	Pottery, teeth
3	20–30 cm	Black, moist sediment mixed with limestone. Coarse texture, dense and clayey.	Pottery, bones, teeth, lithic
4	30–40 cm	Black, moist sediment, coarse in texture. Dense and hard.	Pottery, bones, teeth
5	40–50 cm	Black, moist sediment. Dense and coarse.	Pottery, bones
6	50–60 cm	Black, dense, moist sediment. Rough and hard texture.	Pottery, bones, charcoal
7	60–70 cm	Brownish black, moist sediment. Coarse and clayey.	Pottery, bones, charcoal
8	70–80 cm	Brownish black, moist sediment. Dense and coarse clayey texture.	Pottery, bones
9	80–90 cm	Brownish black, wet sediment. Dense, coarse, clay.	Pottery, bones, teeth
10	90–100 cm	Brownish black, wet sediment. Coarse clay.	Pottery, bones, teeth, charcoal
11	100–110 cm	Brownish black, wet sediment. Dense, rough, and gritty.	Pottery, human bone, teeth
12	110–120 cm	Brownish black, wet sediment. Dense, rough, and gritty.	Pottery, bones, teeth, charcoal
13	120–130 cm	Brownish black, wet sediment. Dense, coarse clay.	Pottery, bones
14	130–140 cm	Dark brown, wet sediment. Dense, coarse, clay.	None
15	140–150 cm	Brownish black, wet sediment. Coarse clay.	None

Source: Author's summary.

Table 12.2: Radiocarbon determinations from Yomokho 2.

Lab code	Spit	Sample type	14C age	Calibrated BP
ANU-66611	6	Charcoal	354±22 BP	491–422 (43.6%)
				398–316 (51.8%)
ANU-66612	12	Charcoal	1323±23 BP	1297–1246 (55.1%)
				1212–1176 (40.4%)

Note: Calibrated at 2 sigma with OxCal 4.4. using IntCal2020.
Source: Author's summary.

Stone flakes found around the surface of the Yomokho 2 site (Figure 12.3D) are triangular in shape, produced by knapping cores made from chert. The lithic recorded from YMK/STN/KT1 Spit 3 is black and irregular in shape (further analysis is required to describe the geological origin of this artefact). Incomplete butt and blade fragments from stone axes were also found on the surface at Yomokho 2. Based on morphological reconstruction, the fragments derive from bifacial oval-shaped stone axes, formed gradually by following several working processes. The axes were made from peridotite rock like that found in the Cyclops Mountains.

Pig teeth were also collected during the survey and excavation from the Yomokho site. The discovery of pig teeth from this site reveals evidence that either domestic pigs were being kept at the site or that people were hunting feral pigs from the nearby area.

The Tutari megalithic site

This site is located in the Tutari hills, Doyo Lama village, and has been mapped showing six sectors of archaeological interest, denoting the presence of petroglyphs and standing stones (Figure 12.5). The pottery fragments encountered during a survey in Sector 4 at 166 m asl motivated the research team to open a 1 × 2 m excavation (box S6B2), again following 10 cm spits. The surface of the unit was overgrown by weeds and partially covered by eucalyptus tree roots and leaves. S6B2 was only excavated two spits deep: Spit 1 comprised a black topsoil, loose and dry, mixed with roots, overlying a blackish-brown hard and clayey sediment, that in turn overlayed a brown and hard clay; Spit 2 was a reddish-brown clay, hard and dense in texture. Pottery sherds were encountered in the first spit only, and no archaeological material was recovered from the second spit.

Based on the ceramic raw material, and the shapes and designs of rims, the pottery found at Tutari was considered to represent household equipment used for cooking and water storage. Other functions for the pottery at the Tutari site, suggested by indigenous people in the area, may have included ceremonial purposes, given the decorations on the sherds carry a symbolic meaning. X-ray diffraction (XRD) analysis was conducted at the Physics Laboratory, Makassar State University, on one fragment of archaeological pottery from Tutari and one modern sherd from Abar village, where pottery making is still performed today. The aim of the analysis was to determine the clay and non-plastic mineralogy of the sherds, to provide a very provisional understanding about the manufacturing origin of the pottery from Tutari. The results show that the Tutari archaeological pottery and the Abar pottery were mineralogically different (Figure 12.6). This result provisionally suggests that Tutari pottery production was distinct from that at Abar village. It is possible that the pottery from the Tutari site was produced from beyond the Lake Sentani area, or it could be that people using this site were able to make their own local pottery. However, these hypotheses need further investigation, especially because no large prehistoric settlements have yet been found around the Tutari site.

Figure 12.5: Tutari archaeological site map.

Notes: Insets: (A) standing menhirs; (B) excavation box S6B2 in Sector 4 of the site, showing the base of Spit 2; (C–E) petroglyphs at Tutari.

Source: Photos by Hari Suroto and Coralie Girard.

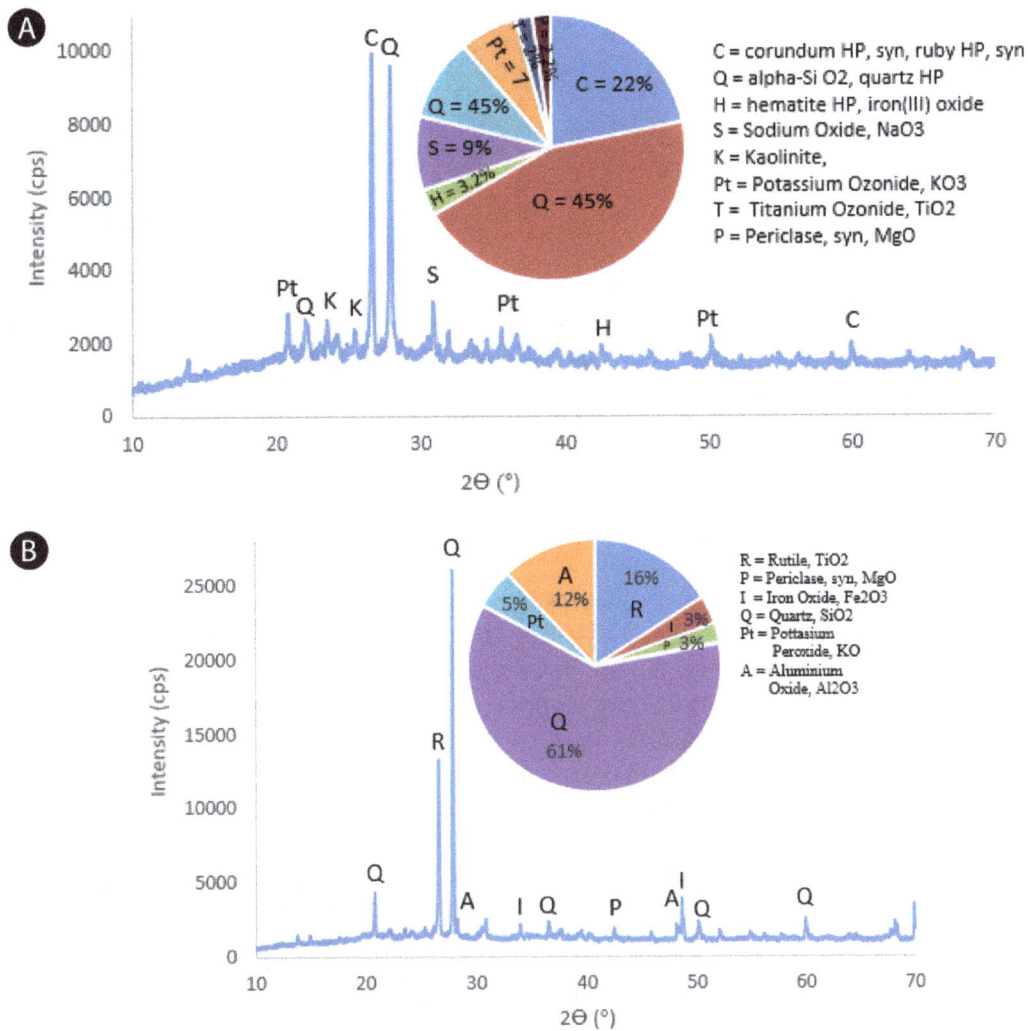

Figure 12.6: XRD results of (A) Tutari archaeological sherd and (B) Abar ethnographic pottery example.

Source: Plots by Hari Suroto.

Other sites around the western part of Lake Sentani

The Warakho site is located at Cape Warakho, Doyo Lama village area. This site is an open site, surrounded by the lake. The site's surface is overgrown by grass and bamboo, and partially overgrown by sago palms and mat-leaf trees. The surface material found at this site includes pottery sherds. In the past, the Warakho site was used as a settlement by the Doyo Lama community's ancestors when they moved from Kwadeware Island.

The Bobu Uriyeng site is located on a hill to the west of Kwadeware Island (Figure 12.7A). Pottery fragments were found during a surface survey on the hilltop, hillsides, and base of the hill. At this site, a bronze axe was accidentally encountered by Obed Wally (a local Sentanian person living in this area) during his gardening activity as he planted *siapu* (a root crop) on the hillside (Figure 12.7B). The bronze axe (13.5 cm long, 9.5 cm wide, and 1.5 cm thick) is crescent-shaped, with the simple wedge gradually developing into a flange. The bronze axe seems to have been produced using the 'cire perdue' wax casting technique.

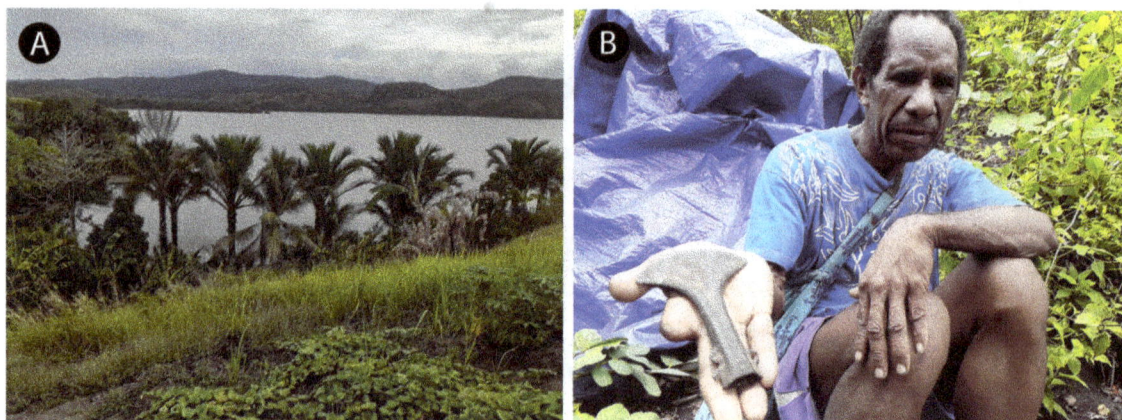

Figure 12.7: Bobu Uriyeng site.
Notes: (A) site surroundings; (B) Obed Wally with bronze axe find.
Source: Photos by Hari Suroto.

The Papua Centre of Archaeology found another site in the western part of Lake Sentani known as the Yope site (Figure 12.8A). *Yope* in the Sentani language means the place located in the bay of the lake. Administratively, it is part of the Dondai village area. The local people at Dondai believe that the Yope site was used as a settlement by their ancestors in the past. Fishermen who used to dive to catch fish found pottery fragments decorated with crocodile motifs and net weights made from burnt clay on the lake floor (Figure 12.8B). Based on the research results and interpretation of the surrounding environment, the Yope site may have been used as a settlement by a community of fishing people in the past, who built stilt houses above the surface of the lake.

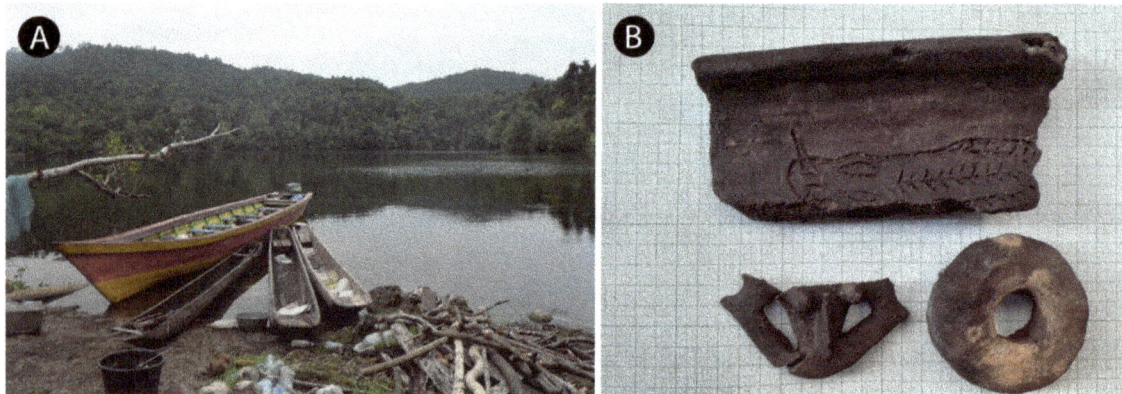

Figure 12.8: Yope site.
Notes: (A) site surroundings; (B) ceramics found by fishermen at Yope.
Source: Photos by Hari Suroto.

The Koning U Nibie site is located at the top of a hill in the Doyo Lama village area (Figure 12.9). Archaeological remains found at the Koning U Nibe Site include a large gabbro boulder that served as a mortar for grinding and a canvas for engravings. The stone mortar consists of a 17 cm semi-hemisphere that had been ground approximately in the centre of the boulder. The engraving is part of the same stone boulder as the mortar. The stone engraving at this site was decorated with geometric designs.

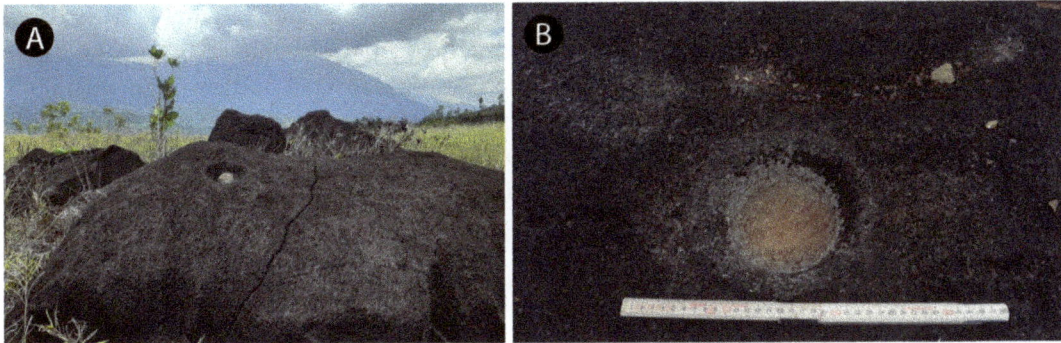

Figure 12.9: Koning U Nibie site.

Notes: (A) large natural mortar stone in wider surroundings; (B) area of wear on mortar stone.

Source: Photos by Hari Suroto.

Figure 12.10: Ayauge site.

Notes: (A) site surroundings; (B) submerged stilt house post; (C) ceramics from Ayauge.

Source: Photos by Hari Suroto.

The Ayauge site is also administratively located in Doyo Lama village area (Figure 12.10). Based on interviews with local people, this site was occupied by the people who moved from Kwadeware to the west. Exploration of the lake floor at this site successfully recovered pottery fragments, bone tools, and an arrowhead made from *soang* wood (*Xanthostemon* sp.). Several house posts made from soang wood have also been found at the Ayauge site, and local people say that this wood was used for making stilt houses in the past. Logs of these trees can last hundreds of years, so traditionally they were used as house posts by the Sentani people.

Discussion

Although research into past human behaviour in the western part of Lake Sentani is ongoing, we can begin to make some tentative statements about past lifestyles by analysing the excavated artefacts, mapping the ecofact distributions, and evaluating the environmental characteristics of the area. At least some periods of the prehistory of western Sentani were characterised by gathering lowland forest and freshwater resources, particularly from Lake Sentani and its surrounding hills. People's choice of settlement location was perhaps related to the central presence of Lake Sentani itself, which provides a ready source of food, including molluscs and fish. Besides that, Lake Sentani is also a source of clean drinking water.

The poles embedded in the water at the Ayauge site are the former pillars of stilt houses used by people in the past and are indicative of a lacustrine way of living. Based on their characteristics, the poles were made from the trunks of soang trees. At the present time, the soang tree only grows around the Cyclops Mountains to the north of Lake Sentani. This shows that humans around Lake Sentani were familiar with the specific wood types that were most useful for house-building components. Besides that, it shows that humans may have travelled around, or beyond, Lake Sentani to acquire the wood from further afield.

At Yomokho 2, the presence of freshwater shellfish further indicates some reliance on local resources from the lake itself. These shell remains were found associated with pottery sherds. However, because no sign of burning was found on the shell surfaces, boiling may have been chosen for shellfish processing in the past.

Prehistoric people's occupation at the Yope site was also based on considerations that the site is close to freshwater food sources such as fish and molluscs. Besides that, the Yope site's environment likely included the presence of good land for sago palms, used by humans as a source for carbohydrates and for construction material. The net weights for fishing found at the Yope site provide evidence of fishing activities in the past. Before the modern net for fishing was developed, the indigenous people in Lake Sentani used nets made from the bark of the *melinjo* tree. The crocodile motifs on the pottery fragments from the Yope site may indicate that the pottery was locally made, related to the current environment of the Yope site as a habitat for crocodiles (*Crocodylus novaeguineae*).

Since the western Sentani sites are located about 20 km from the north coast of New Guinea, prehistoric humans around the lake may have also been familiar with the maritime coast. The finding of marine shells around the settlement at Yomokho 2 suggests that either people were moving between the lake and the coast for shellfish procurement, or that exchange occurred between the people of Lake Sentani and coastal communities. The pottery fragments associated with marine molluscs at this site are considered to have been used for food consumption and cooking in the past. The artefactual findings, including pottery sherds, stone axes, and stone tools used for breaking the sago trunk, provide further evidence of sago processing for food consumption around western Sentani.

This evidence is also supported by the surrounding environment where sago trees are abundantly found today. Stone axes and other stone tools were likely used to cut sago palms, and pottery may have been used as vessels for the sago cooking process.

At Yomokho 2, the hunting (or husbandry) of terrestrial food such as pigs was undertaken to provide much-needed protein. Related to the presence of pigs, O'Connor and colleagues (2011) have stated that there are no scientific data that prove the existence of pigs on New Guinea before 4000 years ago. Although there are no precise data about the time of the introduction of pigs in the New Guinea Highlands, it is likely that they (along with dogs and chickens) were brought into New Guinea by Austronesian speakers between 3500 and 3000 years ago. The pig molars at the Yomokho 2 site, possibly dating before 1300 years ago, may then reflect the long history of Austronesian-speaking influences around the north coast, along with the ready uptake of these animals by locally established non-Austronesian speakers.

In terms of material culture, based on morphological characteristics, the bronze axe found at the Bobu Uriyeng site was identified as Dong Son, a type developed in northern Vietnam from 2400 to 2100 years ago and considered to be the result of a long-distance, down-the-line trade from Southeast Asia in prehistoric times (Swadling 2019). There is evidence of trading activities between Southeast Asia and New Guinea developing after the breakdown of the Lapita trading network about 2500 years ago and other similar bronze axes have previously been found in several locations in the Lake Sentani area (see Wright et al. 2013 for a review), making it distinct from other parts of New Guinea. The mortars and pestles in the Koning U Nibie site were used in food processing by past people. This interpretation was based on the shape analysis, which shows the deep depressions or damage to the area where the grinding and pounding of plant foods occurred. Stone engravings at Koning U Nibie and Tutari share motifs suggesting common designs were used in this part of western Sentani. Finally, based on observations of pottery fragments in the Ayauge site, the pottery thickness from this site has tentative similarities with the pottery found at the Tutari site. It is presently assumed that both potteries were made at the same production centre. This interpretation remains to be tested with further research.

Conclusion

The archaeological sites so far recorded from the western part of Lake Sentani include Yomokho 2, which provides evidence for settlement that occurred at least 1300 years ago (based on surface pottery; Warakho and Yope may be of a similar age). The Tutari site and the Koning U Nibie site present evidence for megalithic and petroglyphic activity which is presently undated. The Bobu Uriyeng site represents the period 2500 years ago when bronze began to be imported into the region. The main reason for selecting Lake Sentani for settlement in the past was presumably related to this area's ideal environmental factors. Lake Sentani provided its inhabitants with readily available freshwater food resources as well as drinking water. Based on the ecofacts and environmental characteristics of the area, human behaviour at the archaeological sites in Lake Sentani's western area was characterised by hunting (or husbandry) and gathering from lowland forest and freshwater zones for food and building resources. Marine shells in archaeological contexts at Yomokho 2 also provide evidence that people were either directly accessing the marine environment for food consumption or that they were trading with coastal groups. Ongoing archaeological research around Lake Sentani is focused on providing clarity about the timing and nature of human occupation in the area, alongside the nature of exchange within and beyond the lake.

References

Balai Arkeologi Jayapura 2010. Penelitian Arkeologi di Kawasan Danau Sentani. Research report. Unpublished. Balai Arkeologi Jayapura, Jayapura.

Dwiastoro, A. 2009. *Doors to the unknown: The story of Sentani in the Regency of Papua*. TSA Komunika, Jakarta.

Lukman, and H. Fauzi 1991. *Laporan Pra Survey Danau Sentani Irian Jaya, dan Wilayah Sekitarnya*. Puslitbang Limnologi-LIPI, Bogor.

Mansoben, J.R. 1995. *Sistem politik tradisional di Irian Jaya*. LIPI-RUL, Leiden.

O'Connor, S., A. Barham, K. Aplin, K. Dobney, A. Fairbairn, and M. Richards 2011. The power of paradigms: Examining the evidential basis for early to mid-Holocene pigs and pottery in Melanesia. *Journal of Pacific Archaeology* 2(2):1–25.

Prasetyo, B. 2001. *Pola Tata Ruang dan Fungsi Situs Megalitik Tutari, Kecamatan Sentani, Kabupaten Jayapura, Provinsi Irian Jaya*. Berita Penelitian Arkeologi No. 3. Departemen Pendidikan dan Kebudayaan, Jayapura.

Revassy, L. 1989. Kepemimpinan tradisional di Pedesaan Irian Jaya: Studi Kasus di desa Ajau Sentani-Jayapura. Unpublished PhD thesis. Fakultas Ilmu Sosial dan Ilmu Politik, Universitas Indonesia, Jakarta.

Suroto, H. 2019. Identifikasi Jejak Hunian Prasejarah di Danau Sentani Bagian Barat. Research report. Unpublished. Balai Arkeologi Papua, Jayapura.

Suroto, H., E.N.I. Djami, and M. Irfan Mahmud 2011. Ekskavasi dan Survei Arkeologi di Kawasan Danau Sentani. Research report. Unpublished. Balai Arkeologi Jayapura, Jayapura.

Suroto, H., K. Fairyo, and A. Putri 2012. Penelitian Arkeologi di Kawasan Danau Sentani. Research report. Unpublished. Balai Arkeologi Jayapura, Jayapura.

Swadling, P. 2019. *Plumes from Paradise: Trade cycles in outer Southeast Asia and their impact on New Guinea and nearby islands until 1920*. Sydney University Press, Sydney. doi.org/10.2307/j.ctv10vkzrf.

Wright, D., T. Denham, D. Shine, and M. Donohue 2013. An archaeological review of western New Guinea. *Journal of World Prehistory* 26(1):25–73. doi.org/10.1007/s10963-013-9063-8.

Zaim, Y. and Haroen 1979. Geologi Tinjau Sepanjang Jalan Genyem-Sentani-Jayapuradan Pulau-Pulau di Danau Sentani. Research report. Unpublished. Pusat Penelitian Arkeologi Nasional, Jakarta.

13

Decorated pottery from the Kayu Batu area, Jayapura

Klementin Fairyo
Translated by Marlin Tolla and Dylan Gaffney

Abstract

Pottery is one of the most frequently recovered artefacts from Papuan archaeological sites. These objects were used by prehistoric people in a variety of ways, such as for cooking, storing food, and also in the sphere of death (e.g. as grave goods). At three burial sites—Gua Tubara, Tubara Sugu, and Aturboyah Suwiyah—located on the shoreline and lying about 10 km from Jayapura city, pottery fragments from grave goods were found associated with human remains. The pottery sherds were richly decorated and most of the surfaces were covered with triangular and straight lines. Other patterns were characterised by design forms like arrows, and horizontal and circular incisions. This chapter provides a preliminary investigation of cultural affiliations of the pottery users and makers through the analysis of the decorative patterns and style of the pottery fragments, interpreted in the context of ethnographic and archaeological sources and additional information collected from local informants to provide complementary information about the pottery typology and morphology.

Abstrak

Gerabah atau tembikar merupakan salah satu jenis artefak yang paling sering ditemukan pada situs-situs arkeologi di Papua. Dalam penggunaanya, diperkirakan bahwa gerabah dimanfaatkan oleh manusia prasejarah pada masa lalu untuk menunjang aktivitas hidup. Hal ini berupa menunjang kegiatan memaasak, digunakan untuk menyimpan makanan serta digunakan sebagai bekal kubur. Bukti ini dapat dilihat pada tiga situs penguburan yaitu: Gua Tubara, Tubara Sugu dan Aturboyah Suwiyah yang terletak di kampung Kayu Batu, sekitar 10 km dari kota Jayapura. Fragmen gerabah tersebut ditemukan berasosiasi dengan rangka manusia pada ketiga situs tersebut. Adapun bentuk pola hias yang terdapat pada fragmen gerabah tersebut antara lain, garis-garis segitiga, garis-garis lurus, motif panah, garis horisontal dan melingkar. Tulisan ini merupakan salah satu langkah awal untuk mengetahui afiliasi budaya pengguna dan pembuat gerabah melalui analisis pola hias, tipologi, morfologi gerabah, yang dianalisis berdasarkan sumber etnografi-arkeologi, serta informasi yang dikumpulkan dari informan lokal.

Introduction

Pottery is often found in archaeological sites and can provide important information about human life in the past; it represents people's knowledge about manufacturing practices, technological functions, the social economy, and culture. As a cultural object, pottery is formed from clay, easy to blend and shape owing to its plasticity, processed by various combinations of techniques, and fired at temperatures of 350–1000 °C. This causes pottery to survive at West New Guinea sites, because it becomes resistant to degradation even in tropical conditions (Atmosudiro 1998, in Sari 2016, 105). Design patterns can be applied to pottery surfaces before the firing process or simply by colouring the pottery surface after firing (Nurhadi 1981, cited in Mene 2014, 70). As Gaffney and Tolla (Chapter 1, this volume) note in their introduction, documenting the pottery sequences of this area, including their form, manufacturing, and decorations, will be crucial for understanding dispersals of Austronesian-speaking groups into the Pacific as well as the origins of later trade networks and ethnographic systems of production and consumption.

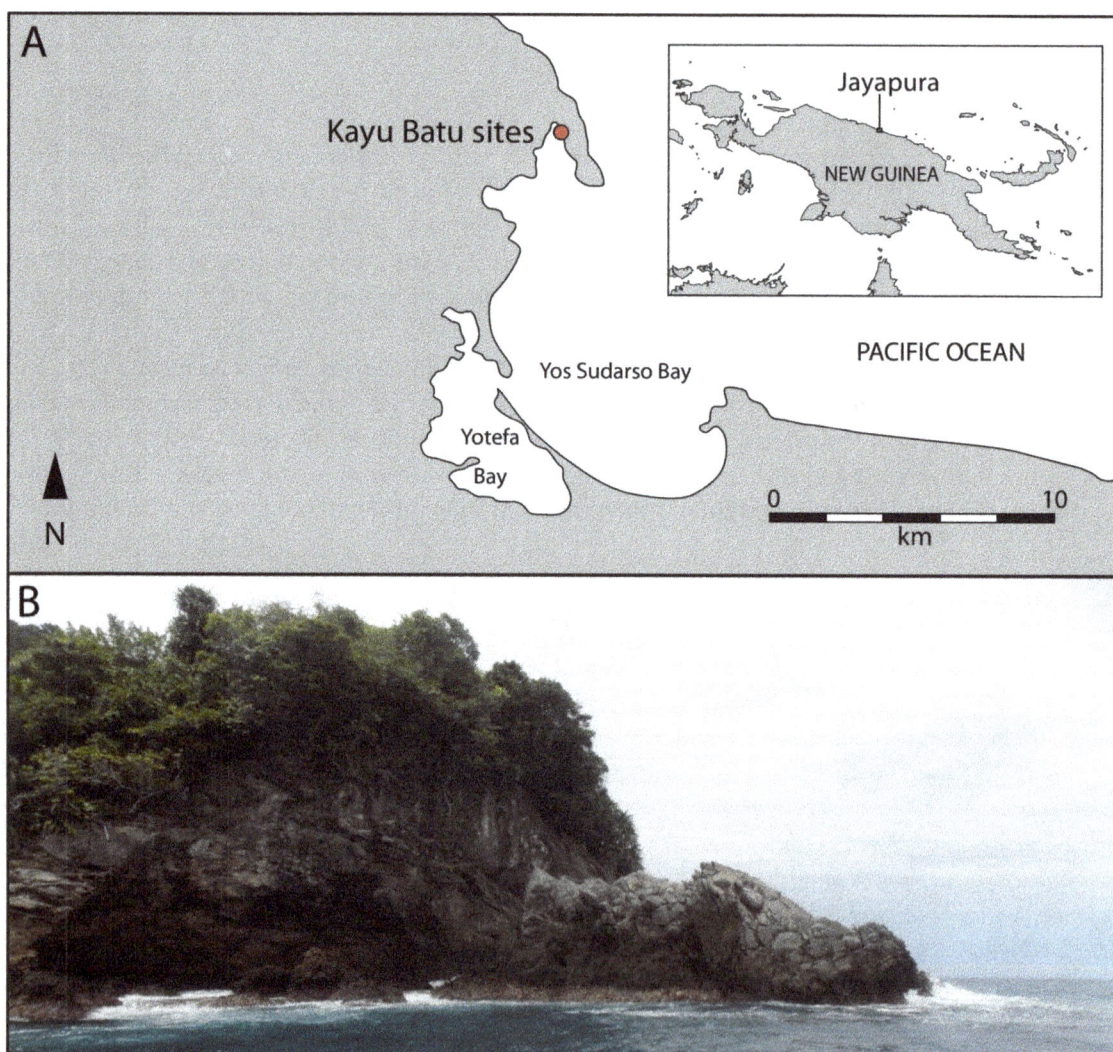

Figure 13.1: Kayu Batu.

Notes: (A) location of Kayu Batu sites near Jayapura; (B) view of Kayu Batu coastline.

Source: Map by Dylan Gaffney; Photo by Balai Arkeologi Papua, 2015.

At three burial sites—Gua Tubara (Tubara Cave), Tubara Sugu, and Aturboyah Suwiyah—located on the shoreline and lying about 10 km from Jayapura city on the north coast of West New Guinea (Figure 13.1), pottery fragments from grave goods were found, associated with human remains. The pottery sherds from the burial sites were richly decorated and most of the surfaces were covered with triangular and straight lines. Other patterns were characterised by design forms like arrows, and horizontal and circular incisions. This chapter aims to investigate cultural affiliations through the analysis of the decorative patterns and style of the pottery fragments, interpreted in the context of ethnographic and archaeological sources and additional data collected from local informants to provide complementary information about the typology, morphology, and decoration of this pottery. The evidence shows that idealised conceptions about life, symbolising the relationships between the living and the afterlife, were presented by the decorative patterns applied to the pottery surface.

Ethnographic and archaeological pottery in West New Guinea

Ethnographically, several traditions of pottery making have recently been practised by indigenous groups in West New Guinea. Owing to its use for roasting sago, one of the primary local plant foods, there continues to be some demand for pottery among communities in West New Guinea's lowlands. In several traditions in Indonesia, pottery vessels have also been used to store human remains (Soejono 1963, 48). In the recent past, pottery traditions in West New Guinea (Indonesian Papua) were practised by indigenous people on Mansinam Island near Manokwari, in the Abar area of Lake Sentani, and Kampung Kayu Batu area near Jayapura; today, only those around Abar have an active potting community (Figure 13.2). Based on morphological analyses, the pottery made in these locations varies substantially in shape. The pottery from Mansinam is dominated by pots used for sago cooking or baking, known locally as *forna*.[1] In Abar, pottery shapes are dominated by jars or *ebe hele* and *sempe*, and plates or *kende* (Maryone 2016, 18). In terms of decorative motifs, the patterns from different locations are also regionally varied. From Mantai Island and Yomokho 2 site at Lake Sentani (see Suroto, this volume), the pottery motifs are characterised by repeated punctations and vertical, horizontal, and wavy lines (Mene 2014). The pottery motifs from Mansinam, in contrast, present a series of parallel lines joined to each other (Balai Arkeologi Papua 2011).

Figure 13.2: Modern pottery making around Abar, Lake Sentani, involving coil forming method.
Source: Photos by Dylan Gaffney.

---

1   Local language words are provided in italics, and Papuan Malay or Indonesian words are underlined, at first mention.

In West New Guinea, prehistoric pottery is particularly distributed in lowland areas, represented at a number of archaeological sites. This pottery is generally found on the north coast of Papua, around Cenderawasih Bay, around the Bird's Neck (for instance at Koan Cave in Nabire), and in the islands of Raja Ampat (for example at Lengsom Cave on Misool island, and Nolol Cave on Salawati island). At these sites, pottery was mostly found associated with human remains, together with grave goods such as glass beads, shell bracelets, and so on. These findings suggest that caves in the past were not merely used as a places for living but also for burial. The pottery fragments at several prehistoric cave sites in West New Guinea represent cultural influences from outside the region that began to spread with the arrival of Neolithic cultures (Soejono 1963, 40). The technology of pottery making itself is considered to have been brought by Austronesian-speaking peoples (Summerhayes 2019). Before the arrival of the Austronesian speakers, the inhabitants of New Guinea spoke non-Austronesian languages but did not produce pottery.

The Kayu Batu study area, Jayapura

Administratively, Gua Tubara, Tubara Sugu, and Aturboyah Suwiyah are located in Kampung Kayu Batu (Kayu Batu neighbourhood), Jayapura city. The original meaning of Kayu Batu is a village or island with the richest fishing ground. It has been transliterated into Papuan Malay but the word Kayu was originally spelled *ka*, which means fish, and *yo*, which means village, while the word Batu indicates the local environment of Kayu Batu which is characterised by rocky terrain, connected to the bay of Port Numbay in Jayapura.

A team from the Balai Arkeologi Papua (Papua Centre of Archaeology) surveyed the Kayu Batu area in 1998 and received information from the local indigenous people about a nearby burial site (Awe 1998, 20). As a response to this survey, in 2015, the Papua Centre of Archaeology resurveyed Kayu Batu and interviewed local people about their culture, especially relating to the meaning of cultural symbols and motifs used in pottery making. The tradition of pottery making has been performed recently by the Kayu Batu groups in this area (Figure 13.3).

During this visit, the Papua Centre of Archaeology team also successfully recorded three burial caves, which are placed a few metres from each other in the same location described in 1998. These sites include the Gua Tubara, Subara Sugu, and Aturboyah Suwiyah caves. From this survey, it was reported that these three burial caves contained human remains and numerous grave goods, including pottery, glass beads, and shell bracelets, which likely relate to the last few centuries before the present (Balai Arkeologi Papua 2015).

Figure 13.3: Recent pot belonging to the Pui clan, Kayu Batu.
Source: Photo by Balai Arkeologi Papua.

Gua Tubara

The Gua Tubara site (East 140° 44'18.4", South 02° 32'54.0") is located in one part of Kayu Batu's small inlets, with the cave entrance facing towards the sea in the west. The cave is today located 13 m above sea level. The site can be reached by following the bay with a boat and climbing the coastal cliffs. The vegetation distributed in the bay includes important economic species such as *matoa* trees and pandanus. The entrance to the cave is broad, and the chamber extends 8 m deep. The cave floor is uneven and dry, with a rough wall, and no rock art or ornaments were found inside. Pottery was found distributed on the cave floor together with human remains, glass beads, and other materials.

Tubara Sugu

Tubara Sugu (East 140° 44'18.5", South 02° 32'07.5") is located about 200 m from Gua Tubara. The entrance of the cave faces to the west, located 18 m above modern sea level. In size, the cave chamber is 8.8 m deep and 2.9 m high. Archaeological findings recovered from the cave surface include human bones, pottery fragments, glass beads, and shells.

Aturboyah Suwiyah

This site is located at East 140° 44'18.7", South 02° 32'10.1". This cave is elongated to the east 25 m, with the entrance being 2.6 m wide and 10 m in height. Nine pottery fragments were found on the cave surface.

Kayu Batu archaeological pottery

Detailed macroscopic analysis of the form, manufacturing marks, and decorative motifs on the archaeological pottery fragments from the Kayu Batu sites were carried out at the Papua Centre of Archaeology offices in Jayapura. Data processing then compared the physical characteristics of the Kayu Batu archaeological pottery with historical and ethnographic literature regarding regional pottery size, form, decoration, and technology, as well as the qualitative information provided by the ethnographic interviews. This allowed the archaeological pottery to be understood in the context of the surrounding natural and social environment. The chapter now presents an analysis of the archaeological pottery from the three Kayu Batu sites in order to examine technological and cultural variation between these wares, as well as to provide a more detailed understanding of how pottery made in the past differed compared with the pottery produced today (see Figure 13.4).

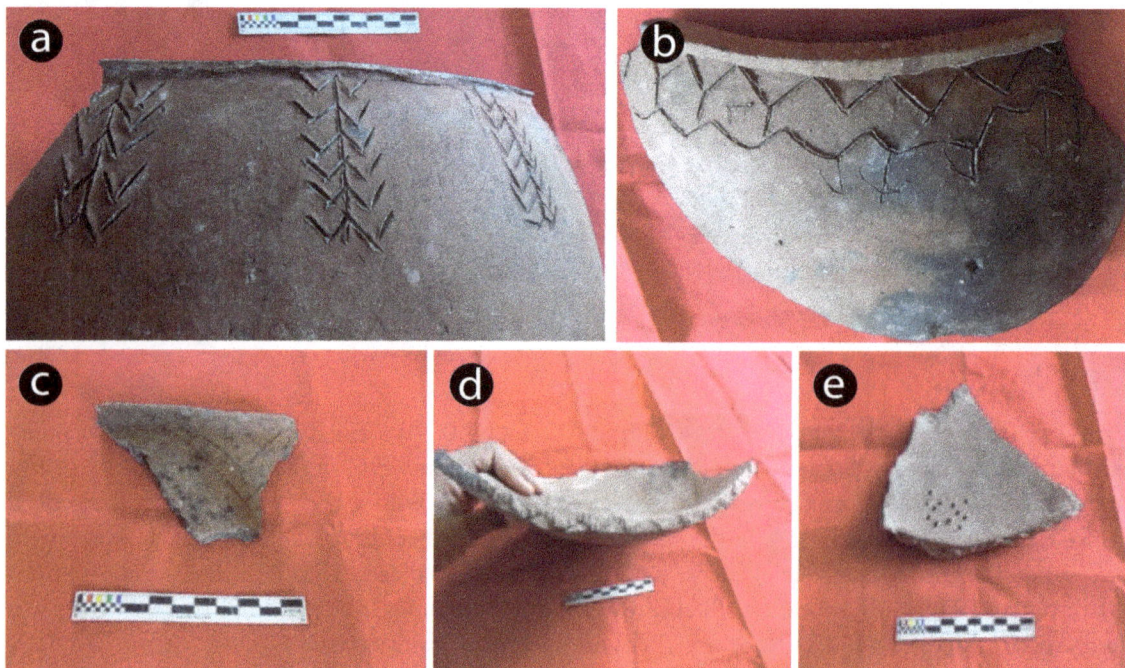

Figure 13.4: Archaeological pottery from the Kayu Batu cave sites.
Notes: (A)–(B) incised lines; (C) incised zig-zags on the rim from Tubara Sugu; (D) incised lip; (E) punctation.
Source: Klementin Fairyo.

The Gua Tubara pottery fragments included 14 rims and three body sherds (Table 13.1). The maximum dimension of these sherds ranged from 59 mm to 165 mm, while the thickness varied from 7 mm to 20 mm. The decorative motifs on the pottery from Gua Tubara included wavy and linear appliqué, and incised repeated dots (punctations).

Table 13.1: Pottery from Gua Tubara.

No	Portion	Length (cm)	Width (cm)	Thickness (cm)	Orifice diameter (cm)	Colour	Core	Motifs	Motif techniques
1	Decorated rim	14.5	23.3	1.0	16	brown, red-slip	brown	horizontal lines, repeated dots	applied, excised
2	Decorated rim	14.2	12.9	1.0	16	red	red	repeated dots	incised
3	Decorated rim	16.5	20.0	1.9	13.5	red	brown	wavy lines	applied
4	Decorated rim	10.0	13.5	1.1	7.5	red	brown	wavy lines	incised
5	Decorated rim	9.3	13.7	1.3	12	brown	black	repeated dots	applied, excised
6	Decorated rim	7.7	7.6	0.7	20	brown	black	wavy lines	applied
7	Decorated rim	6.1	5.8	0.8	20	red	brown	wavy lines	applied
8	Decorated rim	9.5	5.7	1.0	16	brown, red-slip	brown	wavy lines	applied
9	Decorated rim	7.2	8.0	1.1	17	brown	brown	wavy lines	applied
10	Decorated rim	5.7	6.3	1.3	18	brown	brown	wavy lines	incised
11	Decorated rim	6.2	7.2	0.6	10	brown, red-slip	black	wavy lines	applied
12	Decorated rim	4.7	6.0	1.0	15	brown	brown	wavy lines	applied
13	Decorated rim	7.7	5.3	0.6	7	red	black	wavy lines	applied
14	Decorated rim	7.0	6.7	0.7	10	brown	black	wavy lines	applied
15	Decorated rim	4.7	4.8	0.6	13	brown, red-slip	black	wavy lines	applied
16	Plain body	8.3	8.7	1.4	–	brown	black	wavy lines	applied
17	Plain body	5.1	6.2	0.6	–	brown	brown	wavy lines	applied
18	Plain body	2.3	3.2	1.9	–	brown	brown	wavy lines	applied

Source: Author's summary.

Tubara Sugu pottery fragments consisted of two body sherds with motifs, and 15 fragments without motifs. Five rim sherds preserved motifs; eight rim fragments preserved no motifs. Based on the morphological reconstruction, it was established that these fragments were derived from the parts of a globular pot. Manufacturing marks suggest the pot was produced by mixing clay with fine sand using the paddle and anvil technique in the forming process. The motifs added to the pottery surface were created with incised, impressed, excised, and applied techniques (Table 13.2).

Table 13.2: Pottery from Tubara Sugu Cave.

No	Portion	Length (cm)	Width (cm)	Thickness (cm)	Orifice diameter (cm)	Colour	Core	Motifs	Motif techniques
1	Decorated rim	10.0	13.0	0.9	19	brown, red-slip	brown	horizontal lines, repeated dots	applied, excised
2	Decorated rim	7.0	11.8	0.9	22	red	brown	repeated dots	incised
3	Decorated rim	5.1	9.9	0.9	19	red	black	wavy lines	applied
4	Decorated rim	5.1	9.9	0.9	14	brown	brown	wavy lines	incised
5	Decorated rim	14.0	19.6	0.6	17	brown	brown	repeated dots	applied, excised
6	Decorated body	13.0	15.0	0.9	–	brown, red-slip	brown	wavy lines	applied
7	Decorated body	6.1	2.8	0.5	–	brown, red-slip	brown	wavy lines	applied
8	Plain rim	8.0	25.0	2.4	22	red	black	–	–
9	Plain rim	18.5	13.7	2.2	18	red	black	–	–
10	Plain rim	8.0	12.5	1.4	20	red	black	–	–
11	Plain rim	11.0	13.6	1.8	20	red	black	–	–
12	Plain rim	13.5	23.3	1.2	–	red	black	–	–
13	Plain rim	13.3	23.2	1.5	–	red	black	–	–
14	Plain rim	11.0	15.7	1.0	–	red	black	–	–
15	Plain rim	11.4	13.7	1.7	–	red	brown	–	–
16	Plain rim	9.7	13.2	0.9	–	red	brown	–	–
17	Plain body	13.5	16.1	1.5	–	red	brown	–	–
18	Plain body	9.0	10.5	0.6	–	red	black	–	–
19	Plain body	7.8	12.6	0.3	–	red	brown	–	–
20	Plain body	8.3	9.0	0.6	–	red	brown	–	–
21	Plain body	9.1	9.1	1.0	–	red	brown	–	–
22	Plain body	8.2	8.8	0.6	–	red	brown	–	–
23	Plain body	9.2	6.2	0.4	–	red	brown	–	–
24	Plain body	7.7	6.9	1.0	–	brown	brown	–	–
25	Plain body	6.2	8.4	0.5	–	brown	brown	–	–
26	Plain body	6.6	7.2	0.8	–	brown	black	–	–
27	Plain body	5.6	9.0	0.7	–	brown	black	–	–
28	Plain body	6.0	7.5	0.6	–	brown	brown	–	–
29	Plain body	4.0	7.2	0.7	–	brown	brown	–	–
30	Plain body	3.8	5.2	0.5	–	red	brown	–	–

Source: Author's summary.

At Aturboyah Suwiyah, several pottery motifs were described, including anthropomorphic figures, wavy appliqué lines, repeated incised dots (punctuation), and triangles (Table 13.3). The techniques used to apply the motifs were similar to the techniques used for the pottery from Gua Tubara and Tubara Sugu caves. The maximum dimension of pottery ranged from 60 mm to 200 mm, and thickness was between 10 mm and 16 mm.

Table 13.3: Pottery from Aturboyah Suwiyah.

No	Portion	Length (cm)	Width (cm)	Thickness (cm)	Orifice diameter (cm)	Colour	Core	Motifs	Motifs techniques
1	Decorated rim	20.0	27.2	1.2	19	red	brown	arthropods	incised
2	Decorated rim	20.0	25.7	1.1	20	red	brown	wavy lines, repeated dots	applied, impressed, excised
3	Decorated rim	14.6	24.5	1.7	19	red	brown	triangle, wavy lines	incised
4	Decorated rim	8.5	8.0	1.6	16	red	brown	arthropods	incised
5	Decorated rim	6.3	5.2	1.0	8	red	black	wavy lines	applied, impressed
6	Decorated rim	6.9	13.5	1.0	17	red	black	wavy lines, repeated dots	applied, impressed
7	Decorated rim	10.1	13.3	1.3	18	red	brown	arthropods	incised
8	Decorated rim	14.5	12.2	1.1	15	red	brown	wavy lines	applied, impressed
9	Decorated rim	12.0	16.0	1.1	20	red	brown	wavy lines, repeated dots	applied, impressed

Source: Author's summary.

Based on the morphological reconstruction of the pottery, it is clear that the fragments found in the Gua Tubara, Tubara Sugu, and Aturboyah Suwiyah sites are generally globular in form. Based on the raw material, the pottery was made from clay and fine sand temper. The pottery is brown, reddish-brown, and blackish-brown in colour, and some of the pottery has a red-slip surface. The pottery's inner surface colour is not the same as the colour of the outer surface, indicating that the pottery had been fired with inconsistent temperature by using an open firing. The method used to form the pots likely started with a ball of clay that was squeezed and then beaten by the use of a paddle and anvil, while other fingers were held on the outside, forming a flange that becomes the rim or walls of the pot. The paddle and anvil were applied to the pottery from these three sites to draw the clay upwards and thin the walls.

The ornamental patterns applied to pottery at Gua Tubara, Tubara Sugu, and Aturboyah Suwiyah include a wide array of motifs: straight lines, horizontal lines, dots, wavy lines, zig-zags, triangles, and anthropomorphs. In general, these decorative techniques were produced by incised, impressed, excised, and applied decorative techniques (Rangkuti and Pojoh 1991, 24). Wavy lines were generally applied in the zig-zag form; this pattern was arranged in a row following a straight or curved line that was interconnected with another (Toekio 2000, 41). The decoration was applied on a still-wet surface after the forming process was complete. Incision is a simple technique, which only requires scratching a small, thin, sharp, or blunt tool on the pottery's outer surface. The impressed decorative technique can use fingers, nails, stamps, and so on. The excised technique uses tools that are not sharp but have a thin edge. The applied decoration adds additional clay material onto the surface of the pot (Rangkuti and Pojoh 1991, 26–27).

Of the wide variety of decorative patterns on the pottery fragments from these three sites, applied wavy lines were more commonly used than other motifs. Speculatively, the wavy lines may have been inspired by the environment in which the Kayu Batu groups live. The area is marked by a coastal environment where the waves on the sea are seen every day, which could have inspired the pottery makers to apply the forms to the pottery surface. Similar environmental characteristics have been suggested to be reflected in pottery designs from Papua New Guinea (Gaffney 2020; Terrell 2011).

The application of decorative patterns can also be a marker of group identity and social status (Mahmud 2011, 45). The Kayu Batu people consist of three subgroups: the Pui clan, the Makanuai-satu clan, and the Makanuai-dua clan. The Pui clan are seen to be the ancestors of those in Kayu Batu; for this reason, the Pui clan have an elevated position relative to other clans. In terms of social symbolism used in material culture, the Pui clans can use certain symbols that are not permitted to be used by other clans (as seen in other parts of New Guinea, e.g. Mennis 2006). Based on the information obtained from the interview with Mr Obed Pui (a member of the Pui clan), symbols such as lizards and crocodiles are specific cultural figures that belong to the Pui clan, which were applied to the pottery surface as decorations (Figure 13.3). Conversely, the shell decoration applied to pottery refers to the Makanuai-satu clan, while fish images belong to the Makanuai-dua clan.

Based on interviews conducted with the leader of Kayu Batu, we learned that there are several differences between the pottery made in the past compared to the pottery made more recently. These differences are apparently evident in the form of pottery, including the shape and technology. In terms of shape, past pottery is said to have been dominated by bowls, while recent pottery generally forms globular pots and plates. In the past, pottery was said to be fired in the open, whereas in recent times, pottery was fired in a permanent furnace. The motifs applied to the pottery surfaces were also claimed to be different between the past and the present.

Conclusion

The pots from the Gua Tubara, Tubara Sugu, and Aturboyah Suwiyah caves in Kayu Batu neighbourhood, Jayapura, were primarily found in association with human ossuaries and were likely grave goods or offerings. These potsherds are distinct from recent pottery that was produced by Kayu Batu people. The archaeological pottery was produced by adding fine-grained sand temper to clay and using paddles and anvils to shape the vessels into globular pots. Decoration included applied, incised, excised, and stamping techniques. Red-slip was occasionally added, and firing was done in the open. Decorative motifs consisted of the horizontal lines, repeated dots, and wavy lines that characterise Late Holocene post-Lapita pottery produced along the north coast of New Guinea (Gaffney 2020; May and Tuckson 2000; Suroto, this volume; Terrell 2011). These sherds are distinct, in production, form and decoration, from recent pots made in the area. More research is needed to establish the chronology of the Kayu Batu pottery, and by extension pottery from the Jayapura area, in the last millennium before the present. Such research would allow for a refined understanding of when and how pottery manufacture changed through time. Further ethnographic research would also shed light on clan markings and the use of decoration to signal identity—these findings could be insightful for understanding the recent archaeological past.

References

Atmosudiro, S. 1998. Manfaat kajian gerabah masa lalu bagi pengembangan kerajinan tembikar sebagai penunjang industri pariwisata. *Berkala Arkeologi* 18(2):1–11. doi.org/10.30883/jba.v18i2.779.

Awe, R.D. 1998. Penelitian Arkeometri di Situs-Situs Nimboran dan Sekitarnya, Kabupaten Jayapura, Propinsi Irian Jaya. Research report. Unpublished. Balai Arkeologi Jayapura, Jayapura.

Balai Arkeologi Papua 2011. Penelitian Arkeologi di Kawasan Danau Sentani Kabupaten Jayapura. Research report. Unpublished. Balai Arkeologi Papua, Jayapura.

Balai Arkeologi Papua 2015. Eksplorasi Arkeologi dan Etnoarkeologi di Kampung Kayu Batu Kota Jayapura. Research report. Unpublished. Balai Arkeologi Papua, Jayapura.

Gaffney, D. 2020. *Materialising ancestral Madang: Pottery production and subsistence trading on the northeast coast of New Guinea.* University of Otago Studies in Archaeology, No. 29. Archaeology Programme, University of Otago, Dunedin.

Mahmud, M.I. 2011. Jejak Austronesia, Melanesia, dan tradisi sejarah berlanjut di Papua. In M.I. Mahmud and E.N.I. Djami (eds), *Austronesia dan Melanesia di Nusantara: Mengungkap Asal Usul dan Jati Diri dari Temuan Arkeologis,* pp. 43–68. Ombak, Yogyakarta.

Maryone, R. 2016. Perkembangan tradisi pembuatan gerabah abar Sentani. *Papua* 9(1):71–83. doi.org/10.24832/kapata.v10i2.223.

May, P. and M. Tuckson 2000. *The traditional pottery of Papua New Guinea.* University of Hawai'i Press, Honolulu.

Mene B. 2014. Pola hias gerabah dada situs-situs di Kawasan Danau Sentani, Papua. *Kapata Arkeologi* 10(2): 67–76.

Mennis, M.R. 2006. *A potted history of Madang: Traditional culture and change on the north coast of Papua New Guinea.* Lalong Enterprises, Brisbane.

Nurhadi 1981. Gerabah dari Situs Kalumpang Sulawesi Selatan, sebuah analisis pendahuluan. Unpublished master's thesis. Universitas Gajah Mada, Yogyakarta.

Rangkuti, N. and I.H.E. Pojoh 1991. Buku panduan keramik. In Anon (ed.), *Indonesian Field School of Archaelogy Trowulan 1–21 June 1991.* Pusat Penelitian Arkeologi Nasional, Jakarta.

Sari, P. 2016. Temuan gerabah di Grogolan Wetan, sebuah bukti penghunian situs Sangiran pasca Plestosen. *Papua* 8(1):103–110. doi.org/10.24832/papua.v8i1.13.

Soejono, R.P. 1963. Prasejarah Papua. In R.M. Koentjaraningrat (ed.), *Irian Jaya: Membangun Masyarakat Majemuk,* pp. 23–34. Djambatan, Jakarta.

Summerhayes, G.R. 2019. Austronesian expansions and the role of mainland New Guinea: A new perspective. *Asian Perspectives* 58(2):250–260. doi.org/10.1353/asi.2019.0015.

Terrell, J.E. 2011. Wooden platters and bowls in the ethnographic collections. *Fieldiana Anthropology* 2011(42):175–195. doi.org/10.3158/0071-4739-42.1.175.

Toekio, M.S. 2000. *Mengenal Ragam Hias Indonesia.* Angkasa-Indonesia, Bandung.

14

Tracing the remains of World War II on Biak Island

Sonya Kawer and Dylan Gaffney

Abstract

Located in the northernmost part of what is today Papua Province and along the Pacific rim, Biak Island was used as a base for the Japanese and American armies during World War II (WWII). Archaeological surveys have now been conducted around several districts of Biak Island, designed to build a narrative about WWII from the ground up, by examining the distributions of the remains found during fieldwork. The wide array of bunkers, aeroplanes, and amphibious vehicles, and the remains of a now-submerged ship, as well as local toponyms in several areas, make it clear that Biak was a crucial location during WWII, and that the events of the war continue to be resonant for Biakers who live in the area today. It is concluded that the Japanese and American armies used almost the entire land surface of Biak's south-eastern coast as a major base camp. The high value of Biak during WWII was in part related to its location at the crux of Asia and the Pacific, and its geopolitical relevance, especially as a location to establish control in the Pacific theatre.

Abstrak

Terletak di bagian paling utara dari wilayah yang sekarang dikenal sebagai Provinsi Papua, pulau Biak pada masa lalu digunakan sebagai pangkalah tentara Jepang dan Amerika dalam perang dunia II (PD II). Survei arkeologi telah dilakukan di beberapa distrik di pulau ini untuk menarasikan sejarah kependudukan selama perang dunia II ditempat tersebut dengan menganalisis sisa – sisa perlengkapan perang yang masih ditemukan di lapangan. Distirbusi bunker, sisa pesawat terbang, kendaraan amfibi, dan sisa-sisa kapal yang tenggelam, serta toponomi yang ditemukan dibeberapa titik, menjadi bukti kuat akan pentingnya pulau ini pada masa lalu selama perang dunia II, dimana hampir seluruh bagian dari pulau ini digunakan sebagai markas utama kedua negara tersebut di masa lalu. Digunakannya pulau Biak sebagai salah satu markas besar pada perang dunia II diperkirakan didasarkan pada letak geografisnya yang berada di titik pertemuan antara Asia dan Pasifik, serta relevansi geopolitk terutama sebagai lokasi untuk membangun kontrol di kawasan Pasifik.

Introduction

World War II (WWII) was a major conflict in global history that occurred from 1939 to 1945. It was driven by ideological divergences between the several countries in Europe, the Middle East, America, and Asia, and resulted in political and economic instability in many parts of the world (Mawdsley 2009, 3–10; Weinberg 2014, 1–5). In the Pacific, the United States of America, along with its Australian, British, Dutch, Canadian, and New Zealand allies, fought the Japanese Empire for regional hegemony as each side worked to control strategic archipelagos. Cenderawasih Bay (then called Geelvink Bay, part of the Dutch East Indies) was one such archipelago and Biak Island served as a regional headquarters for Japanese and, later, Allied troops, who used the island to exert aerial control over the region (Beevor 2012, 12–45). Biak Island's strategic location in a sheltered bay at the crux of Island Southeast Asia and the Pacific made it an ideal place for the two superpowers to prepare tactics and to implement bombing runs (Smith 1953, 289–394).

An archaeological survey undertaken in 1997 by the Balai Arkeologi Papua[1] (Papua Centre of Archaeology; then called Balai Arkeologi Jayapura) produced the material evidence for Cenderawasih Bay's crucial contribution to the Pacific theatre in the form of military equipment and several buildings used by the Japanese and American armies, found scattered across almost half of Biak Island. In particular, artefacts relating to WWII were found in several locations in Ruar and Sepse villages. In 2016, a Papua Centre of Archaeology research team conducted a further survey, which identified Japanese and American military equipment in several districts in the Biak–Numfor Regency (Balai Arkeologi Papua 2016). These areas included Kota Biak (Biak Town), Biak Timur (East Biak), Oridek, and Kepulauan Padaido (the Padaido Islands). The research in 2016 also succeeded in cataloguing the remains of two major Japanese caves—Binsari in the Sumberker village area and the Japanese heritage cave area in Samofa village—which are located about 5 km from Biak Town. The results of these provisional 2016 surveys and artefact analyses are the focus of this chapter, which first provides historical information about Cenderawasih Bay's role in the Pacific theatre, before seeking to build a picture of Biak's wartime history 'from the ground up', using the archaeological remains as a guide. This picture is then contextualised by wartime archaeology from the wider Asia-Pacific region.

The Pacific theatre

The New Guinea campaign

The Japanese Empire had gained significant ground in China in the years leading up to WWII and held a League of Nations Mandate over several islands in the western Pacific. This territorial expansion was used as a platform to rapidly attack a wide array of Western-controlled/allied nations in Southeast Asia and the Pacific between December 1941 and January 1942, including Hong Kong, French Indochina, Malaya, the Philippines, Guam, the Dutch East Indies, the Australian territories of Papua and New Guinea, and the British Solomon Islands (Rottman 2005). Japanese expansion, although tied to German and Italian aggression in Europe, Southwest Asia, and North Africa, was stimulated by the empire's growing industrial strength and demand for access to commodities like oil, rubber, and tin (Copeland 2011).

1 Bahasa Indonesia words are underlined at first mention.

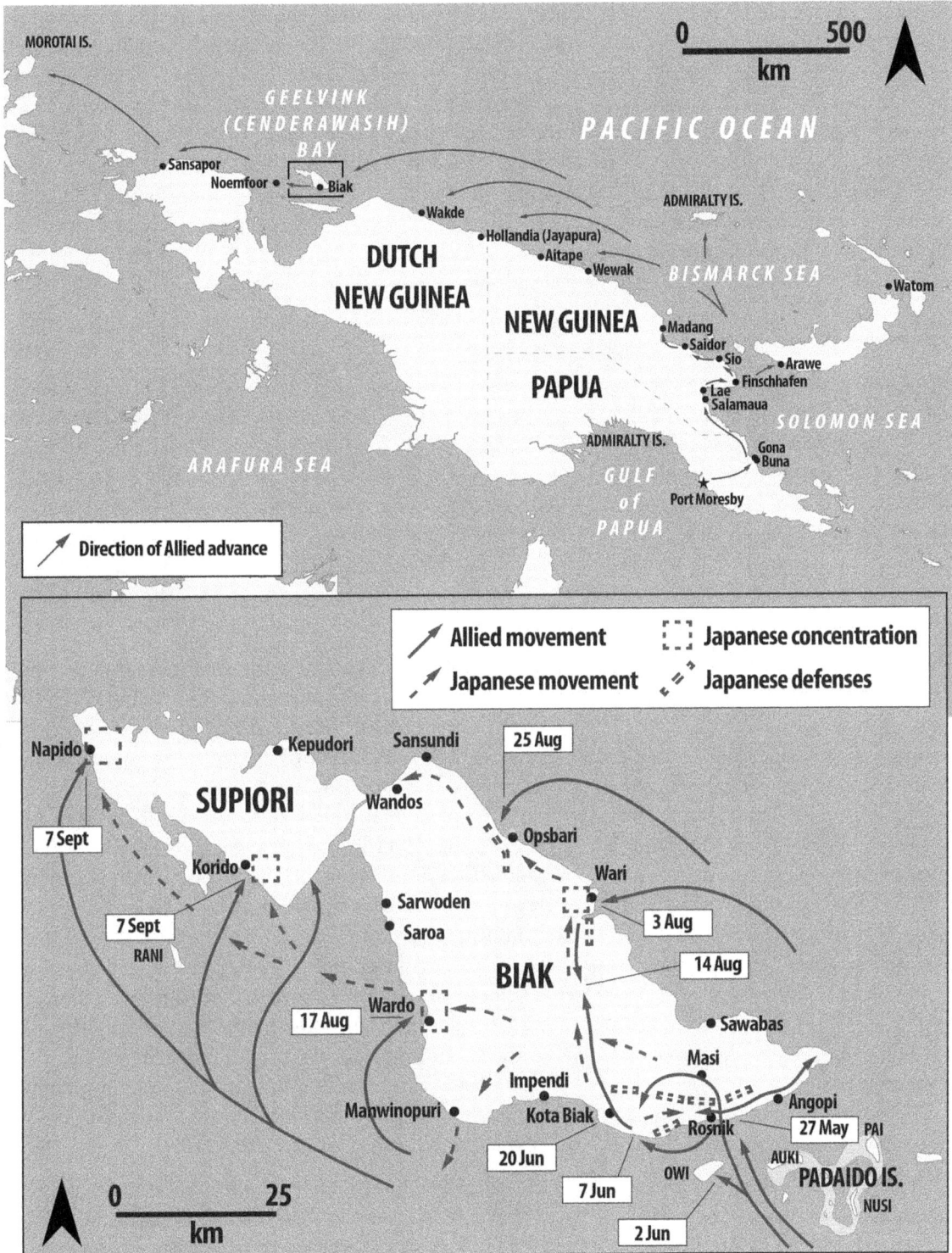

Figure 14.1: The New Guinea campaign.

Notes: above: key sites of conflict during WWII, including Biak in what is now Cenderawasih Bay; below: the Battle of Biak, showing dates of Allied movements and Japanese retreats in 1944.

Source: Dylan Gaffney, redrawn from MacArthur (1966).

New Guinea was quickly identified by Douglas MacArthur, leading the Allied forces from Australia, as a key objective for the recapture of the Pacific. This started with the successful defence of Port Moresby in May 1942, with Allied troops moving westwards to retake Buna-Gona (via the Kokoda track) in January 1943, Lae, Salamaua, and Finschhafen (September–October 1943), Saidor and Sio (January–February 1944), Madang (February–April 1944), Wewak and Aitape (April–May 1944), Jayapura (then Hollandia, April–June 1944), and Wakde (May 1944) along the northern coast of New Guinea (see Figure 14.1). These assaults were increasingly rapid and long-distance, but the tempo was ultimately constrained by the location of Allied airfields on New Guinea and in the Bismarck Archipelago that could support naval operations (Bernstein 1999, 13). As the Allies moved increasingly westwards, they needed new airfields to support their advance.

The Battle of Biak

Biak had been captured by the Japanese in May 1942 and, apart from some early resistance in the form of a guerrilla group that had developed from a local cargo cult (Steenbrink 2010, 316), the island was administered without contest by the Japanese. The development of Biak's defences and infrastructure only started in late 1943 when the Japanese began to realise its potential as a strategic platform to control New Guinea. By 1944, when the Allied fleet advanced towards Cenderawasih Bay (Figure 14.1), it was host to three Japanese airfields at Mokmer, Sorido, and Bosnek (also called Borokoe), and around 12,350 personnel (Bernstein 1999, 20, 32, 38). The island's coral platforms, in contrast to the soft alluvial ground around northern New Guinea, made Biak the most ideal air base between the Bismarck Archipelago and Island Southeast Asia.

The sustained Allied bombing of Biak commenced on 28 April and continued into May of 1944, facilitated by B-24 bombers flying from the Markham Valley and the Admiralties Islands. The first week of May saw intense Japanese retaliation by air, combatted by Allied fighters dispatched from Jayapura, but resistance soon dissipated (Bernstein 1999, 34). From 27 May to 31 August, Allied ground troops numbering 28,580 personnel, supported by 7307 air troops, and offshore naval units, recaptured Cenderawasih Bay, first in the Battle of Biak and then in the Battle of Noemfoor (Bernstein 1999, 35). During the Battle of Biak, the Allies initially underestimated the Japanese numbers because, under the command of Colonel Kuzume Naoyuki, their troops had strategically fallen back to occupy caves and pillboxes around the airfields, but gradually the Allies claimed the island in a bitter contest that lasted several months. According to Allied reports written after the conflict, the core Japanese positions consisted of three cave systems connected by tunnels that could shelter about 1000 people, and these were further protected by the presence of hundreds of smaller entrenched caves along coral ridgelines (Ford 2009). In part, the Allies overcame these defences by pouring gasoline into the windward cave entrances and igniting them with grenades to starve the Japanese of oxygen. The large-scale loss of life and subsequent taking of trophies, including human skulls of enemy combatants, suggests that, by this point in the New Guinea campaign, soldiers on both sides had truly dehumanised each other (Harrison 2006; Scheurer 2015, 10).

The recapture of Biak and its three airfields allowed the Allies to then push into Island Southeast Asia and to run bombing raids to support the recapture of Micronesia. Biak therefore marked a turning point in MacArthur's offensive drive towards the Philippines and eventually Japan itself (Bullard 2010, 28). However, although the occupation of Biak was documented by official war historians (e.g. U.S. Army 41st Division 1944), through interrogations of prisoners of war (e.g. Naval Analysis Division 1946), in personal accounts by individual officers (e.g. Riegelman 1955), and in photographic records (Figure 14.2), the material history of these events, and of life on the island from 1942 to 1945, remains untold. The distribution of wartime remains on Biak and surrounding islands requires documentation because this heritage is now profoundly important to how present-day Biakers define their recent history. Moreover, the island has become an important focus for the repatriation of human remains by both Japan and America. As such, the chapter now turns to the archaeological evidence of wartime occupation in the form of architectural remains and artefact distributions.

Figure 14.2: The Battle of Biak and its aftermath.

Notes: (A) American troops and Sherman tank moving to attack ridge north of Mokmer, 1944; (B) entrance to 'East Caves' east of Mokmer; (C) entrance to 'West Caves' north of Mokmer; (D) Japanese pillbox; (E) American infantry enter Japanese cave on Biak; (F) wrecked bombers at Biak; (G) demolition of American bombers at Sorido airfield, May 1948 (TM-10029866); (H) propellors at Sorido prior to being melted down, 1949 (TM-10029880).

Source: (A)–(E) from the Centre of Military History Archive; (F)–(H) from the Tropenmuseum.

Archaeological sites around south-east Biak

Cenderawasih Bay is host to four large islands: Biak (2455 km²), Supiori (634 km²), Numfor (335 km²), and Yapen (2278 km²). Biak and Supiori effectively form one landmass, separated only by a small channel, less than 100 m wide and today connected by road. The bay also features several smaller islands including Num and the Padaido group. On Biak Island itself, the Biak Town, East Biak, and Oridek districts are formed of numerous <u>kampung</u> (village neighbourhoods), that run relatively contiguously along the island's south-eastern coastal strip, flanked to the north by uplifted limestone coral reefs, and face the Padaido Islands to the south-east. Of these neighbourhoods, several on Biak have so far been surveyed by the Papua Centre of Archaeology: Anggraidi, Sanumi, Mokmer, Orwer, Saba, Sundey, Wisata Binsari, Fandoi, Sorido, and Syabes. During these archaeological surveys, WWII remains were recorded in the field and classified into two site types: (1) built architecture and (2) scatters of fragmentary military equipment. The following section describes the sites recorded around Biak from six areas—Mokmer, Sorido, Orwer, Saba, Sundey, and the Padaido Islands—to provide a representative account of the wartime archaeology of the island (Figure 14.3).

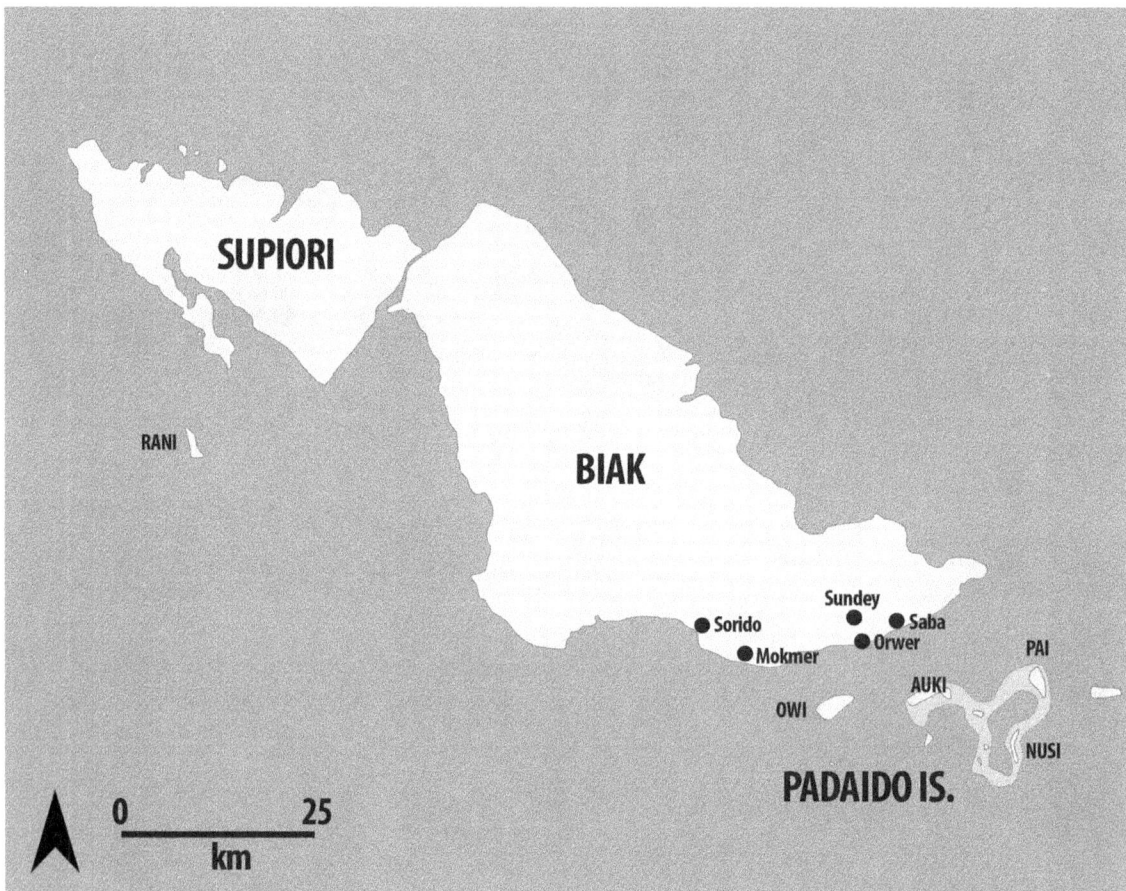

Figure 14.3: The location of survey areas on Biak Island and the Padaido group.
Source: Dylan Gaffney.

Mokmer area

In Biak Town, several sites were recorded around Mokmer and Parai, one of the key strategic landing zones at the Battle of Biak owing to its airfield and defensive position (Table 14.1A). For instance, Mokmer Airfield (S 01° 11'24.0", E 136° 06'27.0") is situated only about 200 m from the present coastline and was the first airfield built by the Japanese (today it is used as an international airport, Frans Kaisiepo International Airport). The original WWII landing strip remains in place but has been extended and widened to accommodate modern passenger jets (Figure 14.4). Farabay, a hill formed of uplifted coral and located to the north of the airfield, was used as a monitoring post by the Japanese army to control Biak, and to support the running of the airfields at Mokmer, Sorido, and Bosnek, and later by the Allies in their naval and air operations around Owi Island (in the Padaido Islands). Allied intelligence maps also record two pockets of caves in the area used for defence by the Japanese; one to the north-west and one to the east of Mokmer Airfield (Figure 14.5). Based on the Papua Centre of Archaeology survey results, there are 14 known bunkers made from natural rock scattered around Farabay Hill, located a few metres from one another. Manggandisapi Cave (S 01° 11'55.7", E 136° 08'37.0") is one such natural cave, part of the eastern pocket of caves, and facing west towards the airstrip (Figure 14.5). It is a small cave with a width of 1.72 m and a height of 1.55 m and was clearly used defensively. Wartime remains were unearthed from this cave, including drinking bottles, broken ceramics, and a part of a soldier's shoes (Table 14.1B; Figure 14.6).

Figure 14.4: Airfields in south-east Biak.
Notes: (A) Borokup Airfield; (B) Sorido Airfield; (C) Mokmer Airfield; and (D)–(F) bunkers in the Mokmer Airfield area.
Source: Photographs by Sonya Kawer.

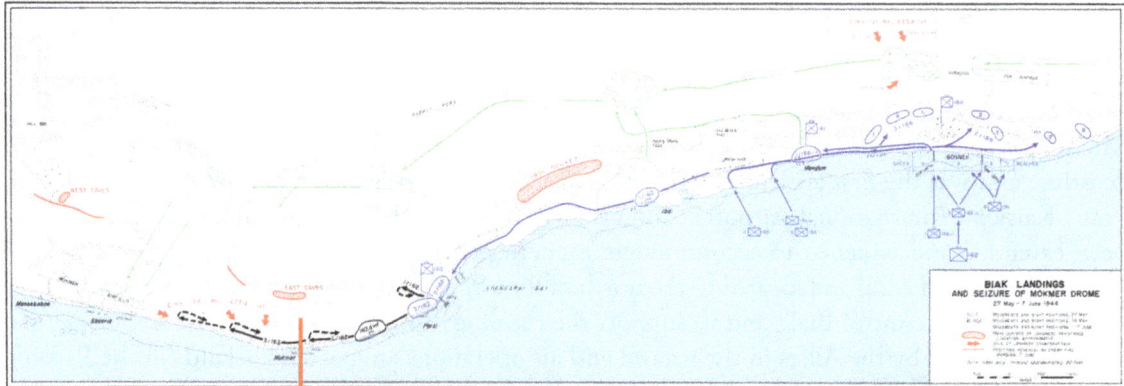

Figure 14.5: Above: Allied intelligence map showing the location of the Japanese-occupied West and East cave systems around Mokmer. Below: Manggandisapi Cave, south of the East Cave system.

Source: Photographs by Sonya Kawer, map from Smith (1953).

Two bunkers have also been recorded just north of Mokmer airstrip. Bunker 1 is located 1 km from the shoreline. The bunker is square and made from metal, facing to the east. Bunker 2 is located a few metres from Bunker 1, with an entrance height of 1.50 m, a width of 0.80 m, and a depth of 3.32 m, placed close to the runway (Figure 14.4).

Binsari in the Sumberker village area and the Japanese heritage cave area in Samofa village represent the two major defensive caves to the west and north of Mokmer. Binsari is a natural cave with a large and spacious chamber. The four walls of the cave contain crevices used to enter the cave. The contents of these caves included bottles, bullets, short buttons, and ceramic fragments (Table 14.1B).

Figure 14.6: Artefacts recovered from wartime archaeological sites on Biak including ordinance, scissors, ceramics, toothbrushes, bullet casings, and glass bottles.

Source: Photographs by Sonya Kawer.

Sorido area

At Sorido, the WWII airfield is still present, but no longer actively in use. In Samofa village, there are several caves and hills that were used as air raid shelters and as gun emplacements by the Japanese. Sorido 1 is a bunker made from a natural cliff, covered by metal building material and located 10 m from the coast. About 15 m from Sorido 1, a rock-shelter that extends 21 m from east to west, faces south and was used as a defence post, evidenced by the remains of weapons and other military equipment found there. Sorido 2 is a raid shelter with an opening 1.5 m in length, 0.8 m wide, and 3.3 m deep.

Orwer area

Orwer village is located in the eastern part of East Biak District. Wartime remains were primarily encountered around caves in the karst, which contained several types of military equipment. At the top of Orwer's karst hill, there is a natural cave called Abyab Mandoryab 1. This cave has a large entrance, 1.40 m high and 1.66 m wide, and it extends 5.11 m in a south-easterly direction. The cave has an uneven floor and is very well lit, although some stalactites are still active. The survey team recorded a military helmet on the cave floor. In Abyab Mandoryab 2 cave, located a few metres from Abyab Mandoryab 1, artefacts included bottles, bullet casings, round plastic from broken oxygen masks, shirt buttons, toothbrushes, cans, plastic boxes, metals, funnels, and army uniforms including helmets and shoe parts.

Sosen Cave is located about 30 m from the Abyab Mandoryab caves. The cave's entrance faces south towards the coast, 0.96 m high, and 5 m wide. Within it were found bullets and explosives.

Saba area

Saba village is located on the coast of Oridek District, facing the Padaido Islands. Five bunkers have been recorded in this area. Bunker 1 (S 01° 09'35.82", E 136° 15'06.4") faces the coast in the south. It was formed by modifying the rock along the coastal strip and breaking into the natural cavity in the limestone (Figure 14.7). The broken opening was then plastered to form a square embrasure (an opening in the bunker from which to shoot) that is 0.65 m high, 1.10 m wide, and 7.00 m long. Inside the cavity, the height of the bunker is 1.50 m. There are seven medium-sized embrasures on either side of the bunker's primary embrasure. Today, the floor inside the bunker is flat, filled with sand and rocks.

Bunker 2 is in line with the first bunker; it was modified from natural boulders. The embrasures are smaller than those of Bunker 1, being 0.50 m high and 0.35 m wide on the eastern side. On the west side, it is connected to a larger embrasure facing the entrance. Bunker 3 is located 7 m from the second bunker, with an embrasure being 1.30 m wide and 0.30 m in height, facing towards the island of Owi at the south-west. The chamber of the third bunker is 3 × 3 m metres. Bunker 4 has two embrasures: one faces to the south-east, being 1.30 m high and 4.10 m wide; the other points to the east, being 0.80 m high and 5.10 m wide.

Bunker 5 is distinct from the first four bunkers, being made from concrete. It is placed in line with Bunkers 1–4, 4 m from the sea. Two embrasures were made with plaster. The first faces south and is 0.30 m high and 0.60 m wide, placed in a low-lying position. The second embrasure is much larger; it faces the south-east, measures 0.50 m high, and 2.10 m wide.

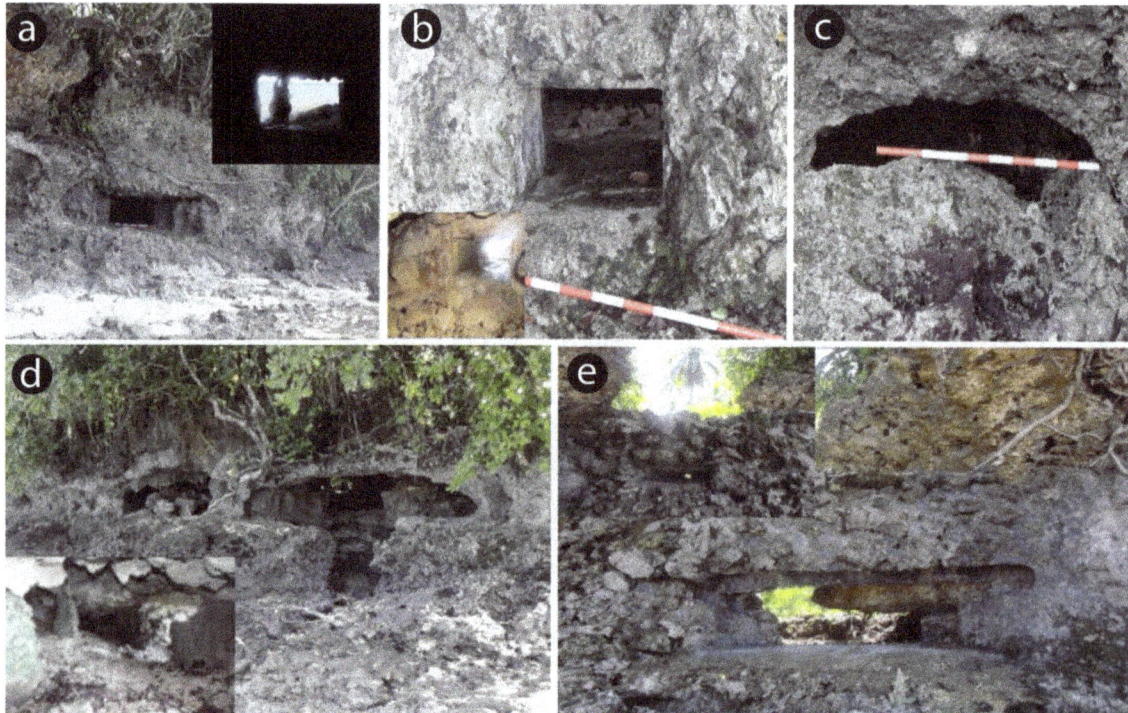

Figure 14.7: Bunkers in the Saba area on Biak Island.
Source: Photographs by Sonya Kawer.

Sundey area

Several caves were also used as Japanese hiding places around Sundey village. Sundey Cave faces north and its entrance, 0.74 m high and 1.26 m wide, is therefore concealed from the coast. The large cave extends 4.9 m into the coral limestone and opens to a second entrance 2.70 m high and 5.00 m wide, facing east. Today, the cave floor is flat and wet, caused by water entering via active stalactites. The archaeological remains distributed on the cave floor confirm its use by the Japanese army during the war. These remains include bottles, cables, drinking glasses, shaving tools, round plastic from oxygen masks, shirt buttons, ammunition, and several pieces of fragmentary metal (Table 14.1C).

These kinds of remains are well known to Biakers who live nearby. For instance, Mr Julianus Masosendifu, a local who lives in Sundey village, found several types of wartime artefacts in the area, including drinking bottles, metal fragments, bullets, shirt buttons, razors, watches, and ceramic marbles. Mr Gerson Rumanasen, another local from Sundey, had collected objects from the forest around the village. These objects include several types of glass bottles in a variety of sizes and two Japanese coins.

The Padaido Islands

The Padaido group consists of several small islands, located between 5 and 45 km south-east of Biak and home to 19 villages. Between the four small islands of Wundi, Urep, Auki, and Nusi is an enormous lagoon and seagrass beds of approximately 530 ha (Kartika et al. 2007, 440). During an archaeological survey for surviving WWII remains, the Papua Centre of Archaeology recorded sites on Auki, Nusi, and Urep islands. On Auki Island were recorded remnants of the former pier, including a 3-m-long wooden pole still embedded in the sea floor (Figure 14.8). On Nusi Island, American-built oil tanks were located, part of a fuel centre to supply military vehicles. Two rusty oil pipelines were found stretching out 100 m into the sea, extending from where the oil tank was once located (S 1° 16'9.455", E 136° 25'0.203"). The pipes were made from metal with a diameter of 0.40 m, with the distance between the two pipes being 1.10 m. In the eastern part of Nusi Island, 10 pier posts emerging from the surface of the water were recorded (Figure 14.8). An aerial bomb was also found in between local people's houses during the survey on Nusi Island and a rusty floating dock was recorded in shallow water between Nusi, Pia, and Pakreki islands (S 1° 15'42.617", E 136° 26'2.436"). On Urep (also known as Ureb, Urip) Island, several WWII remains were recorded, including armoury buildings and four wooden poles, 2.30 m long, embedded into the sea floor about 50 m from today's coast. A former hospital building, 7.15 m × 14.56 m, is also still standing on this island, although its roof has since collapsed.

Figure 14.8: Archaeological remains in the Padaido Islands.

Notes: (A)–(E) pier poles and floating dock; (F) hospital building; (G) oil pipeline; (H) aerial ordinance; (I) armoury building.

Source: Photographs by Sonya Kawer.

Table 14.1A: WWII-era artefacts recorded by site during the Papua Centre of Archaeology surveys on Biak Island, 2016.

Artefact	Para 3	Para 4	Para 5	Para 6	Para 7	Para 8	Para 9	Para 10	Para 11	Para 12	Para 13	Para 14	Para 15	Para 16	Para 17	Para 18	Para 19	Para 20	Para Ceruk	Para 21	Para 22	Para 23	Para 24	Para 25	Para 26	Para 27	Para 30	Para 32	Para 33
Bottle	–	1	–	3	1	–	4	–	–	–	–	–	2	1	1	–	1	–	–	–	2	–	14	4	–	1	–	3	1
Bottle fragment	–	7	–	3	3	5	5	–	2	1	2	6	–	1	–	2	3	4	–	–	–	–	3	–	–	2	–	2	–
Drinking glass (round)	–	–	5	–	–	–	–	–	–	–	–	–	–	–	–	–	1	–	–	–	–	–	–	1	–	–	1	–	–
Drinking glass (rect.)	–	–	–	–	–	–	–	–	–	–	–	–	–	–	–	–	–	–	–	–	–	–	–	–	–	–	–	–	–
Glass bulb	–	–	–	–	–	–	–	–	–	–	–	–	–	–	–	–	–	–	–	–	–	–	–	–	–	–	–	–	–
Glass fragment	–	–	–	–	–	–	–	–	–	–	–	–	–	–	–	–	–	–	–	–	–	–	–	–	–	–	–	–	–
Ceramic fragment	–	–	–	–	–	–	–	–	–	–	–	–	–	–	–	–	–	–	–	–	–	–	2	–	–	–	–	–	–
Scissors	–	–	–	–	–	–	–	–	–	–	–	–	–	–	–	–	–	–	–	–	–	–	–	–	–	–	–	–	–
Spoon	–	–	–	–	–	–	–	–	–	–	–	–	–	–	–	–	–	–	–	–	–	–	–	–	–	–	–	–	–
Knife handle	3	–	–	–	–	–	–	–	–	–	–	–	–	–	–	–	1	–	–	–	–	–	–	–	–	–	–	–	–
Tin can	–	–	3	–	3	–	–	–	–	–	–	–	1	2	–	–	2	–	–	–	–	–	2	–	–	–	1	3	1
Aluminium fragment	–	–	–	–	–	–	–	–	–	–	–	–	–	–	–	–	–	–	–	–	–	–	–	–	–	–	–	–	–
Metal fragment	–	–	–	–	–	–	2	13	–	–	–	–	–	9	–	–	–	2	–	–	–	1	2	–	–	4	2	19	24
Cream box	–	–	–	–	–	–	–	–	–	–	–	–	–	–	–	–	–	–	–	–	–	–	–	–	–	–	–	–	–
Plastic box	–	–	2	–	–	–	–	–	–	–	–	–	–	–	–	–	1	–	–	–	–	–	1	–	–	–	1	–	–
Plastic lid	–	–	–	–	1	–	–	–	–	–	–	–	–	–	–	–	1	–	–	–	–	–	–	–	–	–	–	–	–
Helmet	–	–	–	–	–	–	–	–	–	–	–	–	–	–	–	–	–	–	–	–	–	–	–	–	–	–	–	–	–
Shoe parts	2	15	2	7	3	3	–	3	1	1	–	–	1	5	–	8	4	–	–	–	–	2	–	–	–	1	1	13	3
Button	–	–	–	–	–	2	–	–	–	–	–	–	–	–	–	–	–	–	–	–	–	1	1	–	–	–	–	1	1
Gas mask fragment	–	–	–	–	–	–	–	–	–	–	–	–	–	–	–	–	–	–	–	–	–	–	–	–	–	–	–	1	–
Plastic from mask	–	–	–	–	–	–	–	–	–	–	–	–	–	–	–	–	1	–	–	–	–	–	1	–	–	–	5	–	–
Gun fragment	–	–	–	–	–	–	–	–	–	–	–	–	–	1	–	–	–	–	–	–	–	–	–	–	–	–	–	–	–
Bullet	–	–	–	1	–	–	–	–	–	–	–	–	–	–	–	–	–	–	–	–	–	–	–	–	1	–	–	–	–
Bullet casings	–	–	–	1	–	–	–	–	–	–	–	–	–	–	–	–	–	–	–	–	–	–	–	–	4	3	–	–	–
Explosive	–	–	–	–	2	–	–	–	–	–	–	–	–	–	–	–	–	–	–	–	–	–	–	–	2	–	–	–	–
Cable	–	–	–	–	–	–	–	–	–	–	–	–	–	–	–	–	–	–	–	–	–	1	–	–	–	–	–	–	–
Nail	–	1	–	–	–	–	–	–	–	–	–	–	–	–	–	–	–	–	–	–	–	1	4	–	–	–	–	–	–

	Para 3	Para 4	Para 5	Para 6	Para 7	Para 8	Para 9	Para 10	Para 11	Para 12	Para 13	Para 14	Para 15	Para 16	Para 17	Para 18	Para 19	Para 20	Para Ceruk	Para 21	Para 22	Para 23	Para 24	Para 25	Para 26	Para 27	Para 30	Para 32	Para 33
Battery	-	-	-	-	-	-	-	-	-	-	-	-	-	-	-	-	20	-	-	-	-	-	-	-	-	-	-	-	-
Toothbrush	-	-	-	-	-	-	-	-	-	-	-	-	-	-	-	-	-	1	-	-	-	-	-	-	-	-	-	-	-
Medical tools	-	-	-	-	-	-	-	-	-	-	-	-	-	-	-	-	-	-	-	-	-	-	-	-	-	-	-	-	-
Funnel	-	-	-	-	-	-	-	-	-	-	-	-	-	-	-	-	-	-	-	-	-	2	-	-	-	-	-	-	-
Metal arrow	-	-	-	-	-	-	-	-	-	-	-	-	-	-	-	-	-	-	-	-	-	-	-	-	-	-	-	-	-
Sewing tools	-	-	-	-	-	-	-	-	-	-	-	-	-	-	-	-	-	-	-	-	-	-	-	-	-	-	-	-	-
Razor	-	-	-	-	-	-	-	-	-	-	-	-	-	-	-	-	-	-	-	-	-	-	-	-	-	-	-	-	-
Electric socket	-	-	-	-	-	-	-	-	-	-	-	-	-	-	-	-	-	-	-	-	-	-	-	-	-	-	-	-	-
Coin	-	-	-	-	-	-	-	-	-	-	-	-	-	-	-	-	-	-	-	1	1	-	-	-	-	-	-	-	-
Human bones	-	-	-	-	-	-	1	-	-	-	-	-	-	-	-	18	-	-	8	-	-	-	-	-	-	-	-	-	-
TOTAL	5	26	35	14	13	10	12	16	3	2	2	6	4	19	1	28	35	7	8	1	3	6	30	5	7	11	11	42	30

Source: Authors' summary.

Table 14.1B: WWII-era artefacts recorded by site during the Papua Centre of Archaeology surveys on Biak Island, 2016.

	Manggandi Sapi 1	Mokmer sub	Rumah Radio	G. Binsari	Ceruk Sorido	G. Sanumi 1	G. Sanumi 2	Dekat Bunker	Parit Sanumi	Sanumi Laut	Ibdi Sub 1	Ibdi Sub 2	G. Warbenur	Adibai	G. Wadimor	G. Ruar 1	G. Ruar 2	G. Ruar 5	G. Ruar 6	Kali Ruar	G. Mandon 1	G. Mandon 2	G. Mandon 3
Bottle	3	2	2	1	-	8	1	3	10	-	1	-	2	2	-	-	1	1	-	1	1	2	-
Bottle fragment	1	-	-	1	-	6	2	1	2	-	-	3	-	2	-	-	1	-	6	-	-	2	3
Drinking glass (round)	-	-	-	-	-	-	-	-	-	-	-	-	-	-	-	-	-	-	2	-	-	-	-
Drinking glass (rect.)	-	-	-	-	-	-	-	-	-	-	-	-	-	-	-	-	-	-	-	-	2	-	-
Glass bulb	-	-	-	-	-	-	-	-	-	-	-	-	-	-	-	-	-	-	-	-	-	-	-
Glass fragment	-	5	7	-	-	-	-	-	-	-	-	-	-	-	-	-	-	1	-	-	-	-	-
Ceramic fragment	1	-	-	1	1	-	-	-	2	-	-	-	1	-	-	-	-	-	-	-	11	-	10
Scissors	-	-	-	-	-	-	-	-	-	-	-	-	-	-	-	-	-	-	1	-	-	-	-

	G. Mandon 3	G. Mandon 2	G. Mandon 1	Kali Ruar	G. Ruar 6	G. Ruar 5	G. Ruar 2	G. Ruar 1	G. Wadimor	Adibai	G. Warbenur	Ibdi Sub 2	Ibdi Sub 1	Sanumi Laut	Parit Sanumi	Dekat Bunker	G. Sanumi 2	G. Sanumi 1	Ceruk Sorido	G. Binsari	Rumah Radio	Mokmer sub	Manggandi Sapi 1
Spoon	–	–	–	–	1	–	–	–	–	–	–	–	–	–	–	–	–	–	–	–	–	–	–
Knife handle	–	–	–	–	–	–	–	–	–	–	–	–	–	–	–	–	–	–	–	–	–	–	–
Tin can	–	–	1	–	1	1	1	–	–	4	–	–	–	–	–	–	–	–	–	–	–	2	–
Aluminium fragment	–	–	–	–	–	–	2	–	–	1	1	–	–	–	–	–	–	4	–	–	–	–	–
Metal fragment	–	–	7	3	8	22	11	–	–	–	–	3	–	–	–	–	–	–	3	–	–	2	–
Cream box	–	–	1	–	–	–	–	–	–	–	–	–	–	–	–	–	–	–	–	–	–	–	–
Plastic box	–	–	–	–	3	2	–	–	–	–	–	–	–	–	–	–	–	–	–	–	–	–	–
Plastic lid	–	–	2	1	–	2	1	–	–	–	–	–	–	–	–	–	–	1	–	–	–	1	–
Helmet	–	–	–	–	–	–	–	–	–	–	1	–	–	–	–	–	–	–	–	–	–	–	–
Shoe parts	–	–	–	–	–	–	1	–	–	–	–	–	–	–	–	–	–	–	–	–	–	–	1
Button	1	–	–	1	2	9	1	–	–	–	1	–	–	–	–	–	–	4	–	6	–	–	–
Gas mask fragment	–	–	–	–	–	–	1	–	–	–	–	–	–	–	–	–	–	4	–	–	–	–	–
Plastic from mask	–	–	7	–	3	–	–	–	–	–	–	–	–	–	–	–	–	–	–	–	–	–	–
Gun fragment	–	–	–	–	–	–	–	–	–	–	1	–	–	–	–	–	–	2	–	–	–	–	–
Bullet	1	1	–	1	3	–	2	1	–	–	1	2	6	2	3	2	–	–	–	1	–	–	–
Bullet casings	–	–	2	–	–	1	–	–	–	–	–	–	–	–	1	1	–	–	–	–	–	1	–
Explosive	1	1	1	–	5	1	5	–	–	1	–	–	–	–	–	–	–	–	–	–	–	2	–
Cable	–	–	–	–	–	–	–	–	–	–	–	–	–	–	–	–	–	–	–	–	–	–	–
Nail	–	–	–	–	–	–	–	–	–	–	–	–	–	–	1	1	–	–	–	–	–	–	–
Battery	–	–	–	–	–	–	–	–	–	–	–	–	6	–	–	–	–	15	–	–	–	–	–
Toothbrush	1	–	1	–	–	3	–	–	–	–	–	–	–	–	–	–	–	–	–	–	–	–	–
Medical tools	–	–	–	–	3	–	–	–	–	–	–	–	–	–	–	–	–	–	–	–	–	–	–
Funnel	–	–	–	–	–	–	–	–	–	–	–	–	–	–	–	–	–	–	–	–	–	–	–
Metal arrow	–	–	–	–	1	1	–	–	–	–	–	–	–	–	–	–	–	–	–	–	–	–	–
Sewing tools	–	–	–	–	–	–	–	–	–	–	–	–	–	–	–	–	–	–	–	–	–	–	–
Razor	–	–	–	–	–	–	–	–	–	–	–	–	–	–	–	–	–	–	–	–	–	–	–

	Manggandi Sapi 1	Mokmer sub	Rumah Radio	G. Binsari	Ceruk Sorido	G. Sanumi 1	G. Sanumi 2	Dekat Bunker	Parit Sanumi	Sanumi Laut	Ibdi Sub 1	Ibdi Sub 2	G. Warbenur	Adibai	G. Wadimor	G. Ruar 1	G. Ruar 2	G. Ruar 5	G. Ruar 6	Kali Ruar	G. Mandon 1	G. Mandon 2	G. Mandon 3
Electric socket	–	–	–	–	–	–	–	–	19	–	–	–	–	–	–	–	–	–	–	–	–	–	–
Coin	–	–	–	–	–	–	–	–	–	–	–	–	–	–	–	–	–	–	–	–	–	–	–
Human bones	–	–	–	–	–	–	–	–	–	–	–	–	–	–	–	–	–	–	–	–	–	–	–
TOTAL	6	15	9	10	4	40	3	10	38	2	13	8	8	10	0	1	27	44	39	7	36	5	17

Source: Authors' summary.

Table 14.1C: WWII-era artefacts recorded by site during the Papua Centre of Archaeology surveys on Biak Island, 2016.

	G. Sundey 1	G. Sundey 3	G. Sasler/ Sundey 2	G. Mandaryap 1	G. Mandaryap 2	G. Sosen	P. Urep	P. Wundi	Ansekdo	Kali Warsansan	Nermnu Sup	Nermnu	Wopes	Rosayendi	Supkarkir
Bottle	7	5	1	–	2	–	–	–	–	1	3	–	–	–	–
Bottle fragment	1	–	–	–	4	–	–	–	–	–	–	–	–	–	–
Drinking glass (round)	–	–	–	–	–	–	–	–	–	–	–	–	–	–	–
Drinking glass (rect.)	1	–	–	–	–	–	–	–	–	–	–	–	–	–	–
Glass bulb	–	–	–	–	–	–	–	–	–	–	1	–	–	–	–
Glass fragment	–	–	–	–	–	–	–	–	–	–	–	–	–	–	–
Ceramic fragment	–	–	–	–	–	–	2	–	–	–	–	–	–	–	–
Scissors	–	–	–	–	–	–	–	–	–	–	–	–	–	–	–
Spoon	–	–	–	–	–	–	–	–	–	–	–	–	–	–	–
Knife handle	–	–	–	–	1	–	–	–	–	–	–	–	–	–	–
Tin can	–	–	–	–	–	–	–	–	–	–	–	–	–	–	–
Aluminium fragment	–	–	–	–	–	–	–	–	–	–	–	–	–	–	5
Metal fragment	4	–	2	–	8	–	–	–	–	–	–	–	–	–	–

	G. Sunday 1	G. Sunday 3	G. Sasier/Sunday 2	G. Mandaryap 1	G. Mandaryap 2	G. Sosen	P. Urep	P. Wundi	Ansekdo	Kali Warsansan	Nermnu Sup	Nermnu	Wopes	Rosayendi	Supkarkir
Cream box	–	–	–	–	–	–	–	–	–	–	–	–	–	–	–
Plastic box	–	–	–	–	1	–	–	–	–	–	–	–	–	–	–
Plastic lid	–	–	–	–	–	–	–	–	–	1	–	–	–	–	–
Helmet	–	–	–	1	1	–	–	–	1	1	–	–	–	–	–
Shoe parts	–	–	–	–	1	–	–	–	–	–	–	–	–	–	–
Button	3	–	1	–	6	–	–	–	–	–	–	–	–	–	–
Gas mask fragment	–	–	1	–	7	–	–	–	–	–	–	–	–	–	–
Plastic from mask	1	–	–	–	5	–	–	–	–	–	–	–	–	–	–
Gun fragment	–	–	–	–	–	–	–	–	–	–	–	–	–	–	–
Bullet	–	–	13	–	–	2	4	–	–	–	–	–	–	–	–
Bullet casings	–	–	–	–	1	–	–	–	–	–	–	–	–	1	–
Explosive	–	–	–	–	–	2	–	1	–	–	1	–	–	–	–
Cable	5	–	–	–	–	–	–	–	–	–	–	–	–	–	–
Nail	–	–	–	–	–	–	–	–	–	–	–	–	–	–	–
Battery	–	–	2	–	–	–	–	–	–	–	–	–	–	–	–
Toothbrush	–	–	–	–	2	–	–	–	–	–	–	–	–	–	–
Medical tools	–	–	–	–	–	–	–	–	–	–	201	–	–	–	–
Funnel	–	–	–	–	1	–	–	–	–	–	–	–	–	–	–
Metal arrow	–	–	–	–	–	–	–	–	–	–	–	–	–	–	–
Sewing tools	–	–	–	–	–	–	–	–	–	–	6	–	–	–	–
Razor	–	–	1	–	–	–	–	–	–	–	–	–	–	–	–
Electric socket	–	–	–	–	–	–	–	–	–	–	–	–	–	–	–
Coin	–	–	–	–	–	–	–	–	–	–	1	–	–	–	–
Human bones	–	–	–	–	–	–	–	–	–	–	1	–	–	–	–
TOTAL	22	5	21	1	40	4	6	1	1	2	213	0	0	1	5

Source: Authors' summary.

Discussion

Wartime Biak: Hubs of conflict and refuge

Based on the archaeological surveys conducted by the Papua Centre of Archaeology, two hubs of military activity were uncovered: first, along the south-east coast of Biak, which was established by the Japanese in their occupation and subsequent failed defence of Cenderawasih Bay, and second, in the Padaido Islands, where the Allies located themselves at arm's length from the Japanese and subsequently repaired and restocked ships and aircraft as they moved westwards into Southeast Asia.

Around Mokmer and Sorido, runways, bunkers, and several concrete buildings provide the material evidence for the area's strategic position for the Japanese. The local landscape lends itself to defence, with the airfields being protected by limestone hills that stretch from west to east, and where caves are abundantly found that can be used as bunkers for storing munitions and for shooting from. The elevated position of the uplifted coral also provided perfect vantage points for Japanese machine gunners and snipers during the Allied advance. As such, the presence of bunkers in these areas attests to the Japanese familiarity with the local landscape and suggests Kuzume had good reason to tactically withdraw and lead the Allied troops towards Mokmer. From Mokmer, the Japanese army was ready to attack the enemy from the numerous bunkers that surrounded the airfield.

Larger caves were used to conceal personnel and some caves recorded during survey (e.g. Sundey Cave) were probably chosen because their entrances face away from the coast, being concealed from incoming advances. It is clear from the archaeological remains, including toothbrushes and shaving equipment, found within some of these caves that people lived in them temporarily. Conversely, other bunkers identified along the south-east coast were placed in aggressive locations, a few metres from the shore, to fend off coastal assaults. Many of these caves primarily contained bullet casings and explosives. The positioning of the embrasures in the Japanese bunkers also indicates that they were expecting attacks from the south coast, which is the easiest place to land, and was the focus of Japanese military operations around the airfields. The narrow but wide shape of the embrasures suggests they were designed for the occupation of several combatants using machine guns. Along the coast, the intensity of the defensive infrastructure is clear, with the Japanese installing concrete bunkers to supplement those already carved out of the natural rock. However, as mentioned, during the Battle of Biak many of these frontline bunkers were forfeited in favour of a surprise defence closer to the airfields.

Even after the Allies had captured south-east Biak, Japanese soldiers held out in the northern parts of the island, conducting opportunistic guerrilla attacks. Archaeological surveys previously undertaken by the Papua Centre of Archaeology suggest the north coast of Biak was a key location harbouring the Japanese, about 4000 of which had retreated after Mokmer and the other airfields were captured (Smith 1953, 390). For instance, helmets, medical kits, human bones, and other objects were found scattered around a rock-shelter in Wari village (Balai Arkeologi Papua 2016). Additional information obtained from informants in north Biak confirms that this region, especially around the Korimderi River, was the location of a battle between the American and Japanese armies. The historical sources further indicate that skirmishes occurred along the Waferdori River and the Korim-Sorido where Nermnu, Dofyo Wafor, Wari, and Rosayendi villages are located (Smith 1953).

During and after the Battle of Biak, the Padaido Islands were used by the American army as a forward base to hospitalise crew, repair landing craft, and house officers while the lagoon was used as a temporary naval dock to repair and refuel seaplanes and torpedo boats (United States Government 1947, 310). Following the war, the Dutch military continued to use the base for their own purposes.

The high density of American military remains in the Padaido Islands, particularly including piers and docks, oil tanks, and a hospital, are a testament to these offshore bases being used intensively, first to support combat on Biak and Numfor, and later to facilitate the Allied war effort as it moved into Island Southeast Asia.

Coral islands and the archaeology of the Pacific theatre

Coral islands like Biak and the Padaido group were key stepping stones for the rapid Japanese assault on the Pacific and for the later leapfrogging strategy that the Allies used to reclaim the region. The hard underlying geology and insularity, in part, made these locations favourable in comparison with the softer ground on the New Guinea mainland. Similar defensive positions have been recorded on Watom Island in the Bismarck Archipelago (Petchey 2015), Peleliu Island in Palau (Price and Knecht 2012), Torw, Jalwoj, Mili, and Wija in the Marshall Islands (Christiansen 2002), and Guam and Saipan in the Mariana Islands (Mushynsky 2021; Mushynsky et al. 2018; Taboroši and Jenson 2002). In particular, comparison with the military architecture at these Pacific sites indicates similar Japanese building techniques and defensive strategies (previously synthesised by Rottman 2003). These similarities include the opening of coral limestone crevices to produce inconspicuous complexes of wide, narrow, and low-lying embrasures for machine gunners and riflemen. These defensive positions were distributed with overlapping fields of view so that they formed a continuous defence against enemy landing parties. As noted on Watom Island (Petchey 2015, 47), many of these bunkers had multiple entrances to allow escape if the space was overrun or one entrance collapsed owing to bombardment. Monopolising the higher ground and benefiting from the interplay between these coastal defences and inland strongholds also seems to have been common to the Japanese defensive efforts. The vast extent and intensity of landscape transformation by the Japanese in the Pacific has even led some researchers to describe these locations as island forts (Petchey 2015). On many of these islands, the rapid nature of the conflict and subsequent abandonment has meant that large numbers of military vehicles and weapons were left in situ (although Australian personnel and later Dutch were involved in clean-ups on Biak). Today, military equipment is often found in villages and gardens on these islands and sometimes even repurposed as new tools or kept and sold as souvenirs (Arbay and Laksmono 2020). Several of these sites are conserved locally by people like Yusuf Rumaropen who established a small museum in the 1980s relating to artefacts from Binsari Cave (Arbay 2021). The wartime archaeology on these islands is therefore a salient reminder of a very recent and violent time in the past—for some, within living memory or only a generation removed.

Conclusions

The archaeological record of wartime occupation around Biak demonstrates that Cenderawasih Bay became a high-value area for Japanese control of the West New Guinea region, and was a key location for MacArthur's leapfrogging strategy to retake the Pacific. Biak's south-east coast was especially crucial, providing airstrips that the Japanese could run bombing raids from, and that would later support the Allied advance into Southeast Asia and eventually Japan itself. Offshore islands like those in the Padaido group allowed the Allies to remain at arm's length while repairing equipment and gradually bolstering their supplies over several months during the Battle of Biak, one of the most intense conflicts in the Pacific theatre.

The defensive architecture around the airstrips shows that the Japanese military had become familiar with the local landscape in their two years of occupation and used the sheer limestone slopes along the coast and hidden inland cave systems to their advantage, which especially allowed them to dominate in the early stages of the Battle. Caves, modified and extended where necessary, were a key part of Japanese landscape reworking, and a common strategy employed in other parts of the Pacific to conceal the actual numbers of personnel and avoid bombing runs. The archaeological finds within these cave systems, recorded by the Papua Centre of Archaeology, demonstrate that many larger caves on Biak were occupied and lived in temporarily, while smaller limestone bunkers were used primarily militarily. The presence of small human remains in one tunnel is testament to the strategic weakness of these caves in that numerous Japanese became trapped in them and were starved of oxygen by advancing Allied troops. Many similar human remains previously have been repatriated by the Japanese government.

The wartime archaeology of Biak is only beginning to be recorded in detail and large parts of the island, particularly in the interior, remain archaeologically unexplored. Detailed description of the archaeological artefacts and architecture is the focus of ongoing research and is important, not just for Japanese and American military families that seek to repatriate their war dead, but also for the local Biakers who now see WWII and Biak's role in the conflict as crucial to their own recent history. Further description of the island's archaeological remains, alongside oral histories and people's perception of their heritage landscapes, would provide a more nuanced understanding of indigenous experiences of this conflict (as has been explored in other parts of the Pacific, see Poyer 2022), and how local people have reconstituted these experiences through collecting and repurposing wartime remains.

References

Arbay, E.A. 2021. Development of Biak's war tourism. *Journal of Tourism Destination and Attraction* 9(1):91–98. doi.org/10.35814/tourism.v9i1.1868.

Arbay, E.A. and B.S. Laksmono 2020. Tangible and intangible cultural heritage in support to post-war Biak tourism. *Technium Social Sciences Journal* 14:727–734. doi.org/10.47577/tssj.v14i1.2040.

Balai Arkeologi Papua 2016. Exploration of the Second World War remains in Biak Numfor district. Research Report. Unpublished. Balai Arkeologi Papua, Jayapura.

Beevor, A. 2012. *The Second World War.* Orion Publishing Group Ltd, London.

Bernstein, M.D. 1999. Hurricane at Biak: MacArthur against the Japanese, May–August 1944. Unpublished MA thesis. Department of History, San Jose State University, San Jose.

Bullard, S. 2010. Australia's war in New Guinea, and Australia in the liberation of the Netherlands East Indies. In P. Post, W.H. Frederick, I. Heidebrink, and S. Sato (eds), *Encyclopedia of Indonesia in the Pacific War*, pp. 24–31. Brill, Leiden.

Christiansen, H. 2002. Forgotten and refound military structures in the Central Pacific: Examples from the Marshall Islands. In J. Schofield, W.G. Johnson, and C.M. Beck (eds), *Matériel culture: The archaeology of twentieth-century conflict*, pp. 58–64. Routledge, London. doi.org/10.4324/9780203165744_chapter_6.

Copeland, D.C. 2011. A tragic choice: Japanese preventive motivations and the origins of the Pacific War. *International Interactions* 37(1):116–126. doi.org/10.1080/03050629.2011.546722.

Ford, D. 2009. US assessments of Japanese ground warfare tactics and the Army's campaigns in the Pacific theaters, 1943–1945: Lessons learned and methods applied. *War in History* 16(3):325–358. doi.org/10.1177/0968344509104195.

Harrison, S. 2006. Skull trophies of the Pacific War: Transgressive objects of remembrance. *Journal of the Royal Anthropological Institute* 12(4):817–836. doi.org/10.1111/j.1467-9655.2006.00365.x.

Kartika S.N., A.J. Marshall, and B.M. Beehler (eds) 2007. *The ecology of Papua.* Periplus, Singapore.

MacArthur, D. 1966. *Reports of General MacArthur: The campaigns of MacArthur in the Pacific,* Vol. 1. U.S. Center of Military History, Washington, DC.

Mawdsley, E. 2009. *World War II: A new history.* Cambridge University Press, Cambridge.

Mushynsky, J. 2021. *The archaeology, history and heritage of WWII karst defenses in the Pacific.* Springer, Cham, New York. doi.org/10.1007/978-3-030-67353-6.

Mushynsky, J., J. McKinnon, and F. Camacho 2019. The archaeology of World War II karst defences in the Pacific. *Journal of Conflict Archaeology* 13(3):198–222. doi.org/10.1080/15740773.2018.1583470.

Naval Analysis Division 1946. *Interrogations of Japanese officials.* Vols 1–2. United States Strategic Bombing Survey, U.S. Government Printing Office, Washington, DC.

Petchey, P. 2015. Second World War Japanese defences on Watom Island, Papua New Guinea. *Journal of Conflict Archaeology* 10(1):29–51. doi.org/10.1179/1574077315Z.00000000042.

Poyer, L. 2022. *War at the margins: Indigenous experiences in World War II.* University of Hawai'i Press, Honolulu. doi.org/10.2307/j.ctv2ngx5f5.

Price, N. and R. Knecht 2012. Peleliu 1944: The archaeology of a South Pacific D-Day. *Journal of Conflict Archaeology* 7(1):5–48. doi.org/10.1179/157407812X13245464933786.

Riegelman, H. 1955. *The caves of Biak: An American officer's experiences in the Southwest Pacific.* Dial Press, New York.

Rottman, G.L. 2003. *Japanese Pacific island defenses, 1941–45.* Osprey Publishing, Oxford.

Rottman, G.L. 2005. *The Japanese army in World War II.* Osprey Publishing, Oxford.

Scheurer, H. 2015. A 'gruesome business': Collecting and repatriating Pacific Theater war trophies. Unpublished MH thesis. Department of History, Auburn University, Auburn.

Smith, R.R. 1953. *The war in the Pacific: The approach to the Philippines.* Office of the Chief of Military History, Department of the Army, Washington, DC.

Steenbrink, K. 2010. Christianity. In P. Post, W.H. Frederick, I. Heidebrink, and S. Sato (eds), *Encyclopedia of Indonesia in the Pacific War*, pp. 312–320. Brill, Leiden.

Taboroši, D. and J.W. Jenson 2002. World War II artefacts and wartime use of caves in Guam, Mariana Islands. *Capra* 4:1–8.

United States Government 1947. *Building the Navy's bases in World War II: History of the Bureau of Yards and Docks and the Civil Engineer Corps 1940–1946,* Vol. 2. U.S Government Printing Office, Washington, DC.

U.S. Army 41st Division 1944. History of the Biak Operation 15–27 June 1944. Report to the U.S. Army. Unpublished. U.S. Army, Washington, DC.

Weinberg, G.L. 2014. *World War II: A very short introduction.* Oxford University Press, Oxford. doi.org/10.1093/actrade/9780199688777.001.0001.

15

Agentive seas and animate canoes: Tangible and intangible dimensions of marine voyaging by the Marind-anim of central-southern New Guinea

Ian J. McNiven

Abstract

For the coastal Marind-anim of the south-east corner of West New Guinea (Indonesian Papua), as with other coastal groups of central-southern New Guinea such as the Asmat to the west and Torres Strait Islanders to the east, huge dugout canoes were materially elaborated to various degrees as animate object-beings with social lives intimately connected with the social, spiritual, and ceremonial lives of people. Marind canoe voyaging had technological and cosmological dimensions. The marine realm for the Marind, as with their neighbours, was imbued with sentient and spiritual forces that necessitated ritual intervention and negotiation. The spiritual and ritual dimensions of Marind seascapes and canoe voyaging were given added complexity by associations with large-scale headhunting expeditions to coastal communities to the east (Trans-Fly and Torres Strait). Understanding the long-term history of Marind voyaging beyond oral histories and late nineteenth- and early twentieth-century historical recordings is challenging due to its largely intangible dimensions. The likely absence of preserved canoes necessitates archaeological excavation and dating of materially robust (tangible) proxies of voyaging. In the absence of local stone sources, exotic stone axes and stone club heads traded and raided by the Marind during headhunting expeditions provide such a proxy.

Abstrak

Untuk orang Marind-anim yang menetap di ujung tenggara Papua (Indonesia), seperti kelompok penduduk pesisir di wilayah selatan-tengah Papua Nugini, suku Asmat di barat dan mereka yang berada di selat Torres, perahu yang berukuran besar dibangun dengan menggunakan berbagai macam obyek hidup disekitarnya yang berhubungan dekat dengan suasana sosial, spiritual dan upacara keagamaan mereka. Perahu yang digunakan oleh penduduk Marind dalam berlayar memiliki aspek teknologi dan kosmologis. Kehidupan kelautan bagi penduduk Marind, seperti juga dengan penduduk tetangganya, memiliki rasa mendalam dimana kekuatan spiritual diperlukan untuk negosiasi dan intervensi upacara keagamaan. Pelbagai dimensi keagamaan dan upacara kelautan penduduk Marind dan perjalanan kelautannya makin rumit dengan adanya ekspedisi perburuan kepala yang berskala besar antara orang Marind-Anim dan masyarakat pesisir yang bermukim dibagian timur (Trans-Fly dan selat Torres). Memahami sejarah panjang perjalanan laut yang dilakukan oleh orang Marind dalam bentuk sejarah lisan dan pecatatannya di akhir abad sembilan belas dan awal abad duapuluh sangat sulit dilakukan mengingat besarnya dimensi-dimensi yang tidak tersentuh. Yang tidak ada adalah sisa perahu dari penggalian arkeologi dan sisa bahan yang jelas terlihat sebagai peninggalan perjalanan laut. Tanpa adanya sumber-sumber batuan lokal, maka dengan adanya kapak batu yang eksotis dan kepala-kepala berbatuan yang diperdagangkan dan disita oleh orang Marind selama melakukan peburuan kepala akan bisa dijadikan sebagai wali/proksi.

Introduction

The extraordinary diversity and complexity of the canoes of New Guinea (comprising West New Guinea, or Indonesian Papua, and Papua New Guinea) were first documented by Haddon (1937). More recently, discussions of New Guinea canoes have concerned their ontological status and spiritual, symbolic, and agentive dimensions for groups such as the Asmat (Bigourdan 2006), Torres Strait Islanders (McNiven 2015, 2018), Trobriand Islanders (Campbell 2002; Gell 1998; Munn 1977), and the Murik (Lipset 2014). This chapter extends these discussions to canoes of the Marind-anim of South Papua Province, Indonesia. To understand the anthropomorphic and agentive dimensions of Marind-anim canoes requires broader contextualisation in terms of long-distance voyaging associated with headhunting expeditions. In this sense, Marind-anim canoe use has much in common with other south-coast New Guinea groups such the Asmat to the west and Torres Strait Islanders to the east. More specifically, Marind-anim canoes shared certain aspects of the object-being status of Torres Strait canoes (McNiven 2018) and the cosmological meaningfulness and liminality of Asmat canoes (Bigourdan 2006). This chapter draws on a broad range of published information to elaborate on the embodied cosmological, spiritual, and agentive dimensions of Marind-anim canoes and associated seas.

Marind-anim

Within anthropological literature, the term Marind-anim is often shortened to Marind as *anim*[1] = people/person/human in Marind language (Chao 2021, 248; Olsson 2021, 3). Torres Strait Islanders and some Trans-Fly groups referred to the Marind as the Tugeri, Tuger, or Thuger (Haddon 1891; Hitchcock 2009; Ingui et al. 1991; Laade 1971; Wirz 1933). The territorial domain of the Marind stretches 200 km eastwards along the coast from Selat Muli (Muli Strait, formerly known as Princess Marianne Strait) in the west to 25 km east of Merauke (a town located 100 km along the coast west of the Indonesia–Papua New Guinea border). It extends 200 km inland across swampy lowlands and savannah, taking in the drainage basins of the Bian and Kumbe rivers and the lower reaches of the Merauke (Maro) River (van Baal 1966, 10–11) (Figure 15.1). The Marind comprise three geographically separate languages: 'Coastal Marind' (northern coast and the Kumbe River basin and adjacent coast), 'Bush Marind' (taking in the lower and middle Bian River region and adjacent coast), and 'Bian Marind' (taking in the upper Bian River region) (Olsson 2021, 1, 9, Map 1).

---

1   Throughout this chapter, local language words are italicised at first mention.

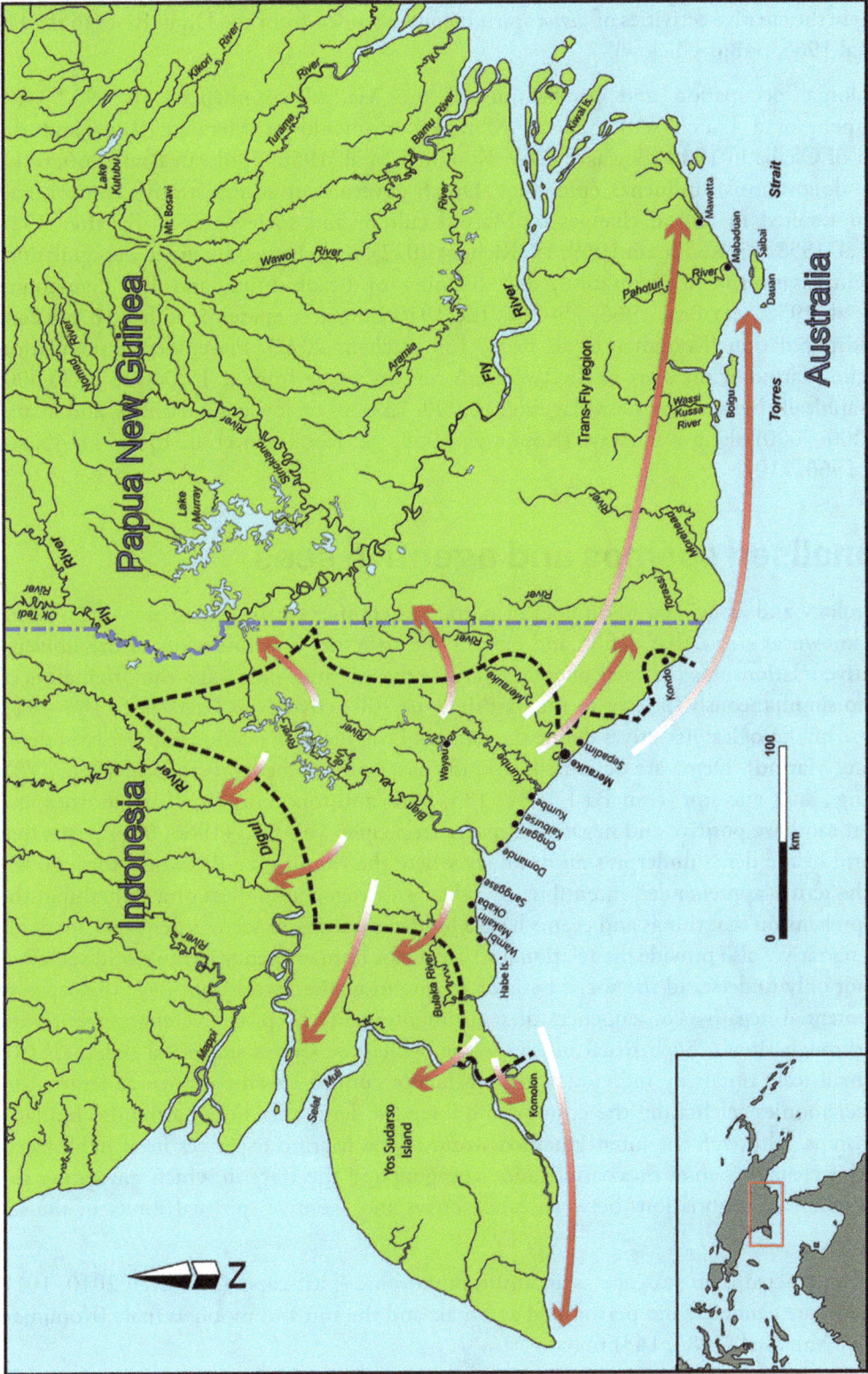

Figure 15.1: Map of central-southern New Guinea.

Note: Figure shows the approximate boundary of Marind (language) territory (black dashed line), schematic routes of headhunting expeditions to documented raiding areas (red and white arrows), and selected place names (including those mentioned in the text).

Source: Artwork by Ian McNiven, after Kooijman (1959, 12), Olsson (2021, Map 2), van Baal (1966), Voorhoeve (1983).

In reality, the Marind 'world' encompassed a much larger area that extended west to Yos Sudarso (formerly Frederik Hendrik) Island, north to the Digul River, and east to the Fly River; areas visited during large-scale headhunting expeditions that could last for months (van Baal 1966, 348). These extra-regional mobility patterns had cosmological referents in numerous Marind mythological narratives where the creative activities of *dema* spirit beings extended from the Digul River to the Fly River (van Baal 1966, 348; see below).

Sustained colonial occupation and pacification of the Marind commenced in 1902 with the establishment of a Dutch settlement at Merauke on the lower Merauke River and the establishment of Okaba in 1908 (Boelaars 1969; Kooijman et al. 1958, 103; van Baal 1966, 681). Diseases (e.g. donovanosis), influenza epidemics, Dutch government administrative control, and missionisation resulted in radical changes to Marind culture and society, especially after 1920 (Kooijman et al. 1958, 53; Kooijman 1959, 19; Richens 2022). Key changes included depopulation, settlement centralisation, Christianisation, and banning of headhunting and key ceremonies (Kooijman et al. 1958; van Baal 1966, 25–26). The 1919 influenza epidemic killed 18 per cent of the Marind population (Kooijman et al. 1958, 163; Richens 2022). Pre-epidemic population estimates of the Marind at the start of the twentieth century range from c. 15,000 to c. 20,000, divided geographically between coastal villages (c. 10,000–13,000) on low coastal dunes, and inland villages (c. 5000–7000) along waterways (Kooijman 1959, 12; Kooijman et al. 1958, 44–45; see also van Baal 1966, 710).

Intentionalised cosmos and agentive seas

Marind cosmology and associated mythological narratives enumerate the emergence of powerful spirit beings known as dema that define and express the structure and intention of the universe and the agentive relationships between phenomena. For the Marind, dema are 'the originators of all things' who simultaneously 'belong to the past' but 'are still active' (van Baal 1966, 180–181). Critically, these mythological narratives define the nature of the agentive relationship between dema and people (i.e. Marind). Dema are described variously as a 'spiritual being' (van Baal 1966, 178), 'mythical being', and 'ancestor' (van Baal 1984, 133) with anthropomorphic characteristics and intentions that can have positive and negative impacts on people. Van Baal (1966, 922) posits that the social world of the dema underpins an ontology where the Marind see the world through the lens of what he terms 'apprehended intentionality'; that is, 'a vague awareness of a something, the undefined apprehension that things and events have a hidden meaning or secret intention'. Yet dema mythological narratives also provide the relational structure for human agency in the world such that the Marind not only understand the social basis of an intentionalised world but have the capacity to alter the potential negative consequences of such intentionality by proactive engagement with dema forces through rituals. Such ritual interventions, while not always successful (Chao 2019), range from small-scale rituals by individuals that influence context-specific events, to large-scale, inter-village ceremonies celebrating the cosmogonic forces of dema that help harmonise human–dema relationships. Although the intentionalised world of the Marind expresses itself in all facets of their life, this chapter focuses on coastal canoe voyaging and the ways in which navigating the seas involved ritualised negotiations between canoe crews and agentive spiritual forces of the sea and cosmos.

The 'Marind constructed their seascape as an anthropomorphic spiritscape' (McNiven 2010, 101). The sea and earth are gendered and personified as female and the sun and moon as male (Kooijman et al. 1958, 71). Van Baal (1984, 143) noted:

The path of the sun is also the path of mankind. Born from a well in the far east as the products of dema who came underground from the far west, the first humans went westward, following the direction of the sun.

When the sun sets daily in the west, it has intercourse with the earth (during the dry season when the sun sets over the land) or sea (during the rainy season when the sun sets over the sea) (Kooijman et al. 1958, 72; van Baal 1966, 213, 256). During the rainy season, the:

> numerous spider-threads floating in the air or hanging suspended from the [coconut] palm trees on the beach at this time of the year are called *kombra-kombra* by the Marind. They are the sperma of the sun, wafted landwards by the wind blowing from the sea. (Wirz 1925, IV:78)

The celestial and cosmological dimensions of this interaction introduce the sea as a vast animate and agentive domain such that canoe voyaging, like all rituals of Marind life, represents an 'intensive co-mingling with the supernatural' by which all Marind feel 'surrounded' (Kooijman et al. 1958, 76). All of the major forces of the sea that impact upon sea voyaging, such as waves, currents, tides, and winds, are animate expressions of the agentive powers and actions of dema.

Yorma is the 'sea déma' who is known for his 'frightening power' and for 'lashing the coast with his mighty waves' (van Baal 1966, 287, 343, 387). His dema father is Desse ('depth') and his dema mother is Dawéna ('who brought forth the ground water') and he was brought up in the interior before he became the dema of the sea (van Baal 1966, 381, 387). Seawater was associated with *nakari* (singular: *nakaru*), 'a term used to denote a kind of female mythical beings, the companions of the more important male déma' (van Baal 1966, 188). Waves are the nakari of Yorma, with two nakari called Karai ('turbid') and Mo ('clear') (i.e. 'qualities' or 'characteristics' of seawater) (van Baal 1966, 189, 383). Jellyfish are also nakari of Yorma (van Baal 1966, 383). During the mythical period of his ascendancy,

> Yorma became a great and dreaded déma; his headgear fluttered in the wind (the foam from the crests of the waves) and his drumming (the roaring of the waves) frightened the villagers, who hid in their huts. (van Baal 1966, 383)

In one extreme case, Yorma obliterated the 'old coastal' village of Imo located near Wambi (van Baal 1966, 383, 661; see also Kooijman et al. 1958, 74).

Yorma resides at the mouth of the Bian River, where a 'big and powerful' and loud bore tide wave up to 1 m high 'betrays his presence' daily and is known to penetrate beyond Kabtel village located 60 km upstream (van Baal 1966, 384). Indeed, Yorma is credited with creating the 'river-valleys' (van Baal 1966, 244, 386, 431). Dabad is a dema 'who lives in a sand-bank' at the mouth of the Merauke River (van Baal 1966, 313). Another dema, Bangréke, 'sets the tidal currents moving in the mouth of the Merauke river' (van Baal 1966, 349). Geurtjens (1929, cited in van Baal 1966, 778) recorded the presence of a dema in Koloi/Koroi Creek at the village of Okaba: 'Whenever there is a strong swell in the mouth of the creek, the déma is stirring up the waves with his hands.'

The island of Habe (Habeeke), located 4.5 km off the north-west mainland coast of Marind territory, was moved into place by dema. In one mythological narrative, the sea eagle dema Bau moved the island 50 km to its current location from its original location at the mouth of the Bian River (Kooijman et al. 1958, 74; van Baal 1966, 392). In another narrative, Habe was part of the mainland near the Fly River before being set adrift by the dema Dawi. Floating westwards, the island was fought over by various other dema before settling in its present position, located 500 km north-west of the Fly River mouth (van Baal 1966, 274–278).

As with Torres Strait Islanders, the Marind had the potential capacity to alter sea conditions by ritual intervention (McNiven 2004). For example, the western Marind mention that Muli-anem is the dema who 'resides in or under the water' of Selat Muli (van Baal 1966, 285, 437). According to Kooijman and colleagues (1958, 73), Muli is 'the dema of the westerly storms'. Up until 1929,

> the crews of canoes going through Strait Marianne [Selat Muli] carefully refrained from throwing any rubbish overboard or, when they started out from a camp on one of the banks of the strait, avoided to make any noise, lest *Yorma* should be enraged. (van Baal 1966, 385)

More generally, van Baal (1966, 878) notes:

> When the sea is turbulent, the waves are conjured by throwing into the water scraps of food over which the following words have been pronounced: '*Wandus! Wandus!* You should lie down!' *Wandus* is the name of a *nakaru* of *Yorma*, the sea déma ... If, on the contrary, one wishes a gale to rise and the waves to do damage to a village or drown a hated sailor, *Yorma* himself is addressed in the spell uttered over the object thrown into the sea: '*Yorma! Yorma!* Kill!'.

Given the formidable power of Yorma, it is no surprise that Wirz (1922, I:124) noted that the 'sea is and remains a foreign and feared element for Marind'.

Animate and agentive canoes

The Marind made and used impressive dugout canoes (*yahun/yavun*—Olsson 2021, 11) for travel along rivers and the coast. In the early twentieth century, Gooszen (1908, cited in van Baal 1966, 22) observed 28 canoes, 20 measuring more than 15 m in length, on the beach fronting Sanggase village. Large canoes could accommodate crews of at least 13 people (Figures 15.2 and 15.3). Marind canoes possessed neither outriggers nor sails (in contrast to Torres Strait Islander canoes—see McNiven 2015), and were propelled with paddles and poles.

According to van Baal (1966, 22, 703–704), the 'best canoes were made inland, along the middle course of the big rivers' (Bian, Kumbe, and Merauke rivers) using stone axes and were purchased directly by coastal Marind venturing upstream (see also Kooijman et al. 1958, 46; van Baal 1982, 92; Verschueren 1970, 47; Wirz 1922, I:123). Inland manufacture was a necessity given that 'large, suitable tree trunks are a rarity on the coast' (Wirz 1922, I:123). A strong association existed between canoe manufacture and headhunting expeditions (van Baal 1966, 424). Indeed, in the early twentieth century, Nollen (cited in van Baal 1966, 703) observed that 'it is curious that they always buy boats when it is the season for headhunting'. Not unexpectedly, the demand for 'big canoes' stopped following government pacification and cessation of headhunting in the early twentieth century (van Baal 1966, 167). Furthermore, Kooijman and colleagues (1958, 107) argue that canoe manufacture and intra-regional and inter-regional canoe mobility by the Marind dramatically decreased during the twentieth century with increasing access to foreign objects (especially tools). That is: 'It was no longer necessary to travel along the coast either for barter or for head-hunting which was now prohibited and a thing of the past'.

Figure 15.2: Marind in canoes meeting the Dutch naval gunboat HMS *Ceram*, the mouth of Merauke River, 1902.
Source: Photo from author's collection.

Figure 15.3: Canoe at the mouth of Merauke River, 1902.
Source: Photo from author's collection, published in Schmeltz (1905, Figure 10).

Marind canoes have a 'tendency towards anthropomorphism', such that 'a canoe is given the shape of a human being' and a 'bow is a human person with a nose and a foot' (van Baal 1966, 869). Wirz (1922, I:XIX, Plate 41) 'interpreted' carved canoe bows in the form of 'human faces' on the lower Kumbe River. The clearest example, with stylised 'eye ridges' and 'nose', is shown in Figure 15.4.3 (Wirz 1922, I:124). Indeed, 'the Marind have made canoes with carved bows' ever since the dema brothers Nazr and Mahu fashioned two canoes with 'bows in the shape of a human face' in preparation for a headhunting expedition to the Digul River (van Baal 1966, 402). Wirz (1922, I:124) adds that the canoe cavity is the 'mouth and stomach' while the 'arched extensions on the boat wall the hands and fingers'. Anthropomorphism of Marind canoes implies a degree of embodiment such that canoes also had agentive qualities and object-being status, as seen in Torres Strait canoes (McNiven 2018).

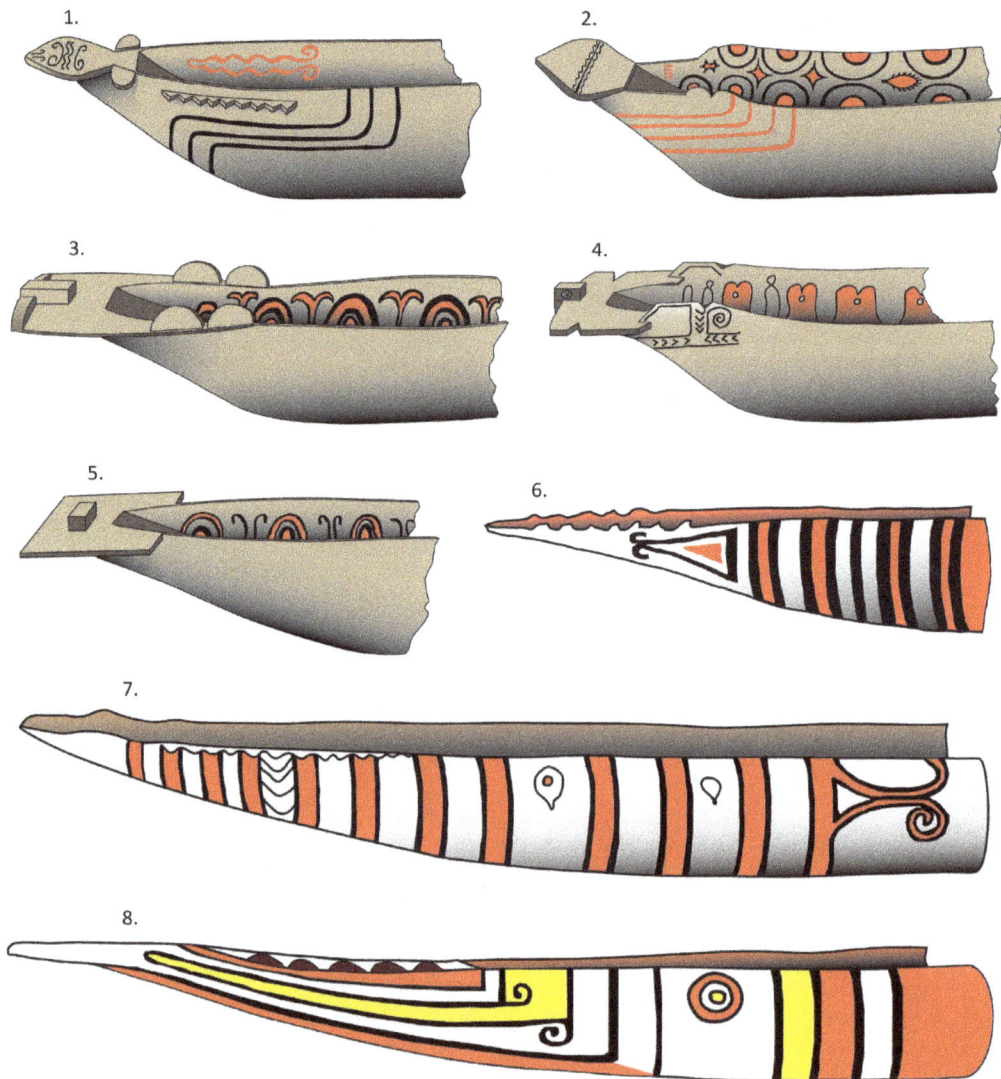

Figure 15.4: Carved and painted bows of Marind canoes.

Notes: (1) and (2) canoe bows in the form of a 'sea turtle', typical of the Merauke River — after Wirz (1922, I:Plates 41.1 and 41.2); (3), (4) and (5) canoe bows in the form of stylised 'human faces', typical of the lower Kumbe River — after Wirz (1922, I:Plates 41.3, 41.4, and 41.5); (6) Marind — after Vertenten (1914, Plate 19.1); (7) west of Bian River — after Vertenten (1914, Plate 19.4); and (8) Kumbe village — after Vertenten (1914, Plate 19.5).

Source: Artwork by Ian McNiven, after Wirz (1922) and Vertenten (1914).

Wirz (1922, I:XIX, Plate 41) also documented Marind canoes with elaborately painted geometric motifs in red (presumably ochre) and black (presumably charcoal) located both inside and outside of the front of canoes (Figure 15.4). Vertenten (1914, 156, Plate 19) documented figurative motifs, including a post-contact motif (sailing ship with flag), on the inside of a Marind canoe (see Figure 15.5). Further examples of painted geometric motifs on the front and rear sections of canoe hulls (e.g. circles and triangles), along with painted and carved figurative motifs (e.g. birds, fish, crocodile, human hand, leaves, crescent moon, evening star) on the outside of hulls, are provided by Vertenten (1914, 155–156, Plate 19) (Figures 15.4.6–15.4.8). In some cases, the inside and outside of Marind canoe hulls beyond bow decorations were painted entirely with red ochre (Figure 15.4.6). Vertenten (1914, 156) observed that canoe bows with vertical stripes were characteristic of areas west of the Bian River and horizontal stripes a feature of the Kumbe and Merauke River areas, which suggests a division between western and eastern Marind canoe decorative conventions (Figures 15.4.7, 15.4.8, and 15.5).

Figure 15.5: Consecration of a Marind canoe, near Sepadim village, 1910–1930.
Source: Tropenmuseum, Amsterdam, TM-10006140.

A strong association existed between canoes and clan identity such that canoes were given subclan dema names and were the 'property of local subclans or men's house communities' (van Baal 1966, 91, 259; 1982, 88; see also Wirz 1934, 147). Van Baal (1966, 179) makes the point that dema 'are the ancestors of the clans and subclans and are associated with their totems'. In this sense, canoes were important symbolic expressions of clan identity, unity, and ancestry (van Baal 1966, 308). It is for this reason that exogamous marriage arrangements were referred to as 'to change canoes' in the coastal villages of Domande, Sanggase, Okaba, and Senegi (van Baal 1966, 84). In the mid-twentieth century, Verschueren observed that the:

> present decrease in the numbers of canoes and drums has obscured the notion of subclan-membership even up to the extent that many young people can no longer find their way in the system. (cited in van Baal 1966, 91)

Few details are available on the ceremonial 'inauguration of a new canoe' (van Baal 1966, 94, 827; Wirz 1922, I:124). Van Baal (1966, 827) noted briefly that 'The new canoe is wetted with *wati* [kava, *Piper methysticum*]. A meal is arranged and a dance performed'. Further details are provided by Corbey (2010, 42–43) in a caption for a photograph of a canoe on the beach near Sepadim, east of Merauke, dated 1910–1930 (Figure 15.5). The caption quotes a 'missionary … thus: "Consecration of a canoe, adorned with fruits … young girls of different age groups symbolize the abundance the canoe would bring the village"'. More generally, van Baal (1966, 93–94) noted that canoes are 'objects of magical incantations in which their names play a part'.

Numerous Marind mythological narratives reference canoes (Kooijman et al. 1958, 72, 75; van Baal 1966, 254, 258–259). These mythological narratives refer to dema travelling in canoes between coastal villages (van Baal 1966, 211, 283, 287, 341, 369, 441, 558) and along and across rivers (van Baal 1966, 311–312, 369–370, 392). For example, the dema brothers Geb and Sami travelled by canoe underground over a distance of 150 km between the coastal villages of Sanggase and Kondo (van Baal 1966, 85). Dema also visited locations beyond Marind territory such as the Digul River to the north-west (van Baal 1966, 368; see below). Mythological narratives also record dema who travelled to Marind territory from the Trans-Fly region using canoes (van Baal 1966, 311; see below). In some cases, particular dema transformed into a canoe, while canoes associated with dema myths transformed into (canoe-shaped) landforms (van Baal 1966, 259, 368). Van Baal (cited in McKinley 2015, 477) added that in some myths, 'canoes turn into serpents when they reach the limits of the known world'. Boelaars (1953, paraphrased in van Baal 1966, 615) recorded a 'public *imo* ceremony' at the village of Wayau on the middle Kumbe River, located approximately 55 km from the coast, that included three male dancers with elaborate figurative headdresses, one of which was a 3.5-m-long canoe decorated with elaborate painted designs and bird-of-paradise feathers. The 'canoe was called *Imo* (déma)' and the ceremony took place 'whenever sickness and death prevailed in the village' (van Baal 1966, 615).

Raised linear garden beds located within swampy depressions between dunes immediately inland of the coast are referred to as '*yavun*, canoe' (van Baal 1966, 874) 'because, in the rainy season, when part of the land is inundated, these beds appear like boats above the surface of the water' (Kooijman et al. 1958, 6). Wati, used in canoe inaugurations (see above), is grown on yavun (Kooijman et al. 1958, 50).

Long-distance canoe voyaging (headhunting expeditions)

The Marind used canoes for maintenance of intra-regional subsistence and social relations, and inter-regional headhunting expeditions. No references were found for the Marind using canoes for offshore fishing. Extensive use of canoes for inland travel was made possible by the low-lying, flat landscape with its myriad waterways that represented something of a complex vascular system, as it did for many groups of central-southern New Guinea (Figure 15.1). Intra-regional voyaging between villages and associated celebrations produced a 'kind of network' which held 'the whole tribe together' in 'relative peace' (van Baal 1966, 68, 695; see also Knauft 1993, 139, 155, 159). Inter-regional voyaging beyond the boundary of Marind territory related to large-scale headhunting expeditions that similarly concerned the reproduction of Marind society. Significantly, no references were found to travels extending inland of Marind territory to the mountainous interior. Among the coastal Marind, canoes were used mostly for long-distance headhunting expeditions, and each canoe held members of one genealogical group (Wirz 1925, III:54). The low waterline of Marind canoes restricted safe open sea travel and Wirz (1933, 109) described the canoes as 'unseaworthy'. MacGregor (1966 [1892], 90) described Marind canoes he observed on the Trans-Fly coast as 'suitable for coast or river work only, and cannot cross any considerable area of deep water unless in perfectly calm weather'.

A Marind 'headhunting expedition was a big undertaking in which several villages used to cooperate' (van Baal 1966, 710). In 1910, 'thousands of Marind set off on a headhunting expedition, departing from about a hundred kilometres of coast' (Corbey 2010, 19). Participants included men, women, children, and their dogs and pigs (van Baal 1966, 713). The expeditions focused on two geographically separated 'headhunting grounds' (*kui-mirav*)—to the north-west (Yos Sudarso Island and Digul River) and to the south-east (Trans-Fly and northern Torres Strait) (van Baal 1966, 24, 677, 696–697, 705). It is also likely that headhunting raids were carried out on neighbouring peoples to the north-east (Schoorl 1993, 8). However, some Marind groups also undertook headhunting raids on their Maklew-anim, Yei-anim, and Kanum-anim neighbours to the immediate north-west, north-east, and south-east, respectively (van Baal 1966, 348, 690, 701, 703–704). For example, around 1917, people of the upper Bian River raided the Yei-anim (Vertenten, cited in van Baal 1966, 704). Headhunting raids between Marind villages were unknown (van Baal 1966; 1996, 183). Peoples who were the focus of headhunting were considered *ikom-anim* (strangers, not human beings) and 'only there to be killed', whereas the Marind considered themselves *anim-ha* (real humans) (van Baal 1966, 402, 695–696; see also van der Kroef 1952, 223). As such, Marind knew when undertaking headhunting expeditions that they were paddling into the world of lesser human beings or indeed non-humans. Van der Kroef (1952, 224) estimated that 'Hundreds, if not thousands have been the victims of head-hunting in these regions'.

Marind headhunting was 'not a matter of revenge or of social conflicts, but ... a religious or ceremonial necessity' (van Baal 1966, 421). A major purpose was to obtain heads, along with the name of the deceased, to be used in naming rituals for boys and girls (van Baal 1966, 135, 461, 676, 709, 753). In contrast to their *boan-igiz* (clan name) and *dema-igiz* (dema-name), a person's *pa-igiz* (head-name) was 'more or less secret and taboo' (van Baal 1966, 135–136) and 'reserved for formal occasions such as initiations' (van Baal, cited in McKinley 2015, 479). According to Olsson (2021, 16), many Marind today 'retain head names that they have inherited'. In the mythological narrative of dema Nazr and Mahu's headhunting raid on a village on the Digul River, Nazr stated that 'it does not matter' if the victim fails to state his name: 'before you cut somebody's head he is bound to say something, and this may be used as a name' (van Baal 1966, 403). In one case, the name translated from the Digul language as 'mother help me' (Corbey 2010, 19). After celebratory feasts, the skulls were placed in the appropriate men's house with jaws the focus of long-term curation, as were cervical (neck) vertebrae (van Baal 1966, 718, 750–751, 885; van der Kroef 1952, 234).

So dominant and feared were the Marind that no records exist of reprisal attacks within Marind territory (van Baal 1966, 24). Van Baal (1966, 24) suggested that this absence of reprisal attacks was aided by the Marind creating a buffer zone of allies, maintained through 'friendly relations with their immediate neighbours'. Yet this interpretation is inconsistent with known occasional raids on the Maklew-anim,

Yei-anim, and Kanum-anim (see above). 'All the neighbouring tribes regarded the Marind as invincible' (Kooijman et al. 1958, 44). However, van Baal (1966, 708) noted that a canoe load of coastal Marind from Wamal village was 'attacked at sea' near Selat Muli (Strait Marianne) by people from Yos Sudarso Island, avenging a headhunting raid (see also Serpenti 1968, 126). Also, a number of cases exist of successful resistance by peoples of the northern Torres Strait and the adjacent Papuan coast against Marind raiders (Beaver 1920, 117–119; Haddon 1891; Hitchcock 2004a, 190; see below).

Western and central Marind headhunting expeditions raided villages on Yos Sudarso Island to the west and the Digul River region to the north during the late dry season, between October and December when the ground is dry and firm and travel is easier (van Baal 1966, 707–709, 715; Serpenti 1968, 125–126; van der Kroef 1952, 226). One expedition in 1912 returned with 90 heads (van Baal 1966, 629, 709). The last recorded Marind headhunting expedition involved the men of Wambi village raiding peoples of the lower Digul River in 1917. This expedition reputedly 'annihilated … one of the Jakai groups of the island Jaar at the mouth of the Digul River' (Kooijman et al. 1958, 121). Van Baal (1966, 707) suggested that it 'is improbable, if not impossible' that the Digul raids were undertaken via the coastal route using canoes. Alternatively, he posited inland expeditions up rivers (using canoes) and overland (on foot), whereupon reaching the Digul River they either made new canoes or used previously cached canoes (van Baal 1966, 707).

Eastern and central Marind headhunting expeditions to the Trans-Fly and northern Torres Strait regions spanned the rainy season, between the end of the dry season (~November) and the start of the next dry season (~July) (van Baal 1966, 707, 715–716). These expeditions became known to the outside world with incursions into the Western Division of British New Guinea, taking in areas from the international border eastwards to the coastal village of Mawatta in the 1880s and 1890s (Hitchcock 2009; MacGregor 1897, 52, 55; Swadling 1996, Fig. 39) (Figure 15.1). As late as November 1900, British government authorities found the headless remains of 15 men, women, girls, and boys from Tugaribio and Gwaigar villages of the Morehead River district that had been decapitated recently by the Tugeri (Murray 1902, xxv). These headhunting grounds were accessed using inland routes and especially along the coast using canoes (Beaver 1920, 117). From mainland camps along the Trans-Fly coast, lethal attacks were launched also against the northern Torres Strait island communities of Boigu (Haddon 1891, 179; Ingui et al. 1991; Le Hunte 1901, 22; MacGregor 1890, 69; Wirz 1933, 109, 120) and Saibai (Le Hunte 1902, xx; Wirz 1933, 119), but not Dauan (Wirz 1933, 119–120). Indeed, '[t]he inhabitants of the northern portion of the Straits have a great dread of them and tell wonderful stories about them' (Haddon 1891, 177; see also Beaver 1920, 119). Haddon (1891, 179) understood that owing to their superior canoes and seamanship, Torres Strait Islanders preferred to violently engage the Tugeri at sea before they arrived on land (see McFarlane 1888, 106–108). In 1887, a group of men from the northern Torres Strait island of Saibai armed with guns travelled to a Marind camp on the adjacent New Guinea mainland where a friendly exchange of objects took place (Haddon 1891, 177–178). Although the eastern Marind mostly undertook these incursions, the western Marind villages of Sanggase and Kaiburse (van Baal 1966, 95), and Okaba and Makalin (Wirz 1933, 113), also participated. Coastal travel between Makalin and Mawatta involved a canoe voyage of ~430 km.

Reliable estimates of the number of Marind participating in Trans-Fly headhunting expeditions range up to 500–600 (MacGregor 1897, 55). As such, large numbers of canoes were involved in these large-scale expeditions. For example, one flotilla recorded on the Wassi Kussa River in 1896 comprised about 75 canoes (Knauft 1993, 156; van Baal 1966, 697). MacGregor (1897, 55) confiscated 48 canoes and destroyed well over five other canoes in 1896. Six years earlier, MacGregor (1890, 71) observed Marind canoes 10–12 m in length in the same area.

Headhunting expeditions appear to have been annual affairs to obtain heads for use in naming young males and females and to steal children and young women to compensate for the high level of sterility among Marind women (Ernst 1979; Knauft 1993, 161–162, 169; Kooijman 1959, 22–23; McKinley 2015; van Baal 1966, 677, 709, 718; van der Kroef 1952). Expeditions could number over 1000 people and included men from numerous villages and often women and children to assist with subsistence tasks and caring for abducted children (Beaver 1920, 117; Knauft 1993, 156; van Baal 1966, 710–713; van der Kroef 1952, 225).

Headhunting expeditions into the Trans-Fly and northern Torres Strait were scheduled to take advantage of seasonal wind and waterway conditions. Le Hunte wrote that the Marind:

> send out several large [headhunting] expeditions every year in various directions, and those that come eastward to us do so at the beginning of the north-west season—about November—and remain hunting and marauding until the south-east season begins—March or April. (Le Hunte 1901, 27; see also Haddon 1891 and Wirz 1933)

If this was the case, then many coastal Marind spent 5–6 months of every year during the wet season living what Wirz (1933, 116) referred to as 'a proper nomadic life' beyond their territory in the coastal and inland areas of south-west Papua New Guinea. Wet season scheduling of expeditions took advantage of flooded swamps and waterways, which facilitated canoe travel. Remarkably, the Marind excavated canals across meander necks along the Bensbach and Morehead rivers of the Trans-Fly as canoeing shortcuts (Garrick Hitchcock pers. comm. 2021).

Although the Trans-Fly was the homeland of numerous coastal and inland groups (Williams 1936), several places (e.g. 'water-courses, sand-banks, hills, coral-reefs and so on') were named by the Marind and had cosmological and ancestral (dema) associations (Wirz 1933, 113). For example, deposits of 'red stones of petrified ferriferous loam' / 'reddish rock (limonite)' exposed within the intertidal zone 'between Mayo and Yavar-makan' on the western Trans-Fly coast of Papua New Guinea are the remains of 'uninitiated' people who were covered with blood and turned to stone by the dema Uaba as punishment for (inappropriate) sexual intercourse with 'initiates' (van Baal 1966, 241, 258; see also Wirz 1933, 112, 117–118).

The westerly and easterly geographical dimensions of Marind headhunting expeditions (and associated canoe voyages) were a critical expression and re-enactment of the fundamental east↔west dialectic in Marind cosmological and mythological travel narratives of dema (see van Baal 1966, 425). McKinley (2015, 452) adds:

> The acquisition of heads from the extreme east and west regions is viewed as a way of reestablishing, on a cosmic level, the living community's sacred ties with these original beings.

Eastward journeys include the dema Gopa (Digul River to the Fly River) and Batend (Okaba area in western Marind territory to the Fly River) (van Baal 1966, 446). For the Marind, 'the world comes to an end' at the Fly River, beyond which 'lies the kingdom of the dead (Hais-mirav)' (Wirz 1933, 120). Van Baal (1996, 184) clarifies:

> The dead are believed to travel underground to the far east, where, like the sun, they will emerge to go to the far west, where, passing the spot where the sun sets, they will go on to the land of the dead which is just beyond.

Analogous eastwards journeys of the Papuan culture hero Sido are told by peoples of the northern islands of Torres Strait. That is, Sido came from 'Kadua' in 'Tuger country' and moved eastwards, visiting Boigu, Saibai, Dauan (leaving a footprint in granite), and other islands of the Torres Strait, before travelling to the island of Kiwai at the mouth of the Fly River where he is killed (Laade 1971, 2–8). Numerous other variants and segments of the travels of Sido over a cumulative distance of

800 km are told by different peoples of south-west Papua New Guinea, including the people of Kiwai, who hold that Sido originated on Kiwai and travelled westwards to Mabaduan (leaving a footprint in granite), and then to Boigu, where he was killed and his spirit returned to Kiwai (Busse 2005; Lawrence 1994, 403–405; 2010, 76–78; Wagner 1972, 1996, 286). Today, near Sagapadi village on Kiwai, an important site linked to Sido is marked by a large tree with 'many stone axe heads' around its base (Lawrence 2010, 78).

Westward journeys of Marind dema include Sosom (brother of Uaba) and Dawi (Wemega [Fly] River to Komolom island), Méru (Fly River to Eromka in western Marind territory), Gerau (Fly River to the upper Kumbe River in eastern Marind territory), Mahu (upper Bian River in central Marind territory to the Digul River), Doreh (Kumbe in eastern Marind territory to the Digul River), and Nazr (south-east corner of Marind territory to the Digul River) (Kooijman et al. 1958, 81; van Baal 1966, 271, 441–442, 446, 448).

Historicising voyaging: Foundations for an archaeology of exotic (traded and raided) stone objects

The final section of this chapter provides preliminary ideas on historicising inter-regional Marind canoe voyaging beyond that known through nineteenth- and twentieth-century historical and ethnographic textual records. Long-term insights into the history of Marind inter-regional canoe voyaging necessitate archaeological evidence. In the likely absence of preserved canoes, archaeological evidence takes the form of ethnographically defined proxies such as stone artefacts obtained during such voyages. Stone objects preserve well in archaeological deposits (e.g. village middens) and it can be predicted that long-term changes in voyaging activities will be expressed through chronological changes in the occurrence and use of stone objects ethnographically known to have been obtained during headhunting expeditions. As the Marind inhabit a stoneless environment, all stone objects within the confines of Marind territory are exotic. Although detailed petrographic descriptions are unavailable for stone objects from within Marind territory, historical and ethnographic information inform hypotheses on potential sources.

Marind territory is 'completely devoid of stony matter except for loose concretions of sand or weathered loam' (van Baal 1966, 16). Living in a stoneless environment, the stone had a special meaning for the Marind as all stone artefacts had to be either imported or obtained directly by either exchange or plunder during headhunting expeditions well beyond their cultural boundaries. Despite an absence of locally available stone, the Marind used stone for tools such as axes (van Baal 1966, 466, 861), club heads (Grottanelli 1951; Kooijman 1952; van Baal 1966, 273), and spearthrower weights (van Baal 1966, 413–415; Wirz 1946, 88–91). The most common reference to stone in ethnographic accounts of the Marind is to hafted stone axes and stone-headed clubs, used in a wide range of violent encounters and ceremonial contexts (van Baal 1966, 22, 732–743). Both types of ground stone implements were 'wealth' objects with a 'practical purpose' (van Baal 1966, 861). Stone club heads were highly prized men's objects and were 'rare' (van Baal 1966, 730). In addition, a range of portable stones are linked to dema while small stones are used in ritual contexts such as rain-making and coconut tree fertility (e.g. van Baal 1966, 182–185, 803, 880–882; Wirz 1946; see also Torrence et al. 2022). Although the Marind used ground stone axes, they did not use flaked stone cutting or scraping tools. Cutting and scraping tools were manufactured from bamboo, marine shells, and boar tusks (Kooijman et al. 1958, 46; van Baal 1966, 313, 907).

The nearest sources of igneous tool stone to the Marind are located in the southern foothills of the central ranges well to the north, and the far northern Torres Strait well to the south-east. Indeed, the northern Torres Strait island of Dauan and the settlement of Mabaduan on the adjacent coast of Papua New Guinea are the only outcrops of igneous stone for an area of ~100,000 km^2 located west of the Fly River and south of the Ok Tedi River (D'Addario et al. 1976; Dow et al. 1986) (Figure 15.1). On the eastern side of the Fly River, igneous outcrops do not occur across an area of ~40,000 km^2 located south of the Ok Tedi River and the Bamu River (Dow et al. 1986) (Figure 15.1).

Wirz (1933, 107) pointed out that apart from the taking of heads and children, the purpose of Marind headhunting expeditions was 'to rob and plunder generally and bring home as much as possible'. Yet Wirz (1933, 107) added that 'these raids were by no means always of a hostile and malignant nature' with many expeditions also involving friendly exchange of objects (see above). McNiven (1998) states that raiding and trading ('enmity and amity') were often two sides of the same coin for communities of Torres Strait and central-southern New Guinea (including the Marind).

Following Wirz (1946, 85), van Baal (1966, 23) ventured that:

> stone axes as well as the stone clubs had to be obtained through trade or robbery during one of their frequent headhunting expeditions. The fact that there are different types of axes and clubs points to a diversity of origin.

Ethnographic information matches geological information, pointing to two potential sources for Marind stone implements—inland regions to the north and Torres Strait to the south-east. In terms of the former, Kooijman and colleagues (1958, 46) noted that the Marind obtained stone axes and club heads from 'inland peoples … by barter or otherwise by robbery'. Wirz (1922, I:112) recorded that the Marind obtained most ovoid- and disc-shaped stone club heads from the Digul River through trading and raiding, while star- and pineapple-shaped stone club heads were obtained through headhunting and were thought by the Marind to come from the upper Fly River. Similarly, Verschueren (cited in van Baal 1966, 730) was informed in 1936 that disc-shaped stone club heads were 'traded, being passed down from the Star Mountains to the south'. Nevermann (1939, 33) was informed that the Marind obtained stone club heads from the Digul River area.

In terms of Torres Strait, van Baal (1966, 699) observed that the 'stone-headed clubs' of the Marind

> are very much like some of the stone clubs of the Torres Str. islands and it is a fair guess that they obtained them from the Fly river district as well as from the interior.

It is unlikely that the Marind obtained tool stone raw materials and/or finished stone tools from Dauan directly, given the absence of historical accounts of visits to the rocky island. Wirz (1933, 121) was of the opinion that while the Marind visited the granite outcrops at Mabaduan, they only viewed the granite hill of Dauan from a distance. It is likely that the Marind obtained stone objects manufactured by Torres Strait Islanders through trading and raiding after they had passed northwards into the hands of Trans-Fly peoples similarly through raiding and trading. Preliminary sourcing studies of stone club heads from Torres Strait and the Torassi or Bensbach River area of the Trans-Fly indicate manufacture from Torres Strait stone (Hitchcock 2004b; McNiven 1998; McNiven and von Gnielinski 2004). Whether or not Marind stone objects are similarly manufactured from Torres Strait stone and/or other sources such as Mabaduan or to the far north on the fringes of the central highlands is a question for future research.

As an aside, it is probable that Marind headhunting trips to the Trans-Fly region also provided an opportunity to obtain spiritually charged ochre for ceremonial use. For example, MacGregor (1897, 54) noted that among the wide range of objects taken from the raided Marind camp on the Wassi Kussa River in 1896 were 'bundles of clay' and woven bags containing what Torrence and colleagues (2022, 273, Table 5) described as 'raw material: mineral/pigment', including 'red ochre'. MacGregor (1897, 56) added that '[t]here was such a quantity of this clay in their baggage, and it was so carefully wrapped up that it is manifest they put much value on Wassi Kussa clay'. In what may be a reference to the intertidal deposits of red limonite created by the dema Uaba (see above), MacGregor (1898, 39, italics added) posited:

> On the foreshore there were stones of the peculiar kind found so plentiful in the Tugeri camp, when these were driven out of the Wasi Kussa. *To obtain these stones may probably have been one of the reasons for the incursions of these tribes along the coast eastward.*

Conclusion

Canoe travel for the Marind involved paddling through seas infused with powerful spiritual forces and associated dema beings that required respect, referential acknowledgement, and propitiation through ritual. In addition, the east–west orientation of canoe voyages to the headhunting grounds of the Trans-Fly and Torres Strait mirrored the alignment of cosmological and celestial forces and the legendary ancestral travels of dema. As Knauft (1993, 137–138) noted, the 'Marind objectified themselves as creative embodiments who continued the dema's restless wanderings and vital energy'. In common with their cultic ceremonies, Marind long-distance canoe voyages were not only 'a celebration and re-creation of the Marind cosmos' (Knauft 1993, 149), but in combination with headhunting and acquisition of heads for initiations, a fundamental re-creation of the Marind and humanity itself. That a cosmologically ordained link existed between dema, eastern voyaging to the Trans-Fly and Torres Strait, and potential stone procurement is indicated by the east-to-west travelling dema Sosom, a 'giant' (height of a 'coconut tree') 'made of stone' (van Baal 1966, 267). In another account, Sosom is said to reside in 'subterranean waters' at Mabaduan, the only source of igneous stone across the Trans-Fly (Viegen 1923, 393). It may also be no coincidence that an important rain-making ritual of the Marind during the 'rainy season' (the time of Trans-Fly headhunting expeditions) involved 'the use of big stones which are rolled up and down a miniature canoe imitating the roar of thunder' (van Baal 1966, 881–882; Torrence et al. 2022, 274).

Referential and ritual relationships between Marind and dema were recursive, as they provided a means for both Marind and dema to reassert and reaffirm their agency in an intentionalised cosmos. Within an aquatic and especially marine context, the agency of Marind canoe crews was shared with canoes whose anthropomorphic bows imply a form of embodied agency akin to that seen with Torres Strait canoes (McNiven 2018). Indeed, Marind agency within an intentionalised cosmos was shared with, and mediated by, dema spirit beings and canoe object-beings.

Archaeological recovery and dating of stone objects (and pigments) from coastal Marind villages sourced to Torres Strait (and the Trans-Fly coast, e.g. Mabaduan) will shed light on the history and time depth of long-distance headhunting voyages. Such insights can be augmented by the excavation of old village/campsites used by Marind raiding parties across the Trans-Fly region (coast and inland) recalled in local oral histories and historical documents (e.g. Hitchcock 2009; MacGregor 1890, 69; 1898, 39; Torrence et al. 2022; Wirz 1933). When undertaken in collaboration with contemporary Marind communities, this research can be expanded to include oral histories and perspectives on Marind voyaging to the northern Torres Strait and the cultural significance of canoes and stone objects, especially stone objects housed in overseas museums.

Acknowledgements

Thanks to Dylan Gaffney and Marlin Tolla for the kind invitation to contribute to this volume. Garrick Hitchcock provided helpful and thought-provoking comments on an earlier draft of this chapter.

References

Beaver, W.N. 1920. *Unexplored New Guinea*. Seeley, Service & Co. Ltd, London.

Bigourdan, N. 2006. Physical and spiritual voyages: An ethno-archaeological approach to the study of Asmat canoes (Irian Jaya, Indonesia). *Bulletin of the Australasian Institute for Maritime Archaeology* 30:62–75.

Boelaars, J. 1953. *Nieuw-Guinea, Uw Mensen Zijn Wonderbaar*. P. Brand, Bussum.

Boelaars, J. 1969. South-western Irian missionary activities, 1905–1966. *Euntes Docete* 22:241–264.

Busse, M. 2005. Wandering hero stories in the Southern Lowlands of New Guinea: Culture areas, comparison, and history. *Cultural Anthropology* 20(4):443–473. doi.org/10.1525/can.2005.20.4.443.

Campbell, S.F. 2002. *The art of Kula*. Berg, Oxford.

Chao, S. 2019. Wrathful ancestors, corporate sorcerers: Rituals gone rogue in Merauke, West Papua. *Oceania* 89(3):266–283. doi.org/10.1002/ocea.5229.

Chao, S. 2021. Children of the palms: Growing plants and growing people in a Papuan Plantationocene. *Journal of the Royal Anthropological Institute* 27(2):245–264. doi.org/10.1111/1467-9655.13489.

Corbey, R. 2010. *Headhunters from the swamps: The Marind Anim of New Guinea as seen by the missionaries of the Sacred Heart, 1905–1925*. KITLV Press and C. Zwartenkot Art Books, Leiden.

D'Addario, G.W., D.B. Dow, and R. Swoboda 1976. *Geology of Papua New Guinea. 1:2,500,000 Map*. Australian Bureau of Mineral Resources, Canberra.

Dow, D.B., G.P. Robinson, U. Hartono, and N. Ratman 1986. *Geological map of Irian Jaya, Indonesia*. 1:1,000,000 scale. Sheets 1 & 2. Geological Research and Development Centre, Bandung.

Ernst, T.M. 1979. Myth, ritual, and population among the Marind-anim. *Social Analysis* 1:34–53.

Gell, A. 1998. *Art and agency: An anthropological theory*. Oxford University Press, Oxford; New York. doi.org/10.1093/oso/9780198280132.001.0001.

Geurtjens, H. 1929. Het taboeschap bij bevallingen op Zuid-Nieuw-Guinea. *Mensch en Maatschappij; Tweemaandelijksch Tijdschrift voor Sociale Wetenschappen* 5:119–132.

Gooszen, A.J. 1908. Nederlandsch Zuid-Nieuw-Guinea. De strandbewoners van Zuid-Nieuw-Guinea en hunne dorpen. *Tijdschrift van het Koninklijk Nederlandsch Aardrijkskundig Genootschap* 25:683–700.

Grottanelli, V.L. 1951. On the 'mysterious' Baratu clubs from central New Guinea. *Man* 51:105–107. doi.org/10.2307/2793639.

Haddon, A.C. 1891. The Tugeri head-hunters of New Guinea. *Internationales Archiv für Ethnographie* 4:177–181.

Haddon, A.C. 1937. *Canoes of Oceania. Volume II. The Canoes of Melanesia, Queensland, and New Guinea*. Bernice P. Bishop Museum Special Publication 28. Bishop Museum, Honolulu.

Hitchcock, G. 2004a. Wildlife is our gold: Political ecology of the Torassi River borderland, Southwest Papua New Guinea. Unpublished PhD thesis. School of Social Science, The University of Queensland, Brisbane.

Hitchcock, G. 2004b. Torres Strait origin of some stone-headed clubs from the Torassi River, southwest Papua New Guinea. *Memoirs of the Queensland Museum Cultural Heritage Series* 3(1):305–313.

Hitchcock, G. 2009. William Dammköhler's third encounter with the Tugeri (Marind-anim). *The Journal of Pacific History* 44(1):89–97. doi.org/10.1080/00223340902900894.

Ingui, A., I. Banu, J. Matthew, G. Matthew, C. Gibuma, M. Gibuma, A.P. Matthew, K. Waireg, and I. Tom 1991. Traditional warfare. In Boigu Island Community Council (ed.), *Boigu: Our history and culture*, pp. 78–84. Aboriginal Studies Press, Canberra.

Knauft, B.M. 1993. *South Coast New Guinea cultures: History, comparison, dialectic.* Cambridge University Press, Cambridge. doi.org/10.1017/CBO9780511621741.

Kooijman, S. 1952. The function and significance of some ceremonial clubs of the Marind-anim, Dutch New Guinea. *Man* 52:97–99. doi.org/10.2307/2793498.

Kooijman, S. 1959. Population research project among the Marind-anim and Jeeo-nan peoples in Netherlands South New Guinea: Summary of a report. *Nieuw-Guinea Studiën* 3:9–34.

Kooijman, S., M. Dorren, L. Veeger, J. Verschueren, and R. Luyken 1958. Report of the investigation into the problem of depopulation among the Marind-anim of Netherlands New Guinea. South Pacific Commission Population Studies S.18 Project. Noumea, New Caledonia.

Laade, W. 1971. *Oral traditions and written documents on the history and ethnography of the Northern Torres Strait Islands, Saibai—Dauan—Boigu. Vol. 1. Adi—Myths, legends, fairy tales.* Franz Steiner Verlag GMBH, Wiesbaden.

Lawrence, D. 1994. Customary exchange across Torres Strait. *Memoirs of the Queensland Museum* 34(2): 241–446.

Lawrence, D. 2010. *Gunnar Landtman in Papua 1910 to 1912.* ANU ePress, Canberra. doi.org/10.22459/GLP.02.2010.

Le Hunte, G.R. 1901. Appendix E. Despatch reporting visit of inspection to the western portion of the Possession. In *Annual report on British New Guinea from 1st July, 1899, to 30th June, 1900: with appendices*, pp. 21–30. Government Printer, Melbourne.

Le Hunte, G.R. 1902. The Tugeri raids and the Netherlands government. In *Annual report on British New Guinea from 1st July, 1900, to 30th June, 1901, with appendices*, pp. XIX–XXI. George Arthur Vaughan, Government Printer, Brisbane.

Lipset, D. 2014. Living canoes: Vehicles of moral imagination among the Murik of Papua New Guinea. In D. Lipset and R. Handler (eds), *Vehicles: Cars, canoes, and other metaphors of moral ambivalence*, pp. 21–47. Berghahm, New York and Oxford. doi.org/10.1515/9781782383765-004.

MacGregor, W.M. 1890. Appendix I: Despatch reporting visit of inspection to the districts lying west of the island of Dauan. In *Annual report on British New Guinea from 1st July, 1889, to 30th June, 1890; with appendices*, pp. 69–75. James C. Beal, Government Printer, Brisbane.

MacGregor, W.M. 1897. Appendix K: Despatch reporting expedition undertaken to repel Tugeri invaders. In *Annual report on British New Guinea from 1st July, 1895, to 30th June, 1896, with appendices*, pp. 52–56. Edmund Gregory, Government Printer, Brisbane.

MacGregor, W.M. 1898. Appendix C: Despatch reporting visit of inspection to Western Districts of the Possession. In *Annual report on British New Guinea from 1st July, 1897, to 30th June, 1898; with appendices*, pp. 39–41. Edmund Gregory, Government Printer, Brisbane.

MacGregor, W.M. 1966 [1892]. Sir William MacGregor to Sir Henry Norman. Despatch respecting expedition undertaken to repel Tugeri invasion, 5th July 1892. In P.W. van der Veur (ed.), *Documents and correspondence on New Guinea's boundaries*, pp. 90–93. Australian National University Press, Canberra. doi.org/10.1007/978-94-015-3706-3_35.

McFarlane, S. 1888. *Among the cannibals of New Guinea*. Presbyterian Board of Publication and Sabbath-School Work, Philadelphia.

McKinley, R. 2015. Human and proud of it! A structural treatment of headhunting rites and the social definition of enemies. *HAU: Journal of Ethnographic Theory* 5(2):443–483. doi.org/10.14318/hau5.2.031.

McNiven, I.J. 1998. Enmity and amity: Reconsidering stone-headed club (*gabagaba*) procurement and trade in Torres Strait. *Oceania* 69:94–115. doi.org/10.1002/j.1834-4461.1998.tb02697.x.

McNiven, I.J. 2004. Saltwater people: Spiritscapes, maritime rituals and the archaeology of Australian Indigenous seascapes. *World Archaeology* 35(3):329–349. doi.org/10.1080/0043824042000185757.

McNiven, I.J. 2010. 'Oh wonderful beach': The Marind-anim of Papua and ethnographic foundations for an archaeology of a littoral sea people. *The Artefact* 33:91–108.

McNiven, I.J. 2015. Canoes of Mabuyag and Torres Strait. *Memoirs of the Queensland Museum—Culture* 8(1):127–207.

McNiven, I.J. 2018. Torres Strait canoes as social and predatory object-beings. In E. Harrison-Buck and J.A. Hendon (eds), *Relational identities and other-than-human agency in archaeology*, pp. 167–196. University of Colorado Press, Denver. doi.org/10.5876/9781607327479.c008.

McNiven, I.J. and F. von Gnielinski 2004. Manufacture of stone club heads from Dauan Island, Torres Strait. *Memoirs of the Queensland Museum, Cultural Heritage Series* 3(1):187–200.

Munn, N.D. 1977. The spatiotemporal transformations of Gawa canoes. *Journal de la Société des Océanistes* 33(54-55):39–53. doi.org/10.3406/jso.1977.2942.

Murray, C.G. 1902. Report of Resident Magistrate, Western Division, on visit with the Resident of Dutch New Guinea to the Tugeri tribe. In *Annual report on British New Guinea from 1st July, 1900, to 30th June, 1901; with appendices*, pp. xxi–xxvi. George Arthur Vaughan, Government Printer, Brisbane.

Nevermann, H. 1939. Die Kanum-irebe und ihre Nachbarn. *Zeitschrift für Ethnologie* 71:1–70.

Olsson, B. 2021. *A grammar of Coastal Marind*. Mouton Grammar Library 87. De Gruyter, Berlin/Boston. doi.org/10.1515/9783110747065.

Richens, J. 2022. *Tik Merauke: An epidemic like no other*. Melbourne University Press, Melbourne. doi.org/10.2307/jj.1176760.

Schmeltz, J.D.E. 1905. Beiträge zur ethnographie von Neu-Guinea. X Die stämme in der nachbarschaft des Merauke-flusses. *Internationales Archiv für Ethnographie* 17:194–220.

Schoorl, J.W. 1993. *Culture and change among the Muyu*. KITLV Press, Leiden.

Serpenti, L.M. 1968. Headhunting and magic on Kolepom (Frederik-Hendrik Island, Irian Barat). *Tropical Man* 1:116–139.

Swadling, P. 1996. *Plumes from Paradise: Trade cycles in outer Southeast Asia and their impact on New Guinea and nearby islands until 1920*. Papua New Guinea National Museum, Boroko.

Torrence, R., S.M. Davies, M. Quinnell, and J. Philp 2022. War and peace: Two radically different encounters with the Marind-Anim. *Memoirs of the Queensland Museum—Culture* 13:247–286.

van Baal, J. 1966. *Dema: Description and analysis of Marind-Anim culture (South New Guinea)*. Martinus Nijhoff, The Hague.

van Baal, J. 1982. *Jan Verschueren's description of Yéi-nan culture: Extracted from the posthumous papers.* Verhandelingen van het Koninklijk Instituut voor Taal-, Land- en Volkenkunde 99. Martinus Nijhoff, The Hague. doi.org/10.1163/9789004287303.

van Baal, J. 1984. The dialectics of sex in Marind-anim culture. In G.H. Herdt (ed.), *Ritualized homosexuality in Melanesia,* pp. 128–166. Paperback edition. University of California Press, Berkeley. doi.org/10.1525/9780520341388-004.

van Baal, J. 1996. Marind-anim. In D. Levinson (ed.), *Encyclopedia of world cultures*, Volume 2, pp. 182–185. Macmillan Reference USA, New York.

van der Kroef, J.M. 1952. Some head-hunting traditions of Southern New Guinea. *American Anthropologist* 54(2.1):221–235. doi.org/10.1525/aa.1952.54.2.02a00060.

Verschueren, J. 1970. Marind-anim land tenure. *New Guinea Research Bulletin* 38:42–59.

Vertenten, P. 1914. Zeichen- und Malkunst der Marindinesen (Bewohner von Niederländisch Süd-Neu-Guinea). *Internationales Archiv für Ethnographie* 22(4):150–164.

Viegen, R.P. 1923. Les sociétés secrètes des Marind. *Semaine d'Ethnologie Religieuse* 3:384–399.

Voorhoeve, C.L. 1983. South-eastern Irian Jaya. In S.A. Wurm and S. Hattori (eds), *Language atlas of the Pacific area. Pt. 1. New Guinea Area, Oceania, Australia.* Pacific Linguistic Series C, 66–67. Australian Academy of the Humanities in collaboration with the Japan Academy, Canberra.

Wagner, R. 1972. *Habu: The innovation of meaning in Daribi religion.* The University of Chicago Press, Chicago and London.

Wagner, R. 1996. Mysteries of origin: Early traders and heroes in the Trans-Fly. In P. Swadling, *Plumes from Paradise: Trade cycles in outer Southeast Asia and their impact on New Guinea and nearby islands until 1920,* pp. 285–298. Papua New Guinea National Museum, Boroko.

Williams, F.E. 1936. *Papuans of the Trans-Fly.* Clarendon Press, Oxford.

Wirz, P. 1922. *Die Marind-anim von Holländisch-Süd-Neu-Guinea. I. Band. Teil I. Die Materielle Kultur de Marind-anim. Teil II: Die religiösen Vorstellungen und die Mythen der Marind-anim, sowie die Herausbildung der totemistisch-sozialen Gruppierungen.* L. Friederichsen & Co., Hamburg. doi.org/10.1515/9783111588902.

Wirz, P. 1925. *Die Marind-anim von Holländisch-Süd-Neu-Guinea. II. Band. Teil III. Das Soziale Leben der Marind-anim. Teil IV. Die Marind-anim in ihren Festen, ihrer Kunst und ihren Kenntnissen und Eigenschaften.* Kommissions-Verlag L. Friederichsen & Co., Hamburg.

Wirz, P. 1933. Head-hunting expeditions of the Tugeri into the Western Division of British New Guinea. *Tijdschrift voor Indische Taal-, Land- en Volkenkunde* 73:105–122.

Wirz, P. 1934. The social meaning of the sept-house and the sept-boat in Dutch and British New Guinea. *Tijdschrift voor Indische Taal-, Land- en Volkenkunde* 74:140–148.

Wirz, P. 1946. Einiges ilher die Steinverehrung und den Steinkult in Neuguinea. *Verhandlungen der Naturforschenden Gesellschaft in Basel* 57:75–117.

16

Carving time: Axes and ancestrality in Asmat, West New Guinea

Tom Powell Davies

Abstract

Asmat, like many Papuan people, are often typecast by non-Papuans as 'living in the Stone Age'. Likewise, in the art market for woodcarving, which is central to Asmat peoples' access to money, the use of stone tools is viewed as a marker of objects' authenticity. While social scientists frequently push back against these stereotypes, it is often unclear how Papuan people themselves think about stone tools in the present. In this ethnographically grounded chapter, I analyse how contemporary Asmat stone tool usage inflects Asmat thinking about ancestral history, particularly as it is informed by ritual feasting. I then consider how increasing integration within a money economy is transforming Asmat peoples' use of stone tools in bride price and compensation payments. At stake, in this analysis, is how tools figure in Asmat conceptualisations of personhood, kinship, and temporality as it is being reshaped in the present in the context of the region's increasing incorporation within broader macrostructural orders.

Abstrak

Suku Asmat seperti halnya orang Papua lainnya sering sekali mendapatkan stigma sebagai orang yang masih hidup di 'Zaman Batu' oleh orang non-Papua. Sebagaimana seni uki kayu yang merupakan sumber penghasilan masyarakat Asmat, penggunaan alat batu dalam keseharian merupakan sebuah kemurnian dari budaya mereka. Walaupun begitu, pemikiran tersebut sering disanggah oleh para ilmuwan terkait dengan perspektif orang Papua sendiri mengenai tidak adanya penjelasan yang dalam mengenai keberadaan alat batu dalam budaya mereka pada masa sekarang. Dalam tulisan yang menggunakan data etnografi ini, saya mempertimbangkan bagaimana peningkatan ekonomi mengubah penggunaan alat batu serta mempengaruhi pola pikir suku Asmat tentang sejarah leluhur mereka terkati dengan ritual budaya. Selain itu, pertimbangan mengenai peningkatan penggunaan uang yang telah mengubah penggunaan alat batu oleh masyarakat Asmat terutama dalam proses pembayaran mas kawin dan kompensasi. Yang menjadi penekanan dalam analisis ini adalah tentang peranan alat dalam konseptualisasi orang Asmat terutama mengenai personalitas, kekerabatan, dan temporalitas yang sedang dibentuk di masa kini dalam konteks meningkatnya penyatuan wilayah kedalam tatanan struktural makro yang lebih luas.

Introduction

In 2015, a group of Asmat junior high school students visited the Asmat Museum of Culture and Progress (AMCP) in the town of Agats, where I was conducting fieldwork.[1] The students drifted around the museum, eying its collection of woodcarvings with polite disinterest. They eventually gathered around a modest cabinet in one corner containing stone axes gathered by Catholic missionaries and visiting 'Western' benefactors during the 1970s (Figure 16.1, see also Konrad and Sowada 2002a, 367–371). In contrast to the museum's other collections, the students examined the axes with intense interest, whispering to each other, and letting out poignant sighs resonant with emotional identification.

Figure 16.1: Cabinet of stone tools at the Asmat Museum of Culture and Progress.
Source: Photograph by Joshua Irwandi.

This chapter interrogates the students' response to the museum and its collections.[2] Why were they drawn to these stone tools, and so moved by them? Unpacking the students' responses addresses a gap in understanding Papuan techniques and temporality. Papuans are often derided by non-Papuan others as 'living in the Stone Age'. Contemporary anthropologists rightly condemn this stereotype. However, it is often unclear in anthropological critiques how Papuan people themselves think about,

---

1   The museum was founded in 1973 by the Agats-Asmat Catholic diocese. The museum aims, to quote the region's first bishop (Sowada 1972, 54–56), to prevent Asmat people from 'los[ing] a sense of identity and contact with their own history' through the collection, preservation and display of Asmat material culture, conceptualised as 'art'. On the museum's history, see Stanley (2012, 112–142); on its contemporary inter-ethnic dynamics, see Powell Davies (2016); for an indigenous account, see Biakai (2002).

2   This chapter is founded on 24 months of fieldwork in Asmat.

and with, stone tools in the present. This account of stone tools' mediation of social relationships proceeds in three sections. First, I analyse the 'Stone Age' trope and review existing critiques of it, asking how the stereotype shapes Papuan people's interactions with inter-ethnic others, and their incorporation within broader structural orders. I then sketch the place of stone tools in Asmat life, before examining their embeddedness in approaches to time and social relationality. Finally, I highlight systematic mismatches between Asmat and non-Papuan ideas about, and engagement with, stone tools. While non-Papuans often view stone tools as a marker of primitivity, for Asmat people, stone tools index the heightened capacities of their 'ancestors' (*tisir uu*[3] secret people) who worked efficaciously without contemporary labour-saving devices in ways considered impossible today. Stone tools, here, are not simply practical instruments, but rather devices for thinking about socio-history. Tools offer Asmat people a haptic connection with ancestral spirits, which they frequently leverage, especially in rituals. Thus, stone tools' association with the past is simultaneously a condition of future communal viability.

'Living in the Stone Age': A primitivist stereotype

Papuan people are often typecast as living in the 'Stone Age'. In this view, Papuans inhabit a primitive, ancient condition distant from those stereotyping them (Stasch 2015, 65). Such a categorisation combines romance and racism in volatile ways (Rutherford 2018, x). The concept of the 'Stone Age' derives from early nineteenth-century Danish Museum curator Christian Jürgensen Thomsen (Trigger 2006, 121–129). Thomsen categorised human endeavour into different ages of technological sophistication by separating objects found at different depths in archaeological excavation into discrete eras of tool use. Here, the materiality of artefacts was seen to typify different stages of linear human development, from the Stone, Bronze, and Iron Age(s). Their categorical distinctiveness was communicated through the organisation of items from each age into separate museological displays. In the nineteenth century, anthropologists began using this model of linear progress to categorise the societies they studied, which appeared as living fossils from the perspective of European modernity (Tylor 1871, 23–24). The idea that contemporary non-Western others somehow live in the past is a general feature of an orientalising, 'Western' colonial imaginary (Said 2003 [1978], 234). Applying this normative time schema to living people denies their coevalness with the ascriber (Fabian 1983). This temporal othering articulates with a popular 'Western' binarism between the categories of 'culture' and 'nature', such that Papuans are viewed as somehow closer to, and in harmony with, the latter (Lemonnier 2004, 81). Indeed, as Rupert Stasch (2015, 66–67) observed, at least since the Cook voyages, the indigenous inhabitants of West New Guinea (Indonesian Papua) have been viewed as 'the ultimate paragon of primitivity', both through a pejorative racial distinction between a more 'advanced' Polynesia and an 'inferior' Melanesia (Douglas 2008, 8), and in comparison with New Guinea's more accessible eastern half. The 'Stone Age' trope is often imbricated with other stereotypes of primitivity in ways that give them overall coherence. These might include an emphasis on bodily nakedness (Stasch 2014a); or in areas where they are worn, genital coverings such as the koteka (penis gourd) (Munro 2015, 169), which are often viewed by outsiders as a form of 'uncivilised' sexual display. Along Papua's south-west coast, cannibalism tropes particularly mediate non-Papuan understandings of the region. Asmat people, for example, became internationally known for their pre-colonial headhunting practices following the disappearance of Michael Rockefeller (1967) in the area while collecting for the Museum of Primitive Art in 1961. Here, contemporary Asmat are defined by an obsolete practice never directly witnessed by outsiders.

---

3   Indigenous Keenok words are italicised, while Bahasa Indonesia and common Papuan Malay words are underlined, at first mention. Other languages (such as Dutch) use single quote marks at first mention.

Above all, the prospect that Papuan people might be 'living in the Stone Age' is underpinned by a fetishisation of tools, viewed as markers of technical and cultural evolution. A vivid example of the temporal model at the heart of this trope is the partially Asmat-focused 1961 Academy Award–winning documentary *Le Ciel et la Boue* (*The Sky Above, The Mud Below*, directed by Pierre Dominique Gaisseau), analysed by Sophie Hopmeier (2020).[4] Though ostensibly a record of a seven-month-long 1000 km expedition northwards from Papua's south-west coast, this journey through space is presented as an expedition into the deep past, in the words of the film's narrator, to 'observe a strange and fossilised way of life before it finally disappeared; to show the men of the twentieth century their still-living ancestors'. The film's mobilisation of the science fiction trope of time travel, in which 'men of the Space Age meet men of the Stone Age', presents the journey into the interior as a trip back to the past, using tools as icons of different ages (see also Lemonnier 2004, 81).

The 'Stone Age' discourse affects Papuan lives in several ways. First, the trope is often deployed to manage closeness and distance in interactions suffused with asymmetrical power. Danilyn Rutherford (2018, 7–8, 66), for example, analysing colonial encounters in 1930s Wissel Lakes, traces how imagining that their Papuan aides lived 'in the Stone Age' helped Dutch colonists come to terms with their own incompetence in an unfamiliar environment, transforming an 'uncomfortable sharing of circumstances' into an imagined relation of kinship, in which Papuan people were 'relations', but distanced by virtue of being from the past.

Second, the trope has allowed policymakers to disregard the lives of Papuans in their decisions. Paradigmatically, in 1961, during an international dispute over the sovereignty of present-day Indonesian Papua, President John F. Kennedy set aside Papuan interests in favour of the broader objectives of US foreign policy by dismissing Papuans as 'living, as it were, in the Stone Age', in a temporally distanced condition only tenuously connected to modernity (Webster 2013, 9).

Third, the trope instantiates what Stasch (2015, 77–79) has termed 'ideologies of unequal human worth', which structure Indonesian Papua's contemporary inter-ethnic field. Here, the perception that Papuan people are the nation's <u>orang asli</u> (original people) is not simply a romantic notion, but rather a tool of state formation, in which Papuan 'primitiveness' is not just the opposite of 'civilisation', but rather, something that demands 'development' (<u>kemajuan</u>). Crucially, perceptions of an association between Papuans' 'Stone Age' condition and ancient forms of warfare, such as headhunting, obscure more structural forms of violence that Papuans encounter in the name of development transformation (Kirsch 2010, 10).

Finally, the 'Stone Age' trope is central to how Papuan life and material culture is commodified. While Papuan 'primitivity' is marketed through travel writing (Stasch 2011) and tourism (Stasch 2014b, 2017), in Asmat, this primarily centres around the art market for woodcarvings (Powell Davies 2021b, 145–193). Here, the historical use of 'Stone Age' tools to make carvings is a marker of authenticity, and with it, price.

While contemporary academics have frequently written against the 'Stone Age' stereotype, their critiques at times reiterate the trope. As Pierre Lemonnier (2004, 83) observes, anthropologists and historians seeking to combat 'Western' fantasies of the 'Stone Age' are frequently also 'hunting for authenticity' in their attempts to imagine pre-colonial Melanesian worlds. Likewise, archaeological analyses that approach Melanesian lifeworlds as 'Neolithic technical systems' offering insights into the living conditions of the deep European past (Pétrequin and Pétrequin 2020, 3) come awkwardly close to reaffirming the 'Stone Age' stereotype.

---

4   For a narrative account of the film expedition, see Saulnier (1961).

Anthropologists' critiques are also complexified by how their Papuan interlocutors engage with the stereotype and leverage it to their own ends. Amid the mistrust that characterises Papua's overall inter-ethnic order (Andersen 2015), there is a pattern of Papuans viewing other Papuan groups as 'primitive' or 'backwards'. Thus, the Asmat with whom I work self-identify as *Keenok*, or 'real people' (*Kee* = people, *nok* = real), implying that others are less than human. This inter-group categorisation articulates with an uneven colonial socio-geography, in which some inhabitants of the island are more incorporated within the orbit of metropolitan centres than others (Lemonnier 2004, 79), and therefore consider themselves to be more advanced (see e.g. Rutherford 2018, 120–121). Furthermore, while non-Papuan others have often used the 'Stone Age' trope to create distance, Papuans, particularly along the south coast, have used it to draw others into their orbit by self-lowering to create relations of patronage (Knauft 2002, 40). Here, the trope is integrated into indigenous 'demand sharing' (Peterson 1993) strategies, in which those without food, money, or other valued articles request them from anyone who might have them (and can reasonably be approached), with extreme social and ethical costs for those who withhold what they have. Thus, when engaging with government officials, my Asmat interlocutors frequently signalled their lack of access to the industrially produced tools that they would like to receive, such as chainsaws and motor boats, by conspicuously using their indigenous, hand-made counterparts, such as stone axes and dugout canoes (Powell Davies 2021b, 72–75; cf. Stasch 2021a). Another aspect, examined below, is how Papuan people, such as the students examining the axes in the museum, view stone tools as temporal icons and mediators of social relations.

One way of addressing the 'Stone Age' stereotype's resistance to critique, and its embeddedness in Papuan social fields, is to examine the denial of Papuan coevalness (following Fabian 1983) as a representation, and study how it intersects with the temporal organisation of present-day Papuan life. This strategy was employed by a group of contemporary ethnographers in an edited volume that gives a valuable overview of contemporary anthropological approaches to the 'Stone Age' trope in Indonesian Papua (Slama and Munro 2015). What is not always clear, however, from these otherwise helpful accounts, is how Papuan people themselves think about tools and time.

Stone tools in Asmat

This research takes place in the Asmat region, particularly the north-western Sawa Erma area. Asmat is home to approximately 110,000 people living across 25,000 km² of low-lying riverine mangrove swamp stretching along New Guinea's south-west coast and inland to alluvial lowlands beneath mountains to the north.[5] Asmat people live in and around villages of between 120 and 2000 people, with settlements generally decreasing in population further inland. Unlike New Guinea's north-west coast, Asmat was not incorporated within the 'Spice Islands' regional trade system controlled by the powerful Maluku Islands (Swadling 2019 [1996]). Permanent colonial presence in Asmat began in 1953 with the arrival of Catholic missionaries and Dutch colonial officers (Zegwaard n.d.), prior to the Indonesian takeover in 1963 (Drooglever 2009, 624).[6] Asmat people are famous in museum worlds for their woodcarving, and for the flamboyant ritual feasts of which it was a part, historically undertaken as a prelude to headhunting raids enacting revenge and mourning (Zegwaard

---

5   Region size and population estimates depend on the administrative unit used to define 'Asmat'. The population estimate given derives from the regency government's 2020 census (BPS Kabupaten Asmat 2021, 36). Estimates of its geographical footprint range from between 25,000 km² for the Agats-Asmat Catholic Diocese (de Hontheim 2011, 51) to 31,983.43 km² for the regency governmental area (BPS Kabupaten Asmat 2021, 5). Today, perhaps 10 per cent of the area's population are settlers from elsewhere in Indonesia (cf. Ananta et al. 2016), although they mostly live not alongside Asmat villagers but at separate state administrative 'district' settlements.

6   For an account of missionary Protestantism elsewhere in Asmat, see de Hontheim (2011).

1959). Daily subsistence generally follows a 'hunter-gatherer' pattern, centred around fishing and processing sago, while coastal tides make soil saline such that gardening is a minimal feature of food production regionally (van Arsdale 1978, 454). Virtually all Asmat groups trace their origins back to a shared settlement on a tributary of the Sirets River named Amumpun, from which Asmat people's ancestral forebears (*tisir uu*, secret people) migrated to their present locations through a fractious process of fission and dispersal (see also Konrad and Sowada 2002b, 94–95; Mansoben 1974a, 9–12; Voorhoeve 1986, 81–96). This history of shared residence lends unity to villagers' interpretations of 'Asmat' as a category.[7] Ritual life is framed around conventions established at that time, a foundational temporal schema in Asmat historical consciousness often mobilised by missionaries attempting to situate Catholicism in locally meaningful terms (Powell Davies and Hopmeier 2020).

Categorising Asmat as 'Stone Age' is ironic, given that it is an alluvial swamp almost entirely without stone. Both historically and in the present, there has been little exchange of stone tools between highland and south-west lowland communities, which are separated by inhospitable central mountain range headwater areas (Pétrequin and Pétrequin 2020, 187). Tool making and circulation is predominantly an intra-Asmat affair. Collecting stone for axes was and is a heroic feat requiring paddling large distances, often past hostile settlements, to the region's foothills. Even those living closest to headwater areas organised stone-gathering trips as highly guarded expeditions (Pétrequin and Pétrequin 2020, 189–190). At upland riverbanks, cobbles are chosen for their naturally preformed shape, then taken back to settlements and hammer-dressed (pecked) into axes with oval cross-sections. This is less efficient than flaking, but allows Asmat people to use any variety of stone, giving independence from particular stone-gathering sites and trade relationships (Konrad and Ligabue 1996, 54–56). Historically, axes were hafted through insertion into wooden handles often longer than those used elsewhere in Indonesian Papua, recalling the handgrip spacing of paddles (Pétrequin and Pétrequin 2020, 35). Hafted stone axes were used to clear settlement sites; construct architecture such as feast houses, and dugout canoes; fell and process sago trees; split deadwood for firewood (tasks now undertaken with steel axes); as well as for marriage and compensation payments (see below).[8] Woodcarvings were shaped and incised with seashells and bevelled cassowary bone knives, with unhafted stone axes used as mallets. Both historically and today, men use axes to fell large trees, while women use them to split firewood and process sago.

Historically, stone was sometimes traded between upstream and downstream Asmat settlements. Those upstream swapped stone, red ochre, and cane arrows for triton shells obtained downstream (Eyde 1967, 15–17), although people also obtained these materials independently. Such transactions often crossed lines of enmity and were mediated by people who had been taken as war captives from one settlement to another, or who had forcibly adopted the names and kin relations of a victim from another settlement via headhunting (Mansoben 1974a, 21–22). However, the relations these exchanges produced were thin. Asmat people tend to remember not the history of the transactions, but rather, the heroic stone collectors who travelled to the edge of their regional world to gather materials, implicating the axe-making process with broader experiences of social spacetime. For example, one elderly interlocutor who made such journeys in the early years of Indonesian rule was locally famous for his travels to the region's peripheries. Villagers listened avidly as he described river journeys, enumerating the number of riverbends one must paddle to reach various far-flung settlements—knowledge that guided early international tourist visitation upon the region's reopening in the early 1990s. Johsz Mansoben (1974a, 22) noted that in Sawa Erma, by 1974, the

---

7   For Sawa Erma villagers, the origin of the category 'Asmat' is obscure, and viewed simply as their 'international name' (nama secara internasional). I employ the category heuristically.

8   While axes were used to shape and finish canoes and drums, they were hollowed out using fire. For historical data on bride price payments see Mansoben (1974b, 53–54), Trenkenschuh (1982b, 31–32), and van der Wouw (1974, 6–8).

stone was no longer a focus of inter-settlement trade. Indeed, during fieldwork trips upstream between 2015 and 2018, my interlocutors were incredibly excited to collect stones for axe-making but did so directly from riverbanks rather than via exchange. As of 2018, two senior men in Sawa Erma regularly made stone axes: one as compensatory wealth items for his younger relatives, in case 'there ever is trouble', while the other for sale to visiting tourists for locally large sums. David Eyde (1967, 15), who conducted fieldwork with upstream Asmat in 1960, described axe-making as 'one of the major "leisure" occupations, especially of the older men'. In contemporary Sawa Erma, it is unclear if young men were learning this skill; however, taboos around women witnessing axe-making made the task more suited to time-rich elderly men without young families. The axes, shaped with metal hammers (Figure 16.2), were made with preforms obtained by relatives who had travelled upstream to the settlement of Mumugu Batas Batu to labour on the Trans-Papua Highway, a state infrastructure project connecting Asmat to Wamena via a 270-km road. Here, the opening of Asmat to previously distant city centres did not cause the end of stone axe production, but rather stimulated it.

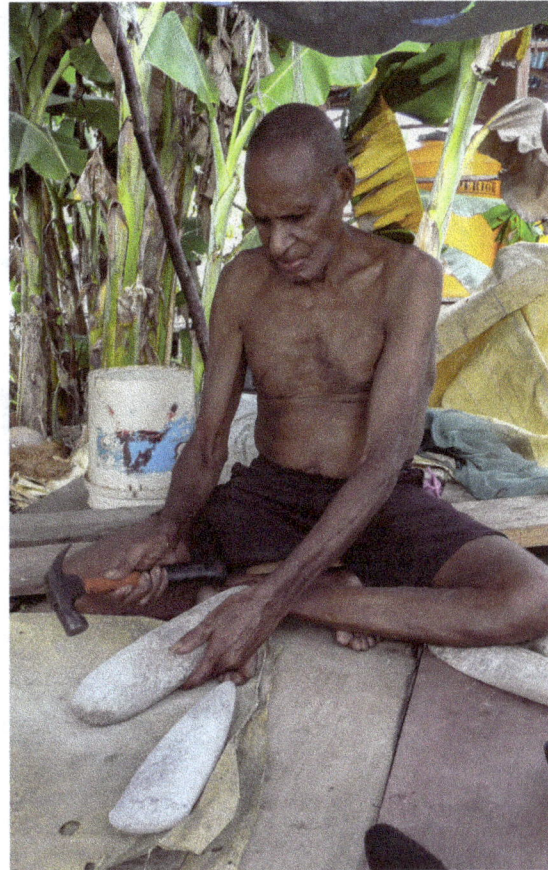

Figure 16.2: An Asmat axe-maker in the villages of Sawa Erma, 2017.

Source: Photograph by Paul Hopmeier.

Periodising pre-colonial Asmat as 'Stone Age' is also undermined by the fact that, as elsewhere in Indonesian Papua, metal was used prior to colonisation (Rutherford 2018, 5). Indeed, the first Asmat shield known to have been collected, by Dutch expeditionary forces along the Bets (formerly Kampong) River in 1904–05, was clearly carved with a metal tool, indicating the use of metal prior to this purportedly 'first contact' (Lamme and Smidt 1993, 139). Similarly, a carrying bag collected around 1910 contained two chisels with metal blades (Hoogerbrugge 1973, 28). While this could be interpreted as evidence of non-European trade, my interlocutors report that their forebears extracted nails from shipwrecks that washed up on the south coast and then reshaped them using water and stone, until their tips resembled the bevelled shape of a cassowary bone dagger (Figure 16.3, cf. Schneebaum 1983, 8 for a similar account). This strategy of demolishing built structures to extract their metal components was witnessed during the early colonial period. In 1928 three Asmat parties raided the Kamoro settlement of Atuka, demolishing a newly opened school and a Chinese trade store, plank by plank, to extract the nails (Trenkenschuh 1982a, 26). Papuan people's 'thirst for iron' was often interpreted by colonial actors as evidence of their primitivity (Rutherford 2018, 98–99). However, for Asmat people, for whom inequitable distribution is problematic, colonists' reluctance to share tools equally was viewed as immoral behaviour (Zegwaard n.d., 63).

Figure 16.3: An Asmat carver holds a chisel made from a nail in Koba village, 2015.

Source: Photograph by the author.

Axes and ancestrality

Examining how Asmat people think about the pathway from 'stone to steel' speaks to a central challenge for ethnohistory or accounts of colonialism and 'social change': how to reconcile understanding the broad sweep of these macrostructural changes with their concrete implications for people's daily lives. Stone axes, as both icons of these larger shifts and tools in daily use, allow us to bridge these scales. Thus, in Asmat, tools are constantly used to fabricate the infrastructure of the lived world (canoes, paddles, houses, woodcarvings), while at the same time, are central to how people think about identity, relations with ancestral spirits, and socio-history.

Asmat thinking about tools is embedded in their understanding of personhood. Human life, from an Asmat perspective, is animated by three types of spirit.[9] While Asmat people generally do not theorise the relationship between these spirit agencies abstractly, any disharmony or separation between them is understood to be a cause of human illness and death. The first is *karo*, a reincarnated spirit, often in the form of a tiny frog, which catalyses conception (see also Zegwaard 1990). The second is *jip*, a type of life force, which one can have more or less of, and underpins the unity of the body. The third is *ndumup*, a type of double or doppelganger associated with thinking, which can bilocate. Ndumup spirits also animate non-human life, albeit in differently organised ways. When a person uses a tool, their ndumup is thought to infuse it. For example, one interlocutor, when showing me his collection of axes and other tools, emphasised that if anyone took them without permission, excepting his son, they would become ill, as a result of his ndumup embodied in the instruments. This association between a tool's user, and their ndumup's agency, is evident in mourning. After a person dies, and the three spirits that animated them separate, the deceased's belongings are destroyed to prevent his or her now-wandering ndumup from returning and 'pulling' family members to join him/her in death. Wealth items, however, such as stone axes, are given to the deceased's in-laws as payment for taking care of mortuary rites, and therefore are some of the only items that pass between generations. The association between touch and a person's ndumup highlights Asmat people's broader interest in indexicality, and tendency to view items as signs of the acts and relations that produced them.

This spirit-imbued quality of tools is leveraged in woodcarving. While woodcarving is often categorised in the 'West' as 'art', for Asmat people it is used to mediate social relationships. Woodcarvings are prototypically made as a component of ritual feasts, which aim to establish and leverage relations with the ndumup of deceased forebears and other non-human agencies in support of the maker's plans. Carving is a semiotically dense act. Carvers contact and propitiate multiple ndumup simultaneously by making forms and incising motifs (*vô*) 'correctly'. This catches the attention of the ndumup represented through wood's materiality, as a felled tree's ndumup remains in the wood, and via naming carvings after deceased relatives (Powell Davies 2021b, 159–167). However, tool use also imbues woodcarvings with ndumup. For example, one interlocutor visited the extensive collection of Asmat woodcarvings at the 'Tropenmuseum' (now 'Wereldmuseum') open storage facility in Amsterdam (Figure 16.4). Walking amid hundreds of Asmat carvings dating to the earliest colonial expeditions (Veys 2018), the ndumup of their makers reportedly talked to him. Here, the makers' physical touch, mediated by tools, entered the wood, such that those spirits were still in the vicinity of the carvings 100 years later. Today, steel axes are predominantly used for quotidian activities. However, carvers still routinely use stone axes as mallets, in a process they describe as <u>ukir roh</u> (carving spirits), in which their ndumup enters the object with every strike (Figure 16.5).[10]

---

9   For an extended account, see Powell Davies (2021b, 153–158).

10   Given their use as mallets, stone axes are today primarily unhafted, a pattern of use that Eyde (1967, 15–16) observed in the central Asmat area as early as 1960–1962.

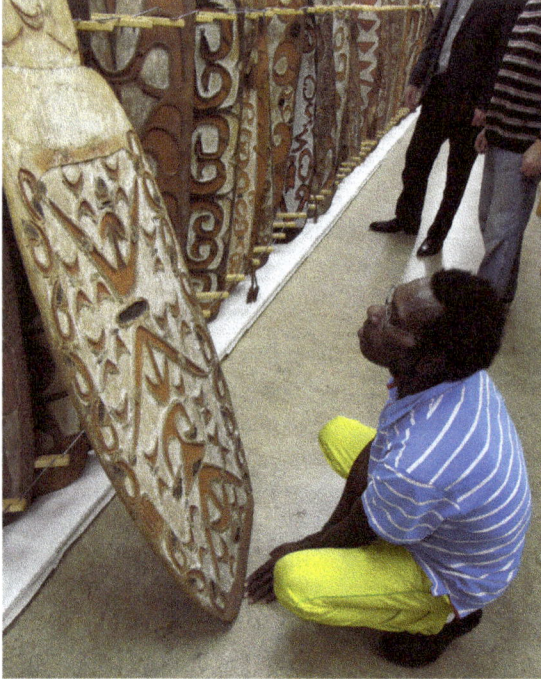

Figure 16.4: A villager from Sawa Erma visits the collection of Asmat woodcarving at the Tropenmuseum, 1999.

Source: Photograph by Roy Villevoye.

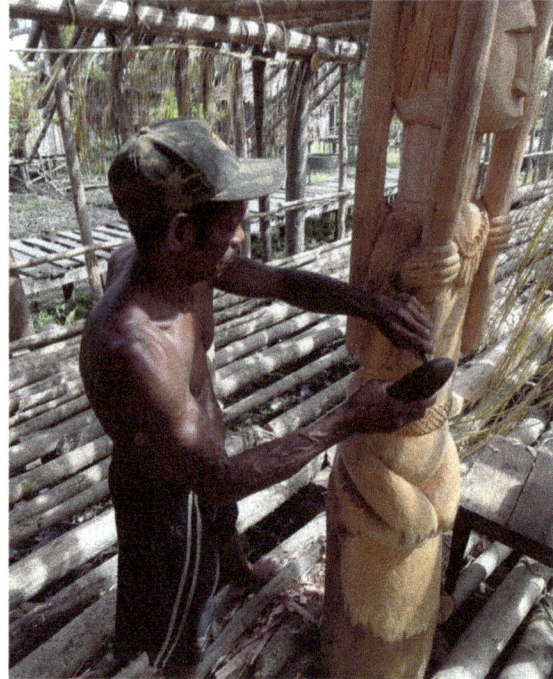

Figure 16.5: An Asmat carver uses a stone axe as a mallet for woodcarving, Sawa Erma, 2017.

Source: Photograph by the author.

My interlocutor's tool-mediated encounter with the spirits of his forebears at the Tropenmuseum raises the question of how Asmat thinking about tool use and social relations articulates with orientations to time and socio-history. Asmat people's relationship to tools and conceptualisation of their regional world is oriented towards their ancestral migration and history of shared residence at the Amumpun settlement. Ritual and woodcarving processes are founded in this temporal schema. 'Correct' actions, which attract spirit agencies, correspond to practices previously enacted by ancestral figures. Another mode of connection with ancestors is through possession of the *tisir pok* (secret tools) they once held, which contain their ndumup. Stone tools are particularly valued as mediators of relations for their hardiness. This was thrown into relief, historically, by traumatic incidents between 1964 and 1974, during 'pacification', in which Indonesian government actors burnt down feast houses, and prohibited the making of carvings associated with them (Sowada 2002; Trenkenschuh 1982a, 31). According to my interlocutors, the burning of feast houses is a wound from which they never fully recovered. The incineration of flammable items kept in feast houses scorched ndumup dating back to Amumpun, some of whom fled far away. This tragedy highlights how fundamentally tools and their use are oriented towards mediating relationships.

The close relationship between tool use and Asmat thinking about regional socio-history was thematised during a community consultation about the Asmat Museum (AMCP) in 2017. A new museum building was being constructed to replace an older facility at risk of flooding due to rising sea levels. There is an awkwardness to Asmat people's involvement with the museum. While established for their benefit, it is owned and funded by the Catholic diocese, and primarily staffed by non-Asmat settlers from elsewhere in eastern Indonesia (Powell Davies 2016; Stanley 2007).[11]

---

11   Although the museum had an Asmat director, Jufentius Biakai, between 1982 and 2005, and currently has an Asmat assistant, David Jimanipits, it has been some years since Asmat voices directed the museum's activities.

As an advisor to the museum, I consulted with Asmat ritual leaders to explore how villagers could be involved in the new building, and feel ownership of it. Leaders from Sawa Erma suggested constructing a monumental hearth—a metonym, in Asmat thought, for a social gathering—inside the museum, above which tools dating back to Amumpun could be stored. Asmat representatives from across the region would deposit tools used by their forebears, from when they last resided in one shared settlement, at this symbolic hearth. Ritual leaders, here, envisaged leveraging tools' haptic connection with an ancestral past to foster future collaboration between Asmat people, thereby renewing relations from one end of their regional world to another.

Having sketched how Asmat thinking about tools articulates with understandings of socio-history, and how this in turn shapes engagement with the museum, we can return to the school students' poignant examination of the museum's collection of stone tools described in the opening vignette. How does connection with the past via tools, and the relationships it affords with spirits in the present, shape how Asmat people feel about their social world today? One temptation is to assume that Asmat people view the transition from 'stone (tools) to steel' as an icon of colonisation. Indeed, I did occasionally hear people make this association, presenting the condition of being without industrially produced tools as typifying the era 'before the government entered'. However, as Marilyn Strathern (2013 [1990], 161–166) observed, 'first contact' situations often made more decisive impressions on colonisers than Melanesian people, for whom, in many cases, 'before' and 'after' colonisation is not the most fundamental temporal distinction. Indeed, Asmat people have historically been nimble in locating the ultimate origin of industrially produced tools in their own ancestral history (Zegwaard 1978 [1949]), treating the appearance of goods as evidence of their own power. Most fundamentally, contemporary Asmat thinking about stone tools evokes a double movement of nostalgic sympathy. Like the school students in the museum, my interlocutors view their ancestral forebears' use of stone with simultaneous pity and awe. Pity, on the one hand, because they did not have access to contemporary labour-saving tools, which make work <u>ringan</u> (light). Awe, on the other, at how strong, excited, and coordinated ancestral forebears must have been to successfully enact large-scale cycles of ritual fabrication, despite the limitations of their tools (for a parallel Rai Coast, Papua New Guinea example, see Nombo and Sisau 2013). Stone, here, is not an index of primitivity, but rather of the strength required to use it.

Asmat carvers' use of 'modern' industrially produced chisels alongside 'traditional' stone axes as mallets (Figure 16.5) seems like a potent image of social 'change' and 'continuity' developing hand in hand. Having noted how densely the 'Stone Age' trope mediates inter-ethnic interaction, I now conclude by asking how Asmat stone-focused approaches to social relations articulate with the broader macrostructural orders in which they are increasingly incorporated.

While one senior man in Sawa Erma regularly makes stone axes as wealth items for his younger relatives, a shift has recently begun away from stone, towards money, as a medium of compensation. According to one interlocutor, this transition began around 2015, corresponding with dramatic macrostructural transformations in the character of the Indonesian state at its outer rural periphery, via policies oriented towards administrative and fiscal 'decentralisation'. From 2014, President Joko Widodo instituted large-scale infrastructure projects at the nation's margins to support <u>pemberdayaan masyarakat</u> (community empowerment). Grants are disbursed to the village level, to be organised and implemented by villagers themselves (Sari 2018, 1). Asmat villagers, who in their daily lives have little access to money outside of that yielded by selling fish or woodcarvings to Indonesian settlers, suddenly have unprecedented access to large amounts of cash via the grant process (Powell Davies 2021a; Stasch 2021b). Cash has been integrated into the exchange in other Melanesian settings for some decades. However, in a 'demand sharing' social world such as that of the Asmat, money given in compensation cannot be easily stored but rather is 'eaten' at once, divided until it is finished. Ritual leaders in Sawa Erma have lectured villagers that money, unlike stone, is not durable. However, despite this sage advice, a number of marriage-related infringements that I witnessed in 2017–2018 were settled via the payment of millions of Indonesian rupiah. Asmat people's ongoing capacity to negotiate the complex social situations for which compensation is called is therefore becoming entangled with state development policy in ways that villagers do not control.

Just as the pathway from 'stone to steel' is not viewed by Asmat people as iconic of colonisation in any straightforward way, neither are stone and money treated as symbols of different eras. However, each type of value, derived from the periphery of the regional world, is understood to have different mediatory affordances. Asmat people's orientation to money follows the semiotics of foodstuffs rather than tools. While money, like fish and sago, has a ndumup master-spirit that directs its distribution, cash's circulation does not connect villagers to the ndumup of its previous users in the way that tools elicit indexical associations with ancestral forebears. When money is used as compensation, therefore, it does not attract the attention of ancestral agencies in the way that axes do, thereby undercutting the ancestral relations potentially activated through ritual transactions at a time when they are needed most.

Thus, tools in Asmat are not simply practical instruments but rather mediate social relations. Stone axes also shape Asmat thinking about time, connecting villagers to their ancestral past and the horizon of the regional world in ways that support efficacious social action in the present. While non-Papuans have often viewed using stone tools as evidence of primitivity, for Asmat people, their history of use is proof of their forebears' strength. This suggests that the study of contemporary Papuan stone tool use is not a project of salvage ethnography. Instead, it highlights how Papuan people are inventively grappling with history in ways that draw the power of ancestral relations into the future, albeit in an unequally structured inter-ethnic field.

References

Ananta, A., D.R.W.W. Utami, and N.B. Handayani 2016. Statistics on ethnic diversity in the land of Papua, Indonesia. *Asia & the Pacific Policy Studies* 3(3):458–474. doi.org/10.1002/app5.143.

Andersen, B. 2015. *Papua's insecurity: State failure in the Indonesian periphery*. East–West Center, Honolulu.

Biakai, Y. 2002. The Asmat Museum. Why so important? In U. Konrad, A. Sowada, and G. Konrad (eds), *Asmat: Perception of life in art*, pp. 65–68. B. Kühlen Verlag, Mönchengladbach.

BPS Kabupaten Asmat 2021. *Kabupaten Asmat Dalam Angka: Asmat Regency in Figure 2021*. Kabupaten Asmat, Agats.

de Hontheim, A. 2011. *Devil chasers and art gatherers: Intercultural encounters with the Asmat*. E.M.E. (Éditions Modulaires Européennes) and InterCommunications, Fernelmont and Paris.

Douglas, B. 2008. Foreign bodies in Oceania. In B. Douglas and C. Ballard (eds), *Foreign bodies: Oceania and the science of race 1750–1940*, pp. 3–30. ANU ePress, Canberra. doi.org/10.22459/FB.11.2008.01.

Drooglever, P. 2009. *An act of free choice: Decolonization and the right to self-determination in West Papua*. Oneworld Publications, Oxford.

Eyde, D.B. 1967. Cultural correlates of warfare among the Asmat of south-west New Guinea. Unpublished PhD thesis. Department of Anthropology, Yale University, New Haven.

Fabian, J. 1983. *Time and the Other: How anthropology makes its object*. Columbia University Press, New York.

Hoogerbrugge, J. 1973. An evaluation of present-day Asmat woodcarving. *Irian: Bulletin of West Irian Development* 2(1):24–35.

Hopmeier, S.K. 2020. An in/divisible whole: Time, space, and technologies of mediation in the Musée de l'Homme. Unpublished PhD thesis. Department of Film Studies, University of St Andrews, St Andrews.

Kirsch, S. 2010. Ethnographic representation and the politics of violence in West Papua. *Critique of Anthropology* 30(1):3–22. doi.org/10.1177/0308275X09363213.

Knauft, B.M. 2002. *Exchanging the past: A rainforest world of before and after.* The University of Chicago Press, Chicago and London.

Konrad, G. and G. Ligabue 1996. Stone tools and ritual stones: Production and trade. In G. Konrad and U. Konrad (eds), *Asmat: Myth and ritual the inspiration of art*, pp. 45–63. Erizzo Editrice, Venezia.

Konrad, U. and A. Sowada 2002a. The collection of the museum of Agats. In U. Konrad, A. Sowada, and G. Konrad (eds), *Asmat: Perception of life in art: The collection of the Asmat Museum of Culture and Progress*, pp. 111–381. B. Kühlen Verlag, Mönchengladbach.

Konrad, U. and A. Sowada 2002b. A key for appreciating the art of the twelve major Asmat groups. In U. Konrad, A. Sowada, and G. Konrad (eds), *Asmat: Perception of life in art: The collection of the Asmat Museum of Culture and Progress*, pp. 94–109. B. Kühlen Verlag, Mönchengladbach.

Lamme, A. and D. Smidt 1993. Collection: Military, explorers and anthropologists. In D.A.M. Smidt (ed.), *Asmat art: Woodcarvings of southwest New Guinea*, pp. 137–147. George Braziller Inc, New York.

Lemonnier, P. 2004. The hunt for authenticity. *The Journal of Pacific History* 39(1):79–98. doi.org/10.1080/00223340410001684868.

Mansoben, J.R. 1974a. Sawa Erma: A brief history of settlement, warfare and economic change. In M.T. Walker (ed.), *Asmat Papers Part I*, pp. 5–28. Universitas Cenderawasih, Jayapura.

Mansoben, J.R. 1974b. Some notes on Keenok social structure. In M.T. Walker (ed.), *Asmat papers,* Part I, pp. 39–56. Universitas Cenderawasih, Jayapura.

Munro, J. 2015. 'Now we know shame': *Malu* and stigma among Highlanders in the Papuan diaspora. In M. Slama and J. Munro (eds), *From 'Stone-Age' to 'Real-Time': Exploring Papuan temporalities, mobilities and religiosities*, pp. 169–194. ANU Press, Canberra. doi.org/10.22459/FSART.04.2015.07.

Nombo, P. and P. Sisau 2013. Mi sori long ol: Seeing the ancestors in the collection. In L. Bolton, N. Thomas, E. Bonshek, J. Adams, and B. Burt (eds), *Melanesia: Art and encounter*, pp. 92–95. The British Museum Press, London.

Peterson, N. 1993. Demand sharing: Reciprocity and the pressure for generosity among foragers. *American Anthropologist* 95(4):860–874. doi.org/10.1525/aa.1993.95.4.02a00050.

Pétrequin, P. and A.M. Pétrequin 2020. *Ecology of a tool: The ground stone axes of Irian Jaya (Indonesia).* Oxbow Books, Oxford & Philadelphia. doi.org/10.2307/j.ctv138wsr5.

Powell Davies, T. 2016. Objects of knowledge: Truth, in/commensurability and social relations at the Asmat Cultural Festival. Unpublished MRes thesis. Department of Social Anthropology, University of Cambridge, Cambridge.

Powell Davies, T. 2021a. Sago versus rice and the reorganisation of ritual spacetime: Competing modes of dependency in an age of decentralisation in Asmat, Indonesian Papua. *Oceania* 91(2):216–235. doi.org/10.1002/ocea.5306.

Powell Davies, T. 2021b. The three hearths: Custom, church and state as colliding orders of time and space in Asmat, Indonesian Papua. Unpublished PhD thesis. Department of Social Anthropology, University of Cambridge, Cambridge.

Powell Davies, T. and S.K. Hopmeier 2020. *Church and the ancestors: Sacred Pir Mats from Asmat, Papua, Indonesia*. Museum of Archaeology and Anthropology, University of Cambridge, Cambridge.

Rockefeller, M.C. 1967. *The Asmat of New Guinea: The Michael C. Rockefeller Expeditions 1961*. A.A. Gerbrands (ed.). The Museum of Primitive Art, New York.

Rutherford, D. 2018. *Living in the Stone Age: Reflections on the origins of a colonial fantasy*. The University of Chicago Press, Chicago and London. doi.org/10.7208/chicago/9780226570389.001.0001.

Said, E.W. 2003 [1978]. *Orientalism*. Penguin Books, London.

Sari, Y.I. 2018. The building of 'monuments': Power, accountability and community driven development in Papua Province, Indonesia. Unpublished PhD thesis. Crawford School of Public Policy, The Australian National University, Canberra.

Saulnier, T. 1961. *Headhunters of Papua*. Crown Publishers Inc, New York.

Schneebaum, T. 1983. Some thoughts on tools and changing carvings in Asmat. *Pacific Arts Newsletter* 16(January):7–14.

Slama, M. and J. Munro 2015. From 'Stone-Age' to 'Real-Time': Exploring Papuan temporalities, mobilities and religiosities—an introduction. In M. Slama and J. Munro (eds.), *From 'Stone-Age' to 'Real-Time': Exploring Papuan temporalities, mobilities and religiosities*, pp. 1–37. ANU Press, Canberra. doi.org/10.22459/FSART.04.2015.01.

Sowada, A. 1972. A museum of heritage and development in Asmat. *Irian: Bulletin of West Irian Development* 1(1):53–56.

Sowada, A. 2002. The decline, suppression and rejuvenation of Asmat culture and art. An historical approach. In U. Konrad, A. Sowada, and G. Konrad (eds), *Asmat: Perception of life in art: The collection of the Asmat Museum of Culture and Progress*, pp. 47–68. B. Kühlen Verlag, Mönchengladbach.

Stanley, N. 2007. Can museums become Indigenous? The Asmat Museum of Culture and Progress and contemporary Papua. In N. Stanley (ed.), *The future of indigenous museums: Perspectives from the Southwest Pacific*, pp. 190–204. Berghahn Books, New York and Oxford. doi.org/10.1515/9780857455727-014.

Stanley, N. 2012. *The making of Asmat Art: Indigenous art in a world perspective*. Sean Kingston Publishing, Canyon Pyon.

Stasch, R. 2011. Textual iconicity and the primitivist cosmos: Chronotopes of desire in travel writing about Korowai of West Papua. *Journal of Linguistic Anthropology* 21(1):1–21. doi.org/10.1111/j.1548-1395.2011.01080.x.

Stasch, R. 2014a. Toward symmetric treatment of imaginaries: Nudity and payment in tourism to Papua's 'Treehouse People'. In N. Salazar and N.H.H. Graburn (eds), *Tourism imaginaries: Anthropological approaches*, pp. 31–56. Berghahn Books, New York and Oxford. doi.org/10.1515/9781782383680-004.

Stasch, R. 2014b. How an egalitarian polity structures tourism and restructures itself around it. *Ethnos* 80(4): 524–547. doi.org/10.1080/00141844.2014.942226.

Stasch, R. 2015. From primitive other to Papuan self: Korowai engagement with ideologies of unequal human worth in encounters with tourists, state officials and education. In M. Slama and J. Munro (eds), *From 'Stone-Age' to 'Real-Time': Exploring Papuan temporalities, mobilities and religiosities*, pp. 59–94. ANU Press, Canberra. doi.org/10.22459/FSART.04.2015.03.

Stasch, R. 2017. Dramas of otherness: 'First contact' tourism in New Guinea. *HAU: Journal of Ethnographic Theory* 6(3):7–27. doi.org/10.14318/hau6.3.003.

Stasch, R. 2021a. Self-lowering as power and trap: Wawa, 'white', and peripheral embrace of state formation in Indonesian Papua. *Oceania* 91(2):257–279. doi.org/10.1002/ocea.5310.

Stasch, R. 2021b. Anarchists for the state: From egalitarian opacity to anticipating thoughts of the powerful. *Ethnos* 88(4):724–748. doi.org/10.1080/00141844.2021.2007155.

Strathern, M. 2013 (1990). Artifacts of history: Events and the interpretation of images. In *Learning to see in Melanesia: Lectures given in the Department of Social Anthropology, Cambridge University, 1993–2008*, pp. 157–178. Hau Masterclass Series, Manchester.

Swadling, P. 2019 [1996]. *Plumes from Paradise: Trade cycles in outer Southeast Asia and their impact on New Guinea and nearby islands until 1920*. Sydney University Press, Sydney. doi.org/10.30722/sup.97817433 25445.

Trenkenschuh, F. 1982a. An outline of Asmat history in perspective. In F. Trenkenschuh (ed.), *An Asmat sketchbook, No 1 & 2*, pp. 25–38. Crosier Missions, Hastings.

Trenkenschuh, F. 1982b. Some additional notes on Zegwaard from a 1970 vantage. In F. Trenkenschuh (ed.), *An Asmat sketchbook, No 1 & 2*, pp. 31–38. Crosier Missions, Hastings.

Trigger, B.G. 2006. *A history of archaeological thought*, 2nd Edition. Cambridge University Press, Cambridge. doi.org/10.1017/CBO9780511813016.

Tylor, E.B. 1871. *Primitive culture: Researches into the development of mythology, philosophy, religion, art and custom*, Vol. 1. John Murray, London.

van Arsdale, P.W. 1978. Activity patterns of Asmat hunter-gatherers: A time budget analysis. *Mankind* 11(4):453–460. doi.org/10.1111/j.1835-9310.1978.tb01183.x.

van der Wouw, A. 1974. The Asmat people of the Casuarinen Coast. *Irian: Bulletin of Irian Jaya Development* 3(1):1–20.

Veys, F.W. 2018. Papua collections in the Netherlands: A story of exploration, research, missionization, and colonization. In L. Carreau, A. Clark, A. Jelinek, E. Lilje, and N. Thomas (eds), *Pacific presences: Oceanic art and European museums*, Vol. 1, pp. 127–164. Sidestone Press, Leiden.

Voorhoeve, C.L. 1986. We, people of one canoe—they, people of wood: Two Asmat origin myths. *Irian: Bulletin of Irian Jaya* 14:79–125.

Webster, D. 2013. Self-determination abandoned: The road to the New York Agreement on West New Guinea (Papua), 1960–62. *Indonesia* 95(1):9–24. doi.org/10.1353/ind.2013.0006.

Zegwaard, G.A. 1959. Headhunting practices of the Asmat of Netherlands New Guinea. *American Anthropologist* 61(4):1021–1041. doi.org/10.1525/aa.1959.61.6.02a00080.

Zegwaard, G.A. 1978 [1949]. The myth of Famiripitsj. In F. Trenkenschuh (ed.), *An Asmat sketchbook, No. 6*, pp. 100–103. Crosier Missions, Hastings.

Zegwaard, G.A. 1990. Spirit children. In T. Schneebaum (ed.), *Embodied spirits: Ritual carvings of the Asmat*, pp. 71–75. Peabody Museum of Salem, Salem.

Zegwaard, G.A. n.d. Geschiedenis van de Katholieke Missie in Het Asmat Gebied. Manuscript. Unpublished. MSC Missiehuis, Tilburg.

17

Shell material culture in the West New Guinea Highlands: An ethnographic kaleidoscope

Beatrice Voirol

Abstract

In the focus of this contribution are the three most common seashells in the West New Guinea Highlands: *Nassarius* spp., *Cypraea* spp., and *Melo* spp. From five different perspectives, the deep meanings of the shells in West New Guinea Highlands culture are closely looked at: alternative geographies, trade chains, questions of value, and of gender, as well as sacralising processes are discussed with a focus on these shells. The chapter brings together the results of a several-months-long field study along with ethnographic information from early contact times. It involves local perceptions of shells of Mee people in the far west of the Highlands, the Dani people in the Baliem Valley as a centre point of the Highlands, and the Lani people in between, as well as of the Yali in the east and the Eipo in the far east of this mountain range. This contribution connects the past with the present.

Abstrak

Bab ini menjelaskan tiga jenis kerang yang paling umum ditemukan di Dataran Tinggi Papua bagian barat yaitu Nassarius *spp,* Cypraea *spp, dan* Melo *spp. Terdapat lima perspektif terkait keberadaan kerang dalam budaya suku-suk di Dataran Tinggi Papua antara lain: alternatif, rantai perdagangan, hal yang berkaitan dengan nilai, gender, serta sakralisasi. Tulisan ini adalah perpaduan antara hasil penelitian lapangan yang dilakukan selama beberapa bulan di wilayah ini yang dipadukan dengan data etnografi pada masa lalu. Selain itu, persepsi lokal 4 suku dalam hal ini suku Mee yang berdiam di ujung barat Dataran Tinggi, suku Dani di Lembah Baliem, suku Lani yang bermukim diantara suku Dani dan Mee, serta suku Yali di bagian timur dan Eipo di ujung timur pegunungan dipaparkan dalam tulisan ini. Data masa lalu dan masa kini mengenai kerang dihubungkan dalam tulisan ini.*

Introduction

Mostly originating from the coast, shells were, and still are, highly desired objects for the West New Guinea Highlands people. Their colour, texture, and haptics make them unique and different from other materials found in the Highlands. Their faraway and often unknown places of origin have led to different appropriation processes. This contribution brings together results of a several-months-long field study along with ethnographic information from early contact times. It involves local perceptions of shells of Mee[1] people in the far west of the Highlands, the Dani people in the Baliem Valley as a centre point of the Highlands, and the Lani people in between, as well as of the Yali in the east and the Eipo in the far east of this mountain range (Figure 17.1). This contribution connects the past with the present. In focus are the three most common seashells in the West New Guinea Highlands: *Nassarius* spp., *Cypraea* spp. (or the well-known cowrie), and *Melo* spp. Whereas *Nassarius* spp. and *Cypraea* spp. are small shells—with *Nassarius* spp. being clearly the smaller of the two—*Melo* spp. shells are significantly bigger, up to 50 cm in size. Alternative geographies, trade chains, questions of value and of gender, as well as sacralising processes are discussed in this chapter with a focus on these three different seashells.

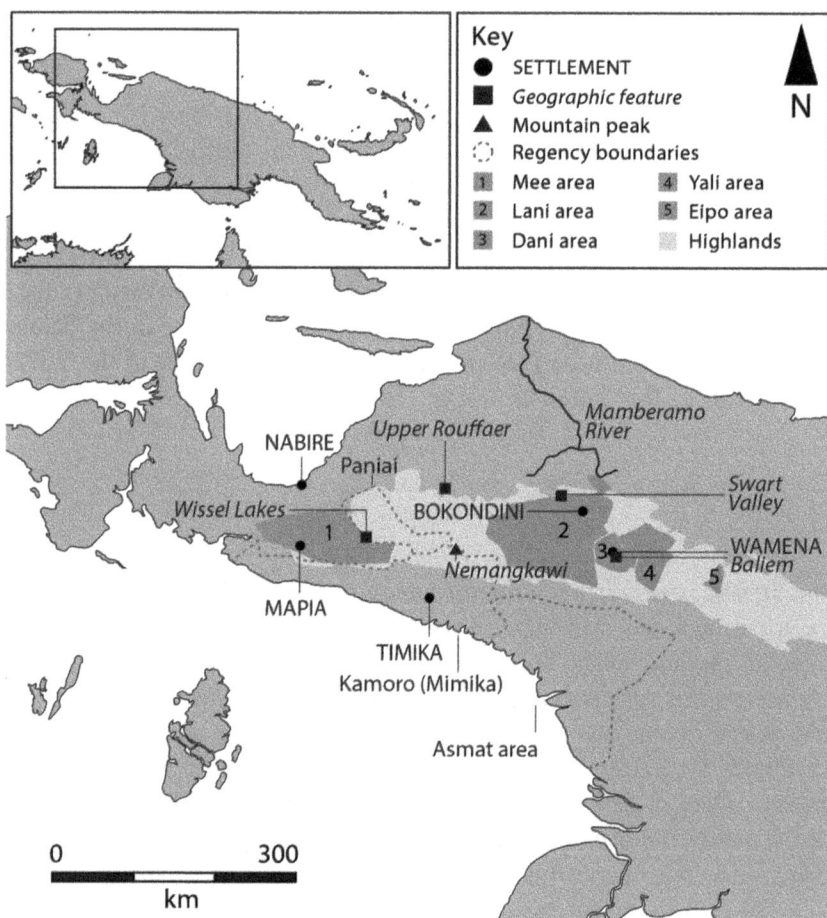

Figure 17.1: Map of West New Guinea Highlands showing key places mentioned in the text.
Source: Map by Dylan Gaffney.

---

1   I call the people Mee because local people asked me to refer to them in this way, but in the ethnographic literature they are named Kapauku or Ekari.

Localising shells

> Geography … is a body of knowledge and an order of knowledge, which requires the same kind of critical theorization as any other body of knowledge. Geography as an epistemic category is in turn grounded in issues of positionality. (Rogoff 2000, 21)

According to ethnographic documentation, seashells from the south and north coast of New Guinea have taken various routes into the central mountain range of New Guinea (Figure 17.2). The shells travel 300–400 km until they reach the Highlands of the western part of New Guinea (Pétrequin and Pétrequin 2006, 53). In the past, only a few people in the Highlands knew about the sea and the animals living in the shells. Although people today have knowledge of the sea, alternative geographies do still exist. Particular places, like lakes or mountains, are believed to be the shells' origins. These locations are meaningful and connected with the ancestors, marked by ponds, mountains, lakes, and rocks.

Figure 17.2: Weathered *Melo* shell on the beach of Bayun, south coast of Papua. Probably *Melo amphora*.

Source: Photo by Beatrice Voirol.

Lake Koma, for instance, situated somewhere between the mountain Nemangkawi/Puncak Jaya and the town of Timika, lies outside the settlement area of the Lani people. Lani people are important intermediate trading partners in the Highlands exchange, connected through a wide network of kin and trade relationships. Frequent visits to kin and trade partners in other hamlets are common up to today. Young men sometimes extend their trips to visit Lake Koma to collect a *meli*[2] (Aria Gorek,

---

2   Local language words are provided in italics, and Bahasa Indonesia or Papua Malay words are underlined, at first mention.

Materi Dupir Kogoya, Toengen Mori, Tebarkwe Tabuni, Jonas Tabuni pers. comm. 2005). Trips outside the settlement area are always risky, as Lani men cannot rely on the hospitality of their kin. Geographical markers, such as walking distances and descriptions of villages and caves are fundamental (see Figure 17.3). According to tales about Lake Koma, men collected and ate the molluscs that lived in the lake and retained the shells. Returning from their expedition, men hid the shells because of their high value (Toengen Mori, Jonas Tabuni, Aweris Morip pers. comm. 2005). With a meli, a young man could gain wealth and pay the bride price. During my fieldwork, I was not able to verify the location of this lake; however, it may be obscured by a large system of caves in the area. It is possible that there is a freshwater shell present in Lake Koma that Lani people perceive resembles the marine *Melo* shell and that this freshwater variety has been assigned to the same cultural category. It may also be possible that, for Lani men, Lake Koma represents the place where coastal *Melo* shells are acquired, but that the lake itself is not the immediate source.

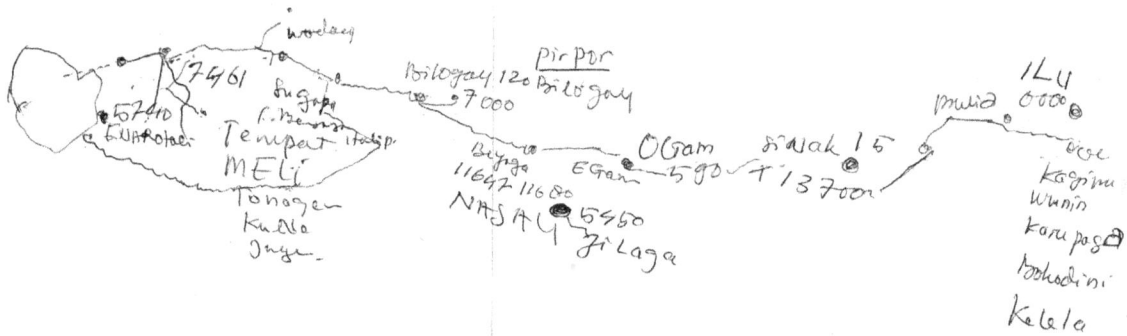

Figure 17.3: This 'treasure chart' portrays a modern version of intertribal trade.

Notes: The chart reproduces data in the form of a schematic map. It is also a mental map with internalised knowledge, a product of the visits of Philippus Weya, a Lani man, in Ilaga with his father many years ago. The map shows places only known by the elders where the *Melo* shell could be found.

Source: Map by Philippus Weya and Beatrice Voirol.

Conceptions of cardinal points help to localise and understand the landscape of shells (Voirol 2009, 182–202). The cardinal points 'east' and 'west' are two completely different concepts for Yali people. The Yalimo, the place where Yali people live, was shaped by Yeli, a giant and ancient tree somewhere in the 'east'. When Yeli was felled, its 'blood' spread and created mythical ponds. After Yeli's transformation into a pig, it travelled 'west', creating the Yalimo's geography (Zöllner 1977, 58–60). Yali people perceived the 'west' as a more economic space. Trade between Yali and the Dani, their neighbours in the 'west', intensified after pacification in the late 1960s and early 1970s. Shells coming from the 'west' were used to acquire pigs and for the production of jewellery. In contrast, shells originating from the 'east' were powerful and sacred. They had to be stored in the men's house. *Melo* shells present in this mythical landscape came from the ancestors (Herman Soneak pers. comm. 2005). Due to their lustre, they could be easily recognised and they had to be paid for with pig fat (Pileko Iohame and Sewena Kawak pers. comm. 2005). In Yalimo there existed different conceptions of the *Melo* shell: the one from the east, *weremolo*, was considered sacred while the *Melo* from the west, meli, was a trading good and currency that the missionaries used to pay locals (Herman Soneak pers. comm. 2005).

The high and fissured mountains of the Baliem Valley play a key role in the conception of the origin of the *Melo*, *Nassarius*, and *Cypraea* shells in this area. On the summit of the mountain Mu lived a snake called Mano. The snake's movement made the earth move. The ancestors called the snake and ate it. After this, the first men built a house on the mountaintop. When they finished they called Mano again. When three snakes came, the men killed them all and cooked them with vegetables and a large pig. They defecated into a little pond. After 10 months *Melo*, *Nassarius*, and *Cypraea* shells appeared in this pond (Yos Itlai pers. comm. 2005). For taking shells, pigs had to be given in return because it was the pigs' blood that made the shells white (Enno Malawa pers. comm. 2005). It is clear that there are numerous ways that West New Guinea Highlanders locate shells in their cultural geography; many of these alternative geographies contradict ethnographic documentation and are tightly linked with etiological stories.

Trading shells

> It was of uttermost interest to us to find out how these people living in the heart of New Guinea came into possession of this Cowrie. (Wirz 1931, 71, author's translation)

Studies on Papua New Guinea Highlands exchange (e.g. Hughes 1977; Nihill 1996; Strathern 1971; Wiessner and Tumu 1998) have shown that shells played a crucial role in local trade; however, the nature of shell exchange in the West New Guinea Highlands is less well documented. In the recent past, the north-west coastlines of New Guinea were part of a trade network with the Indonesian archipelago, subordinated by the sultan of Tidore. They traded with plumes of birds of paradise (Swadling 1996), nutmeg, tortoiseshell, pearls, trepang (sea cucumbers), and slaves (Kocher Schmid 1987, 332–333). However, until the beginning of the twentieth century, when several expeditions to the interior took place (see Ballard 2000; Ballard et al. 2001; Taylor 2006a, 2006b, 2006c; Wirz 1931; Wollaston 1912), little to nothing was known of the West New Guinea Highlands. The expeditions revealed that West New Guinea mountain people possessed things from far away that they must have traded—seashells were the proof. Explorers started to understand that Highlanders were not confined to isolation. The anthropologist Paul Wirz complained that he could hardly leave his tent without exchanging pigs, food, or jewellery offered by locals (Wirz 1924, 120). Little by little, a picture was painted of the vast trade chain, running from west to east along the Highlands. People were 'fond of travelling' along this route (Le Roux 1948–50, 321–367), circulating commodities such as *Nassarius*, *Cypraea*, *Melo*, stone axes, tobacco, salt, pigs, and feathers. In this commodity barter, single items were usually exchanged for single items, for instance, a *Melo* shell was usually exchanged with a pig (Voirol 2009, 90–91).

At the beginning of the 1960s, it became clear that one trading route led from the Mimika region on the south coast northwards to the Paniai region. The local Mee people traded the shells eastwards, across the highland range as far as the Baliem Valley and beyond (Pospisil 1963, 337–340). The Dani living in the Baliem Valley traded extensively with the Yali people from the north-east, but also with the Lani people of the west (Heider 1970, 25–26).

> Most of the raw materials essential to Dani technology are indigenous to the Konda Valley environment, but two primary elements in the technological array—stones and shells—must be imported. (O'Brien 1970, 43)

The Baliem Valley seemed to be an epicentre for trading, which was pictured as a sort of paradise, where pigs abounded (Peters 1975, 72).

At least five trading routes (Hampton 1999, 278–279) existed by the time of first contact with outsiders: the connection from Mimika on the south coast to Paniai in the far west of the Highlands (Pospisil 1963, 337–340; O'Brien 1970, 44–46; Pétrequin and Pétrequin 2006, 156–161), from the north coast (Nabire) to Paniai, from the Asmat region in the south via the Baliem Gorge to the Baliem Valley (Gajdusek et al. 1978, 61), from the Asmat area in the south northwards to Sela east of the Baliem Valley (Pétrequin and Pétrequin 2006, 159; Konrad et al. 1981, 27–28), and finally from the mouth of the Mamberamo River on the north coast to the Bokondini area.

In addition to the known routes, shells might have found other 'ways' of being exchanged. Highland people, as trans-regional organised actors, with their high interest in negotiating and high mobility, were and still are incredibly interconnected. Shells are the material evidence for these connections.

Valuing shells

> as commodities travel greater distances … knowledge about them tends to become partial, contradictory, and differentiated. But such differentiation may itself … lead to the intensification of demand. (Appadurai 1986, 56)

Already in the late nineteenth century, there was a fascination in European academia for non-European forms of money. Shells were defined as a prototypical form of money in traditional societies (Finsch 1914; Schmeltz 1894; Schneider 1905; Wirz 1931). Following the categorisation of 'primitive money' in the middle of the twentieth century (Dalton 1965; Einzig 1966; Quiggin 1949), 'jewellery' and 'money' were often mentioned in the same breath. Later studies revealed an extraordinary interest in the economy of Melanesian societies (Akin and Robbins 1999). Exceptional in this case were the Mee people. The *Cypraea* fulfilled the conditions of 'money'. The use of money had diverse local features: only a special *Cypraea* species—*Cypraea moneta*—were accepted as money. However, several years of special treatment, like burying the shells, were needed to transform the shells into money (Dubbeldam 1964; Pospisil 1963, 301–305; Pospisil 1978 [1963], 18–21).

> cowrie shells functioned as a medium of exchange, a measure of value and a means of payment; at the same time, cowries were seldom kept as a form of savings, but this was partly because the Kapauku people disapproved of hoarding. (Yang 2019, 207)

Colonial administration staff and missionaries opened new channels for already-known commodities. Quickly they realised that indigenous people highly valued shells. The desired shells were collected on the coast and brought to the Highlands. For Europeans, the value of the shells was seemingly disproportionate: a Highland man had to work for up to a month to acquire a shell that was bought by a missionary at a low cost somewhere on the coast. The demand for shells was high, and more and more shells were brought to the Highlands.

> Cowrie shells were introduced in 'a quantity beyond control,' as unknown quantities were brought to the northeastern Highlands (probably after 1910), 6000 shells to the Swart Valley in 1920–1921, 5000 to Upper Rouffaer in 1926, 1200 to Mappia and Tapiro in 1936, 10,000 to the West-Central Highlands in 1939, unknown quantities in 1938–939 by the Archbold expedition, many boxes by the Dutch government to the Wissel Lake area after 1938 and during the war against the Japanese, and a few hundred kilos by the Dutch Government to the Baliem Valley after 1956. A total of 400 cowries shells amounted to one pound, so a few hundred kilos meant more than 160,000 cowries. (Yang 2019, 208)

Gradually the value of the circulating shells decreased in the first half of the twentieth century, mainly close to mission stations and colonial posts (see Hughes 1978, 312 for the Highlands of PNG; Triesch 2003, 35). An important effect of Dutch administration and proselytisation was a pacification process in the West New Guinea Highlands. The efforts to produce a more peaceable and controllable Highlands had far-reaching consequences for the social structure of the West New Guinea Highlands, as ancient war confederations lost their purpose. Seeing it from an economic point of view, pacification led to an intensification of trading.

Mee people, and specifically their leaders, *tonowi*, handled the large import of *Cypraea* to the Highlands by European expeditions very astutely. Not only did they fear that shell money would be devalued, they also feared that their social structure would be changed, as mostly young men were employed and paid by outsiders. To stabilise the currency and to maintain their status, tonowi implemented a new monetary system. Imported shells could only be used for ordinary transactions and intertribal trade. For transactions that were socially and culturally crucial to the community, for example buying pigs to pay the bride price, only the traditional 'old' money could be used. With these measures, the shell currency was in use until the 1950s, when it finally was devaluated during the introduction of the Dutch New Guinea gulden and later the Indonesian rupiah (Yang 2019, 208–209).

The focus on *Cypraea* led people to forget about other shells, like the *Melo* shell in Mee society. The handling of *Melo* shells was regulated by two functions. *Daa pakoba* was sacred. It was not allowed to touch the ground and people had to approach with respect. Its origin was explained differently from *piyo pakoba* that spread along the well-known trading routes and came from the Kamoro people living on the south coast (Pospisil 1963, 337). Daa pakoba had always been there, as the ancestors passed them down to the Mee. Daa pakoba was excluded from the economic process and remained in the sacred sphere. It was deployed in case of illness, hunger, or imminent death. Its value as a ritual object was important in such a manner that expressing its value in economic terms was impossible. Through these social restrictions, the *Melo* shell was protected in this ritual sphere from commoditisation; if this sacral sphere was violated then illness, infertility, and death impended. A careful handling of the shell was rewarded with prosperity and wealth (Voirol 2009, 92–93).

Figure 17.4: *Melo* **sp. necklace, Dani people, Baliem Valley, Papua Pegunungan, Indonesia. Collection Irene Glock, before 2011; Vb 34841.**

Source: Photo by Omar Lemke; © Museum der Kulturen Basel.

Shells were even known in remote mountain valleys of the Eipo people in the far east. The *Melo* shell was highly respected and rare (Koch 1984, 28), but in relation to the two other shells, *Cypraea* and *Nassarius,* its purpose and use was unclear. The *Nassarius* had a huge importance for Eipo people. They were used as trimming for the headband, *barateng,* worn by men and sometimes by women during ceremonies. They were important for dancing and used in compensation payments along with pigs (Koch 1984, 28, 31; Volker Heeschen pers. comm. 2006). The *Cypraea* were sewn on necklaces, *kattum,* and were highly valued (Gerd Koch pers. comm. 2004; see Figure 17.4). They also featured in the songs of the Eipo, where important objects were enumerated.

'Value implies comparison' (Graeber 2001, 42): while shells were once symbols of great value, today they stand for the abolishment of social hierarchies. Social changes led to a commoditisation of shells; their value as sacral or status objects has become obsolete. However, even as a commodity their value adumbrates. Today, the price for which a necklace is offered to tourists or in intertribal trade gives a hint on how valuable these shells used to be. In remote places, a small piece of shell could be worth more than a complete necklace in Wamena in the orbit of tourism. There, shell necklaces have turned into souvenirs for tourists. Elderly indigenous men, in particular, are not pleased with the selling of the necklaces because, for them, their social and ritual value is still much more important than money (Voirol 2009, 94).

Gendering shells

> On the black breasts lay bibs made up of the white faces of minute snail shells: the largest bibs contained hundreds of snails. Most of these were fastened to the throat by a collar of white cowrie shells, and some of the men wore, in addition, a section of the huge baler shell, called *mikak*; this spoonshaped piece, eight inches long or more, was worn with its white concave surface upward, just beneath the chin. Over the centuries, the shells had come up from the coast on the obscure mountain trade routes; they were the prevailing currency of the valley, and a single mikak would purchase a large pig. (Matthiessen 2003, 11–12)

In the Highlands, war was imposed on the men by their ancestor spirits. Shells played an important role in this context. The quotation above draws on the shell's role in the context of war. Two different types of shell adornments are mentioned: the bib, with hundreds of small *Nassarius* shells, and the *mikah* necklace, a lancet-shaped middle piece of *Melo* shell, worn with the concave side towards the outside. Through a hole, this central piece is attached to a string or a braided band. The band could be decorated with small *Nassarius* shells. Sometimes, apart from the centrepiece, small rectangular pieces of *Melo* shells were added to the left and right. The mikah necklace provided protection to its owner. It made the skin of the warrior 'slippery' so that spears could hardly enter the body (Uamu Kurusi, Jonggongginia, Tabernak Kembo pers. comm. 2005).

A Dani tale that describes a footrace of a bird and a snake deals with the issue of war metaphorically. It questions whether men are like birds that have to die, or like snakes that shed their skin and live forever. In the story, the bird won the race, and therefore men have to die. Moreover, weapons and jewellery that were lost during fighting were called dead birds.

A Dani battle was also the perfect opportunity to decorate, and the preparations were crucial. On the eve of a battle, a ceremony was held; all utensils were prepared, and the help of the ancestors was requested. A pig had to be slaughtered, and the meat was distributed among the men and ancestors. On the morning of the battle, men covered their bodies and weapons with pig fat. Pig fat was said to make a man handsome. After adding ash to the fat, the mixture was smeared on the warrior's hair, face, and body. Then, pieces of jewellery were put on, feathers were plugged in the warrior's hair, furs were attached as ornamentation on the forehead, the hair was covered with a net, and armbands and necklaces from shells were put on (Gardner and Heider 1969, 3, 95; Heider 1979, 93).

On the one hand, jewellery is a distinctive attribute of the sexes, because women seldom adorn in West New Guinea Highlands (Heider 1969, 384). On the other hand, war was firmly anchored in the culture of Highlands people in New Guinea and war was crucial for gender identity. Masculinity was indoctrinated through the men's house collective. It emphasised factors like success in war, the achievement of political goals within the alliance, skilled behaviour, public speaking, relationships with several trading partners, acquired knowledge through initiation, male handsomeness that involved adorning and cosmetic measures, charisma, and social networking through polygynous marriage arrangements (Knauft 1997, 233–236, 240).

Without war, opportunities to adorn are missing in the present day. One recent exception was the war festival, a format that was designed for tourists and was active until some years ago. Mock fights were held to demonstrate to tourists visiting the Baliem Valley how battles were fought in ancient times. Tourists could buy shell necklaces, like a mikah, from local vendors in Wamena, the capital of the Baliem Valley. Moreover, without war, masculinity is in crisis. Today, masculinity in the West New Guinea Highlands is defined mainly through the possession of money and consumer goods (Knauft 1997, 237–242; Voirol 2009, 40). In everyday life, although young men might still possess knowledge about the mikah necklace, they are unlikely to wear one except in rare circumstances such as Independence Day parades (Figure 17.5).

Figure 17.5: Young man with paper mikah at a procession for Indonesian National Day, 17 August 2005 in Wamena.

Note: In using a paper mikah the young man is referring to the form and meaning of the mikah, but is substituting shells with another material, paper.

Source: Photo by Beatrice Voirol.

Sacralising shells

> The shiny objects show the important connection between sheen, pig fat, and wealth. As there was no ritual that could have been conducted without pig fat, the sheen of this object is brought out by pig fat and was renewed from time to time. From their sheen, the prosperity of the whole community was dependent. (Zöllner 1977, 329–330, author's translation)

The destruction of powerful objects, like shells, was a common practice in the course of Christianisation that developed its own dynamic from west to east along the highland range of West New Guinea. In 1957, the first community in the West New Guinea Highlands burned sacred objects (Larson 1962, 54). Gradually, events involving the mass destruction of traditional powerful objects became larger and more common. Up to a thousand people could be present at such events, which were mostly initiated by indigenous people under mission influence. Salvation was a strong motivation.

Later, ideas of material wealth were connected with the destruction of the objects. In this thinking, becoming Christian meant also acquiring all of the European goods (O'Brien 1962, 59–60; O'Brien and Ploeg 1964, 284–285; Giay and Godschalk 1993, 334; Jaarsma 1997, 81).

At a certain point, this conflagration reached the Yalimo, where the sacred nets of the Yali were the target. The sacred nets were considered indispensable for the wellbeing of the community. They served the prosperity as they guaranteed a good harvest, the thriving of pigs, success in war, as well as healthiness and protection. The meaning, function, and composition of the nets could be different from men's house to men's house. However, the nets usually contained objects like leaves, bones of tree-kangaroos, relics from initiations, parts of forest animals, rattling fruits of a tree, and *Melo* shells. A common factor of the nets was their power. They had to be controlled because they were potentially dangerous. Therefore, the nets were kept in the sacred men's houses, because only initiated men knew how to deal with them, and experts could channel their power for sorcery. The power of the nets was boosted when presented in rituals, and touching the nets served to empower men (Zöllner 1977, 262, 331). The sheen of the *Melo* shell was a central aspect of this power. *Melo, Nassarius,* and *Cypraea* belonged to the category of shiny objects. Lustre was something very special to Yali people and shells were therefore precious. Lustrous qualities were seen as a talismanic power. Closely connected with lustre is the use of pig fat. In a men's house in which shiny objects were kept in pig fat, men were not allowed to drink water or burn leaves because this would extinguish the lustre and the power of those objects (Pileko Iohame and Sewena Kalak, Arkilaus Iohame pers. comm. 2005; Zöllner 1977, 308). The cutting of the *Melo* shells could only be done by an expert. With the help of pig fat, a black stone, and magic, the expert cut the shell in seclusion, respecting certain taboos (In Tengeli pers. comm. 2005). Lustre was the sign that ancestors were benevolent and this secured prosperity for the whole community (Triesch 2003, 34).

Between the arrival of the first missionaries[3] to the Yalimo in 1961 and the destruction of the first nets as visible signs of conversion, several years had passed. In the conception of Yali people, the power of the nets was too comprehensive, and they feared severe impacts when burning the nets. Some villages fought with weapons for the preservation of the nets, for there existed beliefs that if foreign men came to Yalimo and burned the sacred nets, then a huge waterfall would come over the earth (Zöllner 1977, 82–83). However, in the end people decided to burn their sacred nets. Once the decision was made, the process of burning the sacred nets was unstoppable (Klaus Reuter pers. comm. 2007). In 1969, the first nets were burned on the visit of people from the Baliem Valley. The course of action in the burnings of sacred objects in Yalimo was always similar (Zöllner 1977, 13, 43–45, 298, 331). Local men collected the sacred nets from the men's houses, opened them, and explained the objects in the nets and the connected rituals to the whole community. Through opening up the sacred nets in front of women and children, the power of those objects was lost, and the nets were destroyed afterwards.

The *Melo* shell can be seen as an example of a powerful object that, in the course of proselytisation, lost its effect and was replaced by Christian beliefs that were closely linked to the missionaries that brought the new religion to the Yali. The missionaries projected their ideas of salvation, and their return to Europe in the 1980s was dramatic for local people (Siegfried Zöllner pers. comm. 2008). Therefore, in crisis situations even today the *Melo* shell is sometimes sadly missed by Yali people (Voirol 2009, 76).

---

3   Now United Evangelical Mission (UEM), previously Rhenish Mission Society.

Conclusion

> The shell is striking because it is white and shiny. White is always a beautiful colour and has a high value … this white shininess. And sometimes it becomes apparent that people are very aware of colours, although they possess few adjectives that describe colour. Or that they perceive physically that someone is adorned. One can suddenly see this in the songs about a young man or woman that is wearing beautiful adornments. (Volker Heeschen. pers. comm. 2006, author's translation)

Shells are fascinating aspects of New Guinea's material culture. Through sensory perception, the material characteristics of shells, like brightness, shininess, gloss, and whiteness, come to the fore. These characteristics had, and in some places continue to have, an effect on people that extends beyond all possible Western classifications of value. Shells present themselves as a class of their own as they offer so many possibilities to understand meaning and appropriation beyond their scientific definition. Moreover, shells are special to West New Guinea Highlands people because they are closely linked to ancestors, ritual life, and landscape. In this region with so many ethnic groups, which were often in conflict, shell exchange connected people that came from completely different linguistic and cultural backgrounds. The value of shells was hard to express. Some people indicate that possessing shells in pre-colonial and colonial times was like having a lot of money today (Philippus Weya pers. comm. 2005). In this way, shell valuables provided a means to participate in all sorts of social, cultural, and economic interactions. Shells were also fundamental to male beauty, and male beauty in turn was embedded in a much wider social context. This is demonstrated by the close connection between shells and pigs—or, more specifically, pig fat—in rituals. As a means of empowerment and protection, many shells have lost their effect during colonisation and proselytisation. Sometimes the efficacy of shells is missed dearly by old people in the Highlands.

References

Akin, D. and J. Robbins (eds) 1999. *Money and modernity: State and local currencies in Melanesia.* University of Pittsburgh Press, Pittsburgh.

Appadurai, A. 1986. Introduction: Commodities and the politics of value. In A. Appadurai (ed.), *The social life of things: Commodities in cultural perspective*, pp. 3–63. Cambridge University Press, Cambridge. doi.org/10.1017/CBO9780511819582.003.

Ballard, C. 2000. Collecting Pygmies: The 'Tapiro' and the British Ornithologists' Union Expedition to Dutch New Guinea, 1910–1911. In M. O'Hanlon and R.L. Welsch (eds), *Hunting the gatherers: Ethnographic collectors, agents and agency in Melanesia, 1870s–1930s*, pp. 127–154. Berghahn Books, New York; Oxford. doi.org/10.1515/9780857456915-009.

Ballard, C., S. Vink, and A. Ploeg 2001. *Race to the snow: Photography and the exploration of Dutch New Guinea, 1907–1936.* KIT Publishers, Amsterdam.

Dalton, G. 1965. Primitive money. *American Anthropologist* 67:44–65. doi.org/10.1525/aa.1965.67.1.02a 00040.

Dubbeldam, L.F.B. 1964. The devaluation of the Kapauku cowrie as a factor of social disintegration. *American Anthropologist*, 66(4):293–303.

Einzig, P. 1966. *Primitive money in its ethnological, historical and economic aspects.* Pergamon Press, Oxford.

Finsch, O. 1914. *Südseearbeiten: Gewerbe – und Kunstfleiß, Tauschmittel und Geld der Eingeborenen auf der Grundlage der Rohstoffe und der geographischen Verbreitung.* Friederichsen, Hamburg.

Gajdusek, D.C., W.C. Leysohn, R.L. Kirk, N.M. Blake, B. Keats, and E.M. McDermid 1978. Genetic differentiation among populations in Western New Guinea. *American Journal of Physical Anthropology* 48:47–63. doi.org/10.1002/ajpa.1330480109.

Gardner, R. and K.G. Heider 1969. *Dugum Dani. Leben und Tod der Steinzeitmenschen Neuguineas.* Brockhaus, Wiesbaden.

Giay, B. and J.A. Godschalk 1993. Cargoism in Irian Jaya today. *Oceania* 63:330–344. doi.org/10.1002/j.1834-4461.1993.tb02427.x.

Graeber, D. 2001. *Toward an anthropological theory of value: The false coin of our own dreams.* Palgrave, New York NY. doi.org/10.1057/9780312299064.

Hampton, O.W. 1999. *Culture of stone: Sacred and profane uses of stone among the Dani.* Texas A&M University Press, College Station.

Heider, K.G. 1969. Attributes and categories in the study of material culture: New Guinea Dani attire. *Man* 4:379–391. doi.org/10.2307/2798113.

Heider, K.G. 1970. *The Dugum Dani. A Papuan culture in the Highlands of West New Guinea.* Wenner Gren Foundation, New York.

Heider, K.G. 1979. *Grand Valley Dani: Peaceful warriors.* Case Studies in Cultural Anthropology. Holt, Rinehart & Winston, New York.

Hughes, I. 1977. *New Guinea Stone Age trade: The geography and ecology of traffic in the interior.* Terra Australis 3. Department of Prehistory, Research School of Pacific Studies, The Australian National University, Canberra.

Hughes, I. 1978. Good money and bad: Inflation and devaluation in the colonial process. *Mankind* 11:308–318.

Jaarsma, S.R. 1997. Ethnographic perceptions of cargo: Fragments of an intermittent discourse. In T. Otto and A. Borsboom (eds), *Cultural dynamics of religious change in Oceania.* pp. 67–85. KITLV Press, Leiden. doi.org/10.1163/9789004454194_009.

Knauft, B. 1997. Gender identity, political economy and modernity in Melanesia and Amazonia. *The Journal of the Royal Anthropological Institute* 3:233–259. doi.org/10.2307/3035018.

Koch, G. 1984. *Malingdam. Ethnographische Notizen über einen Siedlungsbereich im Oberen Eipomek-Tal, Zentrales Bergland von Irian Jaya (West-Neuguinea), Indonesien.* Reimer, Berlin.

Kocher Schmid, C. 1987. Traditioneller Handel in Neuguinea. In M. Munzel (ed.), *Neuguinea. Nutzung und Deutung der Umwelt,* Band 1, pp. 331–347. Museum für Völkerkunde, Frankfurt am Main.

Konrad, G., U. Konrad, and T. Schneebaum 1981. *Asmat. Leben mit den Ahnen. Steinzeitliche Holzschnitzer unserer Zeit.* Friedhelm Brückner, Glashütte.

Larson, G.F. 1962. The fetish burning movement among the Western Dani Papuans. In *Working papers in Dani ethnology,* No. 1, pp. 54–58. United Nations Temporary Executive Authority in West New Guinea, Hollandia.

Le Roux, C.C.F.M. 1948–50. *De Bergpapoea's van Nieuw-Guinea en Hum Woongebiet.* E.J. Brill, Leiden.

Matthiessen, P. 2003. *Under the mountain wall: A chronicle of two seasons in Stone Age New Guinea.* Vintage, London.

Nihill, M. 1996. Beyond bodies: Aspects of the politicisation of exchange in the South-West Highlands of Papua New Guinea. *Oceania* 67:107–126. doi.org/10.1002/j.1834-4461.1996.tb02586.x.

O'Brien, D. 1962. Nativistic movements. In *Working papers in Dani ethnology*, No. 1, pp. 59–60. United Nations Temporary Executive Authority in West New Guinea, Hollandia.

O'Brien, D. 1970. The economics of Dani marriage: An analysis of marriage payments in a Highland New Guinea society. Unpublished PhD thesis. Department of Anthropology, Yale University, New Haven.

O'Brien, D. and A. Ploeg 1964. Acculturation movements among the Western Dani. *American Anthropologist* 66 (4.2):281–292.

Peters, H.L. 1975. Some observations of the social and religious life of a Dani-Group. *Irian: Bulletin of Irian Jaya Development*, 4(2): 1–198.

Pétrequin, A.-M. and P. Pétrequin 2006. *Objets de Pouvoir en Nouvelle-Guinée: Catalogue de la Donation Anne-Marie et Pierre Pétrequin.* Musée d'Archéologie nationale de Saint-Germain-en-Laye, Paris.

Pospisil, L. 1963. *Kapauku Papuan economy.* Yale University Publications in Anthropology 62. Department of Anthropology, Yale University, New Haven.

Pospisil, L. 1978 [1963]. *The Kapauku Papuans of West New Guinea.* Holt, Rinehart and Winston, New York.

Quiggin, A.H. 1949 *A survey of primitive money: The beginning of currency.* Methuen & Co. Ltd, London.

Rogoff, I. 2000. *Terra Infirma: Geography's visual culture.* Routledge, London.

Schmeltz, J.D.E. 1894. *Schnecken und Muscheln im Leben der Völker Indonesiens und Oceaniens: Ein Beitrag zur Ethnoconchologie.* Brill, Leiden. doi.org/10.1163/9789004598959.

Schneider, O. 1905. *Muschelgeld-Studien.* Engelmann, Dresden.

Strathern, A. 1971. *The rope of the Moka: Big-men and Ceremonial Exchange in Mount Hagen New Guinea.* Cambridge University Press, Cambridge. doi.org/10.1017/CBO9780511558160.

Swadling, P. 1996. *Plumes from Paradise: Trade cycles in outer Southeast Asia and their impact on New Guinea and nearby islands until 1920.* Papua New Guinea National Museum, Boroko.

Taylor, P.M. 2006a. Introduction: Revisiting the Dutch and American New Guinea Expedition of 1926. In P.M. Taylor (ed.), *By aeroplane to Pygmyland: Revisiting the 1926 Dutch and American Expedition to New Guinea.* Smithsonian Institution Libraries, Digital Editions, Washington, DC.

Taylor, P.M. 2006b. Assembling, assessing and annotating the source materials for the study of the 1926 expedition. In P.M. Taylor (ed.), *By aeroplane to Pygmyland: Revisiting the 1926 Dutch and American Expedition to New Guinea.* Smithsonian Institution Libraries, Digital Editions, Washington, DC.

Taylor, P.M. 2006c. Western New Guinea: The geographical and ethnographic context of the 1926 Dutch and American expedition. In P.M. Taylor (ed.), *By aeroplane to Pygmyland: Revisiting the 1926 Dutch and American Expedition to New Guinea.* Smithsonian Institution Libraries, Digital Editions, Washington, DC.

Triesch, C. 2003. *Schneckenreich und Federschön. Schmuck im Hochland von West-Neuguinea. Völkerkundemuseum der Archiv- und Museumsstiftung Wuppertal.* Hausdruckerei der VEM, Wuppertal.

Voirol, B. 2009. *Sich windende Wege. Ethnografie der Melo-Schnecke in Papua, Indonesien.* Universitätsverlag Goettingen, Goettingen.

Wiessner, P. and A. Tumu 1998. *Historical vines: Enga networks of exchange, ritual and warfare in Papua New Guinea.* Smithsonian Institution Press, Washington, DC.

Wirz, P. 1924. *Anthropologische und ethnologische Ergebnisse der Central Neu-Guinea Expedition 1921–1922.* Nova Guinea 16. Brill, Leiden.

Wirz, P. 1931. *Im Lande des Schneckengeldes. Erinnerungen und Erlebnisse einer Forschungsreise ins Innere von Holländisch-Neuguinea.* Strecker und Schröder, Stuttgart.

Wollaston, A.F.R. 1912 *Pygmies & Papuans: The Stone Age to-day in Dutch New Guinea.* Smith, Elder and Co., London. doi.org/10.5962/bhl.title.21534.

Yang, B. 2019. *Cowrie shells and cowrie money: A global history.* Routledge, London. doi.org/10.4324/9780429489587.

Zöllner, S. 1977. *Lebensbaum und Schweinekult. die Religion der Jalî im Bergland von Irian-Jaya.* Theologischer Verlag Brockhaus, Wuppertal.

18

Meege as bride price in Mee culture, central ranges of West New Guinea

Martinus Tekege
Translated by Marlin Tolla and Dylan Gaffney

Abstract

Bride price payment is one of the most highly cherished practices in many societies around the globe, used as a basis to validate customary marriages. This includes the Mee people who inhabit the central ranges of West New Guinea and who use cowrie shells, or *meege,* as a groom's payment to the bride's family before they are formally recognised as husband and wife. In recent years, the practice of bride price has generated debate among Mee groups in relation to its legitimacy and relevance in the modern era. Besides that, in some cases, the bride price is seen by some people from outside these groups as an outdated practice that promotes male domination. The limited information about bride price practices presented in academic literature, especially from Papuan societies like the Mee who are closely tied to this tradition, may narrow the discussion about it. Therefore, this study's purpose is to fill the gap by describing, from a personal perspective, the experiences and views of Mee people regarding how meege are used as a marriage payment in their tradition. Based on this study, the meege not only acts as a payment from the groom to the bride's family, but also as a symbol of the union and togetherness between two different families who become as one.

Abstrak

Pembayaran mas kawin sebagai salah satu persyaratan legalitas suatu perkawinan dalam beberapa populasi di dunia, merupakan sebuah tradisi yang dijunjung tinggi pada masa lalu serta masih belanjut hingga masa kini. Tradisi ini dapat kita lihat dalam kehidupan suku Mee yang mendiami pegunungan tengah Papua dimana kerang berjenis cowrie atau dalam bahasa Mee disebut Meege merupakan salah satu komoditas pembayaran mas kawin pengantin pria kepada keluarga perempuan sebagai persyaratan mutlak sebelum diakui secara resmi oleh pemuka adat. Dalam beberapa tahun terakhir, penggunaan mas kawin dalam budaya orang Mee, telah menjadi perdebatan diatara kelompok-kelompok suku Mee sendiri terkait legitimasi serta relevansinya di era modern sekarang ini. Selain itu, dalam beberapa kasus, mas kawin dipandang sebagai hal yang perkawinan mendorong dominasi laki-laki dalam sebuah. Pembayaran mas kawin dengan penggunaan Meege/Kerang merupakan salah satu tradisi budaya yang memiliki nilai-nilai luhur yang tidak ternilai dimana informasi mengenai tradisi ini masih sangat jarang diketahui oleh masyarakat luas terutama melalui jurnal dan buku ilmiah. Oleh karena itu, tulisan ini dimaksudkan untuk memperluas pandangan tentang tradisi budaya yang masih berlaku dalam sebuah komunitas terutama untuk memahami nilai-nilai luhur yang terdapat didalamnya. Berdasarkan analisis yang dilakukan terhadap tradisi penggunaannya, maka diketahui bahwa meege tidak hanya berfungsi sebagai alat transaksi dalam prosesi adat perkawinan, namun lebih dalam dari hal tersebut adalah sebagai simbol penyatuan dan kebersamaan antara dua keluarga dari latarbelakang yang berbeda, menjadi satu dalam sebuah perkawinan.

Introduction

Marine and freshwater molluscs are commonly utilised by people in West New Guinea for a wide variety of purposes. As a food source, molluscs have been incorporated as an important part of subsistence for tens of millennia, as evidenced at many archaeological sites in the region (Szabó and Amesbury 2011). Owing to the exceptional colours, shapes, and other aesthetic features of shells, they have not only played an important role as a food source but have also been used to signify value, status, magic, currency, and so on (Gaffney et al. 2019). In many parts of the world, including Africa, Asia, and also in New Guinea, marine shells in particular have been used as a symbol of stratification, as a currency, and for bride price (Szabó 2018; Trubitt 2003). Specifically, the type of shells commonly used for currency around New Guinea, and further afield, is the cowrie (*Cypraea moneta*). In the present day, molluscs continue to be used as an essential part of cultural activities by the groups living in the New Guinea Highlands, including the Mee people (see also Voirol, this volume). This chapter describes the Mee groups, and the nature of their shell use and bride price practices, from a personal perspective.

The Mee groups

The Mee are one of several ethnolinguistic groups that occupy the central ranges of Central Papua Province, living around 1765 m above sea level around the Kamu Valley where the Paniai, Tage, and Tigi lakes are located. The valley system is bordered by a wide array of neighbouring groups: Puncak Jaya Regency to the east is inhabited by Moni, Damal, and Wolani groups; the north borders with Nabire Regency where Wate, Ause, and Tuggare groups live; to the south live Amungme and Kamoro groups; in the west are Fakfak and Kaimana regencies where the Iresim, Yamur, and Semini people live.

The Mee became known to the international community when the Catholic missionary Father Tilemans first came into contact with the Mee leader Auky Tekege in the Mapiha mountains in 1932. This encounter was followed by the pilot Frits Wissel who accidentally came across the Paniai Lakes on 31 December 1933, during the Colijn-led expedition to the Carstensz Pyramid (Nemangkawi or Puncak Jaya) (Douw 2012, 4).

The Mee language (also known as Ekari, Ekagi, and Kapauku in the anthropological and linguistic literature) is a 'Papuan' (i.e. non-Austronesian) language, which is divided into Simori and Yabi dialects (Hidayah 2015, 157), spoken by different groupings living in different parts of the valley system (Boelaars 1950, 103). The word *Mee*[1] denotes people who have a sense of humanity, are wise in thinking and making decisions, and are brave. The Mee people maintain patrilineal lineages where men play an important role in every decision. Members of the community who are born from the same family line are joined in one clan by using specific totemic symbols on their bodies.

---

1   At first mention, Mee words are italicised and common Papua Malay and Indonesian words are underlined.

In general, daily life for the Mee is consumed by farming in the valley area: commodities such as root crops (yams and taro), bananas, and other green vegetables are the main plants grown. Apart from farming, the Mee people also hunt in the forests and fish in the lakes. Keeping and raising pigs is almost universally practised by members of the Mee groups. This is because pigs are generally used for social purposes in cultural events. Today, the Mee trade commodities including pigs, chicken, sweet potato, yam, taro, rabbits, and other produce: traditional trade is a long-established practice that uses shell money as a medium of exchange.

Marine shell exchange and use

Among Mee groups, several mollusc varieties, including both bivalves and gastropods, are used for specific activities and carry important values: (a) mud snails (Nassariidae) known as *dau dagege* are used for traditional clothing, especially covering the genitals of men, as an accessory for the string of musical instruments, and also as money shells; (b) clams (*Tridacna* spp.) are employed as a container for food storage and as a plate to serve food on; (c) cone shells (Conidae), known as *paga dau*, are used as bracelet jewellery; (d) abalone (Haliotidae) are used for spoons; (e) cowrie shells (*Cypraea moneta*), known as *meege*, are used as a medium of exchange and bride price (Figure 18.1). At present, the Mee people continue to use mollusc shells as important goods in their culture; however, it is increasingly less common than in the past.

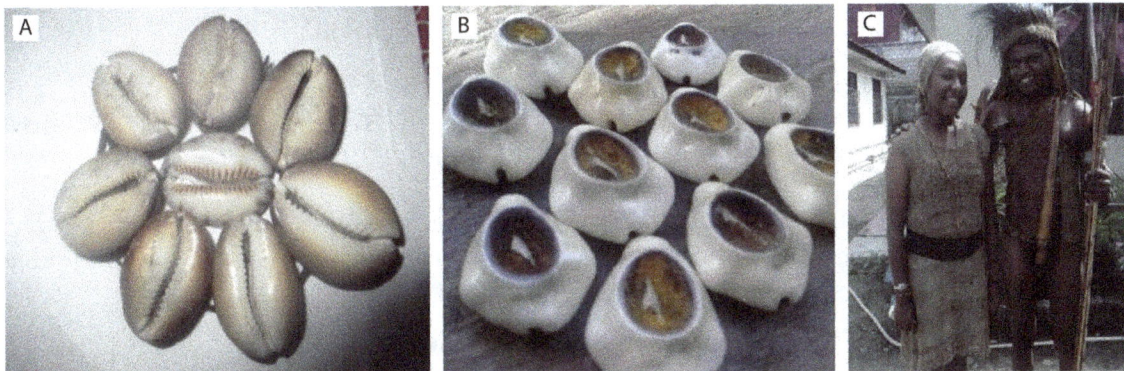

Figure 18.1: Meege shells and their use in marriages.
Notes: (A) Front of *Cypraea moneta* or meege; (B) reverse of *Cypraea moneta* or meege; (C) Mee bride and groom.
Source: Martinus Tekege.

Several types of shells are a legacy of trade and cultural activities among the Mee groups, as they are among neighbouring groups including Moni people. Shells were highly prestigious objects in the deeper past, and in recent decades up until the present. Most shells in the central range had a coastal origin, which was a result of the contact between the groups from the highlands and people from the northern and southern coasts. Marine shells are therefore evidence for the cross-regional network that existed between the coast and the highlands, which included Mee people. Marine shells were obtained by barter from groups around the northern coast of New Guinea, primarily around Cenderawasih Bay, but also including those from Nabire, Waropen, and those around the southern coast at Kokonau. More recently, cowries were also obtained by barter with the Biakers, and also with Waris people in Keerom Regency near Jayapura. The cowries that are acquired from the Waris people are named *meege Waris*.

Several rules govern this barter process, in particular stipulating which type of object can be exchanged for another. Meege can be only exchanged with pigs and chickens, while dau dagege only with rabbits, and paga dau can be exchanged only with salt and tobacco. In the barter process, the Mee people were skilled at discriminating between the type of cowries that were collected live from the seabed and those cowries that were collected as shells from the seashore. Those cowries freshly collected from the seabed are considered the best quality, while the shells collected from the shore are classified as bad quality by Mee people. Beyond these categories of quality, several types of meege are distinguished based on colour. These include *aguwa, bomoyebado, yoobado, bodiyabado, daudedege, warissbado*, and so on. The type of cowrie shell that is used as a money shell has usually been modified on the dorsum (top or back) by making a hole in the middle and smoothing it to produce a flat and smooth surface, in the past using stone tools (Figure 18.1).

Meege and marriage

Marriage among the Mee groups is a sacral celebration that not only unites two different families but also is an expression of a spiritual experience that needs to be celebrated through several steps, which involve the process of presenting a bride price. Like other groups in West New Guinea that are required to provide bride price before a marriage takes place, the Mee groom provides a bride price composed primarily of meege. These objects are needed to obtain the legitimisation from the bride's family. In general, there will be a conflict between the two families if the amount and the quality of meege do not sufficiently match the bridal family's request. Such a conflict between families will also cause the postponement of the marriage.

Unlike other groups in the central range where pig is a vital object that needs to be presented by a groom on the marriage day, in the Mee culture the *ekina* (pig) is not mandatory and instead the meege and dau dagege are used as bride price. One meege is equal to 100,000 Indonesian Rupiah (about 10 Australian dollars, as of 2020). The value of paga dau is lower than that of meege; 50 pieces of paga dau are equal to 100,000 Indonesian Rupiah. The subtypes of cowrie shells that have the lowest values are *bomoye,* yoobado, bodiyabado, and *hei bado.*

According to the rules of Mee culture, the groom needs to prepare the bride price before proposing to the woman he wants to marry. The meege do not necessarily only come from the groom himself, collected during his life, but also from all the members of the groom's family, which can include his mother or father's family, his close friends, and so on. Often parents, brothers, sisters, cousins, and other family members sacrifice their own precious meege for their son or brother to begin the new life journey through marriage. Therefore, meege collected among friends and family and used for bride price become the symbol of togetherness upon which the Mee culture rests. The nature of togetherness that is applied in the process of collecting the meege is a reflection of the philosophy that has been adopted by the Mee people for many generations, known as *ebaamukaii.* The ebaamukaii is essentially a significant message handed down from Mee generation to generation that encourages us to establish togetherness, cooperation, and connectedness between members of the family.

The amount of bride price is decided by the bride's family and relatives. The amount of meege that a Mee woman requires for the marriage to go ahead, is, in general, 50 meege, but this can increase or decrease depending on the discussions between the family of both parties. If the expected meege is available from the groom's side, the next step is for the groom's family to invite the woman and her family to accept the bride price with a marriage ceremony, which is followed by the traditional wedding party.

In several cases, if a couple is already living in the same house and has a child before the bride price is given, the man still needs to provide the bride price to the woman's family. This is based on the consideration that the bride price is a symbol of a happy family, and that it provides good luck for the family itself. A woman who has been living together with a man will be left with unhappy feelings until the man pays the bride price to the woman's family; thus, the man and his family are still required to pay a bride price as a symbol of responsibility to the woman's family.

On the day that the meege is delivered to the bride's family house, the meege will be presented on an open-mat and a *Tonawii* will provide information about its value. In Mee culture, there are a group of people named Tonawii, who have a special ability to assess the value of meege that are brought before the bride's family, examining the shells based on their shape, colour, and quality of the cut marks. This specialised skill possessed by the Tonawii is passed down from generation to generation along the family line until the thirteenth generation. Based on the work of the Tonawii, the result is announced to the bride's and groom's families so that both sides will then decide if the value matches the price requested by the bride's family.

Tonawii, together with the village or clan leader, are allowed to hold the *utepota* or the traditional wallet where the meege are kept. Excluding these two types of community member, none are allowed to hold or keep the utepota. The utepota is made of bark from the *genemo* tree, which is the same material that the Mee use for making <u>noken</u> (string bags) and for providing house-building material. Utepota vary in size but are smaller than noken; however, similar to noken, utepota are also knitted by women using traditional methods.

In the process of delivering the bride price, the two families' relatives, as well as all the community members who have a relationship to the groom and bride, will come and bring produce that will be used for <u>barapen</u> (cooking using heated stones). In Mee culture, the marriage ceremony is one of the important life events that must be celebrated, because marriage is about good things; therefore, the barapen is needed as a sign of a happy celebration. The foods that are brought for the barapen include pigs, yams, taro, and other green vegetables that are gathered from the gardens by Mee women. Simultaneously, the men have a duty to collect wood and stones as a medium to cook the meat and vegetables. All these objects are brought forth on the day when the groom's family brings their bride price to the bride's family home. After the bride price is accepted by the bride's family, the food cooked with the barapen is shared among all the people who attended the event.

In Mee culture, meege as a bride price is not only a compensation to the bride's family because the woman moves to live with her husband and his family group, but it also serves as a sign of unity of the two different families. Through marriage, the two different families become one in a new network of relationships, both economic and social. Besides that, the payment of the bride price is a sign of the groom's ability to care for the bride as well as their future children. After the marriage, the meege are saved by the bride's brothers or used to help other members in the family line that so that in future they can find a bride.

Lastly, there are also some strict rules about who Mee people can marry. In Mee tradition, family members are forbidden to marry the neighbouring Moni people. This is based on a story that the Moni people derive from the brother of the Mee people, who were together in prehistoric times. According to story, Mee and Moni lived together in the past and shared their life together as brothers in a cave. Mee, being the older brother, later left the cave and expanded outside to the area around the Paniai Lakes, where the Mee people live today. This event was followed by Moni, the younger brother, who came to live beside the Mee people. Because of this relatedness, Mee and Moni are forbidden to marry. If these rules are broken, then one of the partners will be stricken with sickness and death. This tradition continues to be adhered to today by the Mee and Moni.

Conclusion

The bride price for the Mee people takes the form of cowrie shells known as meege. Meege have a long history, being traded from the north and south coast in the prehistoric past and into the present time. As a bride price, meege is a symbol of the union between two different families and is essential to producing a happy marriage. The action of providing bride price is deeply woven into Mee identity, which revolves around the philosophy of ebaamukaii and stipulates that the togetherness of the family comes first. Ebaamukaii is manifested in the process by which family and friends of the groom collect meege to pay the bride price and celebrate with a large feast to mark the occasion.

References

Boelaars, J.H.M.C. 1950. *The linguistic position of South-Western New Guinea*. E.J. Brill, Leiden. doi.org/10.1163/9789004645455.

Douw, I. 2012. *Pupu Papa: Tanah di Bawah Gumpalan Awan Putih Sejarah Asal-Usul Orang Mee di Tanah Papua*. Udayana University Press and Absolute Media, Denpasar and Yogyakarta.

Gaffney, D., G.R. Summerhayes, K. Szabo, and B. Koppel 2019. The emergence of shell valuable exchange in the New Guinea Highlands. *American Anthropologist* 121(1):30–47. doi.org/10.1111/aman.13154.

Hidayah, Z. 2015. *Ensiklopedi Suku Bangsa di Indonesia*. Yayasan Pustaka Obor Indonesia, Jakarta.

Szabó, K., 2018. Shell money and context in Western Island Melanesia. In L. Carreau, A. Clark, A. Jelinek, E. Lilje, and N. Thomas (eds), *Pacific presences: Oceanic art and European museums*, Vol. 2, pp. 25–38. Sidestone Press, Leiden.

Szabó, K. and J.R. Amesbury 2011. Molluscs in a world of islands: The use of shellfish as a food resource in the tropical island Asia-Pacific region. *Quaternary International* 239(1–2):8–18. doi.org/10.1016/j.quaint.2011.02.033.

Trubitt, M.B.D. 2003. The production and exchange of marine shell prestige goods. *Journal of Archaeological Research* 11(3):243–277. doi.org/10.1023/A:1025028814962.

19

Muyu noken (*men*): Shifting economic opportunities and cultural values among string bag makers and users in Merauke, southern New Guinea

Veronika Triariyani Kanem
Translated by Marlin Tolla and Dylan Gaffney

Abstract

Noken are customary, neatly woven string bags made from natural fibres of plants and tree bark, which play a key role in the identity-making of many indigenous Papuans. In 2012, the United Nations Educational Scientific Cultural Organization (UNESCO) designated noken as an intangible cultural heritage of Indonesia and added it to the 'urgent safeguarding' program list. Since the designation of the noken as an intangible cultural heritage from Eastern Indonesia, the production of noken in West New Guinea (Indonesian Papua) has dramatically increased, primarily to meet the demands of the tourism industry. Although this renewed support for noken has provided good opportunities for indigenous women to generate household income, some communities—including Muyu women in Merauke in southern New Guinea—have raised concerns about the importance of preserving the traditional knowledge of noken making, because only a few older women focus intensively on producing the bags, while young women face structural barriers or have no time to learn the craft. Another challenge, in relation to urban fashion and styles, is the influx of imported mass-produced bags from Java and Makassar, which has led to many young people wearing modern bags rather than the noken. This study focuses on noken and the changing lives of indigenous Muyu women in Merauke who make and distribute the bags, known locally as *men*, since the UNESCO intervention. It presents a personal perspective and preliminary ethnographic information to explore the life experiences of noken women as the primary bag makers, the gender roles produced and maintained by noken, and the current challenges experienced by the noken makers.

Abstrak

Noken adalah tas anyaman yang terbuat dari bahan serat alami tanaman dan kulit kayu yang dikenal sebagai tas tradisional yang memainkan peranan penting dalam pembentukan identitas bagi masyarakat asli Papua. Pada tahun 2012, badan Perserikatan Bangsa Bangsa dalam hal ini UNESCO yang bergerak di bidang pendidikan, ilmu pengetahuan dan kebudayaan menetapkan noken sebagai warisan budaya tak benda dari Indonesia bagian timur. Selain itu, noken juga ditetapkan oleh UNESCO sebagai warisan budaya yang terancam punah. Sejak penetapannya sebagai warisan budaya tak benda dari Indonesia, produksi noken telah mengalami peningkatan produksi secara dramatis terutama untuk memenuhi permintaan industri pariwisata. Walaupun kondisi tersebut telah memberikan peluang yang baik bagi perempuan asli Papua untuk menghasilkan uang dan meningkatkan pendapatan rumah tangga, beberapa komunitas perempuan seperti orang Muyu yang berdiam di kabupaten Merauke, Provinsi Papua-selatan mengalami beberapa permasalahan terkait dengan produksi noken. Hal ini dilatarbelakangi oleh kurangnya minat anak muda dalam mewarisi keahlian dalam mempelajari seni menganyam noken. Berdasarkan hasil penelitian yang didapatkan, maka diketahui bahwa hanya beberapa perempuan asli Muyu saja yang ahli dalam menganyam noken, itupun didominasi oleh perempuan yang telah berumur. Sehingga dikawatirkan bahwa hal ini bisa menjadi sebuah permasalahan dimasa depan karena karena kurangnya minat generasi muda Muyu untuk mempelajari keahlian tersebut. Tantangan lainnya yang didapatkan terkait dengan pemasaran noken adalah adanya kesenjangan minat terhadap gaya hidup perkotaan di masa sekarang, dimana tas import yang terbuat dari kulit binatang, bahan sintetis, dan material lainnya yang di impor dari luar Papua lebih diminati dibandingkan dengan noken. Penelitian ini berfokus pada noken dalam kehidupan orang Muyu serta membahas tentang peran perempuan Muyu serta tantangan yang dihadapi mulai dari pembuatan hingga proses distribusi noken ke pasar sejak ditetapkannya noken sebagai warisan budaya tak benda oleh UNESCO.

Introduction

A noken[1] is a customary bag from Papua made from woven and knotted bush material, roots, and tree fibres. According to Titus Pekei (director of Gerakan Noken Papua, the Papuan Noken Foundation), the word noken comes from the Biak local language, *ino-kenson* or *inoken*. For many indigenous Papuans, noken are not just ordinary bags, but rather carriers that represent the identity of the Papuan people and a legacy inherited from their ancestors. Apart from being used to transport food, personal items, babies, and pets (dogs or piglets), noken carry a wide array of sociocultural values that are densely embedded in the lives of indigenous Papuans. For example, Marjanto (2013) suggested that a noken represents a mother's womb because the woven bag is elastic, light, and easy to use as a bag for all the daily needs of a family. In addition, from an ecological perspective, the basic materials of noken are natural components obtained from the forest which, when damaged, will decompose easily into soil. Many Papuans believe that this process is similar to the cycle of life. Moreover, noken are used to store and carry items for dowry at engagements or weddings, initiation ceremonies, and peace parties between conflicting tribes, and also used as clothes in women's group religious ceremonies (Marjanto 2013; Ulumuddin 2013).

Since being designated by the United Nations Educational, Scientific, and Cultural Organization (UNESCO) as an intangible cultural heritage on 4 December 2012, noken have received heightened attention from government institutions and the public within Indonesia. As such, noken that were

---

1   At first mention, local language words are italicised and common Papua Malay and Indonesian words are underlined. Other languages (like Tok Pisin) are provided with single quote marks at first mention.

originally woven only to fulfil domestic interests and rituals are now increasingly in demand in the market and can support the household economy. The variety of noken designs is also growing, with new models, colours, and sizes being made. Although noken are increasingly in demand by Indonesians and foreign tourists and this can help the local economy, there are concerns from indigenous Papuans about the importance of maintaining and inheriting noken culture, because a younger generation of Papuans is increasingly not learning to weave.

This chapter represents a personal perspective about the author's home community in Merauke, and provides background to an ongoing indigenous research project being undertaken among Muyu women. The chapter will first review the importance of noken in the lives of indigenous Papuans, exploring the social, economic, and cultural values embedded in noken at a general level. As a source of comparison, it will draw from several studies on Papua New Guinea's (PNG) string bags, conducted by the anthropologist Maureen MacKenzie (1999), which share gendered and sociocultural elements with noken. The chapter will then detail the recent intervention in noken-making made by UNESCO in collaboration with the Indonesian government. The trajectory of noken making following the UNESCO declaration, recent shifts in social and cultural values, and the challenges faced by Muyu communities around Merauke in maintaining the noken weaving culture, will then be explored.

String bags in New Guinea

Across New Guinea, string bag size, shape, and weaving techniques are diverse. Large bags are often used by adults to transport food from the garden, firewood, hunted animals, babies, and piglets. Medium to small bags are often used to keep personal belongings like money, betel nut, books, and so forth. Although string bags are made by women, they are used by almost everybody regardless of gender, age, ethnicity, and religion. Today, men and young people will often use medium or small string bags to put personal items such as cigarettes and tobacco, matches, mobile phones, and money. Schoolchildren use bags to hold books, food, or uniforms. In the mountains, string bags are also used by women as clothes to cover the body, better known as *Sali* (Januar 2017). According to Heider and Gardner (1974), as cited in MacKenzie (1999), string bags are even used by Dani children in the central highlands as a game, when there are no balls or toys nearby. Previous research on string bags in New Guinea has focused primarily on their role in facilitating gift exchanges and in their production and reproduction of gender; two crucial elements in identity formation and relation-making.

Gifting

The Papuans who inhabit New Guinea and its surrounding islands cannot be separated from their connections produced by 'give and take'. Gifting individualised objects can generate status in a way that the exchange of money cannot. In this context, string bags have not conventionally been seen as a commodity that can be sold to generate a profit. I here draw a distinction between trade at the market, which forms a very temporary relationship between the purchaser and the seller, and which dissolves quickly after the sale, and gifting, which forms a more lasting, or delayed, relationship between the giver and the recipient (Strathern 1988).

In the past, string bags would be given to a person or group that has a blood kinship or close contact with the giver, such as family members, friends, and colleagues. Giving a string bag therefore binds and strengthens the relationship and describes the emotional closeness between people, including between mothers and their children (recall that string bags are often used to carry babies and often considered womb-like; see Marjanto 2013). For example, a mother might weave a bag and give it to her child when they grow up and leave to study in the city. The string bag then becomes a material reminder for the child when they miss their family or home. A similar thing happens when a string bag is given to a guest who comes from far away, with the hope that the guest will take the bag with them and always remember the giver.

Through her research with the Telefol in PNG, MacKenzie (1999) describes the relationship between the maker and the recipient of the string bag ('bilum' in PNG). Telefol women would usually produce bilum and give them to their closest connections, such as husbands, children, parents, in-laws, and friends, as a symbol of love and close kinship. In this way, gifting strengthens the sense of solidarity and relationships between groups of women (MacKenzie 1999). For example, when a bride wants to leave her house to live with her husband, her female friends will weave a special bilum which is then filled with household items or utensils in order to support the bride in starting a new life. The person who receives the bilum is expected to remember those who gifted it to her (Andersen 2015).

Gender

MacKenzie (1999) argues that a string bag is not an ordinary object, but rather it is a bag that transcends the life and body of a woman. String bags (noken and bilum) are embedded in the daily life of New Guinea women because the bags are helpful in carrying out productive and reproductive roles. According to Januar (2017), the relationship between mothers, children and string bags has been in formation since infancy because material closeness is created by the woman carrying her child in a string bag slung on her back. When the mother is gardening, the baby will be hung in a string bag from a tree branch to prevent the child from being attacked by animals (Kanem and Norris 2018). Even when the mother is in the process of selling the garden produce at the market, babies are carried by the use of specially designed string bags. In such situations, a strong New Guinea woman can carry three different bags with different contents on her head, such as crops, firewood, and her infant (MacKenzie 1999). As such, it is clear that string bags are both practical objects as well as embedded in the gendered life course of New Guineans.

Women are the primary makers of string bags, involved in the process of collecting raw materials for production, distributing, and marketing to the public. Although bags can be made individually, the process is usually carried out in groups so that women can exchange information, stories, gossip, and encourage each other so that the work of their colleagues can be completed on time. Referring again to the results of MacKenzie (1999, 112), Telefol women and men have very different roles in making bilum, whereby women weave, and men take part in the decorating process and apply these decorations in a separate place from the women. Ornaments used to decorate the bilum include various types of bird feathers or animal bones. Bilum decorated in this way are usually used for ritual events among the Telefol people, while the bilum with no decorations are used in everyday activities such as carrying garden products, transporting babies, and as gifts for relatives. As such, there are complex spatial and interpersonal relationships created during the manufacture and use of string bags that reproduce gender norms and signify gender identities.

UNESCO and state-level interventions in Papuan noken

Given the various functions of noken and the sociocultural significance they are perceived to carry, these objects and the craft of production were listed as an intangible cultural heritage of Indonesia by UNESCO in 2012 (UNESCO 2014). According to a report by the Centre for Research and Development of Indonesian Culture (Pusat Penelitian dan Pengembangan Kebudayaan Indonesia), noken making had slowly begun to disappear, and increasingly few women were practising the craft (Ulumuddin 2013). UNESCO (2012) reported that in many areas, only a small group of elderly women were weaving noken for commercial purposes. Another concern noted by UNESCO was that young people had lost the motivation to acquire knowledge and techniques from their mothers and grandmothers owing to various school activities and new lifestyles in urban areas. It was these public concerns that led UNESCO to designate noken as a heritage that requires urgent protection.

Below are six actions designed to safeguard this intangible cultural heritage based on the UNESCO program, contained in the file 00619 (UNESCO 2012).

1. Inventory of Noken Cultural Heritage; data compilation of noken craftspeople across seven traditional custom areas in Indonesian Papua.
2. Creating noken teaching materials in the form of books, posters, and audio-visual (DVD/CD).
3. Inserting noken into school curriculum as local content.
4. Capacity building for noken craftspeople, through various training and assistance programs.
5. Noken cultural awareness and revitalisation.
6. Promotion of noken by local government.

Since the UNESCO declaration, several provincial and local governments have been aggressively promoting noken as an intangible cultural heritage of Indonesian Papua, providing assistance and training for noken craftspeople and establishing 4 December as Papuan Noken Day. In many ways, the UNESCO and governmental interest in safeguarding 'traditional' noken practices reflects a broader preoccupation with preserving and reifying heritage. As part of this process, heritage itself, tangible or intangible, can be commodified and more easily understood in the context of state-level and regional policy frameworks. However, the UNESCO intervention in noken production does highlight important changes that are taking place in several parts of Indonesian Papua; there are several factors that still require extra attention from local governments and various relevant stakeholders, which will now be examined with a special focus on Muyu weavers around Merauke.

Recent developments concerning *men* string bags in Merauke

Customary production and use of *men* bags

The Muyu people of the southern lowlands of West New Guinea call their string bags *men* in their local language. *Men* are made from tree bark from the species *Gnetum gnemon*, which is spun into yarns and knitted into the bags using needles. Before the presence of iron needles, Muyu women used coconut sticks or chicken quills to help them weave the *men*. The size of *men* bags are various and they have multiple functions. Large *men* string bags are often used to carry food and firewood while the small *men,* also known as *jowotang*, are used to carry money or other personal items. Commonly, children use *men* bags to carry their books, uniforms, and bottled water during school days. Although women are the primary knitters of the bags, males often use them to carry their personal items such as tobacco, matches, and money. In cultural ceremonies, males have been involved in decorating the *men* bags with money, young coconut leaves, and cassowary and cockatoo feathers. Sometimes, males have been involved in collecting the *Gnetum gnemon* fibres when they go hunting, helping their wives or sisters to gather the raw materials for knitting.

The Muyu people analogise *men* bags to *tanakaba* which means pregnant women (Kanem 2021a). The bag looks very small before it is filled and will adjust to become larger in size when it is filled, just like the stages of pregnancy. Like in other parts of New Guinea, among the Muyu, a *men* is a symbol of connection between parents and their children (Kanem 2021a). For example, during a daughter's engagement ceremony or masuk minang, the groom's family will bring new *men* bags containing garden produce such as sago, bananas, taros, and yams and hand them over to the bride's family. The bride's family will also weave a new *men* called *kelokmen*, produced from yellow wood fibres or *nongtimot* in Muyu local language. Before the kelokmen is given to the groom, the bride's family will pray upon the bag and then money will be placed inside it for the new family's supplies. Before the bride leaves the parental household to live with her new husband, her parents will place the kelokmen on their daughter's head (Kanem 2021a). The kelokmen and all the money or goods inside aims to support a new life journey of the newly married couple.

Apart from the masuk minang ceremony, *men* string bags are mostly used in *ketmon* and *danda* dances for welcoming important guests. There are various items placed inside decorated *men* bags for dancing such as food, clothes, and combs. The chosen dancers, which include adult males, females, and young people, will place the *men* bags on their heads and dance along the welcoming procession. Recently, *men* knitting activities have expanded into making traditional attire and dancing accessories among the Muyu community (Figure 19.1).

Figure 19.1: Traditional attire and weaving *men* string bags.

Notes: Left: A Muyu–Mandobo woman wearing a bird feather-decorated noken or *enok* in the Mandobo traditional language as her dancing accessory. Right: a Muyu woman having just finished weaving a *men* string bag in between her trading activities in the Mopah market, Merauke.

Source: Left photo by Kizito Heru, 2021; right photo by Veronika T. Kanem, 2019.

Changing values and relations

After being designated as one of the world's intangible cultural heritages by UNESCO, noken saw a resurgence in demand from different spheres such as tourism, education, and government. Previously, Muyu women bag makers tended to weave *men* part-time, while also being busy housewives, continuing the tradition as an example of Papuan culture for their children (Figure 19.2). Now, by contrast, many women are starting to make *men* bags as their main livelihood because of the inflation of commercial value. At present, *men* bags are made in various models, colours, and sizes to fulfil the market demand and a burgeoning tourist industry (Figure 19.3).

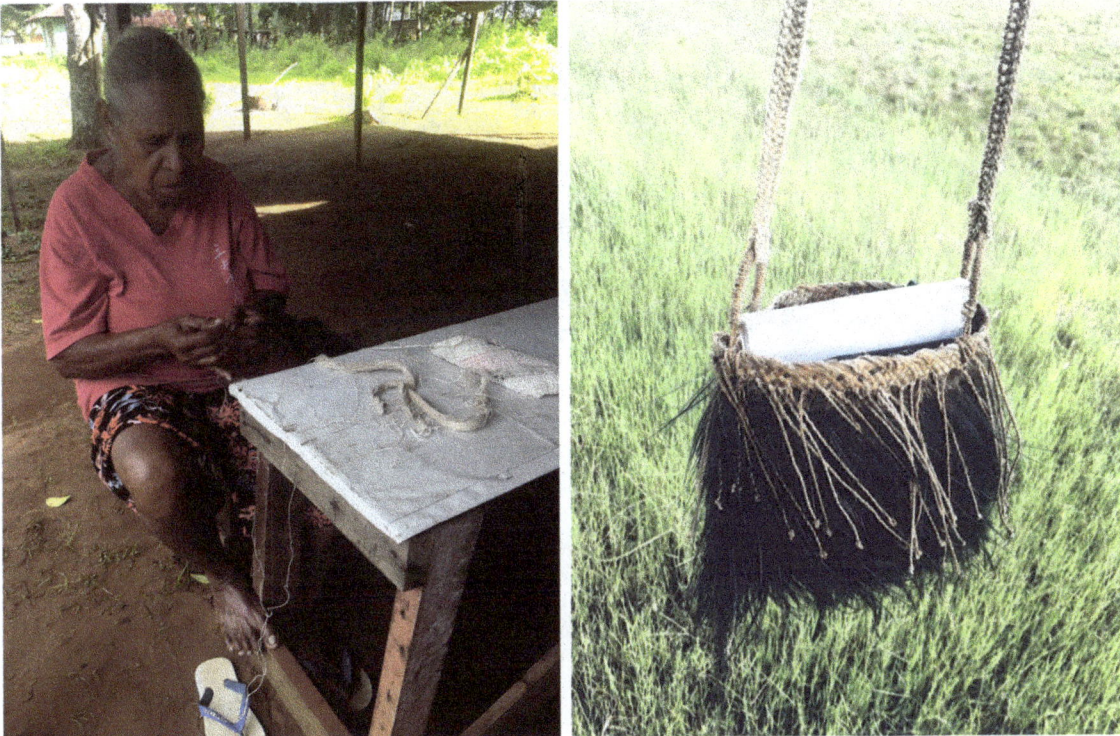

Figure 19.2: *Men* string bags.

Notes: Left: A Muyu woman named Klemensia beginning to weave her *men* string bag in Kelapa Lima, Merauke. Right: a noken from the Marind Kanum tribe, who inhabit the border area of Indonesia and PNG, decorated with cassowary feathers.

Source: Left photo by Veronika T. Kanem, 2022; right photo by Veronika T. Kanem, 2019.

Various micro-enterprise development programs have begun to be offered by government and non-government organisations for noken makers. For instance, support has been provided in the form of grants, loans, training, and facilities for weaving noken from Bank Indonesia and the Papua provincial government during a successful national sports event in Papua Province in 2021 (Sahulteru and Hutubessy 2020). Noken production is also considered to increase household income, which was predicted to reduce poverty in West New Guinea (Dewi et al. 2018). For instance, many mothers in Merauke have been able to send their children to school using the proceeds of noken sales, and more women (mostly single mothers and widows) are able to obtain their household necessities through the income from making *men* bags.

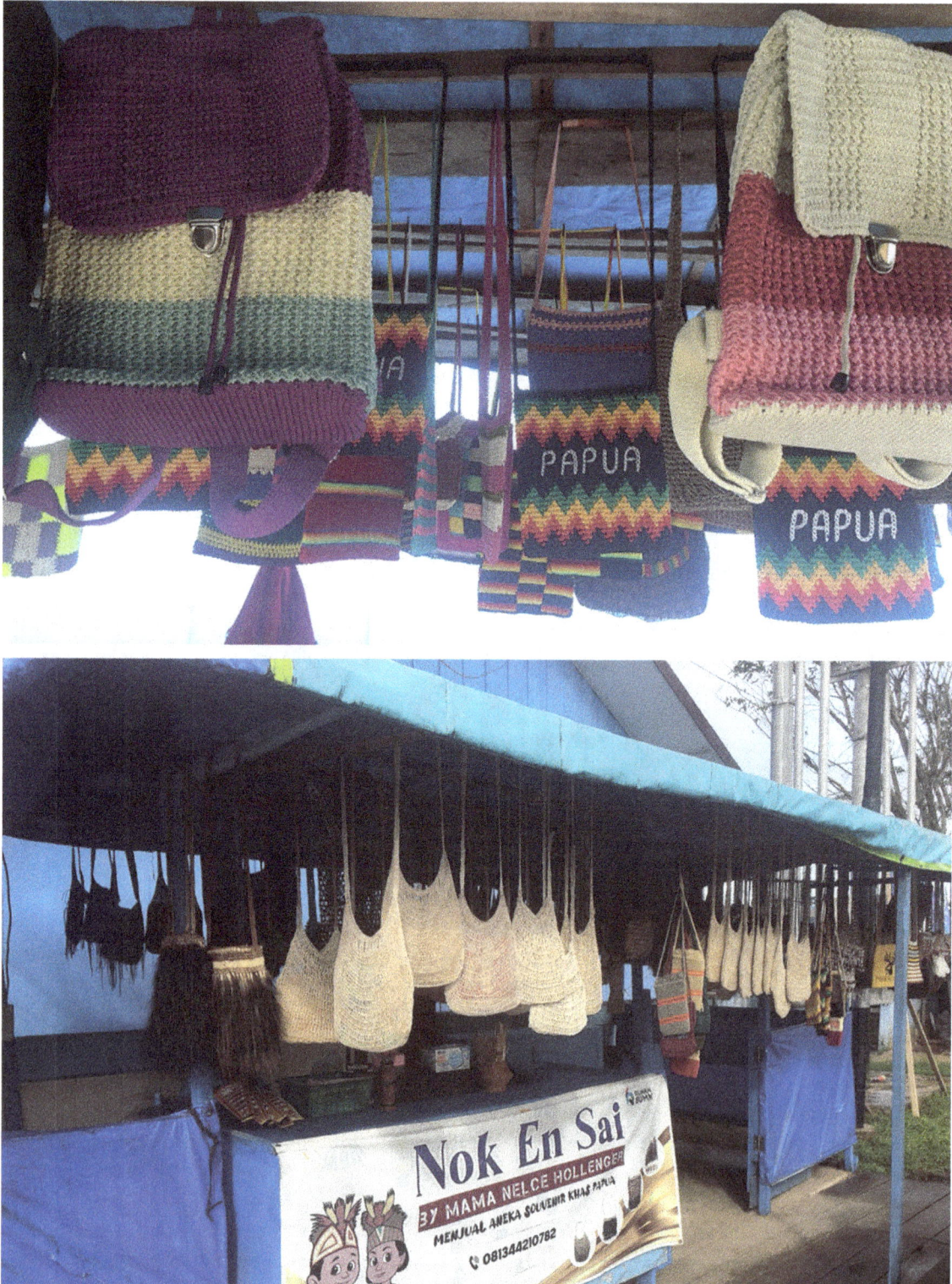

Figure 19.3: Noken bags, a UNESCO-designated example of the world's intangible cultural heritage.

Notes: Above: noken embroidered with the word 'Papua' sold alongside noken in a modern design, both made with synthetic yarn. Below: stalls in Merauke selling noken made from organic and synthetic fibres as souvenirs.

Source: Photos by Veronika T. Kanem, 2022.

Regarding the current rate of development relating to noken weaving in Merauke Regency, several studies including the author's observations in the field demonstrate that although noken revitalisation has encouraged the growth of Papuan women's wealth, there has been a significant shift in the values surrounding noken in everyday life. The shift in question relates to noken manufacture now being considered an activity that can easily generate money which can then be stored, used as capital for further weaving, or distributed and used among kinship networks. This is evident when mothers increasingly weave for direct sales rather than training their daughters to inherit their weaving skills. Additionally, the value of kinship and friendship produced and stored by noken has gradually begun to diminish because noken are less often given to loved ones but must be commoditised and traded for money or other goods. As such, the value and meaning generated through gifting have slowly been replaced with the value of the Indonesian rupiah, notwithstanding the fact that money is increasingly substituted as a material way to generate and transform kinship relations.

Decline in weaving among young women

Recently, fewer young Muyu women have been learning to knit *men* bags. In urban areas, structural barriers to learning are produced by rapidly expanding state interventions and changing social environments. This means that young people are more likely to spend time at school, college, work, or on social media than weaving *men* (Kanem and Norris 2018; Sahulteru and Hutubessy 2020). Some girls who do make *men* bags prefer synthetic materials (see below) and worry that the customary process of spinning wood fibres on their thighs can cause blisters that damage the beauty of their legs. In these urban areas, young people have also started to switch to using modern bags instead of *men* bags because imported bags are considered more stylish; others prefer to wear noken t-shirts to signify their heritage rather than hang the real noken on their necks. As mentioned above, other challenges may be associated with older women devoting more of their time to specialising in the commercial production of noken, monopolising their economic opportunity, but resulting in less time to teach novices.

In villages and rural areas outside of Merauke, many parents send their children to the city to continue their education. Separated from their parents, hometown, and familiar environment, these children begin to leave the practice of weaving string bags behind. The busyness of college means that some teenage girls no longer have the time for holding a needle and thread. In fact, many long to return to spinning yarn, but because of the increasingly heavy burden of education, they are forced to stop. During the Christmas and New Year holidays, many girls return to the village where they have opportunity to resume *men* weaving (Kanem 2021b).

Another change encountered is that, despite intervention from UNESCO and the government, not many schools have included noken weaving studies into the school curriculum. This may relate to the fact that many teachers grow up and train outside of New Guinea and relocate to obtain work. Although several schools in Jayapura have incorporated UNESCO's (2012) suggestions to add noken weaving lessons into their curricula, most schools in Merauke have not implemented it. Thus, the Kementerian Pendidikan dan Kebudayaan (Ministry of Education and Culture) continues to urge all educational institutions in Papua to include noken in their local curriculum, and their hope is that this cultural heritage will be preserved, broadly unchanged, for generations to come.

Shifting materials

Another significant change in noken production can be seen in the basic materials and tools used in the process; some of these changes are driven by a lack of access to organic materials and others by the perceived improved quality of synthetic materials. Customarily, materials derive from plant fibres or tree roots, which are increasingly difficult to obtain, and therefore expensive, in urban areas. For example, mothers from the Muyu and Mandobo groups who have lived in Merauke town for a long time have to order *Gnetum gnemon* wood fibre from Boven Digoel Regency or several villages in the PNG border area (Figure 19.2). One small bundle is initially purchased for IDR 10,000–15,000 (about 1 Australian dollar as of 2020), but this does not include the payment for the car rental services used to obtain the material (Kanem 2021b). In the past, the price of wood fibres was very cheap and easily found at the Mopah Market in Merauke, but now it is rare. One young person named Yohanis, who is the former chairman of the Boven Digoel Student Association, said that recent development in the regency has cleared substantial areas of forest, which has reduced the number of *Gnetum gnemon* trees nearby. People who previously had easy access to the fibre from these trees now must walk substantial distances to obtain these materials. Some even cross the border into PNG. This of course has had a major impact on the price of fibres imported into Merauke, where these materials are increasingly expensive (personal interview with Yohanis, the former chairman of the Boven Digoel Student Association, 2017). In addition to clearing land for housing and office block construction in Boven Digoel, the presence of foreign companies has also had an impact. For example, the presence of oil palm companies in the Boven Digoel Regency and the riverside of the Bian River has cleared a large area of community tropical forest, which has made it difficult for women to access wood fibres to make noken (Chao 2022; Malinda and Yayasan Pusaka Bentala Rakyat 2021).

The difficulty of obtaining natural fibres has forced Muyu women weavers to switch to using synthetic yarn purchased from non-Papuan traders at the market or shops; this is also the case in larger cities like Jayapura (Sahulteru and Hutubessy 2020). Similarly, needles used for weaving and embroidery are increasingly made from modern materials. Usually, Muyu women weavers will modify a broken iron umbrella for use as needles (Kanem 2021b), or use a quill or coconut stick. In the past, before metal was commonly available, Telefol people in central New Guinea used bamboo or animal bones as weaving tools (MacKenzie 1999).

Changes to the basic materials for making knitted bags from organic to synthetic fibres seem normal, commonsense, and do not usually cause problems in Merauke. Muyu weavers no longer need to walk far into the forest to obtain fibres or obtain them from the village at expensive prices. In addition to having a wider array of choices of colours and fibre thicknesses, synthetic yarn is easy to find at the shops and affordable. But without realising it, the shift in these materials has changed the underlying life cycle of noken. This is because what is taken from nature will eventually return to nature and decompose, and likewise, organic noken will one day return to the land (Marjanto 2013, 25). Importantly, the use of *Gnetum gnemon* fibres symbolised a robust connection between the Muyu and their customary forest; a sacred place to trace their ancestors and maintain spirituality. In contrast, synthetic noken, when damaged, will be discarded but do not decompose into the ground.

Changes to noken making are similar to transformations to bilum production in PNG, which is growing rapidly, in part through the use of nylon and synthetic dyes. MacKenzie (1999) argues that the change in the basic materials of string bags, however, has an impact on the quality of the finished product. According to her, natural materials produce a strong bag which is suitable for carrying heavy loads, while bags made of synthetic yarn only emphasise its beauty to elevate the status of its user (MacKenzie 1999, 17). Conversely, Ruscone (2019) perceived that women in PNG have succeeded in incorporating imported materials into every bilum weave and adapted them to models and trends in urban areas as part of their creativity and self-development. Like in West New Guinea, synthetic materials are cheaper and easier to source than organic materials in urban areas. Meanwhile, Bonshek (2010) states that Mondika women who live in the Western Highlands Province of PNG prefer to use synthetic materials because they are more durable and easier to work with when it is wet. The makers state that wood fibres are very difficult to arrange when wet, develop mould easily, and rot quickly.

Discussion and conclusion

Noken carry sociocultural values regarding kinship relations, gender norms, and the life cycle, which become woven into the identity of many indigenous Papuan groups. In addition to their practical everyday function as containers for storing and transporting food ingredients, noken play an important role for mothers by helping them to care for and nurture their children. Owing to the cultural values imbued in noken and the public's concern about the disappearance of the weaving practice among Papuans, the Indonesian government has supported the instatement of noken as an intangible cultural heritage that must receive special attention. After the UNESCO declaration in 2012, noken began to receive attention from various organisations, both domestically and internationally. UNESCO and the government share a preoccupation with avoiding changes to noken making, perceiving such changes as the unfortunate outcome of social and cultural transformations that are moving away from the 'traditional' and towards the 'modern'. However, many of these changes, including a lack of young women learning the craft and lack of access to the usual raw materials (with some materials being prohibitively expensive and new materials being creatively substituted where access is a problem), are themselves partly produced by state expansion, urbanisation, and the emergence of the market economy. As such, important changes are also occurring at the level of governance, whereby listing noken as an intangible heritage and encouraging commercial manufacture is also shifting the custodianship of these practices away from local communities and to the level of the market and the state. It is also unclear if the small number of older women producing noken, reported by UNESCO as a key reason to designate intangible heritage status, reflects a major change from past conditions and whether commercial sales (previously small and now growing) truly index the health of the craft.

The UNESCO intervention certainly has had an impact on the economic growth of Papuan households, because bags which were originally only woven to fulfil domestic and customary needs are now being used as souvenirs that are seeing increased demand in the market. Behind the significant economic development of noken, the value produced by gifting noken—a practice that has deep roots in New Guinea—is slowly starting to be replaced with the commoditised value of money. Increasingly, the drive behind parents weaving noken relates to meeting the target market rather than gifting to kin or training their daughters in the craft to sustain the noken culture.

Several of the safeguarding priorities that were set by the UNESCO nomination file no. 00619 of 2012 have not been fully realised, including the implementation of noken making into school curricula in Merauke and across West New Guinea. Apart from these factors, Muyu parents around Merauke also have concerns that the younger generations, especially young women, are less able, and sometimes less interested, to learn to knit *men* string bags from their parents due to busy study obligations and modern lifestyles in urban areas. Urbanisation and the movement of people from villages to towns are some of the main factors impacting the learning and access to raw materials for making noken. There are few studies that have focused on the process of urbanisation, and its impact on youth and craft making, so it is hoped that this chapter sets the foundation for future study into the ongoing changes surrounding noken in Merauke and West New Guinea more generally.

Acknowledgements

I thank the anonymous reviewer and editors for their constructive feedback on the manuscript.

References

Andersen, B. 2015. Style and self-making: String bag production in the Papua New Guinea Highlands. *Anthropology Today* 31(5):16–20. doi.org/10.1111/1467-8322.12200.

Bonshek, E. 2010. Collecting relations in Melanesia: Making a contemporary collection in the Western Highlands of Papua New Guinea. *Journal of Museum Ethnography* 23:7–20.

Chao, S. 2022. Multispecies mourning: Grieving as resistance on the West Papuan plantation frontier. *Cultural Studies* 37(4):553–579. doi.org/10.1080/09502386.2022.2052920.

Dewi, M.A., M. Sugiarto, and I. Rachmawati 2018. Noken: Women empowerment & tourism industry in Papua. *Advances in Social Science, Education and Humanities Research* 231:225–227. doi.org/10.2991/amca-18.2018.61.

Heider, K.G. and Gardner, R. 1974. *Gardens of war: Life and death in the New Guinea*. Penguin Books, Harmondsworth.

Januar, A. 2017. Fungsi, makna, dan eksistensi *Noken* sebagai simbol identitas orang Papua. *Patrawidya* 18(1):57–70.

Kanem, V. 2021a. Mama Anyam Noken, Mama Merajut Kehidupan. *Noken Post*. nokenpost.com/mama-anyam-noken-mama-merajut-kehidupan/ (site discontinued).

Kanem, V. 2021b. Anyam Noken. Dibalik peluang, ada ancaman pergeseran nilai sosial dan budaya. *Noken Post*. web.archive.org/web/20230610052224/https://nokenpost.com/anyam-noken-dibalik-peluang-ada-ancaman-pergeseran-nilai-sosial-budaya/ (accessed 16 February 2024).

Kanem, V., and A. Norris 2018. An examination of the *Noken* and indigenous cultural identity: Voices of Papuan women. *Journal of Cultural Analysis and Social Change* 3(1):1–11. doi.org/10.20897/jcasc/86189.

MacKenzie, M. 1999. *Androgynous objects: String bags and gender in central New Guinea* Routledge, London.

Malinda, R. and Yayasan Pusaka Bentela Rekyat (eds) 2021. 'Mama ke Hutan': Perempuan Papua dalam Kecamuk Kontestasi Sumber Daya Alam. Report. Unpublished. Yayasan Pusaka Bentala Rakyat, Jakarta. pusaka.or.id/mama-ke-hutan (accessed 2 April 2022).

Marjanto, D.K. 2013. Makna dan fungsi *Noken* dalam kehidupan masyarakat Papua. In H.D. Ismadi (ed.), *Kebudayaan Indonesia: Lestarikan Apa Yang Hendak Dilestarikan?* pp. 22–34. Pusat Penelitian dan Pengembangan Kebudayaan, Badan Penelitian dan Pengembangan Kementerian, Pendidikan dan Kebudayaan, Jakarta.

Ruscone, E. 2019. *Bilum, bilas, bilumwear*: PNG women loop stylish dresses to create new identities. *ZoneModa Journal* 9(2):47–69. doi.org/10.6092/issn.2611-0563/9961.

Salhuteru, A. and F.K. Hutubessy 2020. The transformation of *Noken* Papua: Understanding the dynamics of *Noken*'s commodification as the impact of UNESCO's heritage recognition. *Jurnal Sosiologi Walisongo* 4(2):151–164. doi.org/10.21580/jsw.2020.4.2.5569.

Strathern, M. 1988. *The gender of the gift*. University of California Press, Berkeley.

Ulumuddin, I. 2013. *Noken*: Warisan budaya tak benda masyarakat Papua. In H.D. Ismadi (ed.), *Kebudayaan Indonesia: Lestarikan Apa Yang Hendak Dilestarikan?* pp. 9–21. Pusat Penelitian dan Pengembangan Kebudayaan, Badan Penelitian dan Pengembangan Kementerian, Pendidikan dan Kebudayaan, Jakarta.

UNESCO 2012. Nomination file no. 00619 for inscription on the List of Intangible Cultural Heritage in Need of Urgent Safeguarding in 2012. Report. Unpublished. UNESCO, Paris.

UNESCO 2014. Periodic report no. 00924/Indonesia. Report. Unpublished. UNESCO, Paris.

20

A collection of relationships: Kamoro material culture in the museum

Karen Jacobs

Abstract

Material culture from the Kamoro region on the south-west coast of New Guinea ended up in European ethnographic museums as a result of encounters between Kamoro people and various collectors. As early as 1828, artefacts were acquired during the Triton Expedition for the Wereldmuseum in Leiden, the Netherlands. More material was collected during subsequent expeditions, which found its way into Dutch and British museums. During Dutch colonial times, substantial additions were made by colonial officers, anthropologists, and missionaries. While the Indonesian period between the late 1960s and the 1990s is virtually non-existent in the museum, the Leiden Museum assembled a substantial Kamoro collection during the Kamoro Arts Festival (1998–2006). By focusing in detail on a series of objects in museums, this chapter aims to highlight the Kamoro and European agents involved in collecting processes and their distinct agendas, the long tradition of Kamoro exchange, and the current relevance of museum collections to Kamoro artists. For instance, an armlet collected in 1828 reveals how Kamoro people were continuing an exchange practice established during trade relations with Eastern Indonesia which had been recorded from the seventeenth century onwards. A breast ornament collected by British explorer A.F.R. Wollaston shows how encounters with local communities were not of primary significance to these early expeditions, which were focused instead on the colonial goals of mapping and establishing control over territory. The object was catalogued as 'Utakwa River' after the river that the explorers followed. Naming the makers was not important. Yet this breast ornament, unique in museum collections, inspired Kamoro artists to create similar ornaments to sell at the Kamoro Arts Festival in 2002. An ancestor pole (*mbitoro*) collected by Jan Pouwer in the 1950s indicates how anthropological knowledge was recorded. The encounter with this mbitoro by a group of Kamoro visitors to the Leiden Museum revealed how museum collections are not sets of decontextualised, static objects, but are active links to ancestors. Overall, this chapter demonstrates that Kamoro museum collections of material culture are composed of relationships, past and present. Kamoro museum collections are processes, subject to change as collections are moved or studied, despite their seemingly fixed nature within museums.

Abstrak

Adanya kontak yang dilakukan oleh orang Kamoro yang bermukim di provinsi Papua selatan dengan kolektor berkebangsaan Eropa pada masa lalu mengakibatkan benda-benda budaya tersebut berakhir di beberapa museum etnografi di Eropa. Ekspedisi Triton merupakan salah satu ekspedisi yang dilakukan oleh para pelancong tersebut pada tahun 1828, dimana benda budaya yang dikumpulkan pada masa itu sekarang disimpan di Wereldmuseum, Leiden. Selain itu, beberapa ekspedisi yang dilakukan pada tahun berikutnya berhasil menambah benda-benda budaya orang Kamoro yang kini disimpan di beberapa museum di Belanda dan juga Inggris. Pada masa kependudukan Belanda di Papua, penambahan koleksi benda budaya suku Kamoro dilakukan oleh para perwira militer Belanda, antropolog, serta misionaris. Pada masa peralihan kekuasaan Belanda ke pemerintah Indonesia dalam kurun waktu 1960an hingga tahun 1990an, hampir tidak ditemukan museum di Papua pada masa itu. Pada kurun waktu tahun 1998-2006, para kolektor dari museum Leiden-Belanda berhasil mengumpulkan koleksi budaya suku Kamoro selama festival seni Kamoro. Tulisan ini mengangkat topik mengenai koleksi museum yang merupakan objek budaya orang Kamoro serta permasalahan mengenai kolektor, baik dari suku Kamoro sendiri maupun kolektor berkebangsaan Eropa. Topik ini juga menyoroti mengenai proses serta berbagai macam agenda berbagai pihak yang terlibat dalam proses pengumpulan koleksi, serta kebiasaan yang dilakukan oleh orang Kamoro dalam memperdagangkan benda budaya dan relevansinya dengan para seniman Kamoro pada masa kini. Hal ini bisa terlihat pada koleksi gelang lengan atau gelang tangan suku Kamoro yang telah diperdagangkan sejak tahun 1828 pada saat praktek perdagangan antara penduduk yang berada di Indonesian timur yang telah dimulai sejak abad ketujuh belas dan seterusnya. Selain itu, ornamen dada yang dikoleksi oleh pelancong berkebangsaan Inggris A.F.R. Wollaston menunjukkan bahwa penduduk asli pemilik dari koleksi tersebut merupakan tujuan utama dalam ekspedisi tersebut, melainkan bagaimana memetakan serta membangun kontrol atas wilayah dimana mereka berada. Ornamen dada tersebut dilabeli dengan sebutan 'Sungai Utakwa' yang merupakan sungai yang dilalui oleh para pelancong dalam ekspedisi tersebut. Keunikan ornamen tersebut telah menginspirasi para seniman Kamoro untuk membuat model yang sama yang kemudian dijual di festival seni Kamoro 2002. Selain itu, tiang rumah yang dalam bahasa Kamoro disebut 'mbitoro' yang dikoleksi oleh Jan Pouwer pada tahun 1950an menunjukkan bagaimana pengetahuan mengenai koleksi tersebut direkam berdasarkan studi antropologi. Pengenalan akan 'mbitoro' oleh sekelompok pengunjung di Museum Leiden menguak sebuah fakta bahwa koleksi museum bukanlah sebuah benda statis yang didekontekstualisasikan, tetapi merupakan sarana penghubung antara yang hidup dengan para leluhur. Secara keseluruhan tulisan ini mengungkapkan mengenai makna koleksi pada masa lalu dan masa kini. Koleksi benda Kamoro merupakan sebuah cerminan tentang adanya perubahan makna yang terdapat pada koleksi pada saat dipindahkan termasuk ketika benda tersebut berada dalam sebuah museum.

Introduction

Things made by people from the Kamoro region on the south-west coast of New Guinea ended up in European ethnographic museum collections from the early nineteenth century onwards. The main collections are in various branches of the 'Wereldmuseum'[1]—Leiden, Amsterdam, and Rotterdam— in the Netherlands, and the Cambridge Museum of Archaeology and Anthropology and the British Museum in the United Kingdom. All these collections were acquired for various reasons: to establish contact, as symbols of difference, as scientific data, trophies, souvenirs, gifts, products of conquest

---

1   Indigenous Kamoro words are italicised, and Bahasa Indonesia or common Papuan Malay words are underlined, at first mention. Other languages (such as Dutch) are used with single quote marks at first mention.

and mapping; yet all were the result of encounters with Kamoro people. By focusing on four objects in these museums, chosen to tell the story of different modes of collecting, this chapter takes an object biographical and relational approach to highlight the Kamoro and European agents involved in collecting processes and in shaping the nature and composition of the collections, the long tradition of Kamoro exchange, and the current relevance of museum collections to Kamoro artists.

While this chapter focuses on things in ethnographic museums, it is not about the ethnographic museum as an institution. Yet it is informed by recent and ongoing debates about ethnographic museums as institutions related to the formation of the colonial state and their need to change (Clifford 1988; Lonetree 2012; Phillips 2011), particularly: the nature of museum relationships with communities and related power dynamics; the authority of museums to represent cultures; and issues of ownership, which continue to be questioned in museological theory (Boast 2011; Clifford 1997; Karp et al. 1992; Krmpotich and Peers 2013; Peers 2019; Peers and Brown 2003). Overall, an aspect that has emerged from ongoing attempts to decolonise the museum was the realisation that museums have a social responsibility towards their various museum communities, which requires collaborative and polyvocal approaches (Brown 2017). As this chapter demonstrates, decolonising the museum also involves a critical reading of colonial histories in relation to museum collections. This includes giving voice to the various parties involved in encounters by providing nuanced views on historical processes, how collections were assembled and who was involved, and how these were employed to put forward various agendas. At the core of museology debates are museum collections, which are deeply entangled in value-creation processes that transform over time depending on the context and regime of value in which they are placed (Morphy 2020, 96).

This chapter will therefore follow a biographical and relational approach (Bell 2017; Gosden and Larson 2007; Kopytoff 1986; Moutu 2007) that not only highlights the ways in which objects were exchanged and collected but also how they enter different biographical phases contingent on context and, as such, are at the core of different networks (Latour 2005), assemblages (Bennett 2010), or meshworks (Ingold 2011). While it is important to address and acknowledge the power relations in play that led to the formation of these collections, much can be learned from considering the role of all parties involved in the collecting process. Each object embodies a moment in time, providing a glimpse of what was exchanged and transacted between people and what was at stake. Overall, this chapter demonstrates that Kamoro material culture collections are composed of relationships, past and present, which are key to their initial collecting and, once in the museum, further relationships are established; therefore, these collections should not be considered as static entities but as mobile processes (Driver et al. 2021).

While the indigenous people inhabiting the region from Etna Bay to Otakwa River refer to themselves and their language as Kamoro, there have been various name changes, highlighting the nexus of interest of those doing the naming rather than the indigenous people themselves. The Kamoro are a non-Austronesian linguistic group of approximately 18,000 people. The group of villages in the eastern region of the district (between the Karumuga and Otakwa rivers) sometimes differentiate themselves from other Kamoro with the name Sempan, mainly because of their distinct dialect. *Akwere kamoro*, the Kamoro language, is part of the Asmat–Sempan–Kamoro family (Voorhoeve 2005,148).

Kamoro artefacts were initially acquired during Dutch and British expeditions from 1828 onwards. After a Dutch colonial post was established in the region in 1926, additions to collections were made by named colonial officers, anthropologists, and missionaries who dealt with Kamoro people, whose names were rarely recorded. Before the permanent presence of Dutch administration and mission, Kamoro life was marked by a cycle of feasts that marked important liminal phases celebrating adulthood or death and had significant roles, such as revealing knowledge to uninitiates, the transmission of oral history, and the production of dance and material culture, such as *karapao* (feast houses), *mbitoro* (ancestor poles), *wemawe* (anthropomorphic figures), *yamate* (ceremonial shields), *mbikao* (masks), and *eme* (drums). The complete cycle of the large feasts was stopped rapidly by the Dutch administration. Kamoro themselves, increasingly influenced by Catholicism, also began to consider certain elements of feasts inappropriate (Coenen 1963). However, the feasts did remain important in Kamoro cultural life. While the Indonesian period between the late 1960s and the 1990s is virtually non-existent in museums, a substantial Kamoro collection was purchased during the Kamoro Arts Festival (1998–2006), a festival initiated by the Freeport mining company that began mining the region in 1967 (Leith 2002; Mealey 1996).

Armlet, Leiden, RV-16-514

Figure 20.1: Armlet.
Source: Coll. no. RV-16-514, Collection of the Wereldmuseum.

This armlet at the Wereldmuseum, Leiden, belongs to the oldest known museum collection of Kamoro material culture (Figure 20.1). Made of plaited fibre, wrapped with cloth to which sea snail shells (*Nassarius pullus*) have been attached, it was collected during the 1828 Triton Expedition. Brought to the Netherlands as a curiosity, its collecting circumstances reveal how Kamoro people were continuing an exchange practice established during trade relations with eastern Indonesia, first recorded in the seventeenth century (Swadling 2019, 138). The Triton Expedition was organised as part of Dutch colonial expansion in West New Guinea. Although its south-west coast had been mapped in 1826 by Lieutenant Commander D.H. Kolff, there was no permanent Dutch presence in the region. British interest in West New Guinea pressed the Dutch governor of the Moluccas (now Maluku), Pieter Merkus, to request the establishment of a military post. On 21 April 1828, His Majesty's Corvette *Triton* and Colonial Schooner *Iris* left Ambon for the south-west coast of New Guinea aiming 'to establish a settlement on some convenient spot on the West coast of the island' (Earl 1837, 383). This was east of the current town of Kaimana near an enclosed bay, promptly renamed Triton Bay, where Fort Du Bus was established. On 24 August 1828, the fort's inauguration day, the Dutch formally proclaimed the south-west coast a Dutch possession. However, disease, death, and lack of supplies led to its abandonment in 1836 (Mörzer Bruyns 2019, 39–45).

During their coastal exploration, the Triton Expedition crew stopped twice in the Kamoro region.[2] The first was when the crew thought they had landed at the Oetanata River, which was actually the Wakia. They met Kamoro people, a small delegation of whom navigated them to the mouth of the Oetanata a few days later. While the Kamoro region was not considered practical for establishing a government post due to swampy land and reefs, the crew felt that they had established good contacts with its people. From their first encounter an eagerness to trade became clear to the crew. On their arrival at the Wakia, Kamoro people came out in canoes to greet them: 'each Papuan wanted to praise his weapons and ornaments the most … Hundreds of arrows, bows, spears, nicely carved clubs, paddles, ornaments, etc., were traded', wrote Lieutenant Modera (Modera 1830, 63, author's translation). The taxidermist Salomon Müller described how the Kamoro 'obtain most satisfaction from trade' (Müller 1857, 74, author's translation); trade was a source of excitement, accompanied by loud screaming. He narrates how the Kamoro competed and observed each other's dealings in order to obtain goods quickly. Cloth, knife blades, empty bottles, arrows, and iron tools were the most desirable exchange goods, while mirrors, coral, or copper rings were less interesting to the Kamoro (Müller 1857, 74–75). Not only men had a keen sense for trade; women offered fruit and sago in a similarly excited state (Müller 1857, 68).

While expedition members were fascinated and rather overwhelmed by the Kamoro zeal for trade, the Kamoro themselves were used to exchanging goods with visitors, particularly traders from the Seram (spelled 'Ceram' in older sources) and Aru Islands in Maluku. They integrated the Triton Expedition crew into an already well-established local trade system, aiming to obtain as many goods as possible. The influence of this longue durée trade network became clear from the expedition reports. For example, Abrauw, a Kamoro man who appointed Papuan men to navigate the crew to the Oetanata River, was described as dressing in Malay fashion:

> In his turban he kept a written note to which he seemed to give a lot of significance. It turned out nothing more than some promise of good luck in Malay, probably given to him by a Malay priest, because they traded with people from island Ceram … Our new friend called himself Abrauw and the translator knew him. Abrauw was the chief of the people we had seen around the mouth of the Oetanata in the kampong Oeta. Abrauw had been to Ceram and could speak Malay well. (Modera 1830, 64–65, author's translation)

Not only did some Kamoro travel to Seram, Seram traders regularly visited the Kamoro region, as becomes clear from the description of houses built especially for them. Behind the semi-nomadic longhouses that the Kamoro built on the coast stood 'some empty, slightly decayed Malay houses, which belonged to Ceram traders, who practically annually visited the region and stayed for a while' (Müller 1857, 51, author's translation). This explains Müller's amazement about how quickly the Kamoro accepted and adjusted to the presence of the Dutch crew (Müller 1857, 75). The eastern Indonesian merchants—who adopted the role of rajas—established a trade monopoly, appointing local

---

2   For an overview of Kamoro settlements identified during this expedition, see Modera (1830, 73).

representatives with titles such as <u>kapitan</u>, <u>major</u>, and <u>hakim</u> (judge). Their dealings resulted in the wide distribution of various commodities, such as textiles, beads, and gongs, in return for captured slaves, massoy tree bark, and bird specimens, among other things. They also raised taxes and intermarried with local people (Pouwer 1999, 160; Swadling 2019, 134–151; Vlasblom 2019, 39–60).

The Triton Collection in Leiden consists of various weapons and body ornaments such as armlets, waistbands, penis cases, necklaces, head decorations, arrows, spears, and clubs, all described by the expedition crew in their publications. Müller writes how men were more elaborately adorned than women, with armlets made of boar tusks of fibre. Some had cassowary bird feathers attached, others wrapped with cotton cloth to which shells were attached, like the armlet in focus (Müller 1857, 71). Examples of these armlets have been collected; however, each museum collection is only a selection as not all adornments described went to the museum. For instance, Seram traders gave the women little aprons of horsehair, but only the Kamoro cassowary feather aprons were collected (Müller 1857, 71). In fact, only the type of armlet in focus, wrapped in imported cotton, which must have been obtained from Seram traders, reveals the influence of the trade network with eastern Indonesia in the museum.

Once collected, these objects came to represent a culture distant in time and place; they express the link between collecting and mapping that characterised the spirit of the time. While blanks on maps were filled with every newly mapped region, museums were filled with collected artefacts from these territories. Some objects, including this armlet, were later reproduced in drawings in Modera's publication illustrating his account of the expedition (1830, plate 11, no. 7). In 1869, part of this collection, mostly arrows, was identified as duplicates and exchanged with the British Museum.[3] The nineteenth century was a time of regular exchange between museums to fill gaps in collections, in their mission to represent the world. Initially collected to establish relations with Kamoro people, these objects subsequently furthered relationships with other institutions. However, today these objects are not identified as Kamoro in the British Museum database, being registered only as Oetanata River. The lack of an overarching name to denote the local culture of origin, usually a standard practice in museum classification, and the use of older spelling, makes it hard to find these objects by anyone wanting to connect with Kamoro material culture in museums.

Breast ornament, Cambridge, E 1914.231.98

Similarly, a breast ornament made of bamboo, seeds (*Coix lacryma-jobi*), and fibre (*Hibiscus tiliaceus*) collected by British explorer A.F.R. Wollaston shows how encounters with local communities were not of primary significance to these early expeditions, which were focused on colonial conquest (Figure 20.2). During the early twentieth century, the snow-capped peaks of the central mountain range in Dutch New Guinea, first sighted in 1623 by Dutchman Jan Carstensz from his ship in the Arafura Sea, became the ultimate destination during expeditions to this region. In addition to the snow-covered peak described by Carstensz, now known to be *Nemangkawi*[4] at a height of 4884 m, another was sighted during the Dutch Southwest New Guinea Expedition (1904–05) and named after the reigning queen Wilhelmina, now known to be *Ettiakup*[5] at c. 4700 m (Ploeg and Vink 2001, 13).

---

3   A number of letters in Leiden's correspondence archive relate to this exchange, NL-LdnRMV-A1-1-157/159; 167/168; 202/203 (Leiden correspondence n.d.).

4   Puncak Jaya or Mt Carstensz.

5   Puncak Trikora or Mt Wilhelmina.

Figure 20.2: Breastplate.

Source: Item E 1914.231.98, Courtesy of the Museum of Archaeology and Anthropology, University of Cambridge.

In the early twentieth century, a request to organise a British expedition to form a collection of flora and fauna from the unexplored south-western districts near the central snow range (Rawling 1911, 233) instigated competition between Dutch and British expeditionary teams. While lack of knowledge about this part of their colony generally was a sensitive point, it was the vicinity of the snow-capped mountainous area that led to unease for the Dutch, who had been unable to reach these peaks. The Dutch government allowed access to the British team, but priority was given to a Dutch scientific expedition (led by H.A. Lorentz): 'There were no objections on condition that the expedition would start *after* January the first 1910. The race against the Brits has started' (Gooszen 1913, 645, author's translation, original emphasis).

The Dutch managed to reach the snowfields of Mount Wilhelmina, but not the summit. Having followed Dutch advice to use the Mimika River as a point of entry, the British expedition (1910–11), organised by the British Ornithologist Union, only got halfway to the mountains during their 15 months in New Guinea (Wollaston 1914, 249). Most of the time was thus spent in the Kamoro region, resulting in detailed descriptions of the 'Coast People' (their name was never recorded), and in extensive collections of artefacts presented by the Kamoro. Goods 'were displayed to the best advantage in the obvious hope that they would appeal to us and lead to the clinching of a bargain' (Rawling 1913, 189). The expedition members describe how the Kamoro soon noticed what the team liked and approached them with examples. Wollaston notes how prices increased during these barters:

> The first two [canoes] were bought for a knife apiece, but the price soon rose to an axe for a canoe, and in the course of several months it had still further risen to two axes or even two axes and a knife. (Wollaston 1912, 55)

Trading stopped once the Kamoro had received a steel axe head, as they had obtained what they wanted (Rawling 1913, 155). A high level of Kamoro agency was therefore involved in the collecting process and the resulting collection indicates what they were willing to part with at that time.

During the first British expedition, A.F.R. Wollaston acted as medical officer, entomologist, and botanist, and decided to return to Netherlands New Guinea to follow the Utakwa River (currently Otakwa River) as a pathway to the snow. This was a good strategy, as the Wollaston expeditionary team (1912–1913) reached the snow of the higher Carstensz Mountain on 30 January 1913.[6] Collected during this second British expedition, the breastplate in focus is the only one in the British expedition's collections, which mainly consist of stone axes, bone arrows, wooden spears, clothing, penis cases, and other body decorations.

In the United Kingdom, these collections were used to reinforce stories about adventures in a remote part of the world, where people were still in the 'Stone Age' (Wollaston 1933, 102). The prevailing evolutionist discourse influenced Wollaston considerably. He ignored the fact that the Kamoro region was far from an isolated area, as shown earlier by the armlet, and felt wary of his potential impact on Kamoro culture. For instance, he writes to the Cambridge Museum's curator about a Kamoro club:

> the only reason for my valuing it less than some of the others was that the man from whom I got it had obviously made it with a steel knife, which I had given him a few days before. The other clubs were worthy made and carved with sharp shells, as they had no metal knives except than that they obtained from me or from my party. (Letter Wollaston to Von Hügel, 31 January 1916, MAA archives n.d.)

Wanting to keep the culture unchanged, he suggested isolating a large area: 'to be kept as a native reserve where these people can live their own life, and work out their own destiny, whatever it may be' (Wollaston 1933, 153–155).

This patronising view of the detrimental impact of outside influence on Kamoro culture equally informed the establishment of the Kamoro Arts Festival 90 years later. Between 1998 and 2006 this annual festival was organised by the Freeport mining company, a mine exploiting the region, with the stated purpose 'to help revitalize and revive the Kamoro culture' (PTFI 2000, 1).[7] Festival organisers claimed that Kamoro culture had disappeared due to outside influences and needed restoring in order to reinstate pride in Kamoro culture (PTFI 2000, 2). However, from the first festival in 1998, the Kamoro came up with elaborate dances that re-enacted oral tradition and brought different forms of material culture into play. Many artefacts were sold during the auction. 'Well over twice' the expected number of Kamoro participants attended the festival (PTFI 2000, 6). This wide appearance and enjoyment of Kamoro culture contradicts the opinion that it was 'lost'. Festival organisers might have emphasised the notion of revival because it provided them with a forum for developing business and political relations by being an occasion to entertain important guests and a tool to provide positive publicity in contrast to the critique of its social and environmental issues: 'This is one of the many unsung accomplishments of Freeport Indonesia, completely ignored by the company's critics' (PTFI 2000, 4). The festival was in many ways a continuation of colonial strategies for resource exploitation established in the Kamoro region in the eighteenth to twentieth centuries in order to form relationships with, and generate obligations from, Kamoro people.

---

6   The summit of the Carstensz Peaks was reached in 1936 by A.H. Colijn, F.J. Wissel, and J.J. Dozy.

7   In 1967 the US-based Freeport Mining Company received permission from the Indonesian government to establish what has become the largest gold mine and one of the largest open-pit copper reserves in the world.

Figure 20.3: Beni Aopateyau from Kokonao with a breast plate selected for the auction of the 2002 Kamoro Arts Festival.

Source: Photo by K. Jacobs.

Whatever we may think of the underlying agenda, there is one type of object for which the festival created a renewed market. The organisers distributed copies of Kooijman's book (1984) among Kamoro artists, and the Cambridge breastplate, together with three others in Dutch museums depicted in this book, inspired Kamoro artist Beni Aopateyau to make his own (Figure 20.3). Unique in museum terms and all collected before 1912, no contextual information was collected with these pendants, nor were they described in the expedition reports. Beni Aopateyau mentioned that it concerns decoration for warfare. He made his first one, after copying it from Kooijman's book, for the 2002 festival (Beni Aopateyau, pers. comm. 12 April 2002) and has since become the local specialist maker of breastplates. While his breastplates are now made mostly to be sold to collectors, his work expresses the merging of past and current collecting relationships and their associated power relations, while showing Kamoro pragmatism and resilience concealed in their material culture (see also Jacobs 2012).

Prow ornament, Amsterdam, TM-2229-2

Figure 20.4: Prow ornament.

Source: Coll.no. TM-2229-2, Collection of the Wereldmuseum.

A Dutch administrative post was established in the Kamoro region in 1926 and Mimika was the name given to the colonial district stretching from Etna Bay to Otakwa River. However, during his work in the region from 1935 to 1939, Catholic missionary Petrus Drabbe argued for the use of the term Kamoro, which translates as 'living person', 'in opposition to the dead, ghosts, things, plants and animals', based on conversations with the people inhabiting this region (Drabbe 1947, 158–159).

In order to represent how the formation of museum collections was related to the development of the colonial state during Dutch colonial times, the focus is on a prow ornament in the Wereldmuseum Amsterdam (formerly the 'Koloniaal Museum' and then 'Tropenmuseum'), collected by Carel M.A. Groenevelt (Figure 20.4). His mission coincided with a Dutch yearning to collect as much information as possible from West New Guinea. When Indonesia declared independence on 17 August 1945, it claimed the Dutch East Indies as the new state of Indonesia. Only West New Guinea remained a Dutch foothold as the Dutch wanted to prepare the region for independence. However, the administration was confronted with very little knowledge about the population. Therefore, the 'Kantoor voor Bevolkingszaken' (Bureau of Native Affairs) was established in 1951 and government anthropologists were commissioned to conduct social-scientific research (Gaffney and Tolla, Chapter 2, this volume); another form of collecting, which was accompanied by object collecting (Jaarsma 1991, 130–132). Between 1951 and 1954, Jan Pouwer was employed by the bureau as an anthropologist to conduct research in the region (see below). While government anthropologists were often asked to collect for Dutch museums, these museums also employed specific field collectors.

Based in Hollandia (currently Jayapura) with his wife, Groenevelt became a field collector for the then Tropenmuseum. Between 1951 and 1956, he conducted regular collecting trips around Lake Sentani and to Kamoro and Asmat territory. The Tropenmuseum agreed to accept all the items Groenevelt collected at his stated prices. In return, he was prohibited from collecting for other museums (Letter Bertling to General Secretary 11/01/1952, Tropenmuseum 1952–59). In 1953 a financial shortfall forced the Tropenmuseum to accept the Rotterdam Wereldmuseum as co-sponsor, resulting in competition. From the moment Groenevelt's collection arrived in the Netherlands, both museums had to compromise in dividing the objects. To avoid the 'best' objects being claimed by the Tropenmuseum, Rotterdam curator Victor Jansen introduced the system of sending wish lists to Groenevelt, intending that, if these objects were found, Rotterdam was entitled to them. Many letters included 'a recapitulation of the *special wishes of Rotterdam*' (Letter Jansen to Groenevelt 01/11/1957, Stadsarchief 1957–59, author's translation, original emphasis). Jansen's wishes originated from the desire to fill gaps in the collection after studying other ethnographic collections and books. By having a taxonomic chart of culture in mind, with slots to be filled by objects found in the field, he knew what he wanted:

> The best surprise of the south coast was the plaited crown from the Mimika region, decorated with plumes of the bird of paradise, and worn by the musicians who perform during the nightly dances. This is a long-standing wish coming true! (Letter Jansen to Groenevelt 06/07/1958, Stadsarchief 1957–59, author's translation)

This canoe prow was probably collected in 1952 when Groenevelt shared a journey in the Kamoro region with anthropologist Jan Pouwer:

> Ethnologist Pauwer [sic, Pouwer] on board. When I asked him whether it was possible to disentangle the stems from the canoes he said it was impossible; I spoke then to a few guys and they sawed the figure head off in the open sea … They succeeded and [the look on] Pauwer's [sic] face was worth a Daalder [a Dutch coin]. (Letter Groenevelt to Jager Gerlings 9/11/1952, Tropenmuseum 1952–59, author's translation)

While Pouwer was based in the Kamoro region and had established relationships with the Kamoro which informed his collecting activities, what mattered to Groenevelt was closing a good deal during his brief visit. He was not necessarily interested in collecting contextual information about the objects, something regularly requested by Jansen: 'you only have eye for large aesthetic objects' (Letter Jansen to Groenevelt, 10/09/1958, Stadsarchief 1957–59, author's translation). Groenevelt's letter indicates that Pouwer may have found his actions unethical. It certainly was not common practice to saw off a canoe prow as only two examples are found in museum collections and the practice exposes the audacity of the collectors, perhaps using their commanding position at the time.[8] In contrast, there are many prow ornaments in museum collections of the type that were bound to canoes; these were not permanent features and were therefore easily collectible in comparison. When I asked some Kamoro friends about this in 2011, Yoakim Matameka, Apol Emeyau, and Marcelus Matameka, all experienced woodcarvers, they did not have a strong view on it. They acknowledged that their ancestors would have preferred to make the sale, as these opportunities were rarer than the time necessary for carving (pers. comm. May 2011). The strategic aptitude for trade carries on as much as the skill to produce these carvings.

Mbitoro, Leiden, RV-3070-1

A mbitoro (ancestor pole) collected by Pouwer in Migiwiya village (Kokonao) in 1952 indicates how anthropological knowledge was recorded (Figure 20.5). Employed by the Bureau for Native Affairs, Pouwer's research from July 1951 to May 1954 focused on Kamoro sociality (Pouwer 1955). When collecting material culture, he valued an object for its intrinsic anthropological information rather than its aesthetic value. He also recorded the Kamoro names for the objects he collected.

Mbitoro were, and still are, used in a range of ritual activities. This particular example was made to bid farewell to important deceased people who were depicted on the pole. The mbitoro represents Katiwiuta, a capable woodcarver who died during the Pacific War. Below is Majépia, a woman known for her skilled sago pounding, which helped improve her family's economic situation and earned her a place on the mbitoro. The carver included a small human head at the bottom of the wing-shaped extension, representing his eight-year-old son who had also died during the war (information from series 3070, Leiden series n.d.; also see Smidt 2003, 99). After paying homage to the deceased, the mbitoro would have been left to decay in the bush or sago swamp so that the *kapita* (life force) accumulated in the pole could not harm the living. Instead, Pouwer asked the men of the village to deposit it behind his house. This was done unknowingly to the women who were kept at a safe distance because seeing the pole's pointed end would have made them ill as it is a secret reserved for men. No women were involved in the transporting of the pole either, which was done by building a float of two canoes lashed together to keep the mbitoro's colours intact (Kooijman 1987).

Since its arrival in the 'Rijksmuseum voor Volkenkunde' (later 'Museum Volkenkunde' and now Wereldmuseum), Leiden, this mbitoro has featured in several displays; most recently in the 'Papua Leeft! Ontmoet de Kamoro' (Papua Lives! Meet the Kamoro) exhibition, 14 February – 31 August 2003. While Kamoro people were not much involved in the curatorial process, between 18 May and 5 June 2003, five Kamoro people were invited to the museum, according to the museum's press release, to be 'available to give additional information and explanation with regard to the exhibition'. In addition, the presence of Timo(thius) Samin, Modesta Samin-Etewe, Martinus Neyakowau, Yopi Kunareyau, and Mathea Mamoyau constituted an important statement about their right of self-representation.

---

8   The other prow is at the Museum of Archaeology and Anthropology in Cambridge (Z 9184).

Figure 20.5: Mbitoro.

Source: Coll.no. RV-3070-1. Collection of the Wereldmuseum.

On their first day (18 May 2003) the Kamoro group viewed the exhibition, halting at the first object on display, the mbitoro in focus. Mathea in particular was struck and bewildered while observing the pole, she started shaking and crying, saying that she had seen her ancestors whose spirits resided in the carving. The fact that the mbitoro was collected from her village was not included on the exhibition label. Entering the next exhibition room, the whole group was similarly moved and so emotionally overwhelmed that the visit had to be cut short. There are a plethora of records of similar powerful encounters between descendants of the makers of objects in museums with their ancestors; the fact that things turn into museum objects does not necessarily mean that they lose their agency, particularly to indigenous communities (Dudley 2010; Gell 1998; Schorch et al. 2020; Tapsell 2000). Later conversations confirmed that the Kamoro had felt the presence of their ancestors. Speaking for the group, Timo Samin explained that these objects could never have been kept in a similar manner in their homeland and acknowledged the Dutch for keeping them for so long and looking after his ancestors. He appreciated the exhibition's display manner as they conceived of the museum as an ideal resting place for the artefacts where their agency is sustained. Timo Samin explained how the exhibition stimulated the carvers to make new things—rather than take the collections back home, they wanted exhibition catalogues so the depictions could inspire others. The exhibition was mainly considered a source of inspiration, hence the five Kamoro visitors decided to produce more carvings during the rest of their stay. Each day they installed themselves in the museum to carve. There was no fixed schedule because the Kamoro were free to organise the use of their space. Their carving and plaiting was regularly interspersed with singing and drumming, and they invited members of the public to dance with them, bridging the distance between performers and audience. The encounter with this mbitoro by a group of Kamoro visitors to the Leiden Wereldmuseum revealed how museum collections are not sets of decontextualised, static objects, but are active links to ancestors and relevant inspirations for future creations.

Conclusion

Despite their seemingly fixed status within museums, Kamoro collections of material culture are relational processes. Not just the result of singular encounters, they continue to mediate new social and material relationships. The four objects in focus reveal that a considerable amount of Kamoro agency is concealed in them. The fact that this information is often unknown or silenced in museum documentation, as information from and about collectors is prioritised, does not mean that these Kamoro voices have not spoken.

Once in the museum, these objects become the focus of new relationships, which equally deserve academic attention. Material culture in museums can raise questions about presence and absence. The presence of objects in certain collections can lead to them being of higher status in the eyes of collectors and instigate further collecting endeavours. Far from being a complete snapshot of Kamoro culture in a specific place and time, every collection is a selection only and these selections are produced by the biases of the collectors and local traders involved. The absence of certain types of objects in later assemblages can lead to conclusions of disappearance and the need for revival, which does not necessarily correspond to Kamoro reality.

These museum objects have the potential to create new networks of relationships. While objects are studied, exchanged, loaned, and exhibited, they provide a tangible link with the original makers and users. For Kamoro people, they do not just move physically, they move emotionally too. So far, Kamoro material culture collections have not been subject to repatriation claims, but Kamoro access to them is highly valued and has led to new creations in the form of not only new objects based on the originals but also new technical practices in an attempt to reconstruct the original ways of making things. Kamoro museum collections are therefore complex processes, subject to change as they are used and engaged with.

References

Bell, J. 2017. A bundle of relations: Collections, collecting, and communities. *Annual Review of Anthropology* 46:241–259. doi.org/10.1146/annurev-anthro-102313-030259.

Bennett, J. 2010. *Vibrant matter: A political ecology of things.* Duke University Press, Durham. doi.org/10.2307/j.ctv111jh6w.

Boast, R. 2011. Neocolonial collaboration: Museum as contact zone revisited. *Museum Anthropology* 34(1): 56–70. doi.org/10.1111/j.1548-1379.2010.01107.x.

Brown, A.K. 2017. Co-authoring relationships: Blackfoot collections, UK museums, and collaborative practice. *Collaborative Anthropologies* 9(1/2):117–148. doi.org/10.1353/cla.2016.0013.

Clifford, J. 1988. *The predicament of culture: Twentieth-century ethnography, literature, and art.* Harvard University Press, Cambridge. doi.org/10.4159/9780674503724.

Clifford, J. 1997. *Routes: Travel and translation in the late twentieth century.* Harvard University Press, Cambridge.

Coenen, J. 1963. Enkele facetten van de geestelijke cultuur van de Mimika. Typescript. Unpublished. Omawka, Mimika.

Drabbe, P. 1947. Folk-tales from Netherlands New Guinea. *Oceania* 18(2):157–175. doi.org/10.1002/j.1834-4461.1947.tb00471.x.

Driver, F., M. Nesbitt, and C. Cornish (eds) 2021. *Mobile museums: Collections in circulation*. UCL Press, London. doi.org/10.2307/j.ctv18kc0px.

Dudley, S. (ed.) 2010. *Museum materialities*. Routledge, London.

Earl, G. 1837. Verhaal van eene Reize naar en langs de zuid-west kust van Nieuw-Guinea, gedaan in 1828. Narrative of a voyage along the S.W. coast of New Guinea, in 1828, and communicated by G. Windsor Earl, Esq., M.R.A.S. *Journal of the Royal Geographical Society of London* 7:385–395. doi.org/10.2307/1797534.

Gell, A. 1998. *Art and agency: An anthropological theory*. Oxford University Press, Oxford; New York. doi.org/10.1093/oso/9780198280132.001.0001.

Gooszen, A. 1913. Hoe Nederlandsch Nieuw-Guinea geexploreerd werdt en wordt. *Tijdschrift van het Koninklijk Nederlandsch Aardrijkskundig Genootschap* 30(5):638–651.

Gosden, C. and F. Larson 2007. *Knowing things: Exploring the collections at the Pitt Rivers Museum 1884–1945*. Oxford University Press, Oxford. doi.org/10.1093/oso/9780199225897.001.0001.

Ingold, T. 2011. *Being alive: Essays on movement, knowledge and description*. Routledge, London.

Jaarsma, S.R. 1991. An ethnographer's tale: Ethnographic research in Netherlands (West) New Guinea (1950–1962). *Oceania* 62(2):128–146. doi.org/10.1002/j.1834-4461.1991.tb02384.x.

Jacobs, K. 2012. *Collecting Kamoro: Objects, encounters and representation in West Papua*. Mededelingen van het Rijksmuseum voor Volkenkunde, Leiden 14. Sidestone Press with National Museum of Ethnology, Leiden.

Karp, I., C. Mullen Kreamer, and S. Lavine (eds) 1992. *Museums and communities: The politics of public culture*. Smithsonian Institution Press, Washington, DC.

Kooijman, S. 1984. *Art, art objects, and ritual in the Mimika culture*. Mededelingen van het Rijksmuseum voor Volkenkunde, Leiden, No. 23. E.J.Brill, Leiden. doi.org/10.1163/9789004545106.

Kooijman, S. 1987. Aanvullende gegevens over door Pouwer verzamelde Mimika voorwerpen voor beschrijvingskaarten (pers. In. van P. aan S. Kooijman, d.d. februari 1987). Archival document, series archive, series 3070. Unpublished. National Museum of World Cultures, Leiden.

Kopytoff, I. 1986. The cultural biography of things: Commoditization as process. In A. Appadurai (ed), *The social life of things: Commodities in cultural perspective*, pp. 64–94. Cambridge University Press, Cambridge. doi.org/10.1017/CBO9780511819582.004.

Krmpotich, C. and L. Peers 2013. *This is our life: Haida material heritage and changing museum practice*. Chicago University Press, Chicago. doi.org/10.59962/9780774825429.

Latour, B. 2005. *Reassembling the social: An introduction to actor-network-theory*. Oxford University Press, Oxford. doi.org/10.1093/oso/9780199256044.001.0001.

Leiden correspondence n.d. Correspondence archives containing information related to the collections. Correspondence consulted for this paper: NL-LdnRMV-A1.

Leiden series n.d. Series archives containing information on collection series. Series consulted for this paper: series 16, Series 3070.

Leith, D. 2002. *The politics of power: Freeport in Suharto's Indonesia*. University of Hawai'i Press, Honolulu. doi.org/10.1515/9780824844417.

Lonetree, A. 2012. *Decolonizing museums: Representing Native America in national and tribal museums.* University of North Carolina Press, Chapel Hill.

MAA archives n.d. Series of folders containing notes re the tribes of New Guinea. OA2/11/1.

Mealey, G. 1996 *Grasberg: Mining the richest and most remote deposit of copper and gold in the world, in the mountains of Irian Jaya, Indonesia.* Freeport-McMoRan Copper & Gold Inc, Singapore.

Modera, J. 1830. *Verhaal van eene Reize naar en langs de zuid-westkust van Nieuw-Guinea, gedaan in 1828, door Z.M. Corvet Triton, en Z.M. Coloniale Schoener de Iris.* Vincent Loosjes, Haarlem.

Morphy, H. 2020. *Museums, infinity and the culture of protocols: Ethnographic collections and source communities.* Routledge, London. doi.org/10.4324/9780203705186.

Mörzer Bruyns, W.F.J. 2019. The taking possession of part of New Guinea by the Dutch in 1828, and their contribution to the knowledge of the Arafura Sea. *Great Circle* 41(1):38–59.

Moutu, A. 2007. Collection as a way of being. In A. Henare, M. Holbraad, and S. Wastell (eds), *Thinking through things: Theorising artefacts ethnographically*, pp. 93–111. Routledge, London.

Müller, S. 1857. *Reizen en onderzoekingen in den Indischen Archipel gedaan op last der Nederlandsche Indische regering, tusschen de jaren 1828 en 1836.* Eerste deel. Werken van het Koninklijk Instituut voor Taal-, Land- en Volkenkunde van Nederlandsch-Indië 2. Afd., Afzonderlijke werken. Frederik Muller, Amsterdam.

Peers, L. 2019. Museums and source communities: Reflections and implications. In W. Modest, N. Thomas, D. Prlić, and C. Augustat (eds), *Matters of belonging: Ethnographic museums in a changing Europe*, pp. 37–52. Sidestone Press, Leiden.

Peers L. and A.K. Brown (eds) 2003. *Museums and source communities: A Routledge reader.* Routledge, London.

Phillips, R.B. 2011. *Museum pieces: Toward the indigenization of Canadian museums.* Vol. 6. McGill-Queen's Press-MQUP, Montreal. doi.org/10.1515/9780773587465.

Ploeg, A. and S. Vink 2001. The exploration of South New Guinea and the race for the snow. In C. Ballard, S. Vink, and A. Ploeg (eds), *Race to the snow: Photography and the exploration of Dutch New Guinea, 1907–1936*, pp. 11–16. Royal Tropical Institute, Amsterdam.

Pouwer, J. 1955. *Enkele aspecten van de Mimika-cultuur (Nederlands Zuidwest Nieuw Guinea).* Staatsdrukkerij, 's-Gravenhage. doi.org/10.1525/aa.1956.58.5.02a00260.

Pouwer, J. 1999. The colonisation, decolonisation and recolonisation of West New Guinea. *Journal of Pacific History* 34(2):157–179. doi.org/10.1080/00223349908572900.

PTFI 2000. *Kamoro Kakuru Ndawaitita: The first all-Kamoro festival.* Freeport Public Relations Department, Timika.

Rawling, C. 1911. Explorations in Dutch New Guinea. *Geographical Journal* 38(3):233–255. doi.org/10.2307/1779038.

Rawling, C. 1913. *The land of the New Guinea Pygmies: An account of the story of a pioneer journey of exploration into the heart of New Guinea.* Seeley, Service, London.

Schorch, P., N.M.K.Y. Kahanu, S. Mallon, C. Moreno Pakarati, M. Mulrooney, N. Tonga, and T.Y.P. Kawika Tengen 2020. *Refocusing ethnographic museums through Oceanic lenses.* University of Hawai'i Press, Honolulu. doi.org/10.2307/j.ctvn5twfj.

Smidt. D. (ed.) 2003. *Kamoro art: Tradition and innovation in a New Guinea culture.* KIT Publishers, Amsterdam.

Stadsarchief 1957–59. Correspondence between curator J.V. Jansen and C.M.A. Groenevelt. Archief van het Museum voor (Land- en) Volkenkunde te Rotterdam. Stadsarchief Rotterdam 1407_147.

Swadling, P. 2019. *Plumes from Paradise: Trade cycles in outer Southeast Asia and their impact on New Guinea and nearby islands until 1920.* Sydney University Press, Sydney. doi.org/10.2307/j.ctv10vkzrf.

Tapsell, P. 2000. *Pukaki: A comet returns.* Reed, Auckland.

Tropenmuseum 1952–59. Correspondence Bertling, C.M.A. Groenevelt and J.H. C.Tj. Jager Gerlins about Groenevelt's collecting expedition to New Guinea. Wereldmuseum Amsterdam, former Tropenmuseum, correspondence archive.

Vlasblom, D. 2019. *Papoea: Een geschiedenis.* 2nd edition. Sidestone Press, Leiden.Voorhoeve, B. 2005. Asmat-Kamoro, Awyu-Dumut and Ok: An enquiry into their linguistic relationships. In A. Pawley, R. Attenborough, J. Golson, and R. Hide (eds), *Papuan pasts: Cultural, linguistic and biological histories of the Papuan-speaking peoples,* pp. 145–166. Pacific Linguistics 572. Research School of Pacific and Asian Studies, The Australian National University, Canberra.

Wollaston, A. 1912. *Pygmies & Papuans: The stone age to-day in Dutch New Guinea.* Smith, Elder & Co, London. doi.org/10.5962/bhl.title.21534.

Wollaston, A. 1914. An expedition to Dutch New Guinea. *Geographical Journal* 43(3):248–273. doi.org/10.2307/1778612.

Wollaston, A. 1933. *Letters and diaries of A.F.R. Wollaston.* Cambridge University Press, Cambridge.

21

The prism of respect: Exhibiting a Raja Ampat altar

Fanny Wonu Veys

Abstract

A group of 10 late nineteenth- or early twentieth-century figures from Mayalibit Bay on Waigeo, the largest of the Raja Ampat Islands in Southwest Papua, Indonesia, featured prominently in the exhibition *A Sea of Islands* that opened on 20 February 2020. It was the latest halt in the travels of the group after stopovers in Manokwari, Amsterdam, London, and Paris. One female member of the group even spent more than 70 years in Spain. This chapter traces the politics behind the way this group has been displayed. How do open displays, allowing for a close experience of the objects, versus vitrine displays, putting the objects' security as paramount, compare? Is the whole group, including the ancestor figure with a human skull, appropriate for viewing to everyone or to the selected few? I will demonstrate that the politics of revealing and hiding are about walking the tightrope of respect, honouring the objects, appreciating the materials incorporated, recognising the descendants of the originating communities, and considering the visitors.

Abstrak

Sepuluh patung yang merupakan peninggalan budaya dari masa abad ke-19 dan awal abad ke-20 ditampilkan pada pameran 'A Sea of Islands' pada 20 februari 2020. Patung tersebut berasal dari teluk Mayalibit di Waigeo-Kabupaten Raja Ampat, Provinsi Papua Bara Daya. Patung-patung tersebut telah melalui serangkaian perjalanan dari kepulauan Raja Ampat, kemudian ke Manokwari, hingga sampai di Eropa di kota Amsterdam, London dan Paris. Salah satu dari patung tersebut bahkan telah berada di kota Spanyol lebih dari 70 tahun. Tulisan ini dilakukan untuk menelusuri aspek-aspek yang mempengaruhi dibalik dipamerkannya patung tersebut. Selain itu, tulisan ini juga dimaksudkan untuk membandingkan antara pajangan terbuka dan pajangan tertutup dengan beberapa kriteria yang melekat pada masing-masing faktor, termasuk akses langsung ke objek dan juga faktor keamanan. Selain itu, faktor kepantasan sebagai bahan pajangan menjadi aspek yang menjadi pembahasan didalam tulisan ini. Hal ini terutama dimaksudkan pada bagian tertentu dari objek pajangan tersebut yang dianggap memiliki nilai etik serta kesakralan yang tinggi dimana perlu kiranya diperhatikan dalam sebuah pameran. Berdasarkan hal tersebut maka, tulisan ini mengangkat isu mengenai aspek yang terkait dengan perlakuan rasa hormat serta penghargaan yang perlu diperhatikan dalam sebuah pameran. Tidak hanya itu saja, penghargaan akan bahan-bahan yang digunakan dalam sebuah objek perlu diterapkan serta pengenalan dan pemahaman akan komunitas masyarakat dimana objek tersebut berasal. Melengkapi hal tersebut, faktor seperti pengunjung dan hal-hal yang berkaitan dengan penikmat objek pameran juga perlu kiranya diperhatikan.

Introduction

A group of 10 late nineteenth- or early twentieth-century figures from Mayalibit Bay on Waigeo, the largest of the Raja Ampat Islands in Southwest Papua (Indonesia), featured prominently in the exhibition *A Sea of Islands* that opened on 20 February 2020 (Figure 21.1). The ensemble comprises a central standing male figure and two smaller male figures, each wearing a loincloth and/or headscarf and with spread-out arms. The six female figures have a comb in their hair and hold their palms turned upwards; one figure contains a human skull representing the adopted son of the largest figure. This group (TM-573-36 to TM-573-45) is the only one known to have been preserved in its entirety. The Leiden exhibition *A Sea of Islands* was the latest halt in the group's travels after having made stopovers in Manokwari (1929), Amsterdam (1930), New York (1948), London (2018), and Paris (2019). One of the smaller female figures (TM-573-45) even spent more than 70 years in Spain with a Dutch private collector after having been stolen from the 'Tropenmuseum'[1] display in the early 1940s amid the upheaval caused by World War II. The carving only returned to the institution in 2014 (Sudhölter 2014; Corbey 2017, 58–59).

Figure 21.1: The Mayalibit altar (TM-573-36 to 45) in the exhibition of *A Sea of Islands*, Leiden, 20 February 2020 – 5 April 2021.
Source: Fanny Wonu Veys, 2020.

---

1   Local Raja Ampat words are italicised, and Bahasa Indonesia or common Papuan Malay words are underlined, at first mention. Other languages (such as Dutch and Māori) are used with single quote marks at first mention.

This chapter traces the politics behind the way this group has been displayed. I will demonstrate that the politics of revealing and hiding are about walking the tightrope of respect that oscillates between, but also incorporates, aspects as diverse as appreciating the artistry, reverence for what the figures stand for, thoughtfulness in exhibition conception, recognising the descendants of the originating communities, honouring the ancestral presence, and hearing the queries of Papuan communities.

Appreciating the artistry

In 1929, Johan Christiaan van Eerde (1871–1936), director of the ethnology section of the 'Koloniaal Instituut' (Colonial Institute) in Amsterdam[2] from 1913 until 1936, engaged in a research trip through the various parts of the then Dutch East Indies (contemporary Indonesia) representing the Netherlands in the Pacific Science Congress in Java. In order to fill the gaps in the Colonial Institute collection, he took the opportunity to gather items for this Amsterdam museum, which had opened its doors in 1926 in a brand-new building (Frank 2011, 162). During van Eerde's stopover on Ternate, an island off the west coast of Halmahera in the Moluccas (now Maluku), W.A. Hovenkamp, 'resident' of the Ternate district from 13 July 1926 until May 1931, brought the existence of ethnographic objects in Manokwari, part of his jurisdiction, to van Eerde's attention. Hovenkamp eventually officially donated van Eerde's selection to the Colonial Institute in Amsterdam (Corbey 2017, 34–39; van Eerde 1929, 35). Thanks to Hovenkamp's intervention, van Eerde spent 10 and 11 July 1929 in Manokwari, where a Dutch colonial official guided him to a building known as the 'Museum Manokwari' (van Eerde 1928–1930). When Prince Leopold (1901–1983) and his wife Astrid (1905–1935) of Belgium, the future King Leopold III and Queen Astrid, visited Manokwari in April 1929, newspapers reported on the museum as a place that grouped ethnographic objects (Aneta 1929a; *De Sumatra Post* 1929). Little is known of the exact circumstances of van Eerde's visit except for the description by Jacques Viot (1898–1973), a French modernist author and dealer, of their encounter during his travels. Viot portrayed the Museum Manokwari as 'a very small shack with as sole purpose to hold up the Dutch motto painted above the door "Je Maintiendrai" ["I will maintain", author's translation from French]'. In the little dusty room stood the Mayalibit Bay figures. Even though van Eerde claims that the existence of the museum testifies to the interest for ethnographic objects in the region, Viot's description suggests that the Museum Manokwari was a transit depot for worthwhile art, instead of a museum meant to show the wealth of material culture in western New Guinea (Viot 1932, 53–54; van Eerde 1929, 54).

While the Mayalibit Bay figures were shown without any special deference, they still had an arresting presence, as the altar belongs to the very few pieces in the museum that caught Viot's eyes. He comments on the attractiveness of the figures that exemplify the style of the Raja Ampat Islands. Moreover, van Eerde appreciated the figures enough to make them part of the 89 objects that were shipped to Amsterdam. The philosopher and anthropologist Raymond Corbey (2017), who dedicated a book to Raja Ampat ritual art, believes Assistant Resident A.L. Vink packed and dispatched the objects. This seems unlikely as Vink[3] only started his post on 20 October 1929, four months after van Eerde's visit. Bouwe Jakob Kuik (1898–1942) is reported as being the assistant resident in Manokwari in April 1929 when he participated in a one-month excursion to the Highlands of West

---

2   After a few name changes, the institution settled on the name Tropenmuseum in 1952, integrated in the larger Royal Institute for the Tropics. From 2014, the Tropenmuseum is part of the umbrella organisation named the National Museum of World Cultures (NMVW) together with the Museum Volkenkunde, Leiden, and the Afrika Museum, Berg en Dal. Since 2016 the NMVW has had a close collaboration with the Wereldmuseum in Rotterdam. In October 2023, the abovementioned museums, including Tropenmuseum, were renamed Wereldmuseum.

3   Vink finished his posting in Manokwari on 5 September 1932.

New Guinea (Aneta 1929b; Kuik 1941). Therefore, he is more likely to have met van Eerde and have organised the shipping of the six boxes to the Colonial Institute. The fact remains that the altar was removed from its humble display in the Museum Manokwari and its inherent artistic qualities were deemed worthy enough to be shown in a prestigious institution in the capital city of the colonising motherland, the Netherlands.

Collecting reverence

The altar figures that van Eerde selected were hundreds of kilometres away from the place where they had first been collected by, most probably, administrators or missionaries on Waigeo (Corbey 2017, 34–35, 44). The acquisition of the Mayalibit Bay altar group was part of the collecting practices of the first part of the twentieth century and inextricably linked to the making of the Dutch empire in the east. In the seventeenth century, the Dutch competition with Portugal and Spain for stakes in the spice trade also involved West New Guinea, where not only the aromatic, sweet-smelling massoy bark was obtained, but so too were enslaved people for work on the nutmeg plantations of the Banda islands in the Moluccas. Finally, in 1824, the British acknowledged the Dutch claim to rights over West New Guinea (Vlasblom 2019, 39–47, 51). From then on, exploration, missionisation, and administration, all part of the overarching colonising project, entrenched the Dutch in their most eastern colony.

Perhaps the passion of the Dutch colonial administrators for collecting was triggered because they were surrounded by travellers and scientists who were actively acquiring objects. Furthermore, between 1900 and 1930, many exploratory scientific expeditions took place in West New Guinea, where numerous pieces were brought back, even when the ethnographic items were not the expeditions' main goal (see Corbey 2017, 39–44; Veys 2018a, for details on collecting in the westernmost part of New Guinea). Missionaries also collected ethnographic objects, which they saw as tokens of conversion, often after having encouraged indigenous people to relinquish their artefacts (Jacobs and Wingfield 2015).

It is unclear whether the Mayalibit altar was removed under duress or whether people let go of their ancestral images as part of the recurring religious renewal movements that were characteristic of the Cenderawasih Bay area, but that have also been reported in the Raja Ampat Islands (Kamma 1954). During these events, the indigenous population burned or threw objects into the sea to clear the way for a new religion. Many of the early twentieth-century missionaries interpreted these happenings as a sudden interest in Christianity (Corbey and Weener 2015, 6–7). The 'Utrechtse Zendingsvereniging' (Utrecht Mission Society) missionary Frans van Hasselt, whose background information accompanied the shipment of the Raja Ampat altar and who had worked in the area since 1894, had for example witnessed in 1907 the surrendering of ancestor figures on Biak:

> After my sermon, almost everyone got up, only to come back a short while later with … 68 korwars that people were prepared to relinquish … I had in the past tried several times to buy these images for museums, I even offered large sums for them, but always without success … and now here they lay at my feet and people had brought them willingly to me. (Corbey and Weener 2015, 6–7; van Hasselt 13 May 1908)

While some groups in north Waigeo had already converted to Islam, especially during the last half of the nineteenth century, in the early years of the twentieth century, there was an additional resurgence of Islam conversions among the people of the Raja Ampat Islands which also led to giving up objects that were previously treasured (Corbey 2017, 44; Vlasblom 2019, 37).

These reports of spontaneous surrender are numerous, but there is no evidence that the collecting of the Mayalibit altar happened this way. Even though Raja Ampat narratives are not present, it is likely that the action of collecting was not only proof of conversion for the authorities back in the Netherlands, but also involved capturing some of the reverence felt by the indigenous population for these objects. Indeed, one could argue that the fact that these objects were highly respected instilled in the collector's mind a sense of value that he wished to share with an audience in the Netherlands.

Thoughtful displays?

Upon arrival, the altar pieces were immediately displayed following the instructions detailed on the shipping papers dated 17 July 1929 (Corbey 2017, 40; Lamster 1930). Up to the opening of the Colonial Institute, ethnographic collections would have been held in the rather cramped 'Koloniaal Museum' (Colonial Museum) in Haarlem, together with products and resources from the Dutch colonial empire, including the Caribbean, Suriname, and Indonesia. However, in 1930 visitors to the newly built, imposing, and spacious Colonial Institute in Amsterdam could see the 10 figures as part of the New Guinea Room in the Ethnology Department (Koloniaal Instituut 1930, 110) (Figure 21.2). In those early years of the late 1920s and all through the 1930s, there existed a definite predisposition to exhibit over-modelled skulls, headhunting trophies, and all kinds of weapons. The permanent gallery was entitled 'Anthropology and Prehistory', showing, according to the annual report of 1927, that the New Guinea display presented 'the modern-day Stone Age' (Koloniaal Instituut 1927, 76). The description of this show asserts that the people from New Guinea took up one of the lowest rungs on the evolutionary ladder (van Duuren 2011, 163). This obsession to prove the 'Stone Age' nature of Papuans through the display of skulls might explain the statement on the catalogue cards of January 1930 that the original skull on the figure has been replaced by a random skull of the Museum Manokwari. Where did this information suddenly come from, and does it reflect a reality or a Western obsession with skulls? And was the display of the Mayalibit altar then part of portraying an assumed primitivism?

Figure 21.2: The Mayalibit altar soon after its arrival in Amsterdam in 1930.
Source: Wereldmuseum, TM-60054981.

Since its arrival in Amsterdam, the altar was often exhibited as part of permanent and temporary exhibitions. The abovementioned display, entitled 'Anthropology and Prehistory', lasted until 1946. Just three years after Indonesia's independence (1945), a loan presentation from the Royal Indies Institute Amsterdam travelled to New York to be shown in the Asia Institute. The altar became part of the canon of Indonesian art. In 1966 an exposition called 'Papoea-kunst' (Papuan Art) opened in the 'Rijksmuseum', Amsterdam, focusing on the great artistry of New Guinea art underpinned by the idea that the authentic culture was doomed to disappear due to contact with the West. The Tropenmuseum opened a temporary display of Indonesian art in 1987 entitled *Budaya Indonesia* (Indonesian Culture) setting New Guinea firmly within Indonesia's political and by extension cultural borders (van Brakel 1987, 156, 273). The Tropenmuseum then opened a permanent New Guinea gallery in 1997, where the altar featured prominently. The exhibition was replaced by *Rituals in New Guinea* in 2001, showing the altar within a religious context. During all these display moments the Mayalibit altar functioned in a museum context that wanted to illustrate assumed primitiveness fetishising mystery and intrigue, inferred political and cultural belonging, or adherence to classical anthropological concerns of religion. Considerations of whether the exhibitions treated visitors in a respectful way by showing ancestors and skulls have not been documented, nor has any thought gone into recording the feelings of the descendants of the people who made and used the Mayalibit altar.

Recognising indigenous sensibilities

The history of local and indigenous sensibilities not being accounted for might have led the advisory board to the *Oceania* show that was due to take place in 2018 at the Royal Academy in London (29 September – 10 December 2018) and at the 'Musée du quai Branly' in Paris (12 March 2019 – 7 July 2019) to query the exhibition of such powerful objects. The adopted son of the deity, materialised as a wooden cross-legged and cross-armed figure with a human skull, elicited a lot of discussion among Māori, Samoan, and Hawaiian board members. They had actually advised against the showing of the ancestral skull of the Waigeo group and expressed concern about the possible oversight of indigenous Papuan sensibilities.

The displaying of human remains is regarded as problematic in many parts of Oceania. Likewise, for many present-day European museums and curators, showing human remains feels inappropriate. However, doing justice to historical and contemporary realities also implies looking critically at one's own museum practice while being willing to reconsider it. So, when in 2010 the Tropenmuseum discussed the presence of a significant collection of human remains more generally, the enmeshment of the Tropenmuseum in the science of physical anthropology between 1915 and 1967 was exposed. With its physical anthropology laboratory, collections, and researchers, the Tropenmuseum helped shape ideas on race as a physical and social category. New Guinea was also the focus of this research. As a result of the physical anthropology findings, exhibitions often combined 'evolutionary theories, ideas about progress, about ethnic markers of difference and identity issues' (van Duuren et al. 2010, 57). The conclusion, after examining the Tropenmuseum's involvement with physical anthropology, was that the display of human remains should be done very reluctantly (van Duuren et al. 2010, 58–59).

Discussions with West New Guinea people conducted since my arrival at the National Museum of World Cultures in 2009 had revealed no objections to the respectful display of important ancestors. However, due diligence required further investigation, taking into consideration that the cultural diversity of West New Guinea and the individual personal life stories of Papuan communities in the Netherlands and West New Guinea might yield a panoply of perhaps unreconcilable views.

As the specific collecting place of the altar has not been documented, tracing the object down to particular descendants is challenging. The missionary and anthropologist Freerk Christaan Kamma (Kamma 1948a; Kamma 1948b) who started his missionising work in Cenderawasih Bay and the Raja Ampat Islands in 1931, two years after the altar was removed from the Museum Manokwari, surmised that the objects had originally stood in Linsok, a small village located on the Siam brook on the eastern shore of Mayalibit Bay, close to modern-day Kalitoko village. A small community of people with Papuan ancestry live in the Netherlands. A group of them is committed to museum issues. Our institution thus relied on their network, which extends both within the Netherlands and in Indonesia, including Papua more specifically. Papuans originating from Waigeo and living in the Netherlands, but also people in Waigeo who wanted to comment on the altar, were consulted. Their linguistic affiliation was not shared with us. In the Netherlands, people whose ancestors originate from the Waigeo area as well as from other northern Papuan communities reacted positively, even regarding it as an honour that their ancestors would be exhibited. Individuals in Papua reacted in a very similar way. During the opening ceremony of *A Sea of Islands*, members from the Papuan community expressed feelings of pride upon seeing the altar figures presented outside of a case. However, the ancestral skull figure was placed in a small individual case as a way to protect it against dust and touch from visitors. Interestingly, Papuan visitors explained that this important ancestor was treated in the same way as all the other prestigious objects in the exhibition, which made him even more special among the other figures of the altar. Accidentally, indigenous and material sensibilities coincided.

Out of respect for the Papuan view, the advisory board to the *Oceania* show accepted the altar was going to be on display. However, during the opening of *Oceania* in London one of the women of the Māori delegation made the viewing of the skull figure safe for Māori and wider Polynesian audiences. She deposited a 'rau kawakawa', a wreath made of green leaves, which is often placed on the head by way of mourning. The ritual performed aimed at helping the deceased on his voyage while simultaneously making the exhibition room a safe space. In short, it testified to the ancestral presence while securing the circulation of life (Decottignies-Renard 2020, 246–247). It made it safe for those Pacific Islanders for whom human remains should not be presented and who would consequently not feel a sense of pride in seeing an ancestor on display. It should be noted that, in London, the altar was set in a large glass case among other objects, including the contemporary art portraits of life casts by Māori artist Fiona Pardington, a mourner's hood from the Marind-anim, and a 'malangan' fish from New Ireland. While the space was differently laid out in Paris, the setting of the altar in a large glass case with other objects in its vicinity was reminiscent of the London set-up. By way of contrast, in Leiden, the altar was the focal point of the display in a small intimate room without any Polynesian objects. The exhibition team, of which I was the lead curator, felt a proximity with Polynesian objects would be inconsiderate. The Waigeo people the museum consulted did not experience the London nor the Paris show. Therefore, it is impossible to compare their feelings about the different settings.

Honouring the ancestors

One of the arguments for display was that the altar had always been meant for display. Hence, the Papuan community acknowledged that the historical situation in which the altar would have been presented in an open and honorific way had been taken into consideration in the exhibition *A Sea of Islands*. Typological analyses presented by Uhle (1886), de Clercq and Schmeltz (1893), Serrurier (1898), Nuoffer (1908), Gerbrands (1951), and van Baaren (1968) view the Raja Ampat Islands as the westernmost part of the so-called 'korwar style' area stretching eastwards to the Berau Gulf (MacCluer Gulf). *Korwar* figures (also known under names such as *karwar, koronwar, korovar*) may be carved in standing, squatting, or sitting position, usually have no clear indication of sex, and may incorporate a skull (Baaren 1968, 68). The bodies of the female figures of the altar adhere most closely to the korwar styles. The male figures, with their mobile arms, display characteristics of Malukan carving in the 'mon style'. Mon are representations of spirits that are specific to the cosmologies of Ma'ya and Ambel speakers on the Raja Ampat Islands. However, the altar was, in its use, closely associated with the korwar figures of the Cenderawasih Bay area, and specifically Biak and Numfor Island. The altar functioned as a way to keep the deceased ancestor in close proximity, an ancestor who could be consulted by the villagers or on occasion by a priest. Korwar figures were traditionally displayed in people's houses, as the British ornithologist Francis Henry Hill Guillemard (1852–1933) attested in 1880 when sailing on the 'Marchesa':

> One article of furniture which is found in every room is the *korowaar*, a carved wooden image a foot or so in height … These are not idols, as they have been represented to be by some travellers, but the media by which the living hold communication with, and are kept in memory of, the dead … the image is either placed on the grave or carried to the home of the nearest relation, where it is treated with great respect. On every occasion of importance it is consulted, regarding fishing excursions, sickness, undertaking a journey, and so forth. (Guillemard 1886, vol. 2: 280–281)

According to Corbey, the korwar style used in the altar corresponds to the Biak migrants from the Cenderawasih Bay area that arrived in Linsok, the village from where the altar possibly originates, while the male figures are mon, representing the style of the inland groups, indigenous to Waigeo. Documentation in the past has suggested that the head of the group is the creator god Manseren Nànggi or Lord of the Sky (see Corbey 2017, 58–59; Sudhölter 2014). Many, however, follow Kamma (1978, 178), supported by his observation during his many trips in the Raja Ampat archipelago, who stipulates that the tallest figure is actually Korano Wamurmi, acting as a main mediator between human beings and the paramount deity Manseren Nànggi. Korano Wamurmi would then be accompanied by his two wives, his first and second sons, and their wives. The figure with the skull is the adopted son of the deity and founder of the clan who would later pray at the altar.

Kamma published an image dating to July 1937 with the highly suggestive title of 'The gravity of paganism. Ancestor figure with skull and triton shell, north Waigeo', which shows that mon and korwar figures such as those of the Mayalibit altar were in the early 1930s still displayed and in use (Figure 21.3). René-Primevère Lesson (1794–1849), a pharmacologist and the assistant surgeon on *La Coquille*, captained by Louis-Isidore Duperrey (1786–1865), mentions in November 1823, on the occasion of the ship's stopover in Fafak Bay on the north coast of Waigeo, that all families and individuals owned their own 'fétiches protecteurs' (protector fetishes). Often wrapped in cloth, they were either seated inside the family house or in temples with larger figures (Lesson 1829, 209). Lesson even made a vivid description of one of the larger displays in a dedicated building, which actually resembles largely the Mayalibit altar that is being discussed. He writes:

> we visited a solitary hut, built on trunks driven into the waterbed itself and not essentially different to the huts of the Papuans … it was the temple of the gods that these heathens invoke in their worship or that they hope to entice by their offers. On a kind of altar, arranged in symmetrical tiers, were eleven wooden effigies, painted, roughly carved and covered in dirty rags of different colours; some of these statuettes represented men, others animals and amongst the latter, crocodile shapes were perfectly recognisable. Plates in porcelain from Japan still enclosed food probably placed as sustenance for the supposed gods, because they assume they have the same needs as the humans. All these savage and grotesque divinities have a name; the main one, occupying the middle and higher place, had his hands extended over the five subordinate idols that are placed to the left and to the right; finally the walls of this pagoda were lined with fine mats so boldly painted and made in abundance by these blacks. (Lesson 1839, 87, author's translation from French)

Figure 21.3: View of an altar in north Waigeo showing a mon figure, an ancestral figure, and a triton shell.

Source: Kamma (1953), opposite p. 96.

Figure 21.4: Engraving showing an altar at Fofak, on Waigeo, Raja Ampat Islands.

Notes: The original colour print was published as Plate 27 in Duperry's *Voyage de La Coquille 1822–1825*. Printed by Ambroise Tardieu.

Source: © The Trustees of the British Museum, 2016, 2087.1.

The draughtsman of the Duperrey expedition (1822–1825), Louis-François Lejeune (1775–1848), captured the installation (Figure 21.4). Relying on oral history and family stories, Papuans both from Cenderawasih Bay and from the Raja Ampat Islands assured me that the altar was indeed meant to be seen. So, when it was displayed in this respectful way, many felt a sense of recognition, as their community is often absent from public discourse in the Netherlands. Even after 1962, the year of the Indonesian annexation of the territory, the Dutch entanglement in the area was materialised through museums, which mushroomed from the first half of the nineteenth century onwards, each with its own museological tradition (see Veys 2018a for a short history of Dutch museums with Oceania collections). Despite the fact that Dutch colonial involvement in these Indonesian provinces lasted until 1962, almost 20 years longer than for the other parts of the former Dutch East Indies, the Netherlands seems to have forgotten about its former colony. Schoolchildren and young people barely have an idea that the western part of New Guinea was ever a Dutch colony. While the new Dutch history curriculum aims at including diverse perspectives on the Dutch colonial past and the contribution of women in Dutch historical developments, only one paragraph is dedicated to the former Netherlands New Guinea in the context of Indonesia's struggle for recognition of independence.[4] The paragraph reads:

> New Guinea is only given up in 1962. After a transition period under UN supervision, it is part of Indonesia since 1963, without consideration of the wishes of the Papuans. Hence, the state borders of the current Republic of Indonesia are the same as those of the former Dutch East Indies. (De Commissie Herijking Canon van Nederland 2020, 131, author's translation from Dutch)

On the other hand, older Dutch people who were born and raised in West New Guinea have strong feelings of nostalgia. Museum collections contribute to researching whether Indonesian Papua is subjected to a case of wilful amnesia (Veys 2018b). I believe that amid the political and economic interests and tensions, the Dutch museums can play a role in bringing back memories, with all their nuances, to audiences who, willingly or unknowingly, are suffering from amnesia with regards to West New Guinea.

Hearing queries for respect

Having important material culture on display inspired Eef Mamoribo, an elderly woman originating from Biak, but now part of the Dutch Papuan community, to perform a *wor*, a song accompanied by a handheld drum traditionally performed at ceremonial events or feasts to honour an ancestor or to call for protection in life cycle rituals at the opening of *A Sea of Islands* (Figure 21.5). Through her moving performance, she conveyed feelings of sorrow at her childhood cultural suppression by Dutch missionaries and loss of freedom under historical Dutch and current Indonesian colonisation. Equally important, her song, in the Biak language, which was unfamiliar to most of the guests present, expressed her pride in her Papuan identity and hope that actions carried out today might lead to a brighter future. While speaking for all the Papuan objects on display, she summarised the importance of respect for the viewpoints of those whose voice is not loud, the feelings of those who choose to communicate in a quieter way, those whispering voices that simply ask for respect for ideas of the suppressed. Museums should be places where also those voices are heard, privileging indigenous modes of analysis (Kirsch 2006) in order to achieve a more equitable museum practice that supports 'the enrichment, rather than the authorisation, of collections' where the museum is no longer 'a gatekeeper of authority and expert accounts' (Boast 2011, 67).

---

4   The sovereignty of the Republic of Indonesia was proclaimed in 1945, but only recognised by the Dutch on 27 December 1949 (De Commissie Herijking Canon van Nederland 2020, 131).

Figure 21.5: Eef Mamoribo performing a *wor* during the exhibition blessing.
Source: Photo by Aad Hoogendoorn, 2020.

References

Aneta 1929a. Koloniën. Het Belgische kroonprinsenpaar bij de Papoea's. *Nieuwe Apeldoornsche Courant*, 30 April 1929. resolver.kb.nl/resolve?urn=MMCODA01:000155247:mpeg21:p002 (accessed 9 February 2021).

Aneta 1929b. Wetenschap De Nieuw Guinea-expeditie. *De Maasbode*, 16 April 1929. resolver.kb.nl/resolve?urn=MMKB04:000198225:mpeg21:p009 (accessed 9 February 2021).

Baaren, T.P.V. 1968. *Korwars and korwar style: Art and ancestor worship in North-West New Guinea*. Mouton & Co, Paris, The Hague. doi.org/10.1515/9783111387925.

Boast, R. 2011. Neocolonial collaboration: Museum as contact zone revisited. *Museum Anthropology* 34(1): 56–70. doi.org/10.1111/j.1548-1379.2010.01107.x.

Corbey, R. 2017. *Raja Ampat ritual art: Spirit priests and ancestor cults in New Guinea's far west*. C. Zwartenkot Art Books, Leiden.

Corbey, R. and F.K. Weener 2015. Collecting while converting: Missionaries and ethnographies. In W. van Damme and R. Corbey (eds), *The European scholarly reception of 'primitive art' in the decades around 1900*. Number 12. University of Birmingham, Birmingham.

de Clercq, F.S.A. and J.D.E. Schmeltz 1893. *Ethnografische beschrijving van de west- en noord-kust van Nederlandsch Nieuw-Guinea*. P.W.M. Trap, Leiden.

De Commissie Herijking Canon van Nederland 2020. *Open vensters voor onze tijd. De Canon van Nederland herijkt*. Amsterdam University Press, Amsterdam.

De Sumatra Post 1929. De Belgische bezoekers bij de Papoea's. *De Sumatra Post*, 5 April 1929. resolver.kb.nl/resolve?urn=ddd:011023662:mpeg21:p005 (accessed 9 February 2021).

Decottignies-Renard, L. 2020. L'art de tisser des liens chez les Māori de Nouvelle-Zélande Aotearoa. Analyse des relations entre les vivants et leurs ancêtres par l'intermédiaire des manteaux māori (kākahu) en qualité de trésors ancestraux (taonga). Unpublished PhD thesis. Sciences humaines et sociales – Perspectives européennes UMR 7367 Laboratoire Dynamiques Européennes, Anthropologie sociale et Culturelle, Université de Strasbourg, Strasbourg.

Frank, D. 2011. Oceania in view. In D. van Duuren (ed.) *Oceania at the Tropenmuseum*, pp. 161–178. KIT Publishers, Amsterdam.

Gerbrands, A.A. 1951. Kunststijlen in West Nieuw-Guinea: Een voorlopig onderzoek. *Indonesië* 4:251–283.

Guillemard, F.H.H. 1886. *The cruise of the* Marchesa *to Kamschatka & New Guinea: With notices of Formosa, Liu-Kiu, and various islands of the Malay Archipelago.* J. Murray, London. doi.org/10.5962/bhl.title.23073.

Jacobs, K. and C. Wingfield 2015. Introduction. In K. Jacobs, C. Knowles, and C. Wingfield (eds), *Trophies, relics and curios? Missionary heritage from Africa and the Pacific*, pp. 9–22. Sidestone Press, Leiden.

Kamma, F.C. 1948a. De verhouding tussen Tidore en de Papoese eilanden in legende en historie, I–II. *Indonesië: Tweemaandelijks Tijdschrift Gewijd aan het Indonesisch Cultuurgebied* 2:361–370, 536–559.

Kamma, F.C. 1948b. De verhouding tussen Tidore en de Papoese eilanden in legende en historie, III–IV. *Indonesië: Tweemaandelijks Tijdschrift Gewijd aan het Indonesisch Cultuurgebied* 2:177–188, 256–275.

Kamma, F.C. 1953. *Kruis en Korwar: Een Honderdjarig Waagstuk op Nieuw Guinea.* J.N. Voorhoeve, Den Haag.

Kamma, F.C. 1954. *De Messiaanse Koréri-bewegingen in het Biaks-Noemfoorse Cultuurgebied.* Voorhoeve, Den Haag.

Kamma, F.C. 1978. *Religious texts of the oral tradition from West New Guinea (Irian Jaya), Part B: The threat to life and its defence against 'natural' and 'supernatural' phenomena.* E.J. Brill, Leiden. doi.org/10.1163/9789004669536.

Kirsch, S. 2006. *Reverse anthropology: Indigenous analysis of social and environmental relations in New Guinea.* Stanford University Press, California. doi.org/10.1515/9781503625747.

Koloniaal Instituut 1927. Museum. In Koloniaal Instituut (ed.), *Koninklijke Vereeniging "Koloniaal Instituut" Amsterdam. Negentiende Jaarverslag*, pp. 76–78. Druk de Bussy, Amsterdam.

Koloniaal Instituut 1930. Aanwinsten op ethnografisch en anthropologisch gebied van de afdeeling Volkenkunde. In Koloniaal Instituut (ed.), *Koninklijke Vereeniging "Koloniaal Instituut" Amsterdam. Twintigste Jaarverslag*, pp. 89–218. Druk de Bussy, Amsterdam.

Kuik, B.J. 1941. Verslag van een reis naar het rivierengebied der Jabi's en naar het Jamoermeer, van 5 April 1929 tot 6 Mei 1929, door den assistent-resident t/b. te Manokwari. *Tijdschrift Nieuw-Guinea* 5:245–262.

Lamster, J.C. 1930. Een merkwaardige groep afgodsbeelden. *Tijdschrift van het Aardrijkskundig Genootschap*: 452–458.

Lesson, R.P. 1829. *Voyage Médical Autour du Monde: Exécute sur la Corvette du Roi* La Coquille*, Pendant les Années 1822, 1823, 1824 et 1825 ; Ou Rapport sur l'état Sanitaire de L'équipage Pendant la Durée de la Campagne, avec quelques Renseignements sur des Pratiques Empiriques Locales en Usage dans Plusieurs des Contrées Visitées par L'expédition ; Suivi d'un Mémoire sur les Races Humaines Répandues dans l'Océanie, la Mélanésie et l'Australie.* Roret, Librairie, Rue Haute feuille, Paris.

Lesson, R.P. 1839. *Voyage Autour du Monde Entrepris par Ordre du Gouvernement sur la Corvette La Coquille,* Volume 1. Gregoir, Wouters, & Co., Brussels. doi.org/10.5962/bhl.title.119917.

Nuoffer, O. 1908. *Ahnenfiguren von der Geelvinkbai, Holländisch Neuguinea.* Vol. 12, 2. Abhandlungen und Berichte des Königlichen Zoölogischen und Anthropologischen Museums Dresden. B.G. Teubner, Leipzig.

Serrurier, L. 1898. Die korware oder ahnenbilder Neu-Guinea's: Ein beitrag zur geschichte der bildenden kunst. *Tijdschrift voor Indische Taal-, Land- en Volkenkunde* 40:287–316.

Sudhölter, J. 2014. De dochter herenigd met voorouders. *Trouw,* Tuesday 15 July, p. 6.

Uhle, M. 1886. *Holz- und Bambus-Geräthe aus Nord West Neu Guinea (hauptsächlich gesammelt von A. B. Meyer) mit besonderer Berücksichtigung der Ornamentik.* Vol. VI. Publicationen aus dem Königlichen Ethnographischen Museum zu Dresden. Königlichen Ethnographischen Museum zu Dresden, Leipzig.

van Baaren, T.P. 1968. *Korwars and korwar style: Art and ancestor worship in North-West New Guinea.* Mouton & Co, Paris. doi.org/10.1515/9783111387925.

van Brakel, J.H. 1987. *Budaya Indonesia: Kunst en Cultuur in Indonesië; Arts and Crafts in Indonesia.* Tropenmuseum, Amsterdam.

van Duuren, D., M. Ten Kate, M. Pereira, S. Vink, and S. Legêne 2010. *Physical anthropology reconsidered: Human remains at the Tropenmuseum.* KIT Publishers, Amsterdam.

van Duuren, D. (ed.) 2011. *Oceania at the Tropenmuseum.* KIT Publishers, Amsterdam.

van Eerde, J.C. 1928–1930. *Correspondentie betreffende reizen en reisverslagen. Overzicht van de Studiereis, gemaakt door Nederlandsch-Indië van 4 April tot 21 November 1929 door Prof. J.C. van Eerde, Directeur van de Afdeeling Volkenkunde van het Koloniaal Instituut.* NL-HaNA, Koninklijk Instituut voor de Tropen, 2.20.69, inv.nr. 4484_14; NL-HaNA-KIT-4484_14. Nationaal Museum van Wereldculturen, Amsterdam.

van Eerde, J.C. 1929. Kort verslag nopens de studiereis van den directeur der afdeeling Volkenkunde naar Nederlandsch-Indië (4 April–21 November 1929). In Koloniaal Instituut (ed.), *Koninklijke Vereeniging 'Koloniaal Instituut' Amsterdam. Negentiende Jaarverslag,* pp. 49–60. Druk de Bussy, Amsterdam.

van Hasselt, F. 1908. Frans van Hasselt file. 13 May. 1102-2 *Raad voor de Zending van de Nederlandse Hervormde Kerk.* Het Utrechts Archief, Utrecht.

Veys, F.W. 2018a. Papua collections in the Netherlands: A story of exploration, research, missionization, and colonization. In L. Carreau, A. Clark, A. Jelinek, E. Lilje, and N. Thomas (eds), *Pacific presences: Oceanic art and European museums,* Vol. 1, pp. 169–196. Sidestone Press, Leiden.

Veys, F.W. 2018b. Wilful amnesia? Contemporary Dutch narratives about western New Guinea. In L. Carreau, A. Clark, A. Jelinek, E. Lilje, and N. Thomas (eds), *Pacific presences: Oceanic art and European museums,* pp. 229–234. Sidestone Press, Leiden.

Viot, J. 1932. *Déposition de Blanc.* Librairie Stock, Delamain et Boutelleau, Paris.

Vlasblom, D. 2019. *Papoea. Een Geschiedenis.* Sidestone Press, Leiden.

22

The East and West divide

Roxanne Tsang and Glenn Summerhayes

Abstract

This chapter provides a conclusion and afterword to the book. It evaluates the new evidence presented in this volume from West New Guinea—that is, West Papua—in the context of theoretical and thematic developments in Papua New Guinea. We emphasise there is an 'East and West divide' that has been produced by different colonial histories in West New Guinea and Papua New Guinea, and that this divide has shaped archaeological, anthropological, and related research on the human histories of New Guinea. We revisit the seven key research themes identified in the introduction to this volume, in which Papua New Guinean research has made great strides. These themes include early peopling processes, adaptations and ecological transformations, food production, language dispersals, exchange networks leading into the recent past, contemporary material culture production, and museum collecting and display. We conclude by suggesting ways to improve the inconsistency in research across the East and West divide.

Abstrak

Bab ini merupakan bagian penutup dari buku ini dimana pemaparan atau pengkajian terhadap tulisan-tulisan yang ada dalam setiap bab dirangkum dalam tulisan yang berjudul Papua bagian barat—dalam konteks perkembangan teoritis dan tematis. Tulisan ini menekankan tentang adanya pembagian antara timur dan barat yang awalnya terbentuk sejak masa kependudukan di wilayah ini, Papua New Guinea dan Papua bagian barat. Pembagian kedua wilayah tersebut menjadi cikal bakal penelitian arkeologi, antropologi, dan penelitian yang terkait dengan sejarah kependudukan manusia di Papua. Terdapat tujuh tema penelitian utama yang diidentifikasi dalam buku ini dimana hal ini merupakan sebuah langkah besar dalam lingkup penelitian di wilayah ini. Tema-tema ini meliputi awal kependudukan manusia di Papua, adaptasi dan transformasi ekologi, subsistensi makanan, penyebaran bahasa, sistem pertukaran yang berpijak pada sejarah masa lalu, produksi budaya material kontemporer, serta tema yang berkaitan dengan koleksi museum dan aspek-aspek yang berkaitan dengannya. Berdasarkan hal tersebut maka dapat disimpulkan bahwa perlu adanya langkah – langkah perbaikan terhadap ketidakkonsistenan dalam penelitian di Papua, baik itu di bagian timur maupun wilayah bagian barat.

Introduction

Great strides have been made in understanding the human past of the nation-state of Papua New Guinea. Our models of colonisation, adaptation, subsequent population movements, transformations due to climate change, and the nature of complex exchange systems, to mention only a few, are based on a handful of sites east of the longitude 141st meridian east. This straight line, with the contours of a river, separates Papua New Guinea and West New Guinea (known within Papua New Guinea and internationally as West Papua). This 'East and West Divide', based on the historical events of the mid-twentieth century, has seen one form of colonialism replace another. This geopolitical separation is seen in the trajectory of many academic fields, not least in social and historical disciplines. For instance, archaeology on both sides of the divide progressed at an even pace in the first half of the twentieth century, propelled by administrators and missionaries and the occasional archaeologist/anthropologist, until the first modern archaeological research began in the late 1950s with Sue Bulmer's excavations in the Central Highlands of Papua New Guinea (see Gaffney and Tolla, Chapters 1 and 2 of this volume for West New Guinea and Summerhayes 2021 for Papua New Guinea). In the later twentieth century, great strides were made to the east of the divide, with just a handful of sites allowing archaeological narratives to be constructed and models developed. The legacy of this work in Papua New Guinea is summarised in publications including the recently published *Cambridge History of the Pacific*, which has a chapter dedicated to 50,000 years of the country's history based on archaeological research (Summerhayes 2023). However, to the west, with the exception of Pasveer's (2004) publication of excavations on the Bird's Head, archaeological research was neglected after the Indonesian takeover of West New Guinea in the early 1960s for many reasons that will not be detailed in this chapter. Yet writing a 50,000-year history of a major landmass based on data from only one half of that island demands redressing, a point made by Gaffney and Tolla in their introductory chapter. The island's history is one of interaction from the east into the Pacific and the west into Southeast Asia, not to mention to the south where it was joined to modern Australia for over 80 per cent of the time that humans were present in what was then the continent of Sahul. At present, the deep history of this region is incomplete.

With the above in mind, this present volume is extremely important and a welcome beginning to redress this imbalance and to start to fill in the major holes of our knowledge west of this divide. It also builds on the pioneering work of Pasveer's (2004) excavations on the Bird's Head. The chapters of this volume emphasise the desperate need for much more scholarly research in West New Guinea, not only in archaeology (see Chapter 2), but also in linguistics, where, as Arnold points out, more than half the languages are yet to be studied (see Chapter 3).

Similarly, Chapters 4–6 noted that there has been limited genetic research, which has only been explored at a broad level, and that there are still limited genetic data available for the region. Furthermore, the demography of the region is yet another under-researched theme. As mentioned, given the lack of focused demographic analysis on recent genome data, current research only presents a mixture of new analyses and existing results.

The rest of this chapter will assess the contributions made within this book to the human past of New Guinea by looking briefly at each chapter's impact on key themes described by Gaffney and Tolla in the volume's introduction—themes that were identified in no small part with reference to the more active research tradition in the eastern half of New Guinea and its offshore islands. Here the focus is on early peopling, human adaptation and transformation, food production, language dispersals, exchange networks, recent material culture traditions, and the role of museums.

Early peopling

Papua New Guinea has several archaeological sites that allow us to model these first footprints of humanity. From sites found in the Ivane Valley, located in the central Papuan mountains, some 2000 m above sea level (asl), human occupation has been pushed back to between 49,000 and 44,000 years (Summerhayes et al. 2010). This is at least 10,000 years younger than the purported age of occupation to the south in what is today northern Australia, supposedly dating to between 70,000 and 60,000 years, based on luminescence (Clarkson et al. 2017; Maloney et al. 2018; McDonald et al. 2018; Moss et al. 2017; Vannieuwenhuyse et al. 2017). The location of the Ivane Valley in the central mountains indicates the movement of people inland since the earliest occupation and the exploitation of the local forests. Glimpses into forest use is made possible by starch and macrobotanical analyses of material from the Ivane Valley sites. Analysis of starch on stone tools has identified the use of wild pandanus and yam, while macrobotanical remains have identified pandanus nuts that would have provided protein and oil. The human impact on the environment was felt soon after arrival in the valley, with landscape modification probably produced through ringbarking trees, as evident by the presence of waisted axes and the use of fire (Hope 2009).

Other sites in Papua New Guinea help in modelling this early occupation and provide insights into human management of the landscape. From Bobongara, on the Huon Peninsula, on the east coast of mainland New Guinea, stone tools found on raised terraces dated to over 40,000 years (see Groube et al. 1986). It was argued that waisted axes were used to modify this landscape (Groube 1989). Thirty-five thousand year old sites like Lachitu rock-shelter are also found on the north coast of New Guinea, just to the east of the border with West New Guinea (see O'Connor et al. 2011), and there are a number of locations on the islands to the east in the Bismarck Archipelago and Solomon Islands, like Buang Merabak, Matenkupkum, Kupona na Dari, Yombon, and Kilu Cave (see Summerhayes and Ford 2014 for locations and references).

Sites dating from 25,000 years in age increase in number on mainland Papua New Guinea and the Bismarck Archipelago, providing new glimpses into ancient society at a time of compressed temperature and humidity. These glimpses include evidence for open sea travel, the beginning of a long-distance exchange of obsidian, and evidence of pelagic fishing. There are also indications of overexploitation of marine resources, as evidenced by decreases in shell size at the site of Matenkupkum, that suggest population increases by 20,000 years ago (Gosden and Robertson 1991). Thus, from a limited number of sites in Papua New Guinea, it has been put forward that the increase in the number of archaeological sites across the landscape, the long-distance exchange/ movement of obsidian, and the overexploitation of shellfish all point to the gradual filling up of the landscape at 25,000–20,000 years ago.

West of the border we know little of this time period (see Wright et al. 2013 for a review). From genetic analyses presented by Guy Jacobs and colleagues in Chapter 4, it appears that human populations in New Guinea would have remained relatively small scale and increasingly isolated from Australian groups throughout the Pleistocene. Excavations at Toé Cave, Ayamaru Region, central Bird's Head, have previously yielded the only evidence of Pleistocene occupation dating from 31,040–30,350 years ago. Bones of montane and lowland species of animals have been found at this site (Pasveer 2004), and shifts in the proportion of these different animals contribute to our understanding of the diet of the inhabitants and to changing past climates.

This region and the offshore islands are critical for understanding behavioural processes identified east of the divide. The importance of initial colonisation was outlined in Chapter 7 of the present volume, in which Boesl, Adhityatama, and Wall focus on the submerged landscape at the northern entrance of Sahul. Modelling seafaring in Wallacea and understanding past sea level fluctuation is critical in understanding the entry to the ancient landmass of Sahul. Of note is the authors' focus on the island of Misool as a key entry point of the early colonisers. The area is also an important ecological intersection, Lydekker's Line, which represents the western extent of the Australasian faunal region that would have stimulated adaptations by the colonisers and their descendants. Despite this, Misool remains understudied, especially with regard to the change in landscape over time, and archaeological and palaeoecological research there should be a priority.

Chapter 8 by Gaffney, Tanudirjo and co-authors redresses this imbalance by outlining the archaeological reconnaissance of the northern Raja Ampat Islands, an area previously neglected by archaeologists; the chapter is a breath of fresh air, focusing on this poorly understood area. The Raja Ampat Archaeological Project, which is outlined in the chapter, was specifically set up to redress the paucity of data and is a good start. One hundred and twenty-five new sites from a variety of environments were recorded, an important step for this region that is strategically located as a gateway from Asia to the Pacific. The contribution to understanding the colonisation of this region and subsequent Pleistocene adaptations is now being realised with the depth of occupation only now being identified and extending back over 50,000 years (Gaffney 2021; Gaffney et al. 2023). We wait with bated breath for the full publication of Gaffney's PhD and the results of subsequent excavations.

Human adaptation and transformation

Throughout the Pleistocene and Holocene, there is strong evidence from Papua New Guinea that there were major adaptations to life on islands, in highlands, and among tropical forests (Summerhayes et al. 2017). The genetic insights regarding many of these adaptations, including to lowland malaria, high altitudes, and UV radiation, are presented in new analyses by Attenborough and colleagues in Chapter 6. Alongside these adaptations came human-mediated changes to these environments, as recorded in Papua New Guinea's zooarchaeological and palaeoecological records (Hope and Haberle 2005). What we know about this period of time in West New Guinea is still limited, with sparse traces recorded both in the highlands and on the Bird's Head. Kria Cave and Toé Cave on the Bird's Head, excavated by Pasveer, produced Late Pleistocene and Early to Late Holocene human occupation and rich faunal assemblages. Meanwhile, a high-altitude (3886 m asl) rock-shelter site of Mapala, a northern summit of Mount Carstensz, indicated travel over this mountain range (Hope and Hope 1976, 233).

Up until recently, that was it. This book now adds to the inventory and, with new analyses of fauna and material culture, could address issues such as the nature of environmental interaction, subsistence systems, and human adaptive processes. Here the outstanding chapter by Mene, Setiawan, and Gaffney reports preliminary results on Late Glacial Maximum (LGM) to Late Holocene occupation on the Bomberai Peninsula (Chapter 9). They focus on Andarewa Cave, Fakfak Regency, by presenting the fieldwork results from 2018 to 2021, where two 2 × 2 m units were excavated. In situ excavated material included pottery, shell, stone tools, bone points and jewellery, red and yellow ochre, charcoal, and other ecofacts. Although the full description of what was found will be presented in a later report, radiocarbon dates were presented demonstrating occupation of the site during the LGM, making it the second-oldest reported site in West New Guinea and contemporary with Toé Cave on the Bird's Head (Pasveer 2004). In situ finds extending back to the LGM make this is a major site for New Guinea's past. Radiocarbon estimates for the Terminal Pleistocene/ Holocene transition are also available with abundant faunal material, and with pottery extend to the post-Mid-Holocene according to the authors, more like c. 2000 years ago. There is much for the archaeologist to get their teeth into here including modelling the changing nature of subsistence and people's impact on their environment. Also, the identification of mostly local stone acquisition with imported igneous stone is important in modelling the nature of group mobility and exchange (if any).

Food production

Major advances have been made in the archaeology of the Early and Mid-Holocene in Papua New Guinea, in particular understanding landscape change, the beginnings of agriculture, and the changing levels of interaction between prehistoric communities. With the warming of the planet after the LGM, there was a dramatic increase in the number of archaeological sites, and the intensity of use in these sites, found in Papua New Guinea. The evidence suggests people were returning to higher-altitude sites in the highlands, with subalpine grasses replaced with forest cover, and with that forest cover subsequently cleared in many valley systems (for a review see Hope and Haberle 2005). A few highland sites provide insights into the changing socio-economic dynamics of the Early Holocene. Increases in not only the number of newly visited sites but also the intensity of occupation have been identified previously (Mountain 1991a), while a focus on intensive hunting of bats and forest fauna has been identified from the Terminal Pleistocene into the Mid-Holocene (Gaffney et al 2015, 226). Behavioural transformations are also witnessed by changes in lithic production and procurement, indicating increasingly restricted mobility and territoriality (Gaffney et al. 2015, 226–227). Significant socio-economic changes are also identified from 5050 to 4200 years ago, contemporary with innovations in intensive plant food processing, settlement structures, and regionally networked symbolic social systems (Shaw et al. 2020).

The Holocene also introduced changes to plant production, with the first evidence of agriculture found at Kuk Swamp in the Western Highlands (see Golson et al. 2017). Although Kuk stands alone in its early direct evidence of agriculture, with a number of crops having been identified micro- and macro-botanically, its proximity to other highland sites where intensive plant food production has been inferred through proxy evidence in the Mid-Holocene, plus the evidence of contemporaneously intensive hunting and selective use of animal prey, suggests highland populations practised different forms of subsistence depending on what their environment had to offer. Thus, the nature of human–environment relationships differed across the landscape, even between the same or related groups of people.

Also witnessed during the transition from the Pleistocene to the Holocene was the long-distance movement of objects, as evidenced by New Britain obsidian being found in highland and north coast sites, 800 km from the source (Mountain 1991b; Shaw et al. 2020, 2; Summerhayes 2009; White 1972). Coastal shell is also found in Early and Mid-Holocene highland sites (White 1972). At this time, the appearance of pestles and mortars (used for nut processing) are found at many locations across the landscape, indicating the presence of regional interaction networks not evident in later periods (Swadling 2005, 2017; Swadling and Hide 2005; Swadling et al. 2008). The possible connection between the movement of food production, pestles and mortars, Trans–New Guinea languages, and specific genetic lineages, is noted by Kusuma and colleagues in Chapter 5.

The paucity of West New Guinea archaeology from this period is highlighted when assessing not only the scarce pestle and mortar record, but also the translocation of animals. There is evidence from Papua New Guinea that animals were translocated from the mainland to the Bismarck Archipelago (Summerhayes et al. 2017) and indirect evidence from Indonesia that animals were translocated from mainland New Guinea to islands in the west. Evidence of native New Guinea animals like the wallaby (*Dorcopsis*) and bandicoot were found from 5500–3000-year-old contexts from Halmahera, plus the wallaby was found in Early Holocene contexts from Gebe (Bellwood et al. 1998; Hull et al. 2019). How did they get there from mainland New Guinea, and what are the implications for changes to animal husbandry and hunting?

Although none of the chapters in this volume directly address the origins of agriculture or animal translocation in West New Guinea, Tolla, Roberts, and colleagues' research on prehistoric foodways using stable isotope analysis from sites in lowland areas (Chapter 10) provides important evidence of past diets. Such a technique has been used in Papua New Guinea for a variety of time periods looking at environmental changes or movements of people and animals (e.g. Shaw et al. 2009, 2010, 2011; Roberts et al. 2022, 2023). Tolla and colleagues point out that although people have been exploiting tropical forests in New Guinea for over 45,000 years, we know little about how human diet and subsistence changed from the Pleistocene and into the Holocene in different parts of the island. Their chapter is important primarily for two reasons. First, is the presentation of radiocarbon results from five archaeological sites in the lowland region of Papua and Papua Barat Province, Indonesia. Of the five dates, three had been previously published in Indonesian journals, and two for the first time. They came from sites Yomokho 1, Srobu, Mamorikotey, Karas, and Namatota. Secondly, the authors presented preliminary stable isotope data from human tooth enamel and bones. In their study into diet, they looked at carbon and nitrogen isotope analysis of human bone collagen and enamel apatite and it was hoped this would allow insights into past economies, diet, and changes over time during important parts of climatic change. The chapter highlights the potential of this technique and future research plans.

Language dispersals

The Austronesian-speaking occupation of Near Oceania is an area that desperately needs attention in West New Guinea. As noted by Gaffney and Tolla in Chapter 1 and Arnold in Chapter 3, there are important patterns in the distribution of Austronesian languages around the island that indicate there were arrivals of these speech communities in the Mid- to Late Holocene. These distributions are similarly noted, from a genetic perspective, as presented by Kusama and colleagues in Chapter 5.

From Papua New Guinea, great strides in archaeology have been made not only from the Bismarck Archipelago, but recently from mainland New Guinea. Some 3300 years ago, major introductions from Asia into the western Pacific are seen in terms of the movement of Austronesian-speaking populations who brought with them a Neolithic lifestyle, including pottery, pigs, dogs, chickens, and new varieties of plants. A component of the pottery was highly decorated, mostly with complex dentate-stamped designs. We use the term 'Lapita' to describe this phenomenon. It was these people who went on to colonise Remote Oceania for the first time (areas to the east of the Solomon Island chain), including present-day New Caledonia, Vanuatu, Fiji, Tonga, and Samoa. The descendants of these people went on to colonise the rest of Oceania including Hawai'i, Tahiti, and New Zealand by c. 800 years ago. We now have close to 300 Lapita sites identified throughout this region, including sites along the south coast of Papua New Guinea. Over 110 of these are found in the Bismarck Archipelago and mainland New Guinea (see Bedford et al. 2019 for an up-to-date listing and Kirch 2017 for background).

Links between this Lapita network and mainland New Guinea are now seen with sites along the south Papuan coast and the islands off the south-east coast of Papua New Guinea. Dentate-stamped pottery is also found along the north coast: dentate-stamped surface sherds were found from near

Aitape and another on nearby Ali Island along the Sepik north coast (Terrell and Welsch 1997). It can be assumed that if dentate pottery is found in Aitape, it will be found further west along the West New Guinean coast. The only positive link between the West New Guinea north coast and Lapita is the presence of a greenstone jadeite gouge originating north-west of Lake Sentani, West New Guinea, found on the island of Emirau, New Ireland, associated with Early Lapita pottery (Harlow et al. 2012). To understand what is really happening during this critical period of time, we need an understanding of the archaeology along the north coast of West New Guinea, something we just do not have (although see provisional information presented in Djami and Suroto 2023).

From the above, any evidence of material culture from this period is important! The finding of Late Holocene pottery from Andarewa Cave, Fakfak Regency on the Bomberai Peninsula (Chapter 9), is important. Further refinement of the age of pottery use and identification of production patterns at Andarewa is critical in modelling the nature of Late Holocene society and its relationship to other Austronesian communities further afield. Again, we wait eagerly for further results. Of particular interest is Hari Suroto's chapter (Chapter 12) on prehistoric sites in the western Lake Sentani, and his description and images of decorated pottery. Archaeological research on Lake Sentani has a long history. Finds of ancient bronzes and glass beads all point to contacts with the west. Also, as noted above, a jadeite gouge found at a Lapita site on Emirau, St Matthias Group (Harlow et al. 2012), and sourced to just north-west of Sentani indicates ancient links to the east as well. Suroto's chapter is the product of 13 years of surveys with new sites excavated. Again, what is exciting is the presentation of new data and two radiocarbon dates, indicating settlement at Yomokho 2 in the late second millennium BP. The images of pottery, in particular the appliqué, shows similarities with pottery production further east around the Wewak area. Suroto argues that Lake Sentani was a resource centre for food, water, and building materials. The subsistence practices ranged from fishing to collecting shellfish and gathering sago starch. Trade systems with coastal communities were also indicated by the presence of marine shell, although, as the author points out, this marine shell could also be a product of group mobility. What is needed now is intensive analysis of the pottery with models of production built on petrographic and chemical data, coupled with extensive surveying along the islands off the north coast. There must be late fourth and early third millennium BP sites along this coastline which linked Austronesian movements from west to east. This fieldwork must be of paramount importance.

Exchange networks and the recent past

Our understanding of the last two millennia of human history in Papua New Guinea has seen major advances through an increase in archaeological activity. It paints a picture of strongly defined regionalisation coupled with continuing interactions as seen in complex exchange systems. The analysis of pottery production over long periods of time in many parts of Papua New Guinea and its offshore islands, including, for example, the north Solomons (Wickler 2001), Madang (Gaffney 2020), North Coast (Terrell and Schechter 2011), South Coast (Skelly and David 2017), and south-east Papua (Shaw 2021), has allowed complex trade/exchange models to be developed. This has been made possible by advances in the petrographic and chemical analysis of ceramics. A review can be found in Summerhayes (2023).

Archaeological work in the highlands has identified the introduction of sweet potatoes within the last 300 years (Bayliss-Smith et al. 2005), allowing major changes to the expansion of highland societies into higher altitude settlements and the increasing intensification of production needed for social practices. It has been termed the Ipomoean Revolution (Watson 1965).

The rich archaeology of Papua New Guinea during the last 2000 years can only be replicated in West New Guinea with more intensive archaeological research. Apart from the chapters already described, a step in the right direction is seen in Klementin Fairyo's chapter (Chapter 13) from the Kayu Batu area, Jayapura. The description was offered from surface pottery found in three burial caves near Jayapura (Gua Tubara, Tubara Sugu, and Aturboyah Suwiyah). Fairyo explored the decorated pot sherds by focusing on the characteristics of the design forms (as grave goods) associated with human remains. By exploring the decorations and style of pottery fragments, Fairyo provided insights into the typology and morphology of pots at Kayu Batu. Of note is the use of ethnographic observation in pottery interpretation and comparison between pottery made today and that made in the past. What is needed next is a detailed analysis of pottery production using petrographic and/or chemical characterisation to link this area with north coast systems of information exchange, and to get an idea through excavation of temporal change. As noted in Chapter 1, further methodological developments could also be made in exploring the archaeology of orality at these recent sites, combining information from archaeological material culture with that from oral traditions.

One area that West New Guinea is equal to, or takes the lead over, Papua New Guinea is in the study of rock art, especially around the western coastal margins (see Arifin and Delanghe 2004). Few detailed studies of rock art have taken place in Papua New Guinea, although this is changing with exciting new research along the Sepik and its tributaries (see Tsang et al. 2020, 2021, 2022, 2023). This new research articulates local oral traditions about rock art with the artwork itself for a nuanced understanding of the artworks. The research is also providing new insights into placemaking through rock art, its use and role in society, and how the meanings and artwork can change over time. In this volume, Fairyo (Chapter 11) focused on the rock art of Keerom Regency in Papua Province and described the different types of rock art. It is an important and understudied area located at the border between West New Guinea and Papua New Guinea. The contemporary knowledge relating to the social function and current meaning of the rock art is also described. Figurative and non-figurative rock art and their meanings indicate association with religious beliefs and social communication. In terms of indigenous meanings, the locals associate the rock paintings with symbolic identity and social boundaries. Tsang in Papua New Guinea makes similar observations, and this is one area that joint comparative research would be fruitful.

Another aspect of the recent archaeological record which West New Guinea can contribute to is historical archaeology. As an example, Kawer and Gaffney's (Chapter 14) chapter explored the remains of World War II (WWII) on Biak Island. The island was one of the key American and Japanese bases during WWII. They examined the distribution of objects such as bunkers, airplanes, and their fragmentary remains, to provide a narrative about Biak's recent history. Biak remains an important location for understanding the events of WWII, but its archaeology remains understudied. This chapter stands in contrast with the relative lack of archaeology on war sites across the border (for an exception, see Petchey et al. 2015). In Papua New Guinea, the aim of specialised archaeological visits from Australians, Americans, and the Japanese is almost always to retrieve the human remains of war dead. There are aviation enthusiasts who focus on crashed planes, and collectors looking at war debris (which is protected in Papua New Guinea through legislation), but no systematic academic excavation of wartime sites. Excavation on both sides of the divide has the potential to provide important details about these sites of conflict, as well as information about how local people responded to the conflict.

Materialising culture

An area in which West New Guinea has already made advances is in ethnohistory and material culture studies. McNiven (Chapter 15) examined the tangible and intangible dimensions of marine voyaging by the Marind-anim people of central-southern New Guinea. He focused specifically on agentive seas and animate canoes that were used during various voyaging trips. These voyages were associated with extensive headhunting practices. The author described how the Marind-anim purposely built elaborate canoes imbued with both social and spiritual aspects of their cultural lives for these journeys. This was believed to be necessary for their success in headhunting. Other important chapters include Tom Powell Davies's contribution (Chapter 16), which looked at carved axes as a proxy to understand how the Asmat people engage with ideas about their ancestral history and material culture. Given the challenges of canoe preservation in the tropics, archaeological excavations and dating of stone axes and other material culture around the south coast's former beach ridges and river systems would provide more context and a possible timeframe for when long-distance voyages began to take place and how stone working practices have changed through time. Engaging with Marind-anim and Asmat people about their archaeological heritage might produce interesting and unexpected new insights about the recent history of these practices.

Voirol's contribution (Chapter 17) on shell use in West New Guinea Highlands cultures from an ethnographic perspective demonstrated the social, cultural, and economic importance of seashells in all aspects of Highlands society, especially through trade and exchange interactions. Similarly, Martinus Tekege's chapter (Chapter 18) examined bride price among the Mee people who occupy the central ranges of Papua. The chapter describes the nature of shell use and bride price ceremonies from the author's personal viewpoint. What we need now is a coherent understanding of shell use in the archaeological past as evident by research across the border (see Gaffney et al. 2019).

Kanem (Chapter 19) describes the practice of string bag ('bilum' in Papua New Guinea, noken in West New Guinea[1]) making among her home community in southern West New Guinea, showing how the history of this long tradition is changing in the present day. The ongoing life histories of Papuan material culture—not only canoes, axes, shells, and string bags, but also wooden carvings—is evident and clearly described by Jacobs for Kamoro collections (Chapter 20) and by Veys for Raja Ampat Island collections (Chapter 21).

Museums and collecting

Voirol (Chapter 17), Jacobs (Chapter 20), and Veys (Chapter 21) explore the roles that international museums take in collecting and curating material objects and, increasingly, reuniting Papuan people with their ancestors' cultural traditions. Voirol describes the important information that can be generated when applying an ethnographic, and field-based, approach to museum collections. Jacobs follows the life histories of a small number of Kamoro objects from their place of acquisition to their place of storage in museums so as to illustrate the contingent relationships that have been generated by these collecting practices. Meanwhile, Veys focuses on the politics of displaying West New Guinea material culture in overseas museums, and how these museums are seeking to engage with diasporic and descendent Papuan communities.

---

1   At first mention, common Papua Malay and Indonesian words are underlined, while other languages (such as Tok Pisin) use single quote marks.

The Papua New Guinea National Museum and Art Gallery is the nation's custodian and manager of the country's rich cultural, natural, and contemporary heritage including archaeological remains. An active collecting program for the nation has its roots in the late nineteenth century and has continued ever since. The museum as it stands today was established in 1956 and has developed after independence in 1975 to house many natural, historical, and cultural heritage items and all archaeological material. It is governed by an Act of Parliament and overseen by a Board of Trustees nominated by the government. The day-to-day management is left to the director. The museum regulates all archaeological research in Papua New Guinea, including issuing surveying and excavation permits, which are needed to undertake research, and it also has control of the export of cultural heritage material authorised by an Act of Parliament, the *Papua New Guinea National Cultural Property (Preservation) Act* of 1965, and two other Acts of Parliament: the *War Surplus Materials Act 1952* and the *National Museum and Art Gallery Act 1992*.

By contrast, as mentioned by Gaffney and Tolla in Chapter 2, the few museums in West New Guinea have generally received less funding and less attention at a national level under Indonesian administration. Further development of cultural heritage infrastructure in West New Guinea—including repatriation and donations from museums and private collectors in the Netherlands, America, and elsewhere—will require increased attention in the museums sector.

Conclusions

We have reviewed and made comparisons between Papua New Guinea to the east of the divide and West New Guinea to the west, based primarily on archaeology and cognate disciplines. This volume, however, also touches on politics, ownership, and diversity. These are topics that are equally important across the border and are universal here; however, in West New Guinea, where cultural identity is highly sensitive, ownership takes on a new significance. With this in mind, we conclude by highlighting the major differences in research practice and potential in Papua New Guinea and West New Guinea.

First, in West New Guinea, archaeology and other social and historical disciplines are decades behind what has been developed across the border in Papua New Guinea. We conclude that the main reasons for West New Guinea's stagnant research progress throughout the twentieth century has been related to the current political situation. Researchers and indigenous Papuans cannot be too critical about the recent colonial history of the region and many research projects have been prevented or rejected. On the other hand, Papua New Guinea's archaeological and anthropological research has contributed much more to global knowledge and has developed a stronger tradition of scholarly work, especially providing evidence relating to early human occupation and settlement patterns, the development of cultivation and agriculture, the movement of different language families, the complex development of trade and exchange networks, and the meaningful production and use of material culture.

One way for West New Guinea to begin to contribute in important ways to the global literature would be for indigenous participation in research to be emphasised and encouraged. This is because once people from Papua New Guinea and West New Guinea are both producing research, then they can be motivated, and inspire the next generation to produce their own research. Currently, this is often not the case, as political problems continue to affect Papuans, but it is hoped that current foreign scholars continue to help mentor interested indigenous researchers in pursuit of their own research interests. Furthermore, foreign and indigenous researchers working in West New Guinea and Papua New Guinea should collaborate in their scholarly research because the two areas cannot be separated when answering questions about New Guinea's past.

Acknowledgements

We thank Loretta Hasu for her advice and comments.

References

Arifin, K. and P. Delanghe 2004. *Rock art in West Papua*. UNESCO, Paris.

Bayliss-Smith, T., J. Golson, P. Hughes, R. Blong, and W. Ambrose 2005. Archaeological evidence for the Ipomoean Revolution at Kuk swamp, upper Wahgi Valley, Papua New Guinea. *Oceania Monograph* 56: 109–120.

Bedford, S, M. Spriggs, D. Burley, C. Sand, P. Sheppard, and G.R. Summerhayes 2019. Debating Lapita: Distribution, chronology, society and subsistence. In S. Bedford and M. Spriggs (eds), *Debating Lapita: Chronology, society and subsistence*, pp. 5–33. Terra Australis 52. ANU Press, Canberra. doi.org/10.22459/TA52.2019.01.

Bellwood, P., G. Nitihaminoto, G. Irwin, A. Gunadi, Waluyo, and D. Tanudirjo 1998. 35,000 years of prehistory in the northern Moluccas. *Modern Quaternary Research in Southeast Asia* 15:233–273.

Clarkson, C., Z. Jacobs, B. Marwick, R. Fullagar, L. Wallis, M. Smith, R.G. Roberts, E. Hayes, K. Lowe, X. Carah, S.A. Florin, J. McNeil, D. Cox, L.J. Arnold, Q. Hua, J. Huntley, H.E.A. Brand, T. Manne, A. Fairbairn, J. Shulmeister, L. Lyle, M. Salinas, M. Page, K. Connell, G. Park, K. Norman, T. Murphy, and C. Pardoe 2017. Human occupation of northern Australia by 65,000 years ago. *Nature* 547:306–310. doi.org/10.1038/nature22968.

Djami, E.N.I. and H. Suroto 2023. Distribution of Austronesian languages and archaeology in western New Guinea, Indonesia. *L'Anthropologie* 127(3):103153. doi.org/10.1016/j.anthro.2023.103153.

Gaffney, D. 2020. *Materialising ancestral Madang: Pottery production and subsistence trading on the northeast coast of New Guinea*. University of Otago Studies in Archaeology, No. 29. Archaeology Programme, University of Otago, Dunedin.

Gaffney, D. 2021. Human behavioural dynamics in island rainforests: Evidence from the Raja Ampat Islands, West Papua. Unpublished PhD thesis. Department of Archaeology, University of Cambridge, Cambridge.

Gaffney, D., A. Ford, and G.R. Summerhayes 2015. Crossing the Pleistocene–Holocene transition in the New Guinea Highlands: Evidence from the lithic assemblage of Kiowa rockshelter. *Journal of Anthropological Archaeology* 39:223–246. doi.org/10.1016/j.jaa.2015.04.006.

Gaffney, D., G.R. Summerhayes, K. Szabo, and B. Koppel 2019. The emergence of shell valuable exchange in the New Guinea Highlands. *American Anthropologist* 121(1):30–47. doi.org/10.1111/aman.13154.

Gaffney, D., D. Tanudirjo, E.N.I. Djami, A.R. Macap, and T. Russel 2023. *An archaeology of Waigeo: Raja Ampat islands, West Papua*. University of Otago Working Papers in Anthropology No. 8. Dunedin.

Golson, J., T. Denham, P. Hughes, P. Swadling, and J. Muke 2017. *Ten thousand years of cultivation at Kuk Swamp in the Highlands of Papua New Guinea*. Terra Australis 46. ANU Press, Canberra. doi.org/10.22459/TA46.07.2017.

Gosden, C., and N. Robertson 1991. Models for Matenkupkum: Interpreting a late Pleistocene site from southern New Ireland, Papua New Guinea. In J. Allen and C. Gosden (eds), *Report of the Lapita Homeland Project*, pp. 20–45. Department of Prehistory, Research School of Pacific Studies, The Australian National University, Canberra.

Groube, L. 1989. The taming of the rainforests: A model for Late Pleistocene Forest Exploitation in New Guinea. In D. Harris and G. Hillman (eds), *Foraging and farming: The evolution of plant exploitation*, pp. 292–304. Unwin Hyman, London.

Groube, L., J. Chappell, J. Muke, and D. Price 1986. A 40,000-year-old human occupation site at Huon Peninsula, Papua New Guinea. *Science* 324:453–455. doi.org/10.1038/324453a0.

Harlow, G.E., G.R. Summerhayes, H.L. Davies, and L. Matisoo-Smith 2012. A jade gouge from Emirau Island, Papua New Guinea (Early Lapita context, 3300 BP): A unique jadeitite. *European Journal of Mineralogy* 24(2):391–399. doi.org/10.1127/0935-1221/2012/0024-2175.

Hope, G.S. 2009. Environmental change and fire in the Owen Stanley Ranges, Papua New Guinea. *Quaternary Science Reviews* 28(23-24):2261–2276. doi.org/10.1016/j.quascirev.2009.04.012.

Hope, G.S and S.G. Haberle 2005. The history of the human landscapes of New Guinea. In A. Pawley, R. Attenborough, J. Golson, and R. Hide (eds), *Papuan pasts: Cultural, linguistic and biological histories of the Papuan-speaking peoples*, pp. 541–554. Pacific Linguistics 572. Research School of Pacific and Asian Studies, The Australian National University, Canberra.

Hope, G.S. and J.H. Hope 1976. Man on Mt. Jaya. In G.S. Hope, J.A. Peterson, U. Radok, and I. Allison (eds), *The equatorial glaciers of New Guinea. Results of the 1971–1973 Australian Universities' Expeditions to Irian Jaya: Survey, glaciology, meteorology, biology and paleoenvironments*, pp. 225–238. A.A. Balkema, Rotterdam. doi.org/10.1201/9780203736777-11.

Hull, J.R., P. Piper, G. Irwin, K. Szabó, A. Oertle, and P. Bellwood 2019. Observations on the Northern Moluccan excavated animal bone and shell collections. In P. Bellwood (ed), *The Spice Islands in prehistory: Archaeology in the Northern Moluccas, Indonesia*, pp. 135–166. Terra Australis 50. ANU Press, Canberra. doi.org/10.22459/TA50.2019.10.

Kirch, P.V. 2017. *On the road of the winds: An archaeological history of the Pacific Islands before European contact*, 2nd edition. University of California Press, Oakland. doi.org/10.1525/9780520968899.

Maloney, T., S. O'Connor, R. Wood, K. Aplin, and J. Balme 2018. Carpenters Gap 1: A 47,000-year-old record of indigenous adaptation. *Quaternary Science Reviews* 191:204–228. doi.org/10.1016/j.quascirev.2018.05.016.

McDonald, J., W. Reynen, F. Petchey, K. Ditchfield, C. Bryne, D. Vannieuwenhuyse, M. Leopold, and P. Veth 2018. *Karnatulul* (Serpents Glen): A new chronology for the oldest site in Australia's Western Desert. *PLoSONE* 13(9):e0202511. doi.org/10.1371/journal.pone.0202511.

Moss, P., G. Dunbar, Z. Thomas, C. Turney, and A.P. Kershaw 2017. A 60,000-year record of environmental change for the Wet Tropics of north-eastern Australia based on the ODP 820 marine core. *Journal of Quaternary Science* 32:704–716. doi.org/10.1002/jqs.2977.

Mountain, M.J. 1991a. Bulmer phase I: Environmental change and human activity through the late Pleistocene into the Holocene in the highlands of New Guinea: A scenario. In A. Pawley (ed.), *Man and a half: Essays in Pacific anthropology and ethnobiology in honour of Ralph Bulmer*, pp. 510–520. Polynesian Society, Auckland.

Mountain, M.J. 1991b. Highland New Guinea hunter-gatherers. The evidence from Nombe rockshelter, Simbu, with emphasis on the Pleistocene. Unpublished PhD dissertation. The Australian National University, Canberra.

O'Connor, S., A. Barham, K. Aplin, K. Dobney, A. Fairbairn, and M. Richards 2011. The power of paradigms: Examining the evidential basis for early to mid-Holocene pigs and pottery in Melanesia. *Journal of Pacific Archaeology* 2(2):1–25.

Pasveer, J.M. 2004. *The Djief hunters: 26,000 years of rainforest exploitation on the Bird's Head of Papua, Indonesia*. A.A. Balkema, Leiden. doi.org/10.1201/b17006.

Petchey, P. 2015. Second World War Japanese defences on Watom Island, Papua New Guinea. *Journal of Conflict Archaeology* 10(1):29–51. doi.org/10.1179/1574077315Z.00000000042.

Roberts, P., K. Douka, M. Tromp, S. Bedford, S. Hawkins, L. Bouffandeau, J. Ilgner, M. Lucas, S. Marzo, R. Hamilton, W. Ambrose, D. Bulbeck, S. Luu, R. Shing, C. Gosden, G.R. Summerhayes, and M. Spriggs 2022. Fossils, fish and tropical forests: Prehistoric human adaptations on the island frontiers of Oceania. *Philosophical Transactions of the Royal Society B* 377(1849):20200495. doi.org/10.1098/rstb.2020.0495.

Roberts, P., J. Hixon, R. Hamilton, M. Lucas, A. Ilgner, S. Marzo, S. Hawkins, S. Luu, C. Gosden, M. Spriggs, and G.R. Summerhayes 2023. Assessing Pleistocene–Holocene climatic and environmental change in insular Near Oceania using stable isotope analysis of archaeological fauna. *Journal Of Quaternary Science* 38(8):1267–1278. doi.org/10.1002/Jqs.3555.

Shaw, B. 2021. Palaeolandscapes, radiocarbon chronologies, and the human settlement of southern lowland and Island Papua New Guinea. In M. Carson (ed.), *Palaeolandscapes in archaeology: Lessons for the past and future*, pp. 215–290. Routledge, New York. doi.org/10.4324/9781003139553-9.

Shaw, B., G.R. Summerhayes, H.R. Buckley, and J. Baker 2009. The potential use of strontium isotopes as an indicator of migration in human and pig Lapita populations in the Pacific Islands. *Journal of Archaeological Science* 36:1079–1091. doi.org/10.1016/j.jas.2008.12.010.

Shaw, B., H. Buckley, G.R. Summerhayes, D. Anson, S. Garling, F. Valentin, H. Mandui, C. Stirling, and M. Reid 2010. Migration and mobility at the Late Lapita site of Reber–Rakival (SAC), Watom Island using isotope and trace element analysis: A new insight into Lapita interaction in the Bismarck Archipelago. *Journal of Archaeological Science* 37(3):605–613. doi.org/10.1016/j.jas.2009.10.025.

Shaw, B., H. Buckley, G.R. Summerhayes, C. Stirling, and M. Reid 2011. Prehistoric migration at Nebira, south coast of Papua New Guinea: New insights into interaction using isotope and trace element concentration analyses. *Journal of Anthropological Archaeology* 30(3):344–358. doi.org/10.1016/j.jaa.2011.05.004.

Shaw, B., J. Field, G.R. Summerhayes, S. Coxe, A.C.F. Coster, A. Ford, J. Haro, H. Arifeae, E. Hull, G. Jacobsen, R. Fullagar, E. Hayes, and L. Kealhofer 2020. Emergence of a Neolithic in Highland New Guinea by 5000 to 4000 years ago. *Science Advances* 6(13):eaay4573. doi.org/10.1126/sciadv.aay4573.

Skelly, R. and B. David 2017. *Hiri: Archaeology of long-distance maritime trade along the south coast of Papua New Guinea*. University of Hawai'i Press, Honolulu.

Summerhayes, G.R. 2009. Obsidian network patterns in Melanesia—Sources, characterisation and distribution. *Bulletin of the Indo-Pacific Prehistory Association* 29:110–124.

Summerhayes, G.R. 2021. History of archaeology in Papua New Guinea: The early years up to 1960. In I. McNiven and B. David (eds), *The Oxford handbook of the archaeology of Indigenous Australia and New Guinea*, pp. 85–108. Oxford University Press, Oxford. doi.org/10.1093/oxfordhb/9780190095611.013.3.

Summerhayes, G.R. 2023. New Guinea's past: The last 50,000 years. In P. D'Arcy, R.T. Jones, and K. Matsuda (eds), *The Cambridge history of the Pacific Ocean*, Vol. 1. Cambridge University Press, Cambridge. doi.org/10.1017/9781108539272.024.

Summerhayes, G.R., and A. Ford 2014. Late Pleistocene colonisation and adaptation in New Guinea: Implications for modeling modern human behaviour. In R. Dennell, and M. Porr (eds), *Southern Asia, Australia and the search for human origins*, pp. 213–227. Cambridge University Press, Cambridge. doi.org/ 10.1017/CBO9781139084741.017.

Summerhayes, G.R., M. Leavesley, A. Fairbairn, H. Mandui, J. Field, A. Ford, and R. Fullagar 2010. Human adaptation and plant use in highland New Guinea 49,000 to 44,000 years ago. *Science* 330(6000):78–81. doi.org/10.1126/science.1193130.

Summerhayes, G.R., J.H. Field, B. Shaw and D. Gaffney 2017. The archaeology of forest exploitation and change in the tropics during the Pleistocene: The case of Northern Sahul (Pleistocene New Guinea). *Quaternary International* 448:14–30. doi.org/10.1016/j.quaint.2016.04.023.

Swadling, P. 2005. The Huon Gulf and its hinterlands: A long-term view of Coastal–Highlands interactions. In C. Gross, H.D. Lyons, and D.A. Counts (eds), *A polymath anthropologist: Essays in honour of Anne Chowning*, pp. 1–14. Auckland Research in Anthropology and Linguistics Monograph No. 6. Department of Anthropology, University of Auckland.

Swadling, P. 2017. Early art in New Guinea glimpses from prehistory. In J. Friede, T.E. Hays, and C. Hellmich (eds), *New Guinea Highlands art from the Jolika Collection*. Fine Arts Museums of San Francisco, San Francisco.

Swadling P. and R. Hide 2005. Changing landscape and social interaction, looking at agricultural history from a Sepik–Ramu perspective. In A. Pawley, R. Attenborough, J. Golson, and R. Hide (eds), *Papuan pasts: Cultural, linguistic and biological histories of the Papuan-speaking peoples*, pp. 289–327. Pacific Linguistics 572. Research School of Pacific and Asian Studies, The Australian National University, Canberra.

Swadling, P., P. Wiessner, and A. Tumu 2008. Prehistoric stone artefacts from Enga and the implication of links between the highlands, lowlands, and islands for early agriculture in Papua New Guinea. *Journal de la Société des Océanistes* 126–127(année 2008-1/2):271–292. doi.org/10.4000/jso.2942.

Terrell, J. and E.M. Schechter (eds) 2011. *Exploring prehistory on the Sepik coast of Papua New Guinea*. Fieldiana New series No. 42. Field Museum of Natural History, Chicago. doi.org/10.3158/0071-4739-42.1.fmix.

Terrell, J. and R. Welsch 1997. Lapita and the temporal geography of prehistory. *Antiquity* 71:548–572. doi.org/10.1017/S0003598X0008532X.

Tsang, R., W. Pleiber, J. Kariwiga, S. Plutniak, H. Forestier, P.S.C. Taçon, F.-X. Ricaut, and M.G. Leavesley 2020. Rock art and long-distance prehistoric exchange behavior: A case study from Auwim, East Sepik, Papua New Guinea. *Journal of Island and Coastal Archaeology* 17(3):432–444. doi.org/10.1080/15564894. 2020.1834472.

Tsang, R., L.M. Brady, S. Katuk, P.S.C. Taçon, F.-X. Ricaut, and M.G. Leavesley 2021. Agency, affect and archaeologists: Transforming place with rock art in Auwim, Upper Karawari-Arafundi region, East Sepik, Papua New Guinea. *Rock Art Research* 38(2):183–194.

Tsang, R., S. Katuk, S.K. May, P.S.C. Taçon, F.-X. Ricaut, and M.G. Leavesley 2022. Rock art and (re) production of narratives: A cassowary bone dagger stencil perspective from Auwim, East Sepik, Papua New Guinea. *Cambridge Archaeological Journal* 32(4):547–565. doi.org/10.1017/S0959774322000026.

Tsang, R., S. Katuk, S.K. May, P.S.C. Taçon, F.-X. Ricaut, and M.G. Leavesley 2023. Hand stencils and communal history: A case study from Auwim, East Sepik, Papua New Guinea. *Archaeology in Oceania Journal* 58:115–130. doi.org/10.1002/arco.5287.

Vannieuwenhuyse, D., S. O'Connor, and J. Balme 2017. Settling in Sahul: Investigating environmental and human history interactions through micromorphological analyses in tropical semi-arid north-west Australia. *Journal of Archaeological Science* 77:172–193. doi.org/10.1016/j.jas.2016.01.017.

Watson, J.B. 1965. From hunting to horticulture in the New Guinea Highlands. *Ethnology* 4:295–309. doi.org/10.2307/3772989.

White, J.P. 1972. *Ol Tumbuna: Archaeological excavations in the Eastern Central Highlands, Papua New Guinea.* Terra Australis 2. The Australian National University, Canberra.

Wickler, S. 2001. *The prehistory of Buka: A stepping stone island in the Northern Solomons.* Terra Australis 16. Centre of Archaeological Research, The Australian National University, Canberra.

Wright, D., T. Denham, D. Shine, and M. Donohue 2013. An archaeological review of Western New Guinea. *Journal of World Prehistory* 26(1):25–73. doi.org/10.1007/s10963-013-9063-8.

Contributors

Shinatria Adhityatama: Australian Research Centre for Human Evolution, Griffith University, Queensland, 4111, Australia.

Laura Arnold: Department of Linguistics and English Language, School of Philosophy, Psychology and Language Sciences, University of Edinburgh, Edinburgh, EH8 9AD, United Kingdom, and School of Culture, History and Language, College of Asia and the Pacific, The Australian National University, Canberra, Australian Capital Territory, 2600, Australia.

Robert Attenborough: McDonald Institute for Archaeological Research, Department of Archaeology, University of Cambridge, Cambridge, CB2 3DZ, United Kingdom, and School of Archaeology and Anthropology, College of Arts and Social Sciences, The Australian National University, Canberra, Australian Capital Territory, 2600, Australia.

Fabian Boesl: School of Science, Edith Cowan University, Joondalup, Western Australia, 6027, Australia.

Dominik Bonatz: Department of History and Cultural Studies, Freie Universität, Berlin, 14195, Germany.

Erlin Novita Idje Djami: Research Center for Prehistoric and Historical Archaeology, The National Research and Innovation Agency (BRIN), Jayapura, Papua, 99225, Indonesia.

Klementin Fairyo: Research Center for Sustainable Environmental, Maritime and Cultural Archaeology, The National Research and Innovation Agency (BRIN), Jayapura, Papua, 99225, Indonesia.

Dylan Gaffney: School of Archaeology, University of Oxford, Oxford OX1 2PG, United Kingdom, and Archaeology Programme, School of Social Sciences, University of Otago, 9016, New Zealand.

Guy Jacobs: McDonald Institute for Archaeological Research, Department of Archaeology, University of Cambridge, Cambridge, CB2 3DZ, United Kingdom.

Karen Jacobs: Sainsbury Research Unit for the Arts of Africa, Oceania and the Americas, University of East Anglia, Norwich, NR4 7TJ, United Kingdom.

Sonya Kawer: Research Center for Prehistoric and Historical Archaeology, The National Research and Innovation Agency (BRIN), Jayapura, Papua, 99225, Indonesia.

Pradiptajati Kusuma: Mochtar Riady Institute for Nanotechnology, Tangerang, Banten, 15811, Indonesia.

Mary Lucas: Max Planck Institute for Geoanthropology, Jena, 07745, Germany.

Zubair Mas'ud: Research Center for Prehistoric and Historical Archaeology, The National Research and Innovation Agency (BRIN), Makassar, Sulawesi Selatan, 90242, Indonesia.

Abdul Razak Matcap: Balai Pelestarian Kebudayaan Wilayah XXIII, Manokwari, Papua Barat, 98314, Indonesia.

Bau Mene: Research Center for Prehistoric and Historical Archaeology, The National Research and Innovation Agency (BRIN), Jayapura, Papua, 99225, Indonesia.

Ian J. McNiven: Australian Research Council Centre of Excellence for Australian Biodiversity and Heritage, and Monash Indigenous Studies Centre, Monash University, Clayton, Victoria, 3800, Australia.

Cosimo Posth: Eberhard Karls University, Tübingen, 72074, Germany.

Tom Powell Davies: School of Social Science, University of Queensland, Brisbane, Queensland, 4067, Australia.

Tristan Russell: Archaeology Programme, School of Social Sciences, University of Otago, 9016, New Zealand.

Patrick Roberts: Max Planck Institute for Geoanthropology, Jena, 07745, Germany, and School of Social Science, University of Queensland, Brisbane, Queensland, 4067, Australia.

Adi Dian Setiawan: Research Centre for Archaeometry, The National Research and Innovation Agency (BRIN), Yogyakarta, Daerah Istimewa Yogyakarta, 55171, Indonesia.

Glenn Summerhayes: Archaeology Programme, School of Social Sciences, University of Otago, 9016, New Zealand, and School of Social Science, University of Queensland, Brisbane, Queensland, 4067, Australia.

Hari Suroto: Research Center for Sustainable Environmental, Maritime and Cultural Archaeology, The National Research and Innovation Agency (BRIN), Manado, Sulawesi Utara, 95128, Indonesia.

Daud Tanudirjo: Department of Archaeology, Gadjah Mada University, Yogyakarta, 55281, Indonesia.

Martinus Tekege: Badan Riset dan Inovasi Nasional, Jayapura, Papua, 99225, Indonesia.

Marlin Tolla: Research Centre for Archaeometry, The National Research and Innovation Agency (BRIN), Jayapura, Papua, 99225, Indonesia.

Veronika Triariyani Kanem: Māori and Pacific Studies, Faculty of Arts, University of Auckland, Auckland, 1142, New Zealand.

Roxanne Tsang: Anthropology, Sociology, and Archaeology, School of Humanities and Social Sciences, University of Papua New Guinea, National Capital District, 134, Papua New Guinea.

Beatrice Voirol: Museum der Kulturen, Basel, 4051, Switzerland.

Alexander F. Wall: School of Culture, History and Language, The Australian National University, Canberra, Australian Capital Territory, 2600, Australia.

Fanny Wonu Veys: Wereldmuseum, Leiden, 2312 BS, the Netherlands and Universiteit Leiden, Leiden, 2311 CT, the Netherlands.

www.ingramcontent.com/pod-product-compliance
Lightning Source LLC
Chambersburg PA
CBHW080353030426
42334CB00024B/2861